EARLY MEDIEVAL MORTUARY PRACTICES

Anglo-Saxon Studies in Archaeology and History

14

Edited by
Sarah Semple and Howard Williams

Oxford University School of Archaeology

Published by the Oxford University School of Archaeology
Institute of Archaeology
Beaumont Street
Oxford

Distributed by
Oxbow Books
10 Hythe Bridge Street, Oxford, OX1 2EW, UK
Tel: 01865 241249   Fax: 01865 794449

Distributed in North America by
The David Brown Book Company
PO Box 511, Oakville, CT, 06779, USA

www.oxbowbooks.com

© Oxford University School of Archaeology and individual authors, 2007

ISBN 978 0 947816 15 5
ISSN 0264 5254

A CIP record for this book is available from the British Library

Cover image: Saxon pottery from an early Anglo-Saxon mixed-rite cemetery at Minerva, Alwalton, Cambridgeshire (fig. 42; pp. 238–350)

Typeset by Oxbow Books
Printed in Great Britain by
CPI Antony Rowe, Chippenham

Foreword

Anglo-Saxon Studies in Archaeology and History is an annual series concerned with the archaeology and history of England and its neighbours during the Anglo-Saxon period.

ASSAH offers researchers an opportunity to publish new work in an interdisciplinary forum which allows diversity of length, discipline and geographical spread. Contributions placing Anglo-Saxon England in its international context, including contemporary themes from neighbouring countries, will receive as warm a welcome as papers on England itself.

Papers submitted to ASSAH must be accurate and readable without detailed specialist knowledge. They must conform to the house style of the journal. This format can be seen in both issue 13 and in this volume. A style sheet is available in hard copy or electronic format from the editor. All papers are peer-reviewed.

This volume began its life as the proceedings of a conference entitled 'Early Medieval Mortuary Practices: New Perspectives', organised by Dr. Howard Williams (University of Exeter) and hosted by the Departments of Archaeology and Lifelong Learning at the St Luke's campus of the University of Exeter in February 2004. The proceedings were accepted for publication in *Anglo-Saxon Studies in Archaeology and History* in 2005.

Whilst many of the papers published here derive from the conference, the volume contains additional contributions that serve to consolidate the coverage of the volume and widen its representation of current approaches. The volume is thus a joint-edited, thematic issue, containing a variety of stimulating and challenging perspectives that have a wide application in the method and theory of mortuary archaeology. It is hoped that these will initiate further debate and promote future researches in early medieval funerary studies.

The Editors would like extend their gratitude to the contributors to this volume for their efficiency and commitment during the process of publication. Those who have acted as peer-reviewers for this volume are also to be thanked by the Editors and the Oxford University School for Archaeology, for taking the time to read and comment upon the contributions to this volume. Finally thanks also go to Archaeological Solutions Ltd. Hertfordshire for a generous subvention towards the publications costs.

Finally, from volume 15 onwards, the editorship of the journal will be held jointly by Dr. Helena Hamerow and Dr. Sally Crawford. All papers for consideration should thus be sent to Dr Hamerow using the contact details below.

Sarah Semple
University of Durham
s.j.semple@durham.ac.uk

All papers for consideration should be sent to:

Dr. Helena Hamerow
ASSAH Series Editor
Institute of Archaeology
36 Beaumont Street
Oxford
OX1 2PG

Style sheets available from the Series Editor

Contents

Preface

The conference which forms the basis for this volume, entitled 'Early Medieval Mortuary Practices: New Perspectives', was hosted by the Departments of Archaeology and Lifelong Learning at the St Luke's campus of the University of Exeter in February 2004. It succeeded two extremely influential conferences hosted in the last thirty years, which have produced enduring volumes assessing, analysing and theorizing the evidence for early medieval burials and cemeteries.[1] The Exeter conference built upon these foundations and took research on early medieval burial forward in a range of new directions. After the proceedings were accepted for publication in *Anglo-Saxon Studies in Archaeology and History* in 2005, the volume was enriched by additional contributions that widen the geographical and thematic coverage of the volume and broaden the representation of current approaches.

The volume thus has a broad focus extending beyond Anglo-Saxon England with the inclusion of papers on Scandinavian and Continental topics. In addition, the inclusion of two reports from developer-funded excavations, the mixed-rite cemetery at Alwalton in Cambridgeshire and an inhumation cemetery at Gunthorpe, Cambridgeshire, serve to show how new field-data continues to significantly improve and augment our knowledge and interpretations of early medieval mortuary practices.

The idea for the conference was developed at Cardiff University in 2002–3 by Dr. Howard Williams with support from his colleagues John Hines, Alan Lane and Niall Sharples. His move to Exeter University in the autumn of 2003, involved a re-location of the event, made possible by a kind offer from Derek Gore in the Department of Lifelong Learning to co-host the event and allow free access to a large lecture theatre with modern facilities. The British Academy generously provided a conference grant to assist in the travel and expenses of speakers.

The two days of the conference were made a success through the help of a number of student volunteers from the Department of Archaeology at Exeter: Kirsty Murphy, Helen Rance, Lucy Ryder and Chris Smart. Derek Gore from the Department of Lifelong Learning provided support for the duration of the conference. Guy Halsall and Heinrich Härke are also to be thanked for participating as discussants. Elizabeth Williams provided generous support and acted as registrar for the conference. Most importantly, the speakers are to be thanked for making the event such a positive and informative occasion: Stuart Brookes, Jo Buckberry, Annia Cherryson, Lemont Dobson, Chris Fern, Dawn Hadley, Susanne Hakenbeck, Sue Hamilton, Louise Loe, Marion Manwaring, David Petts, Martin Rundkvist, Sarah Semple, Nick Stoodley and Eva Thäte.

Howard Williams
Sarah Semple

Note

1. Rahtz, P., Dickinson, T. and Watts, L. (eds) 1980. *Anglo-Saxon Cemeteries 1979*, BAR British Series 82, Oxford: BAR; Lucy, S. and Reynolds, A. (eds) 2002. *Burial in Early Medieval England and Wales*, Leeds: Maney.

Contributors

Stuart Brookes
   Institute of Archaeology, University College London, 31–4 Gordon Square, London, WC1H OPY

Jo Buckberry
   Division of Archaeological, Geographical and Environmental Sciences, University of Bradford, Bradford, BD7 1DP

Annia Kristina Cherryson
   School of Archaeology and Ancient History, University of Leicester, University Road, Leicester, LE1 7RH

Zoë Devlin
   School of History and Archaeology, Cardiff University, Cardiff, Wales, CF10 3XQ

Chris Fern
   Fern Archaeology, Bothy East, 1 Pottergate, Gilling East, North Yorkshire, YO62 4JJ

Charles French
   Department of Archaeology, University of Cambridge, Cambridge CB2 3DZ

Rebecca Gowland
   Department of Archaeology, University of Durham, South Park, Durham, DH1 3LE

Dawn Hadley
   Department of Archaeology, University of Sheffield, Northgate House, West Street, Sheffield, S1 4ET

Susanne Hakenbeck
   Department of Archaeology, University of Cambridge, Downing Street, Cambridge, CB2 3DZ

Heinrich Härke
   Department of Archaeology, University of Reading, Whiteknights, Box 227, Reading RG6 6AB

Sue Harrington
   Institute of Archaeology, University College London, 31–34 Gordon Square, London, WC1H OPY

Stephen Harrison
   School of Archaeology, John Henry Newman Building, University College Dublin, Belfield, Dublin 4, Eire

Rik Hoggett
   92 Knowland Grove, Norwich, NR5 8YA

Christine Osborne
   91 Kimberley Road, Lowestoft, Suffolk, NR33 0UB

Philippa Patrick
   Box 234, Addenbrookes Hospital, Hills Road, Cambridge, CB2 2QQ

David Petts
    Department of History and Archaeology, University of Chester, Parkgate Road, Chester, CH1 4BJ

Martin Rundkvist
    Lakegatan 12, SE-13341 Saltsjobaden, Sweden

Nick Stoodley
    Department of Archaeology, King Alfred's College, Winchester, SO22 4NR

Eva Thäte
    1st Floor Flat, 87–89 Kings Road, Reading, RG1 3DD

Howard Williams
    Department of Archaeology, University of Exeter, EX4 4QE

Introduction: Themes in the Archaeology of Early Medieval Death and Burial

Howard Williams

Introduction

The early medieval period (*c.* 400–1100 AD) has been studied by archaeologists through many forms of material evidence: from settlements to sculpture, from pottery to pollen grains. Yet scholars of the period continue to be fascinated and challenged by the rich and complex data from early medieval graves and cemeteries. The aim of this volume is to explore new perspectives applied to this evidence. This introduction aims to set the scene by addressing why graves and cemeteries are such an important archaeological resource for the period. To do this, the chapter considers how studies of early medieval mortuary practices have developed, what themes and ideas are presented by researchers in this volume, and where studies of early medieval graves might develop in the future. Because other papers in this volume address Continental and Scandinavian evidence, this paper will focus its attention on the archaeology of early medieval Britain, especially the furnished burial rites of southern and eastern England from the fifth to seventh centuries AD.

Why Graves?

There are many explanations for the persistent interest in early medieval burials by archaeologists. Certainly the early medieval grave provides a secure and sealed deposit that can contain preserved human remains, artefacts and structures in contextual association with each other. The burial evidence can therefore allow archaeologists to answer innumerable questions about the societies that created them and their changing attitudes towards death and the dead.

There are other reasons for this interest in the early medieval dead. They are 'attractive' as a rare instance where we can directly access early medieval lives. The information their bones provide gives us the perception of intimacy with the past and the stories the dead 'speak' to us and bring the past to life. They provide a materiality, corporeality and, somewhat ironically, they give vitality to the early Middle Ages in a way that cannot be done through either other material remains or through the heavily stylised texts that survive from the period.[2]

This attraction is made stronger through the perception of many that early medieval people are incontrovertibly the ancestors of the modern inhabitants of the British Isles, and that the early Middle Ages was the time when many of the beliefs, practices and traditions that persisted into recent centuries were originated or consolidated, whether from mainly indigenous or intrusive sources.[3]

Through graves we directly come 'face-to-face' with death and the dead. Very few individuals in early twenty-first-century British society have the misfortune to regularly experience death first-hand. Hospitals and undertakers serve to render the corporeality of death distant and manageable and yet death is an obsession of our media. In this environment, ancient graves have an allure unlike any other archaeological data. Hence one might evoke our evolving grisly obsession of British culture with death and commemoration since the Victorian period as a reason for the interest in the archaeology of graves and cemeteries.

Artefacts from burial contexts have an appeal beyond their archaeological value in popular culture. In our society, the material world is cherished and fetishistic obsessions with ancient and precious things abound, manifest (for example) in the increasing popularity of an international trade in illicit antiquities. Building on a long tradition of regarding early medieval artefacts as collector's items; weapons and dress accessories appeal as much as bones to the modern mind. This is especially the case in instances where the volume and quality of grave goods deserve the description of 'treasure'; as with the wealthy, chamber grave recently discovered at Prittlewell in Essex or the contents of St Cuthbert's tomb in Durham Cathedral.[4]

The appeal of mortuary evidence is enhanced by cases where the act of discovering such graves also becomes a story in itself, in which the archaeologist can be portrayed as the pioneer and adventurer. In terms of the accounts of the treasure from mound 1 at Sutton Hoo we can recognise attempts to create the home-grown equivalent to Howard Carter's report on the discoveries in the Valley of the Kings.[5]

Given that the early medieval period as a whole can be characterised as a time of rapid socio-economic, political and religious change and with fragmentary and problematic texts: burials and cemeteries have taken on a special importance by serving to illustrate early medieval history. Graves and other mortuary remains are the intentional outcomes of ritual performances by groups and communities. They are therefore material expressions of public acts and procedures when dealing with the dead. Graves inform us about the traditions, characteristics, structures and diversities of the communities and societies that created them. More specifically they reveal changing early medieval responses to death, dying and the deceased.[6] In turn, the study of these mortuary practices from early medieval Britain can illuminate key themes and debates in the interpretation of burial evidence relevant to all periods and all parts of the globe.

Set against the background of this ongoing research tradition, this volume is about new perspectives on early medieval death and burial, gleaned from new data, methods and theories. To situate the work presented here, let us begin by reviewing the history and development of research into early medieval mortuary practices.

Discoveries, Methods and Theories in Early Medieval Mortuary Archaeology

Discoveries

The roots of early medieval burial archaeology can be found before the advent of archaeology as a discipline: as long ago as the early medieval period itself, both texts and material evidence attest to the occasional practice of exhuming and interpreting the dead. The beginnings of the antiquarian study of early medieval graves are, however, usually charted back to the seventeenth century, with the antiquary Thomas Browne.[7] While Browne (and subsequent pioneers like the barrow-digger Bryan Faussett) attributed the graves they uncovered to the Roman period, James Douglas is often regarded as the first excavator to attribute them correctly to the early medieval period.[8]

During the nineteenth century, cemeteries, burial mounds, tombs and funerary sculpture were investigated and reported in national and local journals and in books. The legacy of the nineteenth century has been a vast data-base of funerary evidence ascribed to the early Middle Ages.[9] While the end of the nineteenth century saw a lull of interest in early medieval graves, the twentieth century saw a renewed interest in early medieval burials and new explorations leading to the discovery of the 'princely' cemetery at Sutton Hoo beginning with excavations in 1938 and 1939.[10]

After World War II, excavations continued and were increasingly recorded by modern contextual standards for both early Anglo-Saxon (or pagan period) and middle Anglo-Saxon (including 'final-phase') cemeteries.[11] Meanwhile later Anglo-Saxon burials were increasingly recovered, recognised and recorded[12] as were burials from other parts of western and northern Britain, from Cornwall to Orkney.[13] Today's scholars have therefore inherited a long tradition of discovering, excavating and interpreting early medieval graves.

Methods and Techniques

In combination with this increasing data-set available for study; methods and techniques for the archaeological investigation of graves have developed too. Eighteenth and nineteenth-century methodologies consisted of either barrow-digging or the exploration of cemeteries following upon accidental discoveries.[14] In both instances, the focus tended to be placed on objects, with only a small selection of scholars exploring the mortuary *context* itself. The study of human remains by trained medical practitioners focused on the misguided study of craniology to discern the race, class and sex of the deceased.[15]

It was only in the 1930s and 1940s that methods of excavation and recording show a demonstrable improvement over the best of the previous century. Early excavations with a detailed record of grave-contexts include the Holywell Row and Burwell cemeteries in Suffolk[16] although the illustration and contextual detail was lacking for most individual burials. The wealth and complexity of the rich assemblage from the chamber within the mound 1 ship burial at Sutton Hoo provided the motivation for more careful recording of contextual information necessary to make detailed inferences.[17] Yet this was very much the exception rather than the rule in the era before the Second World War. In the post-war era, modern scientific archaeology has seen the emergence of earthwork-survey, aerial photography, and more recently, field-walking techniques and geophysical survey as techniques used in the investigation of early medieval cemeteries and their contexts. Meanwhile the advent of metal-detecting as a hobby has provided both new discoveries and new threats to early medieval graves. The recording of graves in-plan with the contextual recording of objects and human remains is now all but universal, yet is only commonplace in excavation reports where grave-goods are recovered.[18] Most recently, we have seen the adoption of GIS in the recording of graves as at West Heslerton, North Yorkshire and the more detailed recording of late fifth and sixth-century graves with multiple plans and sections as at Snape, Suffolk[19]

With the increasing wealth of mortuary evidence, archaeologists have developed refined typologies and chronologies too. For find-less graves, the adoption of AMS radiocarbon dating has been increasingly employed.[20] The raft of scientific methods applicable to early medieval graves has developed tremendously in recent years, from techniques in studying human remains including ageing, sexing, assessing stature, health and disease as well as the study of the ritual technology of cremation.[21] The ability to extract ancient DNA was heralded with enthusiasm but has yet to produce detailed results for either studying population or gender.[22] More positively, studies of bone chemistry have opened up exciting possibilities in the investigation of early medieval migration and diet.[23]

Yet for all this barrage of new methods and techniques, the investigation and excavation of early medieval graves remains something of an 'art'. The discipline continues to rest on the interpretations of human agents during the often complex process of discovering, excavating, recording, analysing and publishing early medieval graves. These choices are not simply a mechanical process of extracting 'facts' from the soil, but the engagement of theories, questions and ideas with the observed material remains.

Interpreting Early Medieval Graves

From its Victorian origins, a racial and religious paradigm has dominated the study of early medieval graves; a desire to identify the history and character of barbarian races, their pagan religious beliefs, and their conversion to Christianity. This was achieved through a series of dichotomies; between pagan Germanic and Christian Celts, between Vikings and Anglo-Saxons. These themes have permeated twentieth-century scholarship as well, but with a more detailed and historical focus upon charting invasion, settlement and conversion. For instance, the influence of culture-history can be recognised in the analyses of brooches and pottery from graves as a means of writing the (pre-) history of the Anglo-Saxons. These approaches might also be regarded as extensions of an 'Anglo-Saxonism' and more broadly across the British Isles, the interaction of imperialism, colonialism and nationalism in the study of early medieval burial evidence.[24]

These culture-histories continue to be popular in some quarters to the present day, but in the post-war era they were augmented by economic and territorial perspectives.[25] Subsequently from the 1970s, some archaeologists adopted the theoretical standpoints of North American and British prehistorians in pursuing an anti-historical, social archaeology.[26] As well as looking for vertical differentiation between rank and status groups, some studies also looked at horizontal differentiation including gender, age, kinship, households and regionality. The pervasiveness of this approach can be recognised in the fact that select cemetery reports of the 1980s and 1990s incorporated their own social analysis; attempting to see patterns in mortuary data as a reflection of the social organisation (or its idealised representation as social structure) of the living society.[27]

The emergence of the post-processual critiques of the New Archaeology focused on the need to recognise the importance of meaning, power, ideology and context in the investigation of past societies. Moreover, these perspectives brought with them a critique of attempts to 'read' social organisation directly and simplistically in the variability of early medieval burial rites. The search for meaning inherent within both artefacts and the burial context involved adopting linguistic, textual, and even poetic analogies for the study of early medieval graves. These approaches emphasised the potential for mortuary ritual to represent, but also to transform, social and political relations.[28] Meanwhile, other scholars focused their attention on the political context of the active and symbolic messages of mortuary practices.[29] Despite these developments, many studies have simply ignored or paid lip-service to these theoretical developments. Numerous analyses continue to be interpreted in traditional cultural and religious terms in many popular studies as well as more detailed scholarly analyses. For some, burial archaeology remains a sub-set of the investigation of early medieval culture-history, religion and church archaeology without recognising or addressing the range of recent debates about the meaningful and discursive nature of mortuary practices.[30]

Debating Early Medieval Mortuary Archaeology

Built upon the rich data of recent excavations, the papers presented here, contain elements of culture-historic, social, symbolic and ideological perspectives combined with the presentation of new perspectives. The volume is arranged in themes rather than by period or region to emphasise the theories explored.

Debating Death and Identity

As noted above, the study of the relationship between burial and identity (whether racial, religious, cultural or social) has been a pervasive theme in early medieval mortuary archaeology since Victorian times. In the first section, five papers discuss different types of relationships between identity and the disposal of the dead in the early Middle Ages.

The contribution by Heinrich Härke addresses directly the thorny topic (and perhaps the most enduring in early medieval burial studies) of ethnicity. He presents a perspective that both rejects a traditional interpretation of early medieval ethnicity as based on racial and tribal origins but equally challenges recent studies that dismiss the usage of ethnicity entirely. Susanne Hakenbeck's paper espouses a local, contextual approach to the construction of identities in early medieval Europe. She charts the use and abuse of ethnicity in past studies of early medieval Bavaria, and considers how instead archaeologists can consider ethnicity as one element of the 'nested identities' communicated through the material culture of early medieval cemeteries. A further form of identity is considered by Rik Hoggett who addresses the link between burial and religious identity. Focusing on East Anglia, Hoggett questions the tendency of recent studies to reject religious explanations and suggests that religious conversion is reflected in changing mortuary traditions. Zoë Devlin's paper augments these discussions by evaluating how social memories were produced and reproduced through early medieval funerals and the material culture used therein. She provides a valuable review of historical and anthropological approaches to social memory and explores the ways in which mortuary practices employed portable objects with particular histories in mediating the retrospective commemoration of identities of the deceased in life, but also prospectively constructing new identities for the dead. The memories constructed through the use of artefacts in mortuary practices were therefore not concerned with directly reflecting static identities but constructing links between past, present and future identities. To put current debates in British and Continental burial archaeology in context, Martin Rundkvist provides an overview of recent Scandinavian first millennium AD mortuary studies, exploring the similarities and differences from the British pattern outlined above.

Burial Rites and Artefacts

The themes of identity and social memory are pursued further in the study of grave goods and burial contexts in six papers. Rebecca Gowland focuses on a critique of traditional concepts of ethnicity, suggesting that we can go 'beyond ethnicity' through a new systematic osteological investigation of entire samples of human remains from cemetery excavations. Additionally, she notes similarities in the signalling of aged and gendered social identities in the burial rites of both late Roman and early Anglo-Saxon cemeteries of southern England that have tended to be ignored in period-specific studies. Chris Fern addresses the role of animal sacrifice in early medieval funerals; comparing and contrasting the ritual killing and disposal of horses from the inhumation and cremation rites of early Anglo-Saxon England and their different Continental influences. Meanwhile, Sue Harrington's paper looks at the evidence from east Kent to illustrate the often-overlooked role of textiles in mortuary practices. Harrington argues that the potential of the careful conservation and analysis of textiles is a richer understanding of the provision of materials in graves. The paper by this author looks at an overlooked category of grave goods, namely the toilet implements of early Anglo-Saxon cremation and inhumation burials. The evidence shows that there was a special significance attributed to toilet implements in post-cremation rites serving to commemorate a new identity for the dead. The last two papers in this section by Jo Buckberry

and Annia Cherryson demonstrate the vast untapped potential of the social analysis of the burial rites of later Anglo-Saxon England. Buckberry combines data from published osteological reports and from her own analyses of the bones from a sample of later Anglo-Saxon graves from Lincolnshire and Yorkshire. She identifies diversity in the spatial organisation, grave forms and structures employed to articulate the status of the deceased. Cherryson also considers middle and late Anglo-Saxon burial rites, but instead of focusing on the contents of graves, she addresses the increasing disturbance of earlier graves during the period by comparing field cemeteries with those found associated with churches. In combination, the six papers illustrate how contextual analyses of burial data are applicable from the late Roman period through to the eleventh century.

Mortuary Practices: Monuments and Landscape

Six papers encapsulate the burgeoning interest in early medieval mortuary monuments and landscapes. A consideration of patterns in burial location in the early medieval landscape of Kent is pursued by Stuart Brookes with the aid of Geographical Information Systems. His study integrates maps, place-names, later medieval historical evidence and the distribution of known cemeteries and settlements to suggest that routes provided a central influence on the positioning and experience of cemeteries by the early medieval population. Meanwhile, Nick Stoodley addresses the connections between authority, territoriality, burial and landscape to consider the phenomenon of cemetery-shift in the seventh century. He develops this through the case study of excavations at two neighbouring cemeteries at Portway Andover. Dawn Hadley explores the often misunderstood issue of burial location from the seventh up to the eleventh centuries AD. She suggests that shifts in burial location were the norm rather than a unique phenomenon of the seventh century.

The next three papers move the focus away from Anglo-Saxon England. The Viking-period re-use of earlier sites and the topographical situation of furnished Viking-period graves is explored by Stephen Harrison. He shows how Scandinavian-style furnished burials may have consciously employed topography and the appropriation of existing native sites to make sociopolitical statements of authority and identity. Eva Thäte's paper looks at Viking-period Scandinavia. She considers the issue of monument reuse but in this paper the focus is on the selective re-use of abandoned house-sites for burial and monument-building. Finally David Petts looks at mythical geographies of burial as portrayed in the literature of early medieval Wales. Rather than seeing the written sources as portraying objectively where and how the elites were buried in the eighth to eleventh centuries AD, Petts argues that both the texts and the mortuary material culture and sculpture of the age were implicated in socio-political discourses.

The Excavation Reports

In addition to the research papers, this volume includes two excavation reports that serve to illuminate the rich new data being produced through ongoing field-based investigation both within the realm of research excavations and rescue-led projects.

Directions in Early Medieval Mortuary Archaeology

What is the future for early medieval mortuary archaeology? It is clear that many of the papers in this volume point research in new directions. Yet it would be amiss for an introduction to this volume that advocates the pursuit of new perspectives not to highlight other areas for potential research. These consist of new directions in mortuary theory, the exploration of the context of mortuary practices in past societies, as well as the study of the history of, popular culture of, and ethical considerations surrounding, early medieval mortuary archaeology.

Mortuary Theory

The last decade of early medieval mortuary archaeology in Britain has seen a series of inter-related new theoretical themes. They have a common focus on the performative and embodied qualities of mortuary practices; the strategic and contextual uses of the arena of death by the living as they experience, engage with, an exploit, mortuary practices. These perspectives promise to situate the interpretation of early medieval death and burial within wider debates in archaeology as well as themes in cognate disciplines such as history, sociology and anthropology.[31]

The issue of mortuary symbolism is by no means done and dusted. Mortuary symbolism – or perhaps more broadly, mortuary significances – have many forms, and therefore more careful considerations of the types of signifier and the range of signified concepts of a particular symbol need to be broadened. Iconic, symbolic and metaphorical messages can be manifest in the material culture deployed in funerals, from portable artefacts to monuments.[32] This is especially true if we consider that, at least some, objects and materials deployed in burials had complex 'biographies' prior to their disposal with the dead; histories that may have informed their role in the funeral.[33] In theorising this, the tendency has been to consider symbolism as largely 'social' in character, pertaining to the identity of the dead person or statements made by mourners about their aspirations and identities. Symbolism liked to eschatology and cosmology requires further attention.[34]

The theme of agency has been mainly explored in studies of prehistoric mortuary ritual although Lucy has incorporated these perspectives in her 'contextual' approach to early medieval cemeteries.[35] Meanwhile, this author has developed a view of early medieval cremation rites that considers both the agency of the living and the dead. The potential for considering objects, cadavers, graves and monuments raised, as having an 'agency' to affect and direct social structures and ideals has yet to be fully explored.[36]

As discussed by Devlin, the relationship between mortuary practices and social memory is central to considering the impact or 'agency' of the rituals surrounding death. Yet the range of media and technologies involved in selective remembering and forgetting during mortuary rituals is only beginning to be explored in early medieval archaeology. Of equal concern is *what* is remembered; whether memories are retrospective or prospective, the media employed in remembering and forgetting (including texts, images, monuments and portable artefacts) and the ways in which different mortuary practices served as divergent and contrasting strategies of commemoration. There is considerable potential in thinking of early medieval mortuary practices as evolving and varying 'technologies of remembrance' in which material culture and the spatial and temporal structuring of the funeral, are carefully employed together with the corpse in order to create memorable experiences and influence the perception of the past and the future through the present.[37]

In this way we can regard mortuary practices as less concerned with the representation of static identities. Through the mortuary process, the identities of both the living and the dead are transformed, not simply composed. Drawing upon anthropological theories of identity, we can consider how early medieval concepts of the person might incorporate 'individual' elements. By this it is meant that qualities of the person are shared between, and exchanged between people, rather than residing in individuals. Anthropological research shows how personhood can operate at a number of scales: personal, social, cosmological and ontological. Therefore, (for example), when archaeologists consider the relationship with animals, objects and monuments in mortuary practices, they are more than substances that 'refer to' or 'represent' individuals. Instead, the material world of death can be considered as contributing towards and even distributing concepts of the person, as considered by Chris Fowler and Jo Brück for later prehistoric Britain.[38]

Without doubt mortuary practices are recognised by many commentators to be more than concerned with the identities of the dead and the living, they are also contexts for mourning. Taking the lead from Sarah Tarlow's discussions of emotion and mortuary practices in post-medieval archaeology, there is potential for considering the range of emotional responses encapsulated within bereavement and mourning practices that may have been stylised and mediated through early medieval material culture associated with the dead.[39]

In combination these themes combine to create something of a check-list of potential areas for future research. Without a meaningful debate over their validity, early medieval mortuary archaeology will not progress into new arenas of research.

Early Medieval Mortuary Archaeology in Context

In addition to these specific theories, there is also the question of how early medieval mortuary archaeology fits into the wider study of the early Middle Ages. There are four areas that require mention here, first the broader stories, narratives or 'meta-narratives' that early medieval graves are slotted into, and serve to enhance. Traditionally, these have been straightforwardly the questions of successive migrations and colonisations by incoming groups, the diffusion of ideas and beliefs, and the evolution of societies into kingdoms.[40] Yet there are other narratives that mortuary archaeology can address. Indeed, it is perhaps a sign of maturity of the subject that a wide range of interpretive frameworks and 'histories' can be written from early medieval graves, and wider contexts can be explored for the significance of mortuary practices of early medieval people.

A clear example of an 'alternative' narrative into which early medieval graves can be discussed is the history of gender relations.[41] Another is the history of settlement and landscape: a story that has tended to be written from settlement evidence rather than burials.[42] To provide one final example, early medieval graves can contribute to wider debates over the social construction of death. Sociologists, anthropologists, historians and psychologists could easily be looking to archaeology for answers and contexts for their perspectives of dying, death and the dead rather than the other way around. This can only begin, however, if archaeologists start to employ their theories, methods and data to address wider inter-disciplinary debates over death across cultures.[43]

The second issue relates to the use of analogy in the interpretation of early medieval graves. While the use of place-name and textual evidence has become common-place in studies of early medieval burials,[44] the use of ethnographies, anthropological and sociological theories have long been entertained in early medieval burial studies, and still there remains a lack of coherent dis-cussions on the integration and assessment of these analogies.[45] Similarly, the use of experimental archaeo-logy in the study of early medieval mortuary practices has untapped potential.[46]

A third issue concerns the critical integration of mortuary theory into the excavation of early medieval graves. Until relatively recently, there has been a tendency for excavation strategies and methods to be situated as static processes that sit outside the research questions being asked. This has been challenged by research-led projects that have served to develop methods and

techniques as an integral part of the fieldwork strategy.[47] Yet in the context of field archaeology, a lack of consideration for mortuary theory might render certain questions unanswerable since the data is not being adequately recorded or even recognised. In short, there is a debate to be held over the extent to which theory, method and data can be separated, and how they relate to each other during cemetery excavations.

A final theme worthy of further consideration is the history of the subject itself. There have been numerous broad summaries on the history of the study of early medieval graves, as with the review above.[48] However, the detailed and contextual analysis of the intellectual and socio-political influences upon their study has yet to be achieved, nor indeed, has it been regarded as a serious avenue of archaeological research. A major landmark in developing such an approach would be more detailed explorations of specific scholars and periods like that conducted recently for Merovingian mortuary archaeology. It remains to be seen if comparable studies are developed to address early medieval Britain.[49]

The Public Archaeology of Early Medieval Graves

So far we have addressed themes related to the inter-pretation of burials themselves, but there are also challenges to be faced in considering how these graves are used in the presentation and education of the public. From the 'theatre' of cemetery excavation where the public can sometimes view the work of the archaeologists, through to the images and accounts of graves in journals and books, early medieval mortuary remains portray the early Middle Ages to the public in many ways. Graves are used in the promotion of early medieval archaeology.[50]

Museums provide one such environment in which early medieval dead are displayed. This is because they contain artefacts from graves and frequently use information provided by human remains to reconstruct the experience of living in the 'Dark Ages'.[51] Equally, museums contain reconstructions of graves themselves, as at Sutton Hoo where the visitor can not only walk around the burial mounds, but the Visitor Centre contains a reconstruction of the chamber within the mound 1 ship-burial.[52]

Similarly, the recently renovated Corinium museum in Cirencester, Gloucestershire has an Anglo-Saxon gallery that is almost exclusively dedicated to the display of finds and contexts uncovered from the sixth and seventh-century cemetery at Lechlade.[53] The centre-piece is a display of a wealthy female burial of the sixth century AD employing the careful reconstruction of her burial posture, appearance (based on forensic reconstruction), costume, grave-goods and structures. Elsewhere in the exhibition, a weapon burial is also portrayed. Here, the public is treated to an exhibition of how the grave was revealed during the archaeological excavation along with the tools of the archaeologist's trade on view.

These exciting displays bring the early medieval dead to life for visitors, providing them with a focus to speculate about the personalities and identities of the dead and the societies in which they lived and died. Moreover, these exhibits attract the audience into the early medieval world of death and the rituals and superstitions that surrounded the transformation and commemoration of the dead. In many ways, the display may be similar to that created in the composition of the grave in the early Middle Ages, affording a tableau which portrays the deceased in an idealised form, and containing many messages to be 'read' by its audience.[54] Yet it remains the case that these displays do not capture the dynamics of the funerary process. They embody the challenge of conveying the actions of early medieval mourners. It is clearly difficult to engage with death today as it may have been experienced by early medieval people. Instead, one is offered a static, seemingly timeless corpse that bears a closer resemblance to medieval effigy tombs than it may do to the multiple staged early medieval funeral. Museums face this challenge, and are answering it in increasingly innovative ways of engaging with the multi-sensory interaction of the living with the dead in past mortuary rituals through illustrations, reconstructions and performances.

It might be worth considering how the representation of early medieval graves forms one facet of the contemporary art of death or art 'against death'. Certainly there are close resemblances between the reconstructed graves from Lechlade and Sutton Hoo with other famous instances of deliberately preserved human remains found across the world from the mummies of Egypt to those of South America.[55] In terms of popular perception, the dead Saxons are being immortalised in a comparable way to these more geographically far-flung vestiges of ancient funerary obsequies. In another sense, one cannot help but notice resemblances with the embalmers art of the modern undertaker, allowing the dead to be displayed to mourners in the open-casket funeral.[56] Equally, one might compare the display of human remains in museums to more extreme uses of the cadaver in art, as with the recent 'Body World' exhibitions, in which Western perceptions and understandings of death, the dead and the body are challenged.[57] In this way, it might be possible to regard the display of the dead as an art-form that prompts engagement with mortality. Therefore, while these displays bring home the positive educational role of museums in facilitating engagement with the past through mortuary remains, simultaneously illustrations and reconstructions of graves may hold a value for today's visitor by depicting death. In a society that rarely sees death in reality since the dead are hidden within hospitals and dealt with by undertakers, can archaeology provide one of the few arenas for intellectual and popular engagements with mortality?[58]

Ethical Debates

The ethics of mortuary archaeology have been dominated by the reburial debate. For the UK, this has impacted on the repatriation and reburial of human and cultural remains held by museums from other parts of the world, notably the Americas and Australasia.[59] Only on occasion has the debate affected the excavation of British burial sites prior to the later and post-medieval periods where objections to excavation are more commonplace. The study of medieval Jewish burials from Jewbury, York are often cited as an example of archaeologists facing protests from a religious minority.[60] It might be thought at first-glance that there are simply no indigenous groups to object against archaeologists digging up and curating the remains of the early medieval dead, and therefore in turn, that ethical considerations and the pressure for re-burial are irrelevant. In fact, neither is the case; there are non-archaeological groups interested in the treatment of human remains from the early Middle Ages, and, in any case, an absence of protest does not mean that ethics are not an issue.[61]

There are certainly many strong strands of argument supporting the excavation, retention, and even the display, of early medieval mortuary remains. Through *Meet the Ancestors* and other media, the early medieval dead have become an integral part of British academic and popular culture.[62] Given the research value of this material, together with the fact that personal identities cannot be known and there is no issue of surviving personal memories of these individuals, it may be argued that there is no debate to be had. Yet, does the antiquity of the material and the lack of a strong indigenous protest movement make research into early medieval mortuary practices free of ethical concerns?

It is this author's contention that there are a range of potential 'stakeholders' in the treatment of early medieval graves of which archaeologists are but one.[63] The most obvious ethical challenges facing archaeologists derive from negotiation with various modern religious groups. Recent guidelines have been agreed upon concerning the best practice for dealing with human remains from Christian burial grounds that exerts a modest degree of pressure for the re-burial of early medieval burial populations. While the guidelines give archaeologists latitude in the treatment of early medieval graves uncovered at sites of religious worship, this does not rule out the likelihood that instances will inevitably occur where Christian communities may express strong concerns and objections to archaeological excavations.[64] Conversely, there seems to be a small but growing voice among neo-pagans concerning the archaeological treatment of early medieval graves, some of whom claim spiritual and ancestral links to an Anglo-Saxon or Viking heritage.[65] Finally, local communities and landowners, aside from any clear religious or political motivations, might voice strong opinions concerning the excavation, curation and display of early medieval remains. This seems to have taken place in Wessex Archaeology's recent investigations of an early medieval burial in Wiltshire leading to the re-interment of the human remains close to the site of discovery.[66]

These voices are not always ones of objection; they can often be strongly on the side of archaeologists. This was the case with the road-widening scheme that threatened the site of the wealthy early seventh-century chamber grave excavated by the Museum of London Archaeological Service in 2004. The early medieval grave's discovery can be linked to the emergence of a sense of pride and identity as well as the environmental concerns of initial road protests.[67]

The archaeological evidence shows us clearly that early medieval people cared for and respected their dead. If archaeologists have any interest in graves as more than a store of human remains that can be subjected for scientific analysis, then there is a need to both respect and appreciate these archaeological contexts as the intentional outcomes of past mortuary rituals and invested with the personalities and emotions of the survivors (see above). For instance, early medieval attitudes can be discerned in the fear or respect for disturbing the dead evident in the low frequency of inter-cutting and disturbed graves at many sites. Yet equally we have many cases where for ritual or practical reasons, graves were re-opened, disturbed and human remains could be curated, suggesting that the early medieval dead could have long and significant material 'afterlives'.[68] Equally, the complexity and heterogeneity of early medieval mortuary practices shows us no single response towards the commemoration and veneration of 'ancestors'. We can identify so many early medieval death-ways, in terms of the deployment of artefacts, structures, technologies, spaces, monuments and the landscape, found in both non-Christian and early Christian communities. It is equally problematic to distinguish and ascribe 'pagan' and 'Christian' labels to the diverse and contingent set of shifting responses to death and disposal that we find in the early medieval archaeological record.[69]

Therefore if we are imposing modern ethics onto the archaeological treatment of early medieval human remains and cultural objects, we cannot entertain the conceit that this has anything to do with the beliefs of early medieval people; it is based on our societies' values and perceptions of the dead. Consequently, archaeologists must challenge the assumptions behind our modern values, especially when they differentiate the treatment of the early medieval dead in terms of perceived religious beliefs and status. This is certainly what has happened, perhaps unwittingly, with the early medieval Christian dead as a consequence of the new guidelines created by English Heritage and the Church of England. Those early medieval graves uncovered at a site of modern worship are being given different ethical treatment to the vast majority of both the early medieval non-Christian and Christian dead who were probably *not* buried in churchyards before the tenth and eleventh centuries AD and for whom no guidelines have been agreed upon.[70] The same debate could be developed along lines of the social identities constructed through early medieval burials. For instance, should the differential treatment afforded to the dead in the past reflect the respect we afford them in the present, or should our judgements provide differential treatment? Certainly we can see both the biases of early medieval and modern people influencing the different responses to the preferential treatment of the Prittlewell chamber grave over other early medieval burials. Would similar attention have been lavished on a find-less cist-burial from Cornwall or Fife, and would the contorted skeleton of an early medieval execution victim found in the ditch of a Norfolk Early Bronze Age barrow attract the same level of respect?[71] Therefore while ethical considerations cannot be dismissed, archaeologists need to rigorously challenge the assumptions and biases that can easily pervade such debates and afford differential treatment to early medieval bodies and grave goods.

In this light it is clear that early medieval archaeologists need to address the ethical issue head-on, developing robust and theorised ethical arguments in support of their activities in order to anticipate the possibility that their activities *will* meet with objections on ethical grounds in certain circumstances.[72] This is particularly important since it might be argued that the early Middle Ages sit on a crucial fault line between ancient and modern perceptions of death and disposal. Ignoring the issue will render early medieval archaeologists enfeebled *when* it arises, especially if this occurs in the media spotlight. Certainly a respect for, and liaison with, the interests of local communities and stakeholders in ancient remains can serve to avoid conflict and enhance the understanding of archaeological research to the wider public, and perhaps render early medieval discoveries an important resource for the promotion of local histories and identities. But there remain problems with accepting a single ethical stance towards early medieval human remains. Certainly re-burial should not be accepted as a 'token' gesture towards political correctness. For this reason, the debate over the ethical treatment of early medieval graves, is likely to become of paramount importance for the future of archaeological research. Without a consideration of these issues, archaeologists working in periods deemed 'safe' from the reburial issue might find themselves forced to accept repatriation and reburial without a fight because of agendas and guidelines imposed upon them by others, or equally may fail in exciting opportunities of including diverse communities and groups in the exploration of this fascinating form of archaeological evidence.

Conclusion

It is hoped that this introduction not only provides a background to current scholarly debate, but also encourages readers and researchers to regard the study of early medieval burial as an exciting and developing field of enquiry in which the more questions we ask open up new avenues of research. Rather than restricting ourselves to age-old questions, the challenge of future research is to both look at old questions in new ways, but also to address new questions in new ways. Which themes addressed here receive consideration and which do not, will be as interesting to chart over the coming decades.

Acknowledgements

Thanks to Heinrich Härke, Martin Rundkvist, Sarah Semple, Faye Simpson and Elizabeth Williams for commenting on earlier drafts of this introduction.

Notes

1. For a recent review, see Lucy 2000; Lucy and Reynolds 2002.
2. For popular engagements with the archaeological discovery of the dead, see Bahn 1996; 2003. For an example of this applied to the early Middle Ages, see Richards 1999.
3. *E.g.* Miles 2005; Pryor 2004.
4. Battiscombe 1956; Webster 1992. On the collecting of early medieval artefacts, see Effros 2003a.
5. For example, the immortalised story of the excavation of mound 1 at Sutton Hoo, see Carver 1998.
6. *E.g.* see Effros 2003b; Halsall 2003.
7. Browne 1658.
8. Douglas 1793.
9. *E.g.* Smith 1856; Wylie 1852.
10. *E.g.* Carver 1998; Leeds and Harden 1936.
11. Meaney and Hawkes 1970.
12. *E.g.* Boddington 1996; Rodwell and Rodwell 1983.
13. Alcock 1992.
14. Lucy 2002; Marsden 1999.
15. Morse 1999.
16. Lethbridge 1931.
17. Bruce-Mitford 1975.
18. *E.g.* compare the recording of graves in the recent unfurnished early medieval cemeteries at Llandough with those from furnished early medieval cemeteries such as at Sewerby: Hirst 1985.
19. Haughton and Powlesland 1999; Filmer-Sankey and Pestell 2001.
20. Hines *et al.* 1999.
21. Mays 1998; McKinley 1994.
22. Lucy 2000.
23. Budd *et al.* 2004; Montgomery *et al.* 2005.
24. Lucy 2002.
25. Bonney 1966.
26. *E.g.* Arnold 1980.
27. Stoodley 1999.
28. Lucy 1998; Pader 1982; Richards 1987.
29. Carver 2000; Halsall 2003.
30. O'Brien 1999.
31. Williams 2005.
32. Andrén 1993.
33. Eckardt and Williams 2003.
34. Oestigaard 2000.
35. Lucy 1998.
36. Williams 2004.
37. Williams 2006.
38. Fowler 2004.
39. Tarlow 1999; Williams 2007.
40. Hills 2003.
41. Stoodley 1999.
42. Rippon 2000.
43. Thompson 2004.
44. Semple 1998; 2004.
45. For a recent discussion of the use of ethnographic analogy for understanding mortuary and ritual practices in past societies, see for example Parker Pearson and Ramilisonina 1998.
46. *E.g.* for cremation experimentations, see McKinley 1997.
47. Carver 2005.
48. Lucy 2002.
49. Effros 2003.
50. For example, see the range of reconstructions involving facial reconstructions, portrayals of funerary scenes and the visual representations of graves discussed by Redknap 2002, 38–44. For the popular representation of early Anglo-Saxon death, see for example: Poulton 1990.
51. *E.g.* West 2000, 9–21.
52. Plunkett 2002. Lucy and Herring's assessment of the portrayal of the early Anglo-Saxons in museum displays focused, as do many museums and open-air centres, on the reconstruction of 'life and material culture'. Yet they do note the potential provided by the reconstruction of the 'Glen Parva lady' at Leicester in stimulating interest in the difference in attitudes to death between the past and present as well as the process of archaeological interpretation: Lucy and Herring 1999, 84.
53. Boyle *et al.* 1998.
54. Carver 2000; Lucy and Herring 1999, 87.
55. Bahn 1996; Bahn 2003; Chamberlain and Parker Pearson 2001.
56. Chamberlain and Parker Pearson 2001, 169–76.
57. Chamberlain and Parker Pearson 2001, 8; Hallam, Hockey and Howarth 1999, 34–42; von Hagaens and Whalley 2001.
58. Jupp and Walter 1999.
59. Fforde, Hubert and Turnbull 2002; Fforde 2004.
60. Lilley, *et al.* 1994.
61. Carroll 2005.
62. Payne 2004; Richards 1999.
63. Fforde 2004.
64. English Heritage/Church of England 2005.
65. Brothwell 2004, 416; Wallis 2001.
66. Carroll 2005; McKinley 2003.
67. Pitts 2006.
68. Härke 2000.
69. Here we might emphasise the critique of the universal use of the term 'ancestors' in both the re-burial debate and in archaeological interpretations of mortuary ritual: see for example Whitley 2002.
70. Hadley 2002.
71. Hirst 2004; MOLAS 2004; Pitts 2006.
72. Brothwell 2004.

Bibliography

Alcock, E. 1992. Burials and cemeteries in Scotland, in N. Edwards and A. Lane (eds) *The Early Church in Wales and the West*, 125–9, Oxbow Monograph, 16, Oxford: Oxbow Books Ltd.

Andrén, A. 1993. Doors to Other Worlds: Scandinavian Death Rituals in Gotlandic Perspective', *Jnl. of European Archaeol.*, **1**, 33–56.

Arnold, C. J. 1980. Wealth and social structure: a matter of life and death, in P. Rahtz, T. Dickinson, and L. Watts (eds) *Anglo-Saxon Cemeteries 1979*, 81–142, BAR British Series, Oxford: British Archaeological Reports.

Bahn, P. (ed.) 1996. *Tombs, Graves and Mummies*, London: Weidenfeld and Nicholson.

Bahn, P. (ed.) 2003. *Written in Bones*, Newton Abbot: David Charles.

Battiscombe, C. F.1956. *The Relics of Saint Cuthbert*, Oxford: Oxford University Press.

Boddington, A. 1996. *Raunds Furnells. The Anglo-Saxon church and churchyard*, English Heritage, Archaeological Report, 7, London: EH.

Bonney, D. 1966. Pagan Saxon burials and boundaries in Wiltshire, *Wiltshire Archaeological Magazine*, **61**, 25–30.

Boyle, A., Jennings, D., Miles, D. and Palmer, S. 1998. *The Anglo-Saxon Cemetery at Butler's Field, Lechlade, Gloucestershire*, Thames Valley Landscapes Monograph No. 10, Oxford: Oxford Archaeology Unit.

Brothwell, D. 2004. Bring out your dead: people, pots and politics, *Antiquity*, **78**(300), 414–18.

Browne, T. 1658. *Hydriotaphia, Urne-Burial, or, a discourse on the Supulchrall Urnes lately found in Norfolk*, London: Brome.

Bruce-Mitford, R. 1975. *The Sutton Hoo Ship-Burial I: Excavations, Background, the Ship, Dating and Inventory*, London: British Museum.

Budd, P., Millard, A., Chenery, C., Lucy, S. and Roberts, C. 2004. Investigating population movement by stable isotopes: a report from Britain, *Antiquity*, **78**(March), 127–41.

Carroll, Q. 2005. Who wants to rebury old skeletons? *British Archaeology*, **82**, 10–15.

Carver, M. 1998. *Sutton Hoo: Burial Ground of Kings?* London: British Museum.

Carver, M. 2000. 'Burial as Poetry: The Context of Treasure in Anglo-Saxon Graves, in E. Tyler (ed.), *Treasure in the Medieval West*, 25–48, York: York Medieval Press.

Carver, M. 2005. *Sutton Hoo: A Seventh-Century Princely Burial Ground and its Context*, London: British Museum.

Chamberlain, A. and Parker Pearson, M. 2001. *Earthly Remains*, London: British Museum Press.

Douglas, J. 1793. *Nenia Britannica*, London: Nichols.

Eckardt, H. and Williams, H. 2003. Objects without a past? The use of Roman objects in early Anglo-Saxon graves, in H. Williams (ed.), *Archaeologies of Remembrance. Death and Memory in Past Societies*, 141–70, New York: Kluwer/Plenum.

Effros, B. 2003a. Memories of the Early Medieval Past: Grave Artefacts in Nineteenth-Century France and Early Twentieth-Century America, in H. Williams (ed.), *Archaeologies of Remembrance: Death and Memory in Past Societies*, 255–80, New York: Kluwer/ Plenum.

Effros, B. 2003b. *Merovingian Mortuary Archaeology and the Making of the Early Middle Ages*, Berkeley: University of California Press.

English Heritage/Church of England. 2005. *Guidance for best practice for treatment of human remains excavated from Christian burial grounds in England*, London: English Heritage/Church of England.

Filmer-Sankey, W. and Pestell, T. 2001. *Snape Anglo-Saxon Cemetery: Excavations and Surveys 1824–1992*, East Anglian Archaeology Report, 95, Ipswich: East Anglian Archaeology.

Fforde, C. 2004. *Collecting the Dead: Archaeology and the Reburial Issue*, London: Duckworth.

Fforde, C., Hubert, J. and Turnbull, P. (eds) 2002. *The Dead and their Possessions: Repatriation in principle, policy and practice*, London: Routledge.

Fowler, C. 2004. *The Archaeology of Personhood*, London: Routledge.

Hadley, D. M. 2002. Burial Practices in Northern England in the Later Anglo-Saxon Period, in S. Lucy and A. Reynolds (eds) *Burial in Early Medieval England and Wales*, 209–28, Society for Medieval Archaeology Monograph, 17, Leeds: Maney.

Hallam, E., Hockey, J. and Howarth, G. 1999. *Beyond the Body: Death and Social Identity*, London: Routledge.

Halsall, G. 2003. Burial Writes: Graves, Texts and Time in Early Merovingian Northern Gaul, in J. Jarnut and M. Wemhoff (eds) *Erinnerungskultur im Bestattungsritual*, 61–74, Munich: Wilhelm Fink.

Härke, H. 2000. The Circulation of Weapons in Anglo-Saxon Society, in F. Theuws and J. L. Nelson (eds), *Rituals of Power From Late Antiquity to the Early Middle Ages*, 377–99, Leiden: Brill.

Haughton, C. and Powlesland, D. 1999. *West Heslerton: The Anglian Cemetery Volume i The Excavation and Discussion of the Evidence*, 2 vols., London: English Heritage.

Hills, C. 2003. *Origins of the English*, London: Duckworth.

Hines, J., Høilund Nielsen, K. and Siegmund, F. (eds) 1999. *The Pace of Change: Studies in Early-Medieval Chronology*, Oxford: Oxbow.

Hirst, S. 1985 *An Anglo-Saxon Inhumation Cemetery at Sewerby East Yorkshire*, York University Archaeological Publications, 4, York: York University.

Hirst, S. 2004. *The Prittlewell Prince: the Discovery of a Rich Anglo-Saxon Burial in Essex*, London: Museum of London.

Holbrook, N. and Thomas, A. 2005. An Early-medieval Monastic Cemetery at Llandough, Glamorgan: Excavations in 1994, *Medieval Archaeology*, **49**, 1–92.

Jupp, P. and Walter, T. 1999. The healthy society: 1918–98, in P. Jupp and C. Gittings (eds), *Death in England*, Manchester: University of Manchester Press.

Leeds, E. T. and Harden, D. 1936. *The Anglo-Saxon Cemetery at Abingdon, Berkshire*, Oxford: Ashmolean.

Lethbridge, T. C. 1931. *Recent Excavations in Anglo-Saxon Cemeteries in Cambridgeshire and Suffolk*, Cambridge: Cambridge Antiquarian Society Quarto Publications. New Series, No. III

Lilley, J. M., Stroud, G., Brothwell, D. R. and Williamson, M. H. 1994. *The Jewish burial ground at Jewbury*, The Archaeology of York, 12/3, York: CBA

Lucy, S. 1998. *The Early Anglo-Saxon Cemeteries of East Yorkshire*, BAR British Series, 272, Oxford: British Archaeological Reports.

Lucy, S. 2000. *The Anglo-Saxon Way of Death*, Stroud: Sutton.

Lucy, S. 2002. From Pots to People: Two Hundred Years of Anglo-Saxon Archaeology, in C. Hough and K. A. Lowe (eds), *'Lastworda Betst' Essays in memory of Christine E. Fell with her unpublished writings*, 144–8, Donnington: Shaun Tyas.

Lucy, S. and Herring, C. 1999. Viewing the 'Dark Ages': The Portrayal of Early Anglo-Saxon Life and Material Culture in Museums, in N. Merriman (ed.), *Making Early Histories in Museums*, 74–94, Leicester: Leicester University Press.

Lucy, S. and Reynolds, A. (eds) 2002. *Burial in Early Medieval England and Wales*, Leeds: Maney.

Mays, S. 1998. *The Archaeology of Human Bones*, London: Routledge.

Marsden, B. 1999. *The Early Barrow Diggers*, Stroud: Tempus.

McKinley, J. 1994. *The Anglo-Saxon Cemetery at Spong Hill, North Elmham. Part VII: The Cremations*, East Anglian Archaeology, 69, Dereham: East Anglian Archaeology.

McKinley, J. 1997 Bronze Age 'Barrows and Funerary Rites and Rituals of Cremation, *Proceedings of the Prehistoric Society*, **63**, 129–45.

McKinley, J. 2003. A Wiltshire 'Bog Body'? Discussion of a Fifth/Sixth Century AD Burial in the Woodford Valley, *Wiltshire Archaeological and Natural History Magazine*, **96**, 7–18.

Meaney, A. L. and Hawkes, S. C. 1970. *Two Anglo-Saxon Cemeteries at Winnall*, Society for Medieval Archaeology Monograph Series, 4, London: SMA.

Miles, D. 2005. *The Tribes of Britain: Who are we? And Where do we come from?* London: Weidenfeld and Nicholson.

MOLAS, 2004. Prittlewell: Treasures of a King of Essex, *Current Archaeology*, **16**(190), 430–36.

Montgomery, J., Evans, J. A., Powlesland, D. and Roberts, C. A. 2005. Continuity or Colonization in Anglo-Saxon England? Isotope Evidence for Mobility, Subsistence Practice, and Status at West Heslerton, *American Jnl. of Physical Anthropology,* **126**, 123–38.

Morse, M. 1999. Craniology and the Adoption of the Three-Age System in Britain, *Proc. Prehistoric Soc.,* **65**, 1–16.

O'Brien, E. 1999. *Post-Roman Britain to Anglo-Saxon England: Burial Practices Reviewed,* BAR British Series, 289, Oxford: British Archaeological Reports

Oestigaard, T. 2000. Sacrifices of Raw, Cooked and Burnt Humans, *Norwegian Archaeological Review,* **33**(1), 41–58.

Pader, E. J. 1982. *Symbolism, social relations and the interpretation of mortuary remains,* British Archaeological Reports International Series, 130, Oxford: British Archaeological Reports.

Payne, S. 2004. Handle with care: thoughts on the return of human bone collections, Antiquity, **78**(June), 419–20.

Parker Pearson, M., Van de Noort, R. and Woolf, A. 1993. Three men and a boat: Sutton Hoo and the East Anglian Kingdom, *Anglo-Saxon England,* **22**, 27–50.

Parker Pearson, M. and Ramilisonina, 1998. Stonehenge for the ancestors: the stones pass on the message, *Antiquity,* **72**(December), 308–26.

Pitts, M. 2006. Bling King's Last Battle, *British Archaeology,* **88**, 40–43.

Plunkett, S. 2002. *Sutton Hoo,* London: The National Trust.

Poulton, R. 1990. *Saxon Secrets in Surrey,* Woking: ExxonMobil.

Pryor, F. 2005. *Britain AD,* London: Harper Collins.

Redknap, M. 2002. *Re-Creations: Visualizing Our Past,* Cardiff: National Museums and Galleries of Wales/Cadw.

Richards, J. D. 1987. *The Significance of Form and Decoration of Anglo-Saxon Cremation Urns,* BAR British Series, 166, Oxford: British Archaeological Reports.

Richards, J. 1999. *Meet the Ancestors,* London: BBC.

Rippon, S. 2000. Landscapes in transition: the later Roman and early medieval periods, in D. Hooke (ed.), *Landscape: the richest historical record,* 42–62, Amesbury: Society for Landscape Studies.

Rodwell, W. and Rodwell, K. 1983. St. Peter's Church, Barton-upon-Humber: Excavation and Structural Study, 1978–81, *Antiquaries Jnl.,* **62**(II), 283–315.

Semple, S. 1998. A Fear of the Past: the place of the prehistoric burial mound in the ideology of middle and later Anglo-Saxon England, *World Archaeol.,* **30**(1), 109–26.

Semple, S. 2004. Illustrations of damnation in late Anglo-Saxon manuscripts, *Anglo-Saxon England,* **32**, 231–45.

Smith. C. R. 1848. Warwickshire Antiquities, *Collectanea Antiqua,* **1**, 33–48.

Smith, L. 2004. The repatriation of human remains – problem or opportunity, *Antiquity,* **78**(June), 404–12.

Stoodley, N. 1999. *The Spindle and the Spear,* BAR British Series, 288, Oxford: British Archaeological Reports.

Tarlow, S. 1999. *Bereavement and Commemoration*, Oxford: Blackwell.

Thompson, V. 2004. *Dying and Death in Later Anglo-Saxon England,* Woodbridge: Boydell.

von Hagens, G. and Whalley, A. 2001. *Körperwelten: Catalogue on the Exhibition,* Heidelberg: Institute for Plastination.

Wallis, R. 2001. Waking Ancestor Spirits: Neo-Shamanic Engagements with Archaeology, in N. Price (ed.), *The Archaeology of Shamanism,* 213–30, London: Routledge.

Webster, L. 1992. Death's Diplomacy: Sutton Hoo in the Light of Other Male Princely Burials, in R. Farrell and C. Newman de Vegvar (eds), *Sutton Hoo: Fifty Years After,* 75–82, Oxford: Oxbow.

West, S. 2000. *Understanding West Stow*, Norwich: Jarrold.

Whitley, J. 2002. Too many ancestors, *Antiquity,* **76**(March), 119–26.

Williams, H. 2004. Death Warmed Up: the agency of bodies and bones in early Anglo-Saxon cremation rites, *Jnl. Material Culture,* **9**(3), 263–91.

Williams, H. 2005. Review article: rethinking early medieval mortuary archaeology, *Early Medieval Europe,* **13**(2), 195–217.

Williams, H. 2006. *Death and Memory in Early Medieval Britain,* Cambridge: Cambridge University Press.

Williams, H. 2007. The emotive force of early medieval mortuary partcices. *Archaeological Review from Cambridge* 22.1: 107–23.

Wylie, W. M. 1852. *Fairford Graves,* Oxford: Parker.

Ethnicity, 'Race' and Migration in Mortuary Archaeology: an Attempt at a Short Answer

Heinrich Härke

This is a belated answer to a question from the audience in the last few minutes of the concluding discussion of the Exeter conference. The essence of the question was: 'What is the current state of thinking on the inference of ethnicity and race from archaeological evidence? How can we play the numbers game concerning the relationship between immigrants and natives in the Migration Period?' The question was not directed at anybody in particular, but a reference to my interest in this matter made clear that it was indirectly meant for me. However, it was such a big question on a complex issue that I was unwilling to give an off-the-cuff answer. Having had some time to consider it, I am willing to give it a try now given the continued importance of the question for the study of early medieval mortuary practices. But in relation to the complexity of the question, it will have to be a reasonably short answer – books can be, and have been, written on this question.[1] Inevitably, it will also reflect my own current thinking on this subject more than that of the discipline as a whole, not least because I retained an interest in the archaeological identification of ethnicity and migration throughout the time when these topics were considered to be deeply unfashionable or even objectionable in some quarters of British archaeology. The emphasis will be more on archaeology than physical anthropology in which I cannot claim specialist expertise; mine is therefore a consumer's perspective on skeletal data.

First of all, we need some clarification of the terminology in order to avoid (or remove) confusion. The concept of 'race' was originally meant as a tool of *biological* classification, and if it is used at all (see below), it should be limited to this. Ethnicity, by contrast, is a *cultural* concept, describing perceptions and expressions of group identity as seen by observers or the respective people themselves. Students of the Early Middle Ages will also frequently encounter the term 'tribe': strictly speaking, 'tribes' are units within a segmentary type of *social* organisation, and they should therefore be conceptually distinct from 'racial' and 'ethnic' groups. In addition, names of *language* groups

(Celts, Germani, Slavs, Balts, Turks etc.) are often used in early medieval archaeology as if they reflect biological or cultural group affiliations or even socio-political units – which they do not, neither in principle nor, mostly, in practice.

Unfortunately, recent political terminology has muddied the waters, with 'ethnicity' becoming the politically acceptable term for what used to be called 'race', possibly because the latter term has become tainted with the connotation of racism (as ethnicity has now become tainted by the association with ethnic violence and ethnic cleansing). It does not help that some scholarly texts, particularly history textbooks, still use 'race' to describe culturally or historically defined groups of people.[2] In a more general, but equally wrong sense, 'race' is occasionally used for the entire human species (the 'human race').

'Race' in Archaeology and Physical Anthropology

Let us start with 'race' because the answer to the original question is reasonably straightforward: You *cannot* infer race from archaeological evidence because it is a biological concept, and as such it cannot be inferred from cultural remains. For this, you would need biological evidence, *i.e.* human bones, blood groups, DNA etc. The analysis of skeletal traits, in particular skull shapes (craniology) which were seen as racially diagnostic, underpinned much of the race anthropology of the late nineteenth and early twentieth century. There was also a widespread assumption that, once the traits of a particular 'race' had been established, not only would it be possible to distinguish it from other 'races', but also the 'racial' origins of individuals could be established using their skeletal measurements and ratios.

However, biologists have become very dissatisfied with the concept of race, mainly for two reasons. The first is the vagueness of the concept itself: race was intended to be the highest category of classification below the level of species; but because at this level interbreeding is, by definition, possible, the resulting races were found to have fuzzy boundaries and marked overlaps.[3] The second reason (which often appears to be the more important one in modern attitudes) was the blatant misuse of the concept of race in late nineteenth and early twentieth century scholarship and politics.[4] Today, the concept has been all but abandoned in physical anthropology.[5]

The Archaeological Inference of Ethnic Identity

Ethnicity is a different matter. Because it is a cultural phenomenon, it should, in principle, be possible to infer it from cultural evidence, including archaeological remains. In early medieval archaeology, such inferences have routinely been made using grave-goods, in particular female dress items, to identify 'tribes' (usually meaning ethnic groups) named in the written sources of the period, to follow their migrations, and to identify the 'tribal' affiliations of individuals.

However, this concept has also undergone extensive re-assessment. Historians of the Early Middle Ages have re-thought ethnic identity since the 1960s.[6] As a result, early medieval ethnic identity is now commonly seen as a 'situational construct':[7] it is considered to be not 'in the blood', but 'in the head', and therefore flexible and changeable. The archaeological re-assessment, beginning around 1980, emphasized the role of the elite in creating ethnic identities,[8] and added the point that an indivdual's identity is made up of multiple, intersecting identities (or 'nested identities' as Susanne Hakenbeck put it in her paper at the Exeter conference): age, gender, household, locality and ethnicity. This has created a widespread scepticism among Anglophone archaeologists against the possibility of inferring ethnic identity, and even against the idea that ethnicity may have been important in the past and/or should be an aspect of study now.[9]

It took the ethnic wars of the 1990s in the Balkans, the North Caucasus and Africa to stop this trend.[10] Few will doubt now that ethnicity was an important facet of identity in the Early Middle Ages; and it is widely accepted again that ethnic identity, like other identities, may find an expression through material culture,[11] ritual behaviour and social practices.[12] The historian Peter Heather has critiqued the extreme view that ethnic identity is wholly arbitrary and a simple matter of individual choice. He has stressed that the group must accept an individual's self-identification with that group, or it is meaningless.[13] In the discussion at the Exeter conference, Martin Welch pointed out another important aspect: the concept of the individual used in much of post-processualist theory is a modern one, whereas in the Early Middle Ages, kinship and group affiliation may have been much more important in shaping the material expression of identity (*e.g.* in dress or burial rites).

So, what can we realistically do to infer ethnic groups in the Early Middle Ages? Let us start with a statement of the obvious: right across early medieval Europe, we can observe distinct styles of dress and other material culture at various geographical levels. In many cases, these styles are accompanied by variations and differences in burial rites, domestic architecture and spatial organisation that in some cases extend down to the local level. Some of these differences may be due to environmental and economic factors, but many, perhaps most, are likely to be the expressions or reflections of group identities. There is every reason to believe that the regional identities reflected in the archaeological evidence include ethnic identities the existence of which is known, in principle, from the written sources of the period.

For example, distributions of supposedly 'Lombard', 'Frankish', 'Saxon' etc. brooches coincide quite well with historians' expectations concerning generalized locations and extent of these ethnic groups (which is, of course, why certain brooch styles were given these ethnic labels in the first place). In some cases, distributions of burial rites coincide with these broad patterns. Siegmund has mapped distinctive details of mortuary rites at the cemetery level in western Europe, noting three large regional groups which in his opinion broadly reflect Franks, Alamanni and Old (*i.e.* Continental) Saxons.[14] The distributions of ethnic markers in all these cases have blurred boundaries and some overlaps, which is exactly what one might expect as a result of contact, intermarriage and individual mobility.

All this does not mean that all ethnic groups of this period will show up reasonably clearly in the mortuary (or other archaeological) evidence. Nor does it mean that every individual buried in a distinctive ethnic style thought of herself or himself as belonging to that group. If identity is 'in the head', there is no certain way of knowing if the material culture adopted for the burial of any one individual accurately reflects his or her identity (if, indeed, it can be accurately reflected at all). Somebody buried in Frankish dress in a Frankish cemetery may well come from this, or another Frankish, community, and have considered himself or herself to be Frankish. Alternatively, the community may have decided to bury this individual in Frankish style because of strong normative ideas about dress styles or burial rites. Or the mourners used an ethnically specific burial rite to express a claim to identity and status, irrespective of actual origins.

Given these uncertainties, what are we to make of those early medieval burials which stand out from their local and regional context by dress or equipment apparently signalling a different ethnic background? Such cases include the 'Lombard' princess in one of the burials under Cologne cathedral in the Frankish Rhineland,[15] and the 'Goth' buried in Gloucester among West Saxons.[16] We cannot exclude the possibility that the respective individuals had simply chosen to wear and/or use items different from the style of his or her ethnic group. On the other hand, we have to bear in mind that the concepts of individual dress taste and unfettered free choice are largely post-medieval and, indeed, modern. This, in turn, brings us back to the possibility that such individuals were migrants whose equipment and dress, whether worn in life or only now in death, signaled their distinctive origins. This takes account of the role of mortuary dress and grave-goods as 'metaphors': items that symbolize events in the life of the deceased, and are used by the mourners as a means of memory and remembrance.[17]

Group Affiliation in Physical Anthropology

With the concept of identifiable 'races' having been abandoned by physical anthropologists, any approach to group affiliation has to be based on the concept of populations – local population samples being the skeletons from a single cemetery each, regional populations comprised of the cemeteries of one period in any one region (however defined) each, *etc.*[18] Such populations are not classified according to some predetermined 'racial' criteria. They are, rather, analysed in their own right, each local population characterized in terms of metric and nonmetric traits. These data may then be compared with those of other populations in order to infer differences and similarities and, ideally, a measure of biological distance. This distance reflects the level of genetic exchange between the populations (or more precisely: the samples available from the populations) which are being compared, although it needs to be borne in mind that some data types and traits are modified by, or reflect, environmental stress.

Comparisons of the skeletal data of local and regional populations across western Europe have shown up identifiable and measurable differences between many early medieval populations.[19] These differences are sometimes subtle, but quite often reasonably clear-cut and significant, usually more so with increasing geographical distance. Such similarities and differences can provide us with information about the degree of physical contact between various populations, maintained by intermarriage, individual mobility, migration etc. In the same way that archaeological patterns may be used to identify areas of *cultural* contact, patterns of skeletal data may tell us about areas of *biological* contact (or lack thereof). Thus, Blondiaux has analysed the skeletal data of the cemetery of Vron (Somme, France) and found that its metric patterns do not fit into the regional and chronological context of early medieval northern France.[20] Its closest similarities appear to be to cemeteries in northern Germany, and Blondiaux concluded that Vron represents an immigrant population from that region.

DNA can be used, in principle, for the same purpose.[21]

But the study of ancient human DNA has not yet been very successful for technical reasons; and the growing field of modern DNA analyses is a different matter, located as it is outside the study of burials and cemeteries which is of interest here.

As with archaeological data, there is a much greater uncertainty when it comes to the identification of the group affiliation of individuals through biological data. Identifying skeletal differences between populations is a matter of statistics – it does *not* mean that each individual of population A differs from each individual of population B. In fact, it is much more typical of contemporaneous populations from the same part of the world to overlap in their measurements, even if their averages are sufficiently different. The reason for this is that the frequencies of measurements or traits of each population are spread in a normal (Gaussian) distribution, or 'bell curve'. The greater the similarity between two populations, the greater their overlap. As a rule, therefore, the identification of the origin population of an individual is, at best, difficult; the likelihood of identification depends on good comparative samples; and the result is always a statement of statistical rather than absolute validity. The Ice Man ('Ötzi') from the Tyrolean Alps is perhaps the best known, recent example of an attempt to identify the biological origins of an isolated individual. His skull data were compared with those of more than a hundred prehistoric and later skulls from Alpine and North Italian regions, leading to the suggestion that he belonged to a population from south of the Alpine chain.[22]

Such cases are rare in early medieval archaeology. Here, a bigger issue is the occasional existence of exceptional individuals which fall well outside the distribution of skeletal traits of the local population (*i.e.* cemetery) they have been found in. Early attempts to identify such individuals as migrants have subsequently met with marked scepticism, but in the discussion at the Exeter conference, Jackie McKinley commented that the pendulum is swinging back: the observation of individuals falling outside the pattern of their respective local populations is now accepted again as a starting point for considering the possibility of their foreign origins. The procedure for this is the same as that for studying the similarities of populations: traits and measurements are compared with patterns observed elsewhere, with the aim to see where that individual might fit in best (and certainly better than in his/her local population).

The Identification of Immigrants and Natives

The archaeological identification of migrations is a wide field of debate of its own. Here, as in other areas of the discipline mentioned above, simplistic assumptions which underpinned past approaches have been re-assessed and replaced with more critical perspectives. Thus, the old idea that burial ritual would be one of the most stable elements of culture, and therefore the best indicator of migration,[23] has been replaced by the realization that cultural elements may change during migrations, and that archaeologists should not look for one-to-one correspondences, neither in mortuary ritual nor in other elements, in order to identify migrations and origins of migrants.[24] Having said this, it is clear that in some cases, burial rites and grave-goods can be used convincingly to identify early medieval migrations, but factors such as acculturation and environmental adaptation must constantly be borne in mind. Not all probable migrations show up in the burial record; and not all apparently intrusive burial rites need be those of immigrants. In the Anglo-Saxon case (which remains one of the best case studies of migration, in spite of almost two decades of critical debate),[25] only part of the burial record, that of cremations, is a convincing piece of mortuary evidence in favour of immigration, whilst the equally frequent inhumation rite is open to different interpretations.

Much the same can be said about the identification of migration from the skeletal record. Whilst it is obvious that there were distinct biological populations in early medieval Europe (cf. above), it is equally obvious that not all migrations would show up in the skeletal record, and that by no means all differences between local and regional populations would be the consequences of migrations. Also, existing differences between populations may be blurred by physical changes which may affect migrant populations,[26] and by intermarriage and assimilation.

This brings us to the question of distinguishing immigrants from natives and assessing their numerical proportions. Much of the answer to this question follows directly from what has been said above and in previous sections, but it can be focused down now on cases of immigrants and natives living in close proximity, as they apparently did in most early medieval cases of migration and settlement. Whilst it may seem obvious, it needs to be stated clearly that it is only possible under certain conditions to distinguish immigrants from natives: Both groups need to be archaeologically visible; and the two groups need to be sufficiently different from one another culturally and/or biologically.

These points are important because there are two widespread and frequent problems militating against such distinctions. The first is that of acculturation and assimilation, and to a certain extent, environmental and economic adaptation. Whether immigrants are assimilated into the native population or *vice versa*, or natives adopt the culture of the immigrants or *vice versa*, such processes of convergence will mean that a distinction is only possible in the initial phase(s) – and given the considerable error span of archaeological dating, the duration of this initial contact phase is critical. Separation, segregation or even apartheid (all of them documented for the early middle ages) may considerably extend the time span during which a distinction of immigrants and natives may be possible.

Rapid integration and acculturation (equally well documented for this period) would make a distinction by archaeological or skeletal means virtually impossible, except by the use of stable isotopes (see below). The second problem which is typical of the post-Roman period is the archaeological invisibility of the natives in the wake of social and economic collapse in the Western Roman Empire.[27] And where you can find only immigrants, but not the natives, you cannot infer much about the relationship between the two groups.

The combined use of archaeological and biological data should improve the chances of identifying immigrants, at least in some cases. In other cases, it is quite possible that the use of these two different data sets, each with their own inherent problems and margins of error, may increase uncertainties and error spans. A useful case study of the biological identification of an immigrant population from skeletal data is that of Vron in northern France (cf. above),[28] but this is also a case where archaeology and written sources could be cited in support of the inference of non-local origins, leading to the ethnic identification of the immigrants as Saxons from northern Germany (for other cases of a coincidence of biological and cultural indicators, cf. the discussion of stable isotope analysis below). Incidentally, the Vron case highlights another important point. In initial contact situations as they arise during migrations, there may well be a temporary coincidence of biological populations and ethnic identities (*i.e.* immigrants and natives remain distinct and separate in both, biology and culture), and such a coincidence may be prolonged by social means or political measures (*e.g.* apartheid). The use of both types of data is necessary to identify such situations.

The argument occasionally used against such a procedure, that biological origins do not matter because identity is 'in the head', is a red herring. The comparison of biological origins and cultural expressions can tell us much more about the workings of identity in the context of immigration than either type of evidence could tell us in isolation. To use an entirely fictitious example: A cemetery in which all the deceased had been buried in, say, Japanese style may tell us about uniform expressions of identity in death, but not much else. If, however, one of the skeletons could be identified, with reasonable certainty, as that of a European, we would immediately have a fascinating case study of migration, acculturation and integration, not least because Japanese identity is highly exclusive, and non-Japanese foreigners are hardly ever accepted into it.

In addition, there are cases where cultural and biological data cannot be neatly separated. Diet is such an aspect, but an even clearer, early medieval case in point is artificial skull deformation which is a *cultural* practice typical among nomad elites (Huns, Sarmatians, Alans), but it has to be identified from the *skeletal* remains. The appearance of skull deformation in early medieval contexts of eastern and central Europe is generally interpreted as a sign of nomad immigration, or an indicator of social dominance by intrusive nomad groups.[29] In North American archaeology, artificial skull deformation is used as an identifier of particular cultural groups and their movements.[30]

In Europe, there have been several cases where it has been possible to suggest the existence of post-Roman natives and immigrants in close proximity to one another. In the German Rhineland, this has been achieved via a distinction of the respective burial rites; the two groups have been found partly in separate cemeteries, partly together in cemeteries (such as Krefeld-Gellep) which continued in use from the Late Roman to the post-Roman period.[31] In southwest Germany and northern Switzerland, it has been suggested that immigrants and natives were buried together in the same cemeteries, and their distinction has been attempted with a combination of archaeological and skeletal data.[32] In England, very few post-Roman British cemeteries have been found, with probably the clearest case being Queenford Farm (Oxfordshire) where radiocarbon dates range from the Late Roman to the sub-Roman period and the burial rites are in clear contrast to nearby, contemporaneous Anglo-Saxon cemeteries.[33] My own analysis of the skeletal data of archaeologically defined groups (men with and without weapons) has led to the suggestion that Britons made up a substantial proportion of males (usually buried without weapons) in most early Anglo-Saxon inhumation cemeteries.[34]

Given the relatively few cases of such identifications, the only possible approach to estimating the numerical ratios of immigrants to natives in any area or country is to calculate a local (within-site) or regional (between-sites) ratio and extrapolate from that, taking into account factors such as overrepresentation of one group (usually the immigrants) and invisible enclaves (usually natives). This approach can only produce absolute figures for the two groups if there are already estimates for one of them; otherwise, the ratio is all that can be achieved on the basis of archaeological evidence. Most estimates for the immigration into post-Roman England are little more than intuitive guesswork. A more systematic, recent attempt started out from the ratio of suggested British to Anglo-Saxon men in Anglo-Saxon cemeteries; made allowances for British local and regional enclaves, and for the lower level of immigration outside southern and eastern England; used the latest population estimates for Roman Britain, but assumed a marked decline in the Late Roman and post-Roman periods; and produced an estimate of relative and absolute numbers of immigrants into early post-Roman Britain.[35] Even if the results of such attempts cannot be more than broad estimates, they are still useful as a background for the discussion of relations between the groups, and of processes such as acculturation and assimilation.

For the future, stable isotope analysis offers great promise for the identification of individual migrants and, by extension, of immigrant groups and their numerical proportions in native populations. Stable isotopes create in living beings a signature of trace elements found in their diet and in the local ground water, and some of this signature is preserved permanently (particularly in teeth), irrespective of subsequent mobility. This implies the possibility of identifying first-generation immigrants (but *not* their locally-born descendants) if their stable isotope ratios are different from those of natives, and identifying their area(s) of childhood residence if the ground-water isotope composition of those area(s) differs from that of their settlement area(s).

Whilst most stable-isotope studies have analysed diet,[36] a recent project has specifically focused on migration; the preliminary results confirm that 'it is possible to identify first generation [sic] northern European and Scandinavian immigrants in early medieval England'.[37] In the Anglo-Saxon cemetery of West Heslerton (North Yorkshire), the data suggest a considerable degree of regional (within-Britain) and overseas mobility, with possibly up to seventeen per cent first-generation immigrants from Scandinavia or eastern Continental Europe among the cemetery population.[38] An extension of this project to other Anglo-Saxon cemeteries in eastern England has resulted in the identification of an even greater proportion of first-generation immigrants from across the North Sea.[39] In the case of the Late Saxon and Viking site of Repton (Derbyshire), the isotope analysis shows that the male individuals suggested on archaeological and skeletal grounds to have been Vikings are, indeed, likely to have come from Scandinavia.[40]

Summary

This paper is not so much an attempt to present a particular argument (except, perhaps, concerning the possibility of identifying immigrants and natives), but rather a contribution to conceptual and terminological clarity which is required when dealing with the highly complex issues of cultural and biological affiliations in a period of intersecting and shifting identities.

Concerning the identification of early medieval groups, the different types of evidence show up different aspects: archaeological evidence reflects culture, and thus identities (including ethnic identities); skeletal evidence is biological, and therefore reflects populations. With both types of evidence, the broad inferences of groups are much safer than attempts to identify the group affiliation of individuals. The concept of 'race' cannot be applied to archaeological evidence, and has been abandoned for the interpretation of skeletal evidence.

Using both types of evidence either separately or in conjunction, the identification of immigrant and native populations in early medieval Europe should be possible under certain circumstances, but has rarely been achieved. Proceeding from the mere identification to calculating the approximate ratio of immigrants to natives for any place or region is even more difficult, and depends on more assumptions than some scholars will feel comfortable with. Certainly, the results of such attempts cannot be more than very rough 'guesstimates'. Stable isotope analysis promises a better approach for future migration studies, both in terms of the direct identification of immigrants and their origins, and in terms of the quantification of the ratio of immigrants and natives.

Acknowledgements

I am grateful to Howard Williams for accepting my late contribution for publication, and for his comments on the first draft. I am also indebted to my Reading colleague, Dr Mary Lewis, for reading the draft text and for commenting, in particular, on the physical anthropology sections.

Notes

1. Jones 1997; cf. also Trigger 1978.
2. *E.g.* the 'races' of the Normans, Saxons, Welsh, Flemings *etc.*; Davies 1987, 97, 99, 103; Golding 1994, 94, 179, 188.
3. See Mead, Dobzhansky, Tobach and Light 1968, *passim*; for problems of the concept, cf. *e.g.* Kohn 1995; Orser 2004.
4. Fetten 2002.
5. However, race often still provides a necessary challenge for forensic archaeologists; pers. comm. M. Lewis, Reading.
6. Wenskus 1961; for an overview of the debate see Pohl 1994.
7. Geary 1983.
8. *E.g.* James 1979, elaborating on the key point made by Wenskus.
9. *E.g.* Lucy 1998.
10. Härke 2004; for an earlier re-affirmation see Megaw and Megaw 1996, 1998.
11. Hodder 1982.
12. Jones 1997.
13. Heather 1998.
14. Siegmund 2000.
15. Werner 1964.
16. Hills and Hurst 1989.
17. After B. Solberg; Härke 2003, 114–15.
18. Mays 1998, 74–121; see also Brothwell 1981, particularly 102–109; Czarnetzki, Uhlig, Wolf and Schwarz 1983, 6–9.
19. *E.g.* Rösing and Schwidetzky 1977.
20. Blondiaux 1989.
21. Renfrew and Boyle 2000; for problems see Richards *et al.* 1995; Stoneking 1995.
22. Bernhard 1994.

23. *E.g.* Clarke 1975.
24. Burmeister 2000.
25. Cf. the recent summary by Hills 2003.
26. Boas 1912. I am grateful to Duncan Sayer (Reading) for pointing out to me that this research was undertaken for the US Government (Senate Document 208, 61st Congress, Second Session, 1911).
27. Härke *forthcoming.*
28. Blondiaux 1989.
29. *E.g.* Bóna 2002, 26, 160; Czarnetzki *et al.* 1983, 100–1.
30. *E.g.* the report by C. Bradley on the human remains of the Woods Canyon Pueblo site, at http://www.crowcanyon.org.
31. Ament 1978; Bierbrauer 1996; for Krefeld-Gellep, cf. Pirling 1989.
32. Straub 1956; Huber 1967; Reich 1996.
33. Chambers 1987.
34. Härke 1990, 1992; for critical comments, cf. Tyrell 2000; Lucy 2000, 74.
35. Härke 1999; summarized in Härke 2002.
36. See the overviews by Price 1989; Schoeninger and Moore 1992.
37. Budd, Millard, Chenery, Lucy and Roberts 2004, 139.
38. Ibid., 135; cf. also Montgomery, Evans, Powlesland and Roberts 2005; http://www.dur.ac.uk/p.d.budd/isogeochem/west_hes.html
39. S. Lucy, paper given at the Internationales Sachsensymposium 2004, Cambridge.
40. Budd *et al.* 2004, 137–8; for a similar coincidence of archaeological and stable isotope indicators, see now the analysis of four male individuals from central Europe (Hungary?) buried in the Late Roman cemetery of Winchester-Lankhills; N. Stoodley, paper given at the Internationales Sachsensymposium 2004, Cambridge.

Bibliography

Ament, H. 1978. Franken und Romanen im Merowingerreich als archäologisches Forschungsproblem, *Bonner Jahrbücher*, **178**, 377–94.

Bernhard, W. 1994. Anthropological Studies of the Mummy, *Coll. Anthropol.*, **18**, 241–67.

Bierbrauer, V. 1996. Romanen im fränkischen Siedelgebiet, in *Die Franken: Wegbereiter Europas. Vor 1500 Jahren: König Chlodwig und seine Erben* (exhibition catalogue, Reiss-Museum Mannheim), vol. 1, 110–20, Mainz: Philipp von Zabern.

Blondiaux, J. 1989. Évolution d'une population d'immigrés en Gaule du nord de la fin du IVe siècle à la fin du VIIe siècle: Vron (Somme), in *Actes des 4e Journées Anthropologiques*, 57–71, Dossier de Documentation Archéologiques 13, Paris: CNRS.

Boas, F. 1912. Changes in the Bodily Form of Descendants of Immigrants, *American Anthropologist*, **14**(3), 530–62.

Bóna, I. 2002. *Les Huns. Le grand empire barbare d'Europe (IVᵉ–Vᵉ siècles)*, Paris: Editions Errance.

Brothwell, D. 1981. *Digging up Bones*, London and Oxford: British Museum (Natural History) and Oxford University Press.

Budd, P., Millard, A., Chenery, C., Lucy, S. and Roberts, C. 2004. Investigating Population Movement by Stable Isotope Analysis: a Report from Britain, *Antiquity*, **78**, 127–40.

Burmeister, S. 2000. Archaeology and Migration: Approaches to an Archaeological Proof of Migration, *Current Anthropology*, **41**(4), 539–67.

Chambers, R. A. 1987. The Late- and Sub-Roman Cemetery at Queenford Farm, Dorchester-on-Thames, Oxon, *Oxoniensia*, **52**, 35–69.

Clarke, G. 1975. Popular Movements and Late Roman Cemeteries, *World Archaeology*, **7**(1), 45–56.

Czarnetzki, A., Uhlig, C., Wolf, R. and Schwarz, T. 1983. *Skelette erzählen: Menschen des frühen Mittelalters im Spiegel der Anthropologie und Medizin*, 2nd edit., Stuttgart: Württembergisches Landesmuseum.

Davies, R. R. 1987. *The Age of Conquest: Wales 1063–1415*, Oxford and New York: Oxford University Press.

Fetten, F. 2002. Archaeology and Anthropology in Germany before 1945, in H. Härke (ed.), *Archaeology, Ideology and Society: the German Experience*, 140–79, Gesellschaften und Staaten im Epochenwandel, 7, 2nd edit., Berne and Frankfurt a.M.: Peter Lang.

Geary, P. J. 1983. Ethnic Identity as a Situational Construct in the Early Middle Ages, *Mitteilungen der Anthropologischen Gesellschaft in Wien*, **113**, 15–26.

Golding, B. 1994. *Conquest and Colonisation: The Normans in Britain, 1066–1100*, British History in Perspective ser., New York: St. Martin's Press.

Härke, H. 1990. 'Warrior Graves'? The Background of the Anglo-Saxon Weapon Burial Rite, *Past and Present*, **126**, 22–43.

Härke, H. 1992. *Angelsächsische Waffengräber des 5. bis 7. Jahrhunderts*, Beihefte der Zeitschrift für Archäologie des Mittelalters 6, Cologne and Bonn: Rheinland-Verlag and Habelt.

Härke, H. 1999. Sächsische Ethnizität und archäologische Deutung im frühmittelalterlichen England, *Studien zur Sachsenforschung*, **12**, 109–22.

Härke, H. 2002. Kings and Warriors: Population and Landscape from Post-Roman to Norman Britain, in P. Slack and R. Ward (eds), *The peopling of Britain: the shaping of a human landscape (The Linacre Lectures 1999)*, 145–75, Oxford: Oxford University Press.

Härke, H. 2003. Beigabensitte und Erinnerung: Überlegungen zu einem Aspekt des frühmittelalterlichen Bestattungsrituals, in J. Jarnut and M. Wemhoff (eds), *Erinnerungskultur im Bestattungsritual. Archäologisch-Historisches Forum*, 107–25, MittelalterStudien des Instituts zur Interdisziplinären Erforschung des Mittelalters und seines Nachwirkens, 3, Munich: Fink.

Härke, H. 2004. The Debate on Migration and Identity in Europe, *Antiquity*, **78**, 453–6.

Härke, H. forthcoming. Invisible Britons, Gallo-Romans and Russians: Perspectives on Culture Change, in N. Higham (ed.), *Britons in Anglo-Saxon England*, Manchester: MANCASS.

Heather, P. 1998. Signs of Ethnic Identity: Disappearing and Reappearing Tribes, in W. Pohl and H. Reimitz (eds), *Strategies of Distinction*, 95–111, ESF Transformation of the Roman World ser., 2, Leiden: Brill.

Hills, C., and Hurst, H. 1989. A Goth at Gloucester? *Antiquaries Journal*, **69**(1), 154–8.

Hodder, I. 1982. *Symbols in Action: Ethnoarchaeological Studies of Material Culture*, New Studies in Archaeology ser., Cambridge: Cambridge University Press.

Huber, N. M. 1967. *Anthropologische Untersuchungen an den Skeletten aus dem alamannischen Reihengräberfeld von Weingarten, Kr. Ravensburg*, Naturwissenschaftliche Untersuchungen zur Vor- und Frühgeschichte in Württemberg und Hohenzollern, 3, Stuttgart: Müller & Gräff.

James, E. 1979. Cemeteries and the Problem of Frankish Settlement in Gaul, in P. H. Sawyer (ed.), *Names, words and graves: Early medieval Settlement*, 55–89, Leeds: School of History.

Jones, S. 1997. *The Archaeology of Ethnicity*, London: Routledge.

Kohn, M. 1995. *The Race Gallery: The Return of Racial Science*, London: Jonathan Cape.

Lucy, S. 1998. *The Early Anglo-Saxon Cemeteries of East Yorkshire: an Analysis and Reinterpretation*, BAR British Series, 272, Oxford: Hedges.

Lucy, S. 2000. *The Anglo-Saxon Way of Death: Burial Rites in Early England*, Stroud: Sutton.

Mays, S. 1998. *The Archaeology of Human Bones*, London: Routledge.

Mead, M., Dobzhansky, T., Tobach, E. and Light, R. E. (eds) 1968. *Science and the Concept of Race*, New York and London: Columbia University Press.

Megaw, J. V. S., and Megaw, M. R. 1996. Ancient Celts and Modern Ethnicity, *Antiquity*, **70**, 175–81.

Megaw, J. V. S., and Megaw, M. R. 1998. 'The Mechanism of (Celtic) Dreams?': a Partial Response to our Critics, *Antiquity*, **72**, 432–5.

Montgomery, J., Evans, J. A., Powlesland, D. and Roberts, C. A. 2005. Continuity or Colonization in Anglo-Saxon England? Isotopes Evidence for Mobility, Subsistence Practice, and Status at West Heslerton, *American Journal of Physical Anthropology*, 126, 123–38.

Orser, C. E. 2004. *Race and Practice in Archaeological Interpretation*, Archaeology, Culture and Society ser., Philadelphia: University of Pensylvania Press.

Pirling, R. 1989. *Das römisch-fränkische Gräberfeld von Krefeld-Gellep 1966–1974*, Germanische Denkmäler der Völkerwanderungszeit, B 13, Stuttgart: Franz Steiner.

Pohl, W. 1994. Tradition, Ethnogenese und literarische Gestaltung: eine Zwischenbilanz, in K. Brunner and B. Merta (eds), *Ethnogenese und Überlieferung: angewandte Methoden der Frühmittelalterforschung*, 9–26, Vienna and Munich: Oldenbourg

Price, T. D. (ed.) 1989. *The Chemistry of Prehistoric Human Bone*, Cambridge: Cambridge University Press.

Reich, Y. 1996. Das frühmittelalterliche Gräberfeld von Villigen AG, *Jahrbuch der Schweizerischen Gesellschaft für Ur- und Frühgeschichte*, **76**, 67–118.

Renfrew, C. and Boyle, K. (eds). 2000. *Archaeogenetics: DNA and the Population Prehistory of Europe*, Cambridge: McDonald Institute for Archaeological Research.

Richards, M., Sykes, B. and Hedges, R. 1995. Authenticating DNA Extracted from Ancient Skeletal Remains, *Journal of Archaeological Science*, **22**, 291–9.

Rösing, F. W. and Schwidetzky, I. 1977. Vergleichend-statistische Untersuchungen zur Anthropologie des frühen Mittelalters (500–1000 n.d.Z.), *Homo*, **28**, 65–115.

Schoeninger, M. J. and Moore, K. 1992. Bone Stable Isotope Studies in Archaeology, *Journal of World Prehistory*, **6:2**, 247–96.

Siegmund, F. 2000. *Alemannen und Franken. Archäologische Studie zu Ethnien und ihren Siedlungsräumen in der Merowingerzeit*, Ergänzungsbände zum Reallexikon der Germanischen Altertumskunde, 23, Berlin and New York: W. de Gruyter.

Stoneking, M. 1995. Ancient DNA: How Do You Know when You Have It and What Can You Do with It? *American Journal of Human Genetics*, **57**, 1259–62.

Straub, R. 1956. Zur Kontinuität der voralamannischen Bevölkerung, *Badische Fundberichte*, **20**, 127–37.

Trigger, B. 1978. Race, Language and Culture, in B. Trigger, *Time and Traditions: Essays in Archaeological Interpretation*, 122–31, Edinburgh: Edinburgh University Press.

Tyrell, A. J. 2000. Corpus Saxonum: Early medieval Bodies and Corporeal Identity, in W. O. Frazer and A. J. Tyrell (eds), *Social Identity in Early medieval Britain*, 137–155, London: Leicester University Press.

Werner, J. 1964. Frankish Royal Tombs in the Cathedrals of Cologne and St. Denis, *Antiquity*, **38**, 201–16.

Wenskus, R. 1961. *Stammesbildung und Verfassung*, Cologne and Graz: Böhlau.

Situational Ethnicity and Nested Identities: New Approaches to an Old Problem

Susanne E. Hakenbeck

Traditional approaches to early medieval ethnicity are all too familiar: historical sources tell the story of the barbarian migrations, and archaeological evidence provides the illustrations. Pots, belts and brooches are classified, ordered, dated and plotted to help track the path of these migrations, reinforced by the occasional spectacular burial that can be associated with an historical figure.

Over the years, such approaches have provoked a mass of criticism, ranging from deconstructions of conventional migration stories to questioning whether ethnicity can be assessed at all through material culture.[1] Early medieval ethnicity continues to be of great interest, and even after decades the same research questions incite passionate responses. Arguments about the origins of early medieval tribes have not been settled, invasions and migrations are still matters of debate and controversies arise over dates, types and the meanings of objects.

One reason for this is that the big events – the barbarian migrations, the struggle between the barbarians and the Roman Empire and the subsequent genesis of the early medieval kingdoms – feature in the national narratives of many modern European states. In the political framework of the *Länder,* German regional nationalism, for example, assumes continuity between past and present populations from the early medieval tribes to the present day. Images of the barbarian tribes are a source of popular identity today.[2]

However, another reason for this continuing interest in ethnicity is that it requires us to question fundamentally the nature of identity, the meanings material culture may have had in the past and whether the one depended on the other. Since the simplistic equation of object and ethnic identity has been challenged, attempts to answer these questions have been almost overwhelmed by the complexities of the issues they conjure up. The specific social and historical context of early medieval ethnicity and the role the funerary rite played in its expression and maintenance have to be taken into account. These underlying conceptual complexities are the source for a deeper understanding of early medieval ethnicity.

Objects and Essences

Studies of ethnicity in archaeology have frequently used essentialist concepts of ethnicity combined with simplistic ideas of the role of material culture in the creation or expression of ethnicity. Instead of treating such ideas as constructs of thought created to help understand ethnicity, they have taken on the guise of facts of universal applicability. Traditionally, the dates and tribal names taken from historical sources have provided the framework for studying early medieval archaeology; the historical narrative was the structure into which archaeological evidence had to fit. The function of archaeological evidence was to provide a colourful backdrop to the sequence of historical events and occasionally to fill in gaps in the established knowledge. The primary purpose of distribution maps, for example, was to plot tribal territories more accurately than the written sources were able to.[3]

The concepts of ethnicity that were used were heavily influenced by nationalism and as such were primordialist[4] and essentialist: ethnic groups were considered to be static, clearly definable entities that could be identified objectively by their essence, that is, the combination of language, genetic relatedness and culture that makes up 'who they are'. Societies were thought to be divided into ethnic groups that were mutually exclusive and could be distinguished from each other by their material culture and customs. Central to these assumptions also was the unquestioned belief that ethnic groups could be identified by outside observers on the basis of their distinguishing characteristics. Thus, ethnic groups were thought of as 'closed' entities that could be studied in isolation.[5] Since nations legitimise themselves through a common past and many European national origin myths go back to the early medieval period, the origins and early history of the barbarian tribes have long been of particular importance. The question of the origins of the Bavarians, for example, has occupied researchers for decades.[6]

This has implications for the archaeological study of

material culture, particularly in the context of burial practice. It is assumed that ethnic groups can be clearly identified by their external characteristics such as language and culture. Archaeologically, specific types of objects, commonly brooches, have therefore been interpreted as indicators of ethnicity. When such objects are found in a grave, a connection between them and the ethnicity of their wearer is immediately made. Objects are thus interpreted as having had enduring and exclusively ethnic meanings.

Such 'primordialist' concepts of ethnicity have not remained uncontested and their continued use in archaeology has been thoroughly criticised.[7] As a response, more complex theories of early medieval ethnicity have been developed. Yet, the nationalist narrative is so pervasive that primordialist concepts of ethnicity frequently continue to be an undercurrent even to critical social and contextual mortuary analyses.

Seeds of Change

In the late 1950s a fundamental shift occurred in anthropological theories of ethnicity, from primordialist concepts to social-constructivist ones.[8] Ethnicity was firmly put back into its social and historical context. It was now seen as one social identity among many, and based on self-identification, rather than on an external definition. These new approaches were taken up or paralleled by historical approaches to ethnicity. Many early medieval historians have attempted to move beyond traditional interpretations of the sources and have applied new concepts of ethnicity borrowed from anthropology or sociology. Nevertheless, theoretically reflexive work on ethnicity in early medieval archaeology has remained limited, despite an acknowledgement of these new ideas.[9]

The early medieval historian Reinhard Wenskus took an instrumentalist approach[10] to the formation of ethnic identities. In *Stammesbildung und Verfassung*, Wenskus[11] emphasised the importance of self-identification and of socio-political factors in early medieval ethnogenesis, the process by which ethnic identity was created. He maintained that the political formation of a group had to precede the formation of its ethnic identity. A new ethnic group developed out of several already existing ones. The most powerful and influential among these contributed the 'kernel of tradition' that brought about new ethnic and cultural uniformity. Fundamental to this development was the belief in a common ancestry and a subjective feeling of affinity within the group. Other criteria such as language, culture, law or political institutions were of secondary importance.

Wenskus' work contained the seeds for many theories of early medieval ethnicity that have since been developed.[12] Among these are the concepts of situational identities and nested ethnicities. Their common basis is the notion that individuals had multiple identities, both in terms of ethnicities and of other social identities.

These identities became relevant or active depending on the context of specific social situations. They were also nested, that is, an individual could combine an affinity with the local with tiers of regional and super-regional ethnic identities. Thus, Geary[13] argued that ethnicity had its own specific terminology in the early medieval period, based on origin, customs, language and law and that each of these aspects was relevant in specific social situations, commonly in relation to a person's proximity to a ruler. Ethnic identity therefore became conscious to early medieval writers largely within the context of politics and the interests of lordship. Similarly, Pohl[14] suggested that ethnic interpretations were not unambiguous; individuals could have had multiple ethnic identities and may have chosen to emphasise specific ones depending on the situation and on whom they wanted to distinguish themselves from. Ethnicity was not the only identity a person could express, nor was it the most fundamental one in the early medieval period. According to Amory,[15] regional, professional and institutional loyalties were as important as ethnic affinities, and the early historiographers often attempted to construct new communities by redefining region and profession in ethnic terms.

Pohl[16] opened up the field to studies of early medieval ethnicity based on material culture, by emphasising that ethnic groups not only defined themselves subjectively but that they had to be reproduced in practice, for example, though religious and political rituals, warfare and external symbols. Daim[17] has applied these ideas to material culture: in the same way that a person could have different identities, objects too could have different meanings, based on their different typological characteristics. So the fabric, firing technique, shape or decoration of a pot could each have had different meanings, depending on the context in which these characteristics became relevant.[18]

These approaches set a strong precedent for a more critical and nuanced consideration of early medieval ethnicity in relation to the mortuary context. However, despite new historical approaches and an increasing body of archaeological literature on ethnicity in other periods and areas.[19] the use of archaeology in the study of early medieval ethnicity still remains under-theorised. There has been much critique of traditional uses of archaeology for determining ethnicity, but few attempts have been made to make use of the archaeological evidence in a positive and constructive way. The following case study is an attempt to reconsider early medieval ethnicity through the analysis of two early medieval cemeteries in modern-day Bavaria.

Ethnicity in Action

The cemeteries of Altenerding[20] and Aubing[21] belonged to a group of early medieval cemeteries in the area around Munich in Bavaria in southern Germany (Fig. 1). They were 'row-grave cemeteries' that have been associated

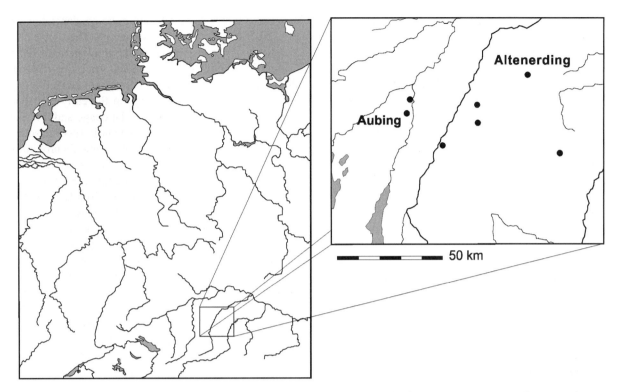

Figure 1. The location of the cemeteries of Altenerding and Aubing and of other cemeteries in the Munich region

with the various groups of barbarians that supplanted Roman authority on the borders of the Empire. They were in use from the mid-fifth to the late seventh centuries AD and are therefore comparable in terms of the presence and distribution of common types of grave goods. The cemeteries contained around 1400 and 900 inhumations respectively and they are also comparable in their sex and age profiles. Because of their size and these fundamental similarities they are well suited for an exploration of ethnic identities. Traditionally these cemeteries and the objects they have produced have been labelled Bavarian. My focus here will be on female graves of the late fifth and first half of the sixth century, particularly on those that were richly furnished, in an attempt to challenge these ascriptions and instead to propose that the burial evidence demonstrates that the funerary rite was used to express situational ethnicity and nested identities.[22]

Brooches

Richly furnished graves from this period typically contained a dress assemblage held together by a pair of large bow brooches worn on the torso and a pair of small brooches worn on the neck or shoulders, beaded necklaces, a belt and knife, and a girdle hanger made up of latch lifters, ornaments and amulets. The overall assemblage and general position of accessories fits with the evidence for costume throughout Belgium, northern France, the Rhineland and southern Germany.[23]

Just as cemeteries have tended to be given ethnic ascriptions based upon the regions in which they are found (*i.e.* Frankish, Alamannic, Thuringian etc.), so the variability of brooch types within them has been used as evidence for ethnic variability. Brooch types were thought to reflect the ethnicity of the wearer. This was based on the assumption that brooches were given to a woman early in life and that they stayed with her throughout her life, right into her grave.[24] Regardless of where the winds of migration period Europe might blow her, a woman's dress accessories would stay the same, through travel, marriage or changing social circumstances. It was also assumed that the identities expressed in the grave were those of the living person, rather than being an interpretation of the deceased through those who buried the dead.

The different brooch types from Altenerding and Aubing have also been interpreted in this way. There were large bow brooches conventionally described as 'Frankish/Alamannic', 'Ostrogothic', 'Langobardic' and 'Thuringian' types (Fig. 2) and a range of small brooches, *i.e.* bird, S- and disc brooches. The small brooch typology is not as detailed as that of bow brooches, however, bird and disc brooches have generally been considered western types, with the greatest concentrations in France and southern Germany, while S-brooches have been thought to be eastern types and have been associated with Langobardic cemeteries.[25] The brooches differ stylistically in their design and distribution patterns, but the terminology by which they are identified is ethnic and based on the historical tribal names. So even within

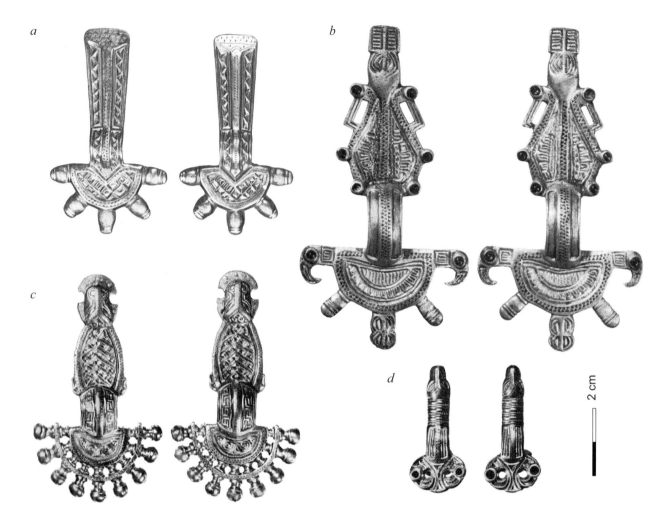

Figure 2. Examples of some of the different types of brooches found in Altenerding: (a) 'Frankish/Alamannic'; (b) 'Langobardic'; (c) 'Ostrogothic'; (d) Thuringian' pairs (from Sage 1984, pls. 186–7)

the apparently neutral and value free activity of creating a brooch typology ethnic interpretations are being made.

Yet, while these brooches are significantly different in style, they were not positioned as part of different styles of costume: bow brooches were always found on or near the pelvis and small brooches in the area of the neck. Also, bow brooches were frequently not paired with their western or eastern European small brooch counterparts. Funerary dress was therefore fairly uniform and corresponded with fashions throughout the area of row-grave cemeteries.[26] It is particularly significant that the bodies in the graves containing 'Ostrogothic' brooches in Altenerding[27] did not wear a *peplos*-style garment, the type of costume that was presumed typical for Ostrogothic Italy,[28] but were buried according to the local fashion.[29]

Brooch types on their own cannot be considered ethnic markers when placed in the context of costume as a whole. However, this does not mean that brooches carried no ethnic meaning at all. They were the most striking objects found in female graves. Their designs were varied and full of complex symbolism, depicting birds with huge beaks, animals with large nostrils and beady eyes and distorted human faces that, like a visual riddle, required some knowledge to understand them. This symbolism may have been associated with the brooches' real or assumed geographical origins. The existence of brooches in a grave therefore meant that their wearer was associated with areas beyond the local, possibly with foreign lands or mythical territories.[30] Brooches were therefore carriers of a common identity that arose out of long-distance connections between populations. A further aspect is that brooches combined meaning about ethnic, gender and status identities; the specific identities they carried were therefore only expressed in the small number of wealthier, or perhaps high status, female graves and the majority of poorly furnished graves was excluded from it.

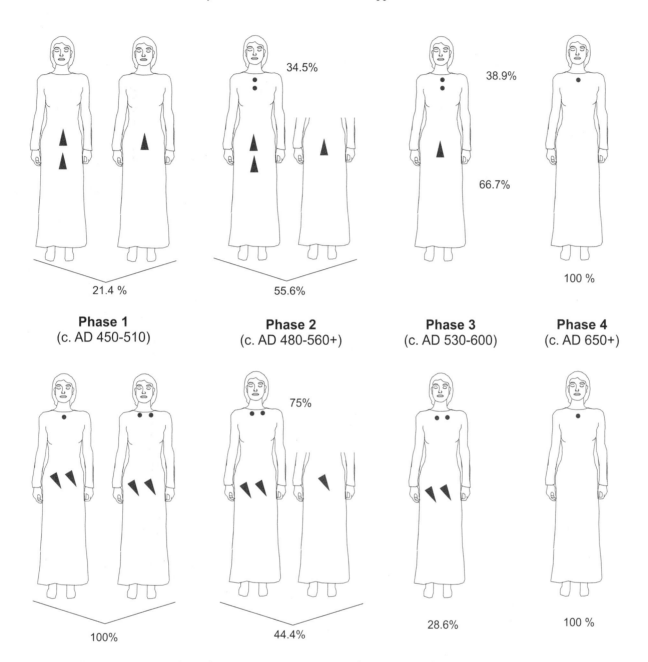

Figure 3. The most common brooch arrangements in Altenerding (top) and Aubing (bottom) over time. Circles represent small brooches, triangles represent bow brooches. The percentages are based on all burials with brooches per phase. Where applicable, percentages for bow brooches and small brooches are given separately

Local Differences

There were also significant differences in the burial rite between the two cemeteries. In Altenerding most of the late fifth- and sixth-century brooches, inclusive of all types, were positioned in a standardised vertical arrangement, with bow brooches worn 'head down' above each other on the pelvis and small brooches above each other on the neck (Fig. 3a). In contrast, in Aubing the standardised arrangement of brooches was two pairs, placed 'head up' horizontally next to each other on pelvis and chest (Fig. 3b).[31] These differences in brooch position imply a visually

striking difference in the way costume was worn, regardless of the type of brooch that held it in place.

There were also differences in the way such an idealised arrangement was maintained. In Altenerding, in cases where only three brooches or single pairs were given into the grave, these were usually positioned to fit in with the ideal vertical alignment even when bow brooches were occasionally positioned head-up rather than head-down. That is, even if a full set was not available, the main focus was on maintaining the vertical line. In Aubing, on the other hand, combinations of

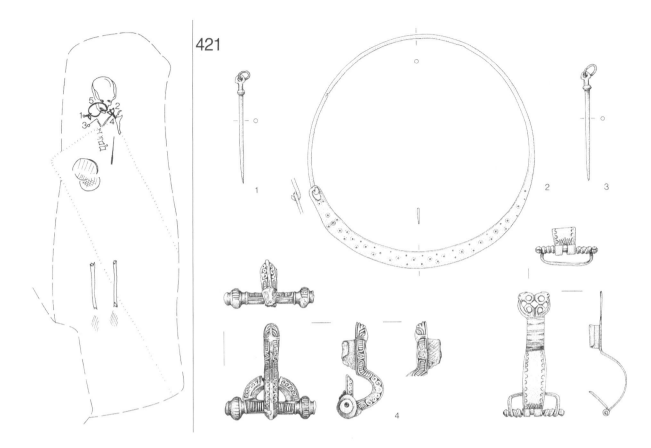

Figure 4. Altenerding, grave 421. The assemblage and position of the grave goods differs distinctly from the typical funerary fashion in Altenerding (from Sage 1984, pls. 54 and 180)

three brooches were less common. If four brooches were not available, two brooches were preferred over three or one, so as not to break the symmetry. The brooch arrangement in Aubing was much more highly regulated and a great number of brooches was positioned in identical ways. These clearly different funerary costumes were established in the late fifth century, when the cemeteries first came into use, and were maintained right into the late sixth century, when the four-brooch costume was transformed into the one-brooch costume.[32] They were expressions of different local identities that were maintained through the specific funerary practices of the two burial communities.

These local differences in costume therefore had the potential to distract from or to subvert the more abstract or symbolic super-regional ethnic meanings of the brooches. In the funeral both aspects of identity were expressed; they represented two opposing and potentially conflicting sources of identity and belonging.

Personal and Social Identities

Conflict may also have arisen between personal and social identities. In Altenerding some graves quite clearly

indicated the presence of a 'foreign' identity while in others there was evidence that the buried individuals might have had a different life-history that was subsumed under the local group identity. In this regard, grave 421 particularly stands out. It dates from the late fifth century and contained the body of a woman of mature age whose grave goods and style of costume were radically different from that of the rest of the cemetery and are unique in southern Germany. The body wore a Scandinavian neck ring, two 'Nörrland-pins' from the Mälar region in Sweden and an unequal pair of cross-bow brooches from the eastern Baltic.[33] The position of the brooches on the shoulders indicates that she wore a *peplos*-style dress (Fig. 4), which at the time was common also in Scandinavia (see note 27). Here a distinctly different and possibly 'foreign' cultural identity is expressed. The persons conducting the funeral made a point of emphasising the otherness of the person that was being buried.

Five female skeletons[34] dating from the late fifth to the early sixth centuries, had artificially deformed skulls,[35] similar to a practice common in eastern or south-eastern Europe which has been associated with the Huns and Avars.[36] The skulls had a very high and elongated forehead and shortened base, which was probably achieved by tight binding during childhood when the bone was still soft (Fig. 5). The funerary dress, however, was no different from that of other female burials in Altenerding. One individual was buried with a pair of 'Frankish/Alamannic' bow brooches, one with two bird brooches and one with a 'Thuringian' brooch. The bird brooches were positioned vertically above each other on the neck and the 'Frankish/Alamannic' brooches were placed 'head-down' vertically above each other on the pelvis. This conformed to the ideal Altenerding brooch arrangement.

In both examples we can assume that the individuals had a personal history that may have been different from that of the people buried around them. The binding of heads and the apparently foreign type of costume indicate that there were influences in the lives of these women that were not present in those of others. The participants in the funerals dealt with such distinct personal histories in different ways, by focusing on differences or on similarities. The woman with 'Scandinavian' costume was portrayed as an outsider while the women with deformed skulls were seen as belonging to the community.

Individuals are bound into society and perform within its structures. Identity is partly determined by a person's life history and experiences, but to a large extent it is shaped by social constraints and expectations. How others see us has a great bearing on how we see ourselves. Society can ascribe an identity and it can force individuals into a place in the social structure that may conflict with their personal histories. In the funerary rite this is taken to its conclusion when the dead body becomes completely objectified through its treatment by the mourners. As a consequence the identity that was ascribed in death may not have matched a person's identity in life. It fulfilled the needs of the burying community in healing the rupture that was caused by a person's death.

Situational Ethnicity and Nested Identities

These examples illustrate that there is no straightforward or direct relationship between material culture and ethnicity. Objects can have many meanings; these meanings can change or be of different relevance in different social situations. But the material environment is an extension of our internal structuring of the world and it also structures our understanding of it. Material culture therefore plays a meaningful role in the expression and maintenance of identities. It is through inconsistencies and oddities in the use of material culture, much more than through the assumed ideal of regulated use, that we can gain an understanding of the complexities of early medieval ethnic identity.

Like the material culture through which it was expressed, ethnicity in Altenerding and Aubing had situational relevance. This means that differences or

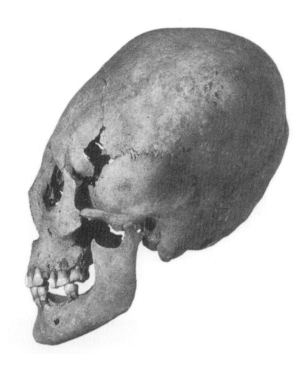

Figure 5. Altenerding, grave 1108. Artificially deformed skull (from Helmuth et al. 1996, pl. 9)

similarities in the funerary practice would have been noticed and become relevant only in relation to the participants' own identities and place in the social structure. For example, members from each of the burial communities might have taken part in the funerals of the other community. The differences in the way in which brooches fastened the funerary dress might have made them aware that they had arrived from different local areas. However, if they were taking part in the funeral of the woman with 'Scandinavian' costume these differences could have retreated into the background in the face of the more obvious differences in dress and accessories that were expressed there.

Funerary dress could convey various meanings at the same time. General similarities in dress and use of brooches were an expression of a super-regional identity, while local differences in the way brooches were pinned created a sense of opposition to funerary customs in other cemeteries and thereby a sense of local identity. Both may have been equally relevant. In Altenerding and Aubing therefore there is evidence for nested identities, ranging from super-regional cultural systems to individuals. The notion of situational ethnicity implies that identities were switched on and off depending on the social context. The concept of nested identities adds to this by being more inclusive: some aspects of identities were brought into sharp focus, while others could only be seen out of the corner of one's eye, but they were there nevertheless.

Such a complex of contrasting and inclusive identities

was not maintained without tensions. We can see such tensions in dealings with individuals that were different in some way, where identities were ascribed in death that may have had less relevance in life. We can also see various levels of conformity in the strength with which fashion ideals were maintained in the two cemeteries. The expression of local funerary fashion in Aubing was much more normative than in Altenerding, where not everyone adhered to the same fashion ideal. Social identities were not accepted or maintained by all with equal conviction. Though identities were pervasive and powerful in determining who a person was and which place he or she occupied in the social structure, there was also evidence that subversive counter-currents were active.

We must bear in mind that the expression of ethnic identity did not take place in a social void. The material culture used for expressing ethnic identity also conveyed meanings about gender, status and age. The boundaries between these different identities were fluid and cannot easily be separated. The above examples make it very clear that the ethnic identities active there were closely related to wealth and status. The majority of female graves in the two cemeteries contained at most a few glass beads, a simple belt buckle and a knife. In the context of a funeral, however, these grave goods did not carry the same wealth of meanings as more richly furnished graves. Similarly, patterns of ethnic identity were quite different in male graves.

Conclusion

The evidence for early medieval ethnicity from Altenerding and Aubing in the late fifth and first half of the sixth century indicates a highly complex network of identities, ranging from the super-regional to the personal and close ties with other aspects of social structure. This study has attempted to build a bridge from increasingly sophisticated historical approaches to early medieval ethnicity to an archaeological one. Archaeologists have legitimately been sceptical about the possibilities of making ethnic interpretations from the archaeological evidence. Too often traditional approaches have not only been simplistic and unsatisfactory but have also been deeply touched by nationalism and even racism. However, there is nothing intrinsically impossible or ideologically reactionary about attempting to understand early medieval ethnicity. Quite to the contrary, only the continued questioning of and questing for it can lead to more appropriate and useful concepts of early medieval ethnicity.

Acknowledgements

I would like to thank Catherine Hills, Howard Williams and an anonymous reviewer for comments on drafts of this text. I am grateful to the Board of Graduate Studies, University of Cambridge, the Cambridge European Trust, Newnham College and the Kurt Hahn Trust for helping to fund my research.

Notes

1. The critical literature on the subject is vast. See Brather 2002; Effros 2003; Hills 2003; Fehr 2004; Härke 2004 for recent discussions and Härke, this volume, for a more optimistic perspective.
2. This is exemplified by the large numbers of visitors to the exhibitions Die Bajuwaren in Rosenheim, Bavaria, in 1988 (Dannheimer 1988) and Die Alamannen in Stuttgart in 1997 (Fuchs 1998).
3. Traditional archaeological approaches to early medieval ethnicity in make up an enormous, and by no means homogeneous, body of work, going back to the mid-nineteenth century. Reviews can be found in Jentgens 2001; Brather 2000; 2002; 2004 and Hakenbeck 2006.
4. Banks 1996; 13; Jones 1997: 65–72.
5. See for example Christlein 1978; Dannheimer and Dopsch 1988; Wieczorek 1996.
6. Menke 1990.
7. Criticism ranges from the general (*e.g.* Shennan 1989; Jones 1997) to specific problems of the interpretation of material culture (*e.g.* Halsall 1992; Effros 2004) or it focuses on the historical background of the field of early medieval ethnicity studies (*e.g.* Brather 2000; 2004). For a more detailed discussion of the critical literature on early medieval ethnicity see Effros 2003, 100–110.
8. Banks 1996.
9. But see Hedeager 2000; Siegmund 2000; Lucy 2002; Hackenbeck 2006.
10. In instrumentalist theories of ethnicity, ethnicity is believed to be socially constructed and that the members of an ethnic group consciously adopt ethnicity as a form of social organisation in

order to serve their economic interests. As such it helps to cement inequalities within society (Banks 1996, 33ff.).
11. Wenskus 1961.
12. See for example Geary 1983; Amory 1993; 1994; Daim 1998; Pohl 1994; 2004; Pohl and Reimitz 1998.
13. Geary 1983.
14. Pohl 1998.
15. Amory 1997.
16. Pohl 1994.
17. Daim 1998.
18. Ibid., 79.
19. *E.g.* Hall 1997; Jones 1997; Bergstøl 2001; Smith 2003.
20. Sage 1984; Losert and Pleterski 2003.
21. Dannheimer 1998.
22. See also Hakenbeck 2004; 2006.
23. Clauß 1987; Martin 1995; 2000.
24. Koch 1998, 70.
25. Haimerl 1998; Martin 2000; Viclitz 2003.
26. Clauß 1987; Martin 1995; 2000.
27. Altenerding: graves 146, 151, 189, 192, 625.
28. In the sixth century, *peplos*-style dresses were still worn in Ostrogothic Italy and further east, in Scandinavia and in Anglo-Saxon England. In western Europe and as far east as Thuringia and Bavaria it had gone out of use by around AD 400. It was replaced by a hybrid of Roman and barbarian dress styles that eventually developed into the four-brooch costume (see Bierbrauer 1971; Böhme 1998; Martin 1995; 2000).
29. These findings are paralleled by Effros's (2004) examples of Visigothic brooches in Frankish cemeteries where there are similar inconsistencies between brooch types and dress styles.

30. There are no 'Bavarian' brooch types. Those that have been identified as having been produced locally (Koch 1998) fall into the general categories of 'Frankish/Alamannic' types.

31. The grave plans for Aubing are only schematic and were probably drawn from sketch plans that are now lost (Dannheimer 1998, 84). The position of the brooches, especially their unusual 'head-up' orientation, may therefore not absolutely be reliable. However, the variability and detail of the drawings justify their use.

32. From the mid-sixth century bow brooches were gradually given up in favour of small brooches. By late sixth century brooches were worn singly, centrally on the chest. This transformation of the four-brooch costume into the one-brooch costume took place across the whole of western Europe (Martin 1995; 2000).

33. Werner 1970; Waller 1972; Schultz-Dörrlamm 1986; Koch 1999

34. Altenerding: graves 125, 513, 1108, 1135, 1350.

35. Helmuth, Ankner and Hundt 1996.

36. Crubézy 1990.

Bibliography

Amory, P. 1993. The meaning and purpose of ethnic terminology in Burgundian laws, *Early Medieval Europe*, 2, 1–28.

Amory, P. 1994. Names, ethnic identity, and community in fifth- and sixth-century Burgundy, *Viator*, 25, 1–30.

Amory, P. 1997. *People and Identity in Ostrogothic Italy, 489–554*, Cambridge: Cambridge University Press.

Banks, M. 1996. *Ethnicity: Anthropological Constructions*, London and New York: Routledge.

Bergstøl, J. (ed.) 2001. *Scandinavian Archaeological Practice – in Theory. Proceedings from the 6th Nordic TAG, Oslo 2001*, Oslo Archaeological Series, 1, Oslo: Universitetet I Oslo.

Bierbrauer, V. 1971. Zu den Vorkommen ostgotischer Bügelfibeln in Raetia II, *Bayerische Vorgeschichtsblätter*, 36, 131–65.

Brather, S. 2000. Ethnische Identitäten als Konstrukte der frühgeschichtlichen Archäologie, *Germania*, 78, 139–77.

Brather, S. 2004. *Ethnische Interpretationen in der frühgeschichtlichen Archäologie*, Ergänzungsbände zum Reallexikon der germanischen Altertumskunde, 42, Berlin: Walter de Gruyter.

Christlein, R. 1978. *Die Alamannen: Archäologie eines lebendigen Volkes*, Stuttgart: Theiss.

Clauß, G. 1987. Die Tragesitte von Bügelfibeln, *Jahrbuch des Römisch-Germanischen Zentralmuseums*, 34, 491–603.

Crubézy, E. 1990. Merovingian skull deformations in the southwest of France, in D. Austin and L. Alcock (eds), *From The Baltic to the Black Sea: Studies in Medieval Archaeology*, One World Archaeology, 18, 189–208, London: Unwin Hyman.

Daim, F. 1998. Archaeology, ethnicity and the structures of identification: the example of the Avars, Caranthians and Moravians in the eighth century, in W. Pohl and H. Reimitz (eds) *Strategies of Distinction. The construction of ethnic communities, 300–800*, Transformations of the Roman World, 2, 71–93, Leiden: Brill.

Dannheimer, H. 1998. *Das bajuwarische Reihengräberfeld von Aubing, Stadt München*, Stuttgart: Theiss.

Dannheimer, H. and Dopsch, H. (eds) 1988. *Die Bajuwaren*, Rosenheim: Ausstellungskatalog Rosenheim/Mattsee.

Effros, B. 2003. *Merovingian Mortuary Archaeology and the Making of the Middle Ages*, Berkeley: University of California Press.

Effros, B. 2004. Dressing conservatively: women's brooches as markers of ethnic identity?, in L. Brubaker and J. M. H. Smith (eds) *Gender in the Early Medieval World* 165–184, Cambridge: Cambridge University Press.

Geary, P. J. 1983. Ethnic identity as a situational construct in the early middle ages, *Mitteilungen der Anthropologischen Gesellschaft in Wien*, 113, 15–26.

Hakenbeck, S. E. 2004. Ethnic tensions in early medieval cemeteries in Bavaria, *Archaeological Review from Cambridge*, 19(2), 40–55.

Hall, J. M. 1997. *Ethnic Identity in Greek Antiquity*, Cambridge: Cambridge University Press.

Halsall, G. 1992. The origins of the *Reihengräberzivilisation*: forty years on, in J. Drinkwater and H. Elton (eds), *Fifth-Century Gaul: A Crisis of Identity?* 196–207, Cambridge: Cambridge University Press.

Hedeager, L. 2000. Migration period Europe: the formation of a political mentality, in F. Theuws and J. L. Nelson (eds), *Rituals and Power*, Transformation of the Roman World, 8, 15–57, Leiden: Brill

Helmuth, H., Ankner, D. and Hundt H.-J. 1996. *Das Reihengräberfeld von Altenerding in Oberbayern* II. Germanische Denkmäler der Völkerwanderungszeit, 18, Serie A. Mainz: Philipp von Zabern

Jones, S. 1997. *The Archaeology of Ethnicity*, London and New York: Routledge

Koch, A. 1998. *Bügelfibeln der Merowingerzeit im westlichen Frankenreich*. Römisch-Germanisches Zentralmuseum. Monographien, 41, Mainz: Verlag des Römisch-Germanischen Zentralmuseums.

Koch, U. 1999. Nordeuropäisches Fundmaterial in Gräbern Süddeutschlands rechts des Rheins, in U. von Freeden, U. Koch, and A. Wieczorek (eds), *Völker an Nord-und Ostsee und die Franken*, 175–194, Bonn: Dr. Rudolf Habelt.

Losert, H. and Pleterski, A. 2003. *Altenerding in Oberbayern*, Berlin, Bamberg and Ljubljana: Scîpvaz/Založba ZRC.

Lucy, S. 2002. Burial practice in early medieval eastern Britain: constructing local identities, deconstructing ethnicity, in S. Lucy and A. Reynolds (eds), *Burial in Early Medieval England and Wales*, 72–87, Society for Medieval Archaeology Monograph, 17, London: SMA.

Martin, M. 1995. Tradition und Wandel der fibelgeschmückten frühmittelalterlichen Frauenkleidung, *Jahrbuch des Römisch-Germanischen Zentralmuseums*, 38, 628–80.

Martin, M. 2000. Späte Völkerwanderungszeit und Merowingerzeit auf dem Kontinent, in H. Beck, H. Steuer, D. Timpe and R. Wenskus (eds), *Fibel und Fibeltracht*, 131–172, Reallexikon der Germanischen Altertumskunde, Berlin: Walter de Gruyter.

Menke, M. 1990. 150 Jahre Forschungsgeschichte zu den Anfängen des Baiernstammes, in H. Friesinger and F. Damm (eds), *Typen der Ethnogenese unter besonderer Berücksichtigung der Bayern*, Part 2, 123–220, Symposium Kloster Zwettl 1986.

Pohl, W. 1994. Tradition, Ethnogenese und literarische Gestaltung: eine Zwischenbilanz, in K. Brummer and B. Merta (eds), *Ethnogenese und Überlieferung*. Angewandte Methoden der Frühmittelalterforschung, Veröffentlichungen des Instituts für Österreichische Geschichtsforschung, 31, 9–26, Wien and München: Oldenbourg.

Pohl, W. 1998. Telling the difference: Signs of ethnic identity, in W. Pohl and H. Reimitz (eds), *Strategies of Distinction. The Construction of Ethnic Communities, 300–800*, Transformation of the Roman World, 2, 17–69, Leiden: Brill.

Pohl, W. 2004. Gender and ethnicity in the early middle ages, in L. Brubaker and J. M. H. Smith (eds), *Gender in the Early Medieval World*, 23–43, Cambridge: Cambridge University Press

Pohl, W. and Reimitz H. (eds) 1998. *Strategies of Distinction*, The Transformation of the Roman World, 2. Leiden, Boston and Köln: Brill.

Sage, W. 1984. *Das Reihengräberfeld von Altenerding in Oberbayern*, Germanische Denkmäler der Völkerwanderungszeit, XIV, Serie A, Berlin: Gebrüder Mann.

Siegmund, F. 2000. *Alemannen und Franken*, Ergänzungsbände zum Reallexikon der Germanischen Altertumskunde, 23, Berlin and New York: Walter de Gruyter.

Smith, S. T. 2003. *Wretched Kush*, London and New York: Routledge.

Wenskus, R. 1961. *Stammesbildung und Verfassung. Das Werden der frühmittelalterlichen gentes*, Graz and Köln: Böhlau.

Wieczorek, A. (ed.) 1996. *Die Franken. Wegbereiter Europas*, Mainz: Philipp von Zabern

Charting Conversion: Burial
as a Barometer of Belief?

Rik Hoggett

This paper explores three ways in which the burial record of Anglo-Saxon East Anglia can be used to chart the spread of Christianity throughout the region. Attention is paid to those material characteristics which typify a Christian burial in the Middle Ages – inhumation, deposition without grave-goods and west–east orientation. It is argued that it is possible to use the adoption of these rites to trace the progress of the conversion, albeit with certain limitations.

Introduction

The following discussion presents one aspect of my doctoral research into the conversion of East Anglia.[1] Approaching the subject from a landscape-archaeological perspective, my work combines the historical and archaeological evidence for the conversion and uses it to examine the role that Christianity played in the numerous social, political, material and landscape changes which occurred during the Anglo-Saxon period. In order to achieve this aim it has been necessary to develop a number of methodologies with which to chart the initial spread of Christianity. Inevitably, given the nature of the surviving material record, funerary archaeology plays a significant role in this research, from the level of individual burial rites through to the wider landscape context of cemeteries.[2]

Limited space dictates a narrow focus and this paper concentrates upon the emergence of the three main material characteristics of the Christian medieval burial rite during the Middle Saxon period, namely inhumation with the absence of cremation, the deposition of the dead without grave-goods, and a west–east orientation to individual graves and cemeteries. The paper aims to assess the use of these criteria in charting the course of the conversion within the East Anglian region.[3] It therefore represents a pilot study instigated to assess the potential of the material evidence for addressing the processes of conversion. It is hoped that future work will incorporate the numerous unpublished sites in the

region's Historic Environment Records (HERs), but this paper focuses on the key excavated sites and makes no claims to be comprehensive. Despite a degree of caution and some provisos, it is argued that all three physical characteristics *can* be demonstrated to have the potential to be useful indicators of the adoption of Christianity, contrary to recent studies that have questioned the use of burial evidence in this way.

Burial and Belief: a Matter
of Grave Importance

The archaeological study of religion, and of conversion in particular, is currently undergoing something of a renaissance, with the recent appearance of a number of publications on the subject.[4] This work has provided many new insights into the nature of conversion and the way in which societies responded to new religious influences. However, while it is certainly true that recent studies of early medieval graves have developed new approaches and interpretations, the vast majority have focused upon the social and political dimensions of burial rather than its religious and cosmological aspects.[5] With the notable exception of a handful of papers, the new thinking in the subjects of burial and religious conversion has yet to seriously converge.[6]

There are several reasons for this lacuna. Studies of Anglo-Saxon burials have traditionally been dominated by the cremations and furnished inhumations of the Early period, with particular attention paid to the many classes of artefact associated with them.[7] This bias is largely due to the archaeological visibility of the material and conversely the unfurnished burials of the period have received little attention, being rendered effectively invisible by a lack of associated artefacts.[8] The problem is compounded in East Anglia, where poor bone preservation results in a number of 'empty graves' in cemeteries, about which very little can be said.[9] As a result of such compartmentalised approaches to the material, it is currently difficult to study the full range of burials throughout the conversion period equally as the later end of the scale is substantially under-represented. Fortunately, this situation is slowly being rectified as more sites are excavated.

Burial evidence is often employed in discussions of Anglo-Saxon religion, although again there is a distinct bias towards the Early material and the evidence that it provides for the nature of Anglo-Saxon paganism.[10] The increase in high-quality excavations and more detailed post-excavation analyses have shed a greater light on the details of the various rites enacted; our understanding of the cremation rite has benefited particularly from this type of work, although inhumation has too.[11] Sites such as Snape (Suffolk) have demonstrated the immense variation that was possible within the broader categories of inhumation and cremation and this variety is argued to be a reflection of the polytheistic and socio-political fragmentation of the Early Anglo-Saxon period in which, as Lucy puts it, 'each community actively created its own burial rite while drawing on common practice'.[12] With regard to the ways in which the burial rite changed over time, we know that inhumation was practised alongside cremation during the Early Anglo-Saxon period, but that it became the sole burial rite by the mid-to-late seventh century. In addition, although inhumation continued to be practised, the nature of the rite changed over time too, most particularly regarding the decreasing deposition of grave-goods.

The large number of known Christian burials excavated from both medieval and post-medieval contexts in this country has increased rapidly over recent decades, demonstrating that unfurnished, supine burial with a west–east orientation was, and continues to be, the normal Christian burial practice.[13] Therefore, with regard to recognising the conversion in the burial record, a simple model has been developed in which Christianity arrived and burial rites were immediately transformed from those of the Early Anglo-Saxon period to those of the Medieval period.[14] In particular, attention has focused upon the change from furnished to unfurnished burial and the increasingly regular adoption of a west–east orientation, both criteria recently described by Arthur MacGregor as being amongst 'the earliest tangible signs of the new religion in the archaeological record'.[15] Although such interpretations persist, they have been demonstrated to be over-simplistic and are increasingly seen as not fitting the available evidence. There are a number of reasons for this change in approach, both theoretical and practical. For example, it has been argued that the absence of cremation does not in itself infer religious affiliation, that furnished burial could be absent in pre-Christian contexts as well as persist in a thoroughly Christian environment, while west–east orientation was common both before and after conversion.[16] Moreover, there are questions about what we mean by 'conversion' as reflected in the burial record: do we mean a change of belief, a change of practice, or simply a politically expedient shift in the symbolism of death?[17]

Consequently, in tandem with the critique of inferring past ethnic groups from early medieval graves, attempting to recognise religious conversion in the burial record has fallen somewhat out of fashion. However, we should be wary of turning the problems in recognising religious change into a wholesale dismissal of religious interpretations. Although the model needs refining, as admitted by Martin Carver (a staunch advocate of the political and ideological messages inherent in early medieval mortuary practices), 'burial rites certainly do change at conversion'.[18] His comments are echoed by Alison Taylor, who has recently observed that 'religious change … is particularly likely to be marked by radical shifts in burial practice'.[19] Fortunately, new developments in our understanding of the conversion process have caused us to revise our expectations of the material record and it is now possible to revisit the burial record and use it with greater success. More traditional models saw conversion as a basic binary opposition – a society was either in one state or another – but this has now been replaced by a much more subtle model in which local trends are adapted and integrated into the Christian doctrine.[20] This aided the progression of new religious ideas, by allowing traditional practices and links to the past to remain, while at the same time furthering the cause. This may well result in a change in the character of the material record rather than its substance. It will inevitably also lead to highly regionalised variations in universal practices.[21] These ideas strike a chord with many of the observations of the changes in burial practices which occurred during the seventh century.

Another difficulty encountered in the more traditional approaches to the study of conversion is the tendency to concentrate upon the conversion of the elite, while paying little heed to the evidence for the wider population. This is a result of using the surviving historical sources as a starting point, many of which were written by, for and about the ecclesiastical and secular elites, and has given rise to a trickle-down model of conversion in which all of the major changes occurred at the top.[22] The archaeological record would seem contradict this, suggesting that religious changes took place at all levels of society and occurred comparatively quickly, primarily during the seventh century.

Reliance on the historical sources to provide a starting point for studying the conversion is in part responsible for the belief that burial evidence has little to contribute to the debate. The historical sources make little or no mention of the early Church's attitude to burial practices and it is argued that they surely would if it was a pertinent issue.[23] Indeed, there is so little documentary evidence that Morris believes 'the written records of the 7th and 8th centuries suggest that pagan burial was not regarded as a danger by the Church, or that if it did present a threat it was low on the list of priorities for elimination'.[24]

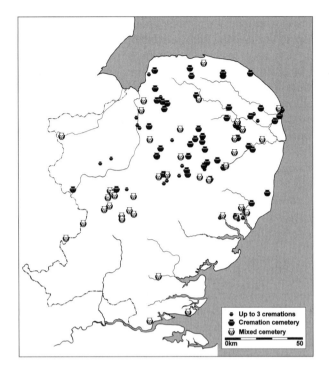

Figure 1. The distribution of cremations in East Anglia

However, there are a lot of things which are not mentioned in the early sources, but which we know from the material record occurred, ranging from the manufacture of individual artefacts through to the management of entire estates. One cannot take an absence of historical evidence as evidence of absence. Although the historical record *is* quiet on the subject of burial, the archaeological record clearly does show that changes in burial practice occurred at the time of the conversion and these require explanation.

Anglo-Saxon East Anglia: the Body of Evidence

Out of necessity any study of the East Anglian region during the Anglo-Saxon period has to be archaeological in nature. Very few pertinent documentary sources have survived, a fact widely attributed to the destructive tendencies of ninth-century Viking raiders within the region.[25] Consequently our main source of documentary evidence for the conversion period in East Anglia is Bede's *Historia Ecclesiastica*, written in a different part of the country over a hundred years after the events it describes.[26] While Bede's all too brief comments have inspired lengthy discussions about the kings Rædwald and Sigeberht, the temple of the two altars and the identity of the individuals buried at Sutton Hoo (Suffolk), beyond drawing our attention to the first half of the seventh century Bede tells us precious little about the wider conversion of East Anglia during this time and in

subsequent decades.[27] In Williamson's words, with regard to understanding the ecclesiastical development of the region 'the evidence of documents will probably contribute little to our understanding in the future: the challenge is one for archaeology to answer.'[28]

Fortunately, we are increasingly well placed to answer this challenge. In direct contrast to its documentary paucity, the burial record of the Anglo-Saxon period within East Anglia is exceptionally rich. Documented accounts of discoveries occur from the mid-sixteenth century onwards and Anglo-Saxon material now accounts for many thousands of entries in the region's HERs.[29] During the last hundred years East Anglia has played host to a number of significant archaeological excavations, almost all of which have been brought to swift publication, at least in catalogue form, and many of which have since become type-sites.[30] Perhaps the most significant contribution to the data set results from the archaeological authorities' good relationships with responsible metal-detector users over the last twenty-five years, now further strengthened under the Portable Antiquities Scheme. To date in Norfolk approximately forty Anglo-Saxon cemeteries have been located through metal-detected finds alone and many more sites lie unrecognised in the numerous reported stray-finds.[31]

Cremation: Gone to Pot

Cremations are among the most archaeologically visible artefacts of the Early Anglo-Saxon period and, within East Anglia at least, have been the subject of recorded discoveries since the sixteenth century when Leland noted 'a great many yerthen pottes' recently dug up in Kenninghall (Norfolk) in his *Itinerary* of *c*.1540.[32] Figure 1 shows the distribution of locatable cremations extracted from the HERs of the East Anglian counties. Following the categories adopted by Myres and Green in their 1973 gazetteer, the 105 identified sites have been subdivided into nineteen sites with less than three cremations, forty-seven with more than three cremations and thirty-nine mixed-rite cemeteries.[33] Although a rather blunt instrument (relative quantities are not represented here) the map clearly demonstrates that cremation was a widely practised rite within the area that now comprises Norfolk and the northern half of Suffolk. Fewer instances occurring further afield and then most often in mixed-rite cemeteries. The discrete nature of this distribution has sparked much debate about the *Adventus Saxonum*, harking back to Bede's observations on the continental origins of the Angles, Saxons and Jutes,[34] but for the purposes of this discussion it is enough to note that the cremation rite was widely practised in the region, for it is its ultimate cessation which primarily interests us here.

The chronology of cremation is of fundamental importance to this discussion, for if it can be demonstrated to have ceased to be practised before the reintroduction of Christianity to these shores, then this is clearly unrelated to the conversion. However, if the rite can be demonstrated to have continued into the early seventh century, then we must at least consider the possibility that its ultimate cessation may be tied into the adoption of Christianity. Unfortunately, as is so often the case, things are not as clear-cut as we would like them to be. Despite the enormous quantity of curated and published material, the precise dating of cremation remains problematic and its chronological cut-off point is rarely discussed in the literature.[35] This uncertainty is largely due to the vast majority of this material, primarily cremation urns, being devoid of archaeological context and, more significantly, any associated finds. Historically the contents of an urn were usually deemed to be useless and discarded, resulting in the loss of a great deal of information.[36] To this day the main source for dating cremations remains the typology of urn styles developed by Myres, who, somewhat surprisingly, himself considered the contents of urns to be 'the least informative … of all the material relics of ancient culture.'[37] Consequently, although comprehensive, Myres' typology actually contains very few absolute dates and the largely stylistic nature of the work has been criticised for its assumption of linear and constant development over time.[38] Richards goes so far as to state that 'one might conclude that the material is undatable.'[39] Fortunately, the increasing number of cremations excavated under modern conditions are enabling more detailed dating to be achieved, both by association and also stratigraphically. The cremation rite can now be demonstrated to extend into the seventh century with some certainty. In particular, most of the examples of cremations contained within copper-alloy vessels can now be dated to the late sixth and seventh centuries, including examples from Illington (Norfolk) and Snape.[40] It is unlikely that these datable examples were isolated cases and we must assume that the more traditional urns also continued to be used at this time, although at present it is difficult to prove this assertion.

This brings us to what seem likely to be among the latest instances of cremation in the archaeological record of East Anglia, the cremations at Sutton Hoo, dated to the first quarter of the seventh century.[41] The fact that the cremation rite was enacted here is perhaps the most telling physical clue in ascertaining the relationship between the end of cremation and the acceptance of Christianity. Over a number of years Martin Carver has promulgated the theory that the Sutton Hoo burial complex represents an overtly political statement of pagan defiance 'provoked by the perceived menace of a predatory Christian mission.'[42] In particular he draws attention to the use of what he takes to be iconic pagan practices at the site: barrow burial, boat burial and cremation.[43] Barrow and boat burials were both very rare, telling us little about the burial practices of the lower echelons of society, but, as we have seen, cremation was widely practised at a grassroots level, making it much more useful in charting the spread of the conversion. It is certainly telling that the last pagan kings of East Anglia

should be among the last to practise cremation in the region.[44] Taking Carver's interpretation to its logical conclusion, cremation became a totemic pagan rite, being flaunted as an act of defiance and resistance. The corollary of this is that the rite was under direct threat from these 'predatory' Christian missionaries and the episode is strongly suggestive of a Christian policy of eradicating cremation, albeit one unrecorded in early documents. Although direct evidence is sparse, the situation is not without precedent: there was a similar cessation of cremation among the Christian populations of the late Roman period, all of whom subsequently inhumed their dead.[45]

This then begs the question why the eradication of cremation should be so desirable to these early Christians? We have seen that one of the means by which Christianity achieved its widespread success was through a deliberate policy of adoption and adaptation of local customs as it expanded into new territories.[46] Yet, while this can be demonstrated to be true for many practices, of which more below, cremation appears to be one practice which was simply not tolerated. Howard Williams has recently outlined an 'ideology of transformation' in which cremation functioned as a mechanism through which the deceased was destroyed and transformed into a new ancestral form.[47] Such ideas would have been fundamentally at odds with the early Christian world-view and, although some ideologies could be assimilated into the emerging doctrine, it would appear that the destruction of the body by fire and its transformation to something Other was not one of them. Indeed, cremation remained an anathema for Anglican Christians until the nineteenth century, for in more recent times it was seen to prevent the possibility of resurrection, for which many believed that the body needed to be kept complete.[48] Stricter still, it was not until 1963 that the Roman Catholic church permitted cremation, although to this day the cremated remains cannot be scattered and must be kept together.[49] This is all suggestive of a strongly ingrained doctrine, which may well have accounted for the disappearance of cremation from the archaeological record in the early seventh century.

To return to the initial problem, with regard to recognising the conversion in the burial record it therefore follows that any cemetery which contains evidence of cremation must represent a community which had yet to adopt Christianity, at least in part, and, where they can be securely dated, these sites can be used to provide something of a *terminus post quem* for the localised adoption of Christianity. Unfortunately individual urns can be very difficult to date, but a broader perspective taking in the wider landscape context of cremation containing cemeteries will hopefully prove enlightening. This is one of the other avenues explored in my doctoral research. While the presence of cremation can be used to demonstrate the continued existence of pagan practices, its absence alone cannot be taken as

Figure 2. The distribution of fifth- to seventh-century inhumations in East Anglia.

conclusive proof of the adoption of Christianity, although it may certainly be used to strengthen the argument. Cremation was only one of many pagan burial rites and due consideration must be given to the clues offered by contemporaneous inhumation rites.

Grave Goods: Taking it With You

It is a commonly held belief that the conversion was responsible for the demise of the practice of burying grave-goods. However, this demise can actually be archaeologically dated to the first half of the eighth century, at least a century after the main period of conversion discussed in the rest of this paper.[50] Clearly then, this event cannot be related to the initial period of conversion, although it is probably related to the subsequent development of churchyard burial and the institutions that accompanied it.[51] Certainly, with the exception of some saints and members of the clergy, the vast majority of the medieval examples of Christian burial are unfurnished.[52] Even if this were not the case, the simple criterion furnished/unfurnished could not be used as an indicator of conversion, because a significant quantity of Early Anglo-Saxon burials were unfurnished anyway or, such as at Snape (Suffolk) and Harford Farm (Norfolk), were furnished with materials which cannot usually be recognised archaeologically.[53] However, given the sheer quantity of material available to study, it would be a counter-intuitive to deny the significance of the

change in the deposition of grave goods. A closer investigation of the material reveals that the practice of furnishing graves did change significantly during the course of the seventh century and this may well be a result of the conversion.

We have already seen that Anglo-Saxon burial studies have historically shown a heavy bias in favour of furnished inhumations and the volume of material involved becomes very clear when one plots its distribution. Figure 2 shows all of the fifth to seventh century inhumations listed in the region's HERs, again broken down into the categories defined by Myres and Green.[54] The locations of 224 sites are shown, 104 with less than three inhumations, 120 with more than three inhumations and the same thirty-nine mixed-rite sites as in Figure 1. Once again we must be aware of the limitations of the method. The discrete distribution exhibited by the cremations is not mirrored here, but this does not mean that regional trends are not present in the material: analyses of individual artefact types would bring them out.[55] The other crucial factor in this distribution is the contribution to the data made by metal detectorists, as many of the sites shown here are only represented by surface scatters and not excavated material.

As one might expect, grave-good assemblages have been studied in considerable detail over the years and are particularly suited to statistical analysis to determine underlying patterns in their deposition. In this manner it has been possible to demonstrate that the gender of the deceased was clearly a determining factor in the composition of grave-goods, for there is a demonstrable correlation between jewellery assemblages and female-sexed burials, while weaponry is strongly associated with male-sexed burials. However, it can equally be demonstrated that it was not the only determining factor, for fifty percent of burials either do not contain sex-specific artefacts or contain no artefacts at all.[56] It has also been demonstrated that the age of the deceased was a factor in structuring their grave-goods and a series of age-related thresholds have been identified at which the composition of the burial assemblage would be changed.[57] Although a similar proportion of cremations contain pyre-goods, it is difficult to interpret them to the same degree because of their incomplete curation and also because of the damage caused by the heat, the selective collection process and the possibility that some artefacts were added to the urn afterwards.[58] The cremated material studied by Julian D. Richards suggested to him that 'very few grave-goods appear to be sex-linked'[59] and that they 'show little or no correlation with a specific age grouping'.[60]

Over the years many authors have commented on the possible ideological reasons behind the provision of pyre- and grave-goods and, although they are many and varied, foremost among them is the suggestion that the deceased was being equipped for an afterlife in which the provided artefacts would prove useful.[61] The trends identified above are clearly indicative of deliberate funerary practices, which in some cases reflected aspects of both the age and sex of the deceased, but there is some mileage in the notion of equipping the dead for an aspired afterlife existence as much as simply reflecting identities held at death by the living person. Many grave-goods are items of dress or ornamentation and so could have simultaneously served to reflect identities in life and in death. The provision of weapons has traditionally been interpreted as the equipping of warriors, although it has been argued that these weapons are symbolic, as they are often not functional weapon sets and the individuals were often too young, old or infirm to use them.[62] The burial of whole animals, especially horses and dogs, is seen as an extension of including personal property in the grave, while the presence of butchered portions of animals and accessory vessels is usually interpreted as evidence of funerary feasting or of food and drink being provided for the deceased.[63] However, all of these practices could have held, at least originally, a pagan religious significance, even if they continued to be practiced after the nominal adoption of Christianity.

So grave-good assemblages can be demonstrated to be highly structured and to symbolically express a number of different messages, but to return to the issue of recognising the conversion in the material record, is this of any use to us? By far the most significant factor in the use of grave-goods is the distinct difference between the burial assemblages of the fifth and sixth centuries and those of the seventh and early eighth. These differences have long been recognised: Lethbridge's excavations at Burwell and Shudy Camps (both Cambridgeshire) in the 1930s provided the stimulus for Leeds's more detailed description of this 'Final Phase' material.[64] Early in the seventh century the character of all of the main grave-good assemblages changed and attention has been drawn to the strong Roman and Byzantine influences visible in the new artefacts. The proportion of unfurnished burials in cemeteries rose and the nature of the non-sex-specific assemblages changed: for example, glass vessels became less popular and bowls more so. Although the same types of weaponry continued to be deposited, the actual number of weapon burials declined significantly until they ceased in the late seventh century. However, jewellery assemblages exhibit the greatest changes: the major Germanic brooch types of the sixth century stopped being used 'almost overnight',[65] as did long strings of beads and many of the girdle items which typified the earlier assemblages. These were replaced by classical-influenced single disc brooches, single pins and pairs of pins, new types of necklaces with pendants and new types of girdle item.[66]

However we wish to read the burial assemblage, the shift from Germanic to Roman/Byzantine influenced grave-goods is striking and requires explanation. Clearly it represents a radical change in wider spheres of influence and the growth of interest in Romanitas could well be ascribed to the arrival of the Church.[67] It would certainly sit comfortably with the idea of a conversion

that took on and adapted existing local practices, changing their character, but not banning them outright. Although this is certainly a possibility, the evidence needs to be viewed within the context of the wider political changes that were afoot during the period; for example, Geake cites the rise of kingship as an equally important factor.[68] These processes are, of course, all bound up together and it is not unreasonable to suggest that, while the presence of Germanic grave-goods signals a non-Christian burial, the presence of Roman/Byzantine grave-goods might actually be an indication of a converting population gradually shifting its allegiance to Rome. This argument has recently been developed by Crawford, who has drawn attention to the explicitly Christian symbolism employed in some of this material, citing it as a clear indication that the new religion was a dominant factor.[69] As was referred to above, detailed study of the later end of the burial spectrum is made difficult by a lack of well excavated sites. Although Geake was able to list a number of East Anglian cemetery sites containing relevant material in her gazetteer, very few sites have been well published, Harford Farm being a notable exception.[70] However, if we accept the possibility that the change in stylistic influence reflects, directly or indirectly, the progress of Christianity, then it could be used as an indicator of the progress of the conversion. These changes in material are also related to a series of changes in cemetery location which fall outside the narrow focus of this paper, the relevance of which to this argument is considered elsewhere.[71]

Burial Orientation: Turning in the Grave

Studies of known examples of Christian burial from both medieval and post-medieval contexts have demonstrated that supine burial orientated west–east was, and continues to be, the norm for Christian burial.[72] Despite being so ingrained in Christian practice, it would appear that the reason for the adoption of this orientation has become obscured by history. It is now generally accepted that the head was placed to the west so that, come the Day of Judgement, the dead would rise up from their graves and face the east.[73] A number of liturgical explanations have been given for the Christian desire to face the east, foremost among them is the expectation that Christ will return from the east on the Day of Judgement.[74] But can the fact that Christian burials are aligned west–east be used to trace the progress of the conversion as some have suggested?[75]

Of course, it does not logically follow that just because all Christian burials are orientated west–east all west–east orientated burials must be Christian and numerous examples of deliberate west–east burials occur in many demonstrably non-Christian contexts from around the world and throughout history. Although liturgy is used to explain the Christian adoption of a west–east alignment, many of the non-Christian examples have been explained as orientation towards the direction of sunrise and/or sunset.[76] That the rising and, perhaps more so, the setting of the sun should become linked with death is not so surprising when one considers how fundamentally important it is to life and we should certainly consider the possibility that burial orientation is another instance of Christianity adopting an already widespread practice and subsequently finding its own justification for it.

Numerous examples of west–east burials occur in many demonstrably pre-Christian cemeteries in East Anglia, such as at Snape and Westgarth Gardens (Suffolk), Bergh Apton and Spong Hill (Norfolk).[77] Clearly then, the adoption of Christian burial practice did not involve the adoption of a new tradition of burial orientation in very many instances, although its meaning may well have been redefined. While the adoption of a west–east alignment is therefore no use as a direct indicator of conversion, the Christian observance is so strict, that we can at least say with certainty that burials which are *not* aligned west–east are demonstrably not Christian. Examples of non-west–east burials can also be found at Snape, Bergh Apton and Spong Hill, and also at Oxborough (Norfolk), where most of the burials were orientated on the prehistoric barrow around which the cemetery clustered.[78]

Conclusions

To date the conversion of Anglo-Saxon East Anglia has received relatively little attention, largely a result of the meagre survival of pertinent historical sources. Any attempt to rectify this situation has to be archaeological in nature and this paper has explored ways in which the period's archaeologically rich burial record could be used to trace the spread of Christianity throughout the region. The cessation of cremation in the seventh century appears to be a result of Christianity and it can be confidently stated that cemeteries which contain cremations represent communities that had yet to convert in their entirety. The absence of cremation does not automatically equate to Christian burial, but it is a necessary criterion. The

deposition of grave-goods did not cease as a result of the adoption of Christianity, but grave-goods became rarer and there was a distinct change in their character from a Germanic to a Roman/Byzantine influence. It is possible that Germanic goods represent non-Christian burials while Roman/Byzantine goods could be seen as an indication of a converted Christian population, but this remains unclear. Unfurnished burial was practiced throughout the period to varying degrees and is not a sound criterion. Finally, while it can be stated that a west–east orientation is a necessary criterion for identifying a Christian burial and that burials which are not orientated west–east are therefore not Christian, west–east burial was also widely practiced throughout the region during the Anglo-Saxon period, effectively ruling it out as an indicator of changing beliefs. Although none of these observations can be applied without provisos, it has at least been possible to demonstrate that material traces of the conversion can be identified in the East Anglian burial record. This is encouraging, because having kept this discussion quite general and limited it to some of the better published examples, it paves the way for a more detailed examination of the East Anglian burial record, published and unpublished. Hopefully the results of this examination will allow a more detailed picture of the spread of Christianity throughout the region to be painted.

Acknowledgements

Thanks are due to my supervisors at the University of East Anglia, Tom Williamson and Stephen Church, and also to Gareth Davies, Sophie Cabot, Trefor Jones, Naomi Payne and particularly Sarah Harrison, all of whom have commented on various versions of this work. I am also grateful to the HER officers for Norfolk, Suffolk, Essex, Cambridgeshire and Hertfordshire who provided the data for the figures. Finally, I must thank Howard Williams for inviting me to contribute this extra paper to his proceedings and for his encouragement throughout the writing process.

Notes

1. I am based at the University of East Anglia, where my research is funded by a postgraduate scholarship from the School of History.
2. A series of papers outlining my various different approaches to this problem, including examinations of the spatial arrangement of cemeteries, their changing locations and their wider landscape context, are currently in preparation.
3. *E.g.* Rahtz 1977; 1978; Rodwell 1989, 157–80; Daniell 1997; Thompson 2004.
4. *E.g.* Morrison 1992; Renfrew 1994; Fletcher 1997; Cusack 1998; Gameson 1999; Insoll 1999; 2001; 2004a and b; Mills and Grafton 2003a and b; Carver 2003.
5. *E.g.* Parker Pearson 1999; Geake 1997; Lucy 1998; 2000; Stoodley 1999; Hadley 2001; Lucy and Reynolds 2002; Effros 2002; 2003; Ravn 2003; Thompson 2004.
6. *E.g.* Meaney 2003; Crawford 2003; 2004.
7. *E.g.* Dickinson 1980; 2002; Scull 2000; Lucy and Reynolds 2002, 1–7; Williams 2002.

8. *E.g.* Boddington 1987; Wade 1997, 48.
9. *E.g.* Bergh Apton (Green and Rogerson 1978); Morning Thorpe (Green, Rogerson and White 1987); Spong Hill (Hills, Penn, and Rickett 1984); Snape (Filmer-Sankey and Pestell 2001).
10. *E.g.* Owen 1981, 67–125; Wilson 1992, 67–172; Arnold 1997, 149–75; Taylor 2001, 139–43; Williams 2001.
11. Wells 1960; McKinley 1989; 1994.
12. Lucy 1998, 49. See also Filmer-Sankey and Pestell 2001, 262–3.
13. *E.g.* Rahtz 1977; 1978; Rodwell 1989; Daniell 1997.
14. Reviewed in Geake 1997, 1–3; Taylor 2001.
15. MacGregor 2000, 221.
16. *E.g.* Daniell 1997; Geake 1997; 1999b; Härke 1992; Kendall 1982; Rahtz 1978.
17. *E.g.* Crawford 2003; 2004; Meaney 2003; Pluskowski and Patrick 2003.
18. Carver 1998a, 14.
19. Taylor 2001, 15.
20. Carver 2003, 4.

21. *E.g.* Carver 1998a; Urbańczyk 1998; 2003; Pluskowski and Patrick 2003.
22. *E.g.* Mayr-Harting 1991; Higham 1997; Yorke 1990; 2003.
23. Wilson 1992, 67–9; Hadley 2001, 92.
24. Morris 1983, 50.
25. Whitelock 1972, 1; Yorke 1990, 58.
26. Whitelock 1972; Yorke 1990, 58–71; Campbell 1996.
27. Williamson 1993, 137–42; Warner 1996, 108–15; Jones 1999, 30–45; Newton 2003.
28. Williamson 1993, 161.
29. Toulmin Smith 1964, 120; West 1998.
30. *E.g.* Caistor-by-Norwich (Myres and Green 1973); Spong Hill (Hills 1977; Hills and Penn 1981; Hills, Penn and Rickett 1984; 1987; 1994); West Stow (West 1985).
31. Newman 1995; Gurney 1997; Geake 2002; Chester-Kadwell 2004; 2005.
32. Toulmin Smith 1964, 120.
33. Figure 1 compiled from HER data for Norfolk, Suffolk, Cambridgeshire, Hertfordshire and Essex up until December 2003. Sites have been defined following the categories set out by Myres and Green (1973, 258–62). Base map after Glazebrook 1997, Fig. 2.
34. *E.g.* Hills 1999.
35. *E.g.* Owen 1981; Wilson 1992; Welch 1992; Lucy 2000; Taylor 2001; Glasswell 2002.
36. Myres 1977; Hills 1980, 197; McKinley 1994, 1.
37. Myres 1969, 13.
38. Myres 1969; 1977; Critiques: Hurst 1976, 294–9; Hills 1979, 324–6.
39. Richards 1987, 25.
40. Myres 1977, 35; Dickinson and Speake 1992; Davison, Green and Milligan 1993; Geake 1999a; Filmer-Sankey and Pestell 2001, 250–5.
41. Carver 1998b.
42. Carver 1998b, 136.
43. Carver 1989; 1998a; 1998b, 134–6.
44. Carver 1989; 1998a.
45. *E.g.* Philpott 1991; Petts 2003, 135–57.
46. *E.g.* Carver 1998a; Urbańczyk 1998; 2003; Pluskowski and Patrick 2003.
47. Williams 2001.
48. Cremation Society of Great Britain 1974; Bynum 1995.
49. Cremation Society of Great Britain 1974.
50. Meaney 1964; Geake 1997.
51. *E.g.* Hyslop 1963; Meaney and Hawkes 1970; Boddington 1990; Hadley 2001.
52. Rodwell 1989, 157–80; Boddington 1990; Geake 2002, 149–52.
53. Filmer-Sankey and Pestell 2001; Penn 2000.
54. Myres and Green 1973, 258–62.
55. *E.g.* Hines 1984.
56. Pader 1982; Brush 1993; Lucy 1998, 43; Ravn 2003.
57. Crawford 1991; Stoodley 1999; 2000.
58. *E.g.* Myres and Green 1973, 77–113; Richards 1987, 126–30; McKinley 1994, 86–92; Williams 2003.
59. Richards 1987, 126.
60. *Ibid.*, 130.
61. *E.g.* Ucko 1969; Bahn 1996; Parker Pearson 1999, 7–11; Taylor 2001, 23–4; Effros 2002.
62. Härke 1989; 1990; 1992.
63. *E.g.* Crabtree 1995; Bond 1996; Williams 2001.
64. Lethbridge 1931; 1936; Leeds 1936, 98–114.
65. Geake 1999b, 204.
66. Geake 1997; 1999b; 2002.
67. Geake 1999b, 209.
68. Geake 1999b, 209–12.
69. Crawford 2003; 2004.
70. Geake 1997, 143–91; Penn 2000.
71. My paper addressing the changing locations of cemeteries is currently in preparation.
72. *E.g.* Rahtz 1977; 1978; Rodwell 1989; Daniell 1997.
73. Dearmer 1949, 432; Rahtz 1978; Kendall 1982; Brown 1983.
74. Rahtz 1978.
75. *E.g.* Hawkes 1976.
76. *E.g.* Ucko 1969; Rahtz 1978, 1–3.
77. Filmer-Sankey and Pestell 2001, 246–48; West 1988, 7–8; Green and Rogerson 1978, 4; Hills, Penn and Rickett 1984, 2–6.
78. Filmer-Sankey and Pestell 2001, 246–48; Green and Rogerson 1978, 4; Hills, Penn and Rickett 1984, 2–6; Penn 2000, 24–5.

Bibliography

Arnold, C. J. 1997. *An Archaeology of the Early Anglo-Saxon Kingdoms*, London: Routledge.

Bahn, P. 1989. *The Bluffer's Guide to Archaeology*, London: Ravette Books Limited.

Bahn, P. G. (ed.). 1996. *Tombs, Graves and Mummies*, London: Weidenfeld and Nicholson.

Boddington, A. 1987. Chaos, disturbance and decay in an Anglo-Saxon cemetery, in A. Boddington, A. N. Garland and R. C. Janaway (eds), *Death, decay and reconstruction. Approaches to archaeology and forensic science*, 27–42, Manchester: University Press.

Boddington, A. 1990. Models of Burial, Settlement and Worship: The Final Phase Reviewed, in E. Southworth (ed.), *Anglo-Saxon Cemeteries: A Reappraisal*, 177–99, Stroud: Sutton.

Bond, J. M. 1996. Burnt offerings: animal bone in Anglo-Saxon cremations, *World Archaeol.*, **28**, 76–88.

Brown, D. 1981. Swastika patterns, in V. I. Evison (ed.), *Angles, Saxons and Jutes*, 227–40, Oxford: Clarendon Press.

Brown, M. A. 1983. Grave Orientation: A Further View, *Archaeol. Jnl.*, **140**, 322–8.

Brush, K. 1993. 'Adorning the Dead: The Social Significance of Early Anglo-Saxon Funerary Dress in England (Fifth to Seventh Centuries AD)', unpublished PhD thesis, University of Cambridge.

Bynum, C. W. 1995. *The Resurrection of the Body*, New York: Columbia UP.

Campbell, J. 1996. The East Anglian See before the Conquest, in I. Atherton, E. Fernie, C. Harper-Bill and H. Smith (eds), *Norwich Cathedral: Church, City and Diocese 1096–1996*, 3–21, London: Hambledon Press.

Carver, M. O. H. 1989. Kingship and material culture in early Anglo-Saxon East Anglia, in S. Bassett (ed.), *The Origins of Anglo-Saxon Kingdoms*, 141–58, Leicester: University Press.

Carver, M. O. H. 1998a. Conversion and Politics on the Eastern Seaboard of Britain; some archaeological indicators, in B. E. Crawford (ed.), *Conversion and Christianity in the North Sea World*, 11–40, St Andrews: University of St Andrews.

Carver, M. O. H. 1998. *Sutton Hoo: Burial Ground of Kings?*, London: British Museum Press.

Carver, M. O. H. (ed.) 2003. *The Cross Goes North*, York: York Medieval Press.

Chester-Kadwell, M. 2004. Metallic Taste: Archaeologists and the Treasure Hunters, in D. A. Barrowclough (ed.), *Our Precious Past*, 49–68, Cambridge: Red Dagger Press.

Chester-Kadwell, M. 2005. Metal-detector finds in context: New light on 'Dark Age' cemeteries in the landscape of Norfolk, *Archaeol. Rev. from Cambridge*, **20**(1), 70–96.

Crabtree, P. J. 1995. The Symbolic Role of Animals in Anglo-Saxon England: Evidence from Burials and Cremations, in K. Ryan and P. J. Crabtree (eds), *The Symbolic Role of Animals in Archaeology*, 200–26, Philadelphia: University of Pennsylvania.

Crawford, S. 1991. When do Anglo-Saxon Children Count?, *Jnl. of Theoretical Archaeol.*, **2**, 17–24.

Crawford, S. 2003. Anglo-Saxon Women, Furnished Burial, and the Church, in D. Wood (ed.), *Women and Religion in Medieval*

England, 1–12, Oxford: Oxbow.

Crawford, S. 2004. Votive deposition, religion and the Anglo-Saxon furnished burial rite, *World Archaeol.*, **36** (1), 87–102

Cremation Society of Great Britain. 1974. *The History of Modern Cremation in Great Britain from 1874*, London: Cremation Society.

Cusack, C. M. 1998. *Conversion among the Germanic Peoples*, London: Cassell.

Daniell, C. 1997. *Death and Burial in Medieval England, 1066–1550*, London: Routledge.

Davison, A., Green, B. and Milligan, B. 1993. *Illington: A Study of a Breckland Parish and its Anglo-Saxon Cemetery*, East Anglian Archaeology Report, 63, Gressenhall: Field Archaeology Division, Norfolk Museums Service.

Dearmer, P. 1949. *The Parson's Handbook (Twelfth Edition)*, Oxford: University Press.

Dickinson, T. 1980. The present state of Anglo-Saxon cemetery studies, in P. Rahtz, T. Dickinson, and L. Watts (eds), *Anglo-Saxon Cemeteries 1979*, 11–33, BAR British Series 82, Oxford: British Archaeological Reports.

Dickinson, T. 2002. Review Article: What's new in early medieval burial archaeology?, *Early Medieval Europe*, **2** (1), 71–87.

Dickinson, T. and Speake, G. 1992. The Seventh-Century Cremation Burial in Asthall Barrow, Oxfordshire: A Reassessment, in M. O. H. Carver (ed.), *The Age of Sutton Hoo*, 95–130, Woodbridge: The Boydell Press.

Effros, B. 2002. *Caring for Body and Soul*, Pennsylvania: Pennsylvania State UP.

Effros, B. 2003. *Merovingian Mortuary Archaeology and the Making of the Early Middle Ages*, London: University of California Press.

Filmer-Sankey, W. and Pestell, T. 2001. *Snape Anglo-Saxon Cemetery: Excavations and Surveys 1824–1992*, East Anglian Archaeology Report, 95, Ipswich: Archaeological Service, Suffolk County Council.

Fletcher, R. 1997. *The Conversion of Europe*, London: HarperCollins

Gameson, R. (ed.). 1999. *St Augustine and the Conversion of England*, Stroud: Sutton Publishing.

Geake, H. 1997. *The Use of Grave-Goods in Conversion-Period England c.600–c.850*, BAR British Series, 261, Oxford: British Archaeological Reports.

Geake, H. 1999a. When Were Hanging Bowls Deposited in Anglo-Saxon Graves?, *Med. Archaeol.*, **43**, 1–18.

Geake, H. 1999b. Invisible kingdoms: the use of grave-goods in seventh-century England, *Anglo-Saxon Stud. in Archaeol. and Hist.*, **10**, 203–15.

Geake, H. 2002. Further response to 'Time please', *Antiquity*, **76**, 386–7

Glasswell, S. 2002. *The Earliest English: Living and Dying in Early Anglo-Saxon England*, Stroud: Tempus

Glazebrook, J. (ed.) 1997. *Research and Archaeology: A Framework for the Eastern Counties. 1. Resource Assessment*, East Anglian Archaeology Occasional Paper, 3, Norwich: Scole Archaeological Committee.

Green, B. and Rogerson, A. 1978. *The Anglo-Saxon Cemetery at Bergh Apton, Norfolk*, East Anglian Archaeology Report, 7, Gressenhall: Norfolk Archaeological Unit.

Green, B., Rogerson, A. and White, S. G. 1987. *The Anglo-Saxon Cemetery at Morning Thorpe, Norfolk*, East Anglian Archaeology, 36, Gressenhall: Norfolk Archaeological Unit.

Gurney, D. 1997. A note on the distribution of metal-detecting in Norfolk, *Norfolk Archaeol.*, **42**, 528–32.

Hadley, D. M. 2001. *Death in Medieval England: An Archaeology*, Stroud: Tempus.

Härke, H. 1989. Early Saxon Weapon Burials: frequencies, distributions and weapon combinations, in S. C. Hawkes (ed.) *Weapons and Warfare in Anglo-Saxon England*, 49–59, Oxford: University Committee for Archaeology.

Härke, H. 1990. "Warrior Graves"? The Background of the Anglo-Saxon Weapon Burial, *Past and Present*, **126**, 22–43.

Härke, H. 1992. Changing Symbols in a Changing Society: The Anglo-Saxon weapon burial rite in the seventh century, in M. O. H. Carver

(ed.), *The Age of Sutton Hoo*, 149–66, Woodbridge: The Boydell Press.

Hawkes, S. C. 1976. Orientation at Finglesham: Sunrise Dating of Death and Burial in an Anglo-Saxon Cemetery in East Kent, *Archaeologia Cantiana*, **92**, 33–51.

Higham, N. J. 1997. *The Convert Kings*, Manchester: MUP.

Hills, C. 1977. *The Anglo-Saxon Cemetery at Spong Hill, North Elmham. Part I: Catalogue of Cremations 20–64 and 1000–1690*, East Anglian Archaeology, 6, Gressenhall: Norfolk Archaeological Unit

Hills, C. 1979. The archaeology of Anglo-Saxon England in the pagan period: a review, *Anglo-Saxon England*, **8**, 297–329

Hills, C. 1980. Anglo-Saxon Cremation Cemeteries, with particular reference to Spong Hill, Norfolk., in P. Rahtz, T. Dickinson and L. Watts (eds), *Anglo-Saxon Cemeteries 1979*, 197–207, BAR British Series 82, Oxford: British Archaeological Reports

Hills, C. 1999. Spong Hill and the Adventus Saxonum, in C. E. Karkov, K. M. Wickham-Crowley and B. K. Young (eds), *Spaces of the Living and the Dead: An Archaeological Dialogue*, 15–26, American Early Medieval Studies, 3, Oxford: Oxbow Books.

Hills, C. and Penn, K. 1981. *The Anglo-Saxon Cemetery at Spong Hill, North Elmham. Part II: Catalogue of Cremations 22, 41 and 1691–2285*, East Anglian Archaeology, 11, Gressenhall: Norfolk Archaeological Unit.

Hills, C., Penn, K. and Rickett, R. 1984. *The Anglo-Saxon Cemetery at Spong Hill, North Elmham. Part III: Catalogue of Inhumations*, East Anglian Archaeology, 21, Gressenhall: Norfolk Archaeological Unit.

Hills, C., Penn, K. and Rickett, R. 1987. *The Anglo-Saxon Cemetery at Spong Hill, North Elmham. Part IV: Catalogue of Cremations 30–2, 42, 44a, 46, 65–6, 2286–799, 2224 and 3325*, East Anglian Archaeology, 34, Gressenhall: Norfolk Archaeological Unit.

Hills, C., Penn, K. and Rickett, R. 1994. *The Anglo-Saxon Cemetery at Spong Hill, North Elmham. Part V: Catalogue of Cremations 2800–3334.* East Anglian Archaeology 67. Gressenhall: Field Archaeology Division, Norfolk Museums Service.

Hines, J. 1984. *The Scandinavian character of Anglian England in the pre-Viking period*, BAR 124, Oxford: British Archaeological Reports.

Hurst, J. G. 1976. The Pottery, in D. M. Wilson (ed.) *The Archaeology of Anglo-Saxon England*, 283–346, Cambridge: University Press.

Hyslop, M. 1963. Two Anglo-Saxon Cemeteries at Chamberlains Barn, Leighton Buzzard, Bedfordshire, *Archaeol. Jnl.*, **120**, 161–200.

Insoll, T. (ed.) 1999. *Case Studies in Archaeology and World Religion*, BAR International Series 755, Oxford: British Archaeological Reports.

Insoll, T. (ed.) 2001. *Archaeology and World Religion*, London: Routledge.

Insoll, T. (ed.) 2004a. *Belief in the Past*, BAR International Series 1212, Oxford: British Archaeological Reports

Insoll, T. 2004b. *Archaeology, Ritual, Religion*, London: Routledge.

Jones, T. 1999. *The English Saints: East Anglia*, Norwich: Canterbury Press.

Kendall, G. 1982. A Study of Grave Orientation in several Roman and post-Roman Cemeteries from Southern Britain, *Archaeol. Jnl.*, **139**, 101–23.

Leeds, E. T. 1936. *Early Anglo-Saxon Art and Archaeology*, Oxford: Clarendon Press.

Lethbridge, T. C. 1931. *Recent Excavations in Anglo-Saxon Cemeteries in Cambridgeshire and Suffolk*, Cambridge Antiquarian Quarto Publications, 3, Cambridge: Bowes and Bowes.

Lethbridge, T. C. 1936. *A Cemetery at Shudy Camps, Cambridgeshire*, Cambridge Antiquarian Quarto Publications, 5, Cambridge: Bowes and Bowes.

Lucy, S. 1997. Housewives, warriors and slaves? Sex and gender in Anglo-Saxon burials, in J. Moore and E. Scott (eds), *Invisible People and Processes*, 150–68, Leicester: University Press.

Lucy, S. 1998. *The Early Anglo-Saxon Cemeteries of East Yorkshire*, BAR British Series 272, Oxford: British Archaeological Reports.

Lucy, S. 2000. *The Anglo-Saxon Way of Death*, Stroud: Sutton Publishing.

Lucy, S. and Reynolds, A. (eds). 2002. *Burial in Early Medieval England and Wales*, Society for Medieval Archaeology Monograph, 17, London: SMA.

MacGregor, A. 2000. A seventh-century pectoral cross from Holderness, East Yorkshire, Med. Archaeol., 44, 217–22.

McKinley, J. I. 1989. Spong Hill Anglo-Saxon Cremation Cemetery, in C. A. Roberts, F. Lee and J. Bintliff (eds), *Burial Archaeology: Current Research, Methods and Development*, 241–8, BAR British Series 211, Oxford: British Archaeological Reports

McKinley, J. I. 1994. *The Anglo-Saxon Cemetery at Spong Hill, North Elmham. Part VIII: The Cremation*, East Anglian Archaeology, 69, Gressenhall: Field Archaeology Division, Norfolk Museums Service.

Mayr-Harting, H. 1991. *The Coming of Christianity to Anglo-Saxon England (3rd edit.)*, Pennsylvania: Pennsylvania State UP.

Meaney, A. 1964. *A Gazetteer of Early Anglo-Saxon Burial Sites*, London: George Allen and Unwin Limited.

Meaney, A. 2003. Anglo-Saxon Pagan and Early Christian Attitudes to the Dead, in M. O. H. Carver (ed.) *The Cross Goes North*, 229–41, York: York Medieval Press.

Meaney, A. and Hawkes, S. C. 1970. *Two Anglo-Saxon Cemeteries at Winnall, Winchester, Hampshire*, Society for Medieval Archaeology Monograph, 4, London: SMA.

Mills, K. and Grafton, A. (eds). 2003a. *Conversion in Late Antiquity and the Early Middle Age*, New York: University of Rochester Press.

Mills, K. and Grafton, A. (eds). 2003b. *Conversion: Old Worlds and New*, New York: University of Rochester Press.

Morris, R. 1983. *The Church In British Archaeology*, CBA Research Report, 47, York: CBA.

Morrison, K. F. 1992. *Understanding Conversion*, London: University Press of Virginia.

Myres, J. N. L. 1969. *Anglo-Saxon Pottery and the Settlement of England*, Oxford: Clarendon Press.

Myres, J. N. L. 1977. *A Corpus of Pagan Anglo-Saxon Pottery of the Pagan Period*, Oxford: Clarendon Press.

Myres, J. N. L. and Green, B. 1973. *The Anglo-Saxon Cemeteries of Caistor-by-Norwich and Markshall, Norfolk*, Reports of the Research Committee of the Society of Antiquaries of London, 30, London: SOA.

Newman, J. 1995. Metal Detector Finds and Fieldwork on Anglo-Saxon Sites in Suffolk, *Anglo-Saxon Stud. in Archaeol. and Hist.*, 8, 87–93.

Newton, S. 2003. *The Reckoning of King Rædwald*, Colchester: Red Bird Press.

O'Brien, E. 1999. *Post-Roman Britain to Anglo-Saxon England: Burial Practices Reviewed*, BAR British Series 289, Oxford: British Archaeological Reports.

Owen, G. R. 1981. *Rites and Religions of the Anglo-Saxons*, London: David and Charles.

Pader, E. J. 1982. *Symbolism, Social Relations and the Interpretation of Mortuary Remains*, BAR International Series 130, Oxford: British Archaeological Reports.

Parker Pearson, M. 1999. *The Archaeology of Death and Burial*, Stroud: Sutton Publishing Limited.

Penn, K. 1998. *An Anglo-Saxon Cemetery at Oxborough, West Norfolk: Excavations in 1990*, East Anglian Archaeology Occasional Papers, 5, Gressenhall: Field Archaeology Division, Norfolk Museums Service.

Penn, K. 2000. *Excavations on the Norwich Southern Bypass, 1989–91. Part II: The Anglo-Saxon Cemetery at Harford Farm, Caistor St Edmund, Norfolk*, East Anglian Archaeology, 92, Gressenhall: Archaeology and Environment Division, Norfolk Museum Service.

Petts, D. 2003. *Christianity in Roman Britain*, Stroud: Tempus.

Philpott, R. 1991. *Burial Practices in Roman Britain*, BAR British Series 219, Oxford: British Archaeological Reports.

Pluskowski, A. and Patrick, P. 2003. 'How do you pray to God?' Fragmentation and Variety in Early Medieval Christianity, in M. O. H. Carver (ed.), *The Cross Goes North*, 29–57, York: York Medieval Press.

Rahtz, P. A. 1977. Late Roman cemeteries and beyond, in R. Reece (ed.) *Burial in the Roman World*, 53–64, CBA Research Report 22, London: CBA.

Rahtz, P. A. 1978. Grave Orientation, *Archaeol. Jnl.*, 135, 1–14.

Ravn, M. 2003. *Death Ritual and Germanic Social Structure*, BAR International Series 1164, Oxford: British Archaeological Reports.

Renfrew, C. 1994. The archaeology of religion, in C. Renfrew and E. B. W. Zubrow (eds), *The Ancient Mind*, Cambridge: CUP.

Richards, J. D. 1987. *The Significance of Form and Decoration of Anglo-Saxon Cremation Urns*, BAR British Series 166, Oxford: British Archaeological Reports.

Rodwell, W. 1989. *Church Archaeology (Revised Edition)*, London: English Heritage/Batsford.

Scull, C. 2000. How the dead live, *Archaeol. Jnl.*, 157, 399–406.

Stoodley, N. 1999. *The Spindle and the Spear*, BAR British Series 288, Oxford: British Archaeological Reports.

Stoodley, N. 2000. From the cradle to the grave: age organization and the early Anglo-Saxon burial rite, *World Archaeol.*, 31, 456–72.

Taylor, A. 2001. *Burial Practice in Early England*, Stroud: Tempus.

Thompson, V. 2004. *Dying and Death in Later Anglo-Saxon England*, Woodbridge: Boydell.

Toulmin Smith, L. (ed.) 1964. *The Itinerary of John Leland Volume 4*, London: Centaur Press.

Ucko, P. 1969. Ethnography and archaeological interpretation of funerary remains, *World Archaeol.*, 1, 262–80.

Urbańczyk, P. 1998. Christianisation of Early Medieval Societies: an Anthropological Perspective, in B. E. Crawford (ed.), *Conversion and Christianity in the North Sea World*, 129–33, St Andrews.

Urbańczyk, P. 2003. The Politics of Conversion in North Central Europe, in M. O. H. Carver (ed.), *The Cross Goes North*, 15–27, York: York Medieval Press.

Wade, K. 1997. Anglo-Saxon and Medieval (Rural), in J. Glazebrook (ed.), *Research and Archaeology: A Framework for the Eastern Counties. 1. Resource Assessment*, 47–58, East Anglian Archaeology Occasional Paper, 3, Norwich: Scole Archaeological Committee.

Warner, P. 1996. *The Origins of Suffolk*, Manchester: University Press

Welch, M. 1992. *Anglo-Saxon England*, London: Batsford/English Heritage.

Wells, C. 1960. A Study of Cremation, *Antiquity*, 34, 29–37.

Wells, C. and Green, C. 1973. Sunrise Dating of Death and Burial, *Norfolk Archaeol.*, 35, 435–42.

West, S. E. 1985. *West Stow: The Anglo-Saxon Village*, East Anglian Archaeology Report, 24, Bury St. Edmunds: Suffolk County Planning Department.

West, S. E. 1988. *The Anglo-Saxon Cemetery at Westgarth Gardens, Bury St. Edmunds, Suffolk*, East Anglian Archaeology Report, 38, Bury St. Edmunds: Suffolk County Planning Department.

West, S. E. 1998. *A Corpus of Anglo-Saxon Material From Suffolk*, East Anglian Archaeology Report, 84, Ipswich: Suffolk County Council.

Whitelock, D. 1972. The pre-Viking age church in East Anglia, *Anglo-Saxon England*, 1, 1–22.

Williams, H. 2001. An ideology of transformation: Cremation rites and animal sacrifice in early Anglo-Saxon England, in N. S. Price (ed.), *The Archaeology of Shamanism*, 193–212, London: Routledge.

Williams, H. 2002. Remains of Pagan Saxondom? – The Study of Anglo-Saxon Cremation Rites, in S. Lucy and A. Reynolds (eds), *Burial in Early Medieval England and Wales*, 47–71, Society for Medieval Archaeology Monograph 17, London: SMA.

Williams, H. 2003. Material culture as memory: combs and cremations in early medieval Britain, *Early Med. Europe*, 12, 89–128.

Williamson, T. 1993. *The Origins of Norfolk*, Manchester: University Press.

Wilson, D. 1992. *Anglo-Saxon Paganism*, London: Routledge.

Yorke, B. 1990. *Kings and Kingdoms of Early Anglo-Saxon England*, London: Routledge.

Yorke, B. 2003. The Adaptation of the Anglo-Saxon Royal Courts to Christianity, in M. O. H. Carver (ed.), *The Cross Goes North*, 243–57, York: York Medieval Press.

Social Memory, Material Culture and Community Identity in Early Medieval Mortuary Practices

Zoë L. Devlin

Introduction

In recent years, the notion that attitudes to the past can be integral to the construction of social identity and community relations has become popular within archaeology and history. In particular, studies have often focused on the idea that a group has a *social memory* which embodies notions of the past that are relevant to the present.[1] Such studies have been wide-ranging, applying the notion of social memory to many aspects of social life in diverse cultures across all historical periods. However, it could be argued that the concept of social memory has the greatest potential when applied to a mortuary context, as in many cultures funerals are key settings for the evocation and manipulation of memories. More specifically, the links between portable artefacts and social memory that have been recently discussed in sociological and anthropological studies may be of particular use in studying early Anglo-Saxon furnished burial rites.

Several archaeological and anthropological studies of funerary behaviour have already recognised the potential of social memory theory to aid our understanding of past mortuary practices.[2] However, the notion of social memory itself is not without its problems, lacking a coherent body of theory and requiring careful consideration before it can be applied to archaeological research. The concept can be found under numerous guises. Social memory can also be collective, popular, imaginative, historical or cultural memory. In addition, the term goes beyond *memory*, incorporating remembrance and commemoration too. As these different terms suggest, there is no single approach to the study of social memory. Across the social sciences, different researchers conceive it in different ways, moulding the concept to fit their methods and theoretical background. Despite some attempts to unify the disparate approaches that exist between and even within disciplines, the study of social memory has been described as 'a non-paradigmatic, transdisciplinary, centreless enterprise'.[3]

Such difficulties challenge archaeologists and historians to set their own agenda in applying social memory theory to the mortuary practices of the early medieval period. Unfortunately, the lack of coherence created by such disparate approaches across the whole of the social sciences has so far not been recognised and therefore not discussed by archaeologists and historians studying social memory. *Memory* is often considered to be something that speaks for itself, that requires no definition. But as will be shown later this approach leaves memory as a vague concept and our understanding of early medieval conceptions of the past suffers because of this. Here it is argued that with a more thorough understanding of the underlying theory, the concept of social memory may prove a productive approach that can help to overcome some of the limitations in theoretical and methodological approaches to early medieval mortuary practices. The aim of this paper is to set out some preliminary arguments from ongoing research on the application of theories of memory to early medieval mortuary practices. It shall firstly discuss the ways in which researchers have previously approached social memory, before attempting a working definition suitable for the study of early medieval burials. Secondly, the paper will examine how objects, and specifically portable grave goods, have a part to play in the processes of social memory in mortuary contexts. Finally, it shall suggest some ways in which these ideas might inform our understanding of early Anglo-Saxon burial practices. The ideas discussed in this paper are developed more fully in the author's doctoral research.[4]

The Concept of Social Memory in the Social Sciences

The popular concept of memory is that of an individual, personal experience centring on the self. In contrast, within the social sciences memory is also seen as having a social aspect in its creation and transmission. The French sociologist Maurice Halbwachs was the first to stress the importance of society in the way memories are formed and recalled.[5] For him, all memories revolve around the concerns and attitudes of the social group, whether the group is a family, a community or a set of work colleagues. For Halbwachs, remembering is shaped by the frameworks of society; only what is relevant to the group is recalled. In this formulation, the individual person has little role in determining what is remembered.

Ironically, Halbwachs' work was forgotten for many years but the recent upsurge in interest in the study of memory in the humanities and social sciences has led to his theories being revived. Influenced by Halbwachs, some researchers argue that the idea dominant in the psychology of memory as an individual mental process tells us little about the way memories are formed and used in social contexts.[6] However, while they agree on following Halbwachs' emphasis on the importance of society in remembering, their definition of social memory varies widely, with no coherent body of theory to explain the influence of society. Researchers refer variously to social, collective, historical, cultural or shared memory, and even those researchers who use the same term differ in how they define it. Some use the terms interchangeably while others distinguish between them or use one only.[7] Still others argue that terms like social memory are too general and prefer more specific terms, such as official memory, vernacular memory, family memory, public memory or popular memory.[8]

Problems with definition do not end with terminology. There is no consensus either on what makes memory social, or on how it works. Some researchers argue that social memory is defined by its content: that it refers to memories of events that are relevant to the group rather than just the individuals that hold them. Memory is therefore something that takes place within individuals but which can have a social function.[9] Other researchers see social memory as something defined not by its content but by its formative process, *i.e.* that it is through social interaction and especially conversation that memories are formed and recalled.[10] Their studies examine the process by which an agreed version of the past is arrived at through discussion and argument. They suggest that language is not simply a window on mental processes but provides the environment in which memories are formed, justified and shared. As such, memories are formulated not within the individual mind but within society.

All these studies draw upon Halbwachs' work for their theoretical background and justification. That Halbwachs' work can provide the basis for so many different understandings of one concept is due to the ambiguities inherent in his work. Halbwachs was in the process of reformulating his arguments when he died; his work was therefore never completed to his satisfaction. In addition, his discussion is affected both by his aims and by the different influences under which he was writing. Halbwachs' intention was not to define the concept of *collective memory* (as he termed it) but to discuss how he saw memory as working in the real world, as opposed to the artificial environment of

contemporary psychology experiments. His discussion was formulated within the functionalist perspective of Durkheim but he had also had an early interest in individual psychology, which continued to influence his work.[11] It is this combination of two very different theoretical perspectives that creates the ambiguity in his work and allows it to be cited in support of widely differing definitions of social or collective memory.[12]

The concept of social memory propounded by Halbwachs and his followers is one that gives society an over-riding influence on remembering at the expense of individual memory. An alternative approach sees social memory as the result of interaction between individuals and society. This view can be summed up in the work of Frederic Bartlett and still has an enormous influence on modern approaches to memory by social and cognitive psychologists.[13] Bartlett's extensive studies found that the personality and emotions of the rememberer, the reason for the reminiscence and the intended audience can all have a strong effect on what is remembered and the form those memories take. In addition, memories are constructed against a background of social and cultural norms, which can affect not only how memories are passed on between individuals but also the way remembering occurs within an individual's mind. Memories are therefore highly selective and context-driven, dependent upon current circumstances for their shape and content. These psychological studies support the importance of society in memory formation and recall but also stress that remembering is centred around the individual. The inherent differences between the sociological and psychological approaches mean it is important for archaeologists and historians to clearly define what they mean by social memory.

The Concept of Social Memory in Archaeology and History

How social *is social memory?*

Archaeologists and historians have been increasingly interested in understanding how the people of early medieval Britain perceived their past and how this perception influenced their present identities and social relationships.[14] The utilization of theories of memory from the social sciences is one way in which this has been approached and social memory in particular has been seen as pivotal to our understanding.[15] Yet with no consensus among social scientists about what social memory is and how it operates in the modern world, how can archaeologists and historians apply it to the early medieval period, where researchers are even further distanced from the people they study? Unfortunately, the lack of clarity in social memory theory has yet to be dealt with directly by archaeologists and historians who use the concept. Despite its perceived importance, many studies of social memory in past societies do not directly discuss what they understand the concept to mean.[16] Social memory is often treated as a given, something that does not require further elucidation or elaboration. Yet the variety of possible approaches to it should make its clear definition a priority.

This lack of explicit discussion on the nature of social memory means that early medievalists might miss the full potential of memory theory to further our knowledge of medieval conceptions of the past. The nature of historical and archaeological material means that some attitude to the past can usually be inferred. The preservation of documents, the association of a site with earlier features of the landscape, the repair and continued use of jewellery, can all be taken as suggesting a wish to remember the past. Conversely, where such things are ignored, destroyed or allowed to decay, researchers speak of the past being *forgotten*.[17] In many studies to date, social memory has been offered as an explanation for a variety of behaviours and cultural expressions within a given society: the form of fairy tales, the violence in Iron Age bog body rituals, the re-use of ancient building material in Byzantine churches, all have been directly attributed to social memory.[18] But as Vinitzky-Seroussi has argued, '…if memory is everything and everything is memory, memory becomes such a catch-all phrase that it loses its significance'.[19] The question is whether the interpretation of this material in the light of social memory theory as it stands can tell us anything new about the past.

The way in which social memory is understood has direct implications for how it is seen to work in past societies. With social memory being potentially visible in all aspects of society, as something that can be applied anywhere and to anything, it becomes an almost passive phenomenon, something that seems to exist independently of the people within a society. A contrasting view sees it not as the end product, something to be studied in and of itself, but as a factor in the way people engage with their past. Ruth M. Van Dyke and Susan E. Alcock see social memory as 'the *construction* of a collective notion (not an individual belief) about the way things were in the past' (author's emphasis).[20] From this perspective, social memory is an ongoing process, active in the construction of the past, rather than something that exists outside the group in its own right. It is something in which members of a society are constantly engaged, requiring mental activity and social interaction on their part, rather than passively accepting what social memory imposes. It is therefore not something which archaeologists and historians need to identify but something that should be understood as instrumental in creating attitudes to the past.

This interpretation inevitably reintroduces the individual as the central figure in remembering, since social memory is the product of the interaction between individuals who have an interest, and a stake, in negotiating the past. Several historians have already questioned the rigid distinction between the recollections of individuals and social memory, arguing that memory is usually a mixture of the two.[21] So if memory *is* an individual phenomenon, in what ways could it be said to be social? Firstly, memory is social in that what is remembered and the form those memories take is largely due to the current social and political context. As we have already seen, researchers have shown that what people remember at any given time is shaped by contemporary social influences.[22] Secondly, events of the past can be remembered by more than one person. Most events are experienced by several people, whether on the scale of the family, community or nation.[23] Finally, memories can be shared with others, whether spoken out loud, written down, or performed.[24] All these aspects of social memory involve the active participation of individuals, since it is they who retain the memories in question and select from them what is relevant to the present. While this may often be done in negotiation with others, it is clear that individual people are central to this process rather than simply subscribing to a dominating external force.

What do we mean by social *memory*?

It is within this interaction between individual recollection and societal concerns that archaeologists and historians can find their definition of social memory. The re-introduction of the individual into our understanding of social memory suggests that there may be temporal limits on that phenomenon. Memories held by individuals imply personal experience and in defining social memory we must ask where that concept ends and other types of cultural knowledge, such as *tradition*, begin. A distinction has already been made between things that are *remembered* from personal experience and that which is *known* about the past through learning. Elizabeth Van Houts distinguished between an 'active memory' of personal experiences, which lasts up to 90–120 years, and knowledge of an older past, which is beyond the re-collection of any living person.[25] Sarah Foot has gone further than this, questioning the existence of a social *memory*, since memory can only occur at the level of the individual. She argues that the idea of a collective past is not *memory* at all but *commemoration*.[26] For her, notions of a collective past can only ever be dependent upon learned knowledge, not remembered personal experience.

Foot discusses this in the context of the disruption of the normal machinery of remembrance of the past by the Viking invasions and the invention of a new past by King Alfred after his victory over the Danes in 878.[27] She argues, convincingly, that this new (written) past, which aimed to unite a diverse people under Alfred's rulership, should not be characterized as social memory since all that the inhabitants of the new Anglo-Saxon kingdom would know of the past was what they had learned from texts rather than experienced personally. Of course, there is no easy distinction between a remembered past and a created, commemorative past like Alfred's, since the two can co-exist and inform each other. Alfred's new written past that was shared among the court did not negate or erase the memories of individuals and communities who remembered the Viking wars.

Where we can see a difference between Alfred's past and a truly remembered one is in its audience and its subscribers. Alfred's past was deliberately created to bind the inhabitants of a newly formed kingdom together by virtue of a common destiny. A remembered past, a social memory, could not be available on such a large scale since only a limited number of people could have experienced the same events and interpreted them in a similar way.[28] This suggests that social memory should not be conceived of simply as anything related to the generic past of a particular group. This is too broad a definition and renders the concept almost meaningless. Rather, it should be considered in terms of what members of the group have themselves experienced and shared with others, for it is this that provides the immediate context for changing roles and relationships within the community. Social memory should therefore be seen as being limited both temporally and spatially. It is also very much context-driven, recalled at a specific time to fulfil a particular need. As such, it is distinct from tradition or knowledge about the past, which can be available on a much larger scale and which may be less dependent on current circumstances for their survival.

Memory and Objects

That there are social influences on memory is indisputable. Memory does not exist purely inside people's heads. It is shaped by, and plays an active part in, social life. Memory forms a part of group relationships. It is therefore implicated in those things that form part of group dynamics: language, rituals, bodily practices and material objects.[29] Within archaeology, the importance of material culture in actively creating and maintaining social relationships and the importance of context in understanding them, is well recognised.[30] More recently, these ideas have been expanded on, with studies tracing the way the meaning of artefacts can alter over time.[31] This biographical approach is based on the work of Igor Kopytoff who argued that an object's meaning and value can change with its context.[32] Since the changes in meaning are cumulative, objects can acquire a biography or life-history so that an object's present significance is related to the people and events with which it was connected in the past. It is argued that since an object's meaning derives from its use within particular social contexts, its biography can reveal social interaction.[33]

A problem with the way the biographical approach has been applied lies in how objects are often treated as an objective 'record' on which the past is 'inscribed'.[34] To fully understand how objects can be related to the past, researchers need to take account of the ways that people participate in its construction. As Arjun Appadurai has argued, past meanings of an object influence how it is perceived and used in the present.[35] But these past interpretations may, just like memory, have been highly selective and related to the present context. The past with which an object was associated may not have included all, or indeed any, of its previous interpretations. For example, the monks of the monastery of Conques recorded their possession of a reliquary, described as the 'A' of Charlemagne in the twelfth century.[36] Charlemagne was believed to have presented this reliquary to the monastery at the time of its foundation. The A symbol was considered proof that Charlemagne had given Conques precedence over all his other foundations. However, Charlemagne was not actually the founder of Conques and the reliquary itself bore no relation to either him or the monastery's foundation. The reliquary's original interpretation – what may be thought of as its true biography – as a symbol of the alpha of Christ, had been forgotten.[37] Instead, a new past was created for the object which set it firmly in the contemporary context of Conques' struggle for supremacy over the rival abbey of Figeac.[38] Objects therefore do not carry an objective record of their past with them for observers to see. Instead, its past is always potentially open to reinterpretation. In this way, the past that archaeologists and historians impute to an object may not be in accord with the biography attributed to it in medieval times. In the creation of an object's biography remembering, forgetting and inventing can play equal roles in an object's biography.

It is clear though that objects can act as a link between past and present and in particular with people or events with which they have been associated, although this link is not always straightforward. Therefore, potentially they are strong conduits of memory. It has been argued that objects have a special resonance with the past. They have a permanence, an *objectivity*, that can long out-last their owners.[39] Objects can therefore provide an enduring link with the dead, acting as a visual mnemonic for those that are gone or for past experiences. Touch can be crucial in connecting with the past as it is the sense most linked to emotion.[40] Physical interaction with objects allows people to directly re-engage with their past in a way that is not possible with more transient experiences such as language or ritual.[41] Modern sociological studies have revealed that everyday objects with which a person regularly interacts are intimately related to the construction of that person's identity.[42] The way people interact with objects helps to create and confirm their identities and their relationships with others. The social philosopher Hannah Arendt argued that, 'the things of the world have the function of stabilising human life, and their objectivity lies in the fact that ... men, their ever-changing nature not withstanding can retrieve their sameness, that is, their identity, by being related to the same chair and the same table'.[43] Objects are instrumental in creating people's identity both practically, through limiting or expanding their abilities, and symbolically, through their relationship with personality and status.[44]

On the other hand, not every object need be associated with memories of people or events. For an object to have significance for the past requires more than mere regular interaction with them. Instead, people have to be prepared to revisit the past events with which the object is associated.[45] Only objects associated with a version of the past relevant to the present can be repositories of memory. In the modern period, for example, there is an emotional and intellectual distinction between antiques and junk that can often bear no relationship to the materials or quality of craftsmanship. In addition, for an object to have importance for memory it must be situated in a social context that marks it out as part of past experience. Several studies have shown how this can involve the removal of the object from its original social context and its placement in a new one.[46] Objects that have been removed from their original context may therefore have special significance for memory. It can be argued that for an object to be associated with memories of the past people's perceptions about it need to change. Such changes can be both triggered by and reflected in alterations in usage and the social context in which the object appears.

Memory and Objects in the Past: Grave Goods and Mortuary Ritual

This paper has argued that archaeologists should avoid interpreting the concept of social memory too broadly and applying it indiscriminately to all aspects of early medieval life and culture. However, the close relationship between memory processes and people's interaction with objects discussed here suggests early Anglo-Saxon funerary practices, in which burial with grave goods is so widespread, might benefit from the application of social memory theory. A number of issues can be raised regarding how the ideas discussed above might relate to such evidence. Firstly, how does social memory come into play during the funeral? How does it mediate the way identities are constructed and reconstructed at this time? The discussion above has revealed that memories can be social when several people remember a past event that they all experienced and where people share their personal experiences with others. Both these aspects of social memory are an integral part of the funeral process. We know from psychological and sociological studies that memories are constructed in the present and as such are influenced by current social and political circumstances. This means that a group's understanding

of its recent past is in a state of flux at the funeral.[47] Memories are being reconstituted and reclaimed by various members of the group as the death of one person leads to identities and responsibilities being renegotiated. The uncertainty generated by the loss of a member of a small community may have resulted in families trying to improve their position by reworking memories of the recent past, either to make themselves seem suitable successors or to denigrate their opponents.

The funeral context therefore presents an opportunity to revisit memories of the past, talking them through or acting them out, and passing them on to others. These could include memories concerning the deceased themselves and their place in the family or community, memories of previous funerals and of other family members, or of major events within the community's past. Funerals present the perfect situation in which to reminisce and rework the past since it is the past with which it is concerned; the central figure, the deceased, is now no longer a part of the present and has no place in the future. In addition, other aspects of life are put on hold for the funeral; the present is interrupted so people can focus on the past. Funerals also represent the ideal context for another aspect of social memory; it is events such as these, where remembering is central, that teach the community's children how to remember. It is through reminiscing with their parents that children learn what is considered worth remembering and the socially acceptable form in which remembering should occur.[48]

Secondly, what part did objects play in this process? Objects at the funeral provided a framework for recall in much the same way as does conversation.[49] The objects chosen to go into the grave acted as a visual mnemonic for the deceased; their presence acted to remind mourners of the deceased in life. Archaeologists cannot know from how large a choice objects were selected for inclusion within the grave but that certain ones were included at all suggests the mourners remembered the deceased in particular ways, choosing objects that seemed most appropriate. The personal belongings of the deceased were closely associated with them through regular use within everyday contexts. These objects were as much a part of them as were their physical remains. In addition, their link to the past and with the deceased was emphasized by their displacement from their usual context and their incorporation within a new one. The objects selected for inclusion in the mortuary rite would therefore have stood out through their dislocation from everyday situations and their appearance in the grave of a loved one. The tableau of the grave, the performance of the burial ritual and the heightened emotions of the mourners combined to actively create new memories in observers.[50]

In a funerary context, social memory is therefore actively involved in creating representations of the past both for the present and for the future. This has previously been discussed in terms of *prospective* and *retrospective* memory by Howard Williams in the context of Anglo-Saxon cremations.[51] He argues in particular that the inclusion of combs in cremation urns provided a material focus for prospective memories, serving to reconstitute and 're-member' the dead in a new form.[52] However, while Williams' analysis fits cremation burials very well, the division between prospective and retrospective memories is perhaps not always a useful one. At the funeral, there is an interaction between the past, present and future through the process of social memory. Prospective and retrospective memories are therefore inextricably intertwined; the form of one affects that of the other. A division between the two forms of social memory also fails to satisfy since it is only a relevant one at the funeral itself. While the funeral would be a focus of remembering in the future, these memories are never static but are constantly being reworked to fit contemporary circumstances. This means that archaeological material represents only the starting point of remembrance, never the finished product. Memories would have continued to be formed and reformed in response to other rituals and community crises. For the early medieval archaeologist studying mortuary practices, social memory theory can give us new insights into the provision of grave goods, revealing how decisions about what to include could be mediated through the act of remembering. Grave goods were not therefore simply chosen to represent a static list of attributes of the deceased, nor was their primary importance to project the power and status of the mourners, whether actual or desired. Instead, the selection of grave goods was related to memories of the past in which the deceased played a part. In turn, the biographies of the grave goods and their relationship to the deceased structured the community's memories of them, placing them firmly in the context of the community's past, present and future. Grave goods did not work alone in this process and so should be placed alongside ritual, language and performance to address how memories of the community's past were altered by the death of one of its members.

Conclusion

Social memory has become a popular way for archaeologists and historians to engage with the past of the societies they study while early medievalists in particular are just beginning to recognise its potential for mortuary archaeology. It seems an appropriate time therefore to consider exactly what the concept means

and how it can be of use in studying archaeological material. We have seen the disparate ways in which the concept is approached within the social sciences. This makes it particularly important for archaeologists, and historians, to define social memory in terms that are meaningful for them. I have argued here that social memory can be used to refer to three aspects of remembering. Firstly, it can refer to the sharing of one person's own memories with others, whether spoken, written or acted out. Secondly, social memory can refer to memories of past events that were experienced by several people together. Finally, when people reminisce together social memory refers to the way the memories are shaped by and are relevant to their current social circumstances.

In each case, social memory is active, not passive, helping to create new ways of seeing the past, present and future. It is not so much the memory itself as how that memory is interpreted, discussed and acted upon that makes it social. It is formed by the process of negotiation and discussion between individuals who have their own ways of seeing the world and their own interests at stake. The end product is a group's understanding of the world and of their place within it, which is at any time open to renegotiation. Archaeologists are in a position to gain a new perspective on social memory since objects are closely implicated in people's social lives and relationships. Mortuary evidence provides the ideal opportunity to examine this since it is at funerals that the past is directly revisited with the aid of objects buried with the deceased. It is through a thorough understanding of what social memory means within a community that archaeologists can open up new perspectives on mortuary practice.

Acknowledgements

The doctoral research on which this paper is based has been funded by the Arts and Humanities Research Council and the British Federation of Women Graduates Charitable Foundation. Grateful thanks are due to Catherine Cubitt, Guy Halsall, Julian D. Richards, Sarah Semple, Howard Williams and the anonymous reviewer for their helpful comments on various drafts of this paper. Thanks also to the conference attendees for their questions and comments which have helped me put my thoughts in order. Any errors remain my own.

Notes

1. For convenience throughout this paper, the terms social memory and collective memory will be used interchangeably although, as will become apparent, not all researchers would follow this. For a selection of studies from across different periods and geographical areas see the edited works of Chesson 2001b; Van Dyke and Alcock 2003a; Williams 2003a.
2. *E.g.* Chesson 2001a; Joyce 2001; Williams 2001; 2003b.
3. Olick and Robbins 1998, 105. Radstone's (2000) edited work attempts to create a concerted multi-disciplinary methodology to memory studies though it still suffers from a lack of theoretical order and clarification; see Vinitzky-Seroussi's (2001) review.
4. Devlin forthcoming.
5. Halbwachs 1992.
6. Gaskell and Wright 1997, 177. See also Middleton and Edwards 1990a; 1990b.

7. Climo and Cattell 2002. For instance, Basabe, Gonzalez and Paez (1997, 147) distinguish between social memory as 'the influence of social factors on individual memory', and collective memory as 'the distributed processes of memory or transactive memory with social functions'. Kujit (2001, 86) even refers to 'individual and collective social memory', although without explaining the distinction.

8. Olick and Robbins 1998, 112.

9. *E.g.* Basabe, Gonzalez and Paez 1997; Bellelli and Amatulli 1997; Crumley 2002.

10. *E.g.* Middleton and Edwards 1990a; 1990b; Pennebaker 1997; Pennebaker and Banasik 1997.

11. Durkheim 1912/1947; Coser 1992, 3.

12. On the one hand, Halbwachs speaks of memory as something possessed and constructed by the group as a whole, for example '... the various groups that compose society are capable at every moment of reconstructing their past' (1992, 182). On the other hand, the importance of the individual in remembering remains inherent in his work: 'While the collective memory endures and draws strength from its base in a coherent body of people, it is individuals as group members who remember' (Ibid, 48).

13. Bartlett 1932, 294–8; see also *e.g.* Baddeley, Conway and Aggleton 2001; Schacter 1995, 1996.

14. *E.g.* Bradley 1987; Holtorf 1998; Williams 1998a; 1998b.

15. For memory in general, see *e.g.* Geary 1994; Innes 1998; Remensnyder 1995, 1996; Van Houts 1999, 2001; Williams 2001. For social memory in particular, see Innes 2001 and n. 1 above.

16. Exceptions include Fentress and Wickham 1992; Holtorf 1998; Innes 1998; Jones 2003; Joyce 2003; McKitterick 2004.

17. See, for example, Geary 1994, especially pp. 23–29, 81–114.

18. For fairy tales and social memory, see Fentress and Wickham 1992. For bog bodies and social memory, see Mike Williams 2003. For re-used ancient building material as vehicles for the transmission of social memory, see Papalexandrou 2003.

19. Vinitzky-Seroussi 2001, 495.

20. Van Dyke and Alcock 2003b, 2.

21. Fentress and Wickham 1992, ix–x; Frisch 1989; Geary 1994, 10–11; Lowenthal 1985, 194–5

22. Babey, Queller and Klein 1998; Bartlett 1932; Clark, Stephenson and Kniveton 1990; Engel 1999; Middleton and Edwards 1990a; Shotter 1990.

23. See *e.g.* studies on the social memory for major events by Igartua and Paez 1997 and Pennebaker and Banasik 1997.

24. See Connerton 1989 in particular for the performance aspects of memory.

25. *I.e.* that memories stretch back up to three or four generations (Van Houts 1999, 6).

26. Foot 1999, 187–8.

27. Ibid., 197–200.

28. This observation clearly does not apply to the modern period where the advent of mass media allows millions to experience events, even if vicariously.

29. Climo and Cattell 2002, 17–21. For the importance of language in memory, see Middleton and Edwards 1990a; 1990b. For memory and bodily practices, see Connerton 1989.

30. *E.g.* Barrett 1994; Greene 1987; Hodder 1982; Parker Pearson 1982; Shanks and Hodder 1995.

31. See *e.g.* Eckardt and Williams 2003; Lillios 1999; Saunders 1999; Seip 1999; Skeates 1995, Williams 2001; Woodward 2002.

32. Kopytoff 1986; see also Appadurai 1986.

33. Gell 1998; Gosden and Marshall 1998.

34. Williams 2001, 40.

35. Appadurai 1986.

36. As discussed in Remensnyder 1995, 157–64; 1996, 897–906.

37. 'I am Alpha and Omega, the beginning and the ending...' (Rev. I.8); 'I am Alpha and Omega, the first and the last...' (Rev. I.11).

38. Remensnyder 1995; 1996.

39. Kwint 1999, 10

40. Pointon 1999, 41; Stewart 1999, 31.

41. Rowlands 1993, 144.

42. Csikszentmihalyi and Rochberg-Halton 1981; Frayling 1999, xiv.

43. Arendt 1958, 137.

44. Csikszentmihalyi and Rochberg-Halton 1981, 53.

45. Engel 1999, 150–1.

46. For instance, Radley (1990) conducted a study on the possessions of the elderly residents of care homes. The elderly residents and a selection of their belongings had been transplanted from one social context to another by their move from their own homes. He found that the social displacement of the objects in this way enhanced their significance as part of their owner's life history. See also Eckardt and Williams 2003; Lowenthal 1985, 240. For the modern period, the most obvious examples are museums and antique shops.

47. Radcliffe-Brown 1922; cited in Bartel 1982.

48. Fivush 1994.

49. See Middleton and Edwards 1990a; 1990b for the importance of conversation in constructing memories.

50. Halsall 2003.

51. Williams 2003b.

52. Ibid, 92.

Bibliography

Appadurai, A. 1986. Introduction: commodities and the politics of value, in A. Appadurai (ed.), *The Social Life of Things. Commodities in a Cultural Perspective*, 3–63, Cambridge: Cambridge University Press.

Arendt, H. 1958. *The Human Condition*, Chicago: University of Chicago Press.

Babey, S. H., Queller, S. and Klein, S. B. 1998. The role of expectancy violating behaviours in the representation of trait knowledge: a summary-plus-exception model of social memory, *Social Cognition*, **16**, 287–339.

Baddeley, A., Conway, M. and Aggleton, J. (eds) 2001. *Episodic Memory. New Directions in Research*, Oxford and London: Oxford University Press.

Barrett, J. C. 1994. *Fragments From Antiquity. An Archaeology of Social Life in Britain, 2900–1200 BC*, Oxford: Blackwell Publishers.

Bartel, B. 1982. A historical review of ethnological and archaeological analyses of mortuary practices, *Jnl. of Anthropological Archaeol.*, **1**, 32–58.

Bartlett, F. C. 1932. *Remembering. A Study in Experimental and Social Psychology*, Cambridge: Cambridge University Press.

Basabe, N., Gonzalez, J. L. and Paez, D. 1997. Social processes in collective memory: a cross-cultural approach to remembering political events, in J. W. Pennebaker, D. Paez and B. Rimé (eds), *Collective Memory of Political Events*, 147–74, Mahwah, New Jersey: Lawrence Erlbaum Associates, Publishers.

Bellelli, G. and Amatulli, M. A. C. 1997. Nostalgia, immigration and collective memory, in J. W. Pennebaker, D. Paez and B. Rimé (eds), *Collective Memories of Political Events. Social Psychological Perspectives*, 209–20, Mahwah, New Jersey: Lawrence Erlbaum Associates, Publishers.

Bradley, R. 1987. Time regained: the creation of continuity, *Jnl of the Brit. Archaeol. Assoc.*, **140**, 1–17.

Chesson, M. S. 2001a. Social memory, identity and death: an introduction, in M. S. Chesson (ed.), *Social Memory, Identity and Death: Anthropological Perspectives on Mortuary Rituals*, 1–10, Archaeological Papers of the American Anthropological Association, 10, Arlington: Virginia.

Chesson, M. S. (ed.) 2001b. *Social Memory, Identity and Death:*

Anthropological Perspectives on Mortuary Rituals, Archaeological Papers of the American Anthropological Association, 10, Arlington: Virginia.

Clark, N. K., Stephenson, G. M. and Kniveton, B. H. 1990. Social remembering: quantitative aspects of individual and collaborative remembering by police officers and students, *Brit. Jnl of Social Psychology*, **81**, 73–94.

Climo, J. J. and Cattell, M. G. 2002. Introduction. Meaning in social memory and history: anthropological perspectives, in J. J. Climo and M. G. Cattell (eds), *Social Memory and History. Anthropological Perspectives*, 1–36, Walnut Creek, California: Altamira Press.

Connerton, P. 1989. *How Societies Remember*, Cambridge: University of Cambridge.

Coser, L. A. 1992. Introduction: Maurice Halbwachs 1877–1945, in M. Halbwachs, *On Collective Memory*, ed., transl. and with an introduction by L. A. Coser, 1–35, Chicago and London: University of Chicago Press.

Crumley, C. L. 2002. Exploring venues of social memory, in M. G. Cattell and J. J. Climo (eds), *Social Memory and History: Anthropological Perspectives*, 39–52, Walnut Creek, California: Altamira Press.

Csikszentmihalyi, M. and Rochberg-Halton, E. 1981.*The Meaning of Things. Domestic Symbols and the Self*, Cambridge: Cambridge University Press.

Devlin, Z. L. forthcoming. *Remembering the Dead in Anglo-Saxon England: Memory Theory in Archaeology and History*, British Archaeological Reports, British Series.

Durkheim, E. 1912/1947. *The Elementary Forms of Religious Life*, New York: the Free Press.

Eckardt, H. and Williams, H. 2003. Objects without a past? The use of Roman objects in early Anglo-Saxon graves, in H. Williams (ed.), *Archaeologies of Remembrance. Death and Memory in Past Societies*, 141–70, New York: Kluwer Academic/Plenum Publishers.

Engel, S. 1999. *Context is Everything: the Nature of Memory*, New York: Freeman and Company.

Fentress, J. and Wickham, C. 1992. *Social Memory*, Oxford: Blackwell Publishers.

Fivush, R. 1994. Constructing narrative, emotion and self in parent-child conversations about the past, in U. Neisser and R. Fivush (eds), *The Remembering Self. Construction and Accuracy in the Self-Narrative*, 136–57, Cambridge: Cambridge University Press.

Foot, S. 1999. Remembering, forgetting and inventing: attitudes to the past in England at the end of the first Viking Age, *Trans. Royal Hist. Soc.*, 6th ser., **9**, 185–200.

Frayling, C. 1999. Preface, in M. Kwint, C. Breward and J. Aynsley (eds), *Material Memories. Design and Evocation*, xiii-xiv, Oxford and New York: Berg

Frisch, M. 1989. American history and the structures of collective memory: a modest exercise in empirical iconography, *Jnl. of Amer. Hist.*, **75**, 1130–55

Gaskell, G. D. and Wright, D. B. 1997. Group differences for memory of a political event, in J. W. Pennebaker, D. Paez and B. Rimé (eds), *Collective Memories of Political Events. Social Psychological Perspectives*, 175–89, Mahwah, New Jersey: Lawrence Erlbaum Associates.

Geary, P. 1994. *Phantoms of Remembrance. Memory and oblivion at the end of the first Millennium*, Princeton, New Jersey: Princeton University Press.

Gell, A. 1998. *Art and Agency: an anthropological theory*, Oxford: Clarendon Press.

Gosden, C. and Marshall, Y. 1999. The cultural biography of objects, *World Archaeol.*, **31**(2), 169–78.

Greene, K. 1987. Gothic material culture, in I. Hodder (ed.), *Archaeology as Long-term History*, 117–30, Cambridge: Cambridge University Press.

Halbwachs, M. *On Collective Memory*, ed., transl. and with an introduction by L. A. Coser, Chicago and London: University of Chicago Press.

Halsall, G. 2003. Burial writes: graves, "texts" and time in early Merovingian northern Gaul, in J. Jarnut and M. Wemhoff (eds), *Erinnerungskultur im Bestattungsritual. Archäologisch-Historisches Forum*, 61–74, Munich: Wilhelm Fink Verlag.

Holtorf, C. 1998. The life-histories of megaliths in Mecklenburg-Vorpommern (Germany), *World Archaeol.* **30**(1), 23–38.

Hodder, I. 1982. *Symbols in Action*, Cambridge and New York: Cambridge University Press.

Igartua, J. and Paez, D. 1997. Art and remembering traumatic collective events: the case of the Spanish Civil War, in J. W. Pennebaker, D. Paez and B. Rimé (eds), *Collective Memories of Political Events. Social Psychological Perspectives*, 79–101, Mahwah, New Jersey: Lawrence Erlbaum Associates.

Innes, M. 1998. Memory, orality and literacy in an early medieval society, *Past and Present*, **158**, 3–36.

Innes, M. 2001. Keeping it in the family: women and aristocratic memory, 700–1200, in E. M. C. Van Houts (ed.), *Medieval Memories. Men, Women and the Past, 700–1300*, 17–35, Harlow: Pearson Education Ltd.

Jones, A. 2003. Technologies of remembrance. Memory, materiality and identity in Early Bronze Age Scotland, in H. Williams (ed.), *Archaeologies of Remembrance. Death and Memory in Past Societies*, 65–88, New York: Kluwer Academic/Plenum Publishers.

Joyce, R. A. 2001. Burying the dead at Tlatilco: social memory and social identity, in M. S. Chesson (ed.), *Social Memory, Identity and Death: Anthropological Perspectives on Mortuary Rituals*, 12–26, Archaeological Papers of the American Anthropological Association, 10, Arlington, Virginia.

Joyce, R. A. 2003. Concrete memories: fragments of the past in the Classic Maya Present (500–1000 AD), in R. M. Van Dyke and S. E. Alcock (eds), *Archaeologies of Memory*, 104–25, Oxford: Blackwell.

Kopytoff, I. 1986. The cultural biography of things: commoditization as process, in A. Appadurai (ed.), *The Social Life of Things. Commodities in a Cultural Perspective*, 64–91, Cambridge: Cambridge University Press.

Kujit, I. 2001. Place, death and the transmission of social memory in early agricultural communitites of the Near Eastern pre-pottery Neolithic, in M. Chesson (ed.), *Social Memory, Identity and Death: Anthropological Perspectives on Mortuary Rituals*, 80–99, Archaeological Papers of the American Anthropological Association, 10, Arlington, Virginia.

Kwint, M. 1999. Introduction: the physical past, in M. Kwint, C. Breward and J. Aynsley (eds), *Material Memories. Design and Evocation*, 1–16, Oxford and New York: Berg.

Lillios, K. T. 1999. Objects and memory: the ethnography and archaeology of heirlooms, *Jnl of Archaeol. Method and Theory*, **6**(3), 235–62.

Lowenthal, D. 1985. *The Past is a Foreign Country*, Cambridge: Cambridge University Press.

McKitterick, R. 2004. *History and Memory in the Carolingian World*, Cambridge: Cambridge University Press.

Middleton, D. and Edwards, D. 1990a. Introduction, in D. Middleton and D. Edwards (eds), *Collective Remembering*, 1–22, London: Sage Publications.

Middleton, D. and Edwards, D. 1990b. Conversational Remembering: a social psychological approach, in D. Middleton and D. Edwards (eds), *Collective Remembering*, 23–45, London: Sage Publications.

Olick, J. K. and Robbins, J. 1998. Social memory studies: from 'Collective Memory' to the historical sociology of mnemonic practices, *Ann. Rev. of Sociology*, **24**, 105–40.

Papalexandrou, A. 2003. Memory, tattered and torn: spolia in the heartland of Byzantine Hellenism, in R. M. Van Dyke and S. E. Alcock (eds), *Archaeologies of Memory*, 56–80, Oxford: Blackwell.

Parker Pearson, M. 1982. Mortuary practices, society and ideology: an ethnoarchaeological study, in I. Hodder (ed.), *Symbolic and*

Structural Archaeology, 99–113, Cambridge: Cambridge University Press.

Pennebaker, J. W. 1997. Introduction, in J. W. Pennebaker, D. Paez and B. Rimé (eds), *Collective Memories of Political Events. Social Psychological Perspectives*, vii–xi, Mahwah, New Jersey: Lawrence Erlbaum Associates.

Pennebaker, J. W. and Banasik, B. L. 1997. On the creation and maintenance of collective memories: history as social psychology, in J. W. Pennebaker, D. Paez and B. Rimé (eds), *Collective Memories of Political Events. Social Psychological Perspectives*, 3–19, Mahwah, New Jersey: Lawrence Erlbaum Associates.

Pointon, M. 1999. Materialising mourning: hair, jewellery and the body, in M. Kwint, C. Breward and J. Aynsley (eds), *Material Memories. Design and Evocation*, 39–57, Oxford and New York: Berg

Radley, A. 1990. Artefacts, memory and a sense of the past, in D. Middleton and D. Edwards (eds), *Collective Remembering*, 46–59, London: Sage Publications.

Radstone, S. (ed.) 2000. *Memory and Methodology*, Oxford and New York: Berg.

Remensnyder, A. G. 1995. *Remembering Kings Past*, Ithaca: Cornell University Press.

Remensnyder, A. G. 1996. Legendary treasure at Conques: reliquaries and imaginative memory, *Speculum*, **71**, 884–906.

Rowlands, M. 1993. The role of memory in the transmission of culture, *World Archaeol.*, **25**(2), 141–151.

Saunders, N. 1999. Biographies of brilliance: pearls, transformations of matter and being, *c.* AD 1492, *World Archaeol.*, **31**(2), 243–57.

Schacter, D.L. (ed.) 1995. *Memory Distortion. How Minds, Brains and Societies Reconstruct the Past*, Cambridge, Massachusetts and London, England: Harvard University Press.

Schacter, D.L. 1996. *Searching for Memory. The Brain, the Mind and the Past*, New York: Basic Books.

Seip, L. 1999. Transformations of meaning: the life history of a Nuxalk mask, *World Archaeol.*, **31**(2), 272–87.

Shanks, M. and Hodder, I. 1995. Processual, post-processual and interpretive archaeologies, in I. Hodder, M. Shanks, A. Alexandri, V. Buchli, J. Carman, J. Last and G. Lucas (eds), *Interpreting Archaeology. Finding meaning in the past*, 3–29, London and New York: Routledge.

Shotter, J. 1990. The social construction of remembering and forgetting, in D. Middleton and D. Edwards (eds), *Collective Remembering*, 120–38, London: Sage Publications.

Skeates, R. 1995. Animate objects: a biography of prehistoric 'axe-amulets' in the central Mediterranean region, *Proc. of the Prehistoric Society.*, **61**, 279–301.

Stewart, S. 1999. Prologue: from the museum of touch, in M. Kwint, C. Breward and J. Aynsley (eds), *Material Memories. Design and Evocation*, 17–36, Oxford and New York: Berg.

Van Dyke, R. M. and Alcock, S. E. (eds) 2003a. *Archaeologies of Memory*, Oxford: Blackwell.

Van Dyke, R. M. and Alcock, S. E. 2003b. Archaeologies of memory: an introduction, in R. M. Van Dyke and S. E. Alcock (eds), *Archaeologies of Memory*, 1–13, Oxford: Blackwell.

Van Houts, E. M. C. 1999. *Memory and Gender in Medieval Europe, 900–1200*, London: Macmillan Press Ltd.

Van Houts, E. M. C. (ed.) 2001. *Medieval Memories. Men, Women and the Past, 700–1300*, Harlow: Pearson Education Ltd.

Vinitzky-Seroussi, V. 2001. Review of *Memory and Methodology*, Susannah Radstone (ed.), *American Ethnologist*, **28**(2), 494–496.

Williams, H. 1998a. Monuments and the past in early Anglo-Saxon England, *World Archaeology*, **30**(1), 90–108.

Williams, H. 1998b. Ancient landscapes and the dead: the reuse of prehistoric and Roman monuments as early Anglo-Saxon burial sites, *Medieval Archaeology*, **41**, 1–32.

Williams, H. 2001. Death, memory and time: a consideration of the mortuary practices at Sutton Hoo, in C. Humphrey and W. M. Ormrod (eds), *Time in the Medieval World*, 35–71, Woodbridge: Boydell and Brewer and York Medieval Press.

Williams, H. (ed.) 2003a. *Archaeologies of Remembrance. Death and Memory in Past Societies*, New York: Kluwer Academic/Plenum Publishers.

Williams, H. 2003b. Material culture as memory: combs and cremation in early medieval Britain, *Early Medieval Europe*, **12**, 89–128.

Williams, M. 2003. Tales from the dead. Remembering the bog bodies in the Iron Age of north-western Europe, in Williams, H. (ed.), *Archaeologies of Remembrance. Death and Memory in Past Societies*, 89–112, New York: Kluwer Academic/Plenum Publishers.

Woodward, A. 2002. Beads and Beakers: heirlooms and relics in the British Early Bronze Age, *Antiquity*, **76**, 1040–47.

Early Medieval Burial Studies
in Scandinavia 1994–2003

Martin Rundkvist

Introduction

To many archaeologists, including myself, graves are a second-rate means to an end. I would gladly swap an entire early medieval cemetery for the telephone number of a single one of its inhabitants. Archaeologists study graves because the people we would like to talk to are all dead.

This means that, generally speaking, archaeologists are not interested in information on graves *per se*, but in making inferences about living societies in the past from their graves. Graves, of course, have great strengths and great weaknesses for this purpose. On one hand, they are often rich closed finds enclosed in intricate structures, which is why archaeologists favour them. On the other hand, graves are anything but people who have suddenly fossilized at their daily chores. All that palaeontologists have to worry about in the interpretation of their dead subjects is taphonomy. The graves that archaeologists study are in fact works of art, portraits to be exact, and we cannot ask the artists if they were photographic realists, expressionists, symbolists, cubists, or what.

This paper attempts a brief overview of analytical, interpretative and synthetic work on early medieval graves in Scandinavia and/or published by Scandinavian scholars from 1994 to 2003.

By the Early Middle Ages I mean (following British terminology) the fifth through the eleventh centuries AD. In Scandinavia, archaeologists call this period the Late Iron Age, a period that is studied and perceived as a period of Prehistory. Thus, in Scandinavia, early medieval graves can only very rarely be linked to any historically attested migrations, wars, kingdoms or royal dynasties. By Scandinavia I mean Denmark, Sweden, and Norway. As can be deduced from their titles, most of the listed works are written in Scandinavian languages, but they often have summaries in English. Although some research by Finnish scholars is reviewed and listed here, this covers only publications in Germanic languages. Publications in Finnish on this topic are not reviewed here.

The text of this paper is followed in the appendix by an annotated bibliography where the listed works are classified according to the main themes they pursue under the overarching subject. In Scandinavia, many useful and innovative studies are produced every year as exam papers by undergraduate and graduate students. In Sweden, those of post-graduate students are printed and widely distributed, but in Denmark and Norway they are not. This means that there are many extensive works on the archaeology of these countries that are only available as photocopies from university departments. These Danish *specialer* and Norwegian *hovedoppgaver* are as a rule not available at Swedish libraries. I have not been able to access them and thus no attempt is made to cover them in the appendix. Only printed monographs and journal articles are listed here.

As will become apparent, the time when Scandinavian archaeology produced all the hot new theory ended more than a century ago. Since the 1970s we have been at the beck and call of Anglo-American theoretical evangelists. Our studies of early medieval graves have consequently followed largely the same lines as American and British work on furnished burial. Nevertheless, even if the broad lines of our thinking will be familiar to British readers, the details and methodology may be worth studying.

My reading in British early medieval burial studies has been limited and I cannot make any detailed comparison between Scandinavian and British work. I do, however, wish to submit that even the most respected British archaeological theoreticians appear to be held in far less awe by their compatriots than by many Scandinavians. A prophet is not without honour, save in his own country, and in his own house.[1]

Religion

The most common theme in Scandinavian burial studies since 1994 has been religion, including cosmology and ritual behaviour. This field of research can be said to by-pass the problematic relationship between living people and their mortuary image, because studies have tended to focus on burial as indicative of religious beliefs and world views that need not reflect living society directly. Since the beginnings of the discipline, many Scandinavian scholars have argued that as graves are works of art and possibly related to beliefs about an afterlife, they are particularly useful as sources on belief systems. It can be argued that if we primarily want to know what people in the past imagined to be true, then we need not bother about what was actually true in their world.

In Scandinavian early medieval studies, there are basically two ways to write about religion: with or without reference to the Old Norse literature of Iceland. High Medieval Iceland where this literature was penned is distant in time, space and religious beliefs from the rich early medieval burial record of, for example, south-east Scandinavia. It would thus be quite defensible on source-critical grounds to ignore the Icelanders and interpret these graves in the light of generalized ethnographic parallels.

However, although the Old Norse texts may not be immediately relevant to Scandinavian early medieval graves, they are in fact closer to them in time and space than any modern ethnography. In the past decade most archaeologists writing about early medieval Scandinavian religion have made use of the texts to some extent despite the biases and problems that they present. One of the most thorough books in this group, Neil Price's award-winning dissertation,[2] covers both Germanic and Saami religion.

Conversion to Christianity has also been intensively studied with the aid of graves.[3] In most of Scandinavia, conversion coincided with the end of cremation and furnished burial and the introduction of westward-orientated inhumation. In many areas burial also moved to churchyards at the time of conversion. However, as elsewhere in northern and western Europe, archaeologists continue to debate the timing of changes in religious belief and how these coincided with changes in mortuary practice. There are areas where pagans and Christians seem to have co-existed as separate organised cultic communities for long periods of time, for instance Gotland and Uppland.

Social Structure: Status, Gender, Age Roles

Social structure is a field where the relationship between mortuary image and living person is important. The Scandinavian consensus seems to be that whereas a single grave may not be a good likeness of its inhabitant, it is worthwhile to identify recurring roles depicted in many graves. These roles may be close to idealized versions of the roles played by living people. Among the dimensions of social structure that have been studied, social inequality, gender and age roles are the most well-researched.

The main developments in these approaches in recent years have been in terms of methodology rather than theory. For example, the application of computer-aided correspondence analysis has provided good tools for the exploration of large data sets. Recurring roles show up as clusters in the scattergrams, often illustrating patterns that are hard to discern in more conventional forms of analysis. Mads Ravn has applied this methodology to the early Anglo-Saxon cremation cemetery at Spong Hill[4] and I have done likewise myself with burials from Gotland.[5] Such statistical approaches are still uncommon, however.

Ethnicity and Territorial Organisation

Scandinavian scholars generally have an up-to-date view of ethnicity. Drawing upon anthropological studies of ethnicity, it is seen as dynamically negotiated and having characteristics both of a situational construct and of *longue durée* culture.

In the Scandinavian context, few archaeologists believe that Swedish, Norwegian or Danish are valid ethnic distinctions when dealing with early medieval graves. The dead are generally conceived of simply as Norsemen, with a myriad of rather similar local identities up to the county level taken for granted. Fredrik Svanberg has pursued this line of inquiry on a detailed level.[6] He has mapped variation in burial ritual and grave goods across south-east Scandinavia and argues for a patchwork quilt of small ethnic territories in the Viking Period.

What interests many scholars is determining whether graves in certain areas contain Norsemen (that is, Germanic speakers), Fenno-Ugric speakers or Slavonic speakers. It is apparently important to distinguish Norsemen from the 'others'. This is largely because of

A) the Saami: Fenno-Ugric-speaking reindeer pastoralists in northern Scandinavia,[7]
B) the Finland Swedes: Swedish-speaking upper-middle class people in coastal Finland,[8]
C) the Western Slavs, who settled along the southern shores of the Baltic Sea in the Early Middle Ages.[9]

Both the Saami and the Finland Swedes are regular features of today's political agenda. The continuing Scandinavian interest in the Western Slavs is an echo of a fierce nineteenth- and twentieth-century debate between German and Slavic-speaking scholars.[10]

Unfortunately, issues of linguistics and ethnicity can never be settled in the absence of relevant written sources. All archaeologists can do is point to similarities and differences in material culture and state their conviction that these differences or similarities are indicative of ethnic and linguistic identities. There is no way to test such propositions.

DNA studies have produced surprising results in this field. Modern Saami are genetically distinct from modern Swedes and Norwegians. A genetic trait confined to modern Saami has been identified in male human bones from two boat graves in southern Sweden.[11] The inhabitants of these boat graves are generally interpreted as high-ranking members of the royal Swedish retinue at Old Uppsala.[12] Apparently some of these Swedish aristocrats were either recruited from among the Saami, intermarrying with the Saami or, at the very least, officially recognizing their children with Saami slaves. (All this pre-supposing, of course, that the sequenced DNA came from the interred individuals and not from someone who has handled their bones.) Birch bark tents found in the graves indicate close contact with the Saami.[13]

These results suggest that the gene pool of early medieval Norsemen was neither homogeneous nor isolated. Neither, it seems, was their ethnic identity and cultural repertoire. Genetic and cultural traits are, of course, mutually independent. The colour of one's skin may influence what pigment one selects for body paint, but it has no bearing upon *e.g.* a society's organisation, architecture or epic poetry.

The past decade saw the tail-end of a research tradition where monumental or uncommonly rich graves were plotted on maps in order to identify early kingdoms and royal seats.[14] This tradition has been somewhat undermined by the realisation that graves are not people. For instance, the nascent Danish kingdom of the eighth century has left ample evidence of high-ranking settlements, proto-urbanisation and large-scale engineering projects, but hardly any rich or monumental graves at all.

Military Organisation

Starting from Danish research into war booty sacrifices, there has been a growing awareness that early medieval warfare was highly organized and geographically far-reaching.[15] Military ranks identified in Continental written sources or from the various equipment quality groups in the war booty sacrifices have been projected onto weapon graves. This is the same problem complex that Heinrich Härke has worked with regarding Anglo-Saxon weapon graves.[16] And again, as he has shown, weapon graves do not contain fossilized warriors. Given this problematic relationship between individual identity and mortuary persona, the potential of early medieval graves for answering questions about military organisation seems limited.

Chronology

As always, graves have been studied for chronological purposes. In this type of research, furnished graves are seen very much in the abstract as closed combinations of contemporaneous artefact types.

Most detailed chronological work in Scandinavia these days is done with computer-aided statistics: mainly correspondence analysis and seriation.[17] There has been an unfortunate tendency for scholars to become blinded

by this technology, overlooking data quality and stringent type definitions.[18] But the chronological framework has been made much more robust in the past few decades.

Fieldwork

I am not aware of any on-going large scale excavation projects targeting early medieval burial sites in Scandinavia. A respectable amount of developer-funded work is conducted each year at small cemeteries, but the way in which these sites are selected means that little of any scholarly note is found. In Scandinavia, archaeologists are employed from the planning stage of (for example) highway and railway projects to steer them away from ancient monuments and help developers avoid expensive and time-consuming excavations. Also, cultural resource management legislation is geared toward preserving sites, which means that developers may not be allowed to use sites with well-preserved monuments even if they are prepared to fund expensive excavations.

Cemeteries of the first millennium AD are by far the most common and clearly visible type of ancient monument in Sweden. Early medieval cemeteries are rarely completely undetectable even when they have been placed under cultivation. This means that early medieval cemeteries are generally discovered before projects have proceeded too far for land development to be avoidable. The typical burial consists of a flat cremation layer on top of the ancient ground surface, covered with a round stone pavement or a small mound. This means that (unlike Anglo-Saxon cemeteries with their urn pits and deep inhumation graves) where cemeteries have been obliterated by cultivation, little survives beneath the plough soil.

For about a century until the 1980s, early medieval archaeology in Scandinavia was strongly involved in cemetery excavations for research purposes, targeting rich and well-preserved sites and accumulating a solid material base.[19] Scholars thus have little need for more burial data of the kind currently produced by developer-funded excavations, and are concentrating their own excavation funding on settlement sites.[20]

It should be emphasized that Scandinavian developer-funded excavations are currently performed to very high standards indeed and are well published with little delay. Osteological analyses are done as a matter of course and include all bones (human and animal osteology are taught as a single subject at Swedish universities). The fact that much of this work receives little scholarly attention is not the fault of the excavation units but of the way sites are selected for excavation. The units are employed to excavate largely unimpressive and already-damaged burial sites.

Fallow Fields

As described above, recent Scandinavian studies of early medieval graves have concentrated on questions about

religion, social structure, ethnicity, territorial organisation, military organisation and chronology. What
interesting and feasible avenues of research, then, are
Scandinavians *not* currently pursuing?

Scandinavian landscape archaeology is not touching
much upon early medieval cemeteries. This is probably
because cemetery siting figured importantly in intensive
studies of settlement structure during the 1960s, 70s
and 80s.[21] During the past decade, early medieval
cemetery siting has been dealt with on a case-per-case
basis, producing many isolated interpretations but little
in the way of large-scale synthesis.

Another unrealized potential lies in the geographical
distribution of the excavated early medieval cemeteries.
Sweden, Norway and Finland all have very low population densities and their populations are strongly
concentrated to a few urban areas. In recent decades,
early medieval cemeteries have mostly been excavated
ahead of land development in modern population centres.

On the other hand, many rural areas that were comparatively densely populated in the Early Middle Ages
are now more or less de-populated. Consequently,
cemeteries in these areas are not being excavated.
Knowledge is therefore patchy regarding geographic
variation in any parameters whose recording requires
modern excavation methods.

The concepts of memory and commemoration, recently popular in British scholarship, are uncommon in
Scandinavian publications of the past decade. Monument
re-use has, however, been an active field of research
since the 1980s, reflecting the popularity of British
theoretical literature. Re-use is generally interpreted as
attempts to appropriate the remains of the past for
political purposes. This manipulation of views of the
past is, however, not commonly thought of as anything
to do with memory *sensu stricto*. After all, the past
represented by ancient monuments lends itself well to
political manipulation precisely because it is time
immemorial.

Conclusion

Where could Scandinavian early medieval burial archaeology be taken in the future? Is there a potential for simply
more of the same, or for new theoretical and methodological developments? Being sceptical about the value
of further theorizing, I wish simply to state my empiricist
credo. To gain new insights into early medieval society
through the period's graves, I believe that we should study
the already available data with the best statistical methods,
study finds and sites with new scientific methods (as is
done *e.g.* at the Archaeological Research Laboratory in
Stockholm), and excavate unusual and well-preserved
cemeteries in areas where there have been few excavations.
At heart, our questions will be the perennial ones of the
humanities. Any surprises will come from the archaeological record.

Appendix

Early Medieval Burial Studies in Scandinavia 1994–2003: a Bibliography

Analytical, interpretative and synthetic work on early medieval graves (fifth to eleventh centuries) in Scandinavia and/or published by Scandinavian scholars, from 1994 to 2003. The list does not cover excavation reports or descriptive finds publications.

Early Medieval burial studies in Scandinavia 1994–2003	Religion	Social structure	Gender	Age roles	Ethnicity	Polit. & territ. org.	Military org.	Chronology
Arrhenius, B. 2002. Kinship and social relations in the early medieval period in Svealand elucidated by DNA, in J. Jesch (ed.), *Scandinavians from the Vendel period to the tenth century. An ethnographic perspective.* Studies in historical archaeoethnology, 5. Woodbridge. [14 pp]	1	1			1			
Artelius, T. 2000. *Bortglömda föreställningar. Begravningsritual och begravningsplats i halländsk yngre järnålder.* Riksantikvarieämbetet, Arkeologiska undersökningar, Skrifter, 36. GOTARC Series B, Gothenburg archaeological theses, 15. Gothenburg. [315 pp]	1							
Arwill-Nordbladh, E. 1998. *Genuskonstruktioner i nordisk vikingatid, förr och nu.* GOTARC Series B, Gothenburg Archaeological Theses, 9. Dept of Archaeology, University of Gothenburg. [291 pp]			1					
Bratt, P. 1996. Storhögar och maktstrukturer i Mälardalen under järnåldern, in A.M. Renck and E. Stensköld, E. (eds), *Aktuell arkeologi,* 5. Dept of Archaeology, University of Stockholm. [24 pp]						1		
Bratt, P. 1999. Storhögar och bebyggelsearkeologi. Några exempel från östra Mälardalen, in P. Bratt and Å. Lundström (eds), *Yngre järnålder och historisk arkeologi.* Stockholm county museum. [20 pp]						1		
Callmer, J. 1994. The clay paw burial rite of the Åland Islands and Central Russia. A symbol in action. *Current Swedish Archaeology,* 2. Swedish Archaeological Society. Stockholm. [34 pp]	1				1			
Carelli, P. 2001. Lunds äldsta kyrkogård – och förekomsten av ett senvikingatida danskt parochialsystem. *Aarbøger for nordisk oldkyndighed og historie,* 2000. Det Kongelige Nordiske Oldskrift-Selskab. Copenhagen. [36 pp]	1					1		
Dommasnes, L.H. 1999. *Tradisjon og handling i førkristen vestnorsk gravskikk 2. Fra Vereide til vikingtid.* Arkeologiske avhandlinger og rapporter, 5. Dept of Archaeology, University of Bergen. [213 pp]	1							
Eisenschmidt, S. 1994. *Kammergräber der Wikingerzeit in Altdänemark.* Universitätsforschungen zur prähistorischen Archäologie, 25. Bonn. [194 pp]		1						
Eisenschmidt, S. 2000. *Grabfunde des 8. bis 11. Jahrhunderts zwischen Kongeå und Eider. Zur Bestattungssitte der Wikingerzeit im südlichen Altdänemark.* University of Kiel.								
Götherström, A. 2001. *Acquired or inherited prestige? Molecular studies of family structures and local horses in Central Svealand during the Early Medieval period.* Theses and papers in scientific archaeology, 4. Archaeological Research Laboratory, University of Stockholm.	1	1			1			
Gräslund, A.-S. 1994. Graves as evidence of Christianisation, in B. Stjernquist (ed.), *Prehistoric graves as a source of information. Symposium at Kastlösa, Öland, May 21–23, 1992.* Conferences, 29. Royal Academy of Letters, History and Antiquities. Stockholm. [9 pp]	1							
Gräslund, A.-S. 2000. The conversion of Scandinavia. A sudden event or a gradual process? *Archaeological review from Cambridge,* 17:2. [16 pp]	1							1
Gräslund, A.-S. 2001. *Ideologi och mentalitet. Om religionsskiftet i Skandinavien från en arkeologisk horisont.* Occasional Papers in Archaeology, 29. Dept of Archaeology, University of Uppsala. [171 pp]	1							1
Hansson, A. 1994. Jämtländska fjällgravar. *Fornvännen,* 89:1. Royal Academy of Letters, History and Antiquities. Stockholm. [11 pp]							1	1
Hansson, M. 1999. Graves, grave-fields and burial customs – variation as theme. A discussion of late Iron Age grave-fields in the inland of Småland. *Lund Archaeological Review,* 1998. Dept of Archaeology, University of Lund. [18 pp]							1	
Hines, J.; Høilund Nielsen, K. and Siegmund, F. (eds). 1999. *The pace of change. Studies in Early-Medieval chronology.* Cardiff Studies in Archaeology. Oxford. [204 pp]								1
Høigård Hofseth, E. 1999. Historien bak handelskvinnan på Kaupang. Kvinnegraver fra vikingtid langs Vestfoldkysten. *Viking. Norsk arkeologisk årbok,* 1999. Oslo. [29 pp]	1	1	1					

Early Medieval burial studies in Scandinavia 1994–2003	Religion	Social structure	Gender	Age roles	Ethnicity	Polit. & territ. org.	Military org.	Chronology
Høilund Nielsen, K. 1995. From artefact to interpretation using correspondence analysis. *Anglo-Saxon Studies in Archaeology and History*, 8. Oxford University Committee for Archaeology. [33 pp]	1							1
Høilund Nielsen, K. 1999. Female grave goods of southern and eastern Scandinavia from the Late Germanic or Vendel Period, in Hines *et al.* 1999. [35 pp]								1
Høilund Nielsen, K. and Jensen, C.K. (eds). 1997. *Burial and society – the chronological and social analysis of archaeological burial data*. Århus University Press. [198 pp]		1						1
Holgersson, M. 2003. Landskapet i människan. Om insjögravar. *Dalarna*, **2003**. Dalarnas fornminnes- och hembygdsförbund. Falun. [10 pp]						1	1	
Isaksson, S. 2000. *Food and rank in early medieval time*. Theses and papers in scientific archaeology, 3. Archaeological Research Laboratory, University of Stockholm.	1	1						
Johansson, Å. 2003. Gravar och gränser. In Anund, J. (ed.). *Landningsplats – forntiden. Arkeologiska fördjupningsstudier kring yngre stenålder, järnålder och historisk tid, inom det område som tas i anspråk för den tredje landningsbanan vid Arlanda flygplats*. Riksantikvarieämbetet, Arkeologiska undersökningar, Skrifter, 49. Stockholm. [22 pp]								1
Jørgensen, L. and Nørgård Jørgensen, A. 1997. *Nørre Sandegård Vest. A cemetery from the 6th–8th centuries on Bornholm*. With contributions by U. Mannering and C. Malmros. Nordiske Fortidsminder series B, 14. Det Kongelige Nordiske Oldskriftselskab. Copenhagen. [243 pp]		1						1
Kristoffersen, S. 1999. Migration Period chronology in Norway, in Hines *et al.* 1999. [22 pp]								1
Kristoffersen, S. 2000. *Sverd og spenne. Dyreornamentikk og sosial kontekst*. Studia humanitatis Bergensia, 13. Kristiansand. [387 pp]		1	1	1		1		1
Lehtosalo-Hilander, P.-L. 2000. *Luistari – a history of weapons and ornaments. Luistari IV.* Suomen muinaismuistoyhdistyksen aikakauskirja, 107. Helsinki. [310 pp]								1
Liljeholm, N. 1999. Gravfält kontra kyrkogård – Bysans kontra Rom? Diskussion kring det senvikingatida begravningsskicket på Gotland utifrån gravfältet Stora Hallvards och Silte kyrkas kyrkogård. *Fornvännen*, **94**. Royal Academy of Letters, History and Antiquities. Stockholm. [16 pp]	1							
Lidén, K.; Isaksson, S. and Götherström, A. 2001. Regionality in the boat-grave cemeteries in the lake Mälaren valley, in B. Arrhenius (ed.). *Kingdoms and regionality. Transactions from the 49th Sachsensymposium 1998 in Uppsala*. Theses and papers in archaeology, B:6. Archaeological Research Laboratory, University of Stockholm. [14 pp]					1			
Lundberg, S. 1997. *Gravmonument i sten från sen vikingatid och äldre medeltid i Västergötland*. Uppsatser från Historiska institutionen i Göteborg, 7. Dept of History, University of Gothenburg. [184 pp]								1
Näsman, U. 1994a. Liv och död. Sydskandinaviska grav- och offerriter från 200 till 1000 e.Kr, in J.P. Schjødt and U. Drobin (eds), *Myte og ritual i det førkristne Norden. Et symposium*. Odense University Press. [22 pp]	1							
Näsman, U. 1994b. The Iron Age graves of Öland – representative of what? On prehistoric graves as a source of information, in B. Stjernquist (ed.), *Prehistoric graves as a source of information. Symposium at Kastlösa, Öland, May 21–23, 1992*. Conferences, 29. Royal Academy of Letters, History and Antiquities. Stockholm. [16 pp]		1						
Neill, T. and Lundberg, S. 1994. Förnyad diskussion om "Eskilstunakistorna". *Fornvännen*, **89**. Royal Academy of Letters, History and Antiquities. Stockholm. [15 pp]	1							1
Nordberg, A. 2002. Vertikalt placerade vapen i vikingatida gravar. *Fornvännen*, **97:1**. Royal Academy of Letters, History and Antiquities. Stockholm. [10 pp]	1							
Nordenstorm, L. 1994. Dödande vid begravningar. Ett inslag i järnålderns gravritualer i komparativ religionshistorisk belysning. *Fornvännen*, **89:4**. Royal Academy of Letters, History and Antiquities. Stockholm. [14 pp]	1							
Nørgård Jørgensen, A. 1999. *Waffen und Gräber. Typologische und chronologische Studien zu skandinavischen Waffengräbern 520/30 bis 900 n.Chr.* Nordiske Fortidsminder Serie B, 17. Det Kongelige Nordiske Oldskriftselskab. Copenhagen. [417 pp]							1	1
Nyqvist, R. 2001. *Landskapet som ram. Hus och grav som manifest*. Urbaniseringsprocesser i Västsverige. Dept of Archaeology, University of Gothenburg. [308 pp]		1						

Early Medieval burial studies in Scandinavia 1994–2003	Religion	Social structure	Gender	Age roles	Ethnicity	Polit. & territ. org.	Military org.	Chronology
Pedersen, A. 1997. Weapons and riding gear in burials. Evidence of military and social rank in 10th century Denmark? In A. Nørgård Jørgensen and B. L. Clausen (eds), *Military aspects of Scandinavian society in a European perspective, AD 1–1300. Papers from an International Research Seminar at the Danish National Museum, Copenhagen 2–4 May, 1996.* [13 pp]	1						1	
Price, N. 2002. *The Viking way. Religion and war in late Iron Age Scandinavia.* Aun, 31. Dept of Archaeology and Ancient History, Uppsala University. [435 pp]	1						1	
Purhonen, P. (ed.). 1996. *Vainionmäki. A Merovingian period cemetery in Laitila, Finland.* National Board of Antiquities. Helsinki. [221 pp]	1	1			1			1
Purhonen, P. 1998. *Kristinuskon saapumisesta Suomeen. Uskontoarkeologinen tutkimus.* (On the arrival of Christianity in Finland. A study in the archaeology of religion.) Suomen muinaismuistoyhdistyksen aikakauskirja, 106. Helsinki. [261 pp]	1				1			
Ravn, M. 1999. Theoretical and methodological approaches to Migration Period burials, in M. Rundkvist (ed.), *Grave matters. Eight studies of First Millennium AD burials in Crimea, England and southern Scandinavia.* B.A.R. International Series, 781. Oxford.	1	1	1					
Ravn, M. 2003. *Death ritual and Germanic social structure (c. AD 200–600).* British Archaeological Reports International Series, 1164, Oxford: BAR [155 pp]	1	1	1	1				
Ringstedt, N. 1997. *The Birka chamber-graves. Economic and social aspects. An analysis based on quantitative methods.* Stockholm Archaeological Reports, 32. Dept of Archaeology, University of Stockholm. [164 pp]		1						
Rundkvist, M. 2003a. *Barshalder 1. A cemetery in Grötlingbo and Fide parishes, Gotland, Sweden, c. AD 1–1100. Excavations and finds 1826–1971.* Stockholm Archaeological Reports, 40. Dept of Archaeology, University of Stockholm. [251 pp]		1						1
Rundkvist, M. 2003b. *Barshalder 2. Studies of Late Iron Age Gotland.* University of Stockholm. [101 pp]	1	1	1	1			1	1
Schanche, A. 2000. *Graver i ur og berg. Samisk gravskikk og religion fra forhistorisk til nyere tid.* Karasjok. [409 pp]	1				1			
Schauman-Lönnqvist, M. 1997. En merovingertida vapengrav från Vemo i Egentliga Finland. *Finskt Museum,* **1994.** Helsinki. [26 pp]							1	1
Schönbäck, B. and Thunmark-Nylén, L. 2002. De vikingatida båtgravarna vid Valsgärde – relativ kronologi. *Fornvännen,* **97.** Royal Academy of Letters, History and Antiquities. Stockholm. [8 pp]								1
Seiler, A. 2001. *I skuggan av båtgravarna. Landskap och samhälle i Vendels socken under yngre järnålder.* Theses and papers in archaeology, B7–8. Archaeological Research Laboratory, University of Stockholm. [165+88 pp]	1						1	1
Shepherd, D. J. 1999. *Funerary ritual and symbolism. An interdisciplinary interpretation of burial practices in Late Iron Age Finland,* British Archaeological Reports International Series, 808, Oxford: BAR [154 pp]	1							
Staecker, J. 1997. Searching for the unknown. Gotland's churchyards from a gender and missionary perspective. *Lund Archaeological Review,* **1996.** [24 pp]	1		1					
Staecker, J. 2000. Die normierte Bestattung. Gotlands Kirchfriedhöfe im Spiegel mittelalterlicher Normen und Gesetze, in D. Ruhe and K.-H. Spiess (eds). *Prozesse der Normbildung und Normveränderung im mittelalterlichen Europa.* Mittelalterzentrum Greifswald. Stuttgart. [41 pp. Largely identical to Staecker 1997a]	1							
Staecker, J. 2001. In atrio ecclesiae. Die Bestattungssitte der dörflichen und städtischen Friedhöfe im Norden, in A. Muntis (ed.). *Lübeck style? Novgorod style? Baltic rim central places as arenas for cultural encounters and urbanisation 1100–1400 AD. Transactions of the central level symposium of the Culture Clash or Compromise (CCC) project held in Talsi September 18–21 1998.* CCC Papers 5. Gotland University College, Centre for Baltic Studies, Visby. Riga. [71 pp]	1							
Staecker, J. 2003. The cross goes North. Christian symbols and Scandinavian women, in M. Carver (ed.), *The cross goes North. Processes of conversion in Northern Europe, A.D. 300–1300.* Woodbridge. [20 pp]	1		1					
Svanberg, F. 2003. *Death rituals in South-East Scandinavia AD 800–1000.* Decolonizing the Viking Age, 2. Acta Archaeologica Lundensia, Series in Quarto, 24. Lund. [350 pp]							1	1

Early Medieval burial studies in Scandinavia 1994–2003	Religion	Social structure	Gender	Age roles	Ethnicity	Polit. & territ. org.	Military org.	Chronology
Thunmark-Nylén, L. 1995a. Vendeltid eller vikingatid? Om datering av gotländska fornfynd kring år 800. *Tor,* **27:2**. Societas Archaeologica Upsaliensis. [73 pp]								1
Thunmark-Nylén, L. 1995b. Churchyard finds from Gotland (11th–12th centuries), in I. Jansson (ed.). *Archaeology east and west of the Baltic. Papers from the Second Estonian-Swedish Archaeological Symposium, Sigtuna, May 1991.* Theses and Papers in Archaeology, New Series, 7. Dept of Archaeology, University of Stockholm. [32 pp]	1				1			
Wagnkilde, H. 1999. Slaviske træk i bornholmske grave fra tiden omkring kristendommens indførelse. En oversigt over gravpladser og skattefund fra 1000–tallet på Bornholm. *META, Medeltidsarkeologisk tidskrift,* **1999:2**. Medeltidsarkeologiska föreningen. Lund. [18 pp]	1				1			
Wagnkilde, H. 2000. Gravudstyr og mønter fra 1000–tallets gravpladser på Bornholm. *Hikuin,* **27**. Højbjerg.	1				1			
Wamers, E. 1994. König im Grenzland. Neue Analyse des Bootkammergrabes von Haiðaby. *Acta Archaeologica,* **65**. Copenhagen [56 pp]						1	1	1
Welinder, S. 1998. The cultural construction of childhood in Scandinavia, 3500 BC – 1350 AD. *Current Swedish Archaeology,* **6**. Swedish Archaeological Society. Stockholm. [21 pp]		1	1	1				
Wienberg, J. 1998. Eskilstunamonumenter i Västergötland. *Fornvännen,* **93:3–4**. Royal Academy of Letters, History and Antiquities. Stockholm. [7 pp]	1							1
Zachrisson, I. 1997. *Möten i gränsland. Samer och germaner i Mellanskandinavien.* Monographs, 4. Museum of National Antiquities. Stockholm. [271 pp]	1	1					1	1

Notes

1. Matt. XIII.57.
2. Price 2003; 2004 award for eminent scholarship of the Royal Academy of Letters, History and Antiquities, Stockholm.
3. *E.g.* Purhonen 1998; Gräslund 2001; Rundkvist 2003b; Staecker 2003.
4. Ravn 1999, 2003.
5. Rundkvist 2003a, 2003b.
6. Svanberg 2003.
7. Zachrisson 1997; Schanche 2000.
8. Purhonen 1996, 134; Ivars and Huldén 2002.
9. Kelm 2000; Roslund 2001.
10. Kilger 1998.
11. Götherström 2001.
12. Ambrosiani 1983; Høilund Nielsen 1997.
13. Zachrisson 1997.
14. Bratt 1996 with refs.
15. Nørgård Jørgensen and Clausen 1997.
16. Härke 2002 with refs.
17. *E.g.* Jørgensen and Nørgård Jørgensen 1997; Høilund Nielsen and Jensen 1997; Hines *et al.* 1999; Nørgård Jørgensen 1999; Rundkvist 2003b.
18. See critique in Rundkvist 2003a.
19. *E.g.* Arbman 1940–43; Petré 1984; Nylén and Schönbäck 1994; Blindheim and Heyerdahl-Larsen 1995; Purhonen 1996; Jørgensen and Nørgård Jørgensen 1997.
20. *E.g.* Jørgensen 1998; Holmquist Olausson and Kitzler Åhfeldt 2002; Stylegar and Skre 2004.
21. Swedish work in this vein surveyed by Broberg 1994.

Bibliography

This section comprises works referred to in the main body of text, published before 1994 or that refer to topics that lie outside the specific area of early medieval burial studies.

Ambrosiani, B. 1983. Regalia and symbols in the boat-graves, in Lamm, J. P. *et al.* (eds).*Vendel Period studies.* Studies, 2. Museum of National Antiquities. Stockholm.

Arbman, H. 1940–43. *Birka. Untersuchungen und Studien 1. Die Gräber.* Royal Academy of Letters, History and Antiquities. Stockholm.

Blindheim, Ch. and Heyerdahl-Larsen, B. 1995. *Kaupang-funnene bind II. Gravplassene I Bikjholbergene/Lamøya. Undersøkelsene 1950–1957. Del A. Gravskikk.* Norske oldfunn, 16. Oldsaksamlingen. Oslo.

Broberg, A. 1994. Mellansvensk bebyggelsearkeologi. En forskningsöversikt med blicken riktad mot 90–talets uppdragsarkeologi. In Andersson, G. *et al.* (eds). *Arkeologi i Attundaland.* Studier från UV Stockholm. National Board of Antiquities. Stockholm.

Härke, H. 2002. Kings and warriors: population and landscape from post-Roman to Norman Britain. In Slack, P. and Ward, R. (eds). *The peopling of Britain: the shaping of a human landscape (The Linacre lectures 1999).* Oxford University Press.

Høilund Nielsen, K. 1997. Retainers of the Scandinavian kings. An alternative interpretation of Salin's style II (sixth-seventh centuries AD). *Journal of European archaeology,* 5:1. European Association of Archaeologists.

Holmquist Olausson, L. and Kitzler Åhfeldt, L. 2002. *Krigarnas hus. Arkeologisk undersökning av ett hallhus i Birkas Garnison. RAÄ 35, Björkö, Adelsö sn, Uppland 1998–2000.* Borgar och befästningsverk i Mellansverige 400–1100 e.Kr. (BMS), vol. 4. Archaeological Research Laboratory, University of Stockholm.

Ivars, A. M. and Huldén, L (eds). 2002. *När kom svenskarna till Finland?* Skrifter utgivna av Svenska litteratursällskapet i Finland, 646. Helsinki.

Jørgensen, L. 1998. En storgård fra vikingetid ved Tissø, Sjælland. En foreløbig præsentation. In Larsson, L. and Hårdh, B. (eds). *Centrala platser, centrala frågor. Samhällsstrukturen under järnåldern. En vänbok till Berta Stjernquist.* Uppåkrastudier, 1. Dept of Archaeology, University of Lund.

Kelm, R. 2000. *Mölleholmen. Eine slawische Inselsiedlung des 11. Jahrhunderts in Schonen, Südschweden.* Report series, 74. Dept of Archaeology, University of Lund.

Kilger, C. 1998. The Slavs yesterday and today. Different perspectives on Slavic ethnicity in German archaeology. *Current Swedish Archaeology,* 6. Swedish Archaeological Society. Stockholm.

Nørgård Jørgensen, A. and Clausen, B. L. (eds) 1997. *Military aspects of Scandinavian society in a European perspective, AD 1–1300. Papers from an international research seminar at the Danish National Museum, Copenhagen 2–4 May, 1996.* Publications from the National Museum, 2. Copenhagen.

Nylén, E. and Schönbäck, B. 1994. *Tuna i Badelunda. Guld, kvinnor, båtar. Västerås kulturnämnds skriftserie.* Västerås.

Petré, B. 1984. *Arkeologiska undersökningar på Lovö 2. Fornlämning RAÄ 27, Lunda.* Studies in North-European archaeology, 8. Dept of Archaeology, University of Stockholm.

Roslund, M. 2001. *Gäster i huset. Kulturell överföring mellan slaver och skandinaver 900 till 1300.* Skrifter utgivna av Vetenskapssocieteten i Lund, 92. Lund.

Stylegar, F. A. and Skre, D. 2004. *Kaupang. Vikingbyen.* Universitetets kulturhistoriske museer. Oslo.

Anglo-Saxon Studies in Archaeology and History 14, 2007

Beyond Ethnicity: Symbols of Social Identity from the Fourth to Sixth Centuries in England

Rebecca Gowland

Introduction

The fourth to sixth centuries have been conceptualised as a time of transition, from the end of Roman Britain to the beginning of the Anglo-Saxon period. During this time there was a profound change in material culture relating to both settlement and burial practice.[1] The perceived mechanism behind this change continues to be vigorously debated, with views ranging 'between population replacement at one end and wholly endogenous change at the other'.[2] While such discussions are crucial to our understanding of this period, they have resulted in a preoccupation with the migration and with ethnic identity.

Generally, the population of fifth- and sixth-century Britain continues to be conceptualized as culturally distinct from that of the fourth century. By assuming such distinctions, comparatively few studies bestride the late Roman/early Anglo-Saxon divide in the same way that they would other periods of transition such as, for example, the Norman Conquest or the Reformation.[3] As recent research has shown, the temporal divisions used in archaeology have, to some extent, actively shaped perceptions of the past. Subsequently, archaeological interpretations can become self-perpetuating and 'constrained by paradigms of their own creation'.[4]

Predicated upon this assumed cultural distinction is a tendency for archaeologists dealing with the Roman-medieval 'transition' to dwell on themes of migration and ethnicity to the exclusion of others. These are themes that do not often feature when comfortably ensconced within a single time period. Firstly, there is a concern with the identification of material indicators of continuity or discontinuity and, secondly, there is a concern with the identification of 'natives' versus 'incomers'.[5] Much of this work in relation to the fourth to sixth centuries has focused on these debates in relation to the burial evidence. First, there have been a number of attempts made to identify an Anglo-Saxon presence in fourth-century Roman Britain through the identification of 'Germanic' burial rites within late fourth-century cemeteries. Correspondingly, the presence of 'Roman' style objects in early fifth- and sixth-century graves have been viewed as indicating a Roman identity or aspiration. Such straightforward culture-historical approaches that correlate burial rites with population movements and ethnicity have received a great deal of criticism, particularly since the 1980s, on both theoretical and more practical grounds.[6] It has been noted that 'Romano-British'/'native' and 'Germanic' identities have been created by archaeologists because of a perceived antithesis between groups with monolithic characteristics that find closer resonance in nineteenth- and early twentieth-century racial stereotypes of 'Celt' and 'Saxon' than may have been relevant in early medieval contexts.[7] While current arguments are much more nuanced than this, there is still a pervasive focus on ethnic ascriptions of 'natives Britons' and 'immigrant Saxons' that is detrimental to a better understanding of the nature of *social* identities and how these may have undergone changes before and after the supposed hiatus of the early to mid-fifth century.

Few archaeologists would doubt that material culture is expressive of social identities when deployed in mortuary contexts. Items of dress have often been regarded as an important means through which many facets of the social personae are constructed and lived during life, and represented in death.[8] Yet even with the rise of social approaches towards portable artefacts in graves since the 1970s, studies have looked at the representation of social structure *within* cultural and chronological groups rather than *between* them. In doing so, archaeologists can begin to examine the burial rites and items of material culture previously described as 'intrusive' in ways other than ascribing ethnic attributions.[9] For example, Eckardt and Williams[10] have recently provided a detailed discussion of the use of Roman artefacts in early Anglo-Saxon graves. They suggest that Roman objects fulfilled a much more symbolic role in the graves of those buried in early Anglo-Saxon cemeteries and that these objects were also important for signifying other aspects of social identity (for example, age and gender).

It is the potential symbolism of such objects in the construction of aspects of social identity that will be explored systematically in this paper. Recent research has shown that grave inclusions vary according to the age and gender of the deceased,[11] and an analysis of grave goods can reveal important social information with respect to the timing of significant age-related milestones and shifts in gendered identity with age. The social construction of age and the changing perceptions of different stages of the life course is an important area of study, but one that has only been addressed more recently.[12] Age and gender identity are inter-twined in complex ways and elucidating the relationship between the two is significant for our understanding of social identity and organization in the past. Yet recent studies have tended to look *within* either late Roman or early Anglo-Saxon cemeteries for evidence of age and gender variability in the provision and representation of identity. In contrast, this study aims to build on these studies and yet provide the first attempt known to this author to systematically compare mortuary variability, in relation to sex and age, from both late Roman and early Anglo-Saxon cemeteries. It will be shown that while there is no straightforward relationship between grave goods and social identity, the analysis reveals significant patterns of deposition. The skeletal evidence plays a crucial role in mortuary analyses; therefore, before discussing the grave goods, the skeletal data recorded for this study will be discussed along with a brief critique of the role of the skeleton in inferring ethnicity.

Skeletal Data and Analysis

Initially, the cemeteries examined in this study involved two clusters of sites of late Roman and early Saxon date, one around Dorchester-on-Thames, the other Winchester (Table 1).[13] These cemeteries were selected because they have been pivotal to the discussion of the Roman to Anglo-Saxon transition and contain burials that are the focus of debate and contention. Unlike previous studies that combine osteological and artefactual data in the analysis of mortuary variability in Roman and early

Anglo-Saxon graves, this author undertook a detailed contextual re-analysis of the skeletal material. This was a substantial task and was deemed essential for a number of reasons. Osteological reports had never been produced for several cemeteries in the study sample (*e.g.* Abingdon and Cassington), while some of the reports available for other sites were in the form of an assessment only (*e.g.* Lankhills) and not sufficiently detailed for an adequate social analysis to be developed. Meanwhile, sites with perfectly good osteological reports (*e.g.* Berinsfield and Worthy Park) were also included in the re-analysis. This was, in part, because osteological techniques have developed substantially over recent years, but, more importantly, to ensure standardised methods of recording between all of the sites and to eliminate inter-observer error. This has been shown to be of particular importance when estimating age-at-death (a key facet of this study), because age estimates can vary profoundly according to the methods used.[14] This problem is exacerbated by the use of differing age categories between osteological reports, making it almost impossible to produce meaningful comparisons of age and sex profiles between cemeteries. Such problems of standardization are currently being addressed by osteologists[15] and hopefully future human bone reports will be much more compatible with each other.

The skeletal samples were examined for differences in growth, dental development and dental wear between Romano-British and Anglo-Saxon populations.[16] The primary aim of this was to ensure that the ageing methods used would be population-specific and thus more reliable. However, it is also interesting to compare the data from different sites. From Table 2, it is clear that not only were the eruption ages remarkably similar between sites of different periods, but so too were the rates of dental wear for the juveniles. These are factors that have been shown to vary between different populations and was the first tentative indication that there were closer connections between late Romano-British and early Anglo-Saxon burial populations than is usually entertained.[17] The data were also divided geographically and dental wear comparisons made between the Hampshire and Oxford-

*Table 1. Archaeological data (NB citations have been provided for those reports used to obtain information on grave goods. All skeletal data was collected through analysis of the remains by the author). *This includes those individuals noted in the report, but also missing and extra individuals identified during the analysis*

Region	Site	Period	No. Ind.
Upper Thames	Berinsfield (Boyle *et al.* 1995)	Early Anglo Saxon	119
Upper Thames	Abingdon (Leeds and Harden 1936)	Early Anglo Saxon	129
Upper Thames	Queensford Farm	Late/Sub Roman	164
Upper Thames	Cassington	Late Roman	63
Hampshire	Lankhills (Clarke 1979)	Late Roman	486*
Hampshire	Worthy Park (Hawkes and Grainger 2003)	Early Anglo Saxon	109
Hampshire	Victoria Road	Late Roman	134
Hampshire	Portway (Cook and Dacre 1985)	Early Anglo Saxon	71
Hampshire	Alton (Evison 1988)	Early Anglo Saxon	50

shire sites. Again the similarity in the eruption and rates of wear is marked. However, the geographical differences between the groups, is greater than that observed between time periods.

Dental development and eruption has a strong genetic component and is only minimally affected by environmental factors.[18] One could, therefore, argue that these results are consistent with what one would expect from a population with no significant 'intrusive' migrant elements. With regard to dental wear, we cannot rule out the possibility of an immigrant group demonstrating indistinguishable wear patterns to the 'natives', particularly if dietary practices were the same. However, this similarity in biological terms provides a broad justification for challenging traditional periods divides and looking at late Roman and early Anglo-Saxon cemeteries for both similarities and differences in the provision of artefacts with the dead

Some previous work has provided similar conclusions. In a complementary study, Lloyd-Jones[19] made a comparison of dental non-metric traits between some of those same late Roman and early Anglo-Saxon cemeteries analysed here. Non-metric traits are natural skeletal variants that are often used in comparisons of skeletal populations to infer ethnicity. Lloyd-Jones[20] found no statistical difference between late Roman and Anglo-Saxon populations with respect to trait expression. As Tyrrell has discussed,[21] certain traits are more valid than others as indicators of heritability. For example, dental traits are more reliable than post-cranial skeletal traits because they are far less affected by environmental factors. Certainly, one does have to treat studies that utilize skeletal markers of ethnicity or 'biodistance' with caution.[22] While trait frequencies vary on a population level, when studying cemeteries, the results may be statistically compromised by the small sample sizes. Furthermore, Tyrrell states:

> Many studies have treated trait frequencies as if they were an archaeological typology, using a mix and match approach to determine if skeletons in a cemetery belonged to related individuals, or to determine the 'ethnic' group to which an individual skeleton belonged. This is unacceptable since not only does it lead to misleading conclusions, but also promises to access information which morphological studies cannot at present ascertain.[23]

On a more theoretical level, such studies also assume a rather homogenous stance with respect to the genetic origins of both groups, viewing them almost as hermetically sealed. Given that 'migration period groups themselves were believed to have been characterized by fluidity and heterogeneity',[24] this seems an unrealistic assumption.[25]

With respect to long bone growth, contrary to the dental evidence, differences were observed between the skeletons

Table 2. Mean ages of wear for each stage of the first permanent molar (M1) with 'known ages', derived from dental development (NB stage 4 has an artificially smaller standard deviation because the upper limits of the age range is beyond the scope of dental development ageing)

M1	STAGE 0		STAGE 1		STAGE 2		STAGE 3		STAGE 4	
Site	Mean	s.d.	Mean	s.d.	Mean	s.d.	Mean	s.d.	Mean	s.d.
RB	5.34	0.46	7.39	1.93	9.25	3.34	14.48	3.95	16.48	1.20
AS	5.44	0.48	7.57	1.94	9.16	2.13	12.73	4.03	16.30	2.08
Hants	5.79	0.87	7.71	1.85	9.29	2.90	14.13	3.71	15.40	1.54
Oxon	5.40	0.57	7.22	2.01	8.65	2.54	12.00	4.26	16.81	2.01
All sites	5.38	0.45	7.50	1.90	9.20	2.73	13.24	4.00	16.35	1.82

Table 3. Mean stature for adult males and females at the sites in the study sample. The present author collected all data and estimates were calculated using the formulae of Trotter and Gleser 1952. Mean stature estimates were not included for Portway and Alton because poor preservation at these sites meant that very few complete long bones were available

Period	Site	Male	Female
Anglo-Saxon	Abingdon	174.4	161.4
Anglo-Saxon	Berinsfield	177.2	164.0
Anglo-Saxon	Worthy Park	173.6	160.3
Romano-British	Cassington	170.5	160.9
Romano-British	Lankhills	171.7	157.8
Romano-British	Queensford Farm	170.3	156.2
Romano-British	Victoria Road	171.2	157.6

at the Romano-British and Anglo-Saxon cemeteries examined for this study. Figure 1 shows that age-specific femur length was slightly greater during the Anglo-Saxon period. However, this should by no means be interpreted as an indication of genetic distance; in contrast to dental development, bone growth is profoundly affected by environmental factors (*e.g.* poor diet and infection) and differences in growth between populations generally relate to these external factors. Mean adult height of both males and females is also greater from the Anglo-Saxon cemeteries in this sample (Table 3) and this factor, together with the long bone growth evidence, argues strongly for a general improvement in health status during the later period.[26] This is given further support from a study by Roberts and Cox (2003) which presents an extensive survey of palaeopathological data over time and finds a general reduction in health stress indicators from the Roman to Anglo-Saxon periods.[27]

When one examines skeletons from different cemeteries it becomes apparent that subtle differences often exist with respect to the suite of morphological characteristics observed. For example, the pubic symphyses in one female population in this study sample were much more gracile (*e.g.* Lankhills and Victoria Road) than those observed at some other cemeteries (*e.g.* Berinsfield and Queensford Mill). Again, this did not seem to relate to period, but rather geography. One cannot put this down simply to the genetic admixture because the environment plays such a strong part in skeletal morphology and populations generally encompass an enormous range of variation that tends to be greater than that observed between populations. Again, our interpretation of the skeletal evidence is coloured by our perceptions of this period. If we were comparing skeletal remains from, for example, the earlier and later Medieval periods, variations are more likely to be ascribed to lifestyle/environmental differences as opposed to genetics. I would argue that we should correspondingly place more emphasis on the impact of shifting external forces in our interpretations of skeletal material from the late Roman to early Anglo-Saxon period.

A more fruitful focus of recent research into the movement of past people has been the use of stable isotopes, in particular those of Strontium and Oxygen. When applied to populations of the fourth to sixth centuries, studies appear to be demonstrating a much more complex pattern of individual and population mobility than that previously suggested through the direct association between grave goods and ethnicity.[28] This work also indicates that grave goods need to be interpreted in more nuanced ways in terms of the identity/ies being expressed and this will be explored further below.

Comparison of Burial Assemblages

Skeletal information and factors relating to the body were entered into a database table and linked relationally to further tables containing information on other grave variables using Microsoft Access™ on a one-to-many basis. The layout of the database was based upon the design produced by Huggett [29] as this allowed a detailed and efficient linking and analysis of both skeletal and cultural variables.

While this research has involved both a considerable amount of skeletal analysis as well as its correlation with mortuary data, the rest of this paper is focused upon the objects themselves and their possible roles in symbolising aspects of social identity in death. Consequently, because there are far fewer grave goods buried with individuals from Romano-British sites, a large proportion of this burial evidence was effectively excluded from the following analysis. The study of Romano-British cemeteries will, therefore, be confined to the proportion of burials at Lankhills with grave goods only, neglecting those in Oxfordshire entirely.[30] This situation is far from ideal and creates certain shortcomings in the discussion below, nevertheless, some broad trends in the provision of artefacts with the dead can be discerned.

It is evident that at both the late Roman and the early Anglo-Saxon cemeteries the grave goods fluctuate in both quantity and type throughout the life course of individuals and between the sexes. Some of these differences have already been noted by researchers addressing Anglo-Saxon and (to a slightly lesser extent) Romano-British cemeteries but have not been compared before.[31]

If one examines the burial ritual surrounding those skeletally immature individuals, usually categorized as children, we can note that at cemeteries of both periods, the goods buried with individuals prior to the age of four years tend to be those described as 'gender neutral' in that they are buried with both skeletally sexed males and females (for example coins and vessels). At both Romano-British and Anglo-Saxon cemeteries there appears to be a shift in social status occurring at about the age of seven to twelve years that coincides with the expression of a more strongly signified gender identity. After the age of approximately four to seven years individuals at Lankhills were buried with large deposits of bracelets, finger rings and necklaces, and these were amongst the richest burials in the entire cemetery.[33] We see a similar pattern at the early Anglo-Saxon cemeteries where at the same age individuals begin to be buried with gendered grave goods.[34] The age of approximately seven years appears to be significant for many temporally and ethnically diverse populations and so we cannot assume this similarity between late Romano-British and early Anglo-Saxon cemeteries reflects cultural continuity, but it does suggest a similar symbolic grammar and social mores may underpin the burial rites in both populations.

Amongst the skeletons usually defined as 'adult' one also sees fluctuations in the deposition of grave goods with regard to age and sex between Lankhills and the

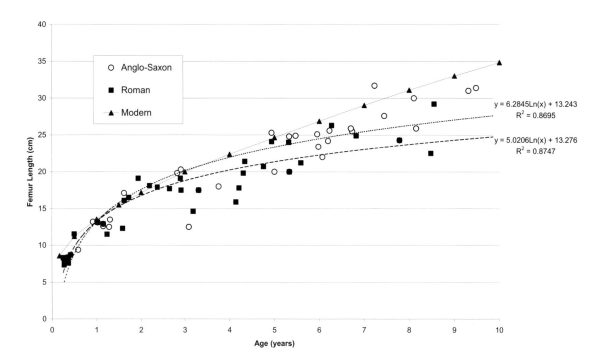

Figure 1. Femur length plotted against dental age for juvenile skeletons at the Anglo-Saxon and Romano-British cemeteries

early Anglo-Saxon cemeteries. The majority of items of personal adornment at the late Roman cemetery of Lankhills were restricted to those young adult females aged eighteen to twenty-four years. Older females, particularly those from the age of thirty-five years and over, were buried with very few items of personal adornment. At the early Anglo-Saxon cemeteries, this pattern is less apparent. Older females tend to be buried with similar assemblages to younger adult females, though they were buried with notably fewer beads and, overall, a smaller average number of brooches.[35]

When one examines specific types of items that were present in cemeteries of both periods some interesting patterns emerge. Bracelets are the most common item of personal adornment recovered from the late Roman cemetery of Lankhills, while from the entire sample of Anglo-Saxon cemeteries only four bracelets were recovered. Three of these were excavated from the Upper Thames sites of Abingdon and Berinsfield and were buried with children aged four to twelve years. The only other bracelet in the Anglo-Saxon sample was recovered from the grave of an adult female from Portway. All bracelets were worn on the right forearm. While bracelets are a rare find in early Anglo-Saxon graves, they have been recovered from settlements.[36] At the Romano-British cemetery of Lankhills, the deposition of bracelets also appears to have been governed, to some extent, by the age and gender of the deceased. No sexed males were buried with bracelets and there is a distinct peak in the quantity of bracelets buried with those aged eighteen

to twenty-four years and also with children aged over four years (Fig. 1). The same is true of many items of personal adornment at the Lankhills site. Comparatively few females over the age of thirty-five years were buried with bracelets and none over fifty years were buried with either bracelets or necklaces.

Finger rings are another item of personal adornment not commonly recovered from Anglo-Saxon burials, but found relatively frequently at Lankhills and Romano-British cemeteries elsewhere in the country. It is notable that seventy-five per-cent of finger rings recovered from the early Anglo-Saxon cemeteries were buried with individuals between the ages of eight to twenty-four years – essentially the same age as those buried with bracelets. They were not buried with individuals younger than eight years of age and no finger rings were recovered from female burials over the age of fifty years. In fact Abingdon is the only site where finger rings were buried with females over the age of twenty-four years. Almost all finger rings were worn on the left hand and none were buried with males.

Like bracelets, finger rings were much more common at late Roman cemeteries. At Lankhills thirty were recovered in all, one of which was buried with a male. As with bracelets and necklaces, the finger rings were buried primarily with those aged four to twelve years and eighteen to twenty-four years of age. Although a substantial proportion of the jewellery buried with individuals below the age of thirteen years was worn, almost all finger rings were unworn (twelve out of the

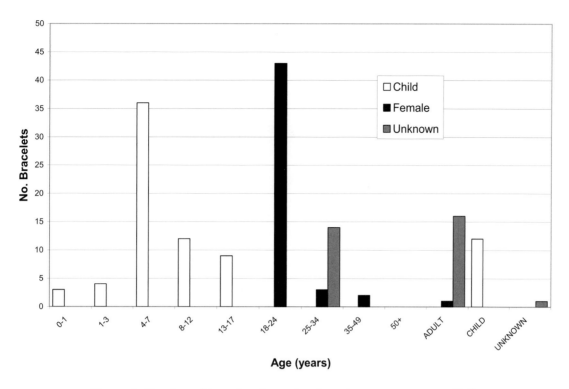

Figure 2. Number of bracelets buried with each age group at Lankhills

thirteen). Perhaps it was culturally inappropriate for this age group to be wearing finger rings; they may have represented a specific relationship/social status during life that they were not yet privy to. Numerous finger rings were also buried with the eighteen to twenty-four year old females and these, with the exception of those buried with one individual, were also unworn. This, however, is consistent with the mode of deposition of other items of personal adornment with this age group, which tend, more often, to be placed in a pile next to the body rather than worn. Several older females were also buried with finger rings, although they were only rarely buried with items of jewellery (see above). In contrast to those finger rings buried with the younger females, they were *always* worn.

It has been suggested that the females buried with worn personal ornaments at Lankhills represent an 'intrusive' ethnic element, possibly linked to Pannonia or Sarmatia.[36] This is based on the large number of bracelets worn on the arms of several individuals, along with necklaces of amber and carnelian beads more commonly seen in Sarmatia.[37] However, when one looks at this group in more detail the situation assumes greater complexity. It is the immature individuals, below the age of twelve years that wear the large quantities of bracelets. The adult females tend to be relatively young (eighteen to thirty-five years) and wear only a couple of bracelets, sometimes worn on different arms (three out of four were also wearing a necklace and one was wearing three finger rings). When discussing these burials, Swift[36]

has suggested that once these women had children, they passed their bracelets to them to wear, keeping only a couple for themselves. The majority of those adult females buried with large deposits of personal ornaments, however, were not wearing them at all and the same is true of many of the immature individuals. The common factor between all of the individuals with jewellery, worn or unworn, is their gender and age (Fig. 2) and I would suggest that it may be these aspects of identity, rather than ethnicity, that are significant. This is also supported to some extent by the Evans *et al.* recent study which examined Strontium and Oxygen isotope samples from the skeletons of these rich female burials.[39] The results revealed that these individuals were more likely to have grown up within Britain rather than the Continent even if the mourners selected elements of mortuary costume from Continental traditions and may have been the descendants of immigrants

In the early Anglo-Saxon cemeteries, it has been shown above that the deposition of relatively rare items such as bracelets and finger rings occurred much more frequently with immature individuals. When we examine the age and sex distribution of those 'Roman' objects or those argued to be of 'Roman style' buried in early Anglo-Saxon graves, a distinctive pattern emerges showing, again, that a much greater proportion were present in the graves of young individuals (Fig. 3). Furthermore, brooch types such as penannular and quoit, which have featured strongly in debates concerning ethnic identity,[40] while buried with all age groups, were most often buried

Rebecca Gowland

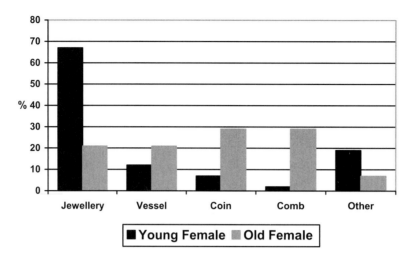

Figure 3. Percentage of the overall quantity of each grave good type buried with females of different ages at Lankhills (younger = 18–34 years, older = 35+ years)

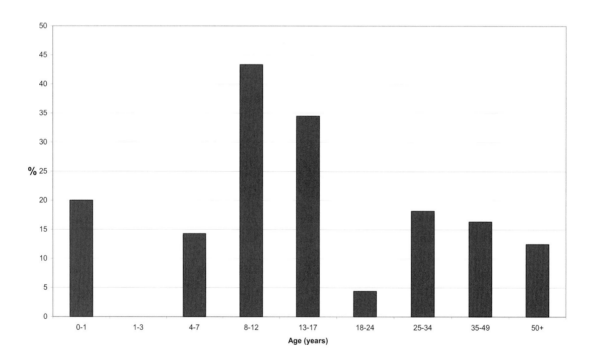

Figure 4. The proportion of items of personal adornment in each age group that may be considered 'Roman' in style or origin buried with individuals at the early Anglo-Saxon cemeteries

with those between the ages of eight to seventeen years. At Portway all 'Roman' style or re-used Roman brooches were buried with individuals between the ages of thirteen to twenty-four years.

Perforated Roman coins were recovered from all early Anglo-Saxon cemeteries and although they were buried with almost all age groups from infancy onwards, there were some age-related biases. For example, at Portway, where they occur most frequently, they were only buried with individuals between the ages of eight to twenty-four years. Overall, very few were buried with individuals

over the age of twenty-five years, and none were buried with females over fifty years. No males were buried with perforated coins. Once more, the repeatedly strong association of these 'Roman' objects in the graves of immature individuals suggests that the 'otherness' that is being constructed here is one that relates to age rather than ethnicity. This is consistent with the proposition of the study by Eckardt and Williams [41] which also suggests that these 'Roman' items in Anglo-Saxon graves could be contributing to the expression and creation of other aspects of social identity.

This analysis has primarily focused on the comparison of items of personal adornment, which has largely precluded a discussion of male burials. There is, however, the issue of cross-bow brooches in the graves of male individuals at the late Roman cemetery of Lankhills. It was unfortunate that because of poor preservation, age-at-death could not be estimated for most of these individuals. However, those that could be aged were found to be over thirty-five years (and usually older). Given the association of these brooches with older males one could surmise that they were associated with positions of power or a status achieved with age, rather than bestowed by birth. This would fit in with the work of others who suggest that such burials reflect a more overt display of power by local leaders by the late fourth century.[42] These objects symbolise not only a masculine identity, but also one that is inextricably and simultaneously linked to age and status.

Conclusion

The term 'transition' has been important in creating a particular perception of the late fourth to sixth centuries AD and our approach to this period has been to look for material vestiges of times past and promises of things to come. Archaeologists have recently questioned this perception and the way that it governs our interpretation of the evidence.[43] By examining age and gender identity at cemeteries either side of the Roman/Anglo-Saxon divide, this research has aimed in some way to avoid the more dominant discourses that have structured the archaeological agenda of the period. While material symbolism may well play an active role in the maintenance of ethnic boundaries, it could equally be used to create other aspects of identity and group identification. The evidence presented here builds upon previous studies that have also sought alternative explanations for the symbolism expressed by grave inclusions of this period and, I would argue, complements the findings of recent Strontium and Oxygen isotope research from the skeletal remains. It has shown that objects previously interpreted as important for the construction of ethnic identity (for example, 'Roman' objects in early Anglo-Saxon graves) may in fact be related more closely to age and gender identity. Distinctive patterns in artefact provision with respect to age and gender have been identified in both late Romano-British and early Anglo-Saxon cemeteries in the sample. While there are some similarities with respect to the timing of these changes, particularly during childhood, there are also some significant differences (for example, there is not such a dramatic reduction in grave goods with older females at the early Anglo-Saxon cemeteries). While comparisons were hampered by the lack of grave good evidence from the Romano-British period, limiting the conclusions drawn, I would argue that this study still provides useful information for inferring changes in social organization over time.

Finally, the brief examination of osteological evidence in this study suggests that future research should aim to forge greater integration between skeletal and artefactual evidence. In so doing, the potential for misinterpretation, particularly with regard to factors such as ethnicity, will be greatly reduced. The skeleton provides a wealth of social information regarding culture, lifestyle, diet, environment and population movement, which, when examined in a contextually sensitive way, can be a powerful investigative tool for illuminating the life-ways and origins of past peoples.[44]

Acknowledgements

This research was undertaken during my PhD at the University of Durham, supported by the AHRB and supervised by Andrew Millard and Sam Lucy, for whose comments I was very grateful. Andrew Millard also helped a great deal with the calculations for the dental eruption and wear. Thanks also to Tim Thompson, John Pearce, Howard Williams, Sarah Semple and an anonymous reviewer whose comments have greatly improved this paper. All errors remain my own.

Notes

1. Esmonde Cleary 1989, 173.
2. Scull 2000, 403.
3. See Esmonde Cleary 2001; Hills 2002; Halsall 1995 for discussion.
4. Jones 1997, 139.
5. See Halsall 1995; Harrison 1999; Esmonde Cleary 1993, 2001.
6. Lucy 1998, 2000, 163–73, see also Moreland 2000.
7. Moreland 2000.
8. Sørensen 2000.
9. See Harrison 1999.
10. Eckardt and Williams 2003.
11. See Sofaer Derevenski 1997a; 1997b.
12. *E.g.* Crawford 1991; 1999; Gowland 2001; Sofaer Derevenski 1997a; 1997b; Stoodley 1999; 2000.
13. Grave good dates for each site were obtained from the following published sources: Abingdon (Leeds and Harden 1936), Berinsfield (Boyle, Dodd, Miles and Mudd 1995), Alton (Evison 1988), Portway (Cook and Dacre 1985), Worthy Park (Hawkes and Grainger 2003), Lankhills (Clarke 1979).
14. See Bouquet-Appel and Massett 1982; Aykroyd, Lucy, Pollard, and Roberts, 1999.
15. Brickley and McKinley 2004.
16. Millard and Gowland 2002.
17. See Hoffman 1979; Holman and Jones 1998.
18. Saunders 2000.
19. Lloyd-Jones 1997.
20. Lloyd-Jones 1997.
21. Tyrrell 2000a; 2000b.
22. Mayall 2000.
23. Tyrrell 2000b, 302.
24. Moreland 2000, 37.

25. See Hills 2001, 57–72 for a discussion of some of these points.
26. Poor health and/or living conditions profoundly affect growth during childhood and ultimately adult stature. See Stinson 2000 for a review of the biological and cultural factors affecting stature.
27. Roberts and Cox 2003.
28. Budd, Millard, Chenery, Lucy, Roberts 2004; Stoodley *in prep*; see also Hills 2002, 63 for a discussion
29. Huggett 1992.
30. See Booth 2001 for a detailed discussion of Romano-British burial rites in Oxfordshire.
31. *E.g.* Crawford 1991; 1999; Stoodley 1999; 2000; Lucy 1998; Philpott 1991; Swift 2000.
32. Gowland 2001.

33. Crawford 1999; Stoodley 1999, 2000.
34. Gowland 2006.
35. Richards 1995, 57.
36. Clarke 1979, 385; see Swift 2000, 42, 72–77 for a detailed discussion of the evidence.
37. Swift 2000, 42.
38. Swift 2000, 42.
39. Evans, Stoodley and Chenery 2006.
40. Eckardt and Williams 2003.
41. Pearce 1999, 164; Halsall 1995.
42. See Harrison 1999.
43. See Halsall 1995.
44. See Larsen 1997; see also papers in Gowland and Knüsel 2006.

Bibliography

Aykroyd, R. G., Lucy, D., Pollard, A. M. and Roberts, C. A. 1999. Nasty, brutish, but not necessarily short: a reconsideration of the statistical methods used to calculate age at death from adult human skeletal and dental age indicators, *American Antiquity*, **64**, 55–70.

Brickley, M. and McKinley, J. I. 2004. *Guidelines to the Standards for Recording Human Skeletal Remains*, IFA Technical Paper, 7, Southampton and Reading: BABAO and IFA.

Bocquet-Appel, J.-P. and Masset, C. 1982. Farewell to palaeodemography, *Journal of Human Evolution*, **11**, 321–333.

Booth, P. 2001. The Late Roman cemeteries of Oxfordshire: a review, *Oxoniensia*, 66, 12–19.

Boyle, A., Dodd, A., Miles, D. and Mudd, A. (eds) 1995. *Two Oxfordshire Anglo-Saxon Cemeteries: Berinsfield and Didcot*, Thames Valley Landscapes Monograph No 8, Oxford: Oxford University Committee for Archaeology.

Budd, P., Millard, A., Chenery, C., Lucy, S. and Roberts, C. 2004. Investigating population movement by stable isotopes: a report from Britain, *Antiquity*, **78**, 127–141.

Chamberlain, A. T. 2000. Problems and prospects in palaeodemography, in M. Cox and S. Mays (eds), *Human Osteology in Archaeology and Forensic Science*, 101–116, London: Greenwich Medical Media.

Clarke, G. 1979. *The Roman Cemetery at Lankhills*, Winchester Studies 3, Pre-Roman and Roman Winchester, Oxford: Clarendon Press.

Cook, A. M. and Dacre, M. W. 1985. *Excavations at Portway, Andover 1973–1975*, Oxford: Oxford University Committee for Archaeology

Crawford, S. 1991. When do Anglo-Saxon children count? *Journal of Theoretical Archaeology*, **2**, 17–24.

Crawford, S. 1999. *Childhood in Anglo-Saxon England*, Sutton: Stroud

Eckardt, H. and Williams, H. 2003. Objects without a past? The use of Roman objects in Anglo-Saxon graves, in H. Williams (ed.), *Archaeologies of Remembrance. Death and Memory in Past Societies*, 141–170, New York: Kluwer/Plenum.

Esmonde-Cleary, A. S. 1989. *The Ending of Roman Britain*, London: Batsford.

Esmonde-Cleary, A. S. 1993. Approaches to the differences between Late Romano-British and Early Anglo-Saxon archaeology, *Anglo-Saxon Studies in Archaeology and History*, **6**, 57–64.

Esmonde Cleary, A. S. 2001. The Roman to medieval transition, in S. James and M. Millett (eds), *Britons and Romans: Advancing the Archaeological Agenda*, 90–97, York: Council for British Archaeology.

Evans, J., Stoodley, N. and Chenery, C. 2006. A Strontium and Oxygen isotope assessment of a possible fourth century immigrant population in a Hampshire cemetery, southern England, *Journal of Archaeological Science* 2006, 265–272.

Evison V. I. 1988. *An Anglo-Saxon Cemetery at Alton, Hampshire*, Hampshire Field Club Monograph 4, Gloucester: Alan Sutton.

Gowland, R. L. 2001. Playing dead: implications of mortuary evidence for the social construction of childhood in Roman Britain, in G.

Davies, A. Gardner, and K. Lockyear (eds), *TRAC 2000. Proceedings of the Tenth Annual Theoretical Roman Archaeology Conference, London 2000*, 152–168, Oxford: Oxbow.

Gowland, R. L. (2006) Ageing the past: examining age identity from funerary evidence, in R. Gowland and C. Knüsel (eds), *The Social Archaeology of Funerary Remains*, Oxford: Oxbow.

Gowland, R. L. and Knüsel, C. J. (eds) 2006. *The Social Archaeology of Funerary Remains*, Oxford: Oxbow.

Halsall, G. 1995. The Merovingian period in north-east Gaul: transition or change?, in J. Bintliff and H. Hamerow (eds), *Europe Between late Antiquity and the Middle Ages*, 38–57, British Archaeological Reports International Series, 617, Oxford: British Archaeological Reports.

Harrison, G. 1999. Quoit brooches and the Roman-Medieval transition, in P. Baker. C. Forcey, S. Jundi and R. Witcher (eds), *TRAC 98. Proceedings of the Eighth Annual Theoretical Roman Archaeology Conference, Leicester 1998*, 108–120, Oxford: Oxbow.

Hawkes, C. S. and Grainger, G. (2003). *The Anglo-Saxon Cemetery in Worthy Park, Kingsworthy, near Winchester*, Oxford University School of Archaeology Monograph No. 59, Oxford: Oxford University School of Archaeology.

Hills, C. 2002. *The Origins of the English*, London: Duckworth.

Huggett, J. 1992. *A Computer-based Analysis of Early Anglo-Saxon Inhumation Burials*, unpublished PhD thesis, North Staffordshire Polytechnic.

Jones, S. 1997. *The Archaeology of Ethnicity*, London: Routledge.

Larsen, C. S. 1997. *Bioarchaeology: Interpreting Behavior from the Human Skeleton*. Cambridge: Cambridge University Press.

Leeds, E. T. and Harden D. B. 1936. *The Anglo-Saxon Cemetery at Abingdon, Berkshire*, Oxford: University of Oxford, Ashmolean Museum.

Lloyd-Jones, J. 1997. Calculating bio-distance using dental morphology, in S. Anderson and K. Boyle (eds), *Computing and Statistics in Osteoarchaeology*, 23–30, Oxford: Oxbow.

Lucy, S. J. 1998. *The Early Anglo-Saxon Cemeteries of East Yorkshire: An Analysis and Re-Interpretation*, British Archaeological Reports British Series, 272, Oxford: British Archaeological Reports.

Lucy, S. J. 2000. *The Anglo-Saxon Way of Death*, Gloucestershire: Sutton.

Mayall, J. T. 2000. Dental morphology: techniques and strategies, in M. A. Katzenberg and S. R. Saunders (eds), *Skeletal Biology of Past Peoples: Research Methods,* 103–134, New York: Wiley-Liss.

Millard, A. and Gowland, R. L. 2002. A Bayesian Approach to the Estimation of Age from Tooth Development and Wear in Humans, *Archaeologia e Calcolatori*, **13**, 197–210.

Moreland, J. 2000. Ethnicity, power and the English, in W. O. Frazer and A. Tyrrell, (eds), *Social Identity in Early Medieval Europe*, 23–52, London: Leicester University Press.

Pearce, J. 1999. *Case Studies in a Contextual Archaeology of Burial Practice in Roman Britain*, unpublished PhD thesis, University of Durham.

Philpott, R. 1991. *Burial Practices in Roman Britain*, British Archaeological Reports British Series, 219, Oxford: British Archaeological Reports.

Richards, J. D. 1995. An archaeology of Anglo-Saxon England, in G. Ausenda (ed.), *After Empire: Towards an Ethnology of Europe's Barbarians*, 51–66, New York: Boydell Press.

Saunders, S. R. 2000. Subadult skeletons and growth related studies, in M. A. Katzenberg and S. R. Saunders (eds), *Skeletal Biology of Past Peoples: Research Methods,* 135–161, New York: Wiley-Liss.

Scull, C. 2000. How the dead live: some current approaches to the mortuary archaeology of England in the fifth to eighth centuries A.D, *Archaeology Journal*, **157**, 399–406.

Sørensen, M. L. 2000 *Gender Archaeology*, London: Polity Press.

Sofaer Deverenski, J. 1997a. Age and gender at the site of Tiszapolgár-Basatanya, Hungary, *Antiquity*, **71**, 875–889.

Sofaer Deverenski, J. 1997b. Linking age and gender as social variables. *Ethnographisch-Archäologische Zeitschrift*, **38**, 485–493.

Stinson, S. 2000. Growth variation: biological and cultural factors, in S. Stinson, B. Bogin, R. Huss-Ashmore, and D. O'Rourke (eds), *Human Biology: an Evolutionary and Biological Approach*, 245–463, New York: Wiley Liss.

Stoodley, N. 1999. *The Spindle and the Spear: A Critical Enquiry into the Construction and Meaning of Gender in the Early Anglo-Saxon Burial Rite*, BAR British Series, 288, Oxford: British Archaeological Reports.

Stoodley, N. 2000. From the cradle to the grave: age organization and the early Anglo-Saxon burial rite, *World Archaeology*, 31, 456–472.

Swift, E. 2000. *The End of the Western Roman Empire*, Stroud: Tempus.

Tyrrell, A. 2000a. *Corpus saxonum*: early Medieval bodies and corporeal identity, in W. O. Frazer and A. Tyrrell (eds), *Social Identity in Early Medieval Europe*, 137–156, London: Leicester University Press.

Tyrrell, A. 2000b. Skeletal non-metric traits and the assessment of inter- and intra- population diversity: past problems and future potential, in M. Cox and S. Mays (eds), *Human Osteology in Archaeology and Forensic Science*, 289–306, London: Greenwich Medical Media.

Transforming Body and Soul:
Toilet Implements in Early Anglo-Saxon Graves

Howard Williams

Introduction – Artefacts in Early Medieval Graves

Recent debates addressing early medieval furnished burial rites have moved away from discussions of religion and culture and have instead been directed towards the contextual study of social structure, symbolism and ideology. The spectacle of the ritual performances involved in creating furnished graves have been likened to theatrical and poetic performances in the sense that they were public spectacles laden with symbolic meanings and political messages in which individual and social identities were portrayed, negotiated and constituted.[1] Portable objects are regarded as having important symbolic and mnemonic roles in these ritual performances as they were selectively incorporated into graves by the mourners to actively convey messages to onlookers as well as mediate a dialogue with the dead. The significance of material culture in mortuary cere-monies was all the more potent because the brevity of the display of artefacts and the cadaver before the grave was covered and the displayed 'image' was concealed and consign to memory.

Most of these discussions concerning burial rites as displays and performances have focused upon the relatively detailed contextual, corporeal and artefactual data found in the inhumation graves of the late fifth- to early eighth-centuries AD. In contrast, the cremation burials of early Anglo-Saxon England (dating from the mid-fifth to the early seventh centuries AD) are generally overlooked because of the seemingly poorer and more fragmented evidence produced by the impact of fire on the remains that were collected and buried within cinerary urns. Yet, because cremation practices involved the systematic transformation of objects and corpses, the consideration of the deployment of artefacts can serve to enhance our understanding of the role of funerary ritual in the mnemonic transformation, as well as the symbolic representation, of social identities in early medieval Britain.[2] Building on earlier publications in which the author has argued for a role for artefacts in the selective

dissolution and reconstitution of identities during the cremation process and their incorporation into cinerary urns,[3] this paper aims to demonstrate that the choice to place toilet implements in early Anglo-Saxon cremation graves was more than a utilitarian practice. It is argued that the commemorative significance of grave goods and the cremation rite as a whole was mediated by these seemingly small and modest objects.

The paper begins by firstly reviewing the toilet implements from a selection of inhumation cemeteries from across England before demonstrating the contrasting character of toilet items found in the broadly contemporary cremation rites. The first-hand examination of the material was not possible for this study, which relies instead on the descriptions found in excavation reports and incorporating data courteously made available by Catherine Hills for the Spong Hill cemetery. An analysis of this data makes it possible to argue that the contrast between the rites indicates a limited significance for inhumation rites, but a central importance for toilet implements in early Anglo-Saxon cremation ceremonies.

Toilet Implements in Early Anglo-Saxon Inhumation Graves

Types

Through a survey of inhumation graves dated to the late fifth and sixth centuries AD published in recent reports, an impression was gained of the frequency and nature of the toilet implements placed with the dead in the furnished burial rites of southern and eastern England. Although no detailed corpus and analysis has yet to be undertaken, the patterns identified here mirror many of those revealed in Nick Stoodley's analysis of the early Anglo-Saxon inhumation rite, the most systematic and comprehensive to date.

Table 1 summarises the instances of the most common toilet implement form, tweezers, in early Anglo-Saxon inhumation graves (Table 1). Other common types found

Table 1. The numbers of tweezers from inhumation graves in the sample of cemeteries investigated

Grave	Age	Sex	Material	State	Length	Tweezer Context
AD 86	40+	f	Fe	broken	24	on chest
AD 72	45+	f	Ae	complete	37	outside left arm
AD 63	45+	m	Ae	broken – half present	?	waist
AD 125	40–45	m	Ae	complete	48	between body and left arm
AN 35	30–35	f	Ae	broken in antiquity, one blade	72	waist
AN 41	young	f	Fe	fragmentary	?	left of waist
AN 2	?	m	Ae	complete	66	right of chest
BD B66/1	adult	f	Ae	complete	33	on skull
BD A23/3	25–30	f	Ae	fragmentary	?	upper chest area
BL 1	adult	f	Ae	complete	49	?
BL 20	adult	f?	Ae	complete	49	?
BL 45	adult	?	Fe	broken	61	waist
BL 58	adult	f	Ae	broken and bent	?	lower end of grave outside right leg
BL 61	adult	?	Ae	fragmentary	?	?
BL 91	adult	f	Ae	?	?	?
BN 3	25–35		Ae	complete	44	between legs
BN 20	19	f	Ae	broken	62	between legs
BN 93	35–45	f	Ae	complete	34	in mouth
CD 10	45+	f	Ae	complete	49	left hip
CD 38	45+	m	Ae	complete	70	outside left femur
CD 63	45+	m	Ae	fragments	?	left upper chest
CD 116	?	?	Ae	broken	?	unclear
CD 163	35–45	f	Ae	broken in antiquity, one blade missing	66	at neck
DB 107	?	?	?	?	?	?
DB 156	?	f	Fe	broken	?	left elbow
DB 41	?	m	Ae	complete	71	left waist
DB 65	45+	m	Ae	complete	75	left waist
DL 81	45–55	m	Ae	?	?	beside head
DL 81	45–55	m	Ae	?	?	left waist
DL 93	40–50	m	Ae	complete	75	left waist
DL 91	?juvenile	m	Ae	?	70	waist area
DL 36	40–50	m	Ae	complete	73	left waist
DL 59	30–40	f	Fe	complete	50	left waist
DL 68	12–14	f	Ae	complete	51	between legs
EH 49	45+	f			58	chest
EM 17	25–35	f	Ae	complete	60	?
EM 90	30–40	f	Ae	broken in antiquity	45	by left hand
EM 95	25–35	f	Ae	broken	43	?
EM 100	30–40	f	Ae	broken	35	?
EM 109	25–35	f	Ae	complete	32	by right shoulder
GC 51	45+	m	Ae	complete	63	at right elbow, under knife, spike & belt frags
GC 140	45+	m	Ae	complete	91	between waist and left arm
LD 25	45+	f	Ae	complete	62	left shoulder
LD 152	40+	f	Ae	complete	36	left of waist
MT 27	older adult	?	Fe	broken – two fragments	?	at waist
MT 45	?	m	Ae	near-complete	57	waist area
MT 65	?	m?	Ae	complete	70	waist
MT 67	?	m	Ae	near-complete	52	centre of grave

Site codes:

AD = *Appledown (Down and Welch 1990)*

AN = *Alton (Evison 1988)*.

BD = *Beckford (Evison and Hill 1995)*.

BL = *Broughton Lodge (Kinsley 1993*

BN = *Berinsfield (Boyle et. al. 1995)*.

CD = *Castledyke South (Drinkall and Foreman 2000)*.

DB = *Buckland, Dover (Evison 1987)*.

DL = *Mill Hill, Deal (Parfitt and Brugmann 1997)*.

EH = *Edix Hill Barrington (Malim and Hines 1988)*

EM = *Empingham (Timby 1996)*.

GC = *Great Chesterford (Evison 1994)*.

LD = *Lechlade (Boyle et. al. 1998)*.

MT = *Morningthorpe (Green and Rogerson 1987)*;

NO = *Norton (Sherlock and Welch 1992)*.

PA = *Portway, Andover (Cook and Dacre 1985)*.

SH = *Spong Hill (Hills, Penn and Rickett 1984)*;

SP = *Snape (Filmer-Sankey and Pestell 2001)*.

SW = *Sewerby (Hirst 1985)*

WD = *Watchfield (Scull 1992)*.

WG = *Westgarth Gardens (West 1988)*

WH = *West Heslerton (Haughton and Powlesland 1999)*.

WK = *Wakerley (Adams and Jackson 1990)*.

Table 1. cont.

Grave	Age	Sex	Material	State	Length	Tweezer Context
MT 78	?	?	Ae	broken	54	centre of grave
MT 87	?	?	Ae	broken	?	centre of grave
MT 148	young adult	f	Ae	complete	73	side of grave
MT 157	?	m	Ae	near-complete	67	centre of grave
MT 251	?	f	Ae	fragmentary	?	centre of grave
MT 281	?	?	Fe	fragmentary	?	centre of grave
MT 288	old mature adult	f	Ae	complete	43	centre of grave
MT 325	young or mature adult	f	Ae	complete	36	middle lower grave
MT 346	?	f	Ae	broken	45	chest area
MT 355	adult	m	Ae	complete	62	waist area
MT 360	?	f	Ae	broken	?	waist area
MT 370	?	f	Ae	fragmentary	?	waist area
MT 416	?	m	Ae	fragmentary	58	waist area
NO 29	25–35	f		broken before burial	60	waist area left of body
NO 78	45–61	m	Ae	complete	62	disturbed
PA 26	55+	m	Ae	complete	62	left waist
PA 53	18–30	f	Ae	complete	45	left hand/ left shoulder
SH27		m	Ae	broken but largely intact	45	not known
SP 18	?	f?	Ae	broken	49	waist
SW 56	?adult	?	Ae	fragmentary	?	top right of grave
WD 11	sub-adult or adult	m	Ae	complete	55	inside lower left arm
WD 14	20–25	f	Fe	fragmented	49	over right clavicle
WD 75	35–40	f	Ae	complete	53	over right ribcage
WG 41	adult	m	Ae	complete	75	waist
WH 2	?	m	Ae	complete	47	centre of grave, next to chest
WH 22	adult	f	Ae	complete	53	waist area
WH 180	adult	?	Ae	fragmented	?	chest area
WH 77	adult?	?	Ae	complete	55	waist area
WH 83	adult	f	Ae	broken	48	side of grave – disturbed
WH 161	adult	?	Ae	fragmentary	?	waist
WH 26	adult	f	Fe	fragmented	69	waist
WH 130	adult	m	Fe	complete	51	centre-left
WK 41			Ae	complete	60	?
WK 51			Ae	complete	55	?

include ear scoops (also called spatulae or miniature spoons), picks (sometimes labelled prickers, pins or tooth-picks), brushes (referred to as cosmetic brush holders) and items described as 'rods' or 'scrapers' (blunt-ended blades comparable to a broken tweezers-blade). These objects are sometimes suspended from loops of iron or copper-alloy wire.[4] By way of illustration, examples of all these types were found during excavations of sixth-century cemeteries at Berinsfield, Oxfordshire and Broughton Lodge in Nottinghamshire (Fig. 1).[5] Less common are finds of miniature weapons, blades, rods, tools and perforated spoons.[6] For example, a miniature iron tool set was found from grave 86 at Appledown consisting of a pair of shears, tweezers, two grades of file, a blade and a point (Fig. 2).[7] It is notable that the majority of these 'miniature' items, when retrieved from dateable contexts, are derived from seventh-century graves rather than those contemporary with cremation burials of the later fifth and sixth centuries.[8] Meanwhile pairs of iron shears mostly date from later seventh- and early eighth-century contexts and are therefore not directly related to the deployment of toilet implements in cremation burials discussed below.[9] They could have been used to cut hair but shears from inhumation graves are too large to have been toilet

implements. A more likely explanation for these items is as tools and symbols connected with textile production (for shearing sheep and/or cutting cloth),[10] although medical functions have also been suggested.[11] Equally important are those types that are rare or absent, notably nail cleaners of Roman type[12] as well as razors and small shears of the types found in cremation burials (see below).

Material and Decoration

The vast majority of toilet sets from inhumation graves were copper alloy. Iron tweezers and toilet sets are known but they constitute a small minority of those found, as are silver toilet implements that are restricted to seventh-century graves.[13] This relative paucity might be partly explained by differential preservation. Cast copper-alloy tweezers sometimes have incised and punched decoration following very closely upon the design of their Roman counterparts, and indeed distinguishing between re-used Roman objects and early Anglo-Saxon examples is problematic (see below).[14] Otherwise toilet sets have no discernible decoration although it is possible that iron toilet implements were decorated but rust has long obscured them.

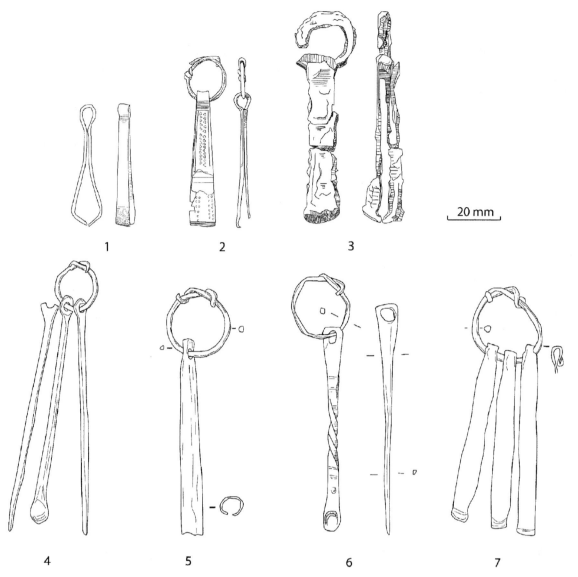

20 mm

1   2   3

4   5   6   7

Figure 1. Examples of tweezers, earscoops, prickers and cosmetic brush-handles from early Anglo-Saxon inhumation graves. 1. Small sheet copper-alloy tweezers from Broughton Lodge grave 20 (Redrawn by the author after Kinsley 1993: 20); 2. large cast coppper-alloy tweezers from Broughton Lodge grave 1 (Redrawn by the author after Kinsley 1993: 100); 3. large iron tweezers from Broughton Lodge grave 45 (redrawn by the author after Kinsley 1993: 130); 4. copper alloy toilet set of ear scoop and two picks from Berinsfield grave 54 (redrawn by the author after Boyle et al. 1995: 179); 5. copper-alloy cosmetic brush-holder from Berinsfield grave 107 (redrawn by the author after Boyle et al. 1995: 191); 6. copper-alloy ear scoop from Norton grave 70 (redrawn by the author after Sherlock & Welch 1992: 172); 7. toilet set of three copper-alloy 'scrapers' from Berinsfield grave 107 (redrawn by the author after Boyle et al. 1995: 191)

Size

Although some artefacts are broken and damaged through centuries of burial, most of the objects recovered from inhumation graves intact are full-sized and are therefore potentially functioning objects. In contrast, clear-cut instances of 'miniature' artefacts are rare.

Functions

We have no direct documentary or visual evidence from early Anglo-Saxon England to confirm how toilet implements were employed. Indeed, it is possible that a single item could have had been utilised for many different tasks. Tweezers could have had craft uses (such as for sewing leather or textile), a suggestion that finds some support in the association of a sewing needle and bronze tweezers within a leather container from grave 56, Sewerby (East Yorkshire).[15] They are equally likely to have been used to remove head, facial, nasal and body hairs as well as splinters, lice and ticks. Ear scoops (spatulas) could

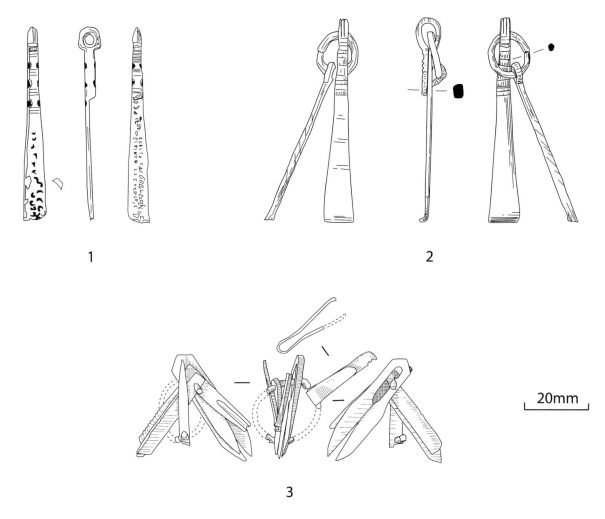

1

2

3

Figure 2. Examples of toilet implements broken in antiquity and miniatures. 1. Cast copper-alloy tweezers broken in antiquity and impressed with semi-circular punchmarks after breakage, from Norton grave 29 (redrawn by the author after Sherlock and Welch 1992: 138); 2. Cast copper-alloy tweezers broken in antiquity with pick from Castledyke South grave 163 (redrawn by the author after Drinkall and Foreman 1998: 189); 3. Iron toilet set from Appledown grave 86 (redrawn by the author after Down and Welch 1990: 72)

have functioned in cleaning out ears and noses but could also have served in applying cosmetics and medicines. Equally, picks might have had numerous functions such as to clean nails, skin and teeth, to lance boils and spots and they may have also been used in tattooing. Scrapers have no self-evident function although they could have been used to scrape and clean skin, shave hair or apply cosmetics. While there must remain uncertainty concerning the precise uses of toilet items, the common theme linking their possible applications is clearly the management and presentation of the body and the treatment of skin and hair in particular. Even some of the miniature 'weapons' and 'tools', although shaped like larger items, could still have functioned to manage hair and skin and need not be 'amulets' if defined as objects with no practical function.[16] However, the form of these 'miniatures', even if employed for grooming, does suggest that toilet implements had more than a prosaic significance

for early medieval people. Indeed, as in many societies, regiments of bodily presentation may have been closely related to managing religious conceptions of pollution and as a means of constituting and displaying social identity.[17]

Condition

Although some artefacts are found in a fragmentary state, there is enough evidence to suggest that they were usually buried intact, with little evidence of deliberate fragmentation or ritual 'killing'. Of the sample of tweezers considered in this study, only a small number display possible evidence of breakage in antiquity, through the presence of only one blade (4/90: 4.4%).[18] A particularly convincing example is from grave 29 of the Norton (Cleveland) cemetery where decorative punch-marks were added to the inside of the single tweezers-blade after breakage (Fig. 2).[19] It is possible

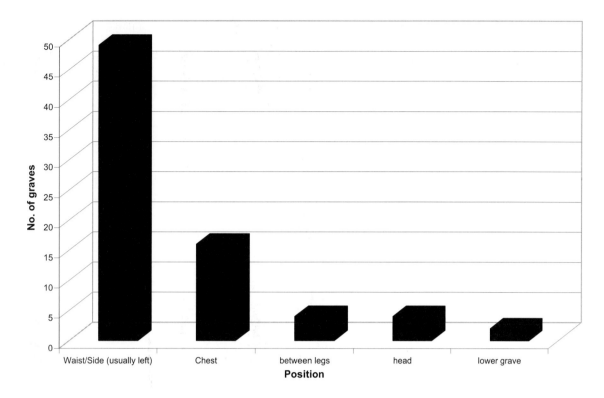

Figure 3. The location of tweezers from early Anglo-Saxon inhumation graves

that the blade was curated after its practical function had ceased because of some personal association with the owner. Alternatively, its curation may have been motivated by a perceived amuletic significance or for more prosaic reasons such as its deployment as a practice-piece for punching or the intention to re-use it as scrap-metal. A toilet set consisting of a broken tweezer-blade and ear scoop from grave 163 at Castledyke South, Barton-upon-Humber (Lincolnshire), suggests that in some instances toilet implements were used as elements of costume and ornament after their functioning lives had ended (Fig. 2).[20]

Owing to the fact that many of the early Anglo-Saxon bronze toilet implements resemble Roman-period objects in terms of form and decoration, it is difficult to ascertain how many of them might have been inherited or re-used following their discovery on Roman sites, or whether the similarities simply reflect comparable technologies available for making these relatively simple objects. Contrary to antiquarian accounts, Roger White, in his study of re-used Roman artefacts in early medieval graves, is sceptical of assigning many from early Anglo-Saxon graves a Roman date. Many are likely to have been of fifth and sixth-century manufacture but inheriting Roman styles either directly from those continuing to circulate or those discovered in the landscape, or indirectly via the influence of Roman material culture styles upon northern Germany and southern Scandinavia in the third and fourth centuries AD. Given their simple form, similarities might

in many cases be coincidental and governed by functional necessity.

Location

There are two main body-areas where toilet implements are found in inhumation graves; by the waist and on the chest. For tweezers, they are most often suspended from the belt, usually on the left side in association with bag collections and knives (Fig. 3). A minority (around 15%) are found in the chest area suggesting that they may have been suspended from the neck. Cosmetic brushes are also found suspended around the neck as at Berinsfield (Oxfordshire). Toilet sets of picks and ear scoops can be often found on the chest suggested suspension in a similar way, as in grave 44 from Portway Andover (Hampshire)[23] and grave 54 from Berinsfield.[24] Whichever position was selected for these items, it is clear that (although many were small) toilet implements were intended as integral and visible parts of early Anglo-Saxon costume. Furthermore, if both locations in the mortuary costume reflect in broad terms the location of these items on the clothing of the living, then it is evident that they were intended to be not only visible, but also accessible for regular use.

While most toilet implements formed a part of mortuary costume, some appear to have been placed in the grave by the mourners. This practice might explain the occasional discovery of tweezers found at the bottom of the grave, upon the skull, and in one case within the skeleton's mouth.[25] Similarly a toilet set of two pins and one ear scoop was found by the knees at grave 27 at Alton (Hampshire).[26] These examples suggest that toilet items were not always a part of costume but they may have had an occasional importance during the final ceremonies associated with the interment of the body.[27]

Combinations

All toilet items can be found singly in inhumation graves. Cosmetic brushes are almost always alone but tweezers can be either placed alone or paired with ear scoops. Meanwhile toilet sets suspended from metal rings usually consist of ear scoops, picks and scrapers. Sometimes there is evidence that multiple objects of the same type were placed in the grave, suggesting that their number had an ornamental or symbolic significance. For example, the three scrapers suspended from a ring from grave 107 from Berinsfield were identical to each other and a distinctive use for each of them is unlikely.[28] Combinations of picks and ear scoops are often discovered in groups of three. Similarly, while a combination of an ear scoop and one pick makes functional sense, often there are two identical picks as in grave 27 from Alton (Hampshire), grave 54 from Berinsfield (Oxfordshire) and grave 11 from Dinton (Buckinghamshire).[29] Audrey Meaney has noted a similar replication of three identical 'latchlifter' keys.[30] Cumulatively, this may indicate an auspicious value was sometimes attributed to combinations of three items suspended from the neck or belt.

Frequency

These toilet implements are relatively infrequent grave goods in inhumation burials when compared with other items suspended from the belt (such as knives) or at the neck (such as brooches, glass beads and pendants). It is important to recognise that the soil conditions may have destroyed many of these small metal items. There is equally no reason why toilet implements could not have been made of organic materials that resultantly do not often survive in archaeological contexts. Yet even in the cemeteries with the most careful and large-scale excavations, accompanied by the best preservation of artefacts, toilet implements are rarely found in more than a handful of graves. Some well-excavated cemeteries, such as Sewerby (East Yorkshire), have failed to produce any toilet sets and only one pair of tweezers.[31] Indeed, their occurrence seems particularly low in cemeteries from eastern England; the areas where toilet implements are commonly found in cremation graves (see below).[32]

Mortuary Variability

The overall infrequency of toilet objects from individual cemetery sites makes it difficult to identify any clear patterns in their provision at the local, contextual level. However, by combining the evidence on a national basis, broad trends can be identified. Matching the results of a more detailed analysis of inhumation graves by Nick Stoodley,[33] these toilet items appear to have been the preserve of adult graves, with very few children interred with them (Fig. 4). This same pattern is evident for tweezers; in the sample of graves with tweezers compiled by this author, they appear most common in adults over 40 years of age.

In terms of the gender of the deceased, ear scoops, picks, brushes and scrapers are associated with female-gendered grave assemblages and osteologically-sexed female skeletons (Fig. 5). Stoodley identified a contrasting male bias for tweezers,[34] although in this study, a bias towards graves with female assemblages was identified. Both Stoodley's and this study agree that both genders could have frequently received these items.[35] The disparity in the precise associations of tweezers between Stoodley's and this author's sample probably arise from the use of different samples, combined with the fact that tweezers appear to have very different gender associations depending upon the individual cemetery. For example, in the east Kent cemetery of Mill Hill, Deal, tweezers have a male bias.[36] However, in other cemeteries, tweezers are found equally with both male and female grave assemblages, as at Morningthorpe (Norfolk),[37] while in further instances they have a strong female association, as is the case for Empingham (Rutland).[38]

A further difference in the provision of tweezers can be identified between the sexes in the sample compiled by this author (Fig. 6). While male and female burials could receive tweezers of all lengths, smaller tweezers (under 50mm in length) are more likely to be associated with female graves while male graves are more likely to receive longer tweezers (particularly 70mm and over). Although this is a trend rather than a hard-and-fast rule, there are also hints that older individuals were interred with longer tweezers than children, sub-adults and young adults. Furthermore, the minority of iron toilet implements are almost always associated with female burials. This suggests that within our archaeological typologies, subtle differences in the meanings and associations of superficially similar artefacts can be identified based upon both size and material. It also suggests that these implements had a role in the construction of social identity (including age, gender and perhaps also social status) through their form, size and use to maintain the body's surface during adulthood.

Summary

Among the furnished inhumation burials of the fifth and sixth centuries AD in southern and eastern England, it appears that toilet and cosmetic implements were a consistent, if uncommon, element of adult burial costume used in the practical management of the body's surface

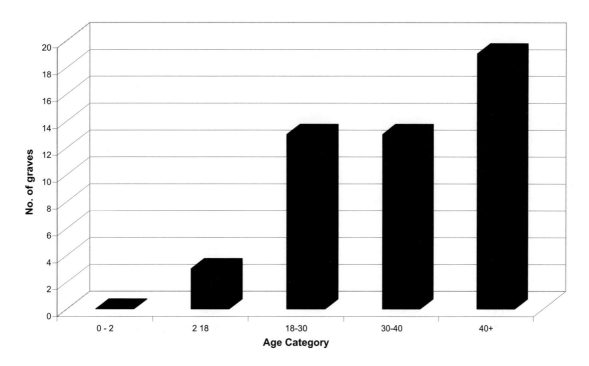

Figure 4. The provision of tweezers vs. age at death in early Anglo-Saxon inhumation graves

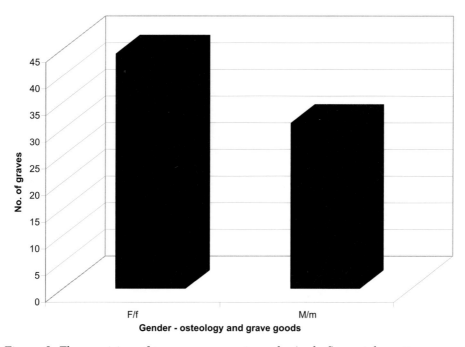

Figure 5. The provision of tweezers vs. sex in early Anglo-Saxon inhumation graves

and appearance and in the enhancement and display of social identity through the medium of the cadaver. Most implements have a clear female bias with the exception of tweezers that can be associated with both genders, displayed on the belt or suspended around the neck.

Toilet Implements in Early Anglo-Saxon Cremation Graves

Having reviewed the evidence for toilet implements in fifth and sixth-century inhumation burials, the study now turns to the cremation burials where a markedly different picture emerges.[39]

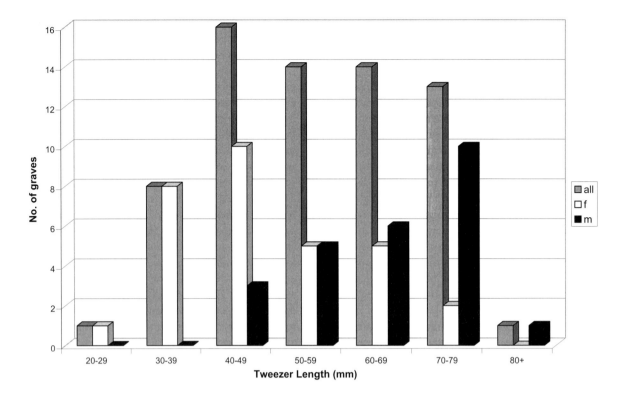

Figure 6. The length of tweezers vs. sex in early Anglo-Saxon inhumation graves

Types

Tweezers are the most common toilet implements items found in cremation graves (Figs 7–11). However, unlike inhumation burials, picks, scrapers, brushes and earscoops are rare finds. Instead, cremations are often found with a distinctive form of razor exhibiting a curved blade and often with a looped handle (Fig. 7).[40] There are a few examples of full-sized shears from cremation burials similar to those uncovered from inhumation graves, however, the vast majority from cinerary urns are much smaller varieties that are rarely paralleled within inhumation contexts (Figs 7 and 8). There are also many 'blades' found in cremation burials; some are clearly broken shears or razors, but others are knives comparable in form to those found in inhumation graves. Other toilet items are rare although miniature tools have been recognised during the excavations at Worthy Park, Kingsworthy (Hampshire), where four graves with toilet sets of up to ten iron miniature implements were recovered (Fig. 8).[41]

Materials and Decoration

Barbara Green constructed a tentative typology for tweezers based on material and size; I – 'functional' bronze of Roman type, II – small bronze tweezers cut from sheet bronze, III – small iron tweezers and IV – large iron tweezers.[42] As discussed above, there are problems associated with a clear definition of 'miniature'

and 'full-sized' items, although Green's typology continues to be employed as a useful guide when studying these objects. Rather than strictly assigning specific implements to one of these four categories, this study instead attempts to recognise trends within the provision of these items in the burial rite.

The materials employed in the manufacture of toilet implements are different in cremation burials from those in inhumation graves. At Spong Hill the distinction is particularly obvious where both inhumation and cremation overlap chronologically. Whereas iron objects were found in the minority in inhumation graves, in this cemetery iron is the predominant material used in the toilet implements found with cremation burials (Figs 12 and 13). This trend is particularly evident for tweezers and shears, and to a lesser extent with razors. Blades can be made of both iron and bronze in almost equal measure. This may suggest a preference for iron items in the cremation rite, although it could reflect the differential melting of copper-alloy implements upon the pyre. Apart from the cast copper-alloy tweezers that display similar decoration to those from inhumation graves (see earlier), toilet implements display no decoration. A further rare category of objects found in cremation burials that are almost unknown in inhumation contexts are bone knives, and it is tempting to postulate that these were further examples of toilet implements, perhaps used especially for the funeral itself.[43]

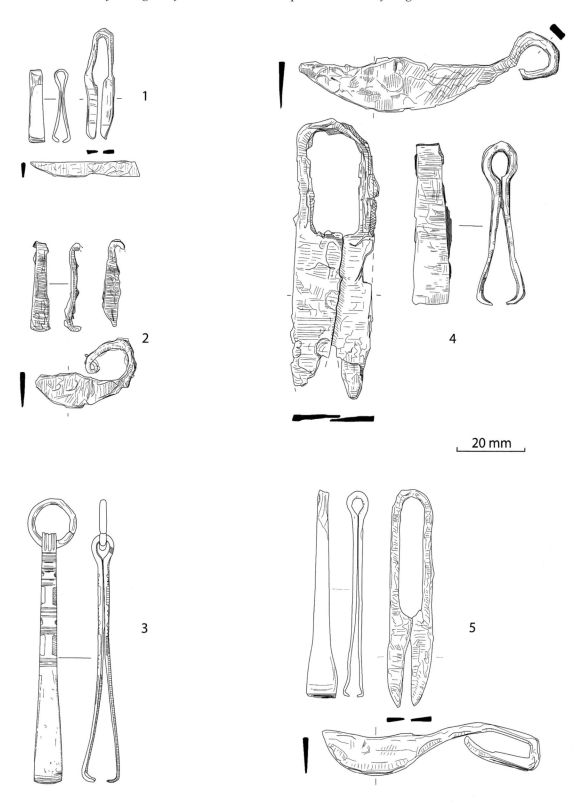

Figure 7. Examples of toilet implements from Spong Hill, Norfolk, including full-sized, small and miniature examples. 1. Sheet copper-alloy tweezers, iron shears and blade/razor from Spong Hill burial 3072 (redrawn by the author after Hills, Penn and Rickett 1987: 211); 2. Iron tweezers, razor and shears (one blade) from Spong Hill burial 2927 (redrawn by the author after Hills, Penn and Rickett 1987: 211); 3. Cast copper-alloy tweezers from Spong Hill burial 2925 (redrawn by the author after Hills, Penn and Rickett 1987: 214); 4. Iron razor, shears and tweezers from Spong Hill burial 2457 (redrawn by the author after Hills, Penn and Rickett 1994: 176); 5. Copper-alloy tweezers, iron razor and iron shears from Spong Hill burial 2898 (redrawn by the author after Hills, Penn and Rickett 1987: 211)

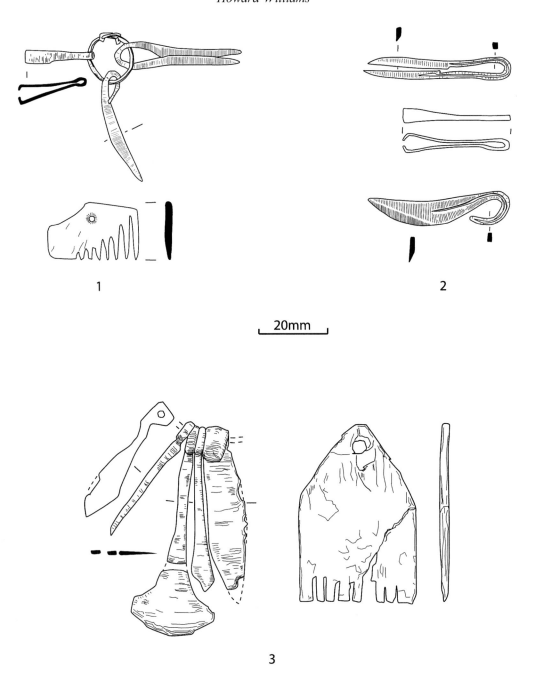

Figure 8. Miniature bronze and iron toilet implements from cremation burials. 1. copper-alloy toilet implements – shears, tweezers and razor – from Newark burial 39 (redrawn by the author after Kinsley 1989: 111); 2. bronze miniature toilet implements – shears, tweezers and razor – from Newark burial 30 (redrawn by the author after Kinsley 1989: 108); 3. four iron miniature toilet implements – a razor, two blades and a 'Thor's hammer' from Worthy Park cremation burial 23 (redrawn by the author after Hawkes and Grainger 2003: 130)

Size

A further contrast between the inhumation and cremation samples concerns the size of toilet implements. Whereas those in inhumation graves are almost all full-sized, cremation graves show a mixture of 'full-sized' and 'miniature' artefacts. In actual fact, there has been no clear definition between what differentiates 'full-sized' from 'miniatures' objects.[44] A brief review of excavation reports identifies an overlap in the length between many of the artefacts labelled 'miniature' and 'full-sized' implements.[45] Moreover, as mentioned above, many of the miniatures, while clearly and deliberately constructed to be small, *could* still have been used to pluck, cut and shave hair.[46] Therefore, this author proposes that in future, we should refer to three sizes of toilet implement: 'functional full-sized', 'functional small' and 'true

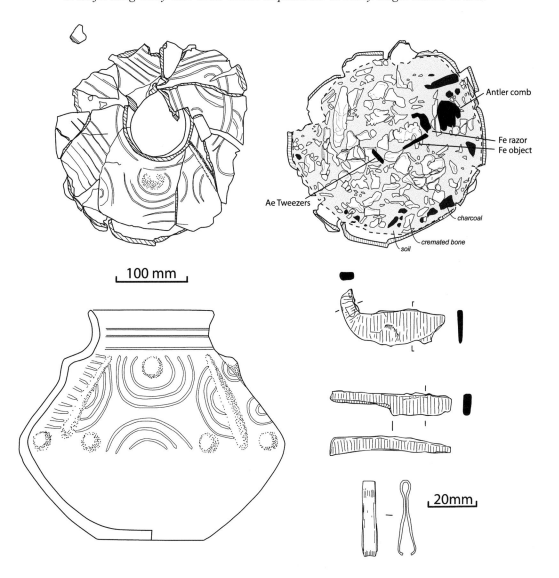

Figure 9. Cremation burial A1419 from Sancton (East Yorkshire) containing the remains of an older subadult. The burial is illustrated in situ *showing the position of the sheet copper-alloy tweezers, iron razor, an iron object that could be a blade, and a bone or antler comb. These items had been placed on the top of the ashes supporting the interpretation that they were added to the ashes* after *the cremation*

miniature', all of which are found in cremation burials. Only a minority of cinerary urns contained 'true miniatures', objects that could never have been functioning items and were of small size. The diminutive form of many objects does preclude the possibility that many items could have been used on a daily basis.

Despite this fact, the inclusion of miniature items hints that the presence of toilet implements had more than a prosaic significance. If not made especially for the funeral, toilet implements may have been items actively selected for deployment in funerals, quite possibly by ritual specialists as well as mourners. A further explanation is suggested below to identify how these miniature objects were connected to the age and sex of the deceased.

Function

As with the items found in inhumation graves, each object need not have had a single use. Both 'functional-full-sized' and 'functional-small tweezers' could have been used to pluck hairs. Similarly despite shears being described as 'miniatures' by Green, many could have been used to pare nails and cut hair and therefore are more appropriately re-labelled as 'functional-small' items. Meanwhile most of the razors, while small in size, were plausibly used in cutting and shaving hair and many can be appropriately attributed the same label 'functional-small'. Admittedly a full re-classification of toilet implements according to size and functionality is outside the remit of this paper, the current 'functional' versus 'miniature' distinction is

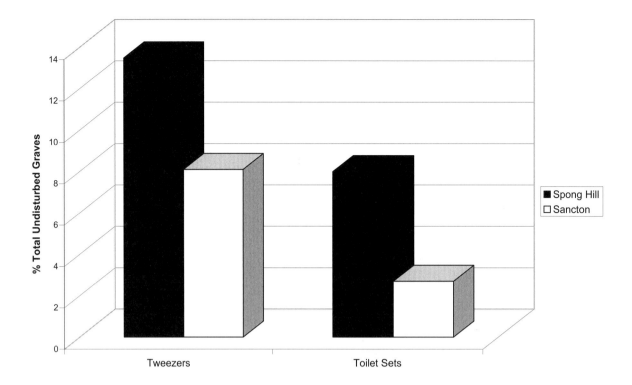

Figure 10. The frequencies of toilet implements from undisturbed early Anglo-Saxon cremation graves from Spong Hill & Sancton

misleading and unhelpful when considering their practical use and potential mortuary significance. Blades are less diagnostic and while some may be knives, others might be broken shears or razors (see below). In each instance an association with the management of hair is likely.

Condition

Owing to the corrosion caused by burial, it is impossible to recognise whether iron toilet implements had been subject to the fire or were added after cremation. Of the bronze toilet implements, it is notable how few reveal the effects of firing. Jackie McKinley has suggested that these smaller items might fall off the funeral pyre and avoid prolonged periods of direct burning.[47] Such a process might explain the fact that copper-alloy artefacts are less common than iron ones. However, the rarity of copper-alloy objects bearing signs of distortion and damage from fire suggests that in many instances, these objects were added to the ashes during the post-cremation rituals.[48] As suggested for bone and antler combs, it is possible that practices varied, with toilet implements sometimes offered as 'pyre goods' and in other funerals they were added at later stages in the ritual process.[49]

There are no examples where it can it be clearly demonstrated that fragmented artefacts were deliberately placed with the dead, although it is extremely difficult in most instances, to discern between 'ritual killing', acci-

dental breakage, the effects of the cremation fire and post-depositional fragmentation.[50] However, it is likely that some of the 'blades' identified are actually broken full-sized shears.[51] If so, then deliberate ritual fragmentation is a possibility, but these broken items could have been re-used effectively as functioning grooming implements when still in circulation.

Location

Very few cinerary urns have survived in a good enough condition and have been excavated and recorded in the necessary detail to make informed comments about the location of toilet implements within them. In some instances from Spong Hill and Sancton, it appears that the toilet implements are found directly above the ashes, suggesting that they were added as a final act during the composition of the burial urn (*e.g.* Fig. 9). However, in other cases recorded at Spong Hill, they are found amidst the ashes and even towards the base of the urns, suggesting the likelihood that they were added to the urn, together with the ashes, at an earlier stage in the post-cremation rites, perhaps during the collecting and sorting of the pyre debris.[52] New excavations are needed that record the location of artefacts within the cinerary urn in order to identify more clearly the ritual practices involved.

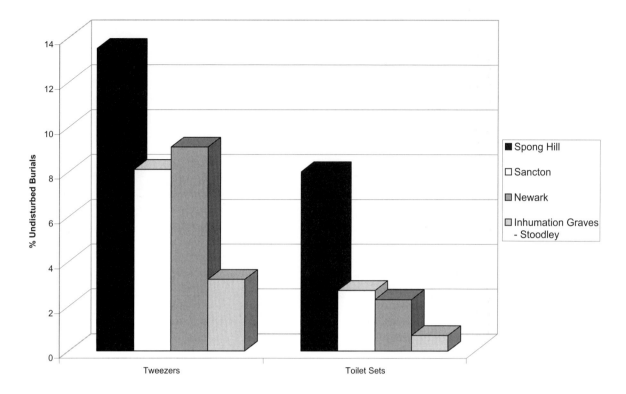

Figure 11. The frequencies of toilet implements from undisturbed early Anglo-Saxon cremation graves from Spong Hill, Sancton and Newark compared with the frequency of tweezers and toilet implements from Nick Stoodley's sample of undisturbed early Anglo-Saxon inhumation graves

Combinations

Whereas tweezers are most often found singly in inhumation graves, within cremation graves toilet implements are either found singly or are found in combinations of two, three or four items. The most common combinations (in descending order of frequency) are (a) tweezers and shears, (b) tweezers and razors, (c) tweezers, shears and razors and (d) tweezers, shears and blades. These combinations indicate that tweezers were the mainstay grooming implement, and that shears, razors and blades were additions to augment the presence of tweezers.

Frequency

The frequency of grave goods varies between cremation cemeteries because of the contrasting recovery methods employed by different excavators but also because of possible variations in burial practices between cemeteries, localities and regions in early Anglo-Saxon England.[53] The well-excavated and recorded samples from Spong Hill and Sancton provide us with the most reliable indication of past mortuary practices (Figs 10 and 11). In these two cemeteries, tweezers are found in a significant minority of graves (found respectively in around 12% and 7% of undisturbed graves). This makes them the most common intact metal artefacts

recovered from cremation burials. Toilet sets from undisturbed burials were also recovered from cinerary urns at these two cemeteries, found in roughly 7% and 2% of graves respectively. While these figures appear low, reflecting the overall scarcity of artefacts in cremation contexts, they are still much higher than the frequency of these items in most contemporary inhumation contexts.

This evidence suggests that toilet implements were either selectively retrieved from the cremation pyres, or that they were deliberately added to the burials after the ashes were collected up. Although, as with all cremation burials, only a minority have grave goods at all, about one in ten of the well-preserved (*i.e.* undisturbed) cremation burials are associated with a toilet implement. Although not the primary focus of this paper, if combs are also considered to be part of the same category of 'objects associated with the body's management in life and death', then the frequency of graves associated with such implements rises considerably.

Mortuary Variability

Unlike the toilet implements within inhumation graves that demonstrate a clear association with adult females (especially for toilet sets), different patterns can be identified in relation to cremation graves.

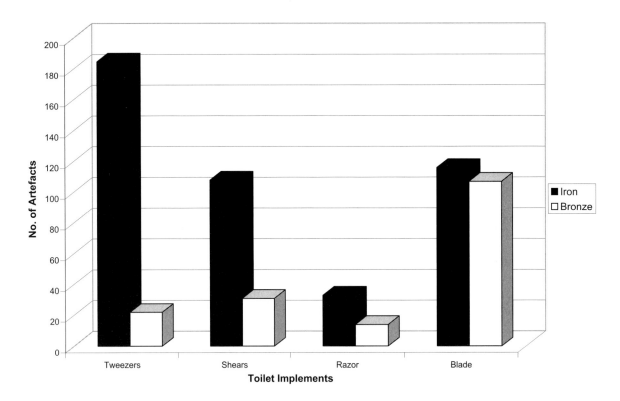

Figure 12. Toilet implement provision vs. materials from early Anglo-Saxon cremation graves at Spong Hill

At Spong Hill, tweezers are found in all age categories, but are less common among infants (following McKinley's definition of 0–4 years of age) than the child (4–12 years of age), subadult (12–18 years of age) and adult (over 18 years) graves (Fig. 14). In contrast, shears are more common in child and sub-adult graves while razors are most common within infant graves. The sample of cremation burials from other cemeteries reveals the same pattern for tweezers and shears, whereas razors have not been discovered within infant graves at other sites (Fig. 15). Therefore, it appears that while all age categories could receive toilet implements, there are different trends in the age-associations of each type of toilet implement.[54]

Evidently, many of those receiving these items in death could not have been individuals who regularly used these same items in life. This stands in contrast to studies of inhumation graves which indicate a clear increase in the number of furnished graves with age, as well as changes in the quality and quantity of the artefacts interred.[55] It also provides a qualification to Sally Crawford's observation which recognised that there were no objects found in child inhumations that were not also common in adult graves.[56] Certainly, Crawford's assertion that children were 'marginal' in early Anglo-Saxon burial ritual seems to be contradicted by the evidence for these cremation urns.[57] It is tempting to consider that these were gifts or offerings by mourners

and/or ritual specialists rather than possessions of the deceased. If so, then the retrospective memory of the deceased when alive may have only been part of the reason for their addition. It is likely that they were objects that served to link the living and the dead, and perhaps serving to create an idealised or even an aspired identity that was only partially or never fully achieved in life. In other words, toilet artefacts were buried with those who had failed to achieve the expected lifecycle route of the ideal social person who would develop through childhood and adulthood to old age before death. This could include many categories of social person, but especially younger individuals. The inclusion of these objects may have been intended to emphasise the posthumous achievement of personhood to facilitate the transformation that cremation was intended to enable for the deceased to become an ancestor and/or reach the next world. This may be a case of artefacts placed with the dead to create a prospective memory for future status in death, rather than a retrospective memory of an identity held by the deceased in life.[58]

Plotting the length of tweezers from Spong Hill against the age of the deceased shows an interesting pattern. Almost all of the particularly small tweezers (measuring from 20 to 40mm in length) were retrieved from infant graves. Children and subadults were most often discovered with tweezers between 30 and 50mm in length, while adults have a broader range of tweezer-

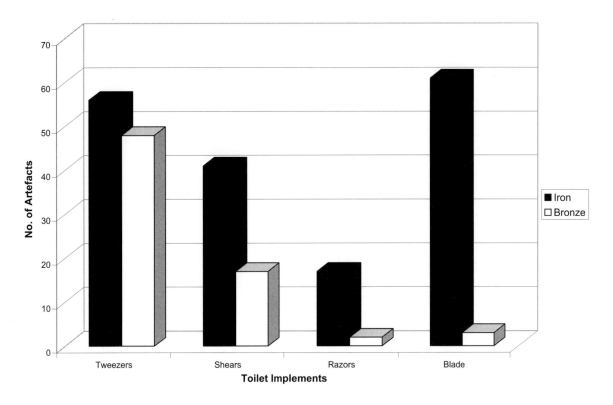

Figure 13. Toilet implement provision vs. materials from cremation graves at other cemeteries

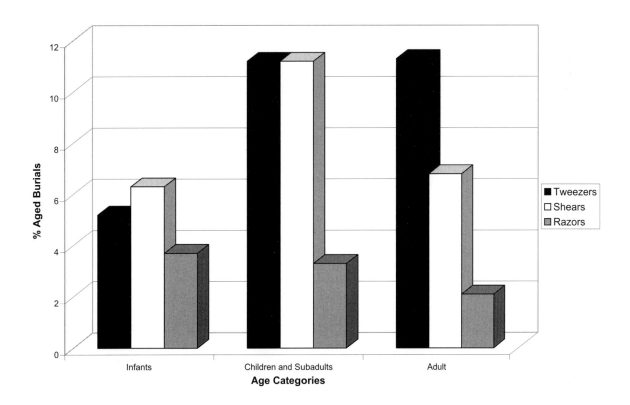

Figure 14. Toilet implement provision vs. age at Spong Hill

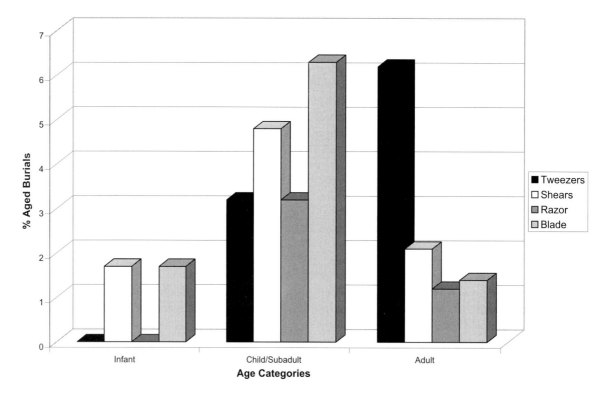

Figure 15. Toilet implement provision vs. age at other cemeteries

lengths over the full range from 10mm to over 90mm, but with most ranging from 30 to 70mm in length (Fig. 16). This indicates that the size of the artefact also articulated the identity of the deceased in a manner that is comparable with that identified by Sally Crawford and Heinrich Härke for the blade-lengths of knives and spearheads in inhumation contexts, and the observations of Julian D. Richards who recognised that the size of cinerary urns broadly correlated with the age of the deceased.[59]

There was also a sex-bias in the provision of toilet implements (Figs 17 and 18). While we have seen a slight female bias with regard to tweezers in inhumation graves, the opposite is the case in cremation burials at Spong Hill. All three main types, tweezers, razors and shears are more common with skeletal remains osteologically assigned to 'certain', 'probable' and 'possible' males rather than their female counterparts. While these are clearly not exclusive markers of male identity, there is a subtle trend evident. A male identity was being emphasised, but toilet implements may have had distinctive roles in association with both male and female individuals. This is supported by the fact that many infants and children received these objects and may indicate that the choice to dispose of these items could have had a broader significance that transcended the precise age and gender of the dead person, perhaps relating to identities constructed at the level of the family, household, community, status or ethnicity.

Summary

Inhumation and cremation rites were associated with toilet implements of different types, materials, sizes, condition, combinations and frequencies (Table 2). This pattern may in part be influenced by chronological variation, since cremation was an earlier burial rite in terms of its overall date-range as well as reflecting a long tradition of placing toilet implements in cinerary urns among the Roman Iron Age cremation cemeteries of northern Germany and southern Scandinavia.[60] There may also be regional patterns, for while tweezers are a consistent grave good in most regions, toilet sets (picks and ear scoops) in inhumation graves are most common in southern England where cremation is less common. Meanwhile inhumation graves appear to have fewer of these items in eastern England where cremation rites are more frequent. Admittedly, further work is needed to plot the chronological and spatial distribution of these finds within individual cemeteries, and to identify different uses of these items between cemeteries to explore the significant of toilet implements in cremation burials further. However the patterns identified so far only serve to emphasise the different ways in which toilet implements were employed in inhumation versus cremation rites. This is particularly evident in cemeteries where both rites are practiced. For instance, at Spong Hill (Norfolk), as described above, we have seen that toilet implements are found in many of the cremation burials, but only one pair of tweezers was recovered from

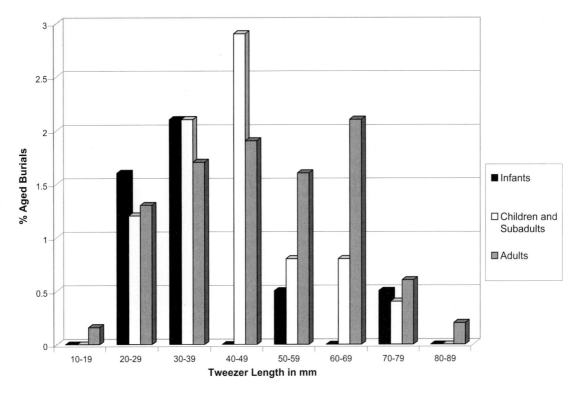

Figure 16. Tweezer length vs. age at Spong Hill

the sixth-century inhumation graves from the same cemetery.[61] Similarly, in mixed-rite cemeteries from southern England such as Saxton Road, Abingdon, bronze full-sized toilet sets accompany inhumation graves whereas those items found in cinerary urns tend to be miniature and made of iron.[62] This distinction is also clear in the differential provision of bone and antler combs between the two methods of disposal; objects again associated with the management of the hair. In a previous study, this author argued that the higher frequency and range of comb-types found in cremation burials was more than the result of differential preservation, but suggested a deliberate connection between the technology of cremation and artefacts associated with hair management.[63]

Theorising Toilet Implements in Early Anglo-Saxon Mortuary Contexts

In contrast to other categories of early medieval grave goods such as brooches and weapons, toilet implements have received limited study including only a tentative typology [64] and sparse interpretation.[65] Having identified a clear distinction between the role of toilet implements in the two modes of disposing of the dead practised in early Anglo-Saxon England, how can we explain this discrepancy?

First and foremost, toilet implements are artefacts connected to the body. More importantly, they are associated with the body's appearance and altering

appearance. In this sense, toilet implements constitute important elements used in 'technologies of remembrance' employed in transforming and managing the body in life and death.[66] There are three interconnected likely uses relating to toilet items in early Anglo-Saxon society that may have linked them to the construction of social identity. These are uses that are simultaneously practical and symbolic and may have contributed to their special significance in cremation rites through the transformation of both the corporeal and metaphysical elements of the deceased. Toilet implements could have been linked to the management of hair through their use to:

1. maintain the body's appearance through regimes and routines of grooming during the person's lifetime.
2. articulate the changes in the person's identity through rites of passage as the social person moves through their lifecycle.
3. alter the appearance of the bodies of mourners as a means of expressing bereavement during funerals.

Each of these uses may have informed the significance of the others, making toilet implements integral to the constitution of social identity including age, gender, status and ethnicity in life and death.[67] However, why have these items been specifically placed with the ashes after cremation? In the light of the theories of mortuary ritual from non-Western societies, building upon the seminal work of Robert Hertz, anthropologists and sociologists

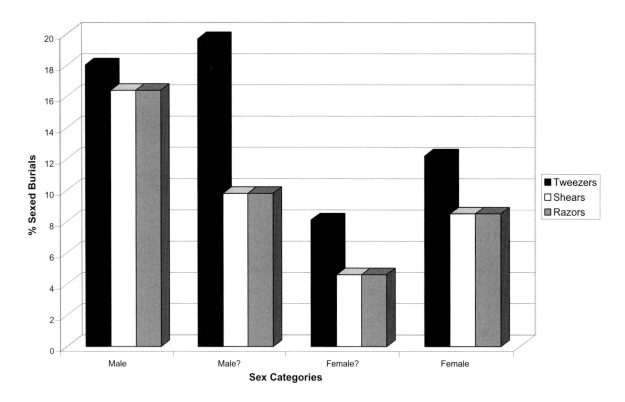

Figure 17. Toilet implement provision vs. sex at Spong Hill

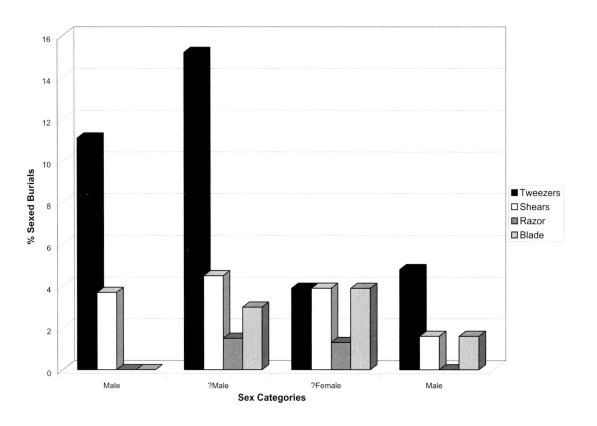

Figure 18. Toilet implement provision vs. sex at other cemeteries

Table 2. The principle differences between the toilet implements found in early Anglo-Saxon cremation and inhumation graves

	Inhumation	*Cremation*
Types	Tweezers, picks, ear scoops, scrapers	Tweezers, razors, shears, Also combs
Material	Cu alloy, some Fe	Fe or Cu alloy
Size	Functional full-size	Functional full-size, functional small & miniature
Functions	Hair, nails, skin & orifice management, cosmetics & medicinal	Hair management
Condition	Most intact, some broken before burial	Many intact, some possible ritual breakage
Location	Suspended from neck or waist	Placed within cinerary urn with ashes
Combinations	Singly or in sets	Singly or in sets
Frequency	Rare	Common
Mortuary Variability – Age	Adult	All age groups Different implements have different age associations Overall, more common with infants & children
Mortuary Variability – Sex	Female bias (toilet sets) Both genders (tweezers)	Slight male bias

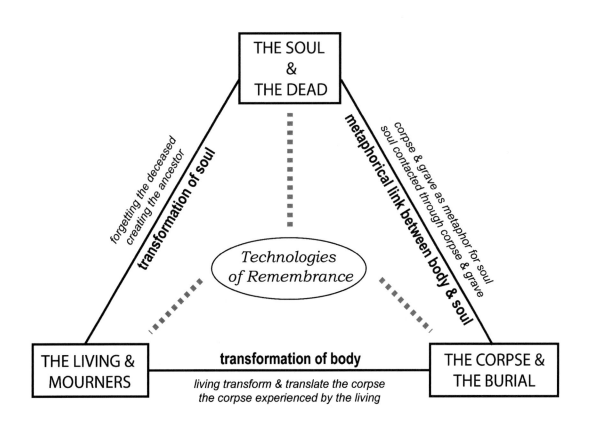

Figure 19. Building on Metcalf and Huntingdon's interpretation of Robert Hertz's formulation of death rituals in non-Western societies, this diagram illustrates the centrality of 'technologies of remembrance' for transforming relations between the living, the body and the soul in early medieval funerals

Figure 20. An artistic impression of the display and dissolution of the body during an early Anglo-Saxon cremation ceremony by Aaron Watson

frequently regard funerals as transitions rather than events. Deaths require rites of separation, a liminal phase and rites of incorporation (Fig. 20).[68] Cremation concerned both ritual display and transformation, focusing upon the dissolution and reconstitution of the body from cadaver to ashes (Fig. 21). This ritual *process* of death would have involved three discrete but related sets of actors: the mourners, the cadaver, and the spiritual elements of the dead (referred to here simplistically as the 'soul'). All of these actors undergo changes in status and relationships during death rituals. Moreover, the transformation in the social, cosmological and ontological state of each affects that of the others. In many societies across the globe including those that employ cremation ceremonies, the management of hair, and in particular the plucking, cutting and shaving of hair among mourners is a means of expressing bereavement as well as managing the physical and spiritual pollution caused by death.[69] At the same time such acts symbolise the transforming identities of mourners during rites of separation, the mediation of the

liminal state, and rites of incorporation. Simultaneously the corpse and the body may have also been regarded as being altered and transformed by these acts. In other words, altering the hair of the corpse and mourners in a comparable fashion could serve to articulate the changing parallel state of the soul or spirit of the deceased. By altering the appearance of mourners and cadaver, such 'magical' acts may have been regarded as essential in order to turn the dead person from the state of a dangerous ghost into the state of benign ancestor. While these themes do not explain the precise deployment of artefacts in early Anglo-Saxon cremation practices, they do provide a broad context for understanding the importance of artefacts connected with hair and the body's surface for transforming and reconstitution of the identities the dead and the living.

Toilet implements were small and modest items, but looked at in this light, they may have had a pivotal and public role in the mortuary rites of early Anglo-Saxon England. In particular, although not as spectacular in

Figure 21. An artistic impression of post-cremation ceremonies in which toilet implements were added to early Anglo-Saxon cinerary urns by Aaron Watson

terms of public display and the dramatic transformation of the body as the cremation itself, the post-cremation rites may have had a central significance in the cremation process; as rites of aggregation that incorporated the body, the soul and the mourners into new identities.[70] This use of material culture is very much about memory; the reconfiguring of how the person was remembered in life and how they were to be remembered in death (Fig. 22). If tweezers, shears and razors were items linked to the transformation, constitution and commemoration of identity through the manipulation of hair in life and death, then their presence in the cinerary urn could have been an act of embodiment; providing both allusions to the past biography of the living person, but also as a corporeal focus for the new ancestral identity created for the dead at the end of the funeral.[71] Therefore, when used in early Anglo-Saxon cremation rituals, the evidence strongly suggests that toilet implements served to affect mourners, the corpse and the soul in parallel and inter-related ways:

MOURNERS: to manage the hair of mourners during the opening stages of the funeral or at the end of the obsequies.

CORPSE: to manage the hair of the cadaver during the preparation of the body for the pyre and to mark the installation of the ashes into a new 'body' formed by the urn and ashes.

SOUL: to articulate the transformation of the deceased's soul from 'ghost' to 'ancestor' (Fig. 22).

Whereas grave goods placed within inhumation graves were also commemorative, the emphasis there was on the composition and brief representation of an idealised identity within the grave. While cremation rites also involved this element during the placing of the body upon the pyre, the emphasis was subsequently focused upon the dissolution and fragmentation of identity brought about by the cremation. Moreover, the cadaver remained a focus of commemoration emphasising its reconstitution during the post-cremation rites. The choice of placing artefacts connected with

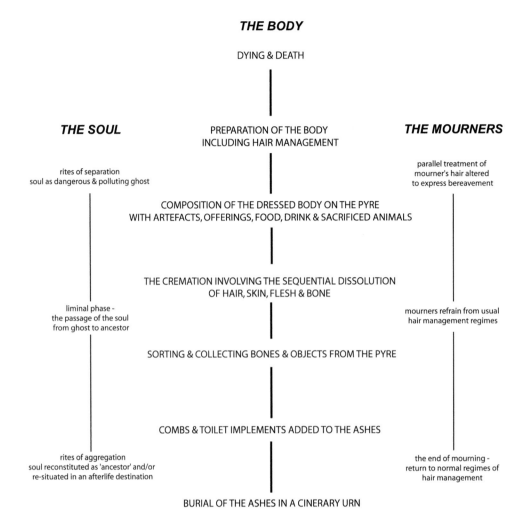

Figure 22. A diagram illustrating the possible roles of hair and toilet implements in the ritual process of early Anglo-Saxon cremation practices

hair in cinerary urns may relate to the fact that the facial and body hair of the corpse is destroyed early on in the cremation process, making artefacts associated with its management an apposite means of symbolising the reconstruction of the body following cremation. The use of toilet implements as grave goods was a mnemonic act by the family members or ritual specialists controlling the cremation ceremony. It articulated the return of the mourners to society with their memories of the deceased, and enabled the dead to inhabit a new identity. Moreover, the evidence suggests that their use could have been reserved for those social actors that needed particular assistance during the transformation from 'ghost' to 'ancestor', including infants and children who had not achieved the (expected or aspired) status of adulthood upon death. Such acts could bind together different conceptions of death as transition; fear of the ghost, veneration of the ancestor, purification, regeneration and soul-journeying. The precise conceptions of death and the dead in this period may elude us, but the

pervasive theme visible in the cremation practices suggests that the dead were regarded as an embodied force long after biological death, requiring transformation and reconstitution focusing upon the body during both cremation and post-cremation ceremonies. Toilet implements were enmeshed in this process as both polluted through association with the mourners and the cadaver, and simultaneously transforming the living and the dead. Perhaps for both reasons they could be regarded as appropriate for burial within the cinerary urn with the ashes.

There remain unanswered questions that provide lines for further enquiry including where, when and how did these practices originate, how different communities developed variations upon this theme, and how the rite changed over time. Yet in the light of the evidence presented in this paper, it is possible to regard toilet implements as more than prosaic and mundane objects in early medieval mortuary practices. They can instead be interpreted as mediating relations between the living and the dead and holding a mnemonic agency, a power to build a new corporeal and metaphysical identity for the dead following the dissolution instigated by the act of cremation. Toilet implements linked together mourners, body and soul and gave commemorative significance to the act of cremation and the subsequent treatment of the ashes. Toilet implements are not best interpreted as the possessions of the dead, gifts from the living or symbols of static identities displayed during the funeral. Tweezers, razors, shears and ear-scoops served to re-create and regenerate the living and the dead – transforming body and soul.

Acknowledgements

Thanks to the audience of the Exeter conference for the range of positive and constructive questions and comments received in response to my paper. I would like to thank Birte Brugmann, Helen Rance, Sarah Semple, Nick Stoodley, Elizabeth Williams and the anonymous reviewer for their invaluable comments on an earlier draft of the paper. Thanks also to Heinrich Härke and Catherine Hills for their support during my doctoral research that provided the initial context for the research from which this article has been developed. Thanks to Aaron Watson for his innovative reconstructions of an early Anglo-Saxon cremation ceremony.

Notes

1. Carver 2000; Halsall 2003; Effros 2003.
2. Richards 1987; 1992; 1995; Ravn 1999; 2003.
3. Williams 2004.
4. Brown 1974; MacGregor and Bolick 1993: 216–28.
5. Boyle *et al.* 1995: 89–90; Kinsley 1993; Malim and Hines 1998: 102.
6. Meaney 1981:148–51. *e.g.* West 1998: 129.
7. Down and Welch 1990: 103.
8. Geake 1997: 100.
9. Geake 1997: 96.
10. *E.g.* Evison 1987: 113; Geake 1997: 96–7; Malim and Hines 1998: 219–220; Penn 2000: 61.
11. Evison 1987: 113.
12. But see West 1998: 233 for a rare instance of possible early medieval provenance.
13. Penn 2000: 59–60.
14. Green in Myres and Green 1973. Penn 2000 notes, they may be copies of Frankish toilet implements (themselves influenced by Roman metalworking) rather than re-used or continuous Romano-British traditions.
15. Hirst 1985: 89; 144.
16. Indeed, many of the miniature tools and weapons cited in Meaney's study are suspended from rings together with functioning toilet implements (Meaney 1981).
17. In many cultures, pollution is symbolically removed through the remove of hair, including the activities of mourners during mortuary contexts; see Bloch and Parry 1982.
18. Alton grave 35, Castledyke grave 163, Empingham grave 90, Norton grave 29.
19. Welch and Sherlock 1992.
20. Drinkall in Drinkall and Foreman 1998: 288–89.
21. White 1988; 149–51.
22. Boyle *et al.* 1995: 89.
23. Cook and Dacre 1985: 92.
24. Boyle *et al.* 1995: 157; 179.
25. Barrington grave 93: Malim and Hines 1998: 81,150. It is possible that the tweezers were originally placed below or above the head.
26. Evison 1988: 78, 113.
27. Similarly the late-addition of a comb for the male weapon burial beneath mound 17 at Sutton Hoo could have been a deliberate last-addition to the burial, contra Carver 1998: 112.
28. Boyle *et al.* 1995: 191.
29. Boyle *et al.* 1995: 179; Evison 1988: 24; 97; Hunn *et al.* 1994.
30. Meaney in Malim and Hines 1998: 274–5.
31. Hirst 1985.
32. The only exception is the exceptionally large inhumation cemetery of Morningthorpe (Norfolk) where, for instance, seventeen graves contained tweezers, although this still represents a small minority of graves Green and Rogerson 1987.
33. Stoodley 1999: 107, 200, 460; Stoodley 2000:
34. Ibid, 31.
35. In the sample of inhumation graves studied containing tweezers, 27 were possible or certain male-gendered graves, 40 were possible or certain female-gendered graves (Table 2).
36. Parfitt and Brugmann 1997.
37. Green *et al.* 1987.
38. Timby 1993.
39. The data used here focuses on the cemeteries of Sancton, Newark and Spong Hill, incorporating material courteously made available for my doctoral research with the kind permission of Dr Catherine Hills; see Hills 1977; Hills and Penn 1981; Hills, Penn and Rickett 1987; 1994; Kinsley 1989; Myres and Southern 1973; Timby 1993.
40. Curved blades of this kind are rare in inhumation graves, but see Parfitt and Brugmann 1997: 174.
41. Grainger and Hawkes 2002. In two of these graves, tentative ascriptions to some of the objects were attempted. In grave C2 were found ten items suspended from a ring, identified as tweezers, spearhead, shears, rod, hook, ear scoop, razor, knife and rod fragment. Meanwhile, the toilet set from grave C23 consists of a razor, two blades and a hammer-shaped tool. All four toilet sets were associated with bone or antler combs; three of which were also miniatures, reminding us that combs, discussed in greater detail elsewhere, should also be considered as a form of toilet implement (see Williams 2003).
42. Green 1973: 105–108.
43. *E.g.* from urn 149 at Sancton: Myres and Southern 1973: 104.
44. *E.g.* Green in Myres and Green 1973; Richards 1987.
45. Although this author has not constructed an alternative typology, he remains sceptical concerning the application of too rigorous a distinction between 'full sized' and 'miniature' implements, both on practical grounds (*i.e.* the current typology does not distinguish between two discrete groups of objects of different sizes) and on theoretical grounds (*i.e.* that both full-sized and miniatures may have been connected in terms of their role at the funeral as argued here – separating them assumes a distinct role or meaning that may not necessarily have existed in the intentions of early Anglo-Saxon mourners since practical function did not necessarily define their only role in funerary commemoration).
46. Contra. Geake 1997: 96.
47. McKinley 1994.
48. Kinsley 1989: 18.
49. Williams 2003.
50. This author is more cautious than Kinsley in attributing fragmentary items to evidence of ritual killing: see Kinsley 1989: 18.

51. Kinsley 1989: 18.
52. A famous example already discussed in print is urn A1242 from Sancton (Fig. 9); see Reynolds 1980; Timby 1993: 336–7.
53. Richards 1987.
54. This contrasts with the claim by Sally Crawford that toilet implements in cremation burials were an exclusive part of 'adult burial ritual'; Crawford 1999: 16; Crawford 2000: 170.
55. *E.g.* Crawford 1999; Harke 1997; Stoodley 1999; 2000.
56. Crawford 1999: 30.
57. Crawford 1999: 30–1.
58. See Hope 1997 for the use of Roman tombstones to commemorate aspired rather than actual identities. See also Martin-Kilcher 2001. Sarah Semple has made the alternative observation to me that some of these items may have had a very practical use in relation to children; as they may have been used to remove ticks and lice for which younger individuals are especially susceptible.
59. Härke 1989; Richards 1987.
60. Hills 1993.
61. Hills, Penn and Rickett 1984.
62. Leeds and Harden 1936.
63. Williams 2003; 2004; forthcoming.
64. Green 1973 in Myres and Green 1973: 105–111.
65. Lethbridge 1951.
66. Jones 2003; Williams 2001.
67. For a comparable discussion of toilet implements in other periods, see N. Crumley and H. Eckardt 2003; Hill 1997; Treherne 1995.
68. Metcalf and Huntingdon 1991: 79–107.
69. There is no space here for reviewing the ethnographic data that supports this assertion. While societies use and perceive cremation in many different ways in different parts of the globe, there are some striking instances of the use of pots and objects in the post-cremation ceremonies to reconstitute the dead into a new body; see Williams 2003 and 2004 for further discussions of this argument.
70. A related argument is explored by John Barrett in relation to tweezers, razors and awls found with early Bronze Age cremation burials; Barrett 1994: 123.
71. This argument is explored further in Williams 2004 and Williams 2006.

References

Adams, B. and Jackson, D. 1990. The Anglo-Saxon cemetery at Wakerley, Northamptonshire, *Northamptonshire Archaeology* **22**, 69–178.

Barrett, J. 1994. *Fragments from Antiquity.* Oxford: Blackwell.

Bloch, M. and Parry, J. 1982. Introduction: death and the regeneration of life, in M. Bloch and J. Parry (eds) *Death and the Regeneration of Life*, Cambridge, Cambridge University Press, 1–44.

Boyle, A., Dodd, A., Miles, D. and Mudd, A. 1995. *Two Oxfordshire Anglo-Saxon Cemeteries: Berinsfield and Didcot.* Oxford: Oxford Archaeological Unit, Thames Valley Landscapes Monograph no. 8.

Boyle, A., Jennings, D., Miles, D. and Palmer, S. 1998. *The Anglo-Saxon Cemetery at Butler's Field, Lechlade, Gloucestershire: Volume 1: Prehistoric and Roman Activity and Anglo-Saxon Grave Catalogue*, Oxford: Oxford Archaeological Unit, Thames Valley Landscapes Monograph No. 10.

Brown, D. 1974. So-called 'needle cases', *Medieval Archaeology* **18**, 151–54.

Carver, M. 1998. *Sutton Hoo. Burial Ground of Kings?* London: British Museum.

Carver, M. 2000. Burial as poetry: the context of treasure in Anglo-Saxon graves, in E. M. Tyler (ed.) *Treasure in the Medieval West*, York: York Medieval Press, 25–49

Cook, A. M. and Dacre, M. W. 1985. *Excavations at Portway, Andover, 1973–1975*, Oxford: Oxford University Committee for Archaeology Monograph No. 4.

Crawford, S. 1999. *Childhood in Anglo-Saxon England.* Stroud: Sutton.

Crawford, S. 2000. Children, grave goods and social status in Early Anglo-Saxon England, in J. Sofaer Derevenski (ed.) *Children and Material Culture.* London: Routledge, 169–79.

Crummy, N. and Eckardt, H. 2003. Regional Identities and Technologies of Self: Nail Cleaners in Roman Britain, *Archaeological Journal* 160, 44–70.

Drinkall, G. and Foreman, M. 1998. *The Anglo-Saxon Cemetery at Castledyke South, Barton-on-Humber.* Sheffield: Sheffield Excavation Reports 6.

Cook, A. and Dacre, M. 1985. *Excavations at Portway, Andover 1973–75.* Oxford: Oxford University Committee for Archaeology Monograph No. 4.

Down, A. and Welch, M. 1990. *Chichester Excavations VII: Apple Down and the Mardens.* Chichester: Chichester District Council.

Effros, B. 2003. *Merovingian Mortuary Archaeology and the Making of the Early Middle Ages,* Berkeley: University of California Press.

Evison, V. 1987. *Dover: Buckland Anglo-Saxon Cemetery.* London: Historic Buildings and Monuments Commission for England Archaeological Report no.3.

Evison, V. 1988. *An Anglo-Saxon Cemetery at Alton, Hampshire.* Stroud: Hampshire Field Club Monograph 4.

Evison, V. 1994. *An Anglo-Saxon Cemetery at Great Chesterford, Essex,* London: Council for British Archaeology Research Report 91.

Evison, V. and Hill, P. 1996. *Two Anglo-Saxon Cemeteries at Beckford, Hereford and Worcester,* London: CBA Research Report 103.

Filmer-Sankey, W. and Pestell, T. 2001. *Snape Anglo-Saxon Cemetery: Excavations and Surveys 1824–1992,* Suffolk County Council: East Anglian Archaeology Report No. 95.

Geake, H. 1997. *The Use of Grave-Goods in Conversion-Period England.* BAR British Series 261, Oxford: British Archaeological Reports.

Green, B., Rogerson, A. and White, S. 1987. *The Anglo-Saxon Cemetery at Morningthorpe, Norfolk.* 2 volumes. Gressenhall: Norfolk Archaeological Unit, East Anglian Archaeology 36.

Hallam, E., Hockey, J. and Howarth, G. 1999. *Beyond the Body: Death and Social Identity.* London: Routledge.

Hallam, E. and Hockey, J. 2001. *Death, Memory and Material Culture.* Oxford: Berg.

Halsall, G. 2003. Burial Writes: Graves, Texts and Time in Early Merovingian Northern Gaul, in J. Jarnut and M. Wemhoff (eds.) *Erinnerungskultur im Bestattungsritual*, 61–74. Munich: Wilhelm Fink,

Härke, H. 1989. Knives in Early Saxon Burials: Blade Length and Age at Death, *Medieval Archaeology* **33**, 144–47.

Härke, H. 1997a. Early Anglo-Saxon Social Structure, in J. Hines (ed.) *The Anglo-Saxons from the Migration Period to the Eighth Century: An Ethnographic Perspective*, 125–70. Woodbridge: Boydell.

Härke, H. 1997b. Material Culture as Myth: Weapon in Anglo-Saxon graves, in C. Kjeld Jensen and K. Høilund Nielsen (eds.) *Burial and Society,* 119–27. Aarhus: Aarhus University Press.

Haughton, C. and Powlesland, D. 1999. *West Heslerton: The Anglian Cemetery,* 2 Volumes, Yedingham: English Heritage.

Hawkes, S.C. and Grainger, G. 2003. *The Anglo-Saxon Cemetery at Worthy Park, Kingsworth near Winchester, Hampshire.* Oxford: Oxford University School of Archaeology Monograph No. 59.

Hill, J. D. 1997 'The end of one kind of body and the beginning of another kind of body'? Toilet instruments and 'Romanization' in southern England during the first century AD, in A. Gwilt and C.

Haselgrove (eds) *Reconstructing Iron Age Societies. New approaches to the British Iron Age*, Oxford, Oxbow Monograph 71, 96–108.

Hills, C. 1993. Who were the East Anglians? In J.Gardiner (ed.) *Flatlands and Wetlands: Current Themes in East Anglian Archaeology.* Dereham. East Anglian Archaeology 50, 14–23.

Hills, C. 1977. *The Anglo-Saxon Cemetery at Spong Hill, North Elmham Part I.* Gressenhall: Norfolk Archaeological Unit, East Anglian Archaeology 6.

Hills, C. and Penn, K. 1981 *The Anglo-Saxon Cemetery at Spong Hill, North Elmham. Part II: Catalogue of Cremations.* Gressenhall: Norfolk Archaeological Unit. East Anglian Archaeology 11.

Hills, C., Penn, K. and Rickett, R. 1984. *The Anglo-Saxon Cemetery at Spong Hill, North Elmham. Part III. Catalogue of Inhumations*, Gressenhall: Norfolk Archaeological Unit. East Anglian Archaeology 21.

Hills, C., Penn, K and Rickett, R. 1987. *The Anglo-Saxon Cemetery at Spong Hill, North Elmham Part IV: Catalogue of Cremations.* Gressenhall, Norfolk Museum Service, East Anglian Archaeology 34.

Hills, C. Penn, K. and Rickett, R. 1994. *The Anglo-Saxon Cemetery at Spong Hill, North Elmham. Part V: Catalogue of Cremations.* Gressenhall, Norfolk Museum Service, East Anglian Archaeology 67.

Hirst, S. 1985. *An Anglo-Saxon Inhumation Cemetery at Sewerby, East Yorkshire.* York: York University Archaeological Publications 4.

Hope, V. 1997. Words and Pictures: the Interpretation of Romano-British Tombstones, *Britannia* **38**: 245–58.

Hunn, A., Lawson, J. and Farley, M. 1994. The Anglo-Saxon cemetery at Dinton, Buckinghamshire, in W. Filmer-Sankey and D. Griffiths (eds) *ASSAH* **7**, Oxford: Oxford Committee for Archaeology, 85–148.

Kinsley, A. 1989. The Anglo-Saxon Cemetery at Millgate, Newark-on-Trent, Nottinghamshire. Nottingham: University of Nottingham.

Kinsley 1993. *Broughton Lodge: Excavations on the Romano-British Settlement and Anglo-Saxon Cemetery at Broughton Lodge, Willoughby-on-the-Wolds, Nottinghamshire 1964–8*, Nottingham: Nottingham Archaeological Monographs 4.

Küchler, S. 2002. *Malanggan: Art, Memory and Sacrifice.* Oxford: Berg.

Jones, A. 2003. Technologies of Remembrance, in H. Williams (ed.) *Archaeologies of Remembrance: death and memory in past societies*, New York: Kluwer/Plenum, 65–88.

Leeds, E.T. and Harden, D. 1936. *The Anglo-Saxon Cemetery at Abingdon, Berkshire.* Oxford: Ashmolean.

Lethbridge, T. C. 1951. *A Cemetery at Lackford, Suffolk.* Cambridge: Cambridge Antiquarian Society. Quarto Publication. New Series. No. VI.

MacGregor, A and Bolick, E. 1993. *Ashmolean Museum Oxford: A Summary Catalogue of the Anglo-Saxon Collections (Non-Ferrous Metals).* BAR British Series 230. Oxford: British Archaeological Reports.

Malim, T. and Hines, J. 1998. The Anglo-Saxon Cemetery at Edix Hill (Barrington A), Cambridgeshire. London: CBA Research Report 112.

Martin-Kilcher, S. 2001. *Mors immatura* in the Roman world – a mirror of society and tradition, in J. Pearce, M. Millett and M. Struck (eds) *Burial, Society and Context in the Roman World.* Oxford: Oxbow, 63–78.

Metcalf, P. and Huntingdon, R. 1991. *Celebrations of Death: The Anthropology of Mortuary Ritual,* 2nd Edition, Cambridge: Cambridge University Press.

McKinley, J. 1994. The Anglo-Saxon Cemetery at Spong Hill, North Elmham. Part VII: The Cremations. Dereham: East Anglian Archaeology 69.

Meaney, A. 1981. *Anglo-Saxon Amulets and Curing Stones.* BAR British Series 96. Oxford: British Archaeological Reports.

Myres, J. N. L. 1977. *A Corpus of Anglo-Saxon Pottery of the Pagan Period*, Cambridge, Cambridge University Press. 2 Volumes.

Myres, J. N. L. and Green, B. 1973. *The Anglo-Saxon Cemeteries of Caistor-by-Norwich and Markshall* London: Society of Antiquaries.

Myres, J. N. L. and Southern, W. H. 1973. *The Anglo-Saxon Cremation Cemetery at Sancton, East Yorkshire* Hull.

Pader, E.J. 1982. *Symbolism, Social Relations and the Interpretation of Mortuary Remains.* BAR International Series 130. Oxford: British Archaeological Reports.

Parfitt, K. and Brugmann, B. 1997. *The Anglo-Saxon Cemetery on Mill Hill, Deal, Kent.* Leeds: Society for Medieval Archaeology Monograph Series No. 14.

Penn, K. 2000. *Norwich Southern Bypass Part II: Anglo-Saxon Cemetery at Harford Farm, Caistor St Edmund.* East Anglian Archaeology 92. Dereham, Norfolks Museum Service.

Price, N. 2002 *The Viking Way.* Uppsala: Uppsala University Press.

Ravn, M. 1999. 'Theoretical and methodological approaches to Migration Period burials', in M. Rundkvist (ed.) *Grave Matters. Eight Studies of First Millennium AD burials in Crimea, England and southern Scandinavia*, BAR International Series 781, 41–56. Oxford: British Archaeological Reports.

Ravn, M. 2003. *Death Ritual and Germanic Social Structure*, Oxford, BAR International Series 1164.

Reynolds, N. 1980. 'The King's whetstone: a footnote, *Antiquity* **54**(212), 232–37.

Richards, J. D. 1987. The Significance of Form and Decoration of Anglo-Saxon Cremation Urns. BAR British Series 166. Oxford: British Archaeological Reports.

Richards, J. D. 1992. Anglo-Saxon Symbolism, in M. Carver (ed.) *The Age of Sutton Hoo.* Woodbridge: Boydell. 131–49.

Richards, J. D. 1995. An Archaeology of Anglo-Saxon England', in G. Ausenda (ed.) *After Empire. Towards an Ethnology of Europe's Barbarians.* Woodbridge: Boydell, 51–66.

Scull, C. 1992. Excavations and Survey at Watchfield, Oxfordshire, 1983–92, *Archaeological Journal* **149**, 124–281.

Sherlock, S. J. and Welch, M. 1992. *An Anglo-Saxon Cemetery at Norton, Cleveland.* London: CBA Research Report **82**.

Stoodley, N. 1999. *The Spindle and the Spear.* BAR British Series 288. Oxford: British Archaeological Reports.

Timby, J. 1993. Sancton I Anglo-Saxon Cemetery. Excavations Carried Out Between 1976 and 1980, *Archaeological Journal* **150**, 243–365.

Timby, J. 1996 The Anglo-Saxon Cemetery at Empingham II. Rutland Oxford: Oxbow Monograph 70.

Treherne, P. 1995. The Warrior's Beauty: the masculine body and self-identity in Bronze-Age Europe, *Journal of European Archaeology* **3:1**, 105–44.

West, S. 1988. *Westgarth Gardens Anglo-Saxon Cemetery Suffolk: Catalogue,* Suffolk County Planning Department, East Anglian Archaeology No. 38.

West, S. 1998. *A Corpus of Anglo-Saxon Material from Suffolk.* Ipswich: Suffolk County Council, East Anglian Archaeology 84.

White, R. 1988. *Roman and Celtic Objects from Anglo-Saxon Graves.* BAR British Series 191. Oxford: British Archaeological Reports.

Williams, H. 2001. Death, Memory and Time: A Consideration of the Mortuary Practices at Sutton Hoo, in C. Humphrey and W.M. Ormrod (eds) *Time in the Medieval World,* York: York Medieval Press, 35–72.

Williams, H. 2003. Material culture as Memory: Combs and Cremation in Early Medieval Britain, *Early Medieval Europe* 12, 2, 89–128.

Williams, H. 2004. Artefacts in Early Medieval graves: A new perspective, in R. Collins and J. Gerrard (eds) *Debating Late Antiquity in Britain 300–700.* BAR British Series 365, 89–102. Oxford: British Archaeological Reports.

Williams, H. 2006. *Death and Memory in Early Medieval Britain,* Cambridge: Cambridge University Press.

Anglo-Saxon Studies in Archaeology and History 14, 2007

Early Anglo-Saxon Horse Burial of the Fifth to Seventh Centuries AD

Chris Fern

The practice of inhuming and cremating animals with the dead was widespread in Europe in the early medieval period. In terms of overall popularity the species that were sacrificed in mortuary rites are (greatest first) sheep/goat, horse, dog, pig, cattle, bear, bird, deer and even fish; though their relative quantities varied considerably between regions and through time (Table 1).[1] For example, animal offerings were particularly popular amongst the cremating communities of the Malären, Sweden, with sheep and dogs the most common sacrifices, whilst horses were by far the most frequent amongst inhuming cultures east of the Rhine.[2] It is important, however, to recognise a distinction between the species in terms of what they constituted as offerings. Examination of animal remains from burials across northern Europe has concluded that cattle, sheep and pig were usually offered in the form of cuts of meat, or immature 'suckling' animals.[3] In contrast, dogs and horses were typically mature individuals buried or cremated 'whole' (but sometimes decapitated or dismembered), that were probably intended as *companion animals* for the deceased.[4] Confirmation of the day-to-day currency of these attitudes is to be found in the early medieval settlement evidence, where the high quantity of butchered sheep, pig and cattle remains indicates their regular consumption, whereas horse and dog bones are fewer, with only the former demonstrating very occasional instances of butchery.[5] For horses this difference may be in part explained by finds of harness equipment in burials across Europe, which indicates their role as a trained riding animal in the period.[6] Exactly what groups had the resources necessary to entertain an equestrian status is indicated by the tendency on the Continent for horse and harness burials to be associated with an elite male martial class, who further emphasised their status by decorating their horse equipment with precious materials and their signature animal art.[7] It is likely that in this context the sacrifice of a riding horse symbolised this class's wealth, and perhaps prerogatives to breed, train and possess quality horses for the activities of warfare and hunting. By comparison, the rite of horse cremation demonstrates a very different character with, in Anglo-Saxon England at

least, offerings appropriate to a far broader social group. This paper seeks to detail these different attitudes towards this specific species within the two early Anglo-Saxon funerary rites, with the ultimate aim of understanding the inspiration and meaning that underlay them.

Anglo-Saxon Horse Burial

The starting point for exploring horse burial in Anglo-Saxon England is Vierck's survey of 1970/71, which identified sixteen cemeteries with inhumed horses, dated between *c*. 450 and 650.[8] Further discoveries and research can now add nine more inhumations of complete horses and two head burials, bringing the total for whole or part-articulated (head or leg) remains in burials to thirty-two (Table 2).[9] The new additions are the whole burials at the cemeteries of: Great Chesterford II (two horses: Essex); Eriswell 046 and 104 (RAF Lakenheath), Icklingham and Sutton Hoo (Suffolk); Saltwood (Kent); West Heslerton (Yorkshire); Witnesham (Suffolk); and finds of horses' heads at Springfield Lyons (Essex) and Snape (Suffolk).[10] Another separate group are the ten human graves, which have been found containing riding gear, but are without horse remains.[11] Also, eleven further cemeteries have produced uncontexted finds of horse equipment that may represent additional horse inhumations or bridle.[12]

Vierck knew of only five cremations with horse. This situation can now be said to have dramatically altered, with the perception of the practice in England as a minority rite no longer appropriate.[13] Indeed, some 227 examples have been identified from the over 2000 cremations at the large cemetery of Spong Hill (Norfolk) alone, with sizeable quantities also recorded at Elsham Wolds (Lincolnshire), Millgate (Nottinghamshire) and Sancton (Yorkshire) (Table 1).[14] At Sancton and Spong Hill horse was the most popular animal sacrifice.[15] In addition, smaller numbers, in most cases single instances, as well as probable identifications (large ungulate remains: horse/cattle), are also known from another eleven sites.[16]

The distribution of horse burials shows distinctive

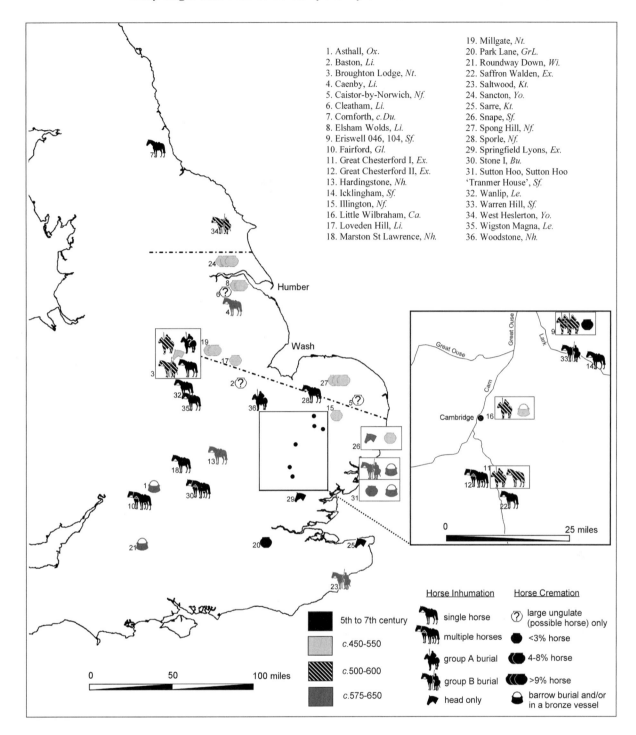

1. Asthall, *Ox.*
2. Baston, *Li.*
3. Broughton Lodge, *Nt.*
4. Caenby, *Li.*
5. Caistor-by-Norwich, *Nf.*
6. Cleatham, *Li.*
7. Cornforth, *c.Du.*
8. Elsham Wolds, *Li.*
9. Eriswell 046, 104, *Sf.*
10. Fairford, *Gl.*
11. Great Chesterford I, *Ex.*
12. Great Chesterford II, *Ex.*
13. Hardingstone, *Nh.*
14. Icklingham, *Sf.*
15. Illington, *Nf.*
16. Little Wilbraham, *Ca.*
17. Loveden Hill, *Li.*
18. Marston St Lawrence, *Nh.*

19. Millgate, *Nt.*
20. Park Lane, *GrL.*
21. Roundway Down, *Wi.*
22. Saffron Walden, *Ex.*
23. Saltwood, *Kt.*
24. Sancton, *Yo.*
25. Sarre, *Kt.*
26. Snape, *Sf.*
27. Spong Hill, *Nf.*
28. Sporle, *Nf.*
29. Springfield Lyons, *Ex.*
30. Stone I, *Bu.*
31. Sutton Hoo, Sutton Hoo
   'Tranmer House', *Sf.*
32. Wanlip, *Le.*
33. Warren Hill, *Sf.*
34. West Heslerton, *Yo.*
35. Wigston Magna, *Le.*
36. Woodstone, *Nh.*

Figure 1. Distribution of horse inhumations and cremations from the fifth to seventh centuries AD

regional trends for the two rites of cremation and inhumation (Fig. 1). Cemeteries which include significant quantities of horse are limited to the regions of the Humber estuary, The Wash and north Norfolk, with the two cemeteries at Sancton and Spong Hill demonstrating around ten-percent horse (as a percentage of the total number of burials).[17] Outside of this region horse cremation is rare, with the majority from mixed rite burial grounds in and around East Anglia, for example, at Little Wilbraham (Cambridgeshire), Snape and Sutton Hoo, and

probably also at Eriswell 104.[18] Most of these are atypical burials, as indicated by their burial under mounds, their use of a bronze container instead of a ceramic urn, and by high status assemblages.[19] It is also only in this eastern region where horse inhumations and cremations have been found together in the same cemetery, as at Sutton Hoo.[20]

In contrast, the density of horse inhumation is greatest within the regions of East Anglia and the Midlands. Additionally, the recent find from Saltwood now takes the distribution of whole horse inhumation south of the

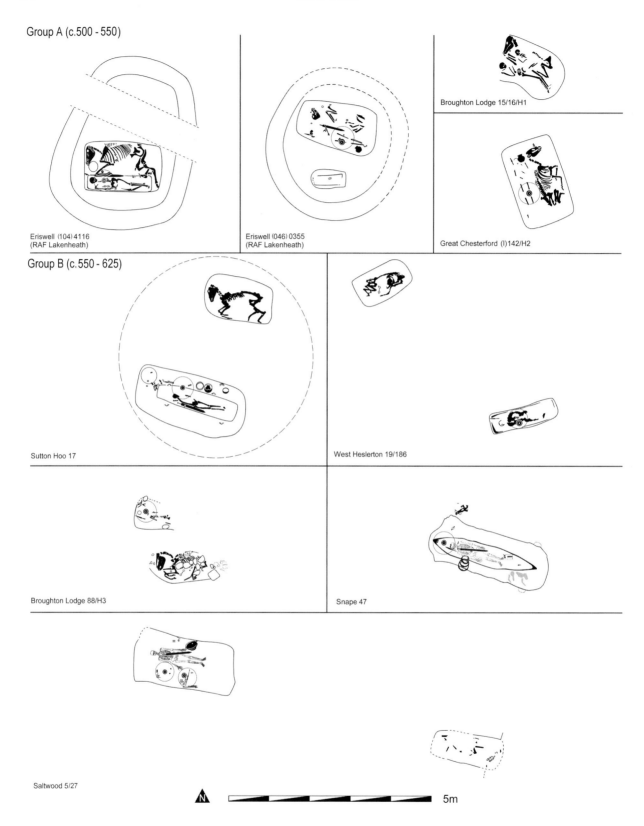

Figure 2. Horse inhumations (Adapted from Carver 1993; Kinsley 1993; Evison 1994b; Haughton and Powlesland 1999; Filmer-Sankey and Pestell 2001)

River Thames.[21] The majority of the sites have revealed only one horse burial, suggesting that the rite was an infrequent occurrence in these burial communities. Rare instances of multiple examples in cemeteries are recorded at Great Chesterford I, Stone I (Buckinghamshire) and Fairford (Gloucestershire), with the most being the five from Broughton Lodge (Nottinghamshire).[22]

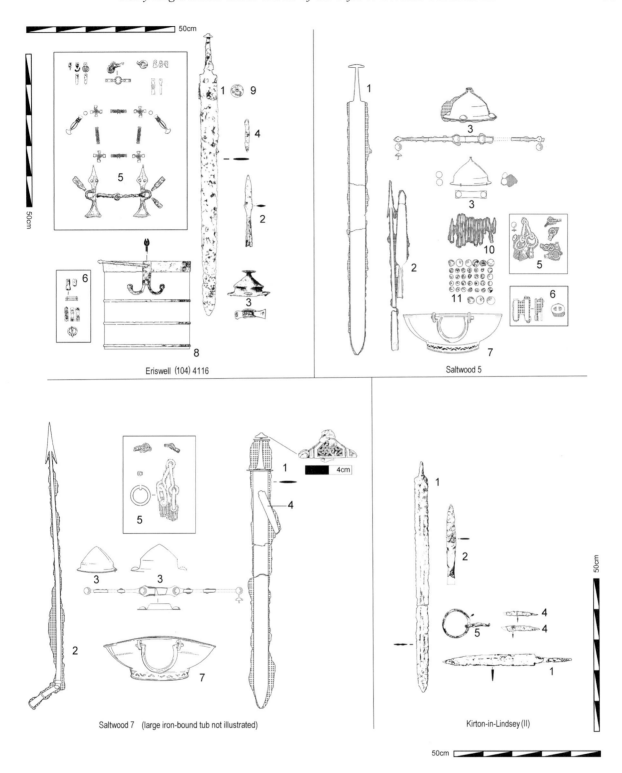

Figure 3. Grave goods with inhumations: 1. sword/seax 2. spear/angon 3. shield 4. knife 5. bridle 6. saddle fittings 7. bronze bowl 8. bucket 9. sword-bead 10. arrows 11. gaming counters

Horses and Harness Equipment in Inhumations

The recent finds of horse inhumations at Eriswell, Saltwood, Sutton Hoo, Snape and West Heslerton, confirm and develop upon Vierck's conclusions that the rite was one reserved principally for male (gendered) adults with weaponry and prestige goods: these include swords, bronze vessels, gaming counters and animal art decorated equipment (Figs 2 and 3; Table 2).[23] Some of the burials are also distinguished by grave furniture, (including coffins and chambers), post-markers, ring-ditches and burial mounds. No examples of horses or riding equipment have been found with infant or juvenile (0–12 years) inhumations. From a consideration of the burial trends within this small corpus, together with the forms of the associated weaponry and art styles, three distinctive groups (A–C) can be identified, which appear on the basis of the current sample to be broadly chronologically sequential.

Group A burials comprise a horse and human in the same large grave (Fig. 2). The horses were interred on their side, with the animal's head at the same end as the deceased's, but with no apparent preference for the animal lying on its left or right side. A further characteristic of this group is the positioning of the head-bridle (and at Eriswell (104) 4116 the saddle) on the horse, as if preparing it for riding. In terms of chronology, the weaponry (including sword-beads) and other objects in these graves suggest that most date to the first half of the sixth century (Fig. 3).[24] More precisely, in line with existing chronological understanding, the Eriswell (104) 4116 burial may be dated to the second quarter of the sixth century on account of its bi-chrome 'Style I' harness fittings and large iron-bound bucket.[25] Broughton Lodge grave 15/16/H1 is of further note, since it contained two human individuals together with a horse: a male without grave goods and an individual in female costume, with a gilt-bronze great square-headed brooch.[26] In this case it would appear that it is the female's status that is being emphasised in an exception to the rule of male prerogative.

Group B burials are characterised by the separate burial of horse and human, with the bridle placed either in the human grave, or with, but not on, the animal (Fig. 2). Since the horse was buried separately the key question is whether or not it can be associated with a particular human burial as a form of 'grave good', or if not, whether it represents an unassociated animal sacrifice.[27] In the case of both Saltwood grave 5 and 27, and Sutton Hoo grave 17, the inhumed horse may be suggested as the *companion animal* to an adjacent weapon burial containing horse harness, aligned 5m and 2m away respectively (Fig. 2).[28] At Sutton Hoo evidence for a single mound covering both burials was also found.[29] Similarly, at Broughton Lodge, horse 3 was found buried next to weapon burial 88; though in this case the head-bridle had been placed in the horse's grave between its legs.[30] The bridle was found in a similar position in West Heslerton grave 186, where the horse may be the *companion animal* to weapon grave 19.[31] Sutton Hoo 17 and Saltwood 5 are dated by their grave goods to between the late sixth to early seventh century; with the C[14] date for the Sutton Hoo 17 horse confirming a date for this grave post-600 (Fig. 3).[32] West Heslerton 19 and Broughton Lodge 88 are dated by their weapon assemblages to the sixth century, and probably to its second half.[33]

As well as whole animals, four horses had been decapitated before burial, although three retained their head-bridles in position.[34] At Snape only the head was buried, in a separate pit adjoining a male boat and weapon burial, which is contemporary with Sutton Hoo 17.[35] In comparison, at Springfield Lyons the horse's head was buried in isolation within a mixed rite cemetery, but is not closely dateable.[36] In a variation of this ritual, with regard to the burial at West Heslerton already mentioned, the horse had been beheaded, but both body and head were buried together.[37] Of note also is Broughton Lodge grave 69/H2, in which only the articulated foreleg of a horse was found by the head of the deceased. However, this grave was heavily disturbed and it is possible that originally an entire horse had accompanied the inhumation.[38]

In contrast to these examples, all from relatively recent excavations with a comprehensive record, the majority of known instances of horse inhumation are antiquarian finds, with varied documentation (Table 2). These records do, nonetheless, give clues as to the burial type and its date, in relation to the groups (A-B) identified above. Little Wilbraham grave 44 is described as '…head to the south, with an iron sword…one iron boss, one spear; close to this [human] skeleton were found the entire remains of a horse; on his head lay the iron bit, with bronze studs and leather of headstall …'.[39] The surviving sword and sword-bead from this burial and this description suggest that it belongs to Group A. Likewise, at Woodstone (Northamptonshire) '…the bones of a horse were found in a grave with those of a man…'.[40] Other descriptions are suggestive of similarities to Group B burials. For example, at Warren Hill (Suffolk), where '…the entire skeleton of a horse, …had apparently been placed in a hole upon its haunches …', 'a few yards' from a weapon burial described as '…just beside the horse, to the west…', which contained a 'basin like' convex shield boss.[41] Similarly, at Wanlip (Leicestershire) limited excavation revealed the remains of a horse buried with a snaffle-bit and two shield bosses, set 'down the slope' from a grave containing a sword, spear and shield.[42] Also suggestive is the iron snaffle-bit and seventh-century gilt-bronze phalera from Hardingstone (Northamptonshire), that are claimed as coming from a single grave, with the former 'said to have been found in the mouth of a horse'; although it is unclear if a human burial accompanied this interment.[43]

There are also horse burials for which a clear association with a specific human grave is problematic, such as Broughton Lodge horse 4, Icklingham and Marston St Lawrence grave 1 (Northamptonshire). At Marston St Lawrence the animal was buried on a different alignment to the two closest human graves: a male with weaponry and a female with jewellery.[44] Yet, like the unassociated Springfield Lyons horse's head, the animal was buried harnessed akin to the Group A burials.

A further group of burials, Group C, are distinctly different in that none contain horse remains, but only horse equipment, which seems to have survived as the symbol of an equestrian status after the abandonment of animal burial.[45] The seventh-century examples of Kirton-in-Lindsey II (Lincolnshire), Bishopsbourne grave 3 (Kent)

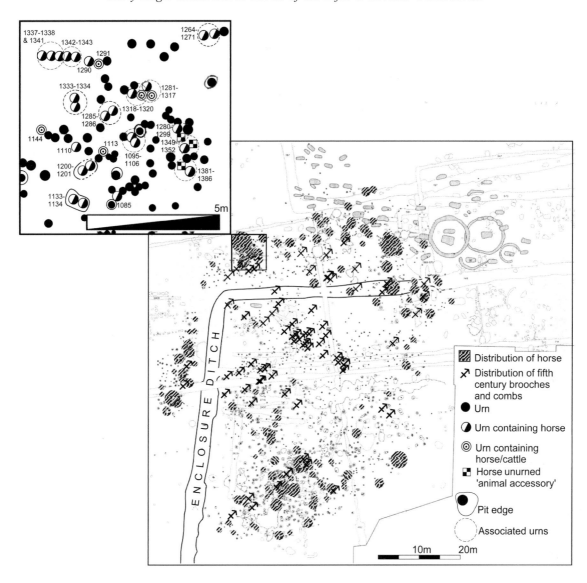

Figure 4. Distribution of horse cremations at Spong Hill compared with finds of fifth-century artefacts (Adapted from Hills 1977; 1981; 1994)

and Saltwood grave 7 (Kent) retain the high status martial associations of the earlier phases of horse burial (Fig. 3, Table 2).[46] However, Garton II grave 10 (Yorkshire) is a notable exception, as it contained two bridles, but was otherwise undistinguished.[47] An earlier burial containing a snaffle-bit is Alfriston grave 91 (West Sussex), a burial with a spear and *francisca* datable to the second half of the fifth century.[48] Also noteworthy is the bit from Loveden Hill (Lincolnshire) that was found associated with a hanging bowl and the remains of a bucket and a spearhead; but which may originally have been part of an exceptional cremation burial that included another hanging bowl, a 'Coptic' bronze bowl, glass vessels and a sword.[49] In addition, bridles have been found in two female burials at East Shefford (Bedfordshire) and Bishop's Cleeve (Gloucestershire), though it seems that in both cases the broken snaffles had been reused as a châtelaine item.[50]

Apart from snaffle-bits, spurs have also been found in a small number of graves. It has been argued elsewhere, however, that only two can be accepted as secure examples.[51] They are Edix Hill grave 88 (Cambridgeshire) and Mill Hill grave 93 (Kent), both male weapon burials of the sixth century, which contained examples of *plattensporen* (disc-spurs).[52]

Horses in Cremations

In most cases of cremation burial in England the burnt remains of the deceased were placed in a single ceramic urn. However, as can be seen from the cemetery plan of Spong Hill, there is a strong tendency for horse cremations (and those of large ungulates) to be represented by paired urns, normally buried together in a single pit (Figs. 4 and 5). This should perhaps be no

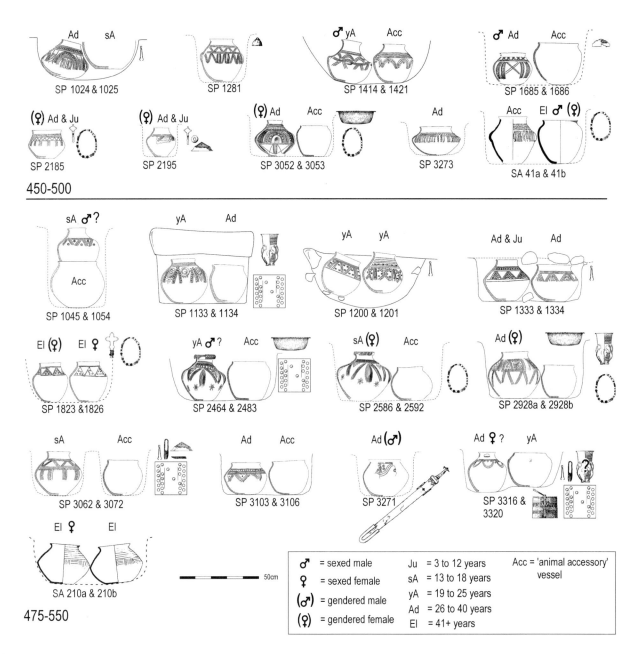

Figure 5. Schematic representations of urned horse cremations, their associated assemblages and gender/sex assignations, with a suggested chronology (Adapted from Myres et al. *1973; Hills 1977; Hills* et al. *1981; 1987; 1994)*

surprise given that the burnt bone of a horse and human(s) cremation can exceed 4500 g.[53] The suggestion that these coupled urns contain the remains of a single funerary episode can be strengthened in some cases. For example, at Spong Hill paired urns 3062/3072 and 1911/1915 each contained one half of a single playing piece.[54] Also, the close similarity of some contiguous vessels at both Sancton (210a/b) and Spong Hill (1200/1201, 1333/1334, 1823/1826, 2563/2564) suggests their simultaneous deposition.[55]

The coupling of the ceramic vessels is also significant (Fig. 5). From the cemeteries of Elsham Wolds, Illington

(Norfolk), Millgate, Sancton and Spong Hill combined there are fifty-four horse cremations that demonstrate the combination of a decorated pot together with an undecorated domestic ware.[56] In twenty of these the deliberate separation of the horse remains from the human had taken place, with the animal deposited in the domestic vessel, and the human in the decorated pot.[57] In a further seven instances the same deliberate separation is observed, but two decorated pots were used.[58] While in twelve cases a decorated vessel was employed for the sorted human remains and the animal remains were deposited either unurned or in a perishable container.[59] The term 'animal accessory' has been used to describe this custom, which in most cases is a phenomenon associated with horse remains.[60] As well as paired examples, in a small number of cases three urns may have been employed. One such is Spong Hill 1754/1756/1757, where two undecorated storage pots were used for the majority of the cattle and horse bone, and one decorated urn for the human.[61] In this instance gaming counters spread between the vessels confirm a single cremation episode.

Regarding the age of the humans cremated with horses, all groups are represented, including a small number of children (3–12 years).[62] Considering biological sex, both males and females have been identified with horse in broadly equal numbers at both Sancton and Spong Hill.[63] But, if gender, as indicated by associated grave goods, is considered then more females are made apparent. Gender has been shown to be strictly aligned to biological sex in the inhumation rite.[64] Indeed, at Spong Hill sexed females have demonstrated a correlation with typically feminine grave goods, such as brooches, multiple beads (constituting necklaces), wrist clasps, ivory bag rings and spindle whorls.[65] Identifying males is more difficult, since weaponry, the typical gender signifier in inhumation burials, is largely absent in the Anglo-Saxon cremation rite.[66] If gender identification is applied to the Spong Hill corpus it has the effect of increasing the number of females with horse to around fifty, as against thirty males. Notably luxury goods, such as bronze vessels and gaming counters appear customary in horse cremations, and occur with both genders in roughly equal numbers; but glass vessels occur with twice as many (sexed or gendered) females as males. Comparing these observations with those gained by Ravn in his social study of Spong Hill, they confirm his findings that horse cremation is to be correlated with gaming counters and glass vessels, but challenge his conclusion that a horse was the signifier of a distinctly male group in the cremation ritual.[67]

Since no detailed chronological studies of the Anglo-Saxon cremation rite have yet been published, dating the phenomenon of horse cremation is difficult. The completely excavated and published site of Spong Hill offers the best opportunity, although the cemetery has yet to be phased chronologically. General empirical observations can be made, however, based on the distribution of horse cremations within the cemetery, as against the earliest datable material culture (Fig. 4). The plan of Spong Hill shows the distribution to be striking, with an almost total absence of horse cremation in the north-west corner of the rectilinear enclosure, where the cemetery's fifth-century material is concentrated, in the form of brooches (Åberg's cruciform Group I, early applied saucer varieties, equal-arm, iron bow, supporting-arm, and tutulus) and barred zoomorphic combs.[68] This material's distribution has been shown to correspond with urn styles that demonstrate strong affinities with fifth-century Continental ceramic traditions, specifically those from Schleswig-Holstein and

Lower Saxony, both in northern Germany.[69] On this basis the central part of the cemetery has been suggested as the initial focus for the burial of immigrants from these regions, which may have come into use as early as the second-quarter of the fifth century.[70] Conversely, in marked contrast horse cremations are focused at the cemetery's edges, in areas characterised both by a greater density of animal cremations generally and an association with chronologically later stamp-linked pottery, which is indicative of developed local ceramic traditions.[71] It may, therefore, be argued that the rite of horse cremation did not arrive at the cemetery with immigrants from northern Germany, but is a trend connected with the cemeteries use by subsequent generations.

Datable finds from the horse cremations themselves are relatively few: items that may indicate a date in the fifth or early sixth century include possible fragments of Roman glass (2638, 2651, and 3235); glass cone beakers (1911, 2672, 3030); a scalloped triangular comb (1686); a possible tutulus brooch (2506); and cruciform brooches of Åberg's Group I/II (2185/2195).[72] In addition, the decoration of some ceramic containers suggests a possible fifth-century date (1024, 1281, 1414, 1421, 1685, 2185, 2195, 3052, 3273). Items that date between the late fifth and the mid-sixth century are: *Typ Brighthampton-Hogom* and *Typ Kempston-Mitcham* sword-fittings (2042, 2099, 2851, 3271); a fragment of florid cruciform brooch (1823); and Type 3 glass claw-beakers (1133, 2921, 2928).[73] Currently, no seventh-century horse cremations can be demonstrated for the Humber-Wash area, yet the rite appears to have functioned as an attribute of high status outside of this region at this time, most conspicuously evidenced in the burial mounds at Sutton Hoo (3, 4 and 7) and Asthall (Oxfordshire).[74]

Horse Inhumation and Cremation Compared

From the above analysis it may be concluded that the rites of horse cremation and inhumation were both in use together in the sixth century, though some horse cremations may be dated to the second half of the fifth century, hinting that this may be the earlier of the two rites in England. They are, however, distinctly different in their social application and demonstrate clear regional distributions. In the Humber-Wash cremating region the sacrifice of a horse with the deceased was not sex specific, and could on rare occasions be attributed to children. Also, at some cemeteries the horse cremation rite could occur with around one tenth of the population and was the most popular animal offering (Table 1). By comparison, the horse (and bridle) inhumation rite is associated predominantly with an exclusive class of male martial elites, as typified by the ostentatious examples at Sutton Hoo, Saltwood and Caenby (Lincolnshire).[75] The lack of a predominant weapon burial status in the cremation ritual may also appear significant, although in Anglo-Saxon England this is a more general contrast between the two rites. However, it is relevant that the horse cremations that lie outside of the Humber-Wash region, but within the predominantly inhuming territories (mainly seventh-century bronze cauldron burials and isolated barrow burials), typically demonstrate a similarly high status to the horse inhumations. The main contrast is therefore regarding the relative popularity of the two rites, with horse burials typically accounting for considerably less than one percent of the buried population in predominantly inhuming regions, but between two- and eleven percent in cremating regions.

There are nevertheless also similarities between the two rites. One is the placing of remains from multiple animals with the deceased. Multiple offerings are common in cremations: at Spong Hill species associated most frequently with horse (greatest first) are sheep, cattle, pig and dog.[76] Likewise, some of the horse inhumations also included a second animal; either a dog or a food offering. A lamb joint was included in the grave in the case of Broughton Lodge 88, Eriswell 4116 and Sutton Hoo 17, while a dog-sized animal was identified in Snape 47.[77] In addition, a possible dog was also recorded by its antiquarian excavator as buried with the horse at Cornforth (Co. Durham).[78]

Another hint of a connection is the single instance of horse decapitation recorded at Sancton, in urn 210a, which echoes the practice in the inhumation rite.[79] Also, in terms of grave-goods, the incidence of gaming counters and feasting vessels (bronze and glass) in both rites may be considered symbolic perhaps of the leisure pursuits of a horse-owning class. Though at the cremation cemeteries of Sancton and Spong Hill these items can only definitely be identified in between twenty- and thirty-percent of burials with horse remains.

The Horse

The killing of a healthy horse, particularly one bred and trained for riding, may be recognised as a significant economic sacrifice and an act of conspicuous consumption. Indeed, where analysis of the inhumed horses has been undertaken, animals at the top end of the early medieval size range are suggested. Five of the eight inhumed horses for which measurements are known were between 13.2 and 14 hands high (*c.* 1.37–1.44 m).[80] This compares favorably against the normal withers height of around 13 hands for mature horses from contemporary settlement sites.[81] In terms of age at death, it appears that most were killed in their prime, at between three-and-a-half and seven years old, although the Snape 47 animal was over twenty.[82] Considering the horses' sex, seven were males, with mares suspected in the cases of Saltwood 27 and West Heslerton 186.[83] This preference for stallions (or geldings) may be because of their larger build, although symbolism, or a conceptual value attached to certain 'pedigree' steeds may also have played a part. The attribution of harness in the inhumation burials makes clear that the sacrifices were trained riding animals, and this is also hinted at by the

vertebral pathology of the Eriswell 4116 and Sutton Hoo 17 animals.[84] The horses typically killed for the inhu-mation rite were therefore an expensive sacrifice chosen for their visual impact, and perhaps their pedigree. As a caveat to this, however, the Eriswell 4116 horse may also have been partially lame and so a preferable offering.[85]

Less can be said for certain of the much larger corpus of horse remains from the more destructive cremation rite, but an overall assessment has suggested that whole, typically young adult individuals are represented, that are thus comparable in age at least to the inhumed examples.[86] Sex could be determined in only a few cases at Sancton and Elsham Wolds by the rare survival of male specific canine teeth.[87] It has proved impossible to discern the build of the horses, though significantly a few individuals at Spong Hill demonstrated pathologies suggestive of their use as working draft animals.[88] Indeed, there is a conspicuous absence of any definite pieces of harness in cremations to signify that the animals were riding stock. Although some iron rings and links at Spong Hill have been suggested as such, it is more likely that these pieces are common female châtelaine items.[89] This absence gives reason to suspect that the meaning of horse sacrifice in the cremation rite was not necessarily the same as for the inhumation rite, *i.e.* as a symbol of equestrianism. Instead, the horse's significance was perhaps more as a totemic species-emblem for a sizeable group within society, which was of modest rather than elite status.[90] Evidence for such a system may be argued from the widespread use of hoof-stamp motifs on ceramics and metalwork in this period, as can be seen on the small-long brooch from grave 69, Great Chesterford I (Fig. 6).[91]

European Horse Burial

In his extensive study of Continental horse burial Müller-Wille demonstrated that the earliest horse inhumations in post-Roman Europe occurred east of the Rhine amongst the Saxons, Thuringians and Lombards in the fifth century; though preceding these were the horse and harness funeral customs of the Huns.[92] However, by the late sixth century and throughout the seventh century the practice was popular particularly amongst the eastern Franks and Alamanni.[93] It is in these latter regions also that horse harness was most commonly deposited in burials.[94] With a few exceptions, notably the fifth-century 'royal' grave of Childeric, with its sacrificial horse pits (and possible horse decapitation), the rites of horse burial and bridle burial did not spread across the Rhine into Roman Catholic Francia.[95] Horse inhumations are also rare in Scandinavia, where instead animal cremation predominated (Table 1). Small numbers only occur from the mid-sixth century, that are attributed to Frankish-Alamannic influence, most famously in the Vendel and Valsgärde aristocratic ship-burials (Sweden).[96]

In most cases a single horse was buried, though two, three and occasionally more occur, sometimes accom-panied by dogs, as well as cuts of meat.[97] Ordinarily, the

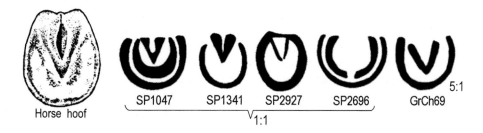

Figure 6   Pottery stamps and a metalworking punch based on the appearance of a horse's hoof (After Hills 1977; 1987; 1994; Evison 1994b)

horse was buried whole, yet decapitated animals are fairly common, particularly in Alamannic and Thuringian cemeteries.[98] In earlier burials there is a greater tendency for the horse and human to be buried in the same grave and for the harness to be placed on the horse, but from *c.* 600 the animal and human are normally in separate burials, with the horse equipment in the human grave.[99] A good example of this is the Alamannic cemetery of Schretzheim (Germany), where separate horse burials, some without heads, have been shown to be the *companion animals* to nearby high status male weapon burials containing bronze vessels and harness equipment of late sixth- and seventh-century date.[100] However, it is frequently the case that horses buried in cemeteries have no obvious association with a specific human grave, although they are still usually buried harnessed.[101] Predominantly the rite was the prerogative of male martial elites and involved the killing of large male stallions in their prime.[102] A notable exception though is that from Zweelou (Netherlands), where a fifth-century Saxon 'princess' was found associated with six horses inhumed in individual pits.[103]

From this brief summary it is clear that the Anglo-Saxon horse inhumation rite shares many features of the Continental custom. Importantly they differ in scale, with the thirty-one Anglo-Saxon horse burials and thirty-eight bridle-sets, comparing with over 700 burials and 600 harnesses known on the Continent.[104] Also, no burials of multiple horses in a single grave have been found in Anglo-Saxon England and no cemetery has produced more than five burials, which is a modest total compared to the twelve from Liebenau (Lower Saxony) and thirty-four from Beckum (Westphalia).[105] There is also a possible chronological difference, since none of the datable Anglo-Saxon inhumations can be placed before *c.*500. Yet, in respect of these variations it is highly probable that the origin of the horse inhumation rite in post-Roman England is, like that of weapon burial, to be sourced from the funerary symbolism of the Continental *Reihengräberzivilisation.* Moreover, in the regions of the rite's greatest popularity in the seventh century, in the kingdoms of the Alamanni and Franks, the martial and equestrian statuses displayed in the rite, became official requirements of office for elites in the earliest law-codes and were given legal protection.[106] Thus, while weapon burial became the essential masculine

celebration of the male kin-group in early medieval Europe, so an equestrian status was employed as a symbol of authority.

The intimacy of these ideological links across the Channel may be argued from the employment in England of the custom of horse decapitation and in the shift *c.* 600 from the burying of the bridled horse in the human grave, to its separate unbridled burial in an adjacent pit, as at Sutton Hoo. Furthermore, the reality of such contact may be demonstrated by the recently discovered Saltwood burials. Both burials have Continental characters, with *angons* buried pointing towards the foot-end of the grave, and shield-bosses of Rhineland type with domed rivets and long grips, as well as arrows in grave 5 (Fig. 3).[107] Also, the 'Style II' silver sword pommel from the Saltwood 7 bridle burial is a seventh-century *Typ Elging-Nusplingen*, of Alamannic or east Frankish character.[108]

The origin of the Anglo-Saxon horse cremation rite is less apparent. The large Migration Period cremation cemeteries of Schleswig-Holstein and Lower Saxony, such as Schmalstede, Süderbrarup, Bordesholm, and Issendorf, which offer some of the best material culture parallels with the Humber-Wash region, have so far produced few animal cremations (most are probably meat offerings) from their many thousands, with horse identified in only two examples (Table 1).[109] However, this pattern fits well with the observations made for the cemetery of Spong Hill, where the period of greatest correlation with these regions, in terms of fifth-century immigrant ceramic traditions and costumes, does not correspond with the chronological spatial distribution of horse cremation. Instead, horse cremation is associated with local ceramic traditions and artefacts datable between the later fifth and sixth centuries.

As an alternative source for the rite of animal cremation Sweden is often cited, since its cemeteries share the aspect of multiple animal offerings as a popular funerary practice, with both meat and *companion animals* (dogs, horses and hawks) represented (Table 1).[110] That the horse cremation rite might potentially reflect Scandinavian influence should perhaps come as little surprise, when we considered that it was also from the late fifth century that eastern England began to adopt many characteristics of Scandinavian material culture, such as wrist-clasps and square-headed brooches.[111]

Exemplary cases of animal and horse cremations are the Swedish 'royal' mounds at Gamla Uppsala, which show that the rite was certainly employed by elite members of society in the early sixth-century.[112] But, amongst the buried 'folk' populations of the region, at the cemeteries of Helgö, Lunda and Viken (Mälaren), horse cremation does not appear to have achieved popularity before the seventh century.[113] As analogies these 'household' cemeteries are nevertheless important, since like Spong Hill and Sancton they demonstrate the use of the horse cremation rite (on the strength of the grave goods) with both adult males and females, though they are considerably smaller in scale. A cemetery of similar size to Spong Hill, with an estimated *c.* 5000–6000 graves is that of Barshalder (Gotland), which demonstrates a comparable material culture of stamped ceramics, gaming sets and glass vessels.[114] Again however, while a high percentage of horse cremations can be demonstrated, with both males and females, only a small number are datable to the Migration Period. Besides these Swedish examples, the cemetery of Lindholm Høje, in Denmark, has also produced a number of horse cremations datable between the fifth and eighth centuries, yet most are marked by ship-shaped stone settings that probably date them to the late seventh or eighth century.[115]

Therefore, in terms of scale and chronology the horse cremations of early Anglo-Saxon England are so far unequalled in contemporary Europe, and as such we should recognise the role of second or third generation local populations in the articulation of this funerary mode and its accompanying beliefs.

Conclusion

In conclusion it can be suggested that across Europe the horse inhumation rite, with its combination of martial, equestrian and wealth symbolism, was used as a statement of authority by a ruling minority. It is possible that viewed within its wider weapon burial context, and alongside the image created by the Continental legal sources, the rite also reflects actual military organization, with small numbers of mounted elites commanding armed groups of men on foot. On another level, the preference for male horses and the strong association of the rite with male inhumations may reflect the conflation of notions of equestrianism and masculinity within these societies. Intriguingly, all these observations find analogy in the equine nomenclature of the Anglo-Saxon mythic-ancestral warrior figures *Hengest* (stallion) and *Horsa* (horse/*equus*), who history records led the invasion of southern England.[116] This is not of course to suggest that the horse inhumations observed above are actual performances of this exact myth, but rather that they may represent funerary enactments of a similar idiom. As 'historic' and mnemonic events we should regard such burials as having had very real significance for the living, as theatrical statements of genealogy, power and social morality.[117] Indeed, the connection between genealogy and ostentatious funerary theatre is demonstrated in the Anglo-Saxon text *Beowulf*.[118] It may have been via the creation and dissemination of such oral genealogies and poetry connected with ruling groups, that elite burial fashions, such as horse and boat burial, were transmitted across Europe.

That the rite was employed as an aspect of social display in England, as on the Continent, may be suggested by the concentrated distribution of horse inhumations in the vicinity of the Rivers Cam and Lark, in East Anglia (Fig. 1). Here a distinct phase of funerary competition between local elite groups is indicated, including the two very similar horse burials from the adjacent Eriswell cemeteries, which we might suppose would have been deliberately intervisible (Fig. 2).

Perhaps because of its contrasting 'popular' character and fire-transforming connotations the animal cremation rite in Europe has attracted very different interpretations from the perspective of cosmological and religious beliefs.[119] Most recently, the Anglo-Saxon rite has been interpreted as a funerary expression of communal animal-human shamanism.[120]

The two very different attitudes towards a single species in the dual funerary cultures of early medieval England are, therefore, also reflected in modern explanations of their meaning. Ultimately, the tension between these two interpretations, of exclusivity on the one hand and communal religion on the other, I would suggest, may find explanation in the different ideological 'pools' of Europe with which they were aligned. Anglo-Saxon horse inhumation appears closely to echo the martial symbolism of the central Continent, while horse cremation finds parallels particularly in Scandinavia, yet crucially in England demonstrates a chronology and popularity that is distinctly insular.

Acknowledgements

The author is grateful to all the individuals and institutions that have provided unpublished information, access to collections, and their time in order to make this study possible. They are: Fleur Shearman and Leslie Webster (British Museum); Susanne Ryder (City of Lincoln Conservation Laboratories); Claire Jones (English Heritage, Fort Cumberland); Kevin Leahy (Scunthorpe Museum); Sue Anderson and John Newman (Suffolk County Council Archaeological Service); Helen Glass (Union Railways South); Robin Bendrey, Martin Carver, Ian Riddler, Terry O'Connor and Sue Tyler. Special gratitude is extended to Malin Holst for her invaluable assistance with German translations, Tania Dickinson for her encouragement, and Emma Fern (née Pettit) and Howard Williams for their incisive comments on the pre-publication draft. Illustrations are by the author except where stated.

Notes

1. Animal inhumations are here considered to be finds of articulated remains, including both whole animals and dismembered parts, but do not include finds of disarticulated bones or teeth which are difficult to disprove as accidental inclusions in grave fills.

2. Müller-Wille 1970/71; Petré 1984, 217; Iregren 1972, Tab. 35; Jonsson 1997, 94.

3. Iregren 1972a, 123; Wahl 1988, 117; Harman 1989, 24; Bond 1994; Kerth 2000.

4. Müller-Wille 1970/71, 130; Harman 1989, 24; Oexle 1984, 141–4; Prummel 1992, McKinley 1994, 94–6; 137; Bond 1996; Kerth 2000, 128.

5. Crabtree 1989, 62, 106.

6. Oexle 1992; Fern 2005.

7. Müller-Wille 1970/71, 141–6; Oexle 1992; Høilund Nielsen 1997, 131–7; Fern 2005.

8. Vierck 1970/71, 189–99, 218–20; see also Pestell 2001; 210–15. The Kemp Town burial is actually a pin made from horse bone, while Reading is a Viking age grave (Welch 1983, Vol. 2, 431–2). Brundcliff is not a 'whole' horse grave as stated by Vierck, but may be an intrusive horse tooth or cremation. Milton-Next-Sittingbourne (I) (an unassociated 'leg') and Breach Down ('jaw') could represent disarticulated residual deposits and so are not counted in this study.

9. '*Whole' horses*: Broughton Lodge 15/16/H1; Broughton Lodge 88/H3; Broughton Lodge H4 (Nottinghamshire); Caenby (Lincolnshire); Cornforth (Co. Durham); Eriswell (046) 0355; Eriswell (104) 4116 (Suffolk); Great Chesterford (I) H1; Great Chesterford (I) 142/H2; Great Chesterford (II) H1; Great Chesterford (II) H1 (Essex); Fairford* (Gloucestershire); Hardingstone (Northamptonshire); Icklingham (Suffolk); Little Wilbraham 44 (Cambridgeshire); Marston St. Lawrence (Northamptonshire); Saffron Walden (Essex); Saltwood 5/27 (Kent); Sporle (Norfolk); Stone (I)* (Buckinghamshire); Sutton Hoo 17 (Suffolk); Wanlip (Leicestershire); Warren Hill (Suffolk); West Heslerton 19/186 (Yorkshire); Wigston Magna (Leicestershire); Witnesham (Suffolk); Woodstone (Northamptonshire) *Heads only*: Broughton Lodge 19/20 (Nottinghamshire); Sarre 271 (Kent); Snape 47 (Suffolk); Springfield Lyons 8577 (Essex) *Leg only*: Broughton Lodge 69/H2 (Nottinghamshire); For all references see Table 2; *Multiple horses are recorded for these sites.

   In addition, very recently part of a possible horse inhumation (117), cut by an Anglo-Saxon cremation grave (108), was discovered by Canterbury Archaeology at Lyminge, Kent. I am grateful to Andrew Richardson and Keith Parfitt for details of this find. If genuine, this burial would take the total number of horse inhumations in England to thirty-three.

10. Meadows 1828, 23; Prigg and Fenton 1888, 71; Hooper 1971; Carver 1993, 11–3, fig. 3; Haughton and Poweslandid 1999, 28–9, 331–3; Filmer-Sankey and Pestell 2001, 102–11, figs. 75–6, 107–10; Fern 2005; Newman *forthcoming*; Powlesland 2006; Tyler and Major 2005, 31–2, figs. 4, 22, 48, pl. II. For information on the unpublished burials at Eriswell 046 and 104 (RAF Lakenheath) I am indebted to Sue Anderson, Jo Caruth and John Newman of Suffolk County Council Archaeological Service; and for information on the unpublished burials at Saltwood my thanks to Helen Glass of Union Railways South, Sue Ryder of the City of Lincolnshire Conservation Laboratories and Ian Riddler.

11. Alfriston 91 (Sussex); Bishopsbourne 3 (Kent); Castledyke 18 (Humberside); Chamberlain's Barn (II) 45 (Bedfordshire); Edix Hill 88 (Cambridgeshire); Garton (II) 10 (Yorkshire); Kirton-in-Lindsey (II) (Lincolnshire); Lovedon Hill HB1/4 (Lincolnshire); Saltwood 7 (Kent); Sarre 28 (Kent). The spur from Linton Heath 18 (Cambridgeshire) is datable by its form to the eighth or ninth centuries, and so is an intrusive find within the burial in which it was found (see Fern 2005).

12. Brixworth (II) (Northamptonshire); Droxford (Hampshire); Duston (Northamptonshire); Eastry (Kent); Faversham (Kent);

Howletts 36 (Kent); Howick (Northumberland); Market Overton (I and II) (Rutland); Milton-Next-Sittingbborne (II) (Kent); Woodstone (Northamptonshire) (see Fern 2005).

13. Sutton Hoo 3, 4 (Suffolk: Gejvall 1975); Little Wilbraham 28.10.1851 (Cambridgeshire: Neville 1852, 23, pls. 16 and 23); Illington 129, 167–8 (Norfolk: Davidson, Green and Milligan 1993).

14. Richards 1987, 125, tab.21; Harman 1989; Bond 1994; 1996; Harman unpublished. I am grateful to Chris Knowles for a copy of Mary Harman's unpublished bone report for Elsham Wolds.

15. Bond 1996, tabs. 1, 2.

16. *Horse*: Asthall (Oxfordshire: Dickinson and Speake 1992); Loveden Hill (Lincolnshire: Wells unpublished a and b; Wilkinson and Noddle unpublished); Park Lane 29 (Surrey: McKinley 2003, 59–60); Roundway Down II (Wiltshire: Robinson 1977/78); Sutton Hoo 7 (Suffolk: Bond 2005); Snape 66 (Suffolk: Filmer-Sankey and Pestell 2001, 258); *Large ungulate only*: Baston 4 (Lincolnshire: Manchester 1976); Caistor-by-Norwich X23 (Norfolk: Myres and Green 1973, 194); Cleatham 71, 242 and 639 (Lincolnshire: Leahy 2003); Eriswell 104 (Suffolk: Newman pers. comm.); Sutton Hoo 5, 6 (Suffolk: Bond 2005); Sutton Hoo 'Tranmer House' (Suffolk: Newman pers. comm.).

17. Bond 1993; 1994; 1996.

18. Neville 1852, 23, pls. 16 and 23; Gejvall 1975; Filmer-Sankey and Pestell 2001, 258; Bond 2005; Newman pers. comm.

19. Asthall; Sutton Hoo 3, 4, 7; Sutton Hoo 'Tranmer House'; Roundway Down II.

20. Carver 2005.

21. The new discovery of a possible Anglo-Saxon horse inhumation at Lyminge (see note 9) should also be noted.

22. Akerman 1842; Wright 1847, 53–4; Kinsley 1993 (graves 15/16/H1, 19/20, 69/H3, 88/H2, H4); Evison 1994b (graves H1, 142/H2).

23. Vierck 1970/71, 218–20; Carver 1993, 11–13, fig. 3; Haughton and Powlesland 1999, 28–9, 331–3; Filmer-Sankey and Pestell 2001, 102–11, figs. 75–6, 107–10.

24. Evison 1967, 64.

25. East 1983, 587; Hines 1997, 230–4, 240; Fern 2005, figs. 5.1, 5.9. The dating of this burial is based on published chronological schemes. However, new work on the chronology of Anglo-Saxon grave goods, particularly in the area of weaponry forms, is currently being undertaken by Karen Høilund Nielsen and Birte Brugmann. Preliminary results have suggested that the combination of Swanton's Type H spearheads and Dickinson and Härke's Group 1/2 shield-bosses may be earlier than previously thought, which may lead to an early sixth-century date for the Eriswell 4116 grave and others. This work has been undertaken in combination with a programme of high-precision radiocarbon dating funded by English Heritage, which will include the Eriswell 4116 horse and rider. As this article was about to go to press the author was given details of the C[14] results for this grave, which suggests that it should indeed be dated earlier, to between 490 and 530 AD (Newman pers. comm.).

26. Kinsley 1993, 30–1.

27. Oexle 1984.

28. Carver 1993, fig. 3.

29. Carver 1993, 11–13.

30. Kinsley 1993, 48, 53–4.

31. Haughton and Powlesland 1999, Vol. 2, 28–9, 331–3.

32. Carver 2005, tab. 9.

33. Kinsley 1993, fig. 80; Haughton and Powlesland 1999, Vol. 1, figs. 46–8.

34. See note 9: Brent 1868, 317; Kinsley 1993, 31–2, 371; Filmer-Sankey and Pestell 2001, 102–11, figs. 75–6, 107–10; Tyler and Major 2005, 31–2, figs. 4, 22, 48, pl. II.

35. Filmer-Sankey and Pestell 2001, 102–11, figs. 75–6, 107–10.

36. Tyler and Major 2005, 31–2, figs. 4, 22, 48, pl. II.

37. Haughton and Powlesland 1999, Vol. 2, 331–3.

38. Kinsley 1993, 46, 60, figs. 23, 78.

39. Neville 1852, 16, pls. 21, 34, 38, 40; Evison 1967, 83, fig. 2.

40. Walker 1899, 354.

41. Prigg and Fenton 1888, 57, 64.

42. Liddle 1979/80.

43. Bateman 1860; Northampton Museum archive.

44. Dryden 1885, 330, pl. 11.

45. Geake 1997, 101.

46. Wright 1844, 253–6; Geake 1997, 160; Fern 2005.

47. Mortimer 1905, 250, figs. 621, 657–66.

48. Welch 1983, Vol. 1, 112, 376, Vol. 2, fig. 38.

49. Fennell unpublished.

50. Peake and Hooton 1915, 112–3; Holbrook 2000, 69, fig. 6.

51. Fern 2005, 61–3.

52. Parfitt and Brugmann, 1997, 153–4, figs. 50, 73; Malim and Hines 1998: 79–80, figs. 3.59–3.60, 3.81; Parfitt, Brugmann and Rettner 2000. This type of spur comprised a short spike with a disc head (like a large drawing pin) that could be pushed through the back of an ankle-strap, boot or shoe, to act as a goad.

53. Harman unpublished: cremation 68 contained 4785 g of bone, identified as a double burial of an adult female, an adolescent and a horse deposited in and around three urns.

54. Hills and Penn 1981, 41–2; Hills, Penn and Rickett 1994, 99–100; McKinley 1994, 93–4.

55. Myres and Southern 1973, 84, fig. 26; Hills 1977, 47, 52, figs 66–7, 71; Hills and Penn 1981, 36–7, fig. 76; Hills, Penn and Rickett 1983, 57–8, fig. 36.

56. *Elsham Wolds (Lincolnshire)*: 133a/b, 269a/b, 290a/b, 315a/b (Harman unpublished; Knowles pers. comm.); *Illington (Norfolk)*: 167/168 (Davidson, Green and Milligan 1993); *Millgate (Nottinghamshire)*: 52/53, 304/305 (Kinsley 1989); *Sancton (Yorkshire)*: 26/a, 41a/b, 129/130, A78/A1443, A1091/A1171 (Myres and Southern 1973; Timby 1993); *Spong Hill (Norfolk)*: 1024/1025, 1045/1054, 1133/1134, 1280/1299, 1297/1308, 1325/1332, 1342/1343, 1616/1621, 1683/1684, 1685/1686, 1719/1724, 1742/1751, 1745/1768/2062, 1784/1785, 1818/1838, 1844/1845, 1851a/b, 1859/1875, 1911/1915, 1979/1980, 1984a/b, 2035/2041, 2065/2070, 2088/a/2124, 2398a/b, 2464/2483, 2497/2519, 2528/2611, 2551a/b, 2575/2576, 2578/2579, 2586/2592/, 2603/2610, 2876/2880, 2928a/b, 3003/3004, 3052/3053, 3062/3072, 3103/3106, 3283/3288, 3310/3311, 3316/3320 (Hills 1977; Hills and Penn 1981; Hills, Penn and Rickett 1987, 1994).

57. *Elsham Wolds*: 315a/b *Spong Hill*: 1045/1054, 1280/1299, 1683/1684, 1685/1686, 1742/1751, 1784/1785, 1818/1838, 1911/1915, 1979/1980, 1984a/b, 2035/2041, 2065/2070, 2464/2483, 2497/2519, 2586/2592, 3052/3053, 3062/3072, 3103/3106, 3283/3288.

58. *Cleatham (Lincolnshire)*: 71/242 (Leahy 2003); *Elsham Wolds*: 50a/b, 91a/b *Sancton*: A1159/A1160 *Spong Hill*: 1414/1421, 1795/1796, 1823/1826.

59. *Elsham Wolds*: 361a/b *Spong Hill*: 1302/1315, 1349/1352, 1381/1386, 1395/1396, 1778a/b, 1835/3332, 1853/3328, 1909/1913, 1942/1943, 2103/2106, 3131/3147.

60. McKinley 1993, 309–310; 1994, 93–94.

61. Hills and Penn 1981, 31–2. Another example is Elsham Wolds 68 (see note 53).

62. *Sancton*: 21, 127 *Spong Hill*: 1778, 1874, 2023, 2181, 2921.

63. McKinley 1994, 99; Bond 1996, 83.

64. Stoodley 1999.

65. McKinley 1994: 88–91; Ravn 2003, 110, 117–8.

66. McKinley 1994: 89.

67. Ravn 1999, 46, 51.

68. Åberg 1926, 28–56; Hills 1977, 31, figs 152, 154–5; 1981.

69. Hills 1977, 31, figs 152, 154; 1993.

70. Hills 1977, 31, figs 152, 154; 1993, 1999.

71. Hills 1977, 31, fig. 153; Hills 1981, 21–2, fig. 3. I am also grateful to Catherine Hills for discussions regarding this point.

72. Åberg 1926, 28–56; Hills 1981; Evison 1994a.

73. Menghin 1983, 336–37, 344–45, Karte 12, 14; Evison 1982, 47–9; 1994a; Mortimer 1996.

74. Dickinson and Speake 1992; Carver 1992; 2005.

75. Jarvis 1850; Carver 1992; 1993; 2005.

76. McKinley 1994, 93.

77. Carver 1993, 11; 2005; Kinsley 1993, 48–9; Filmer-Sankey and Pestell 2001, 111, fig. 75; O'Connor unpublished.

78. Sykes 1866, 150.

79. Bond 1993, 303–4, illus. 25.

80. The horses are Broughton Lodge H1; Eriswell (104) 4116; Great Chesterford H2; Marston St. Lawrence 1; Sutton Hoo 17. Dryden 1885, 330; Harman 1993; Serjeantson 1994; O'Connor 1994; unpublished; Fern 2005, fig. 5.21, tab. 5.3.

81. Crabtree 1989, 56–62.

82. Harman 1993; Serjeantson 1994; O'Connor 1994; unpublished; Davis 2001; Fern 2005.

83. Harman 1993; Serjeantson 1994; O'Connor 1994; unpublished; Haughton and Powlesland 1999, Vol. 2, 331; Davis 2001; Bendrey 2002; Fern 2005.

84. O'Connor 1994; unpublished.

85. O'Connor unpublished.

86. Bond 1994, 123–4.

87. Bond 1993, microfiche M2, 28–9, Harman unpublished.

88. Bond 1994, 124.

89. *Contra* Hills 1999, 153. The pieces in question are iron rings (1469, 2136, 2184), a bronze loop (2963) and a bell (1281). The rings are between 30–40 mm in diameter, which is markedly smaller than the typical 40–60 mm diameter for snaffle rings from horse harness (Fern 2005, tab. 5.1.1). Instead, the rings from the cremations are better compared to those of similar size from female inhumations, such as those in graves 2, 14, 24, 29, 38 and 58 at Spong Hill (Hills 1984), which are probably bag-fittings. Bronze connectors are a feature of Anglo-Saxon harness, employed for example on the Sutton Hoo 17 three-way strap distributor; though significantly the Spong Hill fitting was not found in an urn with horse remains. Bells are an acknowledged part of Continental horse equipment, but in Anglo-Saxon England have not elsewhere been found associated with horse remains, and are conspicuously absent from the corpus of horse and bridle inhumations. Besides these perhaps the most convincing suggestion for a fragment of bridle-bit is the hooked iron fragment from urn 3229. However, this came from an infant cremation, again without horse remains.

90. Richards 1992, 137–41, 145–6; *contra* Ravn 1999, 46, 51; Williams 2001.

91. Evison 1994b, fig. 36. I would like to thank Kevin Leahy for first bringing to my attention the possible significance of these stamps.

92. Müller-Wille 1970/71, 122–4, 148–60, Abb. 1, 20; Bóna 2002, 100–1, 126–9.

93. Müller-Wille 1970/71, 122–4, 148–60, Abb. 1, 20. Further east the practice was also particularly marked in the same period amongst the Avars (for example: Kiss 2001).

94. Oexle, 1984: Fig. 1.

95. Müller-Wille 1970/71, Abb. 1 Oexle 1984: Fig. 1; James 1988, 58–64.

96. Müller-Wille 1999, 10–11, 18, Abb.12.

97. Müller-Wille 1970/71, 127–8, 135–8, Abb. 4–5, 8; Prummel 1992, 137.

98. Müller-Wille 1970/71, 130–2, Abb. 7; Kerth 2000, 128.

99. Oexle 1984, 123, 139.

100. Koch 1977, Vol. 2, Taf. 267.

101. Müller-Wille 1970/71, 138–41.

102. Müller-Wille 1970/71, 141–6; Müller 1980; Oexle 1984, 144–5, Figs 11–2; Oexle 1992, Teil 1, 6–12; Fern 2005, fig. 5.21.

103. van Es and Ypey 1977, Abb. 3.

104. Müller-Wille 1970/71, 124; Oexle 1992, Teil 1, 17.

105. Müller-Wille 1970/71, 127, 206, Abb. 12–4; Kinsley 1993; May 1994.

106. Rivers 1977, 37, 126–7: *Pactus Legis Alamannorum*, XXXV: 'if he [the son] rises against his father forcibly, while his father is still

able to serve the king and lead the army, mount a horse, and fulfil service to the king ... let nothing of the paternal inheritance belong to him, since he has committed an unlawful act against his father'. See also clauses LXI, LXIV and IV.18.
107. Nieveler and Siegmund 1999, 12, fig. 1.9; Spain 2000.
108. Menghin 1983, 326–7, Karte 8.
109. Saggau 1986, 66; Wahl 1988, 117–20, Tab. 39; Bode 1998, 103; Weber 2000, 82; Häßler 2001, 121–91. It should be noted however that the very large corpus from Westerwanna, Lower Saxony, has not been analysed and that future examination of the Issendorf material may yield further examples of horse cremation.
110. For example Hills 1999, 153.

111. Hines 1993; 1997.
112. Duczko 1996.
113. Geyvall and Persson 1970, 232; Ferenius 1971; Iregren 1972a; 1972b, figs 25–26; Pétre 1984a, 88; 1984b, 217.
114. Rundqvist 2003a, 15; 2003b 45–6, 58–9, tabs. 3h, 3v.
115. Ramskou 1976, 135–6.
116. Turville-Petre 1957.
117. Carver 1992, 363–6.
118. Klaeber 1950.
119. Bennett 1989, Richards 1992.
120. Williams 2001.

Bibliography

Akerman, J. Y. 1842. Ancient Fibula found at Stone in Buckinghamshire, *Archaeologia*, **30**, 545–7.

Åberg, N. 1926. *The Anglo-Saxons in England*, Uppsala: Almqvist and Wiksell International.

Bateman, T. 1860. Anglo-Saxon antiquities in the possession of T. Bateman, Esq., *Reliquary*, **1**, 189–90.

Bendrey, R. 2002 (unpublished). Assessment of the animal bone, in *Archaeological Investigations at Saltwood Tunnel, Near Folkstone, Kent*. Detailed Archaeological Works Assessment Report, Vol. 3.

Bennett, A. 1989. Iron Age graves as social and religious symbols, in T. B. Larsson and H. Lundmark (eds), *Approaches to Swedish Prehistory: A spectrum of problems and perspectives in contemporary research*, 367–72, British Archaeological Reports International Series, 500, Oxford: British Archaeological Reports.

Bode, M-J. 1998. *Schmalstede: Ein Urnengräberfeld der Kaiser- und Völkerwanderungszeit*, Urnenfriedhöfe Schleswig-Holstein, 14, Offa-Bücher, 78, Neumünster: Karl Wachholtz Verlag.

Bóna, I. 2002. *Les Huns: Le grand empire barbare d'Europe (IV-V siècles)*, Paris: Errance.

Bond, J. 1993. 'Cremated Animal Bone', in J. Timby, Sancton I Anglo-Saxon Cemetery Excavations Carried Out Between 1976 and 1980, *Archaeol. Jnl.*, **150**, 243–365 (300–9).

Bond, J. 1994. 'Appendix 1: The cremated animal bone', in J. McKinley, *Spong Hill Part VIII: The Cremations*, East Anglian Archaeology, 69, 122–34, Gressenhall: Norfolk Museums Service.

Bond, J. 1996. Burnt offerings: animal bone in Anglo-Saxon cremations, *World Archaeol.*, **28.1**, 76–88.

Bond, J. 2005. The cremated animal bone from Mounds 5, 6 and 7, in M. O. H. Carver, *Sutton Hoo: A Seventh-century princely burial ground and its context*, Reports of the Research Committee of the Society of Antiquaries, 69, London: British Museum Publications.

Brent, J. 1868. Account of the Society's researches in the Anglo-Saxon cemetery at Sarr, *Archaeologia Cantiana*, **7**, 307–21.

Carver, M. O. H. 1992. The Anglo-Saxon Cemetery at Sutton Hoo: an interim report, in M. O. H. Carver (ed.), *The Age of Sutton Hoo: the Seventh Century in North-western Europe*, 343–71, Woodbridge: Boydell Press.

Carver, M. O. H. 1993. The Anglo-Saxon cemetery: an interim report, *Bulletin of the Sutton Hoo Research Committee* **8**, 11–9.

Carver, M. O. H. 2005. *Sutton Hoo: A Seventh-century princely burial ground and its context*, Reports of the Research Committee of the Society of Antiquaries, 69, London: British Museum Publications.

Crabtree, P. J. 1989. *West Stow, Suffolk: Early Anglo-Saxon Animal Husbandry*, East Anglian Archaeology, 47, Gressenhall: Suffolk County Council.

Davidson, A., Green, B. and Milligan, B. 1993. *Illington: a Study of a Breckland Parish and its Anglo-Saxon Cemetery*, East Anglian Archaeology, 63, Gressenhall: Norfolk Museums Service.

Davis, S. 2001. The horse head from grave 47, in W. Filmer-Sankey and T. Pestell, *Snape Anglo-Saxon Cemetery: Excavations and Surveys 1824–1992*, 231–2 , East Anglian Archaeology, 95, Gressenhall: Suffolk County Council.

Dickinson, T. M. and Härke, H. 1992. *Early Anglo-Saxon Shields*, London, *Archaeologia*, **110**.

Dickinson, T. M. and Speake, G. 1992. The Seventh-Century Cremation Burial in Asthall Barrow, Oxfordshire: a reassessment, in M. O. H. Carver (ed.), *The Age of Sutton Hoo: the Seventh Century in North-western Europe*, 95–130, Woodbridge: Boydell Press.

Drinkall, G. and Foreman, M. 1998. *The Anglo-Saxon Cemetery at Castledyke South, Barton-on-Humber*, Sheffield Excavation Reports, 6, Sheffield.

Dryden, H. 1885. Excavation of an ancient burial ground at Marston St. Lawrence, co. Northamptonshire, *Archaeologia*, **48**, 327–39.

Duczko, W. 1996 Uppsalahögarna som symboler och arkeologiska källor, in W. Duczko (ed.) *Arkeologi och miljögeologi i Gamla Uppsala Vol. 2*, 59–93, Uppsala: Uppsala University.

East, K. 1983. The tubs and buckets, in R. Bruce-Mitford *The Sutton Hoo Ship-burial Vol. 3 Pt 2*, 554–94, London: British Museum Publications.

Evison, V. I. 1967. The Dover Ring-Sword and Other Sword-rings and Beads, *Archaeologia*, **101**, 63–118.

Evison, V. I. 1982. Anglo-Saxon Glass Claw-beakers, *Archaeologia*, **107**, 43–76.

Evison, V. I. 1994a. Anglo-Saxon glass from cremations, in C. Hills, K. Penn and R. Rickett, *The Anglo-Saxon Cemetery at Spong Hill, North Elmham, Part V: Catalogue of Cremations*, 23–30, East Anglian Archaeology,67, Gressenhall: Norfolk Museums Service.

Evison, V. I. 1994b. *An Anglo-Saxon Cemetery at Great Chesterford, Essex*, Council for British Archaeology Research Report, 91, London: CBA.

Fennell, K. R. Unpublished. 'Hanging Bowl No. 1 (HB1) Assemblage', Archive report at Fort Cumberland, English Heritage.

Ferenius, J. 1971. *Vårby och Vårberg. En studie i järnålderns bebyggelsehistoria*, Studies in North-European Archaeology Series B, 1, Stockholm: Acta Universitatis Stockholmiensis.

Fern, C. 2005. The Archaeological Evidence for Equestrianism in Early Anglo-Saxon England, *c.* 450–700, in A. Pluskowski (ed.) *Just Skin and Bones? New Perspectives on Human-Animal Relations in the Historic Past*, BAR International Series, 1410, Oxford: British Archaeological Reports.

Filmer-Sankey, W. and Pestell, T. 2001. *Snape Anglo-Saxon Cemetery: Excavations and Surveys 1824–1992*, East Anglian Archaeology, 95, Gressenhall: Suffolk County Council.

Geake, H. 1997. *The Use of Grave-Goods in Conversion-Period England c.600–850*, BAR British Series, 261, Oxford: British Archaeological Reports.

Gejvall, N. G. and Persson, O. 1970. Osteological analysis of the human and animal cremated bones, in W. Holmqvist (ed.) *Excavations at Helgö III*, 227–33, Stockholm: Almqvist and Wiksell International.

Gejvall, N. G. 1975. Identification of cremated bone fragments from Sutton Hoo (1938) Mounds 3 and 4, in R. Bruce-Mitford, *The Sutton Hoo Ship Burial, Vol. 1*, 135–6, London: British Museum Publications.

Harman, M. 1989. Discussion of the finds: cremations, in A. G. Kinsley *The Anglo-Saxon Cemetery at Millgate, Newark-on-Trent, Nottinghamshire*, 23–5, Nottingham Archaeology Monographs, 2, University of Nottingham.

Harman, M. 1993. The animal burials: discussion, in A. G. Kinsley, *Excavations of the Romano-British Settlement and Anglo-Saxon Cemetery at Broughton Lodge, Willoughby-on-the-Wolds, Nottinghamshire 1964–8*, 58–61, Nottingham Archaeological Monographs, 4, University of Nottingham.

Harman, M. unpublished. 'The cremations', Archive report for excavations at Elsham Wolds, 1975–1976.

Haughton, C. and Powlesland, D. 1999. *West Heslerton. The Anglian Cemetery*, Landscape Research Centre Archaeological Monograph Series, 1, Vol. 1 (2 vols.), Nottingham: Technical Print Services.

Häßler, H-J. 2001. *Das sächsische Gräberfeld von Issendorf, Ldkr. Stade, Niedersaschen: Die Brandgräber der Ausgrabungen in den Jahren 1989–1993, 1995 und 1997*, Teil 3, Studien zur Sachsenforshung, 9.3, Oldenburg: Isensee Verlag.

Hills, C. 1977. *The Anglo-Saxon Cemetery at Spong Hill, North Elmham, Part I: Catalogue of Cremations*, East Anglian Archaeology, 6, Gressenhall: The Norfolk Archaeological Unit.

Hills, C. 1981. Barred zoomorphic combs of the migration period, in V. I. Evison (ed.) *Angles, Saxons and Jutes: Essays presented to J. N. L. Myres*, 96–125, Oxford: Clarendon Press.

Hills, C. 1993. Who were the East Anglians?, in J. Gardiner (ed.) *Flatlands and Wetlands: Current Themes in East Anglian Archaeology*, 14–23, East Anglian Archaeology, 50, Gressenhall: Norwich Castle Museum.

Hills, C. 1999. Did the People of Spong Hill come from Schleswig-Holstein?, in *Studien zur Sachsenforschung*, **11**, 145–54.

Hills, C. and Penn, K. 1981. *The Anglo-Saxon Cemetery at Spong Hill, North Elmham, Part II: Catalogue of Cremations*, East Anglian Archaeology, 11, Gressenhall: The Norfolk Archaeological Unit

Hills, C., Penn, K. and Rickett, R 1984. *The Anglo-Saxon Cemetery at Spong Hill, North Elmham, Part III: Catalogue of Inhumations*, East Anglian Archaeology, 21, Gressenhall: The Norfolk Archaeological Unit.

Hills, C., Penn, K. and Rickett, R 1987. *The Anglo-Saxon Cemetery at Spong Hill, North Elmham, Part IV: Catalogue of Cremations*, East Anglian Archaeology, 34, Gressenhall: The Norfolk Archaeological Unit.

Hills, C., Penn, K. and Rickett, R 1994. *The Anglo-Saxon Cemetery at Spong Hill, North Elmham, Part V: Catalogue of Cremations*, East Anglian Archaeology, 67, Gressenhall: Norfolk Museums Service.

Hines, J. 1993. *Clasps; Hektespenner; Agraffen. Anglo-Scandinavian Clasps of Classes A-C of the 3rd to 6th centuries AD: Typology, Diffusion and Function*, Stockholm: Almqvist and Wiksell International.

Hines, J. 1997. *A New Corpus of Anglo-Saxon Great Square-Headed Brooches*, Reports of the Research Committee of the Society of Antiquaries 51, Woodbridge: Boydell Press.

Holbrook, N. 2000. The Anglo-Saxon cemetery at Lower Farm, Bishop's Cleeve: excavations directed by Kenneth Brown, 1969, *Trans. of the Bristol and Gloucestershire Archaeol. Soc.*, **118**, 61–92.

Hooper, B. 1971. A short report of three burials found at Great Chesterford, *Essex Nat.*, **32**, 341–8.

Høilund Nielsen, K. 1996 The burial ground, in E. Johansen and A. Lerche Trolle (eds) *Lindholm Høje. Burial ground and village*, 27–38, Aalborg: Aalborg Historical Museum.

Høilund Nielsen, K. 1997. Animal Art and the Weapon-Burial Rite – a Political Badge?, in C. Kjeld Jensen and K. Høilund Nielsen (eds), *Burial and Society: The Chronological and Social Analysis of Archaeological Burial Data*, 129–48, Aarhus: University Press.

Hyslop, M. 1963. Two Anglo-Saxon cemeteries at Chamberlain's Barn, Leighton Buzzard, Bedfordshire, *Arch J*, **120**, 161–200.

Iregren, E. 1972a. *Vårby och Vårberg II: studie av kremerat människo- och djurbensmaterial från järnåldern*, Theses and Papers in North-European Archaeology, 1, Stockholm: Acta Universitatis Stockholmiensis.

Iregren, E. 1972b. Osteologisk analys av bränt benmaterial från gravfält 57, Viken, Lovö sn, Uppland, in Lamm, J. P. *Undersökningar på Lovö 1958 – 1966*, 102–42, Stockholm University.

James, E. 1988. *The Franks*, Oxford: Blackwell.

Jarvis, E. Rev. 1850. Account of the discovery of ornaments and remains, supposed to be of Danish Origin, in the Parish of Caenby, Lincolnshire , *Arch J*, **7**, 36–44.

Jonsson, R. 1997. The Skeletal Material, in B. Sander, *Excavations at Helgö XIII: Cemetery 116*, 91–6, Stockholm: Almqvist and Wiksell International.

Kerth, Von K. 2000. Die Tierbeigaben aus vier frühmittelalterlichen Gräberfeldern in Unterfranken, *Germania*, **78.1**, 125–38.

Kinsley, A. G. 1989. *The Anglo-Saxon Cemetery at Newark-on-Trent, Nottinghamshire*, Nottingham Archaeology Monographs, 2, University of Nottingham.

Kinsley, A. G. 1993. *Excavations on the Romano-British Settlement and Anglo-Saxon Cemetery at Broughton Lodge, Willoughby-on-the-Wolds, Nottinghamshire 1964–8*, Nottingham Archaeology Monographs, 4, University of Nottingham.

Kiss, A. 2001. *Das Awarenzeitliche Gräberfeld in Kölked-Feketekapu B*, Monumenta Avarorum Archaeologica, 6, Budapest.

Klaeber, F. 1950. *Beowulf and the Fight at Finnsburg*, 3rd Edit., Boston: Heath.

Koch, U. 1977. *Das Reihengräberfeld bei Schretzheim*, Germanische Denkmäler der Völkerwanderungszeit, Serie A, 13 (2 vols.), Berlin: Gebr. Mann Verlag.

Leahy, K. 2003. 'The Cleatham Anglo-Saxon cemetery and its regional context', unpublished PhD thesis, Nottingham University.

Liddle, P. 1979/80. An Anglo-Saxon cemetery at Wanlip, Leicestershire, *Trans. of the Leicestershire Archaeol. and Hist. Soc.*, **55**, 11–21.

Malim, T. and Hines, J. 1998. *The Anglo-Saxon cemetery at Edix Hill (Barrington A), Cambridgeshire*, Council for British Archaeology Research Report, 112, London: CBA.

Manchester, K. 1976. Appendix 1: The Human Remains, in P. Mayes and M. J. Dean, *An Anglo-Saxon Cemetery at Baston, Lincolnshire*, 52–60, Occasional Papers in Lincolnshire History and Archaeology, 3.

May, Von E. 1994. Die Pferdeskelette aus den Pferdgräbern und weitere Tierknochenfunde aus dem Gräberfeld von Liebenau, in H-J. Häßler, *Das sächsische Gräberfeld bei Liebenau, Kreis Nienburg (Weser)*, Teil 5, 133–88, Studien zur Sachsenforschung, 5.4, Hannover: Isensee Verlag.

McKinley, J. I. 1993. 'Animal Accessory Vessels', 309–11, in J. Timby, Sancton I Anglo-Saxon Cemetery Excavations Carried Out Between 1976 and 1980, *Archaeol. Jnl.* **150**, 243–365.

McKinley, J. I. 1994. *The Anglo-Saxon Cemetery at Spong Hill, North Elmham, Part VIII: The Cremations*, East Anglian Archaeology, 69, Gressenhall: Norfolk Museums Service.

McKinley, J. I. 2003. The early Saxon cemetery at Park Lane, Croydon, *Surrey Archaeological Collections*, **90**, 1–116.

Meadows, P. 1828. 'Note', *Gentleman's Magazine*, 98, 23.

Meaney, A. 1964. *A Gazetteer of Early Anglo-Saxon Burial Sites*, London: Unwin.

Menghin, W. 1983. *Das Schwert im Frühen Mittelalter*, Stuttgart: Konrad Theiss Verlag.

Mortimer, J. R. 1905. *Forty Years' Researches in British and Saxon Burial Mounds of East Yorkshire*, London: A. Brown and Sons.

Mortimer, C. 1996. The Florid and Plainer Cruciform brooches, in J. Timby, *The Anglo-Saxon Cemetery at Empingham II, Rutland*, Oxbow Monograph ,70, 38–45, Oxford: Oxbow books.

Müller, H-H. 1980. 'Zur Kenntnis der Haustiere aus Völkerwanderungszeit im Mittelelbe – Saale-Gebiet', *Zeitschrift für Archäologie*, **14**, 145–72.

Müller-Wille, M. 1970/71. *Pferdegrab und Pferdeopfer im frühen Mittelalter*, Berichten van de Rijksdienst voor het Oudheidkundig Bodemonderzoek Jaargang, **20/21.**

Müller-Wille, M. 1999. Das Frankenreich und der Norden. Zur Archäologie wechselseitiger Beziekungen während der Merowinger und frühen Karolingerzeit, in U. v. Freeden, U. Koch and A. Wieczorek (eds) *Völker au Nord- und Ostee und die Franken*, 1–18, Bonn.

Myres, J. N. L. and Southern, W. H. 1973. *The Anglo-Saxon Cremation*

Cemetery at Sancton, East Yorkshire, Hull Museum Publication, 218.

Neville, R. C. 1836. *History of Audley End*, London.

Neville, R. C. 1852. *Saxon Obsequies*, London.

Newman, J. forthcoming. *Anglo-Saxon Cemeteries at RAF Lakenheath, Suffolk*, East Anglian Archaeology, Gressenhall.

Newman, J. 2006. 'Another Anglo-Saxon Horse and Rider Burial from Suffolk', *Saxon* **44.**

Nichols, J. 1807. The History and Antiquities of the County of Leicester, Vol. 4.1, London.

Nieveler, E. and Siegmund, F. 1999. The Merovingian chronology of the Lower Rhine area: results and problems, in J. Hines, K. Høilund Nielsen and F. Siegmund (eds) *The Pace of Change: Studies in Early-Medieval Chronology*, 3–22, Oxford: Oxbow books.

O'Connor, T. 1994. A horse skeleton from Sutton Hoo, Suffolk, U.K., *Archaeolzoologia*, **7.1**, 29–37.

O'Connor, T. unpublished. *Animal bones from Lakenheath, Suffolk (ERL046, 104, 114)*, Archive report to Suffolk County Council Archaeology Unit.

Oexle, J. 1984. Merowingerzeitliche Pferdebestattungen – Opfer oder Beigaben?, *Frühmittelalterliche Studien*, **18**, 122–72.

Oexle, J. 1992. *Studien zu merowingerzeitlichem Pferdegeschirr am Beispiel der Trensen*, Germanische Denkmäler der Völkerwanderungszeit, Serie A, 16 (2 vols.), Mainz: Verlag Philip von Zabern.

Parfitt, K. and Brugmann, B. 1997. *The Anglo-Saxon Cemetery on Mill Hill, Deal, Kent*, Society for Medieval Archaeology Monograph, 14, Leeds: Maney and Son.

Parfitt, K., Brugmann, B. and Rettner, A. 2000. Anglo-Saxon spur from the Mill Hill, Deal, Cemetery, *Kent Archaeol. Rev.*, **140**, 229–30.

Peake, H. and Hooton, E. A. 1915. Saxon graveyard at East Shefford, Berks., *Jnl. of the R. Anthropological Inst.*, **45**, 92–130.

Pestell, T. 2001. Animal Burials, in W. Filmer-Sankey and T. Pestell, *Snape Anglo-Saxon Cemetery: Excavations and Surveys 1824–1992*, 255–9, East Anglian Archaeology, 95, Gressenhall: Suffolk County Council.

Petré, B. 1984a. *Arkeologiska undersökningar på Lovö*, Vol. 3, Studies in North-European Archaeology, 9, Stockholm: Acta Universitatis Stockholmiensis.

Petré, B. 1984b. *Arkeologiska undersökningar på Lovö*, Vol. 4, Studies in North-European Archaeology, 10, Stockholm: Acta Universitatis Stockholmiensis.

Prigg, H. and Fenton, S. 1888. The Anglo-Saxon graves, Warren Hill, Mildenhall, *Proc. of the Suffolk Inst. of Archaeol.*, **6**, 57–72.

Prummel, W. 1992. Early medieval dog burials among the Germanic tribes, *Helinium*, **32**, 132–94.

Ramskou, T. 1976. *Lindholm Høje Gravpladsen*, Nordiske Fortidsminder, B.2, Copenhagen.

Ravn, M. 1999. Theoretical and Methodological approaches to Migration Period Burials, in M. Rundqvist (ed.) *Grave Matters: Eight studies of First Millennium AD burials in Crimea, England and southern Scandinavia*, 41–56, BAR International Series, 781, Oxford: British Archaeological Reports.

Ravn, M. 2003. *Death Ritual and Germanic Social Structure (c. AD 200–600)*, British Archaeological Reports International Series, 1164, Oxford: Archaeopress.

Richards, J. D. 1987. *The Significance of Form and Decoration of Anglo-Saxon Cremation Urns*, British Archaeological Reports British Series, 166, Oxford: British Archaeological Reports.

Richards, J. D. 1992. Anglo-Saxon Symbolism, in M. O. H. Carver (ed.), *The Age of Sutton Hoo: the Seventh Century in North-western Europe*, 131–47, Woodbridge: Boydell Press.

Rivers, T. J. 1977. *Laws of the Alamanns and Bavarians*, Pennsylvania: University Press.

Robinson, P. H. 1977/78. The Merovingian Tremisses from 'Near Devizes': A Probable Context, *The Wiltshire Archaeol. Mag.*, **72/73**, 191–5.

Rundqvist, M. 2003a. *Barshalder 1: A cemetery in Grötlingbo and Fide parishes, Gotland, Sweden, c. AD 1–1100. Excavations and finds 1826–1971*, Stockholm Archaeology Reports, 40, Stockholm: University of Stockholm.

Rundqvist, M. 2003b. *Barshalder 2: Studies of Late Iron Age Gotland*, Stockholm: University of Stockholm.

Saggau, H. E. 1986. *Bordesholm: Der Urnenfriedhof am Brautberg bei Bordesholm in Holstein* Teil 1, Offa-Bücher, 60, Neumünster: Karl Wachholtz Verlag.

Serjeantson, D. 1994. The animal bones, in V. I. Evison, *An Anglo-Saxon Cemetery at Great Chesterford, Essex*, 66–70, Council for British Archaeology Research Report, 91, London: CBA.

Smith, C. R. 1851/52. Notes on Saxon sepulchral remains found at Fairford, Gloucestershire, *Archaeologia*, **34**, 77–82

Spain, S. 2000 'The Shield in Early Anglo-Saxon Kent: A computer-assisted analysis of shield bosses and an investigation into the use of the shield in the burial rite', Unpublished MA dissertation, University of York.

Stoodley, N. 1999. *The Spindle and the Spear. A Critical Enquiry into the Construction and Meaning of Gender in the Early Anglo-Saxon Burial Rite*, BAR British Series, 288, Oxford: British Archaeological Reports.

Swanton, M. J. 1973. *The Spearheads of the Anglo-Saxon Settlements*, Royal Archaeological Institute, London.

Sykes, J. 1866. *Local Records: or; A Historical register of Remarkable Events, which have occurred in Northumberland and Durham, Newcastle-upon-Tyne, and Berwick-upon-Tweed Vol. II*, Newcastle.

Timby, J. 1993. Sancton I Anglo-Saxon Cemetery Excavations Carried Out Between 1976 and 1980, *Archaeol. Jnl.*, **150**, 243–365.

Tyler, S. and Major, H. 2005. *The Early Anglo-Saxon Cemetery and Late Saxon Settlement at Springfield Lyons, Essex*, East Anglian Archaeology , 111, Gressenhall; Essex County Council.

Turville-Petre, J. E. 1957. Hengest and Horsa', *Saga Book*, **14**, 273–90

van Es, v-W. A. and Ypey, J. 1977 Das Grab der 'Pinzessin' von Zweelou und seine Bedeuteung im Rahmen des Gräberfeldes, in *Studien zur Sachsenforschung*, **1**, 97–126.

Vierck, H. 1970/71. Pferdegräber im angelsächsischen England, in M. Müller-Wille, *Pferdegrab und Pferdeopfer im frühen Mittelalter*, 189–99, Berichten van de Rijksdienst voor het Oudheidkundig Bodemonderzoek Jaargang, **20/21.**

Wahl, J. 1988. *Süderbrarup. Ein Gräberfeld der römischen Kaiserzeit und Völkerwanderungszeit in Angeln II: Anthropologische Untersuchungen*, Neumünster: Karl Wachholtz Verlag.

Walker, T. J. 1899. Notes on two Anglo-Saxon Burial-Places at Peterborough, *JBAA*, ns, **5**(55), 343–9.

Weber, M. 2000. *Das sächsische Gräberfeld von Issendorf, Ldkr. Stade, Niedersaschen: Kulturgeschichtliche Studien an den Brandgräbern der Grabungen 1967 bis 1979 in der Zeit der angelsächsischen Landnahme*, Teil 2, Studien zur Sachsenforschung, 9.2, Oldenburg: Isensee Verlag.

Welch, M. 1983. Early Anglo-Saxon Sussex, BAR British Series, 112 (2 vols.), Oxford: British Archaeological Reports.

Wells, C. unpublished a. 'A brief note on some Anglo-Saxon Cremations from Loveden Hill, Lincolnshire', Archive report at Fort Cumberland, English Heritage .

Wells, C. unpublished b. 'Anglo-Saxon Cremations: urns 56/29, 57/41 and Bronze bowls I and II', Archive report at Fort Cumberland, English Heritage.

Williams, H. 2001. An ideology of transformation: Cremation rites and animal sacrifice in early Anglo-Saxon England, in N. Price (ed.) *The Archaeology of Shamanism*, 193–212, London: Routledge.

Wilkinson, L and Noddle, B. unpublished. 'Cremation record report 1972 (Kerr?). C1–1015', Archive report at Fort Cumberland, English Heritage.

Wright, T. 1844. An account of the opening of barrows in Bourne Park, near Canterbury, *Archaeol. Jnl.*, **1**, 253–6.

Wright, T. 1847. On Recent discoveries of Anglo-Saxon Antiquities, *Jnl. Brit. Arch. Assoc.*, **2**, 50–9.

Table 1. Select cremation cemeteries with evidence for animal offerings in Northern Europe in the First Millennium AD: percentages are calculated against the whole buried population analysed (i.e. against the complete number of samples) and not as a species percentage (i.e. against only those cremations containing animal

Cemetery	Region	Date	Burials sampled	No. with animal (%)	Sheep (%)	Dog (%)	Cattle (%)	Horse (%)	Pig (%)	Bear (%)	References
Elsham Wolds	England	425–550	c. 630	c (.30)	'Common'	-	'Present'	23(4)	'Present'	'Present'	Richards 1987; Harman unpublished
Illington	England	425–550	104	21 (20)	7 (7)	1 (<1)	2 (2)	3 (3)	2 (2)	-	Davidson, Green and Milligan 1993
Loveden Hill	England	425–600	169	38 (22)	19 (11)	2 (1)	11 (7)	4 (2)	8 (5)	-	Wilkinson and Noddle unpublished; Wells unpublished (a and b)
Millgate	England	425–550	220	63 (29)	22 (10)	-	7 (3)	14 (6)	12 (5)	-	Harman 1989
Sancton	England	425–550	335	128(38)	26 (8)	3 (<1)	12 (4)	37 (11)	14 (4)	2 (<1)	Bond 1993
Spong Hill	England	425–550	2489	1019 (43)	107 (7)	25 (1)	80 (3)	227 (9)	84 (3)	6 (<1)	Bond 1994
Issendorf (1967–79)	L. Saxony	350–550	2535	18 (<1)	-	-	-	1 (<1)	-	-	Weber 2000
Issendorf (1989–1997)	L. Saxony	350–550	317	30 (7)			Not examined				Häßler 2001
Bordesholm	Schleswig-Holstein	0–550	4688	6 (<1)	-	-	-	-	-	-	Saggau 1986
Schmalstede	Schleswig-Holstein	350–550	295	11 (4)			Not examined				Bode 1998
Süderbrarup (Markt)	Schleswig-Holstein	0–550	763	113 (15)	21 (3)	-	9 (1)	1 (<1)	36 (5)	2 (<1)	Wahl 1988
Lindholm Høje	Denmark	400–800	407	253 (62)	66 (16)	221 (54)	7 (2)	20 (5)	11 (3)	-	Ramskou 1976
Barshalder	Gotland	400–650	59	56(95)	31 (55)	24 (43)	2 (4)	22 (39)	3 (5)	33 (59)	Rundqvist 2003
Helgö 116+150	Mälaren	500–700	23+34=57	49 (86)	24 (42)	20 (35)	9 (16)	7 (12)	3 (5)	10 (18)	Gejvall & Persson 1970; Jonsson 1997
Lunda 27	Mälaren	400–900	145 (18 Viking)	123 (85)	73 (50)	84 (58)	2 (1)	21 (14)	25 (17)	2 (1)	Pétre 1984 Vols. 3 and 4
Varberg 34A/35B/136	Mälaren	400–650	73	25 (32)	18 (25)	24 (33)	3 (4)	2 (3)	4 (5)	-	Iregren 1972a
Viken 57	Mälaren	400–750	21	20 (95)	13 (62)	14 (67)	6 (29)	9 (43)	6 (29)	1 (5)	Iregren 1972b

Table 2. *Inhumations associated with horse burials or harness equipment in early Anglo-Saxon England: spear and shield type identifications are based on Swanton (1973), Dickinson and Härke (1992) and Spain (unpublished). (G) indicates an identification based on gender specific grave goods*

Burial	Group/Date	Horse	Bit/Saddle	Orien.	Sex/Gender (G)	Age	Sword	Spear	Shield	Prestige items	Grave Structure	Other animal	Reference
Broughton Lodge 15/16/H1	A/500–550	Whole	X/-	W/E	Male+Female (G)	Adult+Adult	X	-	-	Great square-headed brooch: Style I	-	-	Kinsley 1993
Eriswell (046) 0355	A/500–550	Whole	X/-	W/E	Male (G)	Adult	X	E2	G2	Sword-bead?	Ring-ditch/Coffin?	-	Newman forthcoming
Eriswell (104) 4116	A/500–550	Whole	X/X	W/E	Male	Adult	X	H2	G2	Bucket/Style I/Sword-bead	Ring-ditch/Coffin	Sheep	Newman forthcoming
Gt Chesterford (I) H2/142	A/500–550	Whole	X/-	S/N	Male	Adult	-	H2	G2	-	-	-	Evison 1994
Little Wilbraham 44	A/500–550	Whole	X/-	S/N	Male (G)	Adult?	X	X	X	Sword-bead	-	-	Neville 1852
Saffron Walden	A/450–600	Whole?	-/-	-	Male?	Adult?	-	-	-	'…in one place, …. the remains of a man and horse, embedded in the chalk, were discovered'	-	-	Neville 1836
Woodstone	A/450–600	Whole?	-/-	-	Male?	Adult?	-	-	-	'…the bones of a horse were found in a grave with those of a man…'	-	-	Walker 1899
Broughton Lodge 88/H3	B/550–600	Whole	X/-	W/E	Male(G)	Adult?	-	X	G3	-	-	Sheep	Kinsley 1993
Saltwood 5/27	B/575–625	Whole	X/X	W/E	Male(G)	Adult?	X	A2-E3	G3bii+G6	Bronze vessel/Gaming counters	Chamber	-	Riddler Pers. Comm
Snape 47	B/575–625	Head	X/-	W/E	Male(G)	Adult?	X	C2+2xD1	G6	Bucket/Gaming counters?	Boat/Posts	Sheep-size	Filmer-Sankey et al. 2001
Sutton Hoo 17	B/575–625	Whole	X/X	W/E	Male(G)	Adult?	X	D2+F1	G6	2Bronze Vessels/2Buckets/Style II/Sword-belt	Mound	Sheep	Carver 1993
West Heslerton 19/186	B/550–600	Head/Whole	X/-	W/E	Male(G)	Adult?	-	C2?	G2	-	Coffin	-	Haughton et al 1999
Alfriston 91	C/450–500		-/-	W/E	Male (G)	Adult	-	C1	-	Francisca	-	-	Welch 1983
Bishopsbourne 3	C/600–650		X/-	S/N	Male (G)		-	X?	G7	Bronze vessel/Bucket/Gaming counters	Chamber/Mound	-	Wright 1844
Castledyke 18	C/625–675		Spur	W/E	-	Sub-adult	-	-	-	-	-	-	Drinkall et al 1998
Chamberlain's Barn (II) 45	C/625–675		X/-	W/E	-	-	-	-	-	-	Ring-ditch/Mound	-	Hyslop 1963
Edix Hill 88	C/575–625		Spur	S/N	-	Adult	-	H2	G3	Bucket	-	-	Malim et al 1998
Garton (II) 10	C/625–675		X/-	W/E	-	Sub-adult	-	-	-	-	-	Sheep/Cattle	Mortimer 1905
Howletts 36	C/450–600		X/-	-	-	-	-	-	-	-	-	-	Meaney 1964
Kirton-in-Lindsey (II)	C/600–650		X/-	-	Male (G)	Adult	X	C5	-	Seax	Mound	-	Geake 1997
Mill Hill 93	C/575–625		Spur	S/N	Male	Adult	X	E3	G6	Glass vessel	-	-	Parfitt et al. 1997
Loveden Hill HB4/1	C/600–650		X/-	-	Male (G)	-	X	X	-	2Hanging bowls/Bucket/Bronze vessel/2Glass vessels	(Cremation)	-	Fennell unpublished
Saltwood 7	C/600–650		X/-	W/E	Male	Adult	X	A2	G3bii+G6	Bronze vessel/Bucket/Style II Pommel	Mound	-	Riddler Pers. Comm
Broughton Lodge 19/20	A?/500–600	Head		W/E	Male+Female (G)	Adult+Adult	-	H3	G2/3?	Bronze vessel	-	-	Kinsley 1993
Broughton Lodge 69/H2	A?/500–600	Foreleg		NW/SE	Male (G)	Adult	-	E2?	X	-	-	-	Kinsley 1993
Broughton Lodge H4	B?/600–650	Whole?	-/X?	W/E	-	-	-	-	-	-	-	-	Kinsley 1993
Caenby	B?/600–650	Whole?		-	Male(G)	Adult?	X	-	-	Drinking assemblage/Style II/Saddle?	Mound	-	Jarvis 1850
Comforth	-/450–600	Whole?	'horse furniture'	S/N?						'…a human skeleton [with] a lance …Another …with a small lance … Eight or nine other sepulchres …in another the bones of a horse, and also perhaps a dog…'			Sykes 1866
Fairford	-/450–600	Whole ?(multiple)	-/X?	NW/SE						'…a quantity of human skeletons, with skeletons of horses…'			Wright 1847; Smith 1851/52
Great Chesterford (I) H1	-/500–600	Whole	-/X?	-	-	-	-	-	-	-	-	-	Evison 1994
Great Chesterford (II) H1	-/450–600	Whole?	-	-	-	-	-	-	-	-	-	-	Hooper 1971
Great Chesterford (II) H2	-/450–600	Whole?	-	-	-	-	-	-	-	-	-	-	Hooper 1971
Hardingstone	B?/600–650	Whole?	X/-	-	-	-	-	-	-	Style II — '…the horse does not appear to refer immediately to any other, but to have been a little apart. …. occupying a place upon the northern verge of the cemetery'	-	-	Bateman 1860
Icklingham	-/450–600	Whole?	-	-	-	-	-	-	-	'…remains of four human skeletons…'	-	-	Prigg 1888
Marston St Lawrence 1	-/450–600	Whole	X/X	NE/SW	-	-	-	-	-	-	-	-	Dryden 1885
Sarre 271	-/450–600	Head?	X/-							'…near the surface human bones, a horse's jaw bone and teeth, and an iron snaffle-bit. A skeleton lay below, entire, with only a broken knife'			Brent 1868
Sporle	-/450–600	Whole?								'Seven skeletons…side by side; round shields…were placed over the faces of some; and spearheads by their sides…beads were on one…a female.'	Mound	'small bones'	Meaney 1964
Springfield Lyons 8577	-/450–600	Head	X/-	-	-	-	-	-	-	-	-	-	Tyler et al. 2005
Stone (I)	-/450–600	Whole ?(multiple)								'…several skeletons of men and horses.'			Akerman 1842
Wanlip	B?/500–600	Whole?	X/-	WNW/ESE	-	-	-	-	-	-	-	-	Liddle 1979
Warren Hill	B?/500–600	Whole?	-/X?	-	-	-	-	-	-	-	-	-	Prigg 1888
Wigston Magna	B?/450–600	Whole?	X/-	-	Male(G)	-	-	-	2xG1	Shield boss: 'basin like', 6'', 5 rivets disc apex	-	-	Nichols 1807
Witnesham	A?/450–600	Whole?	-/X?	-	-	-	-	-	-	'…a human skeleton with that of a horse beside it…several marks of military accoutrements, saddle, stirrups etc.'	-	-	Meadows 1828, 23; Newman 2006

Soft Furnished Burial: an Assessment of the Role of Textiles in Early Anglo-Saxon Inhumations, with Particular Reference to East Kent

Sue Harrington

Introduction

That textiles survive into the British archaeological record as mineral preserved fragments attached to metalwork has long been acknowledged. For example, antiquarians noted them as long ago as the eighteenth century, when excavating early Anglo-Saxon barrow burials. However, the recording of these comparatively significant amounts of textile fragments has been patchy over time. The modern era is fortunate in having a small group of specialists whose ability to analyse these remnants microscopically has added greatly to knowledge of clothing and cloth in the early Anglo-Saxon period. Textiles Research in York and the Manchester Medieval Textiles Project are doing much to raise the profile of this resource, with the production of comprehensive and accessible catalogues of extant examples from the medieval period. Yet, the data is much underused and under-interpreted, with few attempts to connect the evidence to theoretical debates of early medieval mortuary archaeology. Given the ubiquity of woven products in past societies, with their essential roles in societal maintenance and social reproduction, one cannot help but echo Elizabeth Barber's characterisation of textiles in her important review of weaving, cloth and society as the missing data of archaeological research.[1]

A primary focus in textiles studies of the early Anglo-Saxon period to date has been on costume reconstruction in relation to metalwork dress fittings,[2] with very positive results in identifying different feminine dress forms frequently associated with discrete ethnic groups. Attempts to ask more specific questions about the role of cloth and clothing in early medieval mortuary practices should be developed. However, such studies remain a challenge, not only because of the fragmentary evidence, but also because of the way that the evidence is presented in publications. For example, there is often little attempt to synthesise the textiles data with the evidence for weaving technology from the same site. Indeed the technological evidence is often subordinated within other categories; for example, bone spindle whorls discussed as bone-worked objects, not as productive tools in their own right. When the interplay between textiles and their associated technology in the early Anglo-Saxon burial has begun to be explored,[3] it has already suggested a range of complex relationships between those marked as producers of cloth, those who used cloth and the cloth types selected for inclusion in the burial tableau. It is clear from the evidence of bed burials such as at Edix Hill Barrington A, Cambridgeshire[4] and Swallowcliffe Down, Wiltshire[5] that cloth was a component of high status inhumations, although it is difficult to reconstruct the actual usage of textiles in these contexts.

The purpose of this paper is to explore the range of evidence for textiles from the burials of East Kent. In doing so, it is argued that the soft furnishing of graves was more common than has been suggested and that different types of textile artefacts were present in inhumations, including pillows, cloaks, coverings, rugs and bags. 'Soft furnishings' covers many different types of textile object. In modern contexts, the term covers wall and floor coverings, curtains, cushions, bedding, table linen and loose coverings. Their functions in early medieval graves can be defined variously, for example to protect another artefact, to enhance the colour and texture of the burial environment, to cover a space and make it private, to make the old look new or simply to provide comfort and warmth. What is imagined when using the term 'soft furnishings' is not simply cloth serving as a passive backdrop to the bodies and objects placed with the dead. Instead, it encourages us to consider the rich interplay of texture, pattern, colour, motifs and images, all working together to actively enhance and communicate social and symbolic information in the burial context. As Mary Schoeser comments 'at every level of society the use of fabrics in interiors provides a commentary on the interplay of fashion, technology and social change'.[6] If this is as true of mortuary contexts as domestic settings, then the question we must ask is: what were the concepts underpinning the use of soft furnishings in early Anglo-Saxon burial rituals?

The Identification of Textiles
in Early Anglo-Saxon Burials

Before such issues can be explored, it is necessary to look in a more detail at the history of the identification of textiles in burials. Only through understanding the fragmentary nature of the data and ongoing methodological problems that arise when working with this evidence, can we begin to appreciate and interpret the surviving soft furnishings of the inhumation graves from East Kent.

The data referred to throughout is lodged in the East Kent textiles database, which is a related table of ASKED (Anglo-Saxon Kent Electronic Database). ASKED is a collaboratively built research tool, generated by the author and Stuart Brookes at the Institute of Archaeology, University College London, in the period 1999–2001, with guidance from Martin Welch. It comprises the records of over 600 burial sites from East Kent in the period AD 450–725, the full burial records of 3700 individuals found in inhumations, including osteological data and the records of over 10000 objects, including their cultural provenance, together with their positions in the graves. By this means attendant textile fragments are linked to their host objects and can be dated by association.

The Reverend Bryan Faussett first noted the presence of textiles in Anglo-Saxon burials in the mid-eighteenth century during his excavations of the seventh-century barrow cemeteries of East Kent, although the evidence was not published until a century later.[7] A recurrent comment by Faussett in his text for graves at Kingston Down, Barfreston and Sibertswold is to spearheads 'wrapped in or lain upon some coarse cloth'.[8] Through observation of the coarseness of the cloth and the location of the fragment on the artefact, he concluded that many of the weapons were wrapped and deposited outside of the coffin, within the grave. These textiles were in addition to those found within the coffin, which he identified as the remains of clothing, although he appears to have been uncertain whether there might not also have been wrappings associated with some of the objects found on the body.

It was the antiquarian James Douglas, however, who first publicised the extent to which textiles were part of the grave furnishings of the early Anglo-Saxon period. In his *Nenia Britannica* of 1793, Douglas described his opening of one of the barrows in the seventh-century cemetery at Greenwich Park, West Kent, and stated that 'I plainly discerned throughout the whole of the cist very distinct appearances of cloth ... they were of different fineness and textures: some were in the herring-bone and others in the usual square pattern' (these were fragments of twill and of plain weave). In another he noted 'a considerable quantity of woollen cloth sheeting the whole extent of it'.[9]

His detailed examinations of the contents of these burials persuaded him of the following conclusions:

... the preservation of cloth by the rust of the spear is a proof that the body was buried with a vestment. Several specimens of the relics, which have impressions of linen, woollen and silk, of different textures and fineness, indicate that the dead not only had a funeral garment to cover them entirely, but that they were also entombed with their customary apparel when alive.[10]

Following his usual procedure in this matter, he confirmed that these fragments were indeed linen and wool, by burning them and comparing the manner in which they were consumed by the flames. Unsurprisingly, the textiles from these assemblages have not survived into the modern era, save for a dozen threads of a spin-patterned fabric, held in the Ashmolean Museum. Although few threads in number, the combination of sequences of the two different spin directions (z and s), denoting complexity in their manufacture and subtlety in their patterning, is comparable to cloths attached to dress fitments from single graves in the late seventh-century East Kentish cemeteries at Ozengell, Finglesham and Eastry Updown.

Whether Douglas' account was an accurate record of exceptional instances of preservation is uncertain. All fibres are difficult to identify without the aid of a microscope, silk particularly so. It is also accurate to state that, unlike Douglas and Faussett, no modern excavator of early Anglo-Saxon cemeteries has seen the like of these textiles in any grave exposed only to the naked eye. However, no claim can be made for the occupants of the Greenwich Park barrow cemetery as being anything other than ordinary in terms of their assemblages. Although their burial mounds were in a prominent position above the river Thames and lay adjacent to the main route way from Canterbury to London, they were accompanied by nothing remarkable beyond spears, knives, beads, all of which were few in number, and by a single shield boss.

It must be commented though that the best preserved textile fragments do seem to occur within barrows, which operate as both a context for their deposition and as an environment for their preservation. For example, one has only to think of the rich textile remains from Sutton Hoo, Taplow and possibly Broomfield[11] together with the Migration Age Högum mound in Sweden[12] and the ninth-century Oseberg ship in Norway[13] to name the most well-known examples. Elisabeth Crowfoot's interpretation of the Sutton Hoo textile fragments identifies at least some of the fragments as soft furnishings, in the form of wall hangings and rugs, rather than being primarily the remains of wrappings around objects and backdrops for the display of esoteric objects. In earlier Scandinavian burials, it had been the practice to cover the whole contents of a grave with a light cloak or blanket.[14] The practices of the early first millennium AD Romans in soft furnishing their burials have not been researched at the time of writing.[15]

How are we to interpret the remains identified by Faussett and Douglas? There are differences here in what each of the two antiquarian excavators saw within their respective Kentish seventh century cemeteries, although both agreed that the bodies were clothed. Douglas saw layers of cloth throughout the burial, whilst Faussett saw more individualised wrappings around spearheads. However, Douglas also interpreted those fragments attached to spears as the remnants of clothing.

Several questions come out of these records of first-hand observations of textile remnants in barrow burials. First, it must be accurately determined whether objects were wrapped before deposition or whether they were laid out on cloth. If the latter were the case, then the possibility arises that the graves were soft furnished with cloths or textile artefacts, perhaps using valuable or inherited items. Differences in this practice also require further investigation, to consider whether sixth century and non-barrow graves were also vested, as the seventh-century ones clearly had been to some extent. Of more pressing concern is whether we have sufficient evidence to begin to address these questions.

Problems with Textiles Data

There are indeed acute problems when seeking to explore this data. Textiles usually survive in a recognisable form in early Anglo-Saxon burials when in contact with metalwork objects. Whilst it is arguably the case that a few textile fragments might survive on any cemetery site, the amount that is preserved is clearly linked to the amounts of metalwork that were deposited. Thus, there are far more textile fragments from iron- and jewellery-rich East Kent than from any other region.[16] The textile profile for East Kent – that is, the range of types found there – is dominated by plain (tabby) weave, but this may be solely a factor of the numbers of knives, keys and chains clustered together as chatelaines and buried with women, the spaces within which provide an ideal environment for textile survival. So, whilst we have a window into the types of textiles present in the early Anglo-Saxon period, it is a view mainly focused on the cloths associated with the feminine left hip area.

Another problem is the subordinate position that mineral preserved textiles have in relation to their, usually high status, metalwork host objects. When seeking out previously identified textile fragments in museum archives, it has been dispiriting to find, instead of a relatively uncommon z/s 2/2 twill fragment, rather, a rust-like residue in the bottom of the plastic box housing the more common small square headed brooch, the textile around the pin becoming more degraded each time the brooch is removed from its modern packaging for examination.

One can make the same observation regarding spear-heads. As the location of the textile is usually on the socket, that is, the place where the packaging will fit most closely, they are subject to substantial degradation. Furthermore, whereas with brooches one can be fairly certain of their location on the body at the time of burial, with spearheads it is often not possible to ascertain from a publication which face of the blade was uppermost and which edge of the socket was adjacent to the body.

Yet another problem is that many of the textile fragments that were present in the archaeological record have been removed during excavation and conservation. It appeared from examination of all of the extant shield bosses from East Kent cemeteries that there was only one instance of a cloth being laid over the face of them, in the double burial grave 96 at Dover Buckland, dating to the second quarter of the seventh century, and that usually shields represented the final, closing layer in the construction of a masculine burial tableau. However, a group 3 type shield boss, possibly dating to the sixth century and from the unpublished cemetery at Eastbourne, East Sussex, currently undergoing conservation at the Institute of Archaeology University College London, has a fragment of plain woven cloth on the top surface, measuring no more than a half a centimetre across. This single example begins to suggest that other fragments may have been lost over time during conservation processes.

These examples by themselves raise questions as to the amount of textiles that were deposited in inhumations and it is perhaps the case that the more one looks for textiles in the burial during an actual excavation, the more one will see them. A recently examined soil sample from a grave on South Malling Hill near Lewes, East Sussex appears in certain lights to have retained the structure of textile, if not the mineral preserved substance. It looks to consist of 2–3 mm long overlapping threads, although nothing can be determined of the spin direction, weave or fibre.

Where textiles are identified, another problem has been the, often unacknowledged, use of sampling strategies in the post-excavation phases, whereby only the textiles on a selection of host objects are analysed, leaving the more mundane objects such as keys and nails unexamined. One can usually find more fragments extant in the site archive than have appeared in the publication.[17] Given the unevenness in the treatment and recording of textile fragments, what detailed evidence can be determined for soft furnishings in early Anglo-Saxon inhumations?

Findings from the East Kent Textiles Database

The textiles database of ASKED records 720 fragments, from within a total of 3700 graves, the majority of which are the residues of clothing. The data recorded covers weave, spin direction, thread counts per centimetre in the warp and the weft, fibre, the position of the fragment on the host object, the host object and its position in the burial, either on the body or apart from it. Such is the variable condition of the fragments, that few yield a complete dataset. 121 of the fragments, or 17% of the total, were attached to objects that were not in direct contact with the body of the deceased, mainly swords, spears, copper alloy bowls, nails and boxes, thus skewing the dataset towards masculine weapon burials. However, the majority of the clothing evidence is from feminine graves due to the lack of masculine metalwork dress accessories other than belt-buckles and thus fewer opportunities for textile survival.

Within the textiles database, there are 62 spears that are host objects to 67 textile fragments, from graves dating to the period AD525–700. The main textile types found on them are plain weaves and twills, generally but not invariably coarse cloths. Most of the fragments occur singly along one edge of the spearhead socket, which, in the context of their grave plans, suggests they were the result of the placing of the spear next to the clothed shoulder of the interred. Whether or not a coffin was present in the grave does not appear to change the location of the fragments on the spearhead. They still only appear on the blade or the side of the socket. The evidence indicates that if spears were placed on the outside of the coffin and therefore not in contact with clothing, then the coffin itself was probably covered and it was these coverings that provided the source of the fragment.

There are only four cases recorded in the database where there are multiple textile fragments adhering to a spearhead host object. Of these, the spearhead with Broadstairs St Peters (BSP) 53,[18] hosts an exceptionally fine plain weave z/s (count 54/12 threads per centimetre in the probable warp and weft, respectively) along one edge and a medium weight (18/12) plain weave z/z on one face. That with Dover Buckland (DBU) 10[19] had an openly woven (14/10) plain cloth z/z on the socket, a coarse (8/6) plain weave z/z on one face of the blade tip and another plain weave z/z, more closely woven (12/12) and of looser spin, on the other face. The other two examples are from the unpublished excavations at Ozengell (OZE), graves 112 and 172. The former hosts two different qualities of plain weave, whilst the latter has a coarse (10/6) twill z/z on the socket and a coarse and a fine plain weave overlying one another on the blade tip. The evidence here demonstrates that there is no example of the same textile type appearing on the front and the back of the blade, or on both sides of the socket, as might be expected if they had been wrapped on deposition. All of these burials can be dated to the seventh century, with only OZE 112 perhaps slightly earlier.

The double male burial from Dover Buckland (DBU) grave 96 provides evidence, through the identification of additional textile fragments from within the assemblage, to question further the assertion of weapons being wrapped on a consistent basis in early Anglo-Saxon inhumations. Vera Evison[20] interprets the function

of coil-headed iron pins in this and other burials as being to fasten cloth coverings around the spearheads, reflecting a Germanic burial trait that was evidenced by Lyminge grave 1 as present in East Kent since the mid-sixth century.[21] However, this explanation of their usage appears to be at variance to the evidence of two fragments of a particular coarse cloth type (10/8 2/2 twill z/s) present in DBU 96. One fragment is on one of the faces of the coil-headed pin situated adjacent to 96a, whilst the other is on the socket of the spearhead with 96b, suggesting that in this latter instance it was from the shoulder of a cloak. This distribution suggests to me several explanations, none of which necessarily implies wrapping. One is that the men were garbed in similar types of cloaks. Another is that both bodies were covered and tucked in by a single cloth and that the objects were laid adjacent to them on the cloth. 96b's spearhead socket also has a fragment of a closely woven plain cloth (16/16, z/z), together with the imprint of a feather, suggesting that a pillow was placed there. This same cloth type also appears on his knife, although it is not possible to determine if the cloth was on the upper or lower face, that is, whether the knife was laid on the body or on a cloth over it. The same cloth type appears on the upper surface of the shield boss at their feet.

The burial DBU 96 is from the seventh century and unfortunately there is insufficient evidence from spearheads of the sixth century to deduce whether similar uses were made of cloths in earlier burials. However, there is clear evidence that, from the early sixth century onwards, copper alloy bowls were covered by, or wrapped in, cloth. This is demonstrated by the examples from Finglesham 203 and 204, each with several different cloths adhering to them, Finglesham 203 having a rare fragment of Alamannic rosette twill.[22] This trait of wrapping is visible in at least another four East Kentish copper alloy bowls examined in museum archives.[23] Staining on their surfaces suggests that textiles were in contact with them, both around the edges and underneath as pads of cloth. The most closely examined example, from Coombe, Woodnesborough,[24] dates to the late sixth century, with a covering of a finely patterned garment or blanket, similar to a cloth from Broomfield. It is possible that they were also secured around by threads as in the case of the bowl from the Saxon cemetery at Croydon, Surrey.[25]

Traces of textiles are also to be found on the Coptic bowl accompanying the woman uncovered at Sarre (SAR) windmill in 1860,[26] in a burial dating to the first half of the seventh century. The survival of cloth on the inside of a bowl might be due to the weight of soil compressing the cover from above, but the significance of the discovery lies in the fact that it shows that cloths could be used inside the bowl, in this case as a pad to support an assemblage of burnt animal bone. At least three different cloth types were present here showing the potential complexity of textile use in graves.

Hilda Ellis Davidson and Leslie Webster identify the

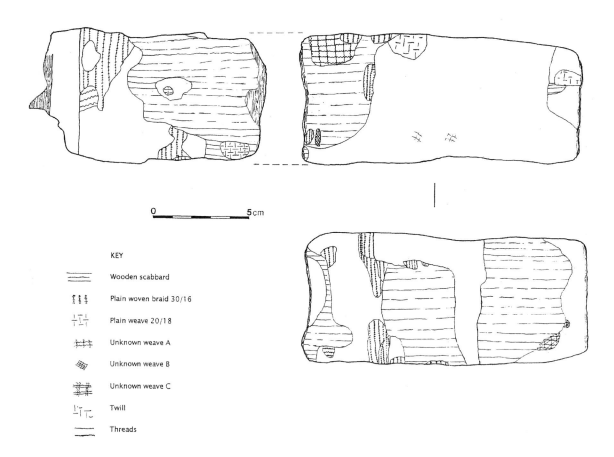

KEY

≣	Wooden scabbard
⌇⌇⌇	Plain woven braid 30/16
⊥⊤⊥	Plain weave 20/18
⊬⊬	Unknown weave A
▦	Unknown weave B
▦	Unknown weave C
⌐⊤⊥	Twill
──	Threads

Figure 1. Textile fragments on both faces of the scabbard and sword from Wickhambreux, Kent

practice of covering copper alloy bowls as analogous to the wrapping of swords, giving an additional protective covering to significant ritual objects.[27] Yet, the assumed practice of wrapping swords can also be questioned. Certainly, much cloth has been found adhering to swords, including the decorative braids and cords around the mouth and upper section of early Anglo-Saxon scabbards and interpreted as a particular cultural trait appearing in the late sixth/early seventh centuries.[28]

The East Kent textiles database records twenty-one fragments adhering to swords from eleven burials, the majority of which are of the late sixth and seventh centuries. The dataset does include some examples from the early to mid sixth century, most notably Finglesham 204,[29] together with Mill Hill Deal graves 81 and 91,[30] and Broadstairs Bradstow School grave 87.[31] The best example is, however, from Wickhambreux, where a large grave of unassociated material was discovered in 1886 and is now held in Maidstone museum.[32] It contained a copper alloy bowl, a sword with a gold stud and scabbard, a garnet-set gold buckle and a glass clawbeaker, again dating probably from the late sixth/early seventh century.

A detailed examination of the Wickhambreux sword textile fragments (Fig. 1), shows fine plain-woven tapes, each probably not more than 6 mm wide, wound overlapping down the length of the scabbard from the mouth for approximately 17 cm. The braids overlie another textile, represented by patches of threads and an unknown weave A, whilst a further textile is visible under the wood of the scabbard on the other side, unknown weave C. On one face, a plain weave is present together with a twill weave and another unknown weave B.

The sequence of deposition in this particular grave is interpreted as the sword being placed into a textile lined scabbard, with the tape round the upper section securing a fine fabric to the outside of the scabbard. The sword and scabbard were probably placed either onto the body and thus in contact with the clothing, or beside it onto a blanket on which the body lay, hence the twill on one face. Also present was a layer of fine quality plain weave and possibly yet another cloth. Taken together, the evidence suggests that the whole sword and scabbard were not wrapped, but were in contact with the layers of textiles, for if it were wrapped, given the good preservation of textiles, traces of the same fabrics should have appeared on both faces of the object.

There is a tantalising textile fragment of cloth to suggest that a whole burial may have been swathed in cloth. It is a piece from the Mill Hill Deal (MHD) cemetery and is hosted by a clench bolt B13 in grave 38,[33] dating to the first half of the sixth century. The fragment of a fine weave, z/? with 20/16 threads per cm, is not in itself particularly remarkable. Its location, however, is on the head of the bolt lying towards the outer face of the burial and suggests that the full extent of cloth may have wrapped over the section of boat timbers placed along one edge of the grave.[34]

Conclusions

The interpretation by archaeologists of certain textile fragments as the cloth wrappings of artefacts is eminently plausible. It is in line with what is known of the practices in the Germanic homelands, suggesting that the objects were conserved in death as they may have been in life, with, in practical terms, the lanolin from wool cloth preventing the oxidisation of the metal, thus keeping them ready for use beyond the burial. This care and attention to objects may have had a bearing on conceptions of the role of objects in commemorating the past and evoking the future.

The burial practices of people in the Saxon and Anglian regions may have been normative and consistently identifiable in this respect. The evidence from East Kent already suggests a more active use of cloth in the burials, as the identity of the cloth itself may have been hidden if it was used solely as a wrapping. What begins to appear to be more probable was that the East Kentish burials were layered with cloth, or that they contained soft furnishings in the form of coverlets, pillows and hangings deployed around the grave, perhaps in the manner of the Sutton Hoo mound 1 burial. The evidence available from mineral preserved textile fragments in East Kent clusters around the period of the late sixth/early seventh centuries, with further examples coming from the mid to late seventh, to contrast with the paucity of data from the early to mid sixth. Why the evidence should be particularly visible at this point in

time is undetermined, although of course it may solely be due to accidents of preservation within graves well furnished with metal objects and placed under barrows. The further question arises as to whether there was a shift in the use of textiles in this period, perhaps away from the wrapping of conserved objects following Germanic cultural traditions in the sixth century to a more conspicuous display and deployment of sumptuous and esoteric cloths in the seventh.

What the evidence suggests is the use of textiles instrumentally in the burial ritual, for example, to close the copper alloy bowl and its contents and the covering of the coffin or the whole uncoffined assemblage. Beyond that, cloth may have been used to construct the burial *tableau*, by providing a layer on which to place the body and a context in which to lay out the other objects, before the 'final curtain'. In this way, the grave assemblage and the attendant rituals may have gained coherence, for the final view of the inhuming community. Whilst this scenario is plausible for weapon burials, it is still an open question as to whether other burials less rich in metalwork were also laid out in such a manner. The seemingly unaccompanied burials in large barrows of the seventh century, for example, may also have been rich in textiles, with the body laid out on and covered by cloths that have not survived. Overall, the evidence suggests that sixth and seventh century society in East Kent was rich in textiles, both in quantity and quality. These furnishings were probably as significant as the curated, imported and locally produced metal objects that now host them. If the interpretation of the wrapping and enveloping of whole assemblages in early East Kentish burial ritual is plausible, then perhaps one can now conceive of textiles as the means through which the transition between life and death was enacted. To subordinate them to their host objects in order of importance and treatment in archaeological excavation, conservation and research is to negate their meaning in the lives and deaths of early medieval people.

Notes

1. Barber 1994.
2. Owen-Crocker 1986.
3. Harrington 2002.
4. Crowfoot 1998.
5. Crowfoot 1989.
6. Schoeser 1989, 9.
7. Faussett 1856.
8. *Ibid.*
9. Douglas 1793, 56.
10. *Ibid*, 90.
11. Crowfoot 1983.
12. Nockert 1991.
13. Sjøvold 1971.
14. Crowfoot 1987, 195.
15. Pers. comm. John-Peter Wild.
16. Bender Jørgensen 1992.
17. Harrington 2003.
18. Crowfoot, n.d.
19. Crowfoot, 1987, 191.
20. Evison 1987, 29, 82.
21. *Ibid.*, 83.
22. Crowfoot 1974.
23. Harrington 2002, 473.
24. Crowfoot 1967.
25. Pers. comm. Martin Welch.
26. Brent, 1860.
27. Davidson and Webster 1967.
28. Cameron 2000.
29. Crowfoot FGL.
30. Fritchie 1997, 254.
31. Harrington 2002, 511.
32. Meaney 1964.
33. Parfitt and Brugmann 1997, 135,199.
34. I am indebted to Stuart Brookes for drawing my attention to this evidence.

Bibliography

Barber, E. 1994. *Women's work: the first 20,000 years*, London: W. W. Norton

Bender Jørgensen, L. 1992. *North European Textiles until AD 1000*, Aarhus: Aarhus University Press.

Brent, J. 1860. Anglo-Saxon relics, Kent. *Gentleman's Magazine*, November, 533–5

Cameron, E. 2000. *Sheaths and Scabbards in England AD 400–1100*, BAR British Series 301, Oxford: Archaeopress.

Crowfoot, E. n.d. The textiles from St Peter's Tip, Broadstairs. Unpublished report.

Crowfoot, E. 1967. The Textiles, in H. Davidson and L. Webster, The Anglo-Saxon burial at Coombe, Kent, 37–39, *Medieval Archaeol.*, **11**, 1–41.

Crowfoot, E. 1974. *Finglesham, Kent: Textiles*, unpublished Ancient Monuments Laboratory Report 1674. English Heritage.

Crowfoot, E .1983. The Textiles, in A.C. Evans (ed.), *The Sutton Hoo Ship Burial*, Vol. 3, 409–79, London: British Museum Publications Ltd.

Crowfoot, E. 1987. The Textiles, in V. Evison, *Dover: Buckland Anglo-Saxon cemetery*, 190–5, Historic Buildings and Monuments Commission for England Archaeological Report, 3. London: HMSO.

Crowfoot. E. 1998. Textiles associated with metalwork, in T. Malim, and J. Hines (eds), *The Anglo-Saxon cemetery at Edix Hill (Barrington A), Cambridgeshire*, 237–47. Council for British Archaeology Research Report, 112.York: CBA.

Crowfoot, E. 1989. The Textiles, in G. Speake, *A Saxon bed-burial at Swallowcliffe Down*, 116–17, English Heritage Archaeological Report 10, London: English Heritage.

Davidson, H. E. and Webster, L. 1967. The Anglo-Saxon burial at Coombe (Woodnesborough), Kent, *Medieval Archaeol.*, **11**, 1–41.

Douglas, Rev. J. 1793. *Nenia Britannica*, London: John Nichols.

Faussett, B. (C. R. Smith, ed.) 1856. *Inventorium Sepulchrale*, London: printed for subscribers.

Fritchie, C. 1997. Textile report, in K. Parfitt and B. Brugmann *The Anglo-Saxon cemetery on Mill Hill, Deal*: 252–57. Society for Medieval Archaeology Monograph No.14, London: SMA.

Harrington, S. 2002. 'Aspects of Gender and craft Production in Early Anglo-Saxon England, with Reference to the Kingdom of Kent', unpublished PhD thesis, University College London.

Harrington, S. 2003. *The Textiles from Five Cemeteries in Hampshire*, unpublished report, King Alfred College Winchester.

Meaney, A.1964. A gazetteer of early Anglo-Saxon burial sites.London: George Allen and Unwin.

Nockert, M. 1991. *The Högom find and other Migration period textiles and costumes in Scandinavia*, Umeå: University of Umea Dept. of Archaeology Riksantikvarieambetet.

Owen-Crocker, G. 1986. *Dress in Anglo-Saxon England*, Manchester: Manchester University Press.

Parfitt, K. and Brugmann, B. 1997. *The Anglo-Saxon cemetery on Mill Hill, Deal*. Society for Medieval Archaeology Monograph, 14, London: SMA.

Schoeser, M. 1989. *English and American textiles from 1790 to the present*, London: Thames and Hudson.

Sjøvold, T. 1971. *The Oseberg find*, Oslo: Universitets Oldsaksammling.

On Sacred Ground: Social Identity and Churchyard Burial in Lincolnshire and Yorkshire, *c.* 700–1100 AD

Jo Buckberry

It has been frequently assumed that, following the conversion of the Anglo-Saxon kingdoms to Christianity and the establishment of monasteries and minster churches during the seventh and eighth centuries, cemeteries were commonly located next to churches.[1] However, following the excavation and publication of several late Anglo-Saxon cemeteries that were not located adjacent to a church, or were adjacent to a church that went out of use during the Anglo-Saxon or medieval period, this interpretation has been recently challenged.[2] In addition, an increasing number of late Anglo-Saxon execution cemeteries, Scandinavian cemeteries and isolated burials have been identified away from church sites.[3] It has also been frequently assumed that late Anglo-Saxon burial practice was relatively uniform and 'egalitarian' in which all social classes were united in death and buried in a manner dictated by the Church.[4] However, recent research has suggested that late Anglo-Saxon period funerary practices remained an important arena for social display as they had been in the fifth, sixth and early seventh centuries,[5] although little systematic work has been undertaken investigating and quantifying the forms and variety of late Anglo-Saxon burial rites.[6] Even less work has been undertaken comparing these different funerary rites with the increasing quantity and quality of osteological evidence for the late Anglo-Saxon period, a methodology that has proved successful in the interpretation of early and mid Anglo-Saxon cemeteries.[7] This paper will attempt to draw these themes together by discussing the range and variation of burial rites within late Anglo-Saxon cemeteries, and investigating the relationship between osteological and funerary evidence within a sample of cemeteries in Lincolnshire and Yorkshire. It will be argued that burial practices were not egalitarian in the late Anglo-Saxon period. Instead, this study reveals that aspects of social identity influenced the choice of burial rites accorded to the deceased. Many of the results presented in this paper arise from a survey of 464 Anglo-Saxon and undated burial sites in Lincolnshire and Yorkshire, of which ninety seven, or 20.9%, dated to the seventh century or later.[8] The paper

will go on to investigate the relationship between the age and sex of the deceased and the different funerary rites present in six cemeteries: York Minster, Swinegate and St Andrew's Fishergate in York; St Mark's Lincoln, St Peter's Barton-upon-Humber and the tenth- to twelfth-century cemetery at Barrow-upon-Humber (formerly mistakenly interpreted as the cemetery of the seventh-century monastery founded by St Chad). These cemeteries were chosen for analysis because they were excavated using modern techniques, skeletal material was reasonably well preserved, large numbers of graves were excavated, and the stratigraphy of the cemetery allowed later medieval burials to be excluded from analysis.

Late Anglo-Saxon Burial Practice

Before exploring the cemeteries in question, let us set the scene by providing an overview of later Anglo-Saxon mortuary practices. A wide variety of burial rites were used during the late Anglo-Saxon period. The archaeological evidence for these practices can be divided into two groups. The first group can be described as *grave types* and relates to the overall structure of the grave and container for the body; for example plain earth graves, coffins, stone-lined graves and sarcophagi. The second group consists of what can be described as *grave variations*, which are found in conjunction with the different *grave types*; for example layers of charcoal, grave markers, grave covers and stones placed around the head (commonly referred to as pillow stones by excavators). For the purposes of this discussion 'pillow stones' will be referred to as 'head support stones' as not all such arrangements included a stone 'pillow' underneath the skull. Here, grave variations are treated separately from grave types as they occur with different grave types (for example head support stones have been found in plain earth graves, coffins and stone-lined graves) and may be found in the same grave as a different grave variation: for example a grave may contain both head support stones and a layer of charcoal.

A wide range of burial rites were used in late Anglo-Saxon cemeteries in Lincolnshire and Yorkshire. The most frequently found grave types are plain earth graves, which are found in high numbers at most cemeteries, although many of these may have once contained organic structures such as coffins that have not survived the burial environment. Evidence from waterlogged sites shows that many coffins were constructed using small wooden dowels, a technique that meant the entire coffin could decay leaving no trace such as iron nails or fittings. Wooden coffins are evident at many cemeteries, including dowel-built coffins,[9] dug-out coffins,[10] nail-built coffins[11] and clinker-built coffins which may have re-used boat parts.[12] Variations on the plain wooden coffin include wooden planks placed either above or below the body and iron-bound coffins, sometimes interpreted as re-used domestic chests.[13] Some of these chests survive with elaborate iron locks.[14]

Stone-lined graves have been found at many cemeteries,[15] as have partial stone-lined graves.[16] Rare grave types include mortar-lined graves identified at York Minster and St Helen-on-the-Walls,[17] and a tile-lined grave excavated at York Minster.[18] Finally, stone sarcophagi have been excavated at York Minster and St Gregory's Kirkdale (North Yorkshire).[19]

Grave variations identified in Lincolnshire and Yorkshire include the use of head support stones, in the form of a pair of stones placed either side of the skull ('ear-muff stones'), a single stone either by the side or behind the skull (often referred to as 'pillow stones'), or a series of three of more stones surrounding the skull (occasionally described as 'head cists'). Arrangements of stones around the head have been identified at many cemeteries including Fillingham (Lincolshire), Kellington (North Yorkshire) and St Martin's Wharram Percy

(North Yorkshire).[20] White quartz pebbles have been found in graves at Kellington[21] and small stones were placed in the mouths, and, in one case, on the eyes of the deceased at Fillingham.[22] The inclusion of charcoal in graves is present in several cemeteries[23] and hazel rods or 'wands' in the grave are evident because of the waterlogged conditions at St Peter's Barton-upon-Humber.[24] At Addingham (West Yorkshire) graves were marked by small mounds of earth and in contrast at Thwing (East Yorkshire) by wooden posts.[25] Plain stone markers and carved or incised stones were utilised at St. Andrew's Fishergate and St Mark's Lincoln respectively.[26] Grave covers could also be plain stone[27] or carved into both simple and complicated designs.[28] The grave cover arrangements at Wharram Percy and York Minster also included head and foot stones.[29] The use of grave markers and grave covers was probably much more widespread than the scant archaeological evidence would suggest, since evidence for grave markers rarely survives in cemeteries due to later disturbance.[30]

Most late Anglo-Saxon cemeteries in Lincolnshire and Yorkshire, both urban and rural, contain two or three different grave types and between one and three grave variations, which were usually only found in a small number of graves at each cemetery (see Table 1). In contrast, the range of grave types and the high number of individuals accorded a more elaborate burial in the cemetery at York Minster is striking. Here, plain earth graves, coffins, iron-bound chests with locks, stone-lined graves, a tile-lined grave, a mortar-lined grave, a stone sarcophagus and two burials on planks, one of which was probably on part of a boat, were excavated. In addition, the cemetery contained a wide range of grave variations: carved stone grave covers, head and foot stones, grave

Table 1. Range of grave types and grave variations present in urban and rural cemeteries in Lincolnshire and Yorkshire

Site	Urban/rural	Grave Types	Grave Variations
Barrow-upon-Humber[31]	Rural	Plain earth graves; stone-lined graves; coffins	Head support stones; charcoal burials; plain stone grave cover
Kellington[32]	Rural	Plain earth graves	Head support stones; white quartz pebbles; probably marked (no inter-cutting)
St Andrew's Fishergate, York[33]	Urban	Plain earth graves, coffins	One grave with head support stone; grave marker
St Mark's Lincoln[34]	Urban	Plain earth graves; stone-lined graves; possible coffins (identified by the presence of iron nails)	Grave markers (including one carved stone upright marker); charcoal burials
St Martin's Wharram Percy[35]	Rural	Plain earth graves; coffins; stone-lined graves	Head support stones; grave covers, grave markers
Tanner's Row Pontefract[36]	Urban	Plain earth graves; coffins; iron-bound coffins (five with locks)	Stones around the shoulders of one individual

markers, head support stones, charcoal burials and several graves contained artefacts including earrings, finger rings, coins, a dress pin and a key.[37]

The diversity in burial practice observed at York Minster may have been partially due to the lack of later burials disturbing the late Anglo-Saxon graveyard, as much of the excavated areas was sealed by the eleventh-century south transept, protecting these burials from later grave digging and possibly enhancing the chances of survival of different types of burial.[38] However, this diversity in burial type is equally likely to reflect the known high status of the York Minster cemetery at this time. St Peter's (York Minster) was a royal foundation and a bishopric, founded by King Edwin in AD 627.[39] Historical records indicate that at least fourteen people of note (royalty, bishops and noblemen) were buried in York, many of whom were probably buried at St Peter's (see Table 2). It is likely that the variation in mortuary practice at York Minster indicates that individuals of a high social status were using both grave form and burial location as a medium for social display. Interestingly many of the more elaborate burials at York Minster were located in groups, with chest burials clustered together to the north east of the excavations (areas SA and SD), and all of the lined

graves, carved grave covers and the sarcophagus located to the north west (excavation area ST).

The range of different grave types seen at cemeteries across the rest of Britain is similar to that seen in Lincolnshire and Yorkshire although some additional grave types have been excavated. Plain earth graves, coffins and stone-lined graves predominate, but other common grave types include iron-bound coffins or domestic chests, some of which had locks; clinker-built coffins and plank burials.[54] More unusual grave types include two graves at Raunds (Northamptonshire) described as having a clay lining,[55] sand-lined graves identified at Winchester Old Minster (Hampshire),[56] a mortar- and stone-lined grave excavated at St Nicholas Shambles, London[57] and the mortar-lined graves excavated at Wells Cathedral (Somerset).[58] Sarcophagi have been excavated at Raunds and Winchester Old Minster[59] and a lead coffin has been excavated at Staple Gardens Winchester.[60] Some stone-lined graves narrowed around the head, mimicking head support stones and occasionally plain grave cuts were shaped to create a recess for the head.[61] Crypts and mausolea may also have been used for burial during the late Anglo-Saxon period as at Repton (Derbyshire).[62] At most of these sites, both urban

Table 2. Documentary evidence of burials at York

Name	Date of Burial	Location of Burial
Æthelhun *Son of King Edwin*	627 × 633	'in the church of York', Rollason suggests St Peter's[40]
Æthelthryth *Daughter of King Edwin*	627 × 633	'in the church of York', Rollason suggests St Peter's[41]
Edwin (head) *King of Northumbria*	633	His head was buried at St Peter's[42]
Ælfwini *Sub-King of Bernicia*	679	Body brought to York, presumably for burial. Rollason suggests at St Peter's[43]
Eadberht *King of Northumbria*	After 738	'in the city of York, in the same chapel' [as his brother Egbert]. Rollason suggests at St Peter's[44]
Egbert *Archbishop, brother of King Eadberht*	After 738	'in the city of York, in the same chapel' [as his brother Eadberht]. Rollason suggests at St Peter's[45]
Eanbald *Archbishop of York*	796	'in the church of the blessed Apostle Peter'[46]
Osbald *King of Northumbria*	799	'in the church of the city of York'. Rollason suggests at St Peter's[47]
Guthfrith *King of Northumbria*	895	'in the high church', Rollason suggests St Peter's[48]
Swein *King of the Danes*	1014	In St Peter's (although other accounts just say at York)[49]
Siward *Earl, founder of St Olave's church*	1055	In St Olave's church[50]
Tostig *Earl of Northumbria*	1066	Buried at York. Possibly at St Peter's or St Olave's[51]
Ealdred *Archbishop of York*	1069	In St Peter's at his bishop's seat[52]
Thomas *Archbishop of York*	1100	In St Peter's next to Archbishop Ealdred[53]

and rural, between two and four grave types and grave variations were present, as shown above for Lincolnshire and Yorkshire (see Table 3). However, a higher proportion of individuals were buried in a wider range of more elaborate graves at the historically attested high-status cemeteries of Winchester Old Minster, Exeter Cathedral (Devon), St Oswald's Minster, Gloucester and Wells Cathedral (Table 4). It is unlikely that everyone buried at these cemeteries were of high social status, however these cemeteries probably attracted a higher proportion of high-status burials than cemeteries attached to a parish church, contributing to the variation in burial forms and the high

Table 3. *Grave types and grave variations present at North Elmham, Raunds, St Nicholas Shambles in London and Staple Gardens in Winchester*

Site	Urban/rural	Grave types	Grave variations
North Elmham (Norfolk)[67]	Rural	Plain earth grave; possible coffins	None reported
Raunds[68]	Rural	Plain earth graves; stone-lined graves, probable coffins; one sarcophagus	Stones placed around the head and elsewhere in the grave; three possible organic pillows; grave covers; grave markers including at least one stone cross
St Nicholas Shambles, London[69]	Urban	Plain earth graves; coffins; stone-lined; stone- and mortar-lined and tile-lined graves; graves with mortar and chalk floor	Head support stones; stones placed in the mouths of the deceased; charcoal burials; Roman tiles placed on the body
Staple Gardens Winchester[70]	Urban	Plain earth graves; coffins; lead coffin	Head support stones; charcoal burials; post holes probably indicative of grave markers; Roman coins placed in the hands or abdominal areas of skeletons

Table 4. *Grave types and grave variations present at Winchester Old Minster, St Oswald's Gloucester, Exeter Cathedral and Wells Cathedral*

Site	Evidence for status	Grave types	Grave variations
Exeter Cathedral[71]	Seventh-century minster; bishopric of western Wessex in seventh to ninth centuries; re-founded by King Athelstan in tenth century	Plain earth graves; coffins; iron-bound coffins	Head support stones; many charcoal burials
St Oswald's Gloucester[72]	New minster founded in Gloucester in the ninth century; housed relics of St Oswald and became more successful than old minster of St Peter's	Plain earth graves; coffins; chests; stone-lined graves	Head support stones; foot support stones; charcoal burials; grave markers; one grave contained a boar's tusk that was probably deposited deliberately
Wells Cathedral[73]	One of three bishoprics in Wessex from AD 909, however many high-status burials may have taken place at neighbouring Glastonbury.[74]	Plain earth graves; coffins; charred boards interpreted as planks; mortar-lined graves; one grave with a mortar floor; shaped plain earth graves with head recesses; stone-lined graves and monolithic stone coffins in the Saxo-Norman period.	Plain stone, shaped and sculpted grave covers; foot stones; one grave has possible head support stones
Winchester Old Minster[75]	Royal foundation; bishopric from seventh century; burial place of the kings of Wessex	Plain earth graves; coffins; chests (some with locks); stone-lined graves; many sarcophagi	Head support stones; charcoal burials; incised grave markers; foot stones; one burial containing a layer of yellow or orange sand

number of elaborate graves within these cemeteries. Charcoal spreads were particularly common at high-status cemeteries, and were present in 57% of graves at Exeter Cathedral, 10% of graves at Winchester Old Minster, 39.3% of graves at Winchester New Minster and 21.4% of graves at St Oswald's Gloucester.[63] Indeed, higher proportions of charcoal burials may be identified during smaller excavations, particularly if the trenches are located close to a church. The charcoal burials at Winchester Old and New Minsters were frequently located close to or inside the minster buildings[64] and all but one of the charcoal burials at St Oswald's Gloucester were located close to the church.[65] Burials with deposits of charcoal were frequently coffined, and many charcoal burials at Exeter Cathedral, Winchester Old Minster, Castle Green Hereford and St Oswald's Gloucester were in iron-bound coffins.[66]

Clusters of elaborate graves, including charcoal burials are also present in several cemeteries. For example, at Raunds burial 5283 had a grave cover and may once have been marked by a stone cross. The burial was located just 2 m from the church, close to the west doorway and was described by Andrew Boddington as a 'founder's grave'. Boddington suggested that the area of the cemetery immediately adjacent to this grave was a particularly prestigious burial location, as burials were particularly dense and a further grave with a carved cover was located in this area.[75] At Winchester Old Minster, sarcophagi and iron-bound coffins, in addition to the charcoal burials mentioned above, were more common both inside and close to the outside of the church and in the vicinity of the grave interpreted as that of St. Swithun. By contrast, in trench XXIX, located to the west of the apse, no stone-lined graves, elaborate coffins or charcoal burials were identified.[76] The area close to the church also contained approximately 20% more males than females.[77] In sum, the evidence from Raunds and Winchester Old Minster shows that elaborate burials were more commonly located close to church buildings or doorways.

Overall the evidence presented thus far indicates that late Anglo-Saxon burial practice was not egalitarian, but rather that the choice of burial ground, location

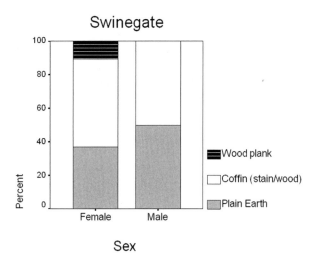

Figure 1. Proportion of males and females accorded different grave types at Swinegate.

within the cemetery and grave form were influenced by the identity of the deceased including the importance of the deceased and their family.

Osteology and Funerary Practice

Osteological evidence of age and sex were compared with the different funerary rites present at York Minster,[78] Swinegate[79] and St Andrew's Fishergate in York,[80] St Peter's Barton-upon-Humber,[81] St Mark's Lincoln[82] and Barrow-upon-Humber.[83] The age and sex of the deceased, ascertained using standard osteological methods,[84] were compared with the grave type, grave variations and grave location.

This study revealed that there was no relationship between the sex of the deceased and grave type at each of the six cemeteries. Most grave types were used for the burial of males and females, in roughly equal proportions. At York Minster males and females were accorded all of the different grave types apart from the use of clinker-built planks; this grave type was only present in one excavated grave at the cemetery, that of an adult male. At

Table 5. Chi-squared tests between sex and grave type

Cemetery	? coffins treated as coffins		? coffins treated as plain earth graves	
	χ^2	p	χ^2	p
York Minster	1.324	1.000	1.312	1.000
Swinegate	2.732	0.311	2.732	0.311
St Andrew's Fishergate	0.008	1.000	0.711	1.000
St Peter's Barton-upon-Humber	0.060	0.977	0.271	0.899
Barrow-upon-Humber	0.769	1.000	2.977	0.269
St Mark's Lincoln	5.530	0.055	1.268	0.444
All six cemeteries combined	0.782	0.938	0.656	0.951

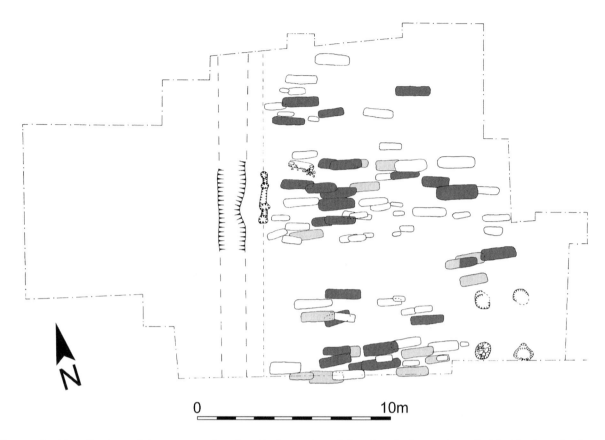

Figure 2. Distribution of the graves of males (dark grey) and females (light grey) at St Mark's Lincoln during Phase VIII. After Gilmour and Stocker 1986, 15.

Swinegate, similar proportions of males and females were buried in plain earth graves and in coffins. However, only two sexed adults were buried with planks in the entire cemetery, both of whom were female (Fig. 1). Very little evidence of different grave types was present at St Andrew's Fishergate, however a small number of graves of both males and females contained tentative evidence of coffins, occasional iron nails or red-brown staining on the bones, indicative of iron, probably nails, in the grave. At Barrow-upon-Humber most of the burials were in plain earth graves, and equal proportions of males and females were buried in more elaborate graves. Only one sexed adult was buried in a stone-lined grave, and this was a male. Many individuals, both male and female were buried with either coffins or planks at St Peter's Barton-upon-Humber. One grave at the cemetery was partially lined with stones; however this was the grave of a child who could not be sexed.[85] At St Mark's Lincoln the majority of burials were in plain earth graves, however small numbers of both males and females were buried with possible coffins (identified by the presence of iron nails in the grave). One grave was lined with stone, and this contained an adult female. Non-significant chi-squared tests support the finding that grave types were not related to the sex of the deceased (see Table 5).

A similar pattern was revealed when grave variations

were compared with the sex of the deceased. Due to the low frequencies of grave variations in most cemeteries, only head support stones at St Peter's Barton-upon-Humber, and charcoal burials at York Minster will be discussed. At St Peter's Barton-upon-Humber, approximately the same proportion of males and females were buried with head support stones. At York Minster, of the fourteen charcoal burials identified, just five adults could be sexed with any certainty: three males and two females. Overall this study showed that most grave types and grave variations were used for equal proportions of males and females at each of the cemeteries, although some of the more unusual grave types were only used for one sex. In these cases no importance should be attached to the fact that, for example, the only sexed adult in a stone-lined grave at Barrow-upon-Humber was male, as any other adults buried in stone-lined graves that either were not excavated, or that could not be sexed accurately, could conceivably be female, redressing this imbalance.

The spatial analysis of burials of males and females revealed that the sex of the deceased did not influence the location of burial within most of these cemeteries. The exception to this was St Mark's Lincoln, where a higher number of males were buried to the north of the probable church dating to Phase VIII (located in the south-east corner of the excavated area), and a higher number of

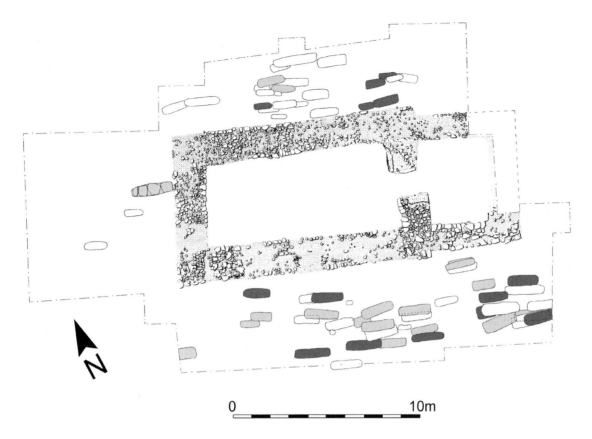

Figure 3. Distribution of the graves of males (dark grey) and females (light grey) at St Mark's Lincoln during Phase IX. After Gilmour and Stocker 1986, 18.

females were buried to the south of the stone church, during Phase IX (Figs 2 and 3 respectively). The sex-related patterning in grave location was not statistically significant when the two phases were treated separately, but was statistically significant when the two phases were combined.[86] As has been previously noted, spatial imbalances between male and female burials have been identified at Raunds and Winchester Old Minster.[87] This evidence indicates that at some cemeteries, male burials were preferentially placed in prestigious areas close to an important grave, structure or the church itself. In most cemeteries, however, the sex of the deceased does not appear to have influenced the choice of grave type, grave variation or the location of the grave within the cemetery.

Most of the different grave types in each cemetery were used for the burial of individuals of most age groups (see Table 6), including the very young and very old, although the more unusual grave types were only used for the burial of individuals within some age groups. At York Minster individuals in all age categories apart from infants were accorded different grave types. In some cases a burial type may have been used for individuals in just one or two age categories, however these were usually the more unusual grave types including the sarcophagus, plank burials, stone-lined graves and chests, all found in only a small number of

graves. Only one infant burial was recorded for York Minster, and this was in a plain earth grave. At Swinegate, individuals in each of the different age groups *including infants* were buried in plain earth graves, coffins or with wooden planks. The only exception to this was for mid-adults, none of whom was buried with a plank. Individuals of all age groups apart from infants were accorded coffined burial at St Andrew's Fishergate and St Mark's Lincoln, even though few coffins were identified at either of these cemeteries. The individuals buried in stone-lined graves at St Mark's include a child and a mid-adult. Most of the burials at Barrow-upon-Humber were in plain earth graves, but once again individuals in all age categories apart from infants could be buried in either a stone-lined grave (child, young adult and older adult) or a coffin (mid-adult and old adult). This evidence shows that individuals in certain age groups were not prohibited certain forms of burial, and no strong relationship between age and grave type was identified (see Table 7). At St Peter's Barton-upon-Humber, where over 600 burials dating to the late Anglo-Saxon period have been excavated, the age-related trend in grave type is, however, clear (Fig. 4). Here, while individuals of all age groups could be buried in plain earth graves, coffins or with planks, individuals were *more likely* to be buried in a more elaborate burial with increasing age.[89] This pattern was duplicated when the data from all of the cemeteries were combined, even if the material from St Peter's (which made up approximately half of the total data set) was excluded (see Table 7). This would suggest that the mourners were more likely to bury older individuals in a more elaborate grave, and/or that those who were buried in more elaborate graves were from social groups more likely to survive to a greater age.

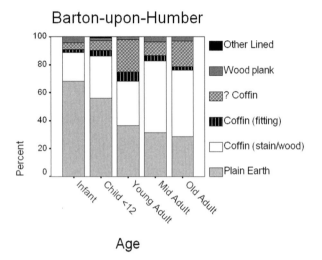

Figure 4. Proportion of individuals of different age groups accorded different grave types at St Peter's Barton-upon-Humber

Table 6. Broad age categories used for the present research[88]

Age Category	Age range
Infant	Up to one year
Child	One to twelve years
Young Adult	Thirteen to twenty five years
Mid Adult	Twenty six to forty five years
Old Adult	Forty six years and older

A range of grave variations were also accorded individuals of all age groups. For example, at York Minster grave covers were found above a young child aged between three and five years, an older child aged between ten and twelve years, an adolescent and several adults. In addition, at St Peter's Barton-upon-Humber, head support stones were found in the graves of individuals of all ages, including two infants, four young children and in one grave containing both a female mid-adult and foetus. Clusters of infant burials in late Anglo-Saxon cemeteries, often located close to the walls of a church, have been frequently discussed in recent research.[90] The location of these burials close to church walls has led to the suggestion that the mourners believed that these infants would be blessed every time rainwater dripped off the church roof onto the graves, and clusters of infant burials have even been used to suggest the location of a lost church, for example at Hartlepool (Cleveland).[91] The tradition of burying infants under the eaves of buildings can be traced back to the Roman period[92] and infant burials were occasionally associated with buildings in early Anglo-Saxon settlements,[93] although obviously burial close to buildings has not been interpreted as a form of symbolic baptism during the Roman or early Anglo-Saxon period. Whatever the intended symbolism of infant burials located close to churches, it appears that at some cemeteries certain types of burial (in this case close to the church walls) may have been seen to be more appropriate for the very young.

The spatial analysis undertaken for the cemeteries investigated in detail identified clusters of infant and, sometimes, child burials at all of the five cemeteries analysed.[94] An increased density of the burials of infants and young children were observed close to the walls of the church at St Peter's Barton-upon-Humber and close to the possible timber church at St Andrew's Fishergate. Many of the infants and young children excavated at St Mark's Lincoln were from graves under the floor of the first stone church, which is believed to be in a slightly different location from the earlier timber church, however this pattern was not statistically significant. It is possible that these burials were protected from disturbance by

*Table 7. Kruskal-Wallis tests between age and grave type. *denotes statistically significant results*

Cemetery	? coffins treated as coffins		? coffins treated as plain earth graves	
	H	p	H	p
York Minster	5.536	0.237	8.041	0.090
Swinegate	4.905	0.086	4.905	0.086
St Andrew's Fishergate	1.900	0.168	0.210	0.647
St Peter's Barton-upon-Humber	32.373	<0.001*	15.630	0.001*
Barrow-upon-Humber	1.907	0.385	2.225	0.329
St Mark's Lincoln	1.941	0.379	0.021	0.885
All six cemeteries combined	41.421	<0.001*	28.672	<0.001*
All except St Peter's Barton-upon-Humber	12.384	0.015*	13.838	0.008*

the floor of the first stone church. At Swinegate, all of the infants and most of the young children were buried in trenches in the southern part of the cemetery.[95] These trenches were noted for the density of burial present and are close to the probable location of St Benet's church, which was not found during the excavations.[96] No strong clusters of infant and child burials were identified at York Minster.[97] The only infant burial excavated was buried in excavation area XK (in the westernmost trench of the excavations), and most of the children (under the age of twelve) were buried in excavation areas ST, SA and SD (located towards the east of the excavations). It was, however, impossible to determine the relationship of the cluster of sub-adult burials to the church, as this has not yet been located archaeologically. No clusters of individuals of older age groups were present at any of the five cemeteries analysed.

Discussion

The present research into late Anglo-Saxon burial rites in Lincolnshire and Yorkshire and comparison with contemporary cemeteries from across Britain has shown that there was a great deal of variation in burial rites during the seventh to eleventh centuries. It is becoming increasingly clear that later Anglo-Saxon burial was not egalitarian and that the Anglo-Saxon Church did not dictate the form that burial should take. Rather, burial continued to be used as a medium for social display, albeit within a more restricted range of burial rites that were appropriate for burials within a Christian cemetery.[98]

Most of the different grave types and grave variations described above are found in cemeteries over a large geographical area. There do not appear to be any strong differences in the numbers and variety of different grave types and grave variations employed in rural and urban cemeteries, however high-status cemeteries such as York Minster, St Oswald's Gloucester and Winchester Old Minster contain both a wider range of different burial rites and a higher number of individuals buried in more elaborate graves, especially close to or inside the church. This is important, as it suggests that the many of the social elite were choosing to bury their dead in the cemeteries attached to high-status churches, and that the funerary practices employed in these burials could be used to emphasise further the status of the deceased and their family. This may have led to the introduction of more innovative burial rites within high-status cemeteries, as the social elite sought to mark the graves of their kin in more elaborate and unusual ways. In less prestigious cemeteries the local elites were also using funerary practice to display the importance and/or wealth of their families. Thus at many cemeteries a small proportion of graves were distinguished by the presence of a burial rite that was more unusual for that cemetery. These types of burial are frequently found in close proximity with each other and often date to quite a short period of cemetery use, for

example the cluster of charcoal burials identified at St Mark's Lincoln.[99] Stone sculpture was also probably used for social display. Freestanding monuments, many of which had a funerary function, are much more common in high-status cemeteries including York Minster and Winchester Old Minster, and most examples of architectural sculpture are also found at high-status ecclesiastical sites.[100] However many churches in Lincolnshire and Yorkshire contained one or two pieces of post-Scandinavian stone sculpture that probably had a funerary function.[101] Graves marked with stone sculpture may have been those of church founders and their families.[102] Other cemeteries contain a larger number of sculpted monuments (although not as many as is found at high-status ecclesiastical sites) including St Mark's Lincoln, St Mary-le-Wigford Lincoln, Creeton, Manton and Stow, all in Lincolnshire[103] and Lythe, St Mary Bishophill Senior in York, Brompton-in-Allertonshire and Stanwick in Yorkshire.[104] These sites have been interpreted as Anglo-Saxon trading centres, leading David Stocker to suggest that the abundance of sculpture at these sites reflects the aspirations of a competitive mercantile elite.[105] The analysis of funerary practices at York Minster, Swinegate, St Andrew's Fishergate, Barrow-upon-Humber, St Peter's Barton-upon-Humber and St Mark's Lincoln has shown that individuals in all age groups could be accorded most of the different grave types and grave variations, but that they were more likely to be buried in a more elaborate manner with increasing age. This indicates that either elaborate burials were more appropriate but not exclusively for older individuals, or that individuals who were buried in more elaborate graves were living longer on average than those buried in plain graves. Spatial analysis has shown that infants and young children were frequently buried in particular locations within the cemetery, and in some cemeteries the graves of infants and young children cluster around the walls of the church.

The present research has also shown that both grave form and grave location were not governed by the sex of the deceased. The only exception to this was for the spatial organisation of graves at St Mark's Lincoln. This lack of sex-related variation in funerary practice is also seen in contemporary cemeteries across Britain, where there is little evidence of burial rite or grave location being influenced by the sex of the deceased. Examples where sex-related patterning in funerary rite have been identified include high numbers of males buried in iron-bound coffins with layers of charcoal at St Oswald's Gloucester and Winchester Old Minster;[106] increased numbers of male burials close to the church at Winchester Old Minster;[107] and the increased proportion of males buried south of the church within the primary zone at Raunds.[108] This indicates that adult males were more likely to be accorded elaborate burial in a prestigious location during the late Anglo-Saxon period, but this was a privilege from which adult females and children were not excluded.

The evidence from late Anglo-Saxon cemeteries contrasts with that from early Anglo-Saxon cemeteries, where sex strongly influenced the choice of grave goods placed in the grave. This would suggest that different aspects of social identity were influencing funerary practice in the eighth to eleventh centuries. Gender does not appear to have been important in determining the form and location of the grave in the later Anglo-Saxon period, although the gender of the deceased may have influenced any rites performed during the funeral that do not leave any archaeological trace.[109] This is, perhaps, not surprising given the decrease in the number of graves in which gender was signalled in the seventh century.[110] This was a period when there was a concomitant emphasis of the masculine gender in more elaborate graves, especially those close to or under barrows.[111] This change was interpreted by Nick Stoodley as a shift in emphasis to the elaboration of the burials of the (usually male) elite, with inheritance and authority passing through the male line.[112] This point was expanded on by Dawn Hadley, who suggested that later Anglo-Saxon burials were not symbolising solely gender (or age), but that family or household status, frequently symbolised through adult male burials, was more important.[113] Hadley has also drawn attention to the masculine symbolism on some tenth-century sculptures and has suggested that these monuments, which are few in number, may have served to commemorate the family as much as individuals,[114] and David Stocker has commented on the symbolism of so-called hogback monuments, many of which have house-like features (including a roof) and which may also have served to commemorate the family or household.[115] This emphasis on family/household or individual status is also evident in the high number of elaborate burials in high-status cemeteries or prestigious locations within cemeteries. The change in social organisation seen through the seventh century towards the increasing importance of household status[116] over and above that of gender eventually led to the lack of gender-specific burial practices in the late Anglo-Saxon period, the occasional association between adult males and particular grave types, the occurrence of clusters of male burials in prominent positions in certain cemeteries and the importance of elaborate burial rites in social display.

Acknowledgements

Permission to study the material from St Peter's, Barton-upon-Humber in advance of publication was granted by Martin Allfrey (English Heritage), Caroline Atkins, Warwick Rodwell and Kirsty Rodwell. Access to material from Swinegate and St Andrew's, Fishergate, York was granted by York Archaeological Trust. For Barrow-upon-Humber, access to the draft excavation report in advance of publication was granted by Humber Archaeology Partnership and access to the skeletal material was given by North Lincolnshire Museum, Scunthorpe. City of Lincoln Archaeology Unit and Lincoln City and County Museum granted access to the archive for St Mark's, Lincoln. In addition, I would like to thank Richard Hall, Christine MacDonnell, Annie Jowett, Christine Kyriacou, Mark Whyman, Jane MacCormish (all from York Archaeological Trust), Dave Evans (Humber Archaeology Partnership), Kevin Leahy (North Lincolnshire Museum), Jen Mann (City of Lincoln Archaeology Unit), Anthea Bolyston (University of Bradford), Tony Wilmott (English Heritage), Ian Roberts (West Yorkshire Archaeology Service), Naomi Field (Lindsey Archaeological Services), Ian Tyers and Cathy Groves (ARCUS Dendrochronology) for their assistance throughout this study. I would like to thank all of the Sites and Monuments and National Monuments Records officers and archaeologists who helped me undertake this study. I am also greatly indebted to Dawn Hadley, Andrew Chamberlain and Annia Cherryson for enlightening discussions about this research, and to Alan Ogden, Howard Williams and the anonymous reviewer for their comments on this paper. Any errors, however, remain my own. This research was funded by a White Rose Studentship awarded by the Universities of Sheffield, York and Leeds.

Notes

1. Meaney and Hawkes 1970, 51; Biddle 1976, 69, but see critiques by Morris 1983; Boddington 1990.
2. Hadley 2000; Lucy and Reynolds 2002.
3. Reynolds 1997; Richards 2002.
4. Hodder 1980, 168; Geake 1997, 127; Tarlow 1997, 139; Carver 1999, 8.
5. Hadley 2000; Hadley 2001; Hadley 2004; Hadley and Buckberry 2005.
6. But see Daniell 1997; Hadley 2001.
7. Lucy 1998; Stoodley 1999a.
8. Of these 29 dated to the mid Anglo-Saxon period, 52 to the late Anglo-Saxon period and 17 dated to the mid to late Anglo-Saxon period, Buckberry 2004, Chapter 3.
9. Rodwell and Rodwell 1982, 301; Bagwell and Tyers 2001.
10. Rodwell and Rodwell 1982, 301; Bagwell and Tyers 2001.
11. Dawes and Magilton 1980, 14; Gilmour and Stocker 1986, 16; Wilmott 1987, 342.

12. Rodwell and Rodwell 1982, 291–2
13. Kjølbye-Biddle 1995, 517; Phillips and Heywood 1995, 83. One of the individuals buried in a chest at York Minster was too tall to fit in the chest, and thus was buried in a flexed position (Phillips and Heywood 1995, 83). This would suggest that the chest had been re-used and was not constructed solely for the purpose of the burial. For other examples of iron bound coffins see Phillips and Heywood 1995, 86–7; Hall and Whyman 1996, 62, 99; Adamson and Abramson 1997, 3–4, 22–3; Hadley 2003, 99.
14. Kjølbye-Biddle 1995, 489; Hall and Whyman 1996, 99.
15. Gilmour and Stocker 1986, 20; Buckberry and Hadley 2001, 11.
16. Reynolds 1979; Dawes and Magilton 1980, 15; Caroline Atkins pers. comm.; Jen Mann pers. comm.
17. Dawes and Magilton 1980, 15; Phillips and Heywood 1995, 85, 88.
18. Phillips and Heywood 1995, 88.
19. Phillips and Heywood 1995, 82; Rahtz and Watts 1997, 422.
20. Bell and Beresford 1987; Mytum 1994, 21; Buckberry and Hadley 2001, 13.

21. Mytum 1994, 21.
22. Buckberry and Hadley 2001, 15–16.
23. Gilmour and Stocker 1986, 16, 20; Phillips and Heywood 1995, 87–8; Grainger unpublished.
24. Caroline Atkins, pers. comm.
25. Adams 1996, 181–2; Geake 1997, 159.
26. Gilmour and Stocker 1986, 21; Stroud and Kemp 1993, 153.
27. Buckberry and Hadley 2001, 11; Grainger unpublished.
28. Bell and Beresford 1987, 58; Beresford and Hurst 1990, 64; Phillips and Heywood 1995, 84.
29. Bell and Beresford 1987, 58; Beresford and Hurst 1990, 64; Phillips and Heywood 1995.
30. Stocker 2000, 180; see also Cherryson this volume.
31. Boden and Whitwell 1979; Buckberry 2004, 31–3, 343–4; Grainger unpublished.
32. Mytum 1994, 21.
33. Stroud and Kemp 1993, 153.
34. Gilmour and Stocker 1986, 15–21; Steane, Darling, Mann, Vince and Young 2001, 284; Buckberry 2004, 30, 186.
35. Bell and Beresford 1987, 56.
36. Wilmott 1986; Wilmott 1987, 342; Geake 1997, 191; Tony Wilmott pers. comm.
37. Phillips and Heywood 1995, 75–92.
38. Phillips and Heywood 1995, 75.
39. Bede **HE** ii, 14; Colgrave and Mynors 1969, 187–9.
40. Bede **HE** ii: 14. Colgrave and Mynors 1969, 187–9; Rollason 1998, 146.
41. *Ibid.*
42. Bede **HE** ii: 20. Colgrave and Mynors 1969, 205; Rollason 1998, 135–6.
43. *Vita Wilfridi* 24. Colgrave 1927, 51; Rollason 1998, 146.
44. ASC 738; Chronicle of Æthelweard 2:15. Whitelock 1955, 161; Campbell 1962, 22; Rollason 1998, 147.
45. ASC 738; Chronicle of Æthelweard 2:15. Whitelock 1955, 161; Campbell 1962, 22; Rollason 1998, 147.
46. History of the Kings. Whitelock 1955, 249; Rollason 1998, 147.
47. History of the Kings. Whitelock 1955, 250; Rollason 1998, 148.
48. Chronicle of Æthelweard 4:3. Campbell 1962, 51; Rollason 1998, 173.
49. Geffrei Gaimar History of the English. Rollason 1998, 174.
50. ASC D 1055. Rollason 1998, 175.
51. William of Malmesbury Deeds of the Kings of England. Rollason 1998, 210.
52. ASC D 1069. Rollason 1998, 198.
53. Chronicle of the Archbishops of York. Rollason 1998, 199.
54. Shoesmith 1980, 36–8; Heighway and Bryant 1999, 208–15; Kjølbye-Biddle 1995, 517; Rodwell 1993, 254; Cramp 1969, 33.
55. Boddington 1996, 41.
56. Kjølbye-Biddle 1992, 227.
57. Schofield, Thompson, Hill and Riviére 1988, 18–19.
58. Rodwell 2001, 65, 67.
59. Boddington 1996, 34; Kjølbye-Biddle 1975, 106–7; Kjølbye-Biddle 1992, 227–8.
60. Kipling and Scobie 1990, 9; Scobie 1994, 6.
61. Shoesmith 1980, 29–30; Rodwell 2001, 65–8.
62. Biddle 1986, 16, 22.
63. Henderson and Bidwell 1982, 154–5; Kjølbye-Biddle 1992, 229; Heighway and Bryant 1999, 202. It should be noted that far fewer graves were excavated at Exeter than at Winchester Old Minster and Winchester New Minster.
64. Kjølbye-Biddle 1975, 106; Kjølbye-Biddle 1992, 229.
65. Heighway and Bryant 1999, 202.
66. Henderson and Bidwell 1982, 154–5; Kjølbye-Biddle 1992, 229; Shoesmith 1980; Heighway and Bryant 1999, 202.
67. Wade-Martins 1980, 188.
68. Boddington 1996, 37–48.
69. Schofield, Thompson, Hill and Riviére 1988, 18–26.
70. Kipling and Scobie 1990; Scobie 1994.
71. Henderson and Bidwell 1982, 152–6.

72. Hare 1999, 33–4; Heighway and Bryant 1999, 202–7.
73. Rodwell 2001, 65–70, 105–10.
74. Rodwell 2001, 2; Annia Cherryson, pers. comm.
75. Kjølbye-Biddle 1975, 98–107; Kjølbye-Biddle 1992, 222–33; Biddle and Kjølbye-Biddle 1995; Tweddle, Biddle and Kjølbye-Biddle 1995 , 273–323.
76. Boddington 1996, 11, 36–7.
77. Kjølbye-Biddle 1975, 98, 105–6; Kjølbye-Biddle 1992, 223, 228.
78. Phillips and Heywood 1995; Buckberry 2004, 25–6, 486–7. All data used for this analysis was obtained from the published excavation report.
79. Pearson 1989; Pearson 1990; Buckberry 2004, 23–5, 485. Excavation data including evidence of funerary practice was obtained from the archive held by York Archaeological Trust. All osteological analysis was undertaken by the present author.
80. Stroud and Kemp 1993; Buckberry 2004, 185. Data for analysis was obtained from the published excavation report, Stroud and Kemp 1993, and from the site archive held at York Archaeological Trust.
81. Rodwell and Rodwell 1982; Buckberry 2004, 30–1, 345–6. Over 600 burials dating to Phase E (up to the twelfth century) were used in this study. Site data for St Peter's Barton-upon-Humber was obtained from Caroline Atkins Consultants with the permission of Warwick Rodwell. Osteological data was taken from the recording forms produced by the late Juliet Rogers, now held by English Heritage at York.
82. Gilmour and Stocker 1986; Steane *et al.* 2001; Buckberry 2004, 28–30, 377. Data used for this analysis was obtained from the published excavation report, Gilmour and Stocker 1986, and from the site archive held at Lincoln City and County Museum.
83. Boden and Whitwell 1979; Buckberry 2004, 31–3, 343–4; Grainger unpublished. Site data was obtained from the excavation archive and draft excavation report, Grainger unpublished, held by Humber Archaeology Partnership and all osteological analysis was undertaken by the present author.
84. As described in Buikstra and Ubelaker 1994.
85. It is generally agreed that it is not possible to sex sub-adult skeletons using the morphology of the bones (Saunders 1992, 4).
86. Phase VIII $\chi^2=5.128$, p=0.105; Phase IX $\chi^2=3.338$, p=0.196; Phases VIII and IX combined $\chi^2=9.648$, p=0.013.
87. Boddington 1996, 13, 36–7, 55; Kjølbye-Biddle 1992, 227.
88. The following age categories were used throughout this research: foetus (less than forty weeks *in utero*); infant (birth to one year, however babies under one month old were occasionally referred to as neonates); young child (one to six years); older child (six to twelve years); adolescent (thirteen to seventeen years); young adult (eighteen to twenty five years); mid-adult (twenty six to forty five years); and older adult (forty six years and older). These age categories were combined as follows for statistical and illustrative purposes: infant (up to one year); child (one to twelve years); young adult (thirteen to twenty five years – this age category included adolescents following research on the Anglo-Saxon age of majority (see Crawford 1991, 19; Keufler 1991, 826)); mid-adult (twenty six to forty five years); and older adult (forty six years and older).
89. $\chi^2=32.373$, p<0.001.
90. Crawford 1993, 88; Lucy and Reynolds 2002, 17–20.
91. Crawford 1993, 88.
92. Watts 1989, 372.
93. Powlesland 1997, 164.
94. Spatial analysis could not be undertaken for the cemetery at Barrow-upon-Humber.
95. St Peter's Barton-upon-Humber: H=8.014, p=0.046; St Andrew's Fishergate (although this cluster was only approaching statistical significance): H=5.936, p=0.051; St Mark's Lincoln: H=6.064, p=0.109; Swinegate: H=14.794, p=0.002.
96. Pearson 1989; Pearson 1990.
97. York Minster: H=1.096, p=0.778.
98. Hadley and Buckberry 2005.

99. Gilmour and Stocker 1986, 16; Hadley 2001, 99.
100. Cramp 1986, 101–2; Sidebottom 2000, 213–4.
101. Richards 2000, 160; Stocker 2000, 180; Stocker and Everson 2001, 224–5.
102. Richards 2000, 160; Stocker 2000, 180.
103. Stocker 2000, 183.
104. Stocker 2000, 204–5.
105. Stocker 2000, 189; Stocker and Everson 2001, 225.
106. Kjølbye-Biddle 1992, 228; Heighway and Bryant 1999, 208–10. It should be noted that the males in elaborate graves and/or buried close to the church at Winchester Old Minster may have been monks.
107. Kjølbye-Biddle 1992, 227.
108. Boddington 1996, 13, 55.
109. Howard Williams, pers. comm.
110. Stoodley 1999b, 101–3.
111. Ibid., 101–3.
112. Ibid., 104–5.
113. Hadley 2004.
114. Ibid.
115. Stocker 2000, 198.
116. Stoodley 1999b, 104–5.

Bibliography

Adams, M. 1996. Excavation of a pre-conquest cemetery at Addingham, West Yorkshire, *Medieval Archaeol.*, **40**, 151–91.

Adamson, C. H. and Abramson, P. 1997. *Thornton Steward to Sowden Beck water pipeline. Archaeological excavation and watching brief for Yorkshire Water Services Ltd*, Unpublished excavation report. Northern Archaeological Associates. Available at Northallerton SMR.

Bagwell, T. and Tyers, I. 2001. *Dendrochronological analysis of a coffin assemblage from Swinegate, York, North Yorkshire, Project Report 575p.* Unpublished dendrochronology report. Sheffield: ARCUS Dendrochronology. Supplied by ARCUS Dendrochronology.

Bell, R. D. and Beresford, M. W. 1987. *Wharram Percy: the church of St Martin*, Wharram: a Study of Settlement of the Yorkshire Wolds Volume III. The Society for Medieval Archaeology Monograph Series No. 11, London: Society for Medieval Archaeology.

Beresford, M. and Hurst, J. 1990. *The English Heritage book of Wharram Percy, deserted medieval village*, London: Batsford.

Biddle, M. 1976. The archaeology of the Church: a widening horizon, in P. Addyman and Morris, R. (eds), *The archaeological study of churches*, Council for British Archaeology Research Report 13, 65–71, London: CBA.

Biddle, M. 1986. Archaeology, architecture and the cult of saints in Anglo-Saxon England, in Butler, L. A. S. and Morris, R. K. (eds), *The Anglo-Saxon Church*, Council for British Archaeology Research Report 60, 1–31, London: CBA.

Biddle, M. and Kjølbye-Biddle, B. 1995. The excavated sculptures from Winchester, in Tweddle, D., Biddle, M. and Kjølbye-Biddle, B. (eds), *Corpus of Anglo-Saxon stone sculpture volume IV: South-East England*, 96–107, Oxford: Oxford University Press.

Boddington, A. 1990. Models of burial, settlement and worship: the final phase reviewed, in Southworth, E. (ed.) *Anglo-Saxon cemeteries: a reappraisal*, 177–99, Stroud: Sutton.

Boddington, A. 1996. *Raunds Furnells. The Anglo-Saxon church and churchyard*, English Heritage Archaeological Report 7, London: English Heritage.

Boden, J. M. and Whitwell, J. B. 1979. Barrow-upon-Humber, *Lincolnshire Hist. and Archaeol.*, **14**, 66–7.

Buckberry, J. L. 2004. 'A social and anthropological analysis of conversion period and later Anglo-Saxon cemeteries in Lincolnshire and Yorkshire', unpublished PhD Thesis, University of Sheffield.

Buckberry, J. L. and Hadley, D. M. 2001. Excavations at Chapel Road, Fillingham, *Lincolnshire Hist. and Archaeol.*, **36**, 11–18.

Buikstra, J. and Ubelaker, D. H. 1994. *Standards for data collection from human skeletal remains*, Arkansas: Arkansas Archeological Survey.

Campbell, A. (ed. and trans.) 1962. *The chronicle of Æthelweard.* London: Thomas Nelson and Sons.

Carver, M. 1999. Cemetery and society at Sutton Hoo: five awkward questions and four contradictory answers, in Karkov, C., Wickham-

Crowley, K. and Young, B. (eds), *Spaces of the living and the dead: an archaeological dialogue*, American Early Medieval Studies 3, 1–14, Oxford: Oxbow.

Colgrave, B. (ed. and trans.) 1927. *The life of Bishop Wilfrid by Eddius Stephanus.* Cambridge: Cambridge University Press.

Colgrave, B. and Mynors, R. A. B. (eds and trans.) 1969. *Bede's ecclesiastical history of the English people.* Oxford: Oxford University Press.

Cramp, R. J. 1969. Excavations at the Saxon monastic sites of Wearmouth and Jarrow Co. Durham: an interim report, *Medieval Archaeol.*, **13**, 21–66.

Cramp, R. J. 1986. The furnishing and sculptural decoration of Anglo-Saxon churches, in Butler, L. A. S. and Morris, R. K. (eds), *The Anglo-Saxon Church*, Council for British Archaeology Research Report 60, 101–4, London: CBA.

Crawford, S. 1991. When do Anglo-Saxon children count?, *Jnl. of Theoretical Archaeol.*, **2**, 17–24.

Crawford, S. 1993. Children, death and the afterlife in Anglo-Saxon England, *Anglo-Saxon Stud. in Archaeology and History,* **6**, 83–91.

Daniell, C. 1997. *Death and burial in medieval England*, London: Routledge.

Dawes, J. D. and Magilton, J. R. 1980. *The cemetery of St Helen-on-the-Walls, Aldwark*, The archaeology of York 12/1. The medieval cemeteries, York: CBA.

Geake, H. 1997. The *use of grave-goods in conversion-period England c. 600–c. 850*, BAR British Series, 261, Oxford: British Archaeological Reports.

Gilmour, B. J. J. and Stocker, D. A. 1986. *St. Mark's church and cemetery*, The Archaeology of Lincoln xiii-i, London: CBA.

Grainger, G. unpublished. *Excavations at St Chads, Barrow-on-Humber, 1977–78*, Draft of unpublished excavation report. Provided by Humber Archaeology Partnership in advance of publication.

Hadley, D. M. 2000. Burial practices in the northern Danelaw, c. 650–1100, *Northern Hist.*, **36**, 199–216.

Hadley, D. M. 2001. *Death in medieval England*, Stroud: Tempus.

Hadley, D. M. 2003. Whitton, Lincolnshire, *Current Archaeol.*, **186**, 234–7.

Hadley, D. M. 2004. Negotiating gender, family and status in Anglo-Saxon burial practices in England c. 600–950, in Brubaker, L. and Smith, J. (eds), Gender in the early medieval world. East and west, 300–900, 301–23, Cambridge: Cambridge University Press.

Hadley, D. M. and Buckberry, J. L. 2005. Caring for the dead in late Anglo-Saxon England, in Tinti, F. (ed.) *Pastoral care in late Anglo-Saxon England*, 121–47, Woodbridge: Boydell.

Hall, R. A. and Whyman, M. 1996. Settlement and monasticism at Ripon, North Yorkshire, from the 7th to the 11th centuries A.D., *Medieval Archaeol.*, **40**, 62–150.

Hare, M. 1999. The documentary evidence for the history of St Oswald's, Gloucester to 1086 AD, in Heighway, C. and Bryant, R. (eds), *The golden Minster. The Anglo-Saxon Minster and later medieval priory of St Oswald at Gloucester*, Council for British Archaeology Research Report 117, 33–45, London: CBA.

Heighway, C. and Bryant, R. 1999. *The golden Minster. The Anglo-Saxon Minster and later medieval priory of St Oswald at Gloucester*, Council for British Archaeology Research Report, 117, London: CBA.

Henderson, C. G. and Bidwell, P. T. 1982. The Saxon Minster at Exeter, in Pearce, S. M. (ed.) *The early Church in western Britain and Ireland*, BAR British Series, 102, 145–75, Oxford: British Archaeological Reports.

Hodder, I. 1980. Social structure and cemeteries: a critical appraisal, in Rahtz, P., Dickinson, T. and Watts, L. (eds), *Anglo-Saxon cemeteries 1979*, BAR British Series, 82, 161–9, Oxford: British Archaeological Reports.

Keufler, M. S. 1991. 'A wryed existence': attitudes towards children in Anglo-Saxon England, *Jnl. of Social Hist.*, **24**, 823–34.

Kipling, R. and Scobie, G. 1990. Staple Gardens 1989, *Winchester Museums Service Newsletter*, **6**, 8–9.

Kjølbye-Biddle, B. 1975. A Cathedral cemetery: problems in excavation and interpretation, *World Archaeol.*, **7**, 87–108.

Kjølbye-Biddle, B. 1992. Dispersal or concentration: the disposal of the Winchester dead over 2000 years, in Bassett, S. (ed.) *Death in towns*, 210–47, Leicester: Leicester University Press.

Kjølbye-Biddle, B. 1995. Iron-bound coffins and coffin fittings from the pre-Norman cemetery, in Phillips, D. and Heywood, B. (eds), *Excavations at York Minster volume 1: from Roman fortress to Norman cathedral*, (2 vols.), 489–521, London: HMSO.

Lucy, S. J. 1998. *The early Anglo-Saxon cemeteries of East Yorkshire: an analysis and reinterpretation*, BAR British Series, 272, Oxford: British Archaeological Reports.

Lucy, S. J. and Reynolds, A. 2002. Burial in early medieval England and Wales: past, present and future, in Lucy, S. J. and Reynolds, A. (eds), *Burial in early medieval England and Wales*, The Society for Medieval Archaeology Monograph Series No. 17, 1–23, London: The Society for Medieval Archaeology.

Meaney, A. L. and Hawkes, S. C. 1970. *Two Anglo-Saxon cemeteries at Winnall, Winchester, Hampshire*, Society for Medieval Archaeology Monograph Series No. 4, London: The Society for Medieval Archaeology.

Morris, R. K. 1983. *The church in British archaeology*, Council for British Archaeology Research Report 47, London: Council for British Archaeology.

Mytum, H. 1994. Parish and people: excavations at Kellington church, *Med. Life*, **1**, 19–22.

Pearson, N. F. 1989. Swinegate excavation, *Interim*, **14**(4), 2–9.

Pearson, N. F. 1990. Swinegate excavation, *Interim*, **15**(1), 2–10.

Phillips, D. and Heywood, B. 1995. *Excavations at York Minster volume 1: from Roman fortress to Norman cathedral* (2 vols.), London: HMSO.

Powlesland, D. 1997. Discussion after Härke, H. Early Anglo-Saxon social structure, in Hines, J. (ed.) *The Anglo-Saxons from the migration period to the eighth century*, 160–9, Woodbridge: Boydell.

Rahtz, P. and Watts, L. 1997. Kirkdale Anglo-Saxon Minster, *Current Archaeol.*, **155**, 419–22.

Reynolds, A. 1997. The definition and ideology of Anglo-Saxon execution sites and cemeteries, in De Boe, G. and Verhaege, F. (eds), *Death and Burial in Medieval Europe, Papers of the Medieval Europe Brugge 1997 Conference*, 2, 33–41, Zellick: Institute voor het Archaeologisch Patrimonium.

Reynolds, N. M. 1979. Saltergate, in C. Colyer and M. J. Jones (eds), Excavations at Lincoln, *Antiquaries Jnl.*, **59**, 84–9.

Richards, J. D. 2000. *Viking Age England*, 2nd edit., Stroud: Tempus.

Richards, J. D. 2002. The case of the missing Vikings: Scandinavian burial in the Danelaw, in Lucy, S. J. and Reynolds, A. (eds), *Burial in early medieval England and Wales*, The Society for Medieval Archaeology Monograph Series No. 17, 156–70, London: The Society for Medieval Archaeology.

Rodwell, K. 1993. Post-Roman burials, in Darling, M. J. and Gurney, D. (eds), *Caister-on-Sea: excavations by Charles Green 1951–55*, East Anglian Archaeology No. 60, 254–5, Gressenhall: East Anglian Archaeology.

Rodwell, W. 2001. *Wells Cathedral: excavations and structural studies, 1978–93*, English Heritage Archaeological Report 21, London: English Heritage.

Rodwell, W. and Rodwell, K. 1982. St. Peter's Church, Barton-upon-Humber: excavation and structural study 1978–1981, *Antiquaries Jnl.*, **62**, 283–513.

Rollason, D. W. 1998. *Sources for York History to AD 1100*, The Archaeology of York 1, York: York Archaeological Trust.

Saunders, S. R. 1992. Subadult skeletons and growth related studies, in Saunders, S. R. and Katzenberg, M. A. (eds), *Skeletal biology of past peoples: research methods*, 1–20, New York: Wiley Liss.

Schofield, J., Thompson, A., Hill, M. and Riviére, S. 1988. The cemetery of St Nicholas Shambles, in White, W. (ed.) *Skeletal remains from the cemetery of St Nicholas Shambles, City of London*, 7–27, London: London and Middlesex Archaeological Society.

Scobie, G. 1994. Staple Gardens 1994, *Winchester Museums Service Newsletter*, **19**, 4–6.

Shoesmith, R. 1980. *Excavations at Castle Green*. Hereford City excavations volume 1, Council for British Archaeology Research Report 36, London: CBA.

Sidebottom, P. 2000. Viking age stone monuments and social identity in Derbyshire, in Hadley, D. M. and Richards, J. D. (eds), *Cultures in contact: Scandinavian settlement in England in the ninth and tenth centuries*, 213–35, Turnhout: Brepols.

Steane, K., Darling, M. J., Mann, J., Vince, A. and Young, J. 2001. *The Archaeology of Wigford and the Brayford Pool*, Lincoln Archaeological Studies, Oxford: Oxbow

Stocker, D. 2000. Monuments and merchants: irregularities in the distribution of stone sculpture in Lincolnshire and Yorkshire in the tenth century, in Hadley, D. M. and Richards, J. D. (eds), *Cultures in contact: Scandinavian settlement in England in the ninth and tenth centuries*, 179–212, Turnhout: Brepols.

Stocker, D. and Everson, P. 2001. Five towns funerals: decoding diversity in Danelaw stone sculpture, in Graham-Cambell, J., Hall, R. A., Jesch, J. and Parsons, D. N. (eds), *Vikings and the Danelaw*, 223–43, Oxford: Oxbow.

Stoodley, N. 1999a. *The spindle and the spear: a critical enquiry into the construction and meaning of gender in the early Anglo-Saxon burial rite*, BAR British Series, 288, Oxford: British Archaeological Reports.

Stoodley, N. 1999b. Burial rites, gender and the creation of kingdoms: the evidence from 7th century Wessex, *Anglo-Saxon Stud. in Archaeology and History*, **10**, 99–107

Stroud, G. and Kemp, R. L. 1993. *Cemeteries of St Andrew, Fishergate*, The archaeology of York 12/2. The medieval cemeteries, York: CBA.

Tarlow, S. 1997. The dread of something after death: violation and desecration on the Isle of Man in the tenth century, in Carman, J. (ed.) *Material harm. Archaeological studies of war and violence*, 133–42, Glasgow: Cruinthne Press.

Tweddle, D., Biddle, M. and Kjølbye-Biddle, B. 1995. *Corpus of Anglo-Saxon stone sculpture volume iv: South-East England*, Oxford: Oxford University Press.

Wade-Martins, P. 1980. *Excavations in North Elmham Park 1967–1972*, East Anglian Archaeology Report No. 9, Norfolk: Norfolk Archaeological Unit.

Watts, D. J. 1989. Infant burials and Romano-British Christianity, *Archaeol. Jnl.*, **146**, 372–83.

Whitelock, D. (ed. and trans.) 1955. *English historical documents c. 500–1042*. London: Eyre and Spottiswoode.

Wilmott, T. 1986. Excavations at Tanners Row, Pontefract: second interim report, *CBA Forum*, **1986**, 20–1.

Wilmott, T. 1987. Pontefract, *Current Archaeol.*, **9**, 340–4.

Disturbing the Dead: Urbanisation, the Church and the Post-Burial Treatment of Human Remains in Early Medieval Wessex, *c.* 600–1100 AD

Annia Kristina Cherryson

The period *c.* 600–1100 AD saw increasing levels of post-burial disturbance of the dead, with the low levels of grave disturbance seen in the seventh and eighth centuries replaced by a higher concentration of intercutting burials in the churchyards of the late Saxon period.

This paper will assess the evidence for post-burial disturbance of the deceased in early medieval cemeteries in Wessex. Particular attention will be given to the differences between the levels of post-burial disturbance seen in field cemeteries and churchyards, as well as to a consideration of the fate of the displaced human remains, from their deposition in charnel pits to the use of displaced skulls to support the skulls of later burials.

The paper will then examine the influence of the Church and the re-emergence of urban centres on the changes in the post-burial treatment of the dead during the early medieval period. Finally, the paper will consider the evidence for the post-burial treatment of the body with respect to both the views of the Church on the treatment of the deceased and the belief in the literal resurrection of the body.

Introduction

'May they rest in peace' is often said of the dead, yet, in reality that rest was often short-lived in the churchyards of medieval England as the skeletal remains of earlier burials were consistently disturbed, displaced and destroyed by the bodies of later generations, tombs or buildings. These high levels of post-burial disturbance appear to have had their origins, as did churchyard burial itself, in the early medieval period. In marked contrast to the infrequent levels of grave disturbance seen in the field cemeteries that preceded and co-existed with these early churchyards, the advent of higher levels of post burial disturbance prompts questions about the role of the Church and the effect of the re-emergence of urban centres in the

transformation in the post-burial treatment of the deceased. Focusing on early medieval Wessex, this study will review the archaeological evidence for post-burial disturbance. The paper will then address whether this shift in the treatment of the dead was related to, and in turn influenced by, changing attitudes towards dying, death and the dead in middle and later Anglo-Saxon England.

Evidence for the Post-Burial Disturbance of the Dead in Early Medieval Wessex

As a part of a broader programme of research into the mortuary practices of early medieval Wessex, an assessment of the levels of post-burial disturbance was undertaken for twenty-one cemeteries in the area considered as the greater Wessex of the later Anglo-Saxon period.[1] For the purposes of this study, Wessex was defined as the counties of Berkshire,[2] Devon, Dorset, Hampshire, Isle of Wight, Somerset and Wiltshire. A descriptive system was used in the analysis, which categorised the levels of disturbance as *none*, *low*, *moderate* and *high* to allow qualitative comparisons between cemeteries.[3] The sites were selected to provide a representative sample of the types of burial grounds in use within the study area between the seventh and eleventh centuries (see Fig. 1 for site locations and Table 1 for a summary of the information for each site). Thirteen of the sites were field cemeteries, not associated with any ecclesiastical buildings. Of these thirteen, eleven were rural burial grounds founded during the late sixth and seventh centuries and were usually relatively short-lived, with ten of the eleven going out of use by or during the eighth century. One slightly atypical cemetery among these eleven sites was the long-lived burial ground of Bevis Grave (Hampshire), which, although founded in the seventh century, continued in use until the tenth.[4] The remaining two field cemeteries included within the study

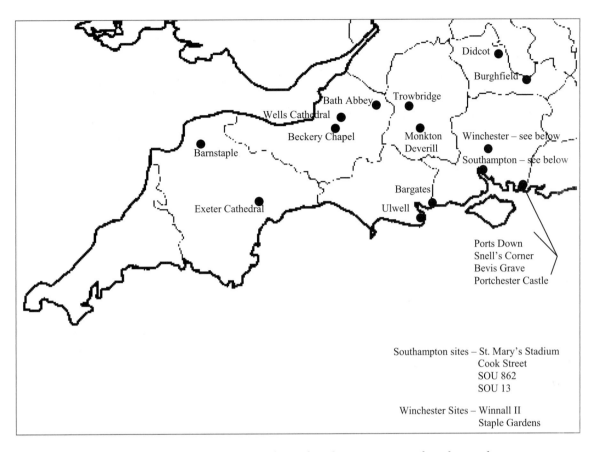

Figure 1. Location map of early medieval cemeteries used in this study

differed from the others in that they were later foundations. One was the small cemetery at Cook Street, which was in use during the eighth century and lay within the middle Saxon emporium of *Hamwic*. [5] The second burial ground is associated with a manorial estate at Portchester, and dates to the eleventh century.[6] Eight cemeteries within this study are either known or strongly suspected to be associated with churches and as such serve as examples of the early medieval churchyards that gradually replaced field cemeteries from the seventh century onwards.[7] Unlike the majority of the field cemeteries that they superseded, many of the churchyards were long-lived with burial continuing throughout the late Saxon period and beyond into the medieval or post-medieval periods. Six of the eight lie within urban centres, while the manorial churchyard at Trowbridge and the monastic cemetery associated with Beckery Chapel are in rural contexts.[8]

There were significant differences seen in the levels of post-burial disturbance in field cemeteries when compared with churchyard cemeteries. In general, lower levels of post-burial disturbance were observed in the thirteen field cemeteries. Seven of the field cemeteries – Bargates; Winnall II; Monkton Deverill; Snell's Corner; Didcot; Burghclere and SOU 862 in Southampton[9] – exhibited no evidence for the post-burial disturbance of graves (Table 1), although a number of these sites had

been subject to disturbance after 1100 AD. The remaining six cemeteries – Ports Down; Ulwell; St. Mary's Stadium; Bevis Grave; Portchester and Cook Street[10] – exhibited low or low-moderate levels of post-burial disturbance (Table 1). Higher levels of post-burial disturbance were observed in the majority of the churchyards, or suspected churchyards, with the study sample.[11] Six of the eight churchyards – Barnstaple; Exeter Cathedral; SOU 13 in Southampton; Staple Gardens in Winchester; Wells Cathedral and Trowbridge (Wiltshire) – exhibited either moderate, moderate – high or high levels of post-burial disturbance.[12] Low levels of post-burial disturbance were observed in the remaining two churchyards – Bath Abbey and the comparatively short lived, monastic cemetery at Beckery Chapel.[13] Density of burial across a churchyard is known to vary with the highest concentration of graves usually found in the vicinity of the church and around important features within the graveyard, such as saint's graves.[14] If only a small part of a churchyard has been excavated, particularly when as at Wells and Exeter the excavated area is adjacent to the church, this may not be entirely representative of the churchyard as a whole.[15] Yet, even with the potential complications caused by variations in burial density, the high levels of post-burial disturbance seen in Wessex's early medieval churchyards is markedly higher than that seen in the field cemeteries that preceeded and co-existed with them.

Figure 2. Grave 49 from the seventh- to tenth-century cemetery of Bevis Grave. This grave has been re-opened twice with the remains of the first two occupants being packed around what was probably a coffin containing the last burial. The skulls from the displaced burials can be seen at the top and upper right of the grave. © Portsmouth Museums and Record Service

The number of burials in a cemetery also appeared to have been an important factor with high levels of post-burial disturbance observed in cemeteries with a large number of burials, while cemeteries containing fewer inhumations often have a lower density of burial and tended to exhibit less evidence for post-burial disturbance. As most of the large cemeteries within the study were the churchyards, many of which were in use for several centuries during the early medieval period and the majority of the field cemeteries are comparatively small and often short-lived, it could be argued that the differences in levels of post-burial disturbance seen among the two types of burial ground can be attributed to disparities in the number of inhumations. Yet the largest of the field cemeteries, the long lived Bevis Grave, still exhibits a lower level of post-burial disturbance than seen in the most of the churchyard cemeteries, although it does have a higher level of disturbance than many of the field cemeteries. This suggests that the number of burials alone does not fully account for the differences seen in the levels of post-burial disturbance between the field cemeteries and churchyards.

The Nature of The Post-Burial Disturbance Seen in the Study Area

The differences between field cemeteries and churchyards were not confined to the level of post-burial disturbance, but also extended to the nature of the post-burial disturbance too. Most post-burial disturbance observed in the field cemeteries was the result of re-using graves. This involved reopening a grave and inserting a secondary or tertiary burial. The remains of the original occupant or occupants were usually either displaced to the sides of the grave, as seen in grave forty-nine at Bevis Grave (Fig. 2) or re-deposited above the later burial as part of the grave fill as with the burials in grave five at Ports Down (Fig. 3).[16] The re-use of graves is usually characterised by the disturbance and displacement of the original occupant. Occasionally, care was taken not to disturb the original occupant when adding additional burials to a grave, as with burials 99 and 100 in the later churchyard at Wells Cathedral.[17] The effort made to avoid disturbing the earlier burial in this case indicates that the motives that lay behind the insertion of an additional burial in this grave may differ from the majority of examples of re-use where the original burials are disturbed.[18]

The factors lying behind the re-use of graves are unclear. Traditionally, they have been interpreted as family plots, and in some cases, especially where later burials have been inserted and efforts have been made not to disturb earlier occupants, this may suggest a recognition and interest in the earlier remains. In many instances, however, this is unlikely due to the lack of interest exhibited towards the original occupant. In these cases, the re-use either represents the accidental disturbance of earlier burials or the purposeful, but not entirely considered re-use of earlier graves based on their utility.[19] A second form of post-burial disturbance, occasionally seen in the field cemeteries, was caused by later burials cutting part of an earlier grave. This intercutting usually resulted in part of the skeletal remains of the earlier burial being displaced while the rest remained in situ, as in grave twenty-nine at Bevis Grave, where the upper part of the skeleton was removed by grave twenty-eight with the lower body left in place.[20] In such instances, a lack of intentionality can be securely suggested.

The churchyard cemeteries exhibited a different pattern of post-burial disturbance. Although examples of the single or double re-use of graves similar to the pattern seen in field cemeteries can be found in churchyards, such as the example from Wells Cathedral (see above), the major cause of the post-burial disturbance in the churchyard resulted from the intercutting of burials. While low levels of intercutting were observed in a few of the field cemeteries, high levels were generally the preserve of the larger, late churchyard cemeteries, such as Staple Gardens in Winchester (Fig. 4), Trowbridge and SOU 13 in Southampton (Fig. 5).[21] At Trowbridge, the earlier burials were interred in rows with later burials inserted between the earlier rows, a process which led to parts of the earlier burials being disturbed.[22] Similarly the rows of burials on either side of the church at SOU 13 had been reworked five times, resulting in the redeposition of a third of all burials, with many others losing parts due to truncation by later graves.[23] In other churchyards, such as Staple Gardens, and Wells Cathedral,[24] the higher density of burials makes it difficult to determine the spatial layout of the cemetery at any given time and whether there was any systematic pattern to the post-burial disturbance.

Figure 3. Grave 5 from the seventh-century cemetery at Portsdown. This grave has been re-used with the remains of the primary burial (indicated by shading) being redeposited above the secondary burial. Redrawn by M. Cherryson from a drawing from the Portsdown archive provided courtesy of Portsmouth Museums and Record Service

Figure 4. Intercutting burials from the ninth- to eleventh-century cemetery at Staple Gardens in Winchester.
© *Winchester Museums Service*

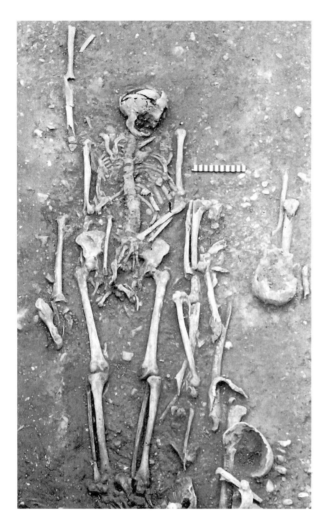

Figure 5. Burial 17 from the eighth- to ninth-century cemetery at SOU 13 in Hamwic *in Southampton. This burial has been cut through the remains of an earlier burial and is surrounded by the remains of at least eight individuals.* © *Southampton City Council Heritage Services*

The buildings and pits associated with domestic and ecclesiastical occupation provided the other major cause of post-burial disturbance during this period. The prevalence of this type of disturbance was usually determined by location rather than the type of cemetery, with much of the evidence for this type of disturbance coming from urban contexts, such as the middle Saxon *wic* site of *Hamwic*. Many of the settlement's early cemeteries were short-lived,[25] and once abandoned, were used for domestic occupation as the settlement expanded during the eighth century.[26] In some cases, little time elapsed between the abandonment of a burial ground and the beginning of the domestic occupation of the area. For example, the earliest evidence for domestic occupation on the site of the late seventh- and early eighth-century St Mary's Stadium cemetery post-dates the graves by at most one or two generations.[27] None of

the ten structures identified at the St. Mary's Stadium site lay over the area of the inhumation cemetery.[28] Yet this does not necessarily mean that the earlier cemetery was being respected as a number of pits were dug in the area of the earlier cemetery with eight of the graves being damaged by subsequent middle Saxon pits.[29] The type of disturbance associated with pits can be seen in Fig. 6, which illustrates part of another *Hamwic* cemetery, the eighth- and ninth-century cemetery SOU 13. A pit cuts through the cemetery in the upper left quarter of the photograph, disturbing grave 30 (the second burial from the left) with the occupant's head being pushed back into the coffin space.[30] The two isolated skulls represent disturbed remains deposited into the pit. One skull is thought to belong to grave 33 (the fourth skeleton from the left) and was probably disturbed when the pit was dug, while the origins of the other skull are unclear. Usually, the disturbance resulting from pits is limited to those parts of the skeleton directly cut by the pit with the rest of the skeleton remaining *in situ*. However, occasionally, the discovery of human remains led to the complete excavation of the grave, as at the richly furnished St Mary's Stadium cemetery. There, the discovery of one end of a grave during the middle Saxon period led to it being completely emptied, probably in the search for grave goods, with the displaced human remains being deposited into the pit, along with the remains of a second individual.[31] While there is substantial archaeological and documentary evidence for grave robbery on the Continent, there is little clear evidence for the practice in early medieval England.[32] It has been suggested that a short late Anglo-Saxon legal text known as *Walreaf*, which defines corpse-robbery as the action of outlaws, may indicate that the practice of grave robbing was not unknown in Anglo-Saxon England.[33]

The tenth and eleventh centuries saw an increasing use of stone for the construction of ecclesiastical buildings and fortifications such as castles. These stone structures all required substantial foundation trenches. When these buildings were located within burial grounds, their construction could result in the substantial disturbance or destruction of human remains unlike wooden buildings that required only superficial foundations. Early medieval churchyards, in particular, were prone to this type of disturbance due to the sporadic rebuilding of ecclesiastical buildings, such as the construction programmes associated with the tenth-century monastic reform and the aftermath of the Norman Conquest. The foundation trenches for the nave of Winchester's new Norman cathedral displaced approximately a thousand burials, whose remains were deposited in one of the robber trenches of the Anglo-Saxon Old Minster.[34] Similarly, a partially excavated charnel pit at Bath Abbey contained the remains of at least thirty-three adults, whose remains are thought to have been disturbed during the construction of the Norman abbey.[35] The Norman Conquest led not only to the rebuilding of

Figure 6 . Depicts part of the eighth- to ninth-century cemetery at SOU 13 in Southampton with several phases of burial shown. There was a lull in the cemetery's use when the pit visible in the upper left of the figure, which disturbed burial 30 (second from left) resulting in the skull being pushed back into the coffin space. Two displaced skulls are also visible at the top of the figure. © Southampton City Council Heritage Services

many ecclesiastical buildings but to the appearance of castles, in both urban and rural locations. Finding room for castles in the crowded urban centres of the eleventh and early twelfth centuries could be difficult and the use of any available open space, which more often than not was the town's burial ground, would have removed the need to destroy property.[36] The association between late Saxon cemeteries and Norman castles is well documented and several examples, all dating to the early twelfth century, are found in the study area at Barnstaple, Trowbridge and Taunton.[37] In the case of both Trowbridge and Barnstaple, it is the defensive banks of the castle which overlie the cemetery, in effect sealing rather than disturbing the late Saxon graves.[38] However, at Barnstaple, there is evidence for the reburial within a single grave of the remains of at least three bodies disturbed by the construction of the moat.[39] Whether the placing of the defensive banks may represent a conscious decision to minimise the damage to the burials caused by the construction of the castle at Barnstaple and Trowbridge is unclear, but the fragmentary evidence from Taunton suggests it was not always an important consideration, with the disturbed and intact remains of the occupants of the late Saxon cemetery

underlying the inner and outer wards of the Norman castle.[40]

All examples of post-burial disturbance considered above are the by-product of other activities, either by the re-use of graves for later interments or the construction of new graves, pits or buildings. Yet, there are a few examples of post-burial disturbance seen in the cemeteries within the study where the primary objective may have been to recover the human remains. Nine of the graves excavated at Barnstaple were completely empty, containing no evidence for the presence of human remains or any indication in the form of nails or wood stains that any coffin may have been present.[41] It has been suggested that the occupants of these graves may have been exhumed, perhaps by their families, and moved to other churchyards before the castle was constructed over the cemetery, a process which echoed the translation of the remains of saints (discussed below).

The ultimate fate of those human remains disturbed by later activities was largely governed by the ease and convenience of disposal. When burials were disturbed by later graves, the displaced remains were either packed around the intrusive body or deposited into the open grave

Figure 7. Depicts the use of two skulls from earlier burials used to support the head of a later burial at Trowbridge mimicking the use of stones to support the head. The practice is found in many late Saxon cemeteries. The burial illustrated here is of medieval date, but the practice is also found in the early medieval phase of the cemetery. © Trowbridge Museum

as it was backfilled. Similarly, those remains disturbed by pits or buildings were often deposited in the pit that disturbed the burial, as at St. Mary's Stadium, or trenches created by the robbing of stone for the new building, as at Winchester.[42] If there was nothing available, then pits may have been dug to take the displaced remains, such as those seen at Portchester Castle, where two burials thought to have been disturbed by the rebuilding of a masonry structure were reburied in small pits.[43] Occasionally, displaced skulls were placed to one or both sides of the head of later burials to support the skull, as can be seen in six graves from the churchyard at Trowbridge (Fig. 7).[44] This echoes of the later Saxon practice of placing stones around the skull.[45] While the vast majority of displaced human remains appear to have been reburied, in some cases it is possible that the skeletal remains ended up simply scattered over the site, often becoming mixed in with the rubbish.[46] Occasionally, disturbed human remains were housed in more elaborate settings as at Wells Cathedral, where a sunken building appears to have been re-used as an Anglo-Saxon ossuary.[47] The structure contained the remains of at least forty-one individuals and the pattern of deposition suggests the bones were deposited over a period of time before the structure was finally sealed in the tenth century.[48] Where the bones originate from is unclear, but the use of the ossuary as a place to deposit disturbed remains from coffins and tombs suggests a deliberate and ritualised treatment of human remains in a post-burial context.

In many of the cases discussed above, the ease of disposal governed the final resting place of skeletons inadvertently disturbed by other activities. However, there are clear cases where human remains appear to have been purposefully exhumed with their final resting place already in mind. The remains of saints but also members of the royalty, aristocracy or clergy could be exhumed and translated to enhance the influence and prestige of a religious house.[49] The acquisition of relics could have a dual religious and socio-political function. For example, when the New Minster in Winchester obtained the remains of St. Judoc from the Continent or when the remains of Birinus (the continental missionary responsible for the conversion of the West Saxons) were moved from Dorchester-on-Thames to the Old Minster in Winchester, the translation enhanced the status of the religious communities and their relationship with secular patrons.[50] A saint's cult could be further promoted by moving their remains to a more prominent position within the church complex or encasing them within elaborate and ornate reliquaries. The remains of St. Swithun were exhumed from their resting place outside the west door of the Old Minster in Winchester in AD 971 and moved to a more prominent location within the church.[51] Shortly after this, part of St. Swithun's body was encased within an ornate reliquary of precious metals and gems.[52] In some cases, the reasons for disturbing the dead may have been more personal. When Edward the Elder's new foundation, the New Minster, was completed, the remains of his father King Alfred were translated from their original resting place in the Winchester's Old Minster to the adjacent new church.[53]

The Role of Church and Town in Changing the Post-Burial Treatment of the Deceased in Early Medieval Wessex

While evidence for the post-burial disturbance of the dead is found throughout the early medieval period in Wessex, it clearly becomes more prevalent in later Saxon church-yards. Moreover, the nature of the disturbance also changes. In the field cemeteries, the most prevalent type of disturbance results from the re-use of graves, with the occasional cutting of one grave by another. The pattern of disturbance seen in the later cemeteries is generally characterised by much higher levels of intercutting of graves combined with less evidence for grave re-use. However, the true level of grave re-use may, in part, be obscured by the higher levels of disturbance seen in these burial grounds. The later cemeteries, particularly those associated with churchyards, are also far more likely to have been disturbed by structural features such as buildings and pits. Finally, the majority of the cemeteries lying within urban contexts seem to be characterised by higher levels of post-burial disturbance, while the majority of rural cemeteries have much lower levels of disturbance.

However, this observation needs to be qualified as the majority of rural burial grounds within this sample are small and can be identified as early field cemeteries, while the majority of urban cemeteries are large and late churchyards. Yet, the difference in the post-burial treatment of human remains in these two distinctive mortuary contexts appears real and genuine.

The higher levels of post-burial disturbance seen in Wessex's churchyards can, in part, be attributed to the Anglo-Saxon Church's increasing concern to separate the sacred from the secular. The late Saxon period saw the increasing definition of churchyard cemeteries as fixed and separate spaces within the landscape, enclosed by boundaries and set apart by consecration.[54] The documentary sources suggest that this custom was well established by the late tenth century.[55] Evidence for the late Saxon policy of enclosing of churchyard cemeteries to define consecrated ground can be seen at Trowbridge. There, the churchyard has a boundary in the form of a ditch and, given the gap between the ditch and the burials, there was probably either a low bank or hedge lying just within the ditch.[56] The enclosing of churchyards served to restrict the space available for burial and resulted in high levels of post-burial disturbance as the number of burials within a cemetery exceeded its capacity. This differs from the earlier field cemeteries which, in general, seem to lack boundaries with burials gradually tapering off towards their peripheries suggesting the absence of a fixed limit for burial.[57] However, the restriction of space available for burial and the cemetery's duration were not the only factors responsible, and the higher levels of post-burial disturbance seen in the Wessex's churchyards can also be seen as a practical response to the processes of urbanisation.

The changes wrought by urbanisation are best illustrated by looking at two cemeteries from the Middle Saxon *wic* site of *Hamwic*. The early eighth-century cemetery at Cook Street lies in the south-west corner of the middle Saxon settlement of *Hamwic*.[58] The cemetery was characterised by low levels of post-burial disturbance and well-spaced burials,[59] and had many features reminiscent of the rural cemeteries of the seventh and eighth centuries.[60] It has been suggested that *Hamwic*'s early burial grounds may have been associated with small rural settlements which pre-dated the trading centre.[61] Alternatively, it is possible that these early burial grounds may have been foundations of new migrants, who recreated the rural cemeteries with which they were familiar with within the new context provided by the *wic*.[62]

The *Hamwic* cemetery, SOU 13, was in use during the eighth and ninth centuries,[63] and must have been founded only one or two generations later than the Cook Street cemetery. This cemetery had a much higher density of burials with high levels of intercutting and had many of the features characteristic of churchyards of the medieval and post-medieval period.[64] The cemetery at SOU 13, unlike that at Cook Street, was in use after the

major expansion of the settlement, which occurred during the mid-eighth century.[65] This was a time when there was increased pressure on space within the settlement. This placed the living and the dead in direct competition for the available space, and this was a competition which the living were always going to win.[66] The restricted space for burial meant that cemeteries, such as SOU 13, were rapidly filled, resulting in the reworking of existing rows of burials causing substantial post-burial disturbance to allow the addition of later burials.[67]

As illustrated above, the late Saxon period saw the increasing restriction of the available space for burial, yet this alone did not create higher levels of post-burial disturbance. Space only became an issue when the number of bodies exceeded the capacity of the cemetery. This suggests that higher levels of disturbance do not directly correlate with the space available for burial, but rather with the number of burials combined with limitations on the space available for burial. The late Saxon period saw not only the restriction of burial ground size, but also an increase in the number of burials in defined burial grounds around churches. This was, in part, the result of the way the Church apportioned rights over burial. Not all churches had associated cemeteries, as the right of burial was the preserve of the minister churches, albeit an increasingly contested one as the number of lay foundations mushroomed in the late tenth and eleventh centuries.[68] As ever greater numbers sought burial by a church on consecrated ground, the restrictions on burial rights had the effects of centralising burial in rural areas at the minister church, and of increasing the numbers of burials at each site. Equally, the higher concentration of people found in late Saxon urban centres would have had a similar effect; increasing the numbers of burials in the cemeteries serving these settlements. Finally, it can be argued that the restriction of space available for burial also served to alter what was perceived to be the capacity of the burial grounds. Burial continued at early medieval churchyards far beyond the point at which it would have stopped in field cemeteries; with a density of burial surpassing anything seen in the earlier field cemeteries.

Discussion

The evidence discussed above indicates that there was a significant shift in the post-burial treatment of the deceased during the early medieval period. The low levels of post-burial disturbance seen in the early field cemeteries examined in this study would appear to indicate that during the sixth and seventh centuries a conscious effort was made to avoid disturbing the remains of the deceased.[69] This supposition is supported by a sixth-century example from outside the study area. During the excavation of the sixth-century Anglian cemetery at West Heslerton in North Yorkshire, excavators discovered evidence that the early medieval grave diggers had inadvertently disturbed an earlier grave not long after burial. They appear to have stopped their excavation and backfilled the grave.[70] Such a response is hard to find in later centuries. By the ninth and tenth century, there appears to have been a shift in policy with the remains of deceased being disturbed to make room for more graves or buildings.

The markedly higher levels of post-burial disturbance associated with the later churchyards were, at least in part, the result of policies pursued by the Church, both by the enclosing of burial grounds and by restricting burial rights to certain churches. Initially, these policies had little effect on the levels of post-burial disturbance as churchyard burial was the preserve of ecclesiastics and those of high status, but as churchyard burial became more widespread, the combination of increasing numbers of bodies and a restricted amount of space of burial resulted in escalating levels of post-burial disturbance. However, the Church was not the only factor, particularly in urban centres, where the pressure on space served to constrain cemetery size. The space available for burial in the earliest urban centres, such as *Hamwic*, was restricted due to competition long before the Anglo-Saxon Church was in a position to dictate the burial mores of the population of Wessex.

This change in the treatment of earlier burials is likely to have been echoed by a shift in attitudes towards the dead and in the role of the body within funerary rites. The increasing proximity of the living and the dead, both within urban centres and within and around the churches that served as religious foci for the living, would have served to increase the living's familiarity with disturbed human remains and perhaps reduce their fear of the dead following decomposition.[71] This is likely to have had an impact on the post-burial treatment of the deceased.

Little is known about the role of the body within funeral rites in early medieval England prior to the arrival of Christianity. The absence of documentary sources for the seventh and even eighth centuries makes the reconstruction of many aspects of the funerary process outside the grave problematic. However, the nature of early Saxon funerary rites suggest that the stage provided by the body displayed within an open grave or the spectacle of the cremation pyre provided important venues for the signalling of social information, the renegotiation of social relationships and as a means for dealing with loss.[72] In contrast, the evidence from the later Saxon period, indicates an increasing trend toward removing the body from view, either wrapped in a shroud or encased within a coffin.[73] This suggests that the focus of the funerary rites and commemoration may have moved away from the body, and perhaps even to some extent the grave. It has even been suggested that by the end of the early medieval period, the enclosed consecrated churchyards had greater importance than the individual graves they contained.[74] While the grave clearly retained its importance at the point of burial, its place as the primary focus for funerary and commemorative activity was increasingly usurped by the buildings and rituals of the Church, a process aided by the development of funerary and commemorative liturgies including the provision of masses for the dead and prayers for the soul of the deceased.[75] In addition, the accumulation of burials both within and around churches may have led to these ecclesiastical buildings, and their associated cemeteries, being increasingly seen as a focus for the remembrance of not only departed individuals, but for an entire community of the dead.[76] Furthermore, the increasing emphasis of the Church on the pastoral care of the soul may have been accompanied by shifting attitudes towards the deceased, changing from fear of the dead to an increasing concern with their fate in the afterlife.[77] It could be argued that this shift away from the grave as the primary focus for funerary and commemorative rites, allied with a decreasing fear of the deceased, may in part explain why the increasing levels of post-burial disturbance seen in late Saxon Wessex were tolerated by the general population.

Despite the shift away from the grave, the body and its afterlife were of increasing concern during the late Saxon period. It is perhaps paradoxical that the very Church whose policies, in part, caused an increase in the level of post-burial disturbance, was one with a belief in bodily resurrection.[78] The picture painted in Aelfric's Homilies, which date to the late tenth century, is one of the transformation of the mortal remains of an individual on the Day of Judgement, with the surviving mortal remains playing an integral part of the process.[79] As such, an important issue was whether the disturbance or destruction of the body after burial would prevent an individual's resurrection. Early medieval thought on the subject was heavily influenced by the fifth-century writings of Augustine of Hippo.[80] In *The City of God against the Pagans* he assures his readers that 'Even if the body has been completely ground to powder in some dreadful accident, or by the ferocity of enemies; even if it has been so entirely scattered to the winds or into the water that there is nothing left of it', this would not prevent its corporeal resurrection.[81] Two centuries later, Augustine's ideas were echoed in Gregory of Tours' History of the Franks which stated that 'He who created man as yet unborn from nothing at all will not find it difficult to replace any lost portions' on the Day of Judgement.[82] In his Easter Day Sermon the Anglo-Saxon Blickling Homilist, writing *c.* AD 1000, painted a similarly reassuring picture for the concerned. On the Day of Judgement, the dead would arise from their graves and 'go forth in judgement in such a fashion as they had previously adorned themselves', even if their bodies had been 'eaten by wild animals, or carried off by birds, or torn by fishes'.[83] In contrast, concern was expressed over disturbing the dead at a number of ecclesiastical councils, such as the sixth-century Council of Mâcon, which decreed that bodies should not normally be displaced to make space for later burials.[84] However, it was the view of Augustine, that the dispersed body would be reconstituted on the Day of Judgement, which appeared in the homilies and sermons of late Saxon England. It is unclear whether the population of late Saxon Wessex were overly concerned with the nuances of eschatology,[85] but they would have been well aware of the high levels of post-burial disturbance seen in many late Saxon churchyards. The unknown author of a late Anglo-Saxon homily wrote about 'when a grave is dug in a minster and bones turn up', in the knowledge that this scenario would be all too familiar to his audience.[86] As such, they may have been concerned about the possible implications that this treatment of the dead had for their resurrection. The Church's reassurances that regardless of the level of a body's fragmentation, it would be restored may have assuaged such fears and it may be that armed with such guarantees that for many, provided the remains of the deceased lay in consecrated ground, it ceased to matter how scattered they were.

Acknowledgements

Thanks are due to the following individuals and institutions, who have generously provided information on unpublished sites and additional information on published sites; John Allen, Barnstaple Museum, Bath Archaeological Trust, Dorset County Museum, Jane Ellis, Exeter Archaeology, Alan Morton (Southampton City Council), Portsmouth City Museum, Royal Albert Memorial Museum and Art Gallery in Exeter, David Rudkin, Graham Scobie, Somerset County Museum, Southampton City Museum, Jenny Stevens, Trowbridge Museum, Wessex Trust for Archaeology, Winchester Museums Service, Karen Wardley.

I would also like to thank Dawn Hadley, Jo Buckberry, Alan Morton, Howard Williams, Sarah Semple and the anonymous referee who have read and commented on various drafts of this paper. Any remaining errors are the author's alone.

This research was funded by a University of Sheffield Studentship and the radiocarbon dating program was funded by an ORADS grant from NERC.

Notes

1. The data in this paper is part of a larger investigation into burial practices in Wessex between 600 and 1100 AD (Cherryson 2005b).
2. For this study, Berkshire's pre-1974 county boundaries were used.
3. Cherryson, 2005a.
4. Rudkin 2001.
5. Garner 1993; 2001; Garner and Vincent 1997.
6. Cunliffe 1976.
7. There is no archaeological evidence for a church associated with the cemetery at Staple Gardens, but as only part of the site has been excavated, the possibility that a church may have been present cannot be excluded. In addition, the cemetery is thought to lie in the vicinity of the medieval church of St. Paul's (Keene 1985, 467). The church is only known from documentary sources and although first mentioned in documents dating to 1256 AD, may well have had Saxon origins. No evidence for an associated church was uncovered during the excavations at Barnstaple, but as with Staple Gardens only part of the site was excavated and it has been suggested that the cemetery was associated with a church (Miles 1986, 73–4).
8. Graham and Davies 1993; Rahtz and Hirst 1974.
9. Jarvis 1983; Meaney and Hawkes 1970; Rawlings 1995; Knocker 1955; Boyle *et al.* 1995; Butterworth and Loeb 1992; Southern Archaeological Services 1998.
10. Corney 1967; Cox 1989; Birbeck 2005; Rudkin 2001, Cunliffe 1976; Garner 1993; 2001; Garner and Vincent 1997.
11. The possibility of churches being present at both Barnstaple and Winchester has been suggested by their excavators – see footnote 7 above for details.
12. Miles 1984; Henderson and Bidwell 1982; Morton 1992a; Kipling and Scobie 1990; Rodwell 2001; Graham and Davies 1993.
13. Bell 1996; Rathz and Hirst 1974.
14. Examples of churchyards with a higher density of burial in the vicinity of the church include Trowbridge (Graham and Davies 1993, 35 and 47), Raunds Furnells (Boddington 1996, 27) and North Elmham (Wade-Martin 1980, 186). A high density of burials was found clustered around the grave of St. Swithun at Winchester (Kjøbye-Biddle 1992, 223).
15. Buckberry this volume.
16. Rudkin 2001; Corney 1967, 23.
17. Rodwell 2001, 67.
18. Stoodley 2002, 114–5.
19. *Ibid.*
20. Rudkin 2001.
21. Winchester Museums Service archive SG84 and SG89; Graham and Davies 1993; Morton 1992a.
22. Graham and Davies 1993, 33.
23. Morton 1992b, 72.
24. Winchester Museums Service archive SG84 and SG89; Rodwell 2001.
25. Morton 1992b, 68.
26. *Ibid.*, 74. Evidence for a similar pattern of earlier cemeteries being over superseded by domestic occupation following the eighth-century expansion of a *wic* has been observed at the Buttermarket cemetery at Ipswich (Scull 1999, 86; Scull and Bayliss 1999).
27. Birbeck 2005, 194 suggest that only a single generation elapsed between the cemetery going out of use and the advent of domestic settlement of the site. However, the possibility that two generations may separate the cemetery from the later settlement cannot be excluded (Alan Morton pers. comm.). The St. Mary's Stadium cemetery was founded while the Southampton area was under Jutish control before the area came under West Saxon control in the late seventh century (Yorke 1995, 59). It has been suggested that the short period of time which elapsed between the cemetery going out of use and the area being built over may represent the West Saxons trying to remove evidence of the earlier Jutish leaders (Birbeck 2005, 194). However, the St. Mary's Stadium cemetery is not the only early cemetery from *Hamwic* to be built over and it may be that these earlier burial grounds were simply forgotten or not respected as the settlement expanded during the eighth century.
28. Birbeck 2005, 194.
29. *Ibid.*, 27, 33.
30. Morton 1992a, 126; A. Morton pers. comm.
31. Birbeck 2005, 33.
32. Effros 2002, 49–61.
33. Wormald 1999, 372.

34. Kjølbye-Biddle 1992, 227.
35. Bell 1996, 51.
36. Examples of the destruction of property to accommodate a castle occurred in a number of urban centre with the number of houses destroyed often recorded in the Domesday Book (Harfield 1991: 373).
37. Hadley 2001, 40; Miles 1986; Graham and Davies 1993; Clements 1984.
38. Miles 1986, 62; Graham and Davies 1993, 63.
39. Miles 1986, 66.
40. Clements 1984. The factors determining what was destroyed or built over to make space for castles within late Saxon urban centres are unclear. In some urban centres property was destroyed while elsewhere cemeteries were built over with varying degrees of displacement and destruction of human remains. It is possible that in some cases that the selection of site used for the location of the new castle was determined by political reasons, perhaps as a slight to the indigenous population, but this is at best speculative and further work on this subject is needed.
41. Miles 1986, 68.
42. Birbeck 2005, 33; Kjølbye-Biddle 1992, 227.
43. Cunliffe 1976, 60–1.
44. Graham and Davies 1993, 41. Another two examples are found at the 4–6 Market Street site in Winchester (Hampshire). The site contains part of the Cathedral cemetery, which was in use from the late tenth to early fourteenth century (Teague 1988, 8).
45. Hadley 2001, 98.
46. Morton 1992b, 74.
47. Rodwell 2001, 75. The sunken building at Wells has been described as a Roman mausoleum by the excavator (*ibid.*, 43), but John Blair has recently suggested that the structure may be no earlier than the ninth or tenth century (Blair 2004, 136).
48. *Ibid.*, 78.
49. Rollason 1986, 32.
50. *Ibid.*, 32 and 36. Sherley-Price 1955, 153.
51. Lapidge 2003a, 285, Lapidge 2003b, 457–9.
52. Lapidge 2003b, 493.
53. Biddle 1976, 314. Edward the Elder's motives for founding the New Minster are unclear. The need for a larger church for the city's growing population, tensions between the king and the bishop of Winchester or to create a new burial place for the West Saxon royal house have all been suggested (*ibid.*, Rumble 2001, 234, Yorke 1984, 67). Whatever Edward the Elder's motives for building the New Minster, the translation of his father's remains to the New Minster, along with the burial of a number of Edward's close relatives – his wife, two of his sons and his brother, served to make the New Minster a royal mausoleum during the tenth century.
54. Thompson 2002, 232.
55. Gittos 2002, 196.
56. Graham and Davies 1993, 37.
57. Gittos 2002, 203.
58. Garner 2001, 189.
59. Although the density of burial may originally have been slightly higher as there was considerable post-medieval disturbance of the site (Garner 2001, 181).
60. Scull 2001, 71.
61. *Ibid.*, 72.
62. Lucy and Reynolds 2002, 13.
63. Morton 1992a. Five burials from this cemetery were dated as part of a programme of radiocarbon dating obtained during the course of this study.
64. Scull 2001, 71.
65. Morton 1992a, 54.
66. Morton 1992b, 75.
67. *Ibid.*, 74–5.
68. Blair 1988, 50.
69. Härke 1997, 165.
70. Haughton and Powlesland 1999, 157.
71. Meaney and Hawkes 1970, 51.
72. Halsall, 1995, 67; Williams 2002, 67.
73. Cherryson 2005b.
74. Ariès 1991, 53.
75. Paxton 1990.
76. Williams 2003, 230, 232.
77. Paxton 1990, 20.
78. Bynum 1995, 10.
79. Thompson 2002, 237.
80. Bynum 1995, 95, 113.
81. Augustine, *De Civitate Dei.* XXII. xxi.; Dyson 1998, 1152.
82. Gregory of Tours, *Historiae Francorum.* XIII. xiii.; Thorpe 1974, 562.
83. *The Blickling Homilist, An Easter Day Sermon.* Swanton 1975, 69.
84. *Concilia Galliae A.* 511–A. 695, Clercq 1963, 247– as referenced in Morton 1992b, 77.
85. The existence of English versions of many religious texts, including Gospels, Psalms and Homilies, by the eleventh century had the potential to make ideas on eschatology more accessible to the laity (Thompson 2004, 4–5).
86. The translated line from the homily Assman XIV is taken from Thompson 2004, 102.

Bibliography

Ariès, P. 1991. *The Hour of our Death*, New York: Oxford University Press (trans. H. Weaver).

Bell, R. 1996. Bath Abbey: some new perspectives, *Bath History*, **6**, 7–24.

Biddle, M (ed.). 1976. *Winchester in the early Middle Ages, An edition and discussion of the Winton Domesday*, Oxford: Clarendon Press.

Birbeck, V. (ed.). 2005 *The origins of middle Saxon Southampton. Excavations at the Friends Provident St Mary's Stadium 1998–2000.* Salisbury: Wessex Archaeology.

Blair, J. 2004. Wells: Roman mausoleum, or just Anglo-Saxon Minster? *Church Archaeology*, **5–6**, 134–137.

Blair, J. 1988. Minster churches in the landscape, in D. Hooke (ed.), *Anglo-Saxon settlement*, 35–58, Oxford: Blackwell.

Boddington, A. 1996. *Raunds Furnells. The Anglo-Saxon church and churchyard*, English Heritage Archaeological Report, 7, London: English Heritage.

Boyle, A., Dodd, A., Miles, D. and Mudd, A. 1995. *Two Oxfordshire Anglo-Saxon cemeteries*, Thames Valley Landscapes Monograph, 8, Oxford: Oxford University Committee for Archaeology for Oxford Archaeological Unit.

Butterworth, C. A. and Lobb, S. J. 1992. *Excavations in the Burghfield area, Berkshire. Wessex Archaeology Report No 1*, Salisbury: Wessex Archaeology.

Bynum, C. W. 1995. *The resurrection of the body in western Christianity, 200–1336*, New York: Columbia Press.

Cherryson, A. K. 2005a. Disturbing the dead: the displacement and destruction of skeletal remains in early medieval Wessex, c.600–1100 AD, in S. Zakrzewski and M. Clegg (eds), *Proceedings of the fifth annual meeting of the British Association for Biological Anthropology and Osteology*, British Archaeological Reports International series Oxford: British Archaeological Reports, 41–49.

Cherryson, A. K. 2005b. '*In the shadow of the Church: Early Medieval burial practices in the Wessex heartlands, c. AD 600–1100*', unpublished DPhil thesis, University of Sheffield.

Clements, C. F. 1984. The inner ward and outer bailey; burials and structures exposed in the 1970s, in P. Leach (ed.), *The archaeology of Taunton. Excavations and fieldwork to 1980*, 26–32, Wessex Archaeological Trust Monograph, 8, Salisbury: Wessex Archaeology.

Corney, A. 1967. A prehistoric and Anglo-Saxon burial ground, Ports Down, Portsmouth, *Proceedings of the Hampshire Field Club and Archaeological Society, 24*, 20–58.

Cox, P. W. 1989. A seventh-century cemetery at Shepherd's Farm, Ulwell near Swanage, Dorset, *Proceedings of the Dorset Natural History and Archaeological Society., 110*, 37–47.

Cunliffe, B. W. 1976. *Excavations at Portchester Castle, Vol. 2., Saxon*, Report of the Research Committee of the Society of Antiquaries of London, 33, London: Society of Antiquaries.

Dyson, R. W. (trans. and ed.), 1998. *Augustine's De civitate Dei*, Cambridge: Cambridge University Press.

Effros, B. 2002. *Caring for the body and soul. Burial and the afterlife in the Merovingian world*, Pennsylvania: Pennsylvania State University Press.

Garner, M. F. 2001. A Middle Saxon cemetery at Cook Street, Southampton (SOU 823), *Proceedings of the Hampshire Field Club and Archaeological Society, 56*, 170–91.

Garner, M. F. 1993. Middle Saxon evidence at Cook Street, Southampton (SOU 254), *Proceedings of the Hampshire Field Club and Archaeological Soc*iety, *49*, 77–127.

Garner, M. F. and Vincent, J. 1997. Further Middle Saxon evidence at Cook Street, Southampton (SOU 567), *Proceedings of the Hampshire Field Club and Archaeological Society, 52*,77–87.

Gittos, H. 2002. Creating the sacred: Anglo-Saxon rites for consecrating cemeteries, in S. Lucy and A. Reynolds (eds), *Burial in early medieval England and Wales*, 195–208, Society for Medieval Archaeology Monograph, 17, London: SMA.

Graham, A. H. and Davies, S. M. 1993. *Excavations in Trowbridge, Wiltshire, 1977 and 1986–1988*, Wessex Archaeology Report, 2, Salisbury: Wessex Archaeology.

Hadley, D. M. 2001. *Death in medieval England*, Tempus: Stroud.

Halsall, G. 1995. *Early Medieval Cemeteries*, Glasgow: Cruithne Press.

Harfield, C. G. 1991. A hand-list of Castles recorded in the Domesday Book. *English Historical Review* 56, 371–392.

Härke, H. 1997. Early Anglo-Saxon social structure, in J. Hines (ed.), *The Early Anglo-Saxons. From the Migration Period to the Eighth Century,* 125–70, Woodbridge: Boydell Press.

Haughton, C. and Powlesland, D. 1999. *West Heslerton. The Anglian cemetery. Volume ii. Catalogue of the Anglian graves and associated assemblages*, Nottingham: Landscape Research Centre.

Henderson, C. G. and Bidwell, P. T. 1982. The Saxon Minster at Exeter, in S. Pearce (ed.), *The Early Church in Western Britain and Ireland*, 145–75, BAR British series, 102, Oxford: British Archaeological Reports.

Jarvis, K. S. 1983. The Bargates Pagan-Saxon cemetery with late Neolithic and Bronze-Age sites, in K. S. Jarvis (ed.), *Excavations in Christchurch, 1969–1980*, 102–35, Dorset Natural History and Archaeological Society Monograph Series, 5, Dorchester: Dorset Natural History and Archaeological Society.

Keene, D. 1985. *Survey of Medieval Winchester,* Winchester Studies 2, part ii and iii. Oxford: Clarendon Press.

Kipling, R and Scobie, G. 1990. Staple Gardens 1989, *Winchester Museum Service Newsletter*, 6, 8–9.

Kjølbye-Biddle, B. 1992. Dispersal or concentration: the disposal of the Winchester dead over 2000 years, in S. Bassett (ed.), *Death in towns*, 210–47, Leicester: Leicester University Press.

Knocker, G. M. 1955. Early burials and an Anglo-Saxon cemetery at Snell's Corner near Horndean, Hampshire, *Proceedings of the Hampshire Field Club and Archaeological Society., 19*, 117–70.

Lapidge, M. (trans.) 2003a. Lantfred of Winchester's Translatio et miracula S. Swithuni, in M. Lapidge (ed.), *The Anglo-Saxon Minsters of Winchester. The cult of St. Swithun. Winchester*

Studies 4.ii, 217–333, Oxford: Clarendon Press.

Lapidge, M. (trans.). 2003b. Wulfstan of Winchester's Narratio Metrica de S. Swithuno, in M. Lapidge (ed.), *The Anglo-Saxon Minsters of Winchester. The cult of St. Swithun. Winchester Studies 4.ii,* 335–551, Oxford: Clarendon Press.

Lucy, S. And Reynolds, A. 2002. Burial in early medieval England and Wales: Past, present and future, in S. Lucy and A. Reynolds (eds), *Burial in Early Medieval England and Wales*, 1–23, Society for Medieval Archaeology Monograph, 17, London: SMA.

Meaney, A. and Hawkes, S. 1970. *Two Anglo-Saxon cemeteries at Winnall, Winchester, Hampshire*, Society for Medieval Archaeology Monograph, 4, London: SMA.

Miles, T. J. 1984. The excavation of a Saxon cemetery and part of the Norman Castle at North Walk, Barnstaple, *Proceedings of the Devon Archaeological Society, 44*, 59–84.

Morton, A. 1992a. *Excavations at Hamwic: Volume 1: Excavations 1946–83, excluding Six Dials and Melbourne Street*, Council for British Archaeology Research Report, 84, London: CBA.

Morton, A. 1992b. Burial in Middle Saxon Southampton, in S. Bassett (ed.), *Death in towns*, 68–77, Leicester: Leicester University Press.

Paxton, F. S. 1990. *Christianizing Death*, London: Cornell University Press.

Rahtz, P. A. and Hirst, S. M. 1974. *Beckery Chapel Glastonbury, 1967–8*, Glastonbury: Glastonbury Antiquarian Society.

Rawlings, M. 1995. Archaeological sites along the Wiltshire section of the Codford-Ilchester water pipeline*, Wiltshire Archaeological and Natural History Magazine, 88*, 26–49.

Rodwell, W. 2001. *Wells Cathedral. Excavations and Structural Studies, 1978–93,* English Heritage Archaeological Report, 21, London: English Heritage.

Rollason, D. 1986. The shrines of saints in later Anglo-Saxon England: distribution and significance, in L. A. S. Butler and R. K. Morris (eds), *The Anglo-Saxon church. Papers on history, architecture and archaeology in honour of Dr. H. M. Taylor,* 32–43, Council for British Archaeology Report, 60, York: CBA.

Rudkin, D. 2001. *Excavations at Bevis' Grave, Camp Down, Bedhampton, Hants.*, Unpublished manuscript held at Fishbourne Roman Palace Museum.

Rumble, A. R. 2001. Edward the Elder and the churches of Winchester and Wessex, in N. J. Higham and D. H. Hill (eds), *Edward the Elder, 899–924*, 230–47, London: Routledge.

Scull, C. 2001. Burials in Emporia in England, in D. Hill and R. Cowie (eds), *Wics: The Early Medieval trading centres of Northern Europe*, 67–74, Sheffield: Sheffield University Press.

Scull, C. and Bayliss, A. 1999. Dating burials of the seventh and eighth centuries: a case study from Ipswich, Suffolk, in J. Hines, K. H. Nielsen and F. Siegmund (eds), *The Pace of Change. Studies in Early Medieval chronology*, 80–8, Exeter: Oxbow Books.

Sherley-Price, L. (trans.). 1955. *Bede. Historia ecclesiastica gentis Anglorum,* London: Penguin.

Southern Archaeological Services. 1998. *Interim report on an archaeological watching brief at 75, Bitterne Road, Southampton*, Unpublished manuscript held at Southampton City Museum.

Stoodley, N. 2002. Multiple burials, multiple meanings? Interpreting the early Anglo-Saxon multiple interment, in S. Lucy and A. Reynolds (eds), *Burial in Early Medieval England and Wales*, 103–21, Society for Medieval Archaeology Monograph, 17, London: SMA.

Swanton, M. (trans. and ed.), 1975. The Blinkling Homilist, An Easter Day Sermon, in M. Swanton (ed.), *Anglo-Saxon Prose*, London: J. M. Dent and Sons, 63–9.

Teague, S. C. 1988. Excavations at Market Street 1987–88, *Winchester Museums Service Newsletter, 2*, 6–8.

Thompson, V. 2004. *Dying and death in later Anglo-Saxon England*, Woodbridge: Boydell Press.

Thompson, V. 2002. Constructing salvation: a homiletic and pentential context for late Anglo-Saxon burial practice, in S. Lucy and A.

Reynolds (eds), *Burial in Early Medieval England and Wales*, 229–40, Society for Medieval Archaeology Monograph, 17, London: SMA.

Thorpe, L.(trans.). 1974. *Gregory of Tours' Historiae Francorum*, London: Penguin Books.

Wade-Martin, P. 1980. *Excavations at North Elmham Park 1967–1972,* East Anglian Archaeology Report, 9, Gressenhall: Norfolk Museums Service.

William, H. 2002. Remains of Pagan Saxondom? – The study of Anglo-Saxon cremation rites, in S. Lucy and A. Reynolds (eds), *Burial in Early Medieval England and Wales*, 47–71, Society for Medieval Archaeology Monograph, 17, London: SMA.

Williams, H. 2003. Remembering and forgetting the Medieval Dead, in H. Williams (ed.), *Archaeologies of Remembrance*, 227–254, New York: Kluwer Academic/Plenum Publishers.

Wormald, P. 1999. *The Making of English Law*, Oxford: Blackwell.

Yorke, B. 1995. *Wessex in the Early Middle Ages*, London: Leicester University Press

Yorke, B. 1984. The bishops of Winchester, the kings of Wessex and the development of Winchester in the ninth and early tenth centuries, *Proceedings of Hampshire Field Club and Archaeological Society,* **40**, 61–70.

Walking with Anglo-Saxons: Landscapes of the Dead in Early Anglo-Saxon Kent

Stuart Brookes

This paper develops the concept of the social and experiential landscape by considering the organisation of funerary monuments with respect to human movement. An analysis of the distribution of Early Anglo-Saxon burials in East Kent demonstrates a close correlation with terrestrial and maritime routeways. Place-name evidence and the topographic positioning of sites are explored to stress the significance of funerary monument visibility. The role of routeways in structuring engagement with the landscape is discussed, with consideration given to how these were increasingly manipulated, restricted and contested by an emergent social order.

Landscapes of Movement

A number of studies have now considered the landscape of burial as evidence of the relationships the living construct with the dead. These studies have shown how the placement, form and use of funerary monuments can be seen as evidence of the ways in which people create and exercise agency on the world around them. Rather than static reminders to the deceased, funerary monuments, in this formulation, are recognised as active media manipulated for the purposes of the living. The practice of funerary deposition always involves decisions and choices, and it is through these choices that people both build the environment they inhabit and create their historical relationship with it.

Recognition of this concept has played an increasing role in the interpretation of the funerary practices of the Early Anglo-Saxons. Beyond more traditional diffusionist explanations, where the landscape context of mortuary remains was used to chart the spatial extent of migratory groups, recent studies have explored the way that funerary practices and relationships to the dead might further be regarded. For example, recent studies have address how burial location might serve to legitimise the strategies of social elites;[1] embody claims and rights over land;[2] as active media in the programme of remembrance and social reproduction;[3] or the crystallisation of ideological

conflicts.[4] Taken together these studies have done much to advance a model of an Anglo-Saxon *Umwelt* (subjective universe) as the projection of perceptions, beliefs and myths on to the physical environment. These studies have highlighted some of the multi-facetted dimensions to landscape, not only by drawing attention to the ways in which sacred places acted as focal points for interpreting the surrounding landscape, but also by considering some of the historical-mythological roles funerary monuments played in their after-life as locales of specialised activities and folklore.[5] In only a few instances, however, has an attempt been made to explore the ways in which mortuary landscape was constructed as part of daily *praxis*.

Using these studies as a point of departure, this paper sets out to develop the concept of the social and experiential landscape by considering the organisation of burial places with respect to both places and traversing the landscape along recognised pathways. The movement of people in landscape is implicitly seen as the basis of many experiential perspectives,[6] and, following Pred,[7] an important element in the creation, maintenance and transformation of social structures. It follows that the placement and organisation of material culture within the perceptual frame of movement offers a way of exploring some of the relationships between the living and the dead. In contrast to a number of previous studies, which have assumed the role of monuments in affecting and guiding movement,[8] this paper will attempt to explore some of the ways in which the siting and visibility of funerary monuments reveal aspects of movement within the landscape.

This approach draws attention to the role of pathways in structuring many of the patterns of Anglo-Saxon everyday life. Although past movement is not exclusive to pathways they provide physical evidence of journeys that have become fossilised through time through habitual use.[9] Moreover, as routeways evidence the structuring of space, they are inseparable from processes of emerging social differentiation.[10] By moving through the landscape along roads; roads act both to mediate the relationship with landscape and become the locus from which interaction of social actors and the structure of the social landscape takes shape. They are, in other words, an important factor in determining the significance of places, and are therefore integral to senses of identity, territoriality and power.[11]

Previous scholarship has made both direct and indirect reference to the importance of roads in social, economic and ideological terms. Who used them and what did movement through the landscape mean? Witney[12] and Everitt,[13] for example, devoted much space to the possible antiquity of the twelfth- and thirteenth-century droves in Kent and their role within the economic web of communications and settlement from the Roman period onwards. Some attempt has also been made, particularly by place-name studies, to stress the importance of Roman roads in the construction of social landscapes.[14] Roads are seen as delimiting boundaries,[15] operating as hundredal meeting places[16] and provide functional benefits to military and economic endeavours.[17] Whilst this important work forms the background to this study, a number of further areas of concern remain. These include the relationship between travelling and experience of landscape, social impacts of movement, and the consequences movement has on the siting of funerary monuments. It is argued that by focusing on an archaeology of movement, insights can be provided, not only into pragmatic relationships between people and landscape, but also the social ordering of space and the ways in which its communities understood their position within it.

With the aim of exploring these themes, this paper considers the topography of movement and burial in East Kent. Large numbers of Early Anglo-Saxon burial sites and routeways that can be considered ancient and potentially contemporary with these funerary grounds provide a substantial data set from which to explore this socialisation of landscape.

Movement and Roads in Anglo-Saxon Kent

At a very generalised level, the Anglo-Saxon settlements of East Kent appear to have appropriated many preexisting topographic features (Fig. 1). Whilst this is not readily demonstrable with regards to settlements *per se*, evidence from the spatial distribution of cemeteries and **OE** place-names suggest that the geometric structure of Roman settlement heavily influenced the shape of the Anglo-Saxon social landscape. In reconstructing this landscape it is important to remember that geomorphological changes in coastal Kent over the past two millennia ensure that the Anglo-Saxon topography and transport geography was somewhat different to that of today. The infilling of the Wantsum Channel[18] and Romney Marsh estuary[19] over the course of the Medieval and Early Modern periods, for example, has done much to negate the importance of riverine and coastal movement in integrating the region. By contrast, the

network of Roman roads radiating out from the *civitas* capital of Canterbury are partially preserved as contemporary routeways and are likely to have operated as important routes throughout the period in question.[20] To these roads can be added a number of paths often claimed to have their origins in prehistoric times.[21] These routes generally follow high-ground for long distances and can be delineated by the close proximity of prehistoric monuments such as Bronze Age round barrows, Roman find-spots along their course and the sometimes partial incorporation within the later Roman road network.[22] However, given the difficulties in dating the origin of these routes, only the most important, the so-called Pilgrim's Way, has been included in the following assessment. Evidence of more localised movement, indicated by subsidiary Roman roads and tracks identified in recent archaeological investigations, has also been discarded, although examples of these, such as the metalled roads uncovered close to the Saltwood cemeteries and at Each End, Ash are tacit reminders of the residual dendritic pattern of communications that may have criss-crossed the Kentish landscape during the Early Anglo-Saxon period.

In addition to this fossilised network of movement, evidence for Anglo-Saxon and Medieval detached pastures revealed from charters and other documentary sources, attest both to the existence of further pathways during the period and the role of these routes in regional economics. Much remarked upon by historians,[23] the extraordinary prevalence of *-den* place-names, compounded by post-Conquest lists of extra-manorial demesne indicate that major estates in coastal areas of Kent counted appurtenant demesne in the Wealden woodland forest for animal pasture amongst their possessions. Thus for example, the thirteenth century archiepiscopal manors of Westgate (Canterbury) included denns in *Betenhame* (Bettenham, in Cranbrook), and *Hatewolden* (High Haldon).[24] Whilst it is often assumed that this system has an Anglo-Saxon ancestry, evidence that earlier estates operated much as their Medieval counterparts is sparse. Of the several hundred denns identified by Witney for the thirteenth century, only forty-eight are mentioned in Domesday Book, and these are not individually named, but included under the heading of the parent manor.[25] Nevertheless, some denns are cited in Anglo-Saxon charters from the mid eighth-century onwards and many of these have been identified with Wealden, and occasionally Blean (S300) place-names.[26] This suggests that dependant pasture formed part of the estate system from at least the eighth century. If this is the case, the example of the holdings of the Bexley manor in AD 814 with lands in the Cray valley and five Wealden denns (S175), probably reflects that of many other estates which are not recorded in the same detail. Even in the absence of conclusive dating this suggests that at least some of the vast number of droves existing as trackways and sunken lanes linking the northern coast with the Weald in the south-west may have

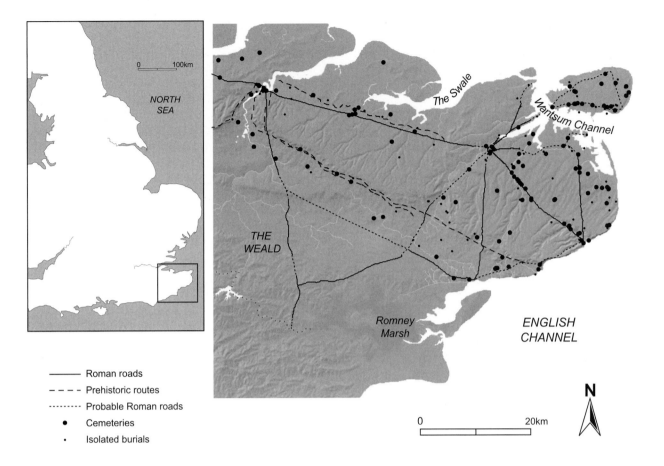

Figure 1. The location of Early Anglo-Saxon funerary monuments in East Kent, showing the reconstructed Wantsum and Romney coastline c. *AD 700 and major Roman and prehistoric routeways*

been used during the Anglo-Saxon period.[27] It follows from this analysis that at least two forms of pedestrian movement, potentially related to different types of routeway, can already be identified. Firstly, the pattern of Wealden transhumance shows the regional movement by people seasonally occupied with stock-rearing between coastal and inland areas. This form of linear movement is in the main distinct from travel along major Roman roads that run perpendicularly to the direction of transhumance. The types of mobility related to these more cyclical routeways are discussed further below.

The Pattern of Funerary Monuments

It is with respect to this transport geography that the distribution of Early Anglo-Saxon cemeteries needs to be considered. The prevalent impression gained from this exercise is that these monuments find close correlation with the fossilised network of Roman communications. Of all 113 burial sites within the case-study area, a significant proportion are located in close proximity to Roman roads, the Pilgrim's Way and the reconstructed coastline. Thirty-five per cent of the sample

lie within a 100 m of these features, half (49%) within 200 m, and nearly a third (61%) within 300 m; figures broadly comparable with the similar statistical analyses by Bonney[28] and Goodier[29] of the relationship of early medieval burials and boundaries. Kolgomov-Smirnov testing comparing actual frequencies with expected random frequencies, proved the statistical significance of these findings, with negative statistical significance noted only at a distances greater than 1400 m.

The clear tendency for funerary sites to be located close to roads or routeways is so persuasive that it is possible to argue that cemeteries not on Roman roads or the coast, mark the course of other contemporary pathways. In support of this theory are eight cemeteries located furthest from the communication network, between 2200 m and 2900 m away. In each instance they correspond either with possible prehistoric routes that were not included in the original calculation, such as the Greenway and North Coast Way, or with droves identified by Witney as part of the later Medieval pattern of transhumance. This suggests that funerary monuments of the sixth and seventh century were sited with respect to the principle routes of movement through the region. One corollary of this view, discussed

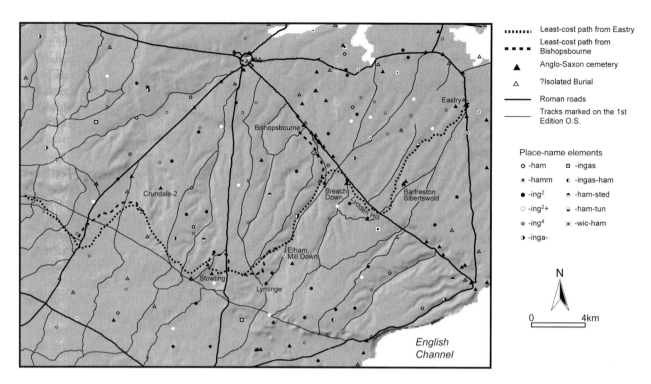

Figure 2. The eastern extent of the least-cost path generated between Eastry, Bishopsbourne and their Wealden denns, projected on an aspect map of the region created from 10m O.S. digital contours

further below, is that routeways may have dictated many of the ways in which funerary monuments were viewed and used, and thereby contributed to the ways in which they became meaningful. Secondly, the relationship between funerary monuments and pathways, in some instances, provides a *terminus ante quem* for their use as communications. The correlation suggests, not only that some of the routeways argued by Witney and Everitt to represent fossilised droves linking the estate centres with appurtenant Wealden pasture in the thirteenth century, may in fact have been used as early as the sixth century, but also that these cemeteries could date the establishment of the system of dependant pasture that was to become so important to later estates.

A 'Low-Cost Path' Test

These observations offer a 'middle-range' theory with which to compare the pattern of Early Anglo-Saxon cemeteries, early place-names and the structure of Middle Anglo-Saxon multiple estates. As parent manors in north Kent are linked with their Wealden outliers along routes of earliest colonisation, these are likely to be governed in-part by functional aspects of accessibility. As such, a predictive model of topographical, least-cost, generated between parent settlement and denn can be compared with the pattern of fossilised paths.

Growing out of site-catchment applications to archaeological research in the 1970s, Cost Surface analysis has

become a mainstay of archaeological GIS applications.[30] By generating a computer model of the landscape as a raster map, costs can be assigned to each cell and accumulated as a travelled path. The route of lowest cost can therefore be calculated with respect to the relevant properties of the terrain, such as slope,[31] visibility,[32] empirical walking effort data,[33] or combinations of the above.[34] Of particular relevance to this discussion is the work of Tyler Bell who has developed an algorithm compiling multiple least-cost paths overlaid as a single road network. This calculation can help to ascertain the optimum route between linked sites as mathematically derived from the tangential slope-aspect of topography.[35]

GIS applications such as this are intimately related with specific technical and epistemological concerns.[36] The use of slope-dependant cost surfaces stresses the reductionist primacy of topography, with little consideration of other factors in determining the location of favoured routes. With this caveat in mind, the mathematical model provided by Bell offers a possible method of exploring specific factors influencing route selection. The anisotropic cost-surface produced takes into consideration certain algorithmic confusion criticised in the case of earlier approaches and offers a simple model of the topographical component influencing optimal paths.

Least-cost path models generated between parent settlements and their historically-attested denns produced a number of notable characteristics of significance to the location of funerary monuments. Firstly, all of the

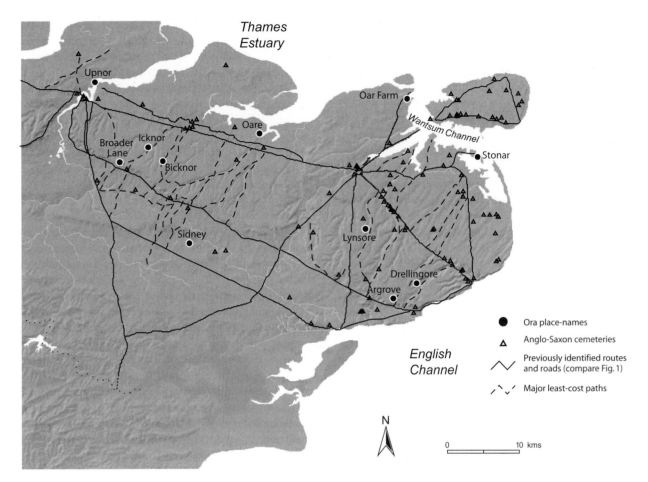

*Figure 3. Map of East Kent showing the distribution of place-names containing the **OE** element* ora *in comparison to main least-cost paths*

paths produced appeared to follow for much of their length known roads, denns or paths (in particular the North Downs trackway[37]), rather than adopting more linear directions of travel – either following the Roman road from Canterbury (Margary 130) or leading directly into the Weald. Instead, the generated optimum paths tend to skirt the northern edge of the Weald before adopting the most direct north-south route to attached denland.

Secondly, there is a close correlation with least-cost paths and routeways hypothesised by more traditional means, but which had not been included in the original statistical survey. For example, the least-cost path joining the settlement at Eastry with its appurtenances at Walkhurst and Sarrenden (Sarnden) in Benenden, along with Henselle and Little Hearsell in Hawkhurst parish[38] roughly follows the potential Roman or prehistoric trackway linking together the known Roman settlements at Eastry and Sibertswold via Thornton Lane and the Thorntonhill trackway,[39] the Nailbourne valley itself, and the course of the North Downs Trackway, known to be marked by a number of important Bronze Age and Anglo-Saxon barrows (Fig. 2).[40] Importantly, this route

highlights the significance in location of several cemeteries lying some distance from major Roman roads. The course of the Thornton Lane trackway leads directly by the Anglo-Saxon burials found at Eastry Mill, to the west of Eastry.[41] The cemeteries of Breach Downs,[42] Elham, Mill Down and Lyminge[43] are close to the Nailbourne valley route, and the ridge-top path from Lyminge into the Great Stour Valley passes closely by the sixth-century cemetery at Stowting, a series of burials on the Wye Down Ridgeway, and through the viewshed of Crundale-2 itself.

Thirdly, the least-resistance paths find close correspondence with routeways indicated by the place-name *ora* (Fig. 3). Possibly derived from either the Latin 'shore' or 'land ahoy', *ora* refers to a flat-topped hill with a shoulder at one or both ends.[44] In Kent, the location of many of the place-names containing *ora* elements are away from Roman roads, but coincident with postulated cross-Down routes, suggesting their likely use as topographical orientation points.

This correlation between predictive models and transport geography is not restricted to terrestrial landforms. I have recently argued that similar evidence suggests that waterborne travel may have also played a significant role in the positioning of funerary monuments.[45] Analysis of the main coastal route around the eastern Kent seaboard was seen to correspond closely not only to the distribution of clinker-boat fragments interred in late sixth- and seventh-century graves,[46] but also with the further *ora* place-names such as Oar Farm and Stonar. Further, it was argued that there was strong evidence to suggest that cemeteries were placed to maximise their visibility to maritime travellers. From a subset of 60 burial sites known to fall within six kilometres of the coast, 90% are visible from the plotted route, and many of these are located at the edges of the produced viewsheds. This indicates, not only a preference for cemeteries to be located on slopes near the crest of hills[47] but also that any above-ground mortuary structure, such as a barrow, would have been sky-lined on a hill top when viewed from the sea.

Communications and Settlements:
the Evidence from Place-names

One explanation for these correlations is that they are merely artefacts of the transport/economic utility underlying settlement hierarchies. Without more archaeological examples of Anglo-Saxon settlements in East Kent it is difficult to assess whether this pattern of cemetery location is not actually that of contemporary settlements located nearby. This lack of evidence can be supplemented by the distribution of 'early' place-names found occurring in written sources up to AD 731.[48] A number of philological investigations have attempted to secure an absolute chronology of place-name elements by comparing these distributions with those of archaeological and geological complexes. Etymologically-defined 'early' place-names have been variously correlated to soil classes,[49] on the assumption that the evolution of settlement developed from more easily worked soils to more marginal areas, or to the pattern established by archaeology.[50] Analyses of this type have recognised the importance and early occurrence of place-names containing topographical elements such as *burh*, *ceaster*, *hām*, *hām-stēde* and *wic* with group elements such as *-ingas*, *-inga-*, and the habitative *-hamm*, belonging to a secondary phase of settlement development.[51]

Despite a general correlation with areas of favoured settlement in Kent (*i.e.* the northern fringe and Holmesdale valley) the pattern of place-names containing early elements such as *-ingas*, *-hām* or *ingahām* is not directly comparable with that of funerary monuments, although they do appear to support a model of settlement evolution into more marginal areas. The distribution of *hām* place-names throughout the north of Kent,[52] and to a certain degree, that of *-ing²* place-names,[53] finds a close correlation with the richer Thanet Bed and Head Brickearth soils of the north coast. Place-names containing the elements *-inga-*, *-ingas*, and possibly *-hamm* alternatively, although

on occasion coincident with Anglo-Saxon cemeteries, in the majority appear to represent a secondary phase of settlement and colonisation, as their distribution is restricted to downland and heavier clay drift soils of the northern coast.[54] Despite a superficial association with Roman roads, as discussed by Dodgson,[55] Kolgomov-Smirnov testing of the distribution of these place-names across East Kent suggests little statistical significance. A similar test of chronologically later *-ingas* and *-ing²* place-names reinforces this negative association.

Visibility

That burial may have been conspicuously sited to take advantage of highly visible locations has was first discussed in 1915.[56] Despite this, Shephard's assertion that barrow siting was determined by the economic forces of land-use has generally held sway.[57] Analysis of a large number of Anglo-Saxon barrow burials throughout both Kent and England led Shephard to stress that the apparent correlation of elevated topography and funerary monuments was a by-product of their position on marginal land.[58] Thus, a distinction was drawn between the position of flat-grave cemeteries such as Bifrons and Howletts on arable Head Brickearth drift, and barrow cemeteries such as the nearby Bishopsbourne and Kingston cemeteries, on Upper Chalk soils less suitable for agriculture.[59]

The demonstrated close association of burial with prevalent routes of communication suggests that additional considerations governed the siting of funerary monuments. Although underlying soils may indeed have determined the form that cemeteries or individual burials took, the significance of these places appears to have been linked to their proximity, and potentially their visibility, from major routeways. Supporting this view is the ubiquity of visible above-ground burial features in Kent in general, not only in the shape of barrow burials, but also in the form of grave-markers such as those recognised from modern excavations at Broadstairs St. Peter's.[60] Whilst it is impossible to gauge just how common these features were, the general impression is that both barrow burials and Shephard's 'flat-grave' cemeteries were distinguished by visible settings; often enhanced by monument construction. Furthermore, given the correlation between routeways and both types of site, it is hard to confine the significance of even smaller scales of barrow to the internal cemetery topography and immediate locality alone.

This suggested emphasis on the visible experience of funerary landscapes is in keeping with a number of recent works that have sought to investigate the significance of Anglo-Saxon ritual sites and monuments with respect to their landscape context.[61] Issues of access and visibility are implicit – if not necessarily addressed – in most of these works, which have done much to emphasise the role of burial places in the spatial ordering

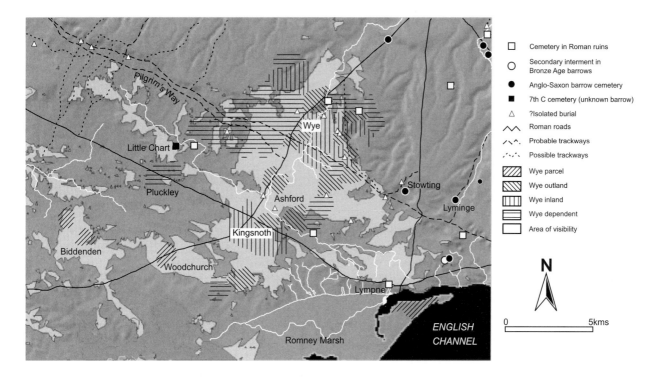

Figure 4. Map of south-east Kent showing the visibility of the landscape from positions two kilometers along the Pilgrim's Way and Roman road from the crossroads at Wye

of landscape. Thus for example, the sitings of burial places have been considered as signifying 'open' or 'enclosed' visible landscapes,[62] within models of territorial demarcation,[63] or in signifying settlement localities.[64] All of these considerations appear relevant in East Kent. Monumental barrow burials such as those of Woodnesborough and Coombe, as well as the cemetery of Sarre for example, seem significantly sited at key points to dominate the visual experience of travellers when moving through the Wantsum Channel. Cemeteries, such as Ozengell, Broadstairs Bradstow School, St Margaret's Bay, Cliffe and many others, are all located on visible spurs above coastal coombs, often overlooking likely landing-places downslope. Significantly, these sites are also usually on inland routeways, and in several cases inland valleys appear to be similarly demarcated by visible funerary monuments. An example is provided by multiple viewsheds produced along the Roman road (Margary 130) and Pilgrim's Way near Wye (Fig. 4). Here, isolated burials seem to enclose Upper Stour valley, occupying visible spurs of the Wye Down and North Down slopes as well as prominent positions to the south at Westwell, Ashford, Brabourne and amongst the Roman ruins at Little Chart. Movement eastwards along the Pilgrim's Way would have revealed to the early medieval traveller similar delineated territories, such as the valleys dominated by the cemeteries at Stowting and Lyminge.

Whilst woodland cover could be seen as a potential problem for seeing some of these monuments, one sug-

gests that the close proximity of cemeteries to identified routes, particularly in inland areas, as well as seasonal variation in vegetation cover, would reduce the impact of trees on site visibility. Trees, rather than restricting the visibility of sites, may have contributed to the significance of burial locations and environs.[65] Interestingly in this regard, viewsheds produced from Wye also find close correlation with the holdings of the medieval manor of Wye.[66] For inland and outland in the Great Stour valley this correlation is likely reflect limits imposed by the local topography. However, the coincidence of islands of visibility such as those around the Roman ruins of Little Chart with the dependant tenure of Pluckley may suggest that intervisibility played some role in determining the pattern of seigneurial holding. Pluckley to the south-west and Kingsnorth to the south, along with the parcel holdings in Woodchurch and Biddenden parishes, remained the only parts of the Weald potentially visible from Wye, and it is these same areas that remain in royal and then ecclesiastical hands until the thirteenth century.[67]

Discussion

In the light of the evidence presented above, it is tempting to suggest that funerary monuments were used to visibly differentiate community territories from as early as the sixth and seventh centuries. Related to this phenomenon may be cases of monument reuse. Most Kentish cemeteries excavated in modern times have revealed fifth-

and sixth-century nuclei associated with prehistoric or Roman monuments (Shephard Types V and VI), indicating the likely proliferation of similar cases of monument reuse amongst the cemeteries excavated in antiquity (*e.g.* Hollingbourne; Lyminge). As many authors have suggested both of Anglo-Saxon and prehistoric burials, it is likely that these monuments, and the associations drawn between them, acted as media through which territorial claims were made by physically naturalising and legitimising some link between past and social present.[68] However, as Shephard[69] has already noted, it is clear that the dialectical relationship between symbolised landscape and society was not static. Thus, in contrast to the reuse of prehistoric features witnessed within fifth- and sixth-century cemeteries, the evidence from such seventh-century settlements as Yeavering,[70] suggests the exclusive appropriation of ancestral links by the aristocracy. Similarly, instead of the group associations fostered by secondary interment within prehistoric and Roman features during the early phase, the conspicuous use of a prehistoric form of mortuary structure i.e. round barrows, restates the symbolic ancestral links of the elite in the seventh century.

Yet as this paper has attempted to demonstrate, this symbolic landscape appears to be tied to routes of movement and the ways in which the landscape was experienced by those travelling through it. In Kent, it seems that an inherited landscape was selectively reused in order to demonstrate the authority of real or imagined elites by the most visible means. Whilst the majority of Bronze Age barrows evident in East Kent appear to have had some Anglo-Saxon reuse, a few, such as those in North Foreland or Eythorne, somewhat removed from the principal routes of communication, have been demonstrated by excavation to have no such evidence.

In keeping, associations between cemeteries and routeways suggest that the emphasis was placed on how landscape was supposed to be experienced and perceived. Further support for this thesis is offered by Kentish law-codes of the seventh century, which offer some evidence of contemporary concerns for the movement of people and goods. The wording of the laws of Æthelberht, and particularly that of Wihtred stress the importance of roads for movement throughout the kingdoms, with heavy penalties being exacted for unannounced travel off the established routes of communication.[71] Ine's code (Ine 20) echoes that of Wihtred (Wihtred 28):

> If a man from afar, or a stranger, quits the road, and neither shouts, nor blows a horn, he shall be assumed to be a thief, [and as such] be either slain or put to ransom.

Specific laws protecting travellers on roads from robbery, as evidenced by Æthelberht 19 and 89, suggest both the importance of safe-transit through the kingdom to the king, and that highway crime was sufficiently common-place that it required explicit measures to be suppressed.

Given the significant number of laws dealing with foreigners, strangers and traders (Æthelberht 19; Hlothere and Eadric 15; Wihtred 4 and 28) it is conceivable that these measures indicate increasing levels of royal control placed on the movement of people and goods through the kingdom; an observation many commentators have associated with tolls and taxation.[72] It is quite clear that roads formed not only the most important routes of movement, with their use actively protected in legislation, but that movement beyond roads was prohibitively dangerous.

More significant from the point of view of monument placement may have been the role that routeways played in peripatetic kingship. If Anglo-Saxon kingdoms, of both the pagan and early Christian period, are to be characterised in a model of gift-mediated patrimony, kings themselves must be seen as the principal agents of communications and social cohesion. Roads therefore play a significant role in facilitating the integration of a territorial region, by aiding the regular physical presence of kings and the concomitant collection of subsistence goods. It is in this context that the clear association of so-called Saxon estate-centres, including the *villa regales* with the prevalent routes of movement is likely to explained.[73]

This concept of direct rule suggests that kings and their retainers were commonly entwined with the geographical encoding of the landscape. Significantly, the ritualisation of long-distance journeys in *Beowulf* suggests that it was the king, or important retainers, and they alone, who could move freely through and beyond the kingdom; a concept potentially underlying the topographical location of a number of postulated vills on tidal inlets.[74] But it also hints at potential conflicts crystallised in the landscape. Examples of this are the restrictions on movement, and specific legislation forcing travellers and foreigners to adhere to routes, detailed in law-codes of the seventh century. It is with respect to these restrictions that the patterns of the visible funerary landscape become significant, as they define not only the established routes through which peers were expected to travel, but also key areas of contested authority. Moreover, as powerful symbols of competing legitimacy, the distribution of these ostentatious burials within the viewshed of travelling kings, aristocrats and foreigners, underline both the territorial claims of the local elite and the fragile basis these claims of landed legitimacy may have had. In other words, routeways became both the conduit of asymmetrical socio-economic relations and the media from which subordinate groups claimed access to holdings and power.

In contrast to this view of in-group competition, the identification of a number of droves and the historically-attested links between regions in Kent suggests that not all middle-distance movement was carried out by elite society. The pattern of denns and droves suggests the existence by the Late Anglo-Saxon period of a regulated network of routes functionally linking mother-settlements in northern Kent with detached Wealden common. Although some concept of serfdom must be expected within this model of estates, this suggests that further restrictions governed the *Umwelt* of servants and lower members of society. Bound both by livelihood and law (Wihtred 10), the experience these populations had of the wider landscape was restricted to the estate and an annual pattern of droving – the seasonal to-ing and fro-ing of the rural economy.

Significantly, proportionately few burials have been identified on these routes, supporting the idea of a hierarchical structure underlying the communication network. In favour of this interpretation, the distribution of royal woods in the Weald form a continuous band along the northern margin following the Roman road from Sutton Valence to Great Chart (Margary 131).[75] These holdings are intersected perpendicularly by Wealden droves leading to common lands beyond. This example emphasises the division of the experiential landscape. On the one hand, it seems that for lower echelons of society, daily praxis and the social construction of the world was defined by the permitted routes of movement, many of which were governed by the economic prerogatives of estate maintenance.

Freemen and the élite, on the other hand, interacted more widely with the landscape, although it seems, still from the locus of the defined routes of communication.

Coming out of this analysis is a definition of Anglo-Saxon space in which conceptions of landscape coincide with the hierarchical nature of social orders. Sea, road and drove are envisaged within a model of stratified geographical movements, schematically relating to the tiers of society. It is as a reflection of this, that they embody crucial aspects of ideology, power and identity.

Acknowledgements

The topographic slope and aspect information used in the generation of least-cost paths was derived in Idrisi from a digital elevation model of East Kent produced at 50m pixel resolution from 10m Ordnance Survey digital contours provided by the Digimap Project (http://edina.ac.uk/digimap/). My thanks go to Tyler Bell and Andrew Bevan for specialist advice in the computation of these. This paper has further benefited from the comments of Martin Welch, Howard Williams, Gustav Milne and an anonymous referee.

Notes

1. Arnold 1980.
2. Shephard 1979.
3. Williams 1998.
4. Carver 2002.
5. *E.g.* Semple 1998; Williams 1999.
6. Tuan 1977; Tilley 1994; Chapman 1997.
7. Pred 1986.
8. See for example Thomas 1993a; 1993b; Barrett 1994; Tilley 1994.
9. Trombold 1991.
10. Pred 1986, 5; Tilley 1994, 31; Witcher 1997, 61.
11. Roads may of course themselves be places with symbolic significance, as is suggested by the close proximity to and orientation of graves such as those from Cottgrave in Nottinghamshire and Churchover in Warwickshire (Meaney 1964, 200, 259). In both cases Roman roads – the Fosse Way and Watling Street respectively – clearly formed the focus for mortuary deposition; the graves at Churchover being interred both within and alongside the road for *c.* a half a mile.
12. Witney 1976.
13. Everitt 1986.
14. Hooke 1985.
15. *Ibid.*, 58.
16. *Ibid.*, 102.
17. Hindle 1993, 48–50.
18. Brookes 2002.
19. Eddison and Green 1988; Rippon 2002.
20. Margary 1948.
21. Though for recent critiques of the antiquity of some of these routes see Turner 1980; Harrison 2003.
22. *E.g.* Margary 1951.
23. *E.g.* Furley 1871–74; Du Boulay 1961; Witney 1976.
24. Du Boulay 1961, 76.
25. Reaney 1961, 72.
26. The earliest mention of a Wealden denn appears in a charter from

762 when the Abbey of St. Augustine received confirmation that Wye was to cede rights of pasture in the wood of Andred in return for the use of half a mill at Chart (Ibid. 71). Denns are also mentioned in the early charters S24; S25; S30.
27. Everitt 1986, Map 1.
28. Bonney 1966; Bonney 1976.
29. Goodier 1984.
30. *E.g.* Vita-Finzi and Higgs 1970; Gaffney and Stanèiè 1991; Gillings and Wheatley 2003.
31. Gaffney *et al.* 1993.
32. Madry and Rakos 1996.
33. Rajala 2000.
34. van Leusen 1999.
35. Bell and Lock 2000.
36. Cf. Llobera 1996.
37. Margary 1951.
38. Witney 1976, 274.
39. O'Grady 1979.
40. Meaney 1964, 142.
41. Hawkes 1979.
42. Meaney 1964, 111.
43. *Ibid.*, 127.
44. Cole 1990.
45. Brookes 2002; *forthcoming* a.
46. Brookes *forthcoming* b.
47. A pattern also recognised of Anglo-Saxon cemeteries in Kent by Richardson 2000.
48. Cox 1976.
49. Wooldridge 1948.
50. *E.g.* Dodgson 1966; Kirk 1972; Cox 1973; Kuurman 1975.
51. Cox 1976; Dodgson 1966.
52. Dodgson 1973.
53. Kirk 1972.
54. *Ibid.*
55. Dodgson 1973, 11–13.

56. Baldwin Brown 1915, III , 142–6.
57. Shephard 1979, 3.9–10.
58. *Ibid.*
59. *Ibid.*, 3.10.
60. Hogarth 1973.
61. *E.g.* Bonney 1966, 1976; Williams 1997, 1999; Lucy 1998; Reynolds 1998.
62. *E.g.* Williams 1999.
63. *E.g.* Bonney 1976; Goodier 1984; Reynolds 1998.
64. Arnold and Wardle 1981.
65. Palaeoenvironmental evidence for post-Roman East Kent is sparse, with a dependency on samples from Sugarloaf Hill, Folkestone or Brook in the Weald, offering little direct or local evidence for the subtlety and patch-work character of the rural scene (Scaife 1987, 125). In very general terms pollen sequences record a reduction of *Quercus* during the Roman/Anglo-Saxon period with an associated expansion of *Corylus, Fraxinus, Fagus* and *Carpinus* secondary woodland, possibly related to either a new phase of community expansion, or, as these species represent the most common coppicing *taxa*, increased woodland management (Scaife 1995, 303–313).
66. Jolliffe 1933, MAP 1.
67. *Ibid.*
68. *Ibid.*; Renfrew 1976; Bradley 1998; Williams 1998.
69. Shephard 1979.
70. Bradley 1987;1993.
71. Law-codes cited here as numbered and translated by Attenborough 1922.
72. *E.g.* Carver 1993; Reynolds 1998, 237.
73. Everitt 1986; Brookes 2002.
74. Brookes *forthcoming* a.
75. Witney 1976, 61.

Abbreviations

S   Sawyer, P. H., 1968. *Anglo-Saxon Charters: an Annotated List and Bibliography*, R. Hist. Soc. Guides and Handbooks, 8, London: R. Hist. Soc.

Bibliography

Arnold, C. J. 1980. Wealth and social structure: a matter of life and death, in P. A. Rahtz, T. M. Dickinson and L. Watts, L. (eds) *Anglo-Saxon Cemeteries 1979*, 81–142, British Archaeological Reports British Series, 82, Oxford: British Archaeological Reports.

Arnold, C. J. and Wardle, P. 1981. Early Medieval settlement patterns in England, *Med Archaeol.,* **25**, 145–49.

Attenborough, F. L. 1922. *The Laws of the Earliest English Kings*, Cambridge: Cambridge University Press.

Baldwin Brown, G. 1915. *The Arts in Early England, III, Saxon Art and Industry in the Pagan Period*, London: J. Murray.

Barrett, J. C. 1994. *Fragments from Antiquity: archaeology of social life in Britain, 2900–1200 BC*, Oxford: Blackwell.

Bell, T. and Lock, G. 2000. Topographic and cultural influences on walking the Ridgeway in later prehistoric times, in G. Lock, (ed.), *Beyond the Map: archaeology and spatial technologies*, 85–100, Amsterdam: IOS Press.

Bonney, D. J. 1966. Pagan Saxon burials and boundaries in Wiltshire. *Wiltshire Archaeol. Mag.,* **61**, 25–30.

Bonney, D. J. 1976. Early Boundaries and Estates in Southern England, in P. H. Sawyer (ed.), *English Medieval Settlement*, 72–82, London: Edward Arnold.

Bradley, R. 1987. Time regained: the creation of continuity, *Jnl. Brit. Archaeol. Assoc.,* **140**, 1–17.

Bradley, R. 1993. *Altering the Earth: The origins of Monuments in Britain and Continental Europe. The Rhind Lectures 1991–92*, Society of Antiquaries of Scotland Monograph Series, 8, Edinburgh: Society Antiquaries Scotland.

Bradley, R. 1998. *The Significance of Monuments*, London: Routledge.

Brookes, S. J. 2002. Landscapes, Communities and Exchange: a reassessment of Anglo-Saxon economics and social change AD 400–900 with special reference to Kent, unpublished PhD Thesis, University College London.

Brookes, S. J. *forthcoming* a. The View from the Sea: maritime migration and the colonised landscapes of Early Anglo-Saxon Kent, in F. Stevens (ed.), *The Archaeology of Water*, London: UCL Press.

Brookes, S. J. *forthcoming* b. Clench-nails from Anglo-Saxon cemeteries in Kent, *International Jnll of Nautical Archaeol.*

Carver, M. O. H. 1993. *Arguments in Stone*, Oxbow Monograph, 29, Oxford: Oxbow.

Carver, M. O. H. 2002. Reflections on the meanings of monumental barrows in Anglo-Saxon England, in S. Lucy and A. Reynolds (eds), *Burial in Early Medieval England and Wales*, Society for Medieval Archaeology Monograph,17, 132–43, London: SMA.

Chapman, J. 1997. Places as timemarks – the social construction of prehistoric landscapes in eastern Hungary, in G. Nash (ed.), *Semiotics of Landscape: archaeology of mind*, 31–45, British Archaeological Reports International Series, 661, Oxford: British Archacological Reports.

Cole, A. 1990. The meaning of the OE place-name element *ora, Jnl. of the English Place-Name Soc.,* **22**, 15–22.

Cox, B. 1973. The Significance of English Place-Names in ham in the Midlands and East Anglia, *Jnl. of the English Place-Name Soc.,* **5**, 15–73.

Cox, B. 1976. The place-names of the earliest English records, *Jnl. of the English Place-Name Society*, **8**, 12–66.

Dodgson, J. McN. 1966. The Significance of the Distribution of the English Place-Name in ingas, -inga- in South-East England, *Med. Archaeol.,* **10**, 1–29.

Dodgson, J. McN. 1973. Place-Names from *ham*, distinguished from *hamm* names, in relation to the settlement of Kent, Surrey and Sussex. *Anglo-Saxon England,* **2**, 1–50.

Du Boulay, F. R. H. 1961. Denns, Droving and Danger, *Archaeologia Cantiana,* **76**, 75–87.

Eddison, J. and Green, C. (eds). 1988. *Romney Marsh: evolution, occupation, reclamation*, Oxford University Committee for Archaeology Monograph, **41,** Oxford: Oxford University Committee for Archaeology.

Everitt, A. 1986. *Continuity and Colonization: the evolution of Kentish Settlement*, Leicester: Leicester University Press.

Furley, R. 1871–74. *A History of the Weald of Kent, with an outline of the Early History of the County*, (2 Volumes. 1871, 1874), Ashford.

Gaffney, V. L. and Stancic, Z. 1991. *GIS approaches to regional analysis: A case study of the island of Hvar*, Znanstveni institut Filozofske fakultete, University of Ljubljana, Yugoslavia: Ljubljana.

Gaffney, V. L., Stancic, Z., Farley, J. *et al.* 1993. Geographical Information Systems, Territorial Analysis and Prehistoric Agriculture on the Island of Hvar, Dalmatia, in M. Fabris I. Kuzma, I. and K. Markova (eds), *Actes du XXIIe Congres International des Sciences Pre- et Protohistoriques, Bratislava, 1–7 Septembre 1991,* 407–15, Institut archeologique de l'Academie Slovaque des Sciences a Nitra: Bratislava.

Gillings, M. and Wheatley, D. 2002. *Spatial technology and archaeology: the archaeological applications of GIS*, New York: Taylor and Francis.

Goodier, A. 1984. The formation of boundaries in Anglo-Saxon England: a statistical study, *Med. Archaeol.,* **28**, 1–21.

Harrison, S. 2003. The Icknield Way: some queries, *Archaeol. Jnl.,* **160**, 1–22.

Hawkes, S. C. 1979. Eastry in Anglo-Saxon Kent: its Importance, and a newly-found Grave, *Anglo-Saxon Studies in Archaeol. and Hist.*, **1**, 81–113.

Hindle, B. P. 1993. *Roads, Tracks and their Interpretation*, London: Batsford.

Hogarth, A. C. 1973. Structural features in Anglo-Saxon graves, *Archaeol. Jnl.*, **130**, 104–19.

Hooke, D. 1985. *The Anglo-Saxon Landscape: the Kingdom of the Hwicce*, Manchester: Manchester University Press.

Jolliffe, J. E. A. 1933. *Pre-Feudal England: The Jutes*, London: Oxford University Press.

Kirk, S. 1972. A Distribution Pattern: -ingas in Kent, *Jnl. of the English Place-Name Soc.*, **4**, 37–59.

Kuurman, J. 1975. An Examination of the *-ingas, -inga-* Place-Names in the East Midlands, *Jnl. of the English Place-Name Soc.*, **7**, 11–44.

Llobera, M. 1996. Exploring the topography of the mind: GIS, social space and archaeology, *Antiquity*, **70**, 612–22.

Lucy, S. 1998. *The Early Anglo-Saxon cemeteries of East Yorkshire*, British Archaeological Reports British Series, 272, Oxford: British Archaeological Reports.

Madry, S. L. H. and Rakos, L. 1996. Line-of-sight and cost-surface techniques for regional research in the Arroux River valley, in H. D. Maschner (ed.), *New Methods, Old Problems. Geographical Information Systems in Modern Archaeological Research*, Southern Illinois University Center for Archaeological Investigations Occasional Paper, 23, 104–26, SIUSAI: Carbondale.

Margary, I. D. 1948. Notes on Roman Roads in East Kent, *Archaeologia Cantiana*, **61**, 126–32.

Margary, I. D. 1951. The North Downs Main Trackway, *Archaeologia Cantiana* **64**, 20–23.

Meaney, A. 1964. *A Gazetteer of Early Anglo-Saxon Burial Sites*, London: George Allen and Unwin.

O'Grady, M. M. 1979. Hedgerows and Tracks, *Archaeologia Cantiana*, **94**, 111–26.

Pred, A. 1986. *Place, Practice and Structure: Social and Spatial Transformation of Southern Sweden*, Cambridge: Polity Press.

Rajala, U. M. 2000. GIS in the analysis of the settlement patterns in central Italy. The possibilities and problems in studying south-east Etruria. *Proceedings of the 15th international congress of classical archaeology, Amsterdam July 12–17, 1998*, 311–313, Amsterdam.

Reaney, P. H. 1961. Place-Names and Early Settlement in Kent, *Archaeologia Cantiana*, **76**, 58–74.

Renfrew, C. 1976. Megaliths, territories and populations, in S. De Laet (ed.), *Acculturation and continuity in Atlantic Europe*, 198–220, Bruges: De Tempel.

Reynolds, A. J. 1998. 'Anglo-Saxon Law and the Landscape', unpublished PhD Thesis, University College London.

Richardson, A. F. 2000. 'The Anglo-Saxon Cemeteries of Kent', unpublished PhD Thesis, University of Cardiff.

Rippon, S. 2002. Romney Marsh: evolution of the historic landscape and its wider significance, in A. Long, S. Hipkin and H. Clarke (eds), *Romney Marsh: Coastal Landscape Change Through the Ages*, 83–99, Oxford: Oxford University Committee for Archaeology.

Scaife, R. G. 1987. A review of the Quarternary plant microfossil and macrofossil research in southern England: with special reference to environmental archaeological evidence, in H. C. M. Keeley (ed.), *Environmental archaeology: a regional review Vol.II*. HBMC occasional paper, 1, 125–179, London: Historical Buildings and Monuments Commission for England.

Scaife, R. G. 1995. Pollen analysis from the Wantsum Channel, in C. Hearne, D. Perkins and P. Andrews, The Sandwich Bay Wastewater Treatment Scheme Archaeological Project 1992–4, *Archaeologia Cantianae*, **115**, 303–13.

Semple, S. 1998. A fear of the past: the place of the prehistoric burial mound in the ideology of middle and later Anglo-Saxon England, *World Archaeol.*, **30**(1),109–26.

Shephard, J. 1979. 'Anglo-Saxon Barrows of the Later 6th and 7th Centuries AD', unpublished PhD Thesis, University of Cambridge.

Thomas, J. 1993a. The politics of vision and the archaeologies of landscape, in B. Bender (ed.), *Landscape: politics and perspectives*, 19–48, Oxford: Berg.

Thomas, J. 1993b. The Hermeneutics of Megalithic Space, in C. Tilley (ed.), *Interpretative Archaeology*, 73–98, Oxford: Berg.

Tilley, C. 1994. *A phenomenology of landscape: places, paths and monuments*, Oxford: Berg.

Trombold, C. D. 1991. *Ancient Road Networks and Settlement Hierarchies in the New World*, Cambridge: Cambridge University Press.

Tuan, Y. 1977. *Space and Place: the perspective of experience*, London: Edward Arnold.

Turner, D. J. 1980. The North Downs Trackway, *Sussex Archael. Collections*, **72**, 1–13 van Leusen, M. 1999. Viewshed and Cost Surface Analysis Using GIS, in J. A. Barcel, I. Briz and A. Vila (eds), *New Techniques for Old Times: CAA98. Computer Applications and Quantitative Methods in Archaeology*, British Archaeological Reports International Series, 757, 215–23, Oxford: British Archaeological Reports.

Vita-Finzi, C. and Higgs, E. S. 1970. Prehistoric economy in the Mount Carmel area of Palestine. Site Catchment Analysis, *Proc. of the Prehistoric Soc.*, **36**, 1–37.

Williams, H. M. R. 1997. Ancient landscapes and the dead, *Med. Archaeol.*, **41**, 1–32.

Williams, H. M. R. 1998. Monuments and the past in early Anglo-Saxon England, *World Archaeol.*, **30**(1), 90–108.

Williams, H. M. R. 1999. Placing the dead: investigating the location of wealthy barrow burials in seventh-century England, in M. Rundkvist (ed.), *Grave Matters: Eight Studies of First.*

Millennium AD Burials in Crimea, England and Southern Scandinavia, British Archaeological Reports International Series, 781, 57–86, Oxford: British Archaeological Reports.

Witcher, R. 1997. Roman Roads: phenomenological perspectives on roads in the landscape, in C. Forcey, J. Hawthorne and R. Witcher (eds), *TRAC 97: proceedings of the 7th Annual* Theoretical Roman Archaeology Conference which formed part of the 2nd International Roman *Archaeology Conference. University of Nottingham, April 1997*, 60–70, Oxford: Oxbow Books.

Witney, K. P. 1976. *The Jutish Forest: a study of the Weald of Kent from 450 to 1380 AD*, London: Athlone Press.

Wooldridge, S.W. 1948. The Anglo-Saxon Settlement, in H. C. Darby (ed.), *An Historical Geography of England before AD 1800*, 88–133, London: Cambridge University Press.

New Perspectives on Cemetery Relocation in the Seventh Century AD: the Example of Portway, Andover

Nick Stoodley

Introduction

Over the last thirty years archaeological investigations in the area known as the Portway, Andover, Hampshire, have produced a range of important Iron Age, Roman and Anglo-Saxon period sites. This article focuses on the relationship between a partially excavated seventh- to earlier eighth-century site at Portway West[1] and the much better known late fifth- and sixth-century cemetery at Portway East[2] to examine the phenomenon of cemetery relocation within a local setting. In the course of so doing the article compares the Anglo-Saxon evidence with that from the Roman and Iron Age sites to suggest a model for the evolution of the Portway land unit and the nature of territorial organisation during the early Anglo-Saxon period.

The cemetery at Portway West was first encountered in 1981 during construction work on the western part of the Portway Industrial Estate (Fig. 1). Only brief details of the burial ground are given here but a full account can be found in Stoodley (2006). In total, seventeen graves were recovered from what is almost certainly a much larger burial ground (Fig. 2). Assuming that the excavated graves belong to the same cemetery it could have covered an area of about 3600 m², roughly similar to Portway East and could thus have contained anywhere between 60 and 100 interments.

The site focuses on a Bronze Age barrow (Homestead Farm Barrow) and is notable because of an intriguing double burial of two decapitated males, plus two pen-annular ditches that were probably associated with Saxon graves. The cemetery appears to exhibit a row-grave arrangement with the graves aligned south-north (heads to the south) and most of the interments extended supine. Grave goods were rare and were limited to just one or two artefacts (the number of interments with objects is six), though grave 6 yielded a more generous assemblage which included a pin and chatelaine (Fig. 3).

Cemetery Relocation and the Final Phase

The character of the objects accompanying grave 6 coupled with the general lack of grave goods indicates that Portway West belongs to a short-lived group of cemeteries traditionally believed to have been established around AD 600 and commonly termed final phase – a term coined in the 1930s by E. T. Leeds[3] to denote the last of the burials accompanied by grave goods. At this time the change was seen often as resulting from the conversion to Christianity which is documented in Bede's Ecclesiastical History. Thus a seemingly neat succession in burial from pagan to Christian could be charted. From the 1930s to the 1980s the model was gradually developed and one key area centred on situations where a final-phase cemetery appeared to replace an earlier 'pagan' burial site. The classic examples are Chamberlain's Barn, Leighton Buzzard (Bedfordshire)[4] and Winnall (Hampshire),[5] and at both sites religious change was considered to be the driving force behind the urge to re-establish and relocate. Since this heyday, the topic of relocation has enjoyed modest attention, but has mainly focussed on the establishment of elite or princely burials sited separately from the rank and file. C. J. Arnold's[6] processual study argued that the establishment of new cemeteries reflected the polarisation of wealth in society, while Helen Geake asked whether the new burial sites and rites were the symbolic manifestations of new cultural and political groups, who also asserted pagan beliefs in opposition to the threat posed by the spread of Christianity.[7]

It was Andy Boddington, nevertheless, who brought the final-phase cemeteries back into focus, and demonstrated that the final-phase model was inherently weak because of the inadequacy of the excavated data.[8] This led him to systematically dismantle the notion that religious motivation was the main reason, thus pointing out that social, economic and landscape issues should also be considered. Unfortunately Boddington's thesis has still to be tested against a large dataset. However,

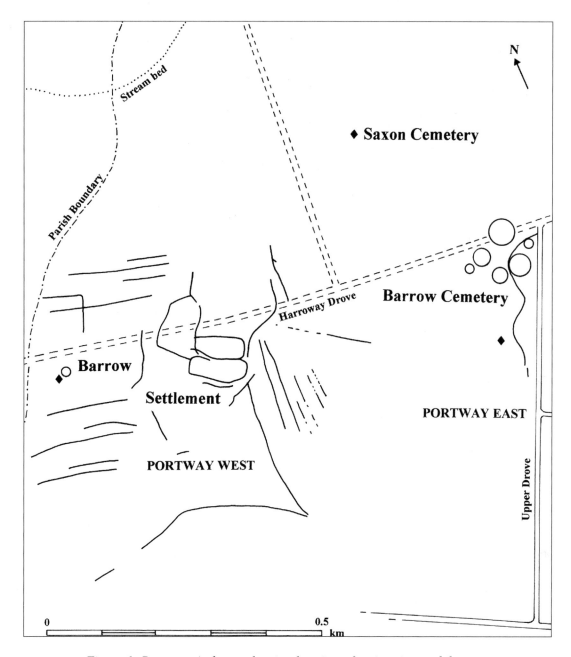

Figure 1. Portway, Andover, showing location of major sites and features

the Portway sites afford an excellent opportunity to revisit this debate and to examine the phenomenon of cemetery relocation at least within a local context.

The evidence provided by the two Portway cemeteries is considerably better than many of the other 'classic' two-cemetery configurations, especially Winnall – of obvious relevance because it is the only other example from Hampshire. Although about half of Winnall II was recovered, the only information surviving from the earlier cemetery (Winnall I), discovered during the construction of a railway line, amounts to just three unstratified shield bosses. Thus Portway places us in a much stronger position to investigate the relationship between two burial

grounds and to explore why, at least at this site, cemetery shift occurred. Did it take place under religious pressure or because of changes to the community's social structure; perhaps it was a result of changing landscape dynamics?

The Two Portway Cemeteries

Portway West lies 800 m to the west of Portway East and close to the presumed course of the Roman road from Silchester to Old Sarum, which gives its name to the area, and just south of the Harrow Way, a prehistoric track way similar to the Ridge Way (Fig. 1). The

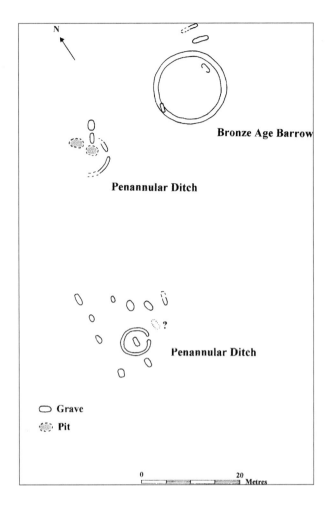

Figure 2. Portway West Anglo-Saxon cemetery: the excavated features

cemeteries were placed in a rich archaeological landscape, with evidence from the Neolithic, Bronze Age, Iron Age and Romano-British periods. The cemetery at Portway East is a mixed rite early Anglo-Saxon cemetery possibly beginning as early as the late fifth century and continuing in use until the late sixth century.

Before we can begin to investigate the reasons why burial shifted to a new site it is necessary to establish that the two were actually related. It is possible that they both belong to different settlements and the relationship is spurious: an artefact of archaeological activity. The physical distance between the two sites is the first matter to be explored. As Table 1 shows, in all but one case, the distances involved demonstrate that it is probably correct to refer to the cemeteries as paired.

Almost all of Portway East seems to have been excavated: the limits were defined on the north, south and east sides. While on the west, some burials may have been lost during the construction of the road, development on the opposite side of the road did not produce any graves.[9] So the possibility that the cemetery at Portway East was part of a longer-lasting burial ground

Table 1. Distance separating paired cemeteries

Eastry	650 m
Winnall	350 m
Long Wittenham	402 m
Leighton Buzzard	73 m
Wakerley	250 m

can be ruled out. The situation at Portway West, however, is not so clear cut: a coherent excavation strategy was not followed, excavation taking place piecemeal during the development of the site.

The Andover Archaeological Society and Test Valley Archaeology Trust have between them examined a large part of Portway West however, discovering evidence of occupation from the Neolithic to the present day, and it is significant that no fifth- and sixth-century material has been recovered. This alone argues against it being part of a larger cemetery with an earlier component. Considering that no positive evidence exists to suggest otherwise, it can be assumed that the two were related.

The next crucial issue concerns when relocation occurred. It is logical to place the foundation of the former shortly after the latter closed; in this way there would be an unbroken sequence of burial from the earlier to the later cemetery. Burial at Portway East continued into the second half of the sixth century as the type C3 spearhead with grave 44, the saucer brooches of seven running-leg design accompanying burial 35, the beads and type C knife in burial 23, and the polychrome beads with burials 9 and 44, demonstrate. Clearly, these are late migration-period burials, yet there is also evidence that prior to the abandonment of this ground, practices one would normally associate with the seventh century were starting to take hold. The clearest example is grave 51, a large pit lying roughly in the centre of the cemetery, which has a shelf along one side of the grave; such structural elements are a feature of seventh-century graves.[10] Moreover, the adult individual, although buried with jewellery, was not equipped with a pair of brooches and a necklace in typical sixth-century style, rather the items consisted of pin and what can be loosely described as a chatelaine, *i.e.* a group of objects suspended from the waist, which concur with the late date suggested by the shelf. The chatelaine consisted of, amongst other items, three iron rings, one of which was fused to an iron rectangular plate, and is not terribly unlike the example from Portway West grave 6, though it is lacking the iron chain. Of further interest is the group of eight graves found on the western extremities of the cemetery. The location of this group may support a late date for their interment and the majority are materially impoverished. Of the eight graves, only three were accompanied by grave goods: grave 64 with a pin, grave 65 with a knife and grave 61 which has a greater number

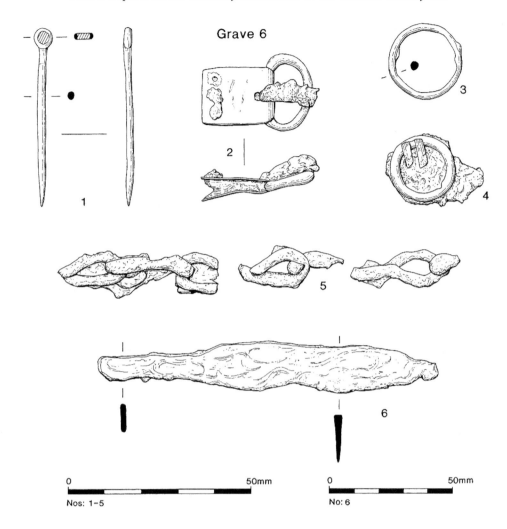

Figure 3. The artefacts from grave 6, Portway West

of objects (necklace of and amber beads plus several pendants comprising copper alloy strips and pierced Roman coins). The latter burial could be of sixth century date given the types of beads and it could be argued that because there are no definitive seventh-century types with any of the interments a similar date might apply to all in the group. Yet the general spartan character of these burials is indicative of a seventh-century date; they are not that dissimilar to the burials from Portway West. Moreover, Northern Hampshire seems to lack the fine assemblages that generally characterise the female burials of the seventh century, like those found in Kent and Wiltshire and it may not be appropriate to expect to find this class of burial in this region. These materially impoverished interments from Portway East therefore might signal a change in female costume in the late sixth and early seventh century that could bridge the transition from the migration to the final phase.

The possible presence of these practices may suggest that Portway East continued into the early seventh century. The implication for burial at Portway West is

that it could have commenced in the first half of the seventh century. Yet the general lack of grave goods, compared to some other final-phase cemeteries such as Winnall II, is notable and may in fact indicate that the cemetery was established later in the seventh century. Recent work utilising the latest developments in radio-carbon dating at the Buttermarket cemetery, Ipswich, have shown that an absence of grave goods cannot be interpreted solely in chronological terms, however.[11]

Cemetery Relocation at Portway

If this chronology is correct then it has important implications regarding the reasons why relocation took place. Most notably, the church could not have been responsible for either the changes to burial practice or the transference of burial. Portway West was probably established before Christianity was even introduced in the area, sometime in the last two thirds of the seventh century, let alone had time to become established. Moreover, the changes to burial rites, often associated with the final phase, had already started to influence practices at Portway East. Long-lasting sites such as Castledyke[12] (Lincolnshire) and Lechlade (Gloucestershire),[13] in use from the late fifth to the late seventh/ early eighth century, demonstrate that changing burial customs do not necessarily result in the establishment of a new burial place. At all these sites clear transformations in burial practice can be observed: the decline of mixed burial practices giving way to inhumation; new dress fashions probably inspired by developments in Kent; a general reduction in grave goods and physical changes to the structure of the grave. These are not abrupt changes; rather they are gradual responses by the community to new cultural influences. To reiterate, changing burial customs or religious factors did not force the closure of Portway East, another event must have prompted the community to abandon this burial ground.

Neither is there any firm evidence to suggest that an evolving social hierarchy and increased wealth was responsible for the shift. The latest burials at Portway East do not exhibit any difference in terms of grave good quality and quantity or grave elaboration to the earliest burials. No complex mid to late-sixth-century chamber graves like those found at Spong Hill, Norfolk[14] exist, which may point to the emergence of local elite. Similarly Portway West has not produced any clear evidence of burial elite which might indicate that a changing social structure prompted the establishment of a new cemetery. It should though be mentioned that grave 11 was surrounded by a modest penannular ditch, which could reflect someone of heightened social importance and thus worthy of having their space within the cemetery demarcated. It is also notable that the area lacks any high-status barrow burials or interments where the individual could be described as unusual in terms of wealth or social standing.

Now that religious and economic motivations can be ruled out the enquiry can be widened to take account of the wider landscape setting of the two sites and especially their relationship to prehistoric monuments. At Portway East the cemetery was discovered about 80 m to the south of a cluster of six middle-Bronze Age round barrows. It is notable that although close to the earlier monuments, the cemetery was not directly related spatially. At Portway West, however, the site is in direct association with a single barrow (Homestead Farm Barrow) of Bronze Age date.[15] Grave 17 was inserted into the ditch floor, it was unaccompanied, but the style of the burial, and sherds of Anglo-Saxon pottery found in the ditch, indicate that it is contemporary with the cemetery. In addition, an empty grave pit was discovered in the barrow and two further graves (1 and 4) were found close to the north-east edge of the barrow.

If the only determining factor in the decision to relocate was a desire to bury one's dead around an earlier monument, perhaps because it served as a visible landscape feature, or helped to promote a link with the ancestors,[16] then why did the community move 800m to the west, when a cluster of six barrows were within a stone's throw of the earlier cemetery?

The answer to this may lie in a consideration of earlier land use patterns and territorial organisation. The Portway cemeteries are on a chalk spur that rises from the river Anton, along which the Harrow Way had connected three prehistoric settlements. The ditched enclosures at Old Down Farm[17] and Portway West,[18] which each cover about 10 acres, were mainly occupied during the Iron Age. In fact recent work on the prehistoric pottery from Portway West has found that the two sites were probably established at roughly the same time (Champion pers. comm.). Both sites have also produced limited evidence for settlement in the Romano-British period.[19] In particular a small collection of Romano-British pottery spanning the whole of the period was recovered from Portway West,[20] while in the same area two extended inhumations interred in wooden coffins and dug into earlier features are probably late-Roman in date (Champion pers. comm.). The settlement at Blendon Drive lies in between the aforementioned sites and saw very limited archaeological investigation, revealing buildings of a probable ditched settlement of the middle/late Iron Age into the early Roman period.[21] An important feature is the Portway East linear ditch, which though undated could have been established during the Iron Age to serve as a boundary between the Blendon Drive and Portway West settlements.[22]

The evidence is sufficient to permit a tentative reconstruction of the prehistoric and possibly the Romano-British land division system at Portway, within which the Saxon evidence can be evaluated. The Portway East linear ditch was still visible in the sixth century AD as the relationship of the Portway East Saxon cemetery to it makes perfectly clear. The fact that the ditch was still serving as a boundary suggests that the prehistoric/ Romano-British pattern strongly influenced the Anglo-Saxon: perhaps indicating continuity of land-use into the post-Roman period. This explanation is preferred over one that sees the ditch being employed in the organisation of the burial ground, perhaps as a simple boundary demarcating the area of the dead. There is precious little evidence for the formal bounding of cemeteries[23] and although numerous early Anglo-Saxon cemeteries were initially sited close to earlier field boundaries and ditch systems, e.g. Berinsfield, they often came to grow over these features suggesting that no firm relationship existed.[24]

Various studies have demonstrated that the Anglo-Saxons commonly utilised long established field patterns, at least until the tenth century,[25] though as Andrew Reynolds points out, the survival of field boundaries does not necessarily mean continuity of cultivation and we should anticipate periods of abandonment.[26] In fact the general scarcity of Romano-British evidence would suggest that these farmsteads went into a decline during the Roman occupation, perhaps as a result of the establishment of large grain producing villas located just to the west on Salisbury Plain. The establishment of the cemetery on the former boundary during the late-fifth century implies that this process was now beginning to be reversed, however, and that the eastern part of this unit was once again under cultivation. The position of the cemetery on a boundary indirectly suggests that the Anton Valley was witnessing other similar processes and that a new form of landownership was being signalled. In fact, evidence for early medieval activity is provided by the Anglo-Saxon settlement at Old Down Farm – directly over the Iron Age settlement. To the west of this site and on the other side of the river, early Anglo-Saxon structures and artefacts have been found at several locations in the village of Charlton:[27] such as a small collection of pottery found at Armstrong Rise and sunken-featured buildings at Goch Way. In addition, sherds of vegetable-tempered pottery and a Saxon bead were recovered from the Foxcotte settlement site,[28] just to the west of Charlton and roughly opposite Portway East. Was it this resurgence in activity that made it necessary to mark the limits of one's territory?

Rather than viewing the linear ditch as primarily demarcating the eastern edge of the cemetery, is it more correct to see the siting of the cemetery as a means to reactivate this earlier boundary? A number of features in the Portway East cemetery may add weight to this hypothesis. In the eastern part of the burial ground, close to the ditch and ringed by a group of graves, are two slots which are traversed by a line of post-holes. These features have never been satisfactorily explained, though it seems certain that they formed a structure contemporary with the burials.[29] A possible reconstruction would see screens or fences placed in the slots in combination with a row of posts. This could have had religious significance and/or it may have acted as a territorial marker. Lying on the cemetery's eastern edge it would have been easily visible from the other side of the ditch and it is notable that it is on the same alignment of the ditch, perhaps another reflection of the line of the boundary ditch (Andrew Reynolds pers. comm.).

It can then be suggested that during the course of the sixth century, and probably in response to an enlarging population, the amount of land being farmed gradually increased until it reached an extent similar to that achieved in the prehistoric/Roman period. Did the increase in territory necessitate that a visible sign of land ownership be established on the western boundary? If it did, it may have been this act which resulted in relocation and burial shifting to Portway West late in the sixth or early seventh century. The cemetery came to focus on the Bronze Age barrow, because yet again this ancient feature would not, on its own, be sufficient. How would people know that this barrow was now marking a land boundary if nothing about it had changed? Like at Portway East, it had to be associated with contemporary activity so that it would be clear to surrounding settlements that it had now become an active symbol marking the new western boundary of this land unit. Indeed, the renaming of prehistoric monuments in the middle and late Saxon periods demonstrates that the appropriation of these features into the early medieval landscape was an established practice.[30] Was this practice taking place at the end of the early Anglo-Saxon period too?

Of course, to be able to assert the above hypothesis with any force the site of the contemporary settlement(s) served by the Portway cemeteries will need to be demonstrated. Without this knowledge, it could be argued that the cemeteries may have been located immediately adjacent to their settlement(s) as opposed to lying at some distance on the land unit's periphery. Although there is no direct evidence for the settlement(s), the evidence from Old Down Farm, Charlton and Foxcotte may allow a tentative suggestion to be made regarding the likely whereabouts of the Portway settlement(s). It is notable that the settlement evidence from the above three sites is located in the valley bottom close to the river (Table 2), whereas both the Portway cemeteries were sited on higher ground and at a much greater distance from the river. This observation is compatible with the evidence from other river valleys in Hampshire, such as the Dever and Itchen, where although in close proximity, the living and the dead did not occupy the same space around a settlement. The dead were deliberately placed above the living, again at a distance of several hundred

Table 2. Anton Valley sites giving height above sea level and distance from water. Note: averages have been given for the three Charlton sites

Site	Height above sea level (metres)	Distance from water source (metres)
Old Down Farm	70	60
Charlton sites	70	120
Foxcotte	67	60
Portway East	85	275
Portway West	90	300

metres away, thus showing a clear separation between the living and the dead.[31] On the basis of this finding it can be suggested that the settlement served by the Portway cemeteries would also have been located in the valley bottom close to the water source. The settlement may in fact be the one indicated by surface finds at Foxcotte, although this site lies on the opposite side of the river. Unfortunately not enough is known about settlement patterns in this part of the county to say whether a settlement and its cemetery(s) would have to be confined to one side of the river. Was the river acting as a boundary as well? Again we cannot be sure. Nevertheless, the evidence does seem to indicate that the cemeteries were peripheral to the land unit – not centrally placed around the settlement; a finding which supports the notion that the burial grounds acted as boundary markers in this period.

That the cemetery at Portway West may have been the western boundary of a land unit is further suggested by the fact that the parish boundary with Penton Mewsey is found just a few metres to the west. A boundary is recorded on the 1857 Ordnance Survey 1" Geological map,[32] which is very similar to the one recorded in 1614, and according to Russel, must represent an estate boundary at that time, perhaps reflecting part of the territory of a more ancient land unit.[33] If parishes were based on secular estates, they should share common boundaries,[34] and the implication here is that the modern boundary is in part a fossilisation of earlier territorial organisation: possibly the western limits of the Portway West prehistoric/Romano-British site, which was re-established, possibly as early as the end of the sixth century, and was responsible for cemetery relocation. Although the idea that a significant proportion of cemeteries were sited on the limits of earlier territorial boundaries which over time became parishes boundaries,[35] cannot be proven statistically,[36] in individual cases where the evidence is expansive, such as here, it is a model which deserves serious consideration.

Conclusion

This study has raised several important questions regarding the final phase, territorial organisation and cemetery relocation. The Portway sites contribute important evidence to the debate about the origins and the chronology of final-phase sites. Geake[37] draws attention to the fact that because earlier and later cemeteries in areas outside Kent have few characteristics in common, it is usual to date them some time apart. However, Portway East seems to show that some features normally associated with the final phase may have been taking hold in the late sixth or early seventh century. The important contribution made by the Portway sites is that this is a much more subtle change than that found later in the seventh century as indicated by the appearance of the wealthy female assemblages typified by the garnet inlaid metal pins and necklets consisting of metal beads and wire rings. Portway may demonstrate a development in burial practice more akin to that identified as having taken place in the late sixth century in the current English Heritage funded project (*Anglo-Saxon England c. 580–720: the Chronological Basis*) – evidence for a progression in burial practice throughout the sixth and seventh centuries. Moreover, if, as seems likely, Portway West was established shortly after burial in Portway East ceased then this would suggest a much earlier date for the establishment of final-phase cemeteries, in Wessex at least, than traditional scholarship has permitted.

The study has suggested that concepts of land ownership and territorial organisation may have been important to rural settlement from the sixth century. By the following century this evidence can be set alongside several other cases which show the increasingly important and varied role that land and property demarcation was now playing. For example, in the Avebury region (Wiltshire) Semple[38] argues that high-status barrow burials were used to demarcate competing territory. While at the other end of the scale the evidence from rural settlements in Hampshire, such as Chalton and Cowdery's Down[39] demonstrates that space was now being ordered within the farmsteads and hamlets of rural southern England. Does the evidence from Portway allow the evolution of an early Anglo-Saxon period land unit to be glimpsed? Can it provide a model that can be used to understand the development of similar examples in terms of their territory and the positioning of sites?

Finally, Portway is important because it has been possible to undertake a detailed investigation into the relationship between a sixth- and a seventh-century cemetery and to evaluate it against the backdrop of the local landscape and evidence of earlier territorial administration. Consequently, the findings have much to contribute to the debate surrounding why cemetery relocation occurred. The findings from Portway broadly confirm Boddington's claim that the reason behind relocation has more to do with the evolution of the landscape than religious factors. But it has discovered that the reasons are considerably more complicated than first imagined. At Portway the evidence should be viewed as reflecting the regeneration of a former landscape: a landscape that was not static, but changed with response to different social and political stimuli.

Acknowledgements

I should like to express my gratitude to Hampshire County Council, especially Dave Allen and Kay Ainsworth, and Wessex Archaeology for their assistance with the material and documentary archives, David Taylor and Rob Read for preparing the illustrations,

Tim Champion for information about the excavation of the Iron Age site at Portway West, Andrew Reynolds for his valuable comments on an earlier version of this paper and Annia Cherryson, Chris Fern and Mark Stedman for discussing the Portway sites with me. Thanks go to

Howard Williams for the invitation to speak at the conference and the opportunity to share my ideas both verbally and in print. Finally I am grateful to the helpful comments and suggestions provided by the anonymous referee.

Notes

1. Cook and Dacre 1985, 3; Stoodley 2006.
2. Cook and Dacre 1985.
3. Leeds 1936, 96–114.
4. Hyslop 1963.
5. Meaney and Hawkes 1970.
6. Arnold 1982.
7. Geake 1992, 91–2.
8. Boddington 1990.
9. Cook and Dacre 1985, 52.
10. Hogarth 1973.
11. Scull and Bayliss 1999, 86.
12. Drinkall and Foreman 1998.
13. Boyle, Jennings, Miles, and Palmer 1998.
14. Hills 1984.
15. Power, unpublished archive report.
16. Härke 1994; Williams 1997.
17. Davies 1979.
18. Champion pers. comm.
19. Dacre unpublished archive report.

20. Millett, unpublished report.
21. Dacre unpublished archive report.
22. Cook and Dacre 1985, 10–11.
23. Hirst 1985, 20–24.
24. Boyle, Dodd, Miles and Mudd 1995.
25. Reynolds 1999, 22.
26. *Ibid.*, 22.
27. Wright 2004.
28. Russel 1985.
29. Stoodley 1999, 131–2.
30. Reynolds 2002 171–194.
31. Hawkes and Grainger 2003.
32. Russel 1985, 150.
33. *Ibid.*, 150.
34. Hooke 1998, 70.
35. Bonney 1966, 1979.
36. Goodier 1984, 12; Reilly 1988.
37. Geake 1997, 11.
38. Semple 2003.
39. Reynolds 2003.

Bibliography

Arnold, C. 1982. Stress as a stimulus to socio-economic change, in C. Renfrew and S. Shennan (eds), *Ranking, Resource and Exchange*, 124–131, Cambridge University Press.

Boddington, A.1990. Models of burial, settlement and worship: the final phase reviewed, in E. Southworth (ed.), *Anglo-Saxon Cemeteries: a reappraisal*, 177–99, Stroud: Sutton.

Bonney, D. J. 1966. Pagan Saxon burials and boundaries in Wiltshire, *Wiltshire Archaeolog. and Nat. Hist. Soc.*, **61**, 25–30.

Bonney, D. J. 1979. Early boundaries and estates in southern England, in P. H. Sawyer (ed.), *English Medieval Settlement*, 41–51, London: Edward Arnold.

Boyle, A., Dodd, A., Miles, D. and Mudd, A.1995. *Two Oxfordshire Anglo-Saxon Cemeteries: Berinsfield and Didcot*, Thames Valley Landscapes Monograph, 8, Oxford: Oxford University Committee for Archaeology?

Boyle, A., Jennings, D., Miles, D. and Palmer, S. 1998. *The Anglo-Saxon Cemetery at Butler's Field, Lechlade, Gloucestershire, Volume I: Prehistoric and Roman activity and Anglo-Saxon Grave Catalogue*, Thames Valley Landscapes Monograph, 10, Oxford: Oxford University Committee for Archaeology.

Cook, A. M. and Dacre, M. W. 1985. *Excavations at Portway, Andover 1973–1975*, University of Oxford Committee for Archaeology Monograph, 4, Oxford: Oxford University Committee for Archaeology.

Dacre, M. undated. *Excavations at Portway Industrial Estate, Andover*, unpublished archive report, Hampshire County Council.

Davies, S. M. 1979. Excavations at Old Down farm, Andover. Part I: Saxon, *Proc. Hampshire Field Club Archaeol. Soc.*, **36**, 161–80.

Drinkall, G. and Foreman M. 1998. *The Anglo-Saxon Cemetery at Castledyke South, Barton-on-*Humber, Sheffield Excavation Reports, 6, Sheffield: Sheffied Academic Press.

Geake, H. 1992. Burial practice in seventh- and eighth-century England,

in M. Carver (ed.), *The Age of Sutton Hoo*, 83–94, Woodbridge: Boydell Press.

Geake, H. 1997. *The Use of Grave-Goods in Conversion-Period England, c. 600–850*, BAR British Series, 261, Oxford: British Archaeological Reports.

Goodier, A. 1984. The formation of boundaries in Anglo-Saxon England: a statistical study, *Medieval Archaeol.*, **28**, 1–21.

Härke, H. 1994. A context for the Saxon barrow, in M. G. Fulford, and S. J. Rippon, Lowbury Hill, Oxon: a Re-assessment of the Probable Romano-Celtic Temple and the Anglo-Saxon barrow, *Archaeol. Jnl.*, **151**, 202–6.

Hawkes, S. C. and Grainger, G. 2003. *The Anglo-Saxon Cemetery at Worthy Park, Kingsworthy, near Winchester, Hampshire*, Oxford University School of Archaeology Monograph, 59, Oxford: Oxford School for Archaeology.

Hills, C. 1984. *Spong Hill Part III: Catalogue of Inhumations*, East Anglian Archaeology, 21, Gressenhall: The Norfolk Archaeological Unit.

Hirst, S. 1985. *An Anglo-Saxon Inhumation Cemetery at Sewerby, East Yorkshire*, York University Archaeological Publications, 4, Leeds: Maney and Son Limited.

Hogarth, A. C. 1973. Structural features in Anglo-Saxon graves, *Archaeol. Jnl.*, **130**, 104–19.

Hooke, D. 1998. *The Landscape of Anglo-Saxon England*, London: Leicester University Press.

Hyslop, M. 1963. Two Anglo-Saxon cemeteries at Chamberlains Barn, Leighton Buzzard, Bedfordshire, *Archaeol. Jnl.*, **120**, 161–200.

Leeds, E. T. 1936. *Early Anglo-Saxon Art and Archaeology*, Oxford: The Clarendon Press.

Meaney, A. L. and Hawkes, S. C. 1970. *Two Anglo-Saxon cemeteries at Winnall, Winchester, Hampshire*, Society for Medieval Archaeology Monograph, 4, London: SMA.

Millett, M. undated. *Romano-British Pottery from Portway, Andover*, unpublished archive report, Hampshire County Council.

Power, S. undated. *A Round Barrow on Portway Industrial Estate, Andover, Hampshire*, unpublished archive report, Hampshire County Council.

Reilly, P. 1988. *Computer Analysis of an Archaeological Landscape*, BAR British Series, 190, Oxford: British Archaeological Reports.

Reynolds, A. 1999. *Later Anglo-Saxon England*, Stroud: Tempus.

Reynolds, A. 2002. Burials, boundaries and charters in Anglo-Saxon England: a Reassessment, in S. Lucy and A. Reynolds (eds), *Burial in Early Medieval England and Wales*, 171–94, Society for Medieval Archaeology Monograph, 17, London: SMA.

Reynolds, A. 2005. On farmers, traders and kings: archaeological reflections of social complexity in early Medieval Europe, *Early Medieval Europe*, **13**(1), 97–118.

Russel, A. 1985. Foxcotte: the archaeology and history of a Hampshire hamlet, *Proc. Hampshire Field Club Archaeol. Soc.*, **41**, 149–224.

Scull, C. and Bayliss, A. 1999. Dating burials of the seventh and eighth centuries: a case study from Ipswich, Suffolk, in J. Hines, K. H.

Nielsen and F. Siegmund (eds), *The Pace of Change: Studies in Early Medieval Chronology*, 80–8, Oxford: Oxbow Books.

Semple, S. 2003. Burials and political boundaries in the Avebury region, North Wiltshire, *Anglo-Saxon Studies in Archaeology and History*, **12**, 72–91.

Stoodley, N. 1999. *The Spindle and the Spear: A Critical Enquiry into the Construction and Meaning if Gender in the Early Anglo-Saxon Burial Rite*, BAR British Series, 288, Oxford: British Archaeological Reports.

Stoodley, N, 2006. Changing Burial Practice in the Seventh Century AD: the Anglo-Saxon Cemetery at Portway West, Andover, *Proc. Hampshire Field Club Archaeol. Soc.*, **61**, 63–80.

Williams, H. 1997. Ancient landscapes and the dead: the reuse of prehistoric and Roman landscapes as early Anglo-Saxon burial sites, *Medieval Archaeol.*, **51**, 1–32.

Wright, J. 2004 Excavation of Early Saxon settlement and Mesolithic activity at Goch Way, near Charlton, Andover, *Proc. Hampshire Field Club Archaeol Soc*, **59**, 116–38.

De Situ Brecheniauc and *Englynion Y Beddau*:
Writing about Burial in Early Medieval Wales

David Petts

Early medieval archaeology has always had an uneasy relationship with textual evidence, bouncing between over optimistic uses of written sources to interpret both events and processes recognised in the archaeological record to the cynical rejection of the value of historical evidence and approaches to the study of material culture.[1] The use of written evidence to illuminate early medieval attitudes and practices surrounding death, burial and commemoration have a particularly long history of use and abuse. All too often, certain prominent texts, such as the Anglo-Saxon poem *Beowulf*, have been employed as illustrations of early medieval burial practices.[2] This approach focuses on extracting nuggets of *realia* from the texts to confirm archaeological interpretations, as if texts record first-hand observations or objective recollections of mortuary practices. Texts are often adduced to supplement archaeological evidence, and in doing so, material culture serves merely as an addendum or illustration to the written sources of the period. A range of early medieval Welsh texts, such as the *Englynion y Beddau*, *Marwnad Cynddylan* and the *Historia Brittonum* have been used in this manner to explicate early Welsh burial practices.[3]

It is important to acknowledge the complexity of such exercises. Whilst documentary evidence may certainly shed light on contemporary and past burial practice in some instances, the relationship between text and practice is a complex one. It is important to understand the social and political context in which the text was produced, the choices and selections made in how mortuary rites are portrayed and the possible literary elaborations to which texts can be subject. Rather than the wholesale adoption or rejection of the written evidence for inform our understanding of early medieval mortuary practices, this paper suggests that a fruitful way forward lies in regarding both as meaningful 'discourses' involving both ideas and practices. In this light, early medieval literature and archaeological evidence were not two separate strands running along in parallel, yet separate, tracks. Instead, as this paper will show, the wider threads of discourse about death and burial that ran through early medieval Welsh society was expressed in a dialogue between the textual record and mortuary practice in a recursive relationship with each other. By exploring the ways in which two texts, the *Englynion y Beddau* and *De Situ Brecheniauc*, wrote about burials and mortuary monuments, I want to try and explore the discursive relationship between text and material culture in early medieval Wales. While this is not the place to review the rich corpus of archaeological evidence for burials, cemeteries as well as inscribed and sculpted monuments of early medieval Wales, the paper hopes to illustrate that both texts, graves and monuments formed part of an emerging ideology and practice about the role of burial and commemoration in society from the ninth to the eleventh centuries AD.

Englynion y Beddau

The text most frequently adduced in discussions of burial in early medieval Wales is the collection of three-line *englynion* (stanzas) known collectively as the *Englynion y Beddau* (Stanzas of the Grave) or *Beddau Milwyr ynys Prydein* (The Graves of the warriors of the Island of Britain).[4] This consists of 73 stanzas describing the mythical burial places of famous, and not so famous, Welsh warriors. The stanzas have been recorded from several sources, but the most extensive collection comes from the *Black Book of Carmarthen*, the earliest version dating from the second quarter of the thirteenth century. Although no known manuscript examples predate AD 1000, consensus, based on the metrical patterns and textual history, points to a ninth/tenth century date.[5]

The verses seem to be full of evidence for burial in barrows and cairns in a variety of topographical locations: on the seashore, on mountains, by rivers, in churches and at fortified sites. It is noticeable, however, that out of all the graves mentioned only six are located in ecclesiastical contexts. Dylan is buried at Llanfeuno which can probably be identified as Clynnog Fawr in

Caernarvonshire[6] and the grave of Ceri Long-sword is placed 'in the churchyard of Corbre' at Heneglwys in Anglesey,[7] Cynon is buried at Llanbadarn,[8] Owain ab Urien at Llanforfael[9] and Llemenig is buried at Llanelwy, probably St Asaph.[10] It is this rarity of church burial that should warn against using the *Englynion y Beddau* for understanding contemporary (ninth/tenth century) burial practice, let alone earlier rites. Whilst it is hard to be certain about the date that churchyard burial became dominant in early medieval Wales, archaeological and written evidence would suggest that it was likely to have been commonplace by the time the *Englynion y Beddau* were composed. The kings of Gwynedd were burying at Llangadwaladr by the end of the seventh century[11] and the crosses from Llantwit Major[12] suggest that it was a royal burial site in the tenth century. Other documentary evidence, such as *De Situ Brecheniauc* and *Cognacio Brychan* suggest that in the tenth century churches were seen as the appropriate place for royal burial. Equally unlike Type 1 stones, the seventh- to tenth-century Type 2 cross-marked stones are found almost exclusively on ecclesiastical sites and excavations at ecclesiastical centres such as Llandough show a long-sequence of burials from the seventh century onwards

It is clear that the *Englynion y Beddau* do not record contemporary burial practices, but neither is there reason to believe that the mortuary practices of earlier generations were being accurately portrayed. This is because while cairns, mounds and graves with structures are known dated to sixth to ninth centuries AD from Wales, they do not correspond in any direct way with the descriptions recorded in the *Englynion y Beddau*, Nonetheless, the source does seem to be deliberately conjure up a vision of monuments that serves to connect the contemporary landscape to a perceived, mythical past. Indeed, it has even been suggested that the use of the old-fashioned three-line englynion form rather than the more usual four-line englynion form was a deliberate 'archaicizing' literary device.[13] If so, then the subject matter and literary style unify to strengthen the message.

There is also other evidence to suggest that this group of poems is not describing a simple historical past, but a more subjective mythic past. Whilst not all of the warriors mentioned in the *Englynion y Beddau* are identifiable, there are at least three groups of recognisable individuals. The first group, and in some ways the most 'historic' are a group of heroes usually identified with the 'Old North', the *gwr y gogledd*: Rhydderch the Generous, Owain ab Urien and Cynon ap Clydno Eidyn.[14] Their historical context is in the northern kingdoms of Strathclyde, Rheged and Gododdin. In the poems, however, they are localised in a Welsh geographical context; Owain ab Urien is buried in Llangorfael and Rhydderch at Aberech.[15]

A second overlapping group includes those associated with the emerging Arthurian cycle, such as Bedwyr, Gwalchmai, Cynon, March and Gwythur,[16] though it is

recorded that the grave of Arthur himself was 'the wonder of the world', as its location was unknown. Again, although perhaps originally from a Northern British context, they too were localised in Wales.

The final group includes individuals who were probably euphemerised pre-Christian gods that may have survived in Christian culture as heroes, such as Dylan and Lleu Lawgyffes.[17] Most of the other names mentioned are otherwise unknown, but Jones has suggested that many of the names were eponyms derived from the names of landscape features. For example, he equates Epynt with the Epynt mountain, near Llangamarch.[18] In other cases individuals are related to well known landscape features:

20 Three graves of three steadfast ones are on a
      conspicuous hill
      in Pant Gwyn Gwynionog
      Mor and Meilu and Madog.

Looking at these groups of identifiable individuals it is clear that many of the stanzas in the *Englynion y Beddau* are not historicizing the Welsh landscape, but mythologizing it. It is one of the few examples of topographical and onomastic lore known from the early Welsh poetic tradition. Two verses describing the route of rivers are found in *Canu Heledd* but there is nothing comparable to the Irish metrical *dindsenchas*. However, there are Irish parallels in a group of tenth century poems from Leinster, such as 'On the Graves of the Leinster Men', written in 972 by Broccán the Pious of the monastery at Clonmore.

A few earlier examples of topographical lore can be found within Wales. The best-known examples are the 'Wonders of Britain' from the *Historia Brittonum*.[19] These *mirabilia* first appear in the Harleian text derived from a redaction of AD 829/30. In this short collection, however, the emphasis is on miraculous properties of certain sites, such as unmeasurable tombs or apples growing on an ash tree, rather than linking the wonders to particular historical or mythical stories.[20] Even when one of the sites is connected with a named individual, such as Amr, son of Arthur,[21] it is the miraculous nature of the site rather than its historical context that justifies its mention. However, these examples are operating in a different genre to the *englynion y beddau* in which the locations are made significant by the presence of the individual warriors, and there is a notable lack of any significant supernatural elements.

This mythologization of the Welsh landscape is best seen in the context of the time in which it was written down. The ninth and tenth centuries were a period of great tension in the Welsh kingdoms, caught between the expanding Saxon kingdoms to the east and the Danes, known as the 'Black Gentiles', threatening from Ireland and Scotland to the west and north. It is noticeable that at least two of the groups of the identifiable individuals in the *Englynion y Beddau*, the Arthurian group and the *gwyr y gogledd*, were known for their struggles against Anglo-Saxon expansion. Arthur was associated with the battles of Badon and Camlan. There is also an explicit reference to the Battle of Camlan in the text:

12 The grave of Osfran's Son is at Camlan,
after many a slaughter;
the grave of Bedwyr is on Tryfan Hill.

It is possible that these graves were believed to have been in Merioneth, where the village of Camlan (SH 85 12), is 12 km south of Llyn Tegid (Bala Lake), which is associated with Morfran, son of Tegid, who was believed to have escaped the Battle of Camlan. Also 18km from Camlan is Twyn where a fourteenth century praise-poem to St Cadfan alluded to Osfran in a positive light.[22]

It is in this context that the stanzas can be best appreciated: they literally write a history of resistance to invaders of the landscape of Wales. Indeed, there is even an overt reference to warfare against the Saxons.

16 Whose is the grave of good repute
who would lead a compact host against Lloegr [England]?
The grave of Gwên, son of Llywarch is this

The warriors with names are eponymous with landscape features were therefore connected to the Welsh countryside onomastically, and there is evidence to suggest that some of the sites mentioned were actually prehistoric monuments: prominent ancient sites whose original construction was lost in time. The description of the graves at Gwanas may suggest that a megalithic chambered tomb was being referred to, possibly one that had been robbed out and explored without notable discoveries:

29 The long graves on Gwanas, –
they who despoiled them did not discover
what they were, what their mission was.

30 The war-band of Oeth and Anoeth came thither
to their man, to their servant;
let him who would seek them dig Gwanas

The possible references to treasure being found in the graves, may suggest the discovery of prehistoric grave-goods, considering the lack of a tradition of grave-goods in early medieval Welsh graves:

60 The grave of Taflogau, son of Lludd is in his homestead yonder,
as he is in his durance,
whoso would dig it would find treasure.

Equally the references to four-sided stone graves may well be better understood as the remains of prehistoric monuments, rather than looking for parallels with Pictish cairns or the early medieval squarebarrows at Tandderwen:

63 Whose is the four-sided grave
with its four stones at its head?
The grave of Madawg, fierce horseman.

Jones has also identified the grave of Dylan, with the standing stone, known as Maen Dylan close to Clynnog Fawr, on the beach between Aberdesach and Pontlyfni. He has also suggested that the three graves of Cynon, Cynfael and Cynfeli, recorded as being on Cefn Celfi[23] may be identified as the three standing stones, on the farm of Cefn Celfi, near Neath.[24]

The poem transforms the landscape of Wales with its landmarks, both natural and prehistoric, into a landscape of resistance to Saxon and Danish incursions. The emphasis on landmarks and legendary heroes with a tradition of defending Wales serves to place the *Englynion y Beddau* as part of the arsenal of literary weapons built by the Welsh in the tenth century against the English and the Vikings. This means that any attempt to use the stanzas as a way to directly understand fifth- to seventh-century burial practice must be carried out with extreme caution. Whilst there may certainly be echoes of earlier burial practices, they are to be understood through a ninth- or tenth-century lens. Whether burial sites of a fifth- to seventh-century date were being accurately remembered or not, it does appears that the composers of the *Englynion y beddau* were interpreting and portraying mortuary monuments in a mythological rather than an 'historical' or 'archaeological' manner.

But how can it help us better understand strategies of mortuary behaviour in ninth- and tenth-century Wales? It seems that this appreciation of the literature as a means by which death and landscape were mythologized, sheds new light on at least one unusual burial site from the period, namely the unique memorial known as the Pillar of Eliseg.[25] This is a curious structure, drawing from a range of traditions in an unusual act of cultural *bricolage* that created a unique memorial. The column may have originally been surmounted by a cross head and is clearly inspired by eighth- and ninth-century Mercian cross-shafts. Like the Mercian monuments, the sculpture may have evoked links with Rome and the Roman past through its form and also the commemorative context of royal power and ecclesiastical patronage. However, the extensive inscription records that it was set up by the King of Powys, Cyngen, who died in 856. It carries a genealogy of the kings of Powys linking them back to the mythical fifth-century British king Vortigern and the Roman imperial usurper Magnus Maximus. It connects this mythical past to the prestige of Cyngen's recent ancestors, recording the success of Cyngen's grandfather, Eliseg, in warfare against the English. In the 840s or early 850s, when it was probably erected, the kingdom of Powys was again suffering from increased pressure from both Anglo-Saxons. Aethelwulf was probably raiding into Powys in 853, and there may have been attacks from the increasingly powerful

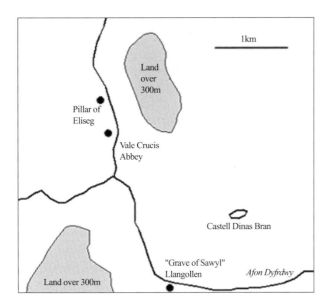

Figure 1. The environs of the Pillar of Eliseg, Denbighshire

kingdom of Gwynedd under the leadership of Merfyn Frych and Rhodri Mawr.[26]

The cross with its surviving commemorative column was only one element of the monument. The stone itself lies on an earth mound – a unique position for a mid-ninth century memorial stone. Antiquarian investigation in the eighteenth century revealed a stone cist and a silver coin. It has been suggested that these were the remains of a prehistoric burial and that it was a case of the early medieval re-use of an earlier medieval barrow.[27] However, there is extensive evidence for early medieval re-use of burials and there is no reason to assume that this burial was not early medieval in date.[28] Consequently, the memorial could have been raised on a site that Cyngen knew (or believed or even invented) as the burial mound of one of his ancestors.

I would argue that as well as using Anglo-Saxon sculptural traditions and Welsh genealogical traditions, this monument also has a dialogue with either the *Englynion y Beddau* or related contemporary traditions which placed the graves of heroes, notably those who had resisted foreign invasion (in this context foreign referring to the English and the kingdom of Gwynedd), at prominent burial mounds. Ultimately, this ideological weapon was not a success; Cyngen was forced into exile where he died. He was the last recorded king of Powys until the last quarter of the eleventh century. Be that as it may, the monument can be interpreted as a statement of resistance to Mercian hegemony, made more effective through its adoption of Mercian commemorative iconography to achieve this.

Intriguingly, one of the *Englynion y Beddau*, interpolated into the body of the Llywarch Hen poems includes references to sites in the vicinity of the Pillar of Eliseg:

Bed Gwell yn y Riw Velen	The grave of Gwell in Y Rhiw Felen
Bed Sawyl yn Llan Gollen	The grave of Sawyl in Llangollen
Gwercheidw llam yr bwch Lloryen	Llorien guards 'roebuck's leap'

This seems to place at least two legendary burial sites in the same general area as the Pillar of Eliseg (Fig. 1). The grave of Sawyll, one of the sons of Lywarch Hen is in Llangollen. Patrick Sims-Williams has pointed out that there was a site named Rhiwfelen only about 5 miles from Llangollen.[29]

Within its more immediate vicinity, the Pillar did not stand alone. Although the adjacent Valle Crucis Abbey was not built until 1201, an earlier settlement stood at the site. Its name, Llanegwestl, is a clear indication that a church also stood in the immediate environs, suggesting that Eliseg's Pillar was only one element of a dispersed elite landscape possibly incorporating both secular residences and a monastic complex.[30] It can be seen that the Pillar of Eliseg was not only drawing on a generalised tradition associating the burials of heroes with mounds and prehistoric monuments, but more importantly, a tradition which was already expressed locally in written and perhaps also in oral traditions. We see here interplay between text and material culture. It is not possible to say which influenced which, rather, together they created a story about the tombs of heroes as guardians of the landscape against foreign incursions to produce a new mythology about the Welsh landscape. This tradition reached into earlier burial traditions and linked them with historical traditions, both oral and textual. It must have influenced the construction and subsequent interpretation of sites such as the Pillar of Eliseg and the other ninth- and tenth-century re-used barrows. For example, the cross-incised stone from Ty'n y Cae, Nefyn (Caernarvonshire) was reputed to have been erected on a mound in which bones had been found.[31] Intriguingly, this stone stood on a boundary between Pistyll and Nefyn parishes. Another example is the ring-cross associated with a probable prehistoric standing stone at Llechgynfarwy.[32]

Without knowing about the *Englynion y Beddau* we cannot fully understand the significance of the inscription and form of the Pillar of Eliseg nor its siting on an earth mound. The textual evidence allows us to move from an abstract concept about the use of a mound as a marker of territoriality,[33] such as is common in interpreting the early medieval use of mounds for burial sites,[34] to a contextually-specific understanding of monument reuse, linking into clearly defined discourses about the relationship between burial, landscape and defence against aggression.

It is important to be aware of the diversity of content within the *Englynion y Beddau*. They should be seen as a collection of poems, rather than a single body of work. As such, despite the theme of burial places that they share, the actual way the theme is explored varies considerably. As has been noted 'the stanzas combine the lore of place-names with lists of heroes… in some the commemoration of the hero being the more important and the location of the grave remaining vague'.[35] These stanzas were clearly exploring a range of issues beyond simply burial, whilst they partly functioned to graft the stories of the past heroes to the present landscape, the situation was not this clear cut. The references to the long graves on Gwanas note that it was not known who was buried there,[36] and many heroes are given no precise burial place. However, whilst some stanzas appear to be 'elegiac poetry for its own sake',[37] there is a still a clear thread running through the verses linking quasi-historical events to real places.

Whilst the *Englynion y Beddau* were ultimately committed to paper it is probable that they were primarily intended to be heard rather than read. Whether recorded on manuscript or committed to memory, the main purpose of the stanzas was to be performed. References in stanza 42–3 mention bardic training, indicating that it is most likely that the poem would have indeed been recited by a bard. In royal household this is most likely to have been either the *pencerdd* (chief poet) or *bardd teulu* (poet of the warband).[38] The role of the *bardd teulu* is significant in this context. The Welsh Law of Hywel Dda record that the bard was to declaim whilst plunder was being divided and or when the bodyguard was setting off on a raid.[39] This declamation was intended to inspire the warrior; the poem to be recited in the Iorweth redaction of the laws was meant to be *Unbeiniaeth Prydain* (The Sovereignty of Britain). It has been suggested that this was an alternate name of the *Armes Prydain*.[40] It is probable that this is precisely the kind of context in which the *Englynion y Beddau* would have been recited. The recorded text suggests that there was an element of interplay between the orator and the audience:

Stanza 46   Whose is this grave and this?
                  Question me for I know it….

As well as providing entertainment, it is likely that such interplay provided a mechanism that prevented the reciter from changing or altering the content of the poem excessively. This control over content is profoundly important if the political and ideological content of the stanzas is acknowledged. In the same way that the audience acted as a control on shifts of content and interpretation in the oral and textual tradition, the same process may well have taken place between the poems and the actual burial record. The burials and the poems both acted as mechanisms that informed the interpretation of the other, but also acted to constrain the way in which they were understood. This recursive ideological buttressing would have acted to check any attempts to contest the political narratives embedded within their structure.

De Situ Brecheniauc and *Cognacio Brychan*

This emphasis on the burial of mythological figures at significant points in the natural landscape and rarely at church sites contrasts with the short sections on burial found in the two early medieval Welsh texts known as *De Situ Brecheniauc* and *Cognacio Brychan* (CB), probably written in or near Brecon. *De Situ Brecheniauc* (DSB) (On the circumstances of Brychan) is first known from a larger manuscript collection that may have been put together around 1200, perhaps at Monmouth Priory (BL Cotton Vespasian A xiv). The *Cognacio Brychan* (CB) (The Kin of Brychan) is only known from a transcript made at Brecon by Sir John Prise (1502–55), but probably originally derived from an earlier lost manuscript, possibly of thirteenth century in date.[41] Although in their current form they are probably date no earlier than the late eleventh century, they deal so specifically with the royal dynasty of Brycheiniog that they were almost certainly compiled at an ecclesiastical centre with close links to the ruling family. Brycheiniog ceased to exists as a polity in the late tenth century, giving a rough *terminus ante quem* for the creation.[42]

Both follow a similar pattern-outlining the circumstances of birth, career and death of the early king Brychan (dated to approximately the sixth century), the

Table 1. Comparison of sections of the 'Brychan documents' dealing with the burial sites of Brychan and his kin. Latin taken from Wade-Evans (1944) and the English translation from Thomas (1994, 137–40)

De Situ Brecheniauc	*Cognacio Brychan*
Sepulchrum Brachan est in insula, que vocatur Enys Brachan, que est iuxta Manniam.	*Brichan iacet in Mynav*
Sepulchrum Rein filii Brachan in Landeuailac	*In valle, qui dicitur Vall[is] Br[I]cha*
Sepulcrum in Kannauc Merther in Brecheniauc	*Anllach iacet ante hostium ecclesie Llanyspidit*
Sepulcrum Anlauch, ante hostium ecclesie de Lanespetit'	*Reyn, filius Brichan, iacet apud Llanvaubo*
	Sepulchrum Kynauc in Merthy Kynauc in Brecheniauc;
The grave of Brachan is in the island called Enys Brachan, which is next to Mannia. The grave of Rein, son of Brachan, in Landeuailac. The grave of Kannauc, Merthir in Brecheniauc. The grave of Anlauch, before the door of the church of Llanspetit .	Brichan lies in Mynau in the valley which is called Vallis Bichan. Anllach lies before the door of the church at Llanyspydyt. Reyn, son of Brychan, lies at Llanvayloc. The grave of Kynauc, in Merthyr Kynauc in Brecheiniawc.

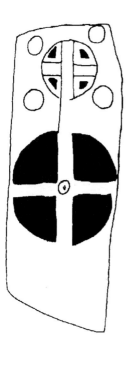

Figure 2. Images of inscribed stones (a) Llandyfaelog Fach (Brecks); (b) Llansbyddyd (Brecks)

founder of the eponymous kingdom of Brycheiniog. Both also contain genealogical material relating to Brychan's descendents. Finally, and importantly for this paper, they also contain similar sections noting the burial places of Brychan and his immediate family.)

Both are very similar, and clearly identify the burial places of the king and his sons. The three sons are of Brychan are all buried in churches. The burial place of Rein has been identified with Llandyfaelog Fach (Brecks) which lies about two miles to the north of Brecon. By the tenth century this was clearly a burial site of some importance because two inscribed stones have been recorded coming from the site. One, now lost, is too poorly known to make any guesses about its date, but the second is an unusual Type 3 stone with a rare depiction of a warrior (Fig. 2a).[43] The grave of Kennauc is found at Merthyr Cynog and Annlauch at *Llansbyddyd*,

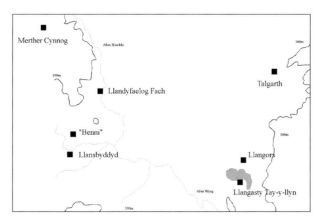

Figure. 3. Location of sites mentioned in Brychan documents

another church that has produced a carved cross stone (Fig. 2b). Both versions record that he was buried *ante hostium* – before the doors. Interestingly, the twelfth-century Life of St Cadog contains a foundation legend for this church, suggesting it was founded by the saint, Brychan's grandson, who was given the land by his grandfather after he was miraculously fed by a mouse that had a cache of wheat concealed within a tumulus nearby.[44]

Several attempts have been made to identify the burial site of Brychan himself (Mannia/Mynau). Charles Thomas suggested that he was buried on Lundy Island before being translated to Hartland.[45] In a review of Thomas's book Philip Bartholomew suggested that the crannog at Llangorse might be a better candidate.[46] This is an equally unlikely location, particularly considering that excavation has shown that the crannog dates to the late ninth or tenth century AD, several hundred years after Brychan's death.[47]

Apart from the site of Brychan's burial, the others are all securely located in the heartland of the kingdom of Brycheiniog, close to other significant ecclesiastical and royal sites (Fig. 3). For example, other sites mentioned in the Brychan documents include 'Garth Matrun' (probably Talgarth), Llansefin, Meidrim, 'Benni' (probably the hillfort near the mouth of the Ysgir). Important ecclesiastical sites mentioned include those noted as burials sites and Llangasty Tal-y-llyn close to Llangorse lake and its crannog. Another reference to the burial site of a king of Brycheiniog is also known, a charter granting *Lann Cors* to Llandaffin which King Awst of Brycheiniog (fl. first half of the eighth century) makes reference to Llangorse as the proposed burial place of himself and his sons.[48]

The most intriguing aspect of these two Brychan texts is the lack of similar, biographical histories of secular figures from this date. Instead, they appear to have many of the hallmarks of contemporary hagiographical writing. Most of our early Welsh hagiographic material belongs to the eleventh to twelfth centuries, such as the *vitae*

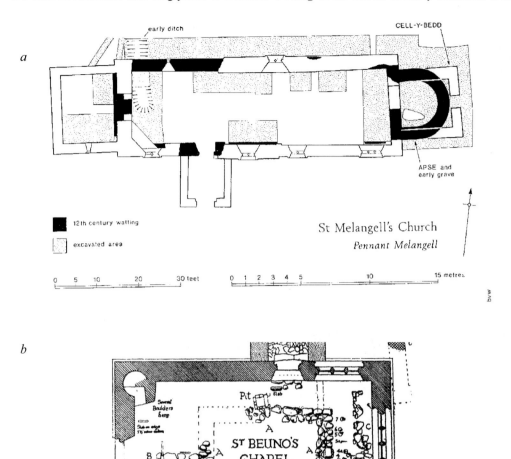

Figure 4. Archaeological evidence for shrines and holy graves (a) Pennant Melangell (Powys); (b) Clynnog Fawr (Caernarvonshire)

incorporated into the Book of Llandaff, Rhigyfarch's Life of St David and Lifris' Life of St Cadog. However, there was certainly an earlier tradition of writing stories about Saints lives; the life of Saint Samson dates to between the seventh and ninth centuries (broadly contemporary with the Brychan documents). Although written in Brittany, probably at Landevennec, the connections between the Breton and Welsh church were extensive. Indeed the author of the Vita claimed to have borrowed from the Acta of Saint Samson, which had been brought overseas by Henoc, the Saint's cousin. It is equally likely that the eleventh to twelfth century Welsh saints lives were drawing on earlier hagiographical material, though clearly rewritten for a contemporary audience.

The broad parallels between the Brychan documents and the saint's life take a number of forms including the emphasis on lineage and ancestry, the recording of

miraculous events and the emphasis placed on recording the death and burial place of the subject.[49] More specifically, the recording of the burial of Brychan's sons in or near a church, clearly reflects the recording of the burial sites of saints within or close to church structures. For example, St Brynach was recorded as being beneath the eastern wall of his church[50] while Gwynllyw was described as being placed either by the wall on the south side of his own monastery[51] or in the floor of the church.[52] Tatheus was also recorded as being buried under the floor of the church.[53] David and Padarn were both buried in the grounds of their monasteries.[54]

Whilst the burials recorded in the Brychan documents appear to reflect burial practices associated with saints in hagiography, what they do not seem to reflect is the burial practice of the sixth century, when Brychan and his immediate family are likely to have had their floruit. Indeed, there is little to suggest that these church sites,

Merther Cynog, Llandyfaelog Fach and Llanysbyddid, were exceptionally early foundations (*i.e.* pre-eighth century). The only tentative evidence for an early establishment of these sites is a lost stone from Llandyfaelog Fach, which is recorded as having the name *CATVC* inscribed upon it.[55]

From what relatively little we know about the graves of holy individuals in the ninth to eleventh century, the documentary evidence appears to be born out in the archaeology (Fig. 4). The tombs of Welsh saints appear to have remained beneath ground, though they may often have been surrounded by a small building or chapel, known as a *capel y bedd* or *cell y bedd*. For example, the excavated shrine of St Melangell at Pennant Melangell shows that the original central burial was placed in an apse at the east end of the church, beneath a large stone slab (and 'ante hostium': before a door). It was not until the twelfth century that the Romanesque shrine that can now be seen was built.[56] The *capel y bedd* of Saint Beuno at Clynnog Fawr in Gwynedd also contained a central focal stone-lined grave, rather than a built shrine.[57]

The presence of a saint's body or relics became an increasingly important way of asserting a sphere of influence over an ecclesiastical property in the ninth to tenth century, as well as becoming increasingly important commodities in their own right. Most of the Saint's lives written in the eleventh and early twelfth century are clearly intended to help validate claims to property and associated rights in the face of increasing pressure from Normans, as well as in internecine tensions over ecclesiastical jurisdiction. For example, the Life of St Cadog ends with a series of charters recording the gifting of land to the saint and his monasteries.[58]

It is in this context that we should see this record of royal burials. The kingdom of Brycheiniog was increasingly under pressure from neighbouring kingdoms from the ninth century onwards. The Welsh annals record battles against Gwent (s.a. 848 *ASC*) and Asser's *Life of Alfred* (ch.80, *c.* 885) records the submission of members of the royal family to Alfred, seemingly an attempt to court protection from the powerful monarch in the face of pressure from the sons of Rhodri Mawr.[59] The area also came under threat in the early tenth century, when the crannog of Llangorse was destroyed by the armies of Lady Aethelflaed of the Mercians.[60]

As well as pressure from rival Welsh kingdoms and Anglo-Saxon armies, there was also the possibility of ecclesiastical rivalry – indeed it is in this context that we should perhaps understand the reference to Llanysbyddid in the Life of St Cadog.[61] Disputes about territory were common between early medieval Welsh monasteries and dioceses.

The descriptions of the burials in the *De Situ Brycheniog and Cognacio Brychan* should not be taken as historically accurate descriptions of the burials of sixth century British nobility. Instead we need to see the text in context; they are attempts to use a burial – actual or believed – as an indicator of the primacy of a claim to control the central heartland of Brycheiniog.

Conclusions

This paper has discussed two broadly contemporary texts, both dealing with the burial of important, secular members of early medieval Welsh society, yet they both seem to be talking about death and burial in contrasting ways. The *Englynion y Beddau* situates elite burial sites away from churches at important points in the landscape, often seemingly associated with prehistoric monuments or significant natural features. The second text, the Brychan documents, firmly locates the burials of Brychan's family in churches, indeed churches that seem to be important ecclesiastical centres on the basis of other early medieval evidence. It records these burials in a document that seems to be drawing on existing hagiographic traditions, and aims to link the secular dynasty of Brycheiniog into traditions of sainthood and saintliness.

How do we reconcile these seemingly contrasting strategies for recording burial sites in early medieval Wales? The simple answer is, we do not have too. It is important to avoid the mind-set that says we can only have one contemporary discourse about burial rites. We have discovered here two complimentary dialogues about death and burial; dialogues that include the practice of burial as well as literary writing about it. It appears that elites in early medieval Wales were creative in seeking sources of ideological legitimation, turning to both martial and ecclesiastical prototypes for defining modes of power. This may well express the tensions between the Welsh nobility and the increasingly powerful Church. By appealing to antiquarian traditions and historical precedents, burial practice and textual descriptions of burial appealed to the past as a source of legitimation for the present.

The production of biographies of individuals and families in the medieval period is closely linked to strategies for ideological and political legitimation.[62] For example, in early medieval Wales, Saint's lives sometimes incorporated grants of land to saints connected to the ecclesiastical institutions that were responsible for the production of the *vita*. In his discussion of the biography of Gruffud ap Cynan, Rhys Jones has noted 'lay biographies also incorporated discourses of power that helped to legitimise certain socio-spatial formations'.[63] The transformation of oral historical and genealogical narratives to textual ones in the ninth to tenth century reflected a wider process of transition from oral to textual in the medieval period.[64] It has often been suggested that the move to written record prevents the manipulation of the information contained within the narrative structure. However, this is not necessarily so; the opposition between 'fluid' oral narrative and 'fixed' textual narrative is not so clear-cut. There are good examples from early medieval Welsh contexts of written versions of the same broad genealogies providing alternate genealogical data.[65] As suggested above the relationship between the bard and his audience may have acted as a constraint on the manipulation of content; equally textual records can be vulnerable to alteration, manipulation and rewriting. In the context of the Brychan documents and the related burial evidence it is likely that the parallel material and textual records both facilitated and constrained political interpretations. The presence of the documentary record has limited attempts to re-interpret the meaning embedded in the ecclesiastical sites (which may have been contested); equally the traditions associated with the sites and their material remains would have acted as a constraint on attempts to rewrite textual histories.

These textual representations of burial combine with varying burial practices to form wider discourses about death and burial in the ninth century Wales. These discourses are intimately related to the ebb and flow of dynastic politics and wider debates about the sources of social power in the region. The tension between the church and the secular elite is partly reflected in the diverging ways in which burial is presented in these two texts. Crucially, these discourses may have served to influence wider attitudes to the production of symbolic places in the early medieval landscape, swinging from the bounded, nodal points formed by early ecclesiastical sites with their tightly defined boundaries to the more diffuse landscapes of mythology and legend, which is

being actively created outside the church. Increasingly, from the tenth to twelfth century the church itself appears to become involved in the struggle to make places outside the bounds of the church itself symbolically important; this is reflected in the increasing emphasis on imbuing meaning on natural sites found in saint's lives of this period. A good example of this can be found in Rhigyfarch's Life of Saint David, when the scene of Nonita's conception is marked by the miraculous appearance of a pair of large stones 'in order to ...declare before hand the significance of her offspring'.[66]

The eighth to tenth century was a fluid and difficult time of the Welsh nobility, faced with increased internal friction combined with renewed external threats from both the Anglo-Saxons and the Vikings. Whilst the church provided important ideological support, it was also posing a threat of its own, with its increased demands for fiscal powers and exemptions from service obligations. By bringing together the evidence from historical texts and archaeological evidence it can be seen that the consequence of this was a period of originality and creativity by the elites when seeking ways to project images in death that implied power and consequence in life.

Acknowledgements

I would like to thank the anonymous referee who saved me from some wilder flights of fancy, and made me think again about the context of production and reproduction of early medieval Welsh literature.

Notes

1. Moreland 2001.
2. Hills 1998.
3. *E.g.* Davies 1996, 185–6.
4. Jones 1967.
5. Jones 1967, 100.
6. *EB* 4.
7. *EB* 5.
8. *EB* 8.
9. *EB* 13.
10. *EB* 50; Jones 1967, 100–1.
11. Nash-Williams 1950, no.13.
12. Nash-Williams 1950, nos 222, 223.
13. Rowlands 1990, 143.
14. *EB* 9–11, 13–14.
15. *EB* 13–14.
16. *EB* 8, 12, 44.
17. *EB* 4, 35.
18. *EB* 26; Jones 1967, 109–10.
19. *HB* 67–75.
20. Roberts 1991, 88–93.
21. *HB* 73.
22. Sims-Williams 1993, 57.
23. *EB* 65.
24. Jones 1967, 113.
25. Nash-Williams 1950, no.182.

26. Maund 2000, 41 Davies 1982, 106–7, *ASC* s.a 853.
27. *E.g.* Edwards 2001.
28. *Ibid.*
29. Sims-Williams 1993, 47.
30. Silvester 2001, 87; Robinson 1998, 194.
31. Nash-Williams 1950, 90, 99.
32. Edwards 2001, 30.
33. *E.g.* Van der Noort 1993; Shepherd 1979.
34. *ibid.*
35. Stephens 1986, 179.
36. *EB* 29–30.
37. Rowlands 1988, 183.
38. Jenkins 2000.
39. *Ibid.*, 149–50.
40. Jenkins 2000, 150.
41. Sims-Williams 1993, 56.
42. Sims-Williams 1992, 56–7; Dumville 1983, 148, n.4.
43. Nash-Williams 1950, 49.
44. *VC* 11; Corner 1988.
45. Thomas 1994, 131–180.
46. Bartholomew 1996.
47. Campbell and Lane 1989.
48. *LL*146.
49. Henken 1991.
50. *VB* 16.
51. *VC* 28.

52. *VG* 10.
53. *VT* 17.
54. *VD* 65; *VP* 29.
55. Nash-Williams 1950, 74, *50*.
56. Britnell 1994a, 1994b.
57. RCAHMW 1960, 36–42.
58. *VC* 55–69.
59. Dumville 1982.

60. s.a. 916 *ASC.*
61. *VC* 12.
62. Jones 2004.
63. *Ibid.*, 461.
64. Clanchy 1993.
65. Thornton 1998.
66. *VS Dauid* 4.

Abbreviations

AC   *Annales Cambriae* (Morris 1980)
ASC   *Anglo-Saxon Chronicle (*Whitelock and Tucker 1961)
EB   *Englynion y Beddau* (Jones 1967)
HB   *Historia Brittonum* (Morris 1980)
LL   *Book of Llandaff* (Evans 1893)
VB   *Vita Bernachius* (Wade-Evans 1944, 2–16)
VC   *Vita Cadocus* (Wade-Evans 1944, 24–142)
VS Dauid *Vita Sancti Dauid* (James 1967)
VG   *Vita Gundleius* (Wade-Evans 1944, 172–94)
VP   *Vita Paternus* (Wade-Evans 1944, 252–69)
VT   *Vita Tatheus* (Wade-Evans 1944, 270–87)

Bibliography

Asser's Life of Alfred = Alfred the Great: Asser's Life of King Alfred trans. S. Keynes and Lapidge, M. (Penguin, 1983).

Bartholomew, P. 1996. Review of Thomas, C., *And Shall These Mute Stones Speak? Post-Roman Inscriptions in Western Britain, Britannia,* **27**, 486–7.

Britnell, W. J. 1994. Saint Melangell's shrine, Pennant Melangell, *Montgomeryshire Collections* (*Transactions of the Powys-land Club*), **82**, 147–66.

Britnell, W. J. 1994. Excavation and recording at Pennant Melangell Church, *Montgomeryshire Collections* (*Transactions of the Powys-land Club*), **82**, 41–102.

Campbell, E. and Lane, A. 1989. Llangorse: a 10th century royal crannog in Wales, *Antiquity,* **63**, 675–81.

Cartwright. J. (ed.) 2003. *Celtic hagiography and saints' cults,* Cardiff: University of Wales Press.

Clanchy, M. 1993. *From Memory to Written Record: England 1066–1307,* Oxford: Oxford University Press.

Corner, D. J. 1988. The Vita Cadoci and a Cotswold-Severn Chambered Cairn, *Bull. Brd. Celtic Stud.* **32**, 50–67.

Davies, E. 1929. *The Prehistoric and Roman Remains of Denbighshire,* Cardiff: William Lewis.

Davies, W. 1982. *Wales in the Early Middle Ages,* Leicester: Leicester University Press.

Dumville, D. 1983. Brittany and 'Armes Prydein Vawr', *Études Celtiques,* **20**, 148–58.

Dumville, D. 1982. The "Six" Sons of Rhodri Mawr: A Problem, in Asser's *Life of King Alfred' Cambrian Medieval Celtic Stud.* **4**, 5–18.

Edwards, N. 2001. 'Stones and Stone Sculpture in Wales: Context and Function' *Medieval Archaeol.* **45**, 15–39.

Evans, J. G. with J. Rhys 1893. *The Text of the Book of Llan Dâv,* Cardiff: National Library of Wales.

Hills, C. 1998. Beowulf and Archaeology, in R. Bjork and J. Niles (eds), *A Beowulf Handbook,* Exeter: University of Exeter Press.

James, J. W. 1967. *Rhigyfarch's Life of St David,* Cardiff: University of Wales Press.

Jenkins, D. (trans.) 1986. *The Law of Hywel Dda: Law texts from Medieval Wales,* Llandysul: Gomer.

Jenkins, D. 2000. *Bardd teulu* and *Pencerdd,* in T. M. Charles-Edwards, M. Owen and P. Russell (eds) 2000. *The Welsh King and his Court,* 142–67, Cardiff: University of Wales Press.

Jones, R. 2004. Medieval Biographies and the geography of power: the *Historia Gruffud vab Kenan, Journal of Hist. Geography,* **30**, 459–69.

Jones, T. 1967. The Black Book of Carmarthen "Stanzas of the Grave", *Proc. Brit. Acad.* **53**, 97–137.

Keynes, S. and Lapidge, M. (trans.) 1983. *Alfred the Great: Asser's Life of King Alfred and other contemporary sources.* Harmonsworth: Penguin.

Henken, E. R. 1991. *The Welsh Saints: A Study in Patterned Lives,* Woodbridge: Brewer.

Maund, K. 2000. *The Welsh Kings,* Stroud, Tempus.

Moreland, J. 2001. *Archaeology as Text,* London: Duckworth Press.

Morris, J. (ed. and trans.) 1980. *Historia Brittonum, British History and the Welsh Annals,* London: Phillimore.

Nash-Williams, V. E., 1950. *The Early Christian Monuments of Wales,* Cardiff: University of Wales Press.

RCHAMW 1960. *An Inventory of the Historical Monuments in the County of Caernarvonshire,* London: HMSO.

Roberts, B. 1991. *Culhwch and Olwen,* The Triad's, Saint's Lives, in R. Bromwich, A. O. H. Jarman and B. Roberts (eds), *The Arthur of the Welsh,* 73–97, Cardiff: University of Wales Press.

Rowland, J. 1988. Genres, in B. F. Roberts (ed.), *Early Welsh Poetry: Studies in the Book of Aneirin,* 179–208, Cardiff: National Library of Wales.

Rowland, J. 1990. *Early Welsh saga poetry: a study and edition of the Englynion,* Woodbridge: D. S. Brewer.

Shephard, J. 1979. The social identity of the individual in isolated barrows and barrow cemeteries in Anglo-Saxon England, in B. Burnham and J. Kingsbury (eds), *Space, Hierarchy and Society,* 47–49, 59, BAR 59 Oxford: British Archaeological Reports.

Silvester, B. 2001. Archaeological works at Valle Crucis Abbey, Denbigh, *Archaeology in Wales,* **41**, 87–92.

Sims-Williams, P. 1993. The provenance of the Llywarch Hen poems: a case for Llan-gors, Brycheiniog, *CMCS,* **26**, 27–63.

Stephens, M. (ed.) 1998. *New Companion to the Literature of Wales,* Cardiff: University of Wales Press.

Thomas, C., 1994. *And Shall These Mute Stones Speak?* Cardiff: University of Wales Press.

Thornton, D. 1998. Orality, literacy and genealogy in early medieval Ireland and Wales, in H. Pryce (ed.), *Literacy in Medieval Celtic Societies,* 83–98, Cambridge: Cambridge University Press.

Van der Noort, R. 1993. The context of the early medieval barrow in Western Europe, *Antiquity,* **67**, 66–73.

Wade-Evans, A. 1944. *Vitae sanctorum britanniae et genealogiae,* Cardiff: University of Wales Press

Whitelock, D. and Douglas, D. C. 1961. *The Anglo-Saxon Chronicle,* London: Eyre and Spottiswood.

Anglo-Saxon Studies in Archaeology and History 14, 2007

Separated from the Foaming Maelstrom: Landscapes of Insular 'Viking' Burial

Stephen H. Harrison

In 1852, an English translation of a Danish text by J. J. A. Worsaae was published in London as *An Account of the Danes and Norwegians in England, Scotland and Wales*.[1] The result of an extended tour in the mid-1840s, Worsaae's work represents one of the first systematic evaluations of the linguistic, historical and archaeological evidence for Scandinavian activity in these islands, although it must be admitted that his treatment of all three forms of evidence was occasionally idiosyncratic.[2] This is particularly true in the case of what was then the comparatively limited corpus of archaeological evidence, and it may have been a desire to expand on discoveries at a handful of Scottish sites such as Castletown (Highland) that led him to propose a series of unexcavated coastal 'barrows' on the shores of the Pentland Firth as 'the last resting-places of the daring Vikings, who, not even in death, could endure to be far separated from the foaming maelstrom.'[3]

Worsaae did not use proximity to the sea as evidence for the 'Viking' origins of burial mounds in any other part of the British Isles, and his treatment of this northern material can be contrasted with his rather more extensive discussion of a series of graves from the area around Dublin. When describing the evidence from College Green and the then newly discovered sites at Kilmainham and the Phoenix Park, he virtually ignored the local topography, instead focusing his attention on the grave goods that allowed these burials to be identified as 'Viking'.[4] It was this latter approach, firmly based on grave contents rather than site, which was to dominate the study of 'Viking' graves for the next century or more, being adopted and modified by insular scholars from Wilde and Anderson to Coffey and Armstrong.[5] These – and other – researchers became progressively more convinced that a distinctive artefact assemblage could be specifically associated with Scandinavian burials, and focused their research on these objects, devoting particular attention to weapons and oval brooches.[6] Today, the term 'Viking grave' is effectively synonymous with furnished burial, although recent

discoveries at sites such as Cnip, Lewis, Western Isles, St Patrick's Isle, Man, and Heath Wood, Derbyshire, have begun to demonstrate that insular Scandinavian communities buried their dead with rather more variety than was once believed.[7]

Given the current emphasis on urban and rural settlement sites in studies of insular Scandinavian activity in the Viking Age, it is easy to forget that as late as the mid-twentieth century the corpus of archaeological evidence was almost entirely dominated by graves. When Shetelig edited the six-volume *Catalogue of Viking Antiquities in Great Britain and Ireland*, for example, approximately half of the Scottish and Irish volumes and a fifth of the English volume were devoted to the evidence from Viking burials, and more specifically their grave goods.[8] The sites of these burials were, in contrast, almost entirely ignored, and it is perhaps indicative of the compilers' priorities that none of the volumes contain maps. While Grieg, Bøe, Bjørn and Shetelig were working under exceptionally difficult circumstances, the *Catalogue*'s vague topographical references stand in marked contrast to the care with which individual artefacts were discussed and identified typologically.[9]

Using the results of this survey, Shetelig was one of the first to argue for a general relationship between these graves and areas of Scandinavian settlement, but the local relationships between individual burials and settlements were generally ignored, and for many subsequent scholars, some elements of the views expressed by Worsaae lingered on.[10] Furnished insular Scandinavian burials were to be associated not with the land but with sea routes, and most, if not all, were to be interpreted as transient features. In this context, detailed discussion of their landscape setting was essentially irrelevant, and even those scholars who followed Shetelig's lead in linking burials to long-term Scandinavian activity tended not to examine individual sites in any detail.[11] Of course, all recent excavation reports and re-evaluations of older finds have included at least some reference to the surrounding topography and 'viewshed', and recent work on Scar, Westness and Pierowall (all Orkney) has given particular attention to the relationship between burial and settlement.[12] As with other time periods, however, there is perhaps a danger that a desire to identify settlements using furnished burials may lead to the latter evidence being used as 'second-rate evidence for the positioning of settlements in the landscape, rather than as first-rate evidence for the positioning of the dead.'[13] A general study of Viking Age burial sites within their associated landscape, while problematic, seems long overdue.

Unfortunately, attempts to study any aspect of furnished insular Scandinavian burials (hereafter FISBs) must first confront a series of difficulties relating to the quality and extent of the available evidence. As highly distinctive monuments, the discovery of individual examples has been (erratically) recorded for several centuries, but these records vary enormously, from a series of highly precise excavations carried out in the last two decades to loose accounts of weapons and other artefacts, with or without associated skeletal material, found (and very often lost) up to 250 years ago. In the northern and western part of these islands, where furnished burial is virtually unknown in the prehistoric Iron Age, any reference to iron objects associated with skeletal material, as at Cornaigbeg, Tiree, in 1794, may provide evidence for one or more FISBs, but such vague references provide little reliable information.[14] In much of England, on the other hand, furnished burial was practiced in the Early Anglo-Saxon period (and occasionally later), and dating ambiguities mean that even comparatively well recorded burials, such as that from Harrold, Bedfordshire, cannot always be assumed to be those of insular Scandinavians.[15] To incorporate such varied evidence within this study, individual burial sites were assigned to one of three groups. 'Definite' burial sites have produced evidence for at least one 'certain' FISB, generally with specific references both to human remains and associated Viking Age artefacts. 'Probable' burials lack one of these two basic criteria (generally specific references to human remains), and consequently 'probable' burial sites are those for which one or more 'probable' graves provided the best evidence for a burial. The third group, 'possible' burial sites, comprise those sites for which the evidence is most tenuous, generally due to the early date or unreliable nature of the available sources, while some of the most obscure references were dismissed as 'unlikely' or entirely rejected. By placing most emphasis on the 'definite' burial sites, but incorporating the evidence provided by 'probable' and 'possible' sites, it was hoped to make maximum use of the available material, and to provide a reasonable assessment of the phenomenon as a whole.[16]

When the evidence from the British Isles is drawn together, including the most recent discoveries at Cumwhitton (Cumbria) and Finglas (Dublin), it would seem that there is evidence for a minimum of 194 sites with FISBs, of which 84 contain at least one definite grave, 55 contain at least one probable grave, and the remaining 55 contain one or more possible graves (Fig. 1). These sites cover most of these islands, from the definite burial at Clibberswick, Shetland, to more ambiguous references to a series of graves around Reading (Berkshire), and from the debated evidence for a possible burial at Caister-on-Sea (Norfolk) to the definite weapon inhumation at Eyrephort (Galway). There is, however, a clear concentration of sites in northern Britain and the Irish Sea basin.[17] Given the quantity of sites, their wide dispersal, and the limited time and funding available for the present (doctoral) project, it was not possible to visit more than a handful of them, but as so many have been removed without leaving any trace, and the surrounding environment has often changed considerably, a map-based approach should not be entirely invalid. This research has focused on the relationship between burial sites and the coast, and their relationship to surrounding higher ground, both aspects of the local environment that can be successfully examined using cartographic evidence, particularly 1:50,000 sheets, with more detailed and/or older maps being consulted where appropriate. This has occasionally produced surprising results, as at Brockhall Eases (Lancashire) where a mid-nineteenth century six-inch sheet showed the precise site of a probable weapon grave rather more than a kilometre from the area with which it was more generally associated.[18] In all cases where burial sites could be determined with reasonable precision, this research provided a general overview of contemporary local topography.

In addition to establishing the precise sites of these individual burials and cemeteries within the modern landscape, however, some consideration was also given to potential changes since the Viking Age. With the exception of a limited number of areas that had experienced extensive quarrying and other earth-moving activity, perhaps most notably Kilmainham, Dublin, it could be assumed that the local topography had not changed substantially, but the same was not necessarily true of the coastline.[19] A number of burials, particularly in northern Scotland, were discovered as a result of coastal erosion, but while this was noted in individual cases, more general evidence suggests that sea level change has been comparatively restricted in all parts of the British Isles in the last thousand years, with the most substantial changes occurring in the comparatively flat landscapes of the east and south coast of England, areas with comparatively few FISBs, most of which are at sites a considerable distance inland.[20] Given the scale at which the study was carried out, it is believed that coastal change has not had a major impact on its results. It can also be argued that while preservation and recovery have undoubtedly affected the distribution pattern, variations in local conditions should not have altered

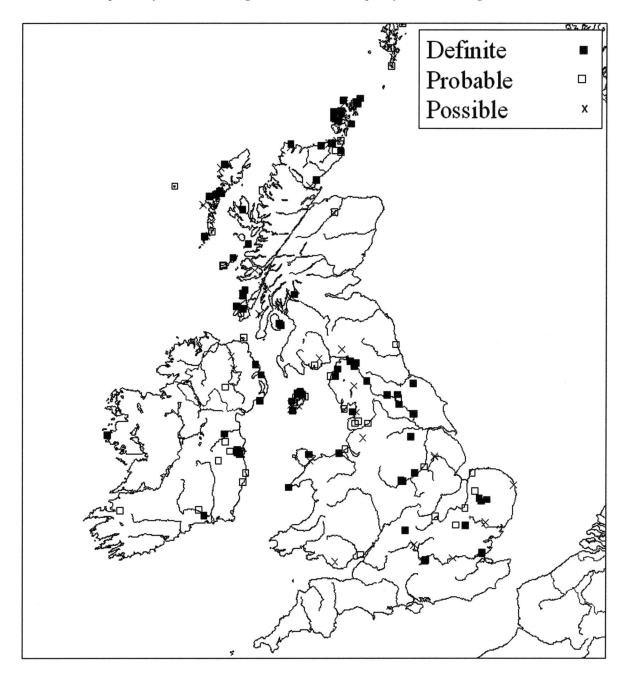

Figure 1. Definite, Probable and Possible Furnished Insular Scandinavian Burial Sites

this pattern out of all recognition. Burials must exist in order to be discovered, and intense activity does not always produce evidence for FISBs.

Given these considerations, the most obvious result of this study is the evidence for a particularly strong relationship between burials and the modern coast, with 113 of 176 sites which can be identified with precision (64%) occurring within 2000 m of the shore, with definite burials having an almost identical ratio (63%), with 41 (50%) of this latter group being less than 500 m from the coast. There are also strong regional variations, par-

ticularly when sites east of the Pennines are compared to those found elsewhere. In Scotland and the Irish Sea basin, 109 of 137 provenanced sites (80%) occur within 2000 m of the shore, while in eastern England, only 3 of 35 (8%) of burials occur in this zone, and only one of these is a definite example. The contrast between the two regions is further emphasised by the fact that 29 of the eastern burials (83%) are more than 10 km from the coast, compared to just 17 (12%) in the western and northern groups, figures confirmed by an examination of definite burials in isolation. While these patterns do, of course, reflect the comparative importance of the Scottish coastal zones and the inland settlement of the Danelaw, the fact that the east coast of England seems to have been almost completely ignored as an area of potential burial suggests that priorities governing the selection of burial sites may have been very different in the two areas.

In the case of coastal burials and in particular those within a few hundred metres of the coast, the majority occur beside small bays, inlets or estuaries, with 52 of the 73 examples north of the North Channel (71%), for example, falling into this category. While some of these burials occur at the heads of bays and inlets, almost three out of four (73%) are positioned close to the ends of beaches or on the slopes of flanking promontories. This distribution may reflect the fact that slightly higher ground tends to occur in these areas, but these graves also consistently avoid hill and promontory summits in favour of sloping land, with two thirds of coastal burials occurring below the 10m contour, and almost none occurring above 20m. As a result, views to and from these sites are normally quite restricted, being confined to the associated inlet and/or the land immediately adjacent to it. Burials at sites commanding extensive views of open sea do occur, but are comparatively rare, comprising approximately 10% of the total. These burials are often comparatively well furnished, however, with boat burials particularly likely to occur at sites with extensive views. The burial at Kiloran Bay, Colonsay (Argyll and Bute) for example, must have looked northwest towards Mull, while that at Càrn a' Bharraich, Oronsay (also Argyll and Bute) looked southeast towards Jura. Similarly, the burial at Balladoole, Man, provided views southwest across the adjacent Bay ny Carrickey towards the Calf of Man and potentially the coast of Ireland.[21] The relationship between well-furnished graves and prominent sites is not entirely consistent, however, and comparatively modestly furnished graves can also be placed in prominent positions, as at Kings Cross Point, Arran (North Ayrshire).[22] Conversely, well-furnished graves have been found at sites on slopes facing away from the open sea, as at Cnip, Lewis, and nearly 90% of coastal burial sites have similarly restricted views.[23]

When those burials located over 2000 m from the coast are examined, they reveal similar topographical preferences. The overwhelming majority of inland burials, comprising 81% of the general total and 88% of definite burials, occur in river valleys, with a definite preference for sites on slightly elevated ground close to their edges but well below the crests of flanking high ground. In scale, these rivers range from the Thames, Trent and Liffey to rather more modest waterways such as the River Ure in North Yorkshire. Although also a church site (see below) the burial at Wensley in the latter river valley is in many ways typical of these 'valley' burials, occurring on a slight rise above the river.[24] A

number of 'coastal' burials set well back from the shore also follow this pattern, as is the case with the probable burials at St John's and the possible burials at Ballabrooie and Balladoyne, all of which are set on slightly elevated land above the floodplain of the river Neb, Man.[25] The altitude of inland sites is obviously higher than coastal sites, but they tend not to be more than 20 m above the river they overlook, and a number occur on the valley floor itself. As with comparable coastal sites, most overlook comparatively restricted areas of their respective valleys, and terrain often conceals the river itself from the burial site. In this context, the cemetery at Heath Wood is as exceptional in its height above the valley floor and its comparatively extensive views as it is distinctive in terms of the burial rituals carried out there.[26] The remaining inland burials do not seem to conform to a definite pattern, although it should perhaps be noted that a number of English burials such as Hesket-in-the-Forest (Cumbria) and Leeming Lane (North Yorkshire) seem to have been placed beside contemporary roadways, and a similar pattern has been suggested for some of the burials around Dublin.[27] It is also possible that burials were placed at fords, but as debates on sites such as Magdalen Bridge (Oxford) demonstrate, it is almost impossible to differentiate between potential grave-goods and more general ritual deposits, or indeed material which was accidentally lost.[28] Consequently, no definite burials at ford sites have been identified to date.

While it seems clear that the majority of FISBs were placed on slightly elevated sloping sites with comparatively restricted views, it must also be remembered that this surrounding physical landscape did not exist in isolation. If 'landscape is an entity that exists by virtue of its being perceived, experienced and contextualised by people',[29] then insular Scandinavian communities must be seen as operating within long established and inhabited landscapes whose extant monuments had a profound effect on their own land use. In Scotland, insular Scandinavian settlements at Buckquoy (Orkney) and the Udal, North Uist (Western Isles) were constructed directly above indigenous settlement sites, and a similar trend can be seen in the case of burial sites.[30] More specifically, 56 of the 194 FISBs (29%) and 30 of 84 definite sites (36%) are located at or directly adjacent to sites used for burial by indigenous groups in the early medieval period. In some cases, perhaps most obviously Dunrobin Castle and Ackergill (both Highland), the indigenous burials occur in mounds, but the overwhelming majority of these reused sites seem to contain east-west unfurnished 'Christian' burials, very often centred on churches.[31] Graves at these near-contemporary indigenous sites occur throughout these islands, with the northernmost example being the Kirk of St Ola (Shetland), but the practice is very much more common in the area south of the North Channel, where all but five of these sites occur (Fig. 2).[32] Although confused stratigraphy and poor recovery conditions mean

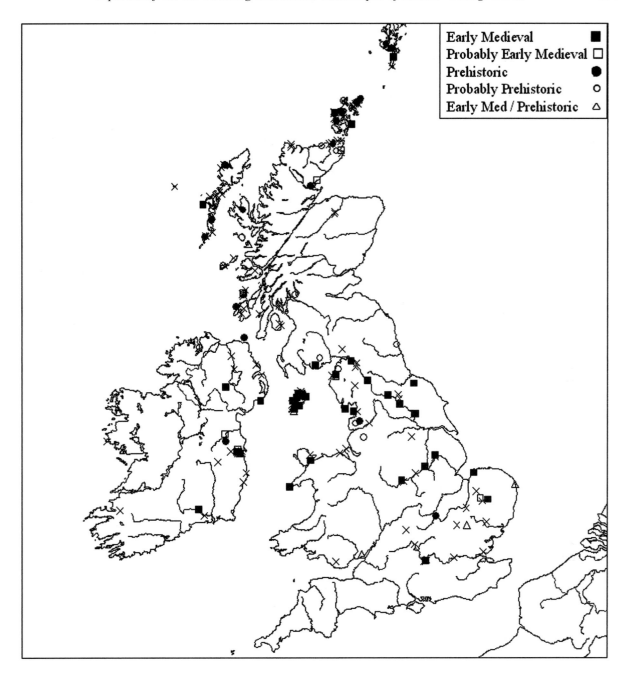

Figure 2. Reuse of Early Medieval and Prehistoric Sites for Furnished Insular Scandinavian Burial

that context and associations are often confused, most archaeologists would agree that the majority of Viking Age weapons from Christian burial sites, together with a similar proportion of dress fastenings, represent disturbed furnished burials at these sites.[33] Shetelig believed the practice of placing such 'pagan' graves in Christian cemeteries was 'peculiar to the British Isles', and although a limited number of examples are now known from Scandinavia, it seems clear that the practice was very much more common on this side of the North Sea.[34]

The precise interpretation of these furnished burials at indigenous sites is the subject of heated debate, with opinions divided as to whether they represent the graves of those who were in the process of assimilating with local population groups, or those who were effectively demonstrating their domination of these same groups. Although the two interpretations are by no means mutually exclusive, in those cases where stratigraphic evidence is available, the relationship of FISBs to extant unfurnished burials varies considerably from place to place. At Balladoole (Man), for example, comparatively recent burials were destroyed during the construction of the mound there, while at St Patrick's Chapel, Heysham (Lancashire), a female burial with a comb formed part of the general pattern of graves in the cemetery.[35] In at least one case, at Repton (Derbyshire), evidence has been found both for extensive disturbance of extant burials and for other furnished burials forming an integral part of a group of unfurnished graves, while a number of other FISBs at the same site seem to have been placed directly outside the extant Anglo-Saxon cemetery.[36] This latter practice can also be seen at Santon (Norfolk), and Kildonnan, Eigg (Highland) and further indicates the potential complexity of the relationship between contemporary indigenous burials and FISBs at these sites.[37] Despite this complexity, however, it seems clear that these burials were deliberately placed at the centre of an extant religious landscape, at sites which were also close to the heart of established, settled landscapes. Perhaps equally importantly, if burial at church sites was indeed a practice particularly associated with elite or dominant groups within local communities, then these insular Scandinavian graves, with their enthusiastic incorporation of other potential high status burial practices (such as lintel graves) must be seen as an attempt to link the insular Scandinavian community to these elites and their areas of authority.[38]

The use of indigenous and Christian sites for furnished burial is, however, only one aspect of a more widespread reuse of sites by insular Scandinavian communities. In addition to those monuments constructed and used by contemporary indigenous groups, the insular landscape also contained many ancient monuments, some of which acted as focal points for FISBs. While this phenomenon has been noted by a number of commentators, particularly Shetelig, few have appreciated its full extent, with no less than 39 examples known, representing 20% of the total corpus of insular burial sites and 18% of definite sites (Fig. 2).[39] In what may perhaps be regarded as its simplest form, weapons (and presumably human remains) were interred within shallow pits dug into the tops of extant mounds. Burials at Tote, Skye (Highland) and Boiden (Argyll and Bute) conform to this pattern, and while the evidence from other sites is not necessarily so clear-cut, it would seem that this particular practice was relatively common.[40] Similar deposits also seem to have been made in prehistoric monuments which had rather different origins, but which may have resembled burial mounds by the Viking Age, such as the burnt mound at Weisdale (Shetland) or the semi-collapsed brochs at Castletown (Caithness), Gurness (Orkney), and perhaps Stenness (also Orkney), where the 'building' within which the burial was placed may have been either a broch or a more recent structure, as at Buckquoy (Orkney).[41] Like those at early medieval sites, FISBs associated 'ancient' sites can also be placed a few metres from the prehistoric monument itself, as certainly occurred at Cnip, Lewis (Western Isles), and may also have occurred at Pierowall, where several graves appear to have respected an extant mound.[42] In at least three cases, at Ospidale (Highland), Ballinaby, Islay (Argyll and Bute) and Ardvouray, Barra (Western Isles),

burials seem to have been associated with standing stones rather than burial mounds, a phenomenon which is particularly interesting when it is realised that Viking Age burials are not normally associated with standing stones in Norway.[43] These, and other less certain examples, together with some recent interpretations of the site at Claughton Hall (Lancashire) suggest that the practice of associating burials with 'ancient' structures was comparatively adaptable rather than inherently conservative.[44]

Given the widespread use of so many different prehistoric monuments as Viking Age Furnished burial sites, it can perhaps be suggested that this site reuse represents something a little more complex than 'common economy' or efforts to 'spare…work'.[45] Site reuse in Anglo-Saxon England, once viewed in a similar way, has more recently been interpreted as an attempt to 'symbolise and maintain relationships with ancient monuments' as part of a more general attempt to reinforce or even manipulate perceptions and memories of the past.[46] Those who created these insular Scandinavian burials, while comparatively new arrivals, may well have had a similar desire to associate themselves with a local past, and their re-use of prehistoric sites, like their re-use of Christian sites, had a potential political significance which extended beyond their own local, insular Scandinavian communities to all those who may have witnessed these burials, or subsequently encountered them in the landscape. The reuse of 'ancient' sites was far from uncommon among indigenous Christian communities in England and Wales, who not infrequently placed churches in old Roman monuments for reasons that 'must go beyond the purely practical'.[47] A number of these sites, such as Caerwent (Glamorgan) and York were subsequently used as sites of probable and possible FISBs, albeit modest ones in the case of York.[48] Rather more direct parallels can be seen in Ireland, where the political and social significance of prehistoric landscapes such as Tara (Meath) to indigenous Christian communities was enormous.[49] Driscoll's recent exploration of the relationship between prehistoric and early medieval monuments in the area around Dunadd and Kilmartin (Argyll and Bute) suggests that such monuments may have had political and social significance in this area too.[50] The fact that one of the prehistoric mounds near Kilmartin was the site of a possible FISB is particularly significant in the present context.[51]

Although there are potential similarities between the reuse of near-contemporary Christian and 'ancient' sites, however, there are also strong differences, particularly where distribution is concerned. It has already been noted that the reuse of early medieval burial sites north of the North Channel is comparatively rare, with only five examples of the practice known, but this situation is effectively reversed south of the Channel, where only twelve examples of burials at purely prehistoric sites are known, of which the evidence from eight is somewhat ambiguous. Thus, while the ratio of reused to 'new' sites in the two areas is directly comparable, with 45% of northern and 52% of southern burials sites associated with either 'Christian' or 'prehistoric' monuments, the monument types reused in the two areas differ greatly (Fig. 2). Explanations of this phenomenon are problematic, if only due to our lack of knowledge of many aspects of early medieval settlement patterns across these islands. It may be, for example, that the lack of reuse of Christian sites in northern and western Scotland reflects a less firmly established church structure in this area, but this cannot be substantiated on current evidence.[52] Suggestions that this pattern reflects the expulsion, or even extermination, of indigenous groups in the north are even more problematic, and the (limited) evidence for the importance of prehistoric monuments to indigenous communities already presented suggests that this explanation is equally problematic.[53] Nor do chronological theories provide any easy solutions to the problem, for while the northern burials are generally early, there are exceptions, and it must be remembered that some of the artefacts found at southern church sites, perhaps most notably Kilmainham (Dublin), are at least as early as any artefacts found in northern or western Scotland. [54]

At a more general level, it has been suggested that the two forms of site reuse can be seen as politically or religiously inspired. Religious explanations for Christian site reuse have already been mentioned, but an opposing theory, which seeks to relate prehistoric site reuse to an active 'pagan' resistance to evangelization has recently begun to gain popularity, particularly in Continental studies.[55] Similar models have been proposed for parts of England, perhaps most notably Derbyshire, where the 'pagan' cremations at the 'new' site of Heath Wood have been contrasted with the inhumations at nearby Repton, with the latter representing some form of 'accommodation' with Christianity and the local polity.[56] While appealing, it is difficult to find clear evidence to support this approach in insular contexts. In particular, if it is assumed that there is a broad relationship between the use of grave goods and religious belief in this period (and the rarity of more than a single generation of FISBs at any one insular site would suggest that there must be), then some differences in the contents of graves at Christian and prehistoric sites should be expected.[57] In practice, the grave goods found at the two site types are almost identical, with weapons being found in equal numbers at both site types, and the average number of artefacts per grave (where this can be established with reasonable confidence) is also virtually identical at reused Christian and prehistoric sites. The contents of more modestly furnished graves are also remarkably similar. It may well be true, for example, that inhumations accompanied by a single ringed pin represent burials in 'Christian' shrouds, but possible burials of this type have been found close to a Bronze Age cairn at Kinnegar (Donegal) as well as at early medieval burial sites such as Brigham (Cumbria) and Ceann Ear, Heisker (Western Isles).[58] Overtly religious symbols, while rare, are also

as likely to occur on reused Christian as prehistoric sites, so that while one of the two certain Thor's hammers from an insular burial context comes from Gurness (Orkney), the other was found in a grave at Repton (Derbyshire).[59] Explicitly Christian imagery from graves is even rarer, and the only example of cross slabs found in direct association with an FISB comes not from a Christian site, but rather the 'new' site at Kiloran Bay, Colonsay (Argyll and Bute), where the east-west chamber has a (possibly reused) cross slab at each end.[60] If the reuse of either site type is a reflection of any major religious or political commitment, this is in no way reflected in the type or quantity of artefacts placed in individual graves.

When examining these two types of site reuse, it is easy to forget that they actually share a great deal in common, in that both seek to associate what is essentially an intrusive burial practice with established monuments within the insular landscape. The role of burials and burial sites as focal points for a community has received considerable attention from commentators in the past, and it can be argued that this is also true in the case of FISBs.[61] While many archaeologists have seen furnished burial as a practice shared by almost all levels of Scandinavian society, more recent Norwegian studies have stressed the comparatively high status of any individual buried with grave goods, and at least one commentator has sought to associate elements of the practice with inheritance or other moments of potential social stress.[62] If insular Scandinavian burials are viewed in the same way, they may represent similar attempts to demonstrate authority and ownership, not merely for the deceased but at least equally importantly for those responsible for the selection of both the burial ritual and the site. Whatever the precise nature of the relationship between insular Scandinavian and indigenous groups, the positioning of graves in the landscape must have been a crucial element in the funeral ritual and the care with which sites were clearly chosen must be seen as a reflection of this. The selection of 'new', 'Christian' and 'prehistoric' sites in different areas can only be seen as the product of a series of local negotiations within and between communities, reflecting social and political relationships at a whole series of levels. The patterns examined here are the result of these individual negotiations, presumably involving differing levels of conflict and compromise, or domination and mediation, but all these sites share a common concern for local landscapes and a desire for burials to be incorporated within them. While this general study cannot hope to examine such local activity, it may at least provide a background against which more geographically focused work may be carried out in the future.

To return to Worsaae's early hypothesis on the site of 'Viking' graves, it seems clear on the basis of current evidence that even coastal sites show far more concern for small inlets than any open 'foaming maelstrom', with only a handful of furnished burial sites overlooking extensive sections of the coast. Indeed, even the inland burials of England seem to follow a similar pattern, typically positioned to dominate limited areas, particularly valleys. The care with which these sites were selected suggests a familiarity with the local environment, and the fact that over half of all burial sites occur at either 'Christian' or 'prehistoric' monuments further illustrates the close links

which those creating these burials had already established with the local polity and landscape. Far from being the last resting places of wandering Vikings, these sites represent specific individuals and communities who sought to make their presence felt at a local level, either through the creation of new monuments or the adaptation of existing ones, and through the shared memory of what was a constantly modified and adapted funerary rite.

Notes

1. Worsaae 1852.
2. For a recent discussion of the Irish section of Worsaae's tour, see Henry 1995.
3. Worsaae 1852, 255.
4. *Ibid.*, 325–31.
5. *E.g.* Wilde 1866; Anderson 1874; Coffey and Armstrong 1910.
6. For an example of this approach, see Curle 1914, 301–15.
7. Dunwell *et al.* 1995; Freke 2002; Richards *et al.* 1995.
8. Shetelig 1940.
9. Grieg 1940; Bøe 1940; Bjørn and Shetelig 1940.
10. Shetelig 1945; 2, 48.
11. *E.g.* Wilson 1976, 97, 99, 101, 104,106.
12. Owen and Dalland 1999, 17–18, 21; Kaland 1993, 308–17; Graham-Campbell and Batey 1998, 54–6.
13. Williams 1997, 2.
14. Sinclair 1794, 402.
15. Eagles and Evison 1970, 42–6; Geake 1997, 61, 71, 126.
16. These categories have been developed as a result of ongoing PhD research by at the Dept. of Medieval History, Trinity College, Dublin. The information and statistics used in this paper are derived from the same source.
17. Anon 1863, 312–14; Graham-Campbell 2001, 115; Darling with Gurney 1993, 45–61, 69–71, 104; Sheehan 1988, 60–72.
18. Edwards 1998, 19.
19. O'Brien 1998, 35.
20. Toomey 1990, 1–16; Devoy 1990, 17–26.
21. Anderson 1907, 443–9; Bersu and Wilson 1966, 1–44.
22. Balfour 1909, 371–5.
23. Welander *et al.* 1987, 147–74.
24. Wilson 1965, 41–2.
25. Megaw 1937, 235; Cubbon 1965, 249–53; Megaw 1940, 11–14.
26. Richards *et al.* 1995, 51–2.
27. Hodgson 1832, 106–9; Anon. 1848, 220–1; Ó Floinn 1998, 137.
28. Blair and Crawford 1997, 135–43; Graham-Campbell 2001, 116–17.
29. Knapp and Ashmore 1999, 1.
30. Ritchie 1977, 175–90; Graham-Campbell and Batey 1998, 173.

31. Close-Brooks 1980, 328–45; Edwards 1926, 16.
32. Shetelig 1945, 4.
33. *E.g.* Wilson 1976, 397; Richards 2000, 149–50.
34. Shetelig 1945, 35.
35. Tarlow 1997, 138–40; Potter and Andrews 1994, 55–134.
36. Biddle and Kjølbye-Biddle 2001, 60–74.
37. MacPherson 1878, 577–97.
38. Blair 1988, 52.
39. Shetelig 1945, 29–30.
40. Lethbridge 1920, 135–6; Stewart 1854, 132–5.
41. Anderson 1874, 549–50; Hedges 1987, 17, 73; Graham-Campbell and Batey 1998, 64; Charleson 1904, 565–6.
42. Dunwell *et al.*, 720; Thorsteinsson 1965, 166, 168–9.
43. Anderson 1874, 551; Anderson 1879, 71; Anon 1864, 229–31; Shetelig 1945, 30.
44. Edwards 1998, 14–15.
45. Ritchie 1977, 190; Shetelig 1945, 29.
46. Williams 1997, 25; Moreland 2001, 41.
47. Blair 1988, 44.
48. Knight 1996, 56–9; Philips and Heywood 1995, 192–3.
49. Herrity 1993, 127–51.
50. Driscoll 1998, 149–51.
51. Graham-Campbell and Batey 1998, 84–5.
52. Dumville 1997, 17.
53. For two recent contributions to this ongoing debate, see Smith 2001 and Bäcklund 2001.
54. Myhre 1993, 190–1.
55. *E.g.* Van de Noort 1993, 71–2.
56. Richards 2003, 173.
57. Gräslund 1987, 85. For comparable discussion of late Anglo-Saxon burials, see Geake 2003, 261.
58. Fanning 1983, 325; Lacy 1983, 66; Anon. 1904, 340; Anon. 1856, 176.
59. Graham-Campbell and Batey 1998, 128; Biddle and Kjølbye-Biddle 1992, 40.
60. Anderson 1907, 447.
61. *E.g.* Pearson 1999, 124–41.
62. Dommasnes 1982, 71; Skre 1997, 42, 44–6.

Bibliography

Anderson, J. 1874. Notes on the Relics of the Viking Period of the Northmen in Scotland, Illustrated by Specimens in the Museum, *Proc. of the Soc. of Antiquaries of Scotland*, **10**, 536–94.

Anderson, J. 1879. Notes on the Contents of Two Viking Graves in Islay, Discovered by William Campbell, Esq., of Ballinaby; with Notices of the Burial Customs of the Norse Sea-Kings, as Recorded in the Sagas and Illustrated by their Grave-Mounds in Norway and in Scotland, *Proc. of the Soc. of Antiquaries of Scotland*, **14**, 51–89.

Anderson, J. 1907. A Notice of Bronze Brooches and Personal Ornaments from a Ship-Burial of the Viking Time in Oronsay, and other Bronze Ornaments from Colonsay. Presented to the National Museum by the Right Hon. Lord Strathcona and Mount Royal, G.C.M.G. With a

Description, from Notes by the Late William Gallowy, of a Ship-Burial of the Viking Time at Kiloran Bay, Colonsay, *Proc. of the Soc. of Antiquaries of Scotland*, **41**, 443–9.

Anon. 1848. Archaeological Intelligence, *Archaeol. Jnl.*, **5**, 220–1.

Anon. 1856. Donations to the Museum, *Proc. of the Soc. of Antiquaries of Scotland*, **2**, 176.

Anon. 1863a. Proceedings of the Society June 10, *Jnl. Brit. Archaeol. Assoc.* **19**, 312–14.

Anon. 1864. Proceedings, *Proc. of the Soc. of Antiquaries of London*, 2nd Ser., **2**, 229–31.

Anon. 1904. Proceedings: Annual Meeting, *Trans. of the Cumberland and Westmoreland Ant. and Archaeol. Soc.* 2nd Ser., **4**, 340.

Bäcklund, J. 2001. War or Peace? The Relations between the Picts and the Norse in Orkney, *Northern Studies*, **36**, 33–47.

Balfour, J. 1909. Notice of a Viking Grave-Mound, Kingscross, Arran, *Proc. of the Soc. of Antiquaries of Scotland*, **43**, 371–5.

Bersu, G. and Wilson, D. 1966. *Three Viking Graves from the Isle of Man*, Society for Medieval Archaeology Monograph 1, London: SMA.

Biddle, M. and Kjølbye-Biddle, B. 1992. Repton and the Vikings, *Antiquity*, **66**, 36–51.

Biddle, M. and Kjølbye-Biddle, B. 2001. Repton and the 'great heathen army', 873–4, in J. Graham-Campbell, R. Hall, J. Jesch and D. N. Parsons (eds), *Vikings and the Danelaw*, 45–96, Oxford: Oxbow.

Bjørn, A. and Shetelig, H. (ed. H. Shetelig). 1940. *Viking Antiquities in England with a Supplement on Viking Antiquities on the Continent of Western Europe*, Viking Antiquities in Great Britain and Ireland 4, Oslo: H. Aschehoug.

Blair, J. 1988. Minster Churches in the Landscape, in D. Hooke (ed.), *Anglo-Saxon Settlements*, 35–58, Oxford: Blackwell.

Blair, J. and Crawford, B. 1997. A Late-Viking Burial at Magdalen Bridge, Oxford?, *Oxoniensia*, **62**, 135–43.

Bøe, J. (ed. H. Shetelig). 1940. *Norse Antiquities in Ireland*, Viking Antiquities in Great Britain and Ireland 3, Oslo: H. Aschehoug.

Charleson, M. M. 1904. Notice of Some Ancient Burials in Orkney, *Proc. of the Soc. of Antiquaries of Scotland*, **38**, 559–66.

Close-Brooks, J. 1980. Excavations in the Dairy Park, Dunrobin, Sutherland, 1977, in *Proc. of the Soc. of Antiquaries of Scotland*, **110**, 328–45.

Coffey, G. and Armstrong, E. 1910. Scandinavian Objects found at Islandbridge and Kilmainham, *Proc. of the R. Irish Acad.*, **28C**, 107–22.

Cubben, A. M. 1965. A Viking Sword from Ballabrooie, Patrick, with Evidence of Pattern Welding, *Jnl. of the Manx Museum*, **6**, 249–53.

Curle, J. 1914. On Recent Scandinavian Grave-finds from the Island of Oronsay, and from Reay, Caithness, with Notes on the Development and Chronology of the Oval Brooch of the Viking Time, *Proc. of the Soc. of Antiquaries of Scotland*, **48**, 292–315.

Devoy, R. J. N. 1990. Controls on Coastal and Sea-Level Changes and the Application of Archaeological-Historical Records to Understanding Recent Patterns of Sea-Level Movement, in S. McGrail (ed.), *Martime Celts, Frisians and Saxons*, 17–26, Council for British Archaeology Research Report, 71, London: CBA.

Dommasnes, L. H. 1982. Late Iron Age in Western Norway. Female Roles and Ranks as Deduced from an Analysis of Burial Customs, *Norwegian Archaeol. Rev.*, **15**, 70–84.

Driscoll, S. T. 1998. Picts and Prehistory: Cultural Resource Management in Early Medieval Scotland, *World Archaeol.*, **30**, 142–58.

Dunwell, A. J., Cowie, T. G., Bruce, M. F., Neighbour, T. and Rees, A. R. 1995. A Viking Cemetery at Cnip, Uig, Isle of Lewis, *Proc. of the Soc. of Antiquaries of Scotland*, **125**, 719–52.

Dumville, D. N. 1997. *The Churches of North Britain in the First Viking Age*, Fifth Whithorn Lecture, Whithor.

Eagles, B. N. and Evison, V. 1970. Excavations at Harrold, Bedfordshire, 1951–53, *Bedfordshire Archaeol. Jnl.*, **5**, 17–5.

Edwards, A. J. H. 1926. Excavation of a Number of Graves in a Mound at Ackergill, Caithness, *Proc. of the Soc. of Antiquaries of Scotland*, **40**, 160–8.

Edwards, B. J. N. 1998. *Vikings in North-West England: The Artifacts*, Lancaster, Centre for North-West Regional Studie.

Fanning, T. 1983. Some Aspects of the Bronze Ringed Pin in Scotland, in A. O'Connor and D. V. Clarke (eds), *From the Stone Age to the 'Forty-Five*, 324–42, Edinburgh: John Donald.

Freke, D. 2002. *Excavations on St Patrick's Isle Peel, Isle of Man, 1982–88 Prehistoric, Viking, Medieval and Later*, Centre for Manx Studies Monograph, 2, Liverpool: Liverpool University Press.

Geake, H. 1997. *The Use of Grave-Goods in Conversion Period England c. 600–c. 850*, BAR British Series, 261, Oxford: British Archaeological Reports.

Geake, H. 2003. The Control of Burial Practice in Anglo-Saxon England, in M. Carver (ed.), *The Cross Goes North: Processes of Conversion in Northern Europe AD 300–1300*, 259–69, York: York Medieval Press.

Graham-Campbell, J. 2001. Pagan Scandinavian Burial in the Central and Southern Danelaw, in J. Graham-Campbell, R. Hall, J. Jesch and D. N. Parsons (eds), *Vikings and the Danelaw*, 105–23, Oxford: Oxbow.

Graham-Campbell, J. and Batey, C. 1998. *Vikings in Scotland An Archaeological Survey*, Edinburgh: Edinburgh University Press.

Gräslund, A. S. 1987. Pagan and Christian in the Age of Conversion, in J. E. Knirk (ed.), *Proceedings of the Tenth Viking Congress, Larkollen, Norway 1985*, 81–94, Oslo: Universitetets Oldsaksamlings.

Grieg, S. (ed. H. Shetelig). 1940. *Viking Antiquities in Scotland*, Viking Antiquities in Great Britain and Ireland, 2, Oslo: H. Aschehoug.

Hedges, J. W. 1987. *Bu, Gurness and the Brochs of Orkney vol.2 Gurness*, BAR British Series, 164, Oxford: British Archaeological Reports.

Henry, D. 1995. *Viking Ireland. Jens Worsaae's Accounts of his Visit to Ireland: 1846–47*. Balgavies: Pinkfoot.

Herrity, M. 1993. Motes and Mounds at Royal Sites in Ireland, in *Jnl of the R. Soc. of Antiquaries of Ireland*, **123**, 127–51.

Hodgson, C. 1832. An Account of Some Antiquities found in a Cairn, near Hesket-in-the-Forest, in Cumberland, in a Letter from Mr. Christopher Hodgson, to the Rev. John Hodgson, Secretary, *Aae*, 1st Ser., **2**, 106–9.

Kaland, S. H. H. 1993. The Settlement of Westness, Rousay, in C. E. Batey, J. Jesch and C. D. Morris (eds), *The Viking Age in Caithness, Orkney and the North Atlantic*, 309–17, Edinburgh: Edinburgh University Press.

Knapp, A. B. and Ashmore, W. 1999. Archaeological Landscapes: Constructed, Conceptualized, Ideational', in A. B. Knapp and W. Ashmore (eds), *Archaeologies of Landscape: Contemporary Perspectives*, 1–30, Oxford: Blackwell.

Knight, J. K. 1996. Late Roman and Post-Roman Caerwent: Some Evidence from Metalwork, *Archaeologia Cambrensis*, **145**, 34–66.

Lacy, B. *Archaeological Survey of County Donegal*, Lifford: Donegal County Council.

Lethbridge, T. C. 1920. A Burial of the Viking Age in Skye, *Archaeol. Jnl.*, **77**, 135–6.

MacPherson, N. 1878. Notes on Antiquities from the Island of Eigg, *Proc. of the Soc. of Antiquaries of Scotland*, **12**, 577–97.

Megaw, B. R. S. 1937. Weapons of the Viking Age found in Man, *Jnl. of the Manx Museum*, **3**, 234–6.

Megaw, B. R. S. 1940. An Ancient Cemetery at Balladoyne, St John's. New Discoveries near Tynwald Hill, *Jnl. of the Manx Museum*, **4**, 11–14.

Moreland, J. 2001. *Archaeology and Text*, London: Duckworth.

Myhre, B. 1993. The Beginning of the Viking Age – Some Current Archaeological Problems, in A. Faulkes and R. Perkins (eds), *Viking Revaluations*, 182–204, London: Viking Society for Northern Research.

O'Brien, E. 1998. A Reconsideration of the Location and Context of Viking Burials at Kilmainham/Islandbridge, Dublin, in C. Manning (ed.), *Dublin and Beyond the Pale Studies in Honour of Patrick Healy*, 35–44, Bray: Wordwell.

Ó Floinn, R. 1998. The Archaeology of the Early Viking Age in Ireland, in H. B. Clarke, M. Ní Mhaonaigh and R. Ó Floinn (eds), *Ireland and Scandinavia in the Early Viking Age*, 131–65, Dublin: Four Courts.

Owen, O. and Dalland, M. 1999. *Scar A Viking Boat Burial on Sanday, Orkney*, Phantassie: Historic Scotland.

Phillips, D. and Heywood, B. 1995. *Excavations at York Minster Vol. I From Roman Fortress to Norman Cathedral*, London: HMSO.

Potter, T. W. and Andrews, R. D. 1994. Excavation and Survey at St Patrick's Chapel and St Peter's Church, Heysham, Lancashire 1977–8, *Antiquaries Jnl.,* **74**, 55–134.

Richards, J. D., Jecock, M., Richmond, L. and Tuck, C. 1995. The Viking Barrow Cemetery at Heath Wood, Ingleby, Derbyshire, *Medieval Archaeol.,* **39**, 51–70.

Richards, J. D. 2000. *Viking Age England*, Stroud: Tempus.

Richards, J. D. 2003. Heath Wood, Ingleby, *Current Archaeol.,* **16**, 170–3.

Ritchie, A. 1977. Excavation of Pictish and Viking-Age Farmsteads at Buckquoy, Orkney, *Proc. of the Soc. of Antiquaries of Scotland*, **108**, 174–227.

Sheehan, J. 1988. A Reassessment of the Viking Burial from Eyrephort, Co. Galway, *Jnl. of the R. Soc. of Antiquaries of Ireland*, **41**, 60–72.

Sinclair, J. 1794. *The Statistical Account of Scotland*, 10, Edinburgh: William Creech.

Shetelig, H. (ed.). 1940. *Viking Antiquities in Great Britain and Ireland*, vols. 1–5, Oslo: H. Aschehoug.

Shetelig, H. 1945. The Viking Graves in Great Britain and Ireland, *Acta Archaeologica,* **16**, 1–55.

Skre, D. 1997. Haug og Grav. Hva Betyr Gravhaugene? In A. Christensson, E. Mundal and I. Øye (eds), *Middelalderens Symboler*, 37–52, Bergen: Senter for Europeiske Kulturstudier.

Smith, B. 2001. The Picts and the Martyrs or Did Vikings Kill the Native Population of Orkney and Shetland? *Northern Studies*, **36**, 7–32.

Stewart, H. J. 1854. Notice of the Discovery of Some Ancient Arms and Armour, near Glenfruin, on the Estate of Sir James Colquhoun of Luss, Baronet, *Proc. of the Soc. of Antiquaries of Scotland*, **1**, 142–5.

Tarlow, S. 1997. The Dread of Something after Death: Violation and Desecration on the Isle of Man in the Tenth Century, in J. Carmen (ed.), *Material Harm: Archaeological Studies of War and Violence*, 133–42, Glasgow: Cruithne.

Thorsteinsson, A. 1965. The Viking Burial Place at Pierowall, Westray, Orkney, in B. Niclasen (ed.), *The Fifth Viking Congress*, 150–73, Tórshavn: Føroya Fornminnissavn.

Toomey, M. J. 1990. Sea-Level and Coastline Changes During the Last 5000 Years, in S. McGrail (ed.), *Maritime Celts, Frisians and Saxons*, 1–16, Council for British Archaeology Research Report, 71, London: CBA.

Van de Noort, R. 1993. The Context of Early Medieval Barrows in Western Europe, *Antiquity,* **67**, 66–73.

Welander, R. D. E., Batey, C. and Cowie, T. 1987. A Viking Burial from Kneep, Uig, Isle of Lewis, *Proc. of the Soc. of Antiquaries of Scotland*, **117**, 147–74.

Wilde, W. 1866. On the Scandinavian Antiquities lately discovered at Islandbridge, near Dublin, *Proc.of the R. Irish Acad.,* **10**, 13–22.

Williams, H. 1997. Ancient Landscapes and the Dead: The Reuse of Prehistoric and Roman Monuments as Early Anglo-Saxon Burial Sites, *Medieval Archaeol.,* **41**, 1–32.

Wilson, D. M. 1965. Some Neglected Late Anglo-Saxon Swords, *Medieval Archaeol.,* **9**, 32–54.

Wilson, D. M. 1975. Scandinavian Settlement in the North and West of the British Isles – An Archaeological Point-of-View, *Trans. Royal Hist. Soc.,* 5th ser., **26**, 95–113.

Wilson, D. M. 1976. The Scandinavians in England, in D.M. Wilson (ed.), *The Archaeology of Anglo-Saxon England*, 393–403, Cambridge: Cambridge University Press.

Worsaae, J. J. A. 1852. *An Account of the Danes and Norwegians in England, Scotland, and Ireland*, London: John Murray.

A Question of Priority: the Re-use of Houses and Barrows for Burials in Scandinavia in the Late Iron Age (AD 600–1000)

Eva Thäte

The last decade has seen a growing debate about the re-use of prehistoric monuments as early medieval burial sites.[1] However, in Scandinavia, archaeological excavations have identified not only the Viking Period re-use of ancient monuments by graves, but also the mortuary re-use of houses. This paper attempts to provide an explanation of the re-use of abandoned dwellings as a selective strategy for commemorating and inventing connections to the past.

Archaeological research has shown that there had not always been a clear distinction between mortuary practices and settlements in early Scandinavia. For instance, it appears that the destruction of houses was sometimes part of burial rituals. At the site of Trappendal in Denmark, a Bronze Age barrow was superimposed on a Bronze Age house which had been burnt down.[2] In Denmark and Sweden, excavations have revealed both Bronze Age and Early Iron Age instances where graves were placed in houses shortly after abandonment. While this pattern seems to decline in the Late Iron Age and is almost non-existent in the Viking Age; the Late Iron Age of Norway has produced numerous examples of houses re-used for burial after intervals of several hundred years. While in Denmark and Sweden the 'short-interval use' of houses for burial has been discussed in a few articles and dissertations,[3] the re-use of ruinous houses has received little attention. What was the significance of abandoned houses as burial sites in Viking-Period Norway? If this re-use was intentional, why were some graves interred in houses while others were interred in earlier barrows?

The Re-Use of Houses in the Late Iron Age in Rogaland (Norway)

Rather than attempting a detailed survey of all Viking-Period burial sites from Norway, this paper will focus upon instances of house re-use in the county of Rogaland in south-west Norway where the evidence is particularly striking. By way of comparison, the evidence for house re-use from excavations at Buckquoy, Orkney will be reviewed to illustrate the wider prevalence of this practice in areas of Norse influence.

Ullandhaug

A clear instance of house re-use was identified during excavations at the site of *Ullandhaug* in Stavanger commune (Fig. 1). At this site excavations revealed a Migration-Period farmstead comprised of three houses which had been burnt down in the sixth century AD. Associated with the houses were several barrows of the Early Iron Age (in this case of the Roman Iron Age and Migration Period). Houses 1 and 3, both long-houses with a length of *c.* 35.0 m (house 1) and 50.0 m (house 3) respectively, contained four Late Iron Age graves. Two Viking Age barrows (barrows 11 and 12; identified on morphological grounds) were superimposed on the ruins of house 1. Barrow 11 was situated over the north-west corner of the house and contained a ship setting for the construction of which stones of the west-wall had been re-used.[4] Barrow 12 – of the same oval shape as barrow 11 – was placed in the south-east corner of the building. Two burials of the Late Iron Age were found in house 3. The first was an inhumation grave of a man (grave I) interred in a substantial 'coffin' (or chamber?) measuring 2.3 m by 1.5 m. This grave was dug into the south-east corner of the building close to one of the entrances. The only artefact found – an axe – dates the grave to the early ninth century AD. Although no traces remained, it is probable that the grave was originally covered by a barrow. The second grave in house 3 was a cremation burial (grave II) placed right in the middle of the western wall of the ruin. It was covered by a small low cairn or stone setting and was associated with some beads that may indicate a female burial of the Late Iron Age. Another burial of a woman was found outside the eastern wall of house 3. It was contemporaneous with grave I inside the house.[5]

What is distinctive about the funerary activity on this site is that while both inhumations and cremations were

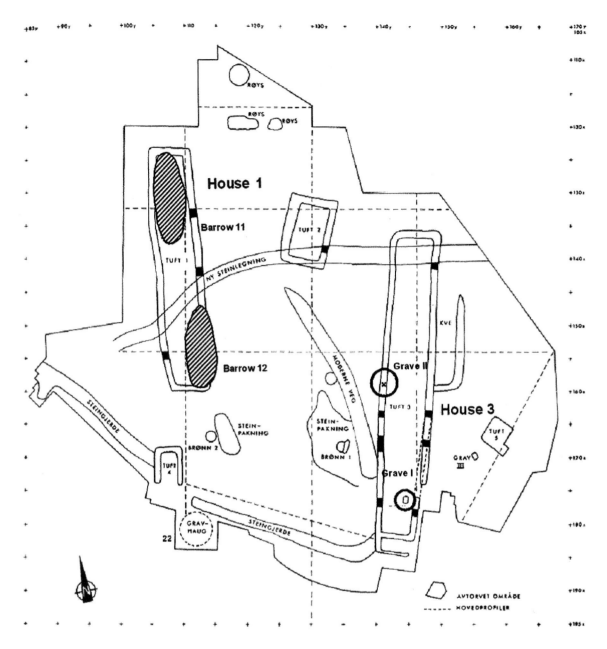

Figure 1. Ullandhaug, Frue landsn., Hetlands pgd., (Stavanger kommune), Rogaland: Position of the Viking-Age graves (black hatching and black circles) in the Migration-period houses (after Myhre 1992, 51, fig. 3). With kind permission of the Arkeologisk museum i Stavanger

interred within the abandoned houses display high-status features including barrows, ship-settings and chamber-graves; the adjacent Early Iron Age barrows remained untouched. This suggests a clear choice was made to associate the dead with houses rather than burial mounds.

Espeland

A different pattern of re-use can be seen at the site of Espeland in Sandnes parish. Here, both houses *and* barrows were re-used for burial (Fig. 2). Three houses were found at this site: House I (in the references also called 'house no. 25') was of Migration Period character while house II should be older since it was covered by a burial mound of the fourth to fifth centuries AD.[6] (House III is not relevant in this context). Houses I and II were located on the northern side of a large burial mound of the pre-Roman Iron Age called 'Medhaug' (13.0 m in diameter and 1.85 m high). The 'Medhaug' as well as the houses had been re-used over time. A cremation burial of the Early Migration Period (about AD 400) was inserted into the 'Medhaug' as a secondary burial. Another grave – probably of the same period – was placed on the north-east longitudinal wall of house II.

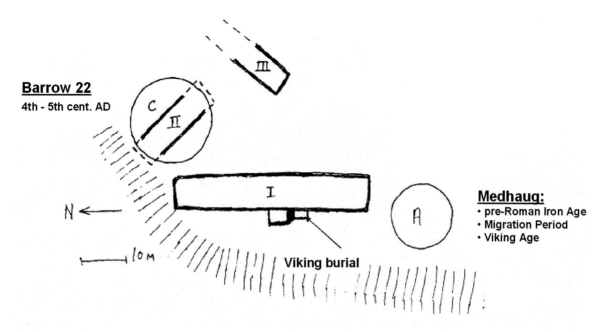

Figure 2. The re-use of houses and barrows at the site of Espeland, Højland sn. and pgd. (Sandnes kommune), Rogaland. House I and III date to the Migration Period, house II dates to the Late Roman Iron Age (after a drawing in Odd Espedals diary, Topographical Archive, Arkeologisk museum i Stavanger). With kind permission of the Arkeologisk museum i Stavanger

The human remains were placed in a small stone cist and covered by a barrow (no. 22) which measured 17.0 m in diameter and was consequently even larger than the pre-Roman Iron Age mound. Its precise location seems deliberate as the barrow was symmetrically positioned on the ruins of house II. Hundreds of years later, in the Viking Period, the 'Medhaug' was again re-used for the cremation burial of a man. Also, house I was re-used by an inhumation grave of an adult male dating to the tenth century AD. He was buried in a stone cist, one side of which was actually a longitudinal wall of the building.[7]

Storsheia

At the site of Storsheia av Store Svela and Vigeså in Bjerkreim parish, six houses (nos. 1–6) were found among *c.* 100 (undated) barrows and clearance cairns.[8] A stone wall enhanced this area of about 400 × 400 m. The dates of the houses are doubtful in some cases but all of them contained artefacts of the Migration Period. However, house 2 was dated by Petersen to the Viking Period on the basis of artefacts recovered from within the building. Similarly, house 4 was supposed to have shown evidence for continuity from the Migration Period to the Viking Period on the basis of the discovery of artefacts of the latter period. However, since the Viking Period artefacts discovered in houses 2 and 4 were soap stone vessels, whetstones and knives which were common

grave goods, it is equally likely that the houses were re-used by furnished graves after a period of abandonment.

More definite evidence for funerary evidence came from Migration Period house 1. Here, a female burial of the ninth century AD was located in the southern longitudinal wall on the east side of the entrance. In house 2, another Viking period grave was placed close to the east entrance of the northern longitudinal wall (Fig. 3). A Late Iron Age round barrow (according to Petersen probably dating to the Viking Age) had its eastern side superimposed on the western transverse wall of late fourth-century house 6.[9] On the bottom of the barrow there was only a dark layer of soil which did not contain any cremated bones, which is reminiscent of the Viking Age barrows at Ullandhaug where graves were not found either.[10] It is possible that these were either burials mounds in which the skeletal material has not survived, or alternatively, they were cenotaphs. In either instance, the aim seems to have been to use the house as a foundation for a burial mound.

Gausel

At *Gausel* in Stavanger parish, the Viking-Period grave of a woman was placed on the foundation wall of the south-west corner of a house of the seventh century AD (Fig. 4). The grave was covered by a cairn, *c.* 7.0 × 4.5 m wide, and 0.15–0.60 m high. Stones of the destroyed wall had apparently been used to build it. For some reason this

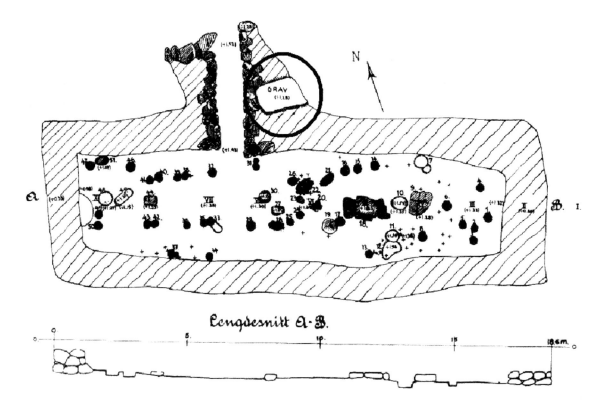

Figure 3. Re-used house II from the site of Storsheia, Bjerkreim sn., Helleland pgd. in Norway: The grave near the entrance is marked with a black circle (after Petersen 1933, Pl. XLVIII)

grave was placed here and not in the nearby cemetery where 98 cairns are recorded. At the same site the wealthiest Viking Age female grave of Rogaland was found: it is called the *Gausel dronningens grav* – 'the grave of the Gausel Queen'.[11] A well-equipped Viking Age boat grave of a man was also discovered recently close to the settlement area where the re-used house had been found. These two wealthy burials suggest that Gausel must have been an important place in the Viking Age, probably a mighty *storgård* ('big farm') and probably a central place.[12]

The Significance of the House in the Archaeological Evidence and Written Sources

Having reviewed the archaeological evidence from four excavations indicating the re-use of abandoned houses for burial in the Viking-Period, we must now attempt to explain this practice. In Norway, one explanation of house re-use appears to be popular, that people placed burials in houses because the ruins were convenient quarries for new cairns. But were the ancient Norwegians really such lazy people?

One point that argues against such a view is the fact that the use of houses for burials was already a common practice in Scandinavia in earlier periods. More precisely,

since the Bronze Age in Denmark, and since the Early Iron Age in Sweden and Norway houses and graves apparently often followed one another in close succession.[13] Moreover, a wider context for the practice can be recognized throughout European prehistory. For example, archaeologists have argued that there was a deliberate resemblance between Neolithic houses and long barrows in northwest Europe.[14] Similarly, at the site of Denstrupvej, Dalbyneder in Randers amt in Denmark the central grave in a mound of the Single-Grave Culture resembled a house.[15] Urns were shaped like houses in the Late Bronze Age and Early Iron Age in various parts of Europe while Etruscan tombs imitated domestic rooms.[16] In subsequent periods, mortuary houses are known from Danish, Norwegian and Continental Late Saxon cemeteries,[17] possibly built for the veneration of the dead and for cult-meals.[18] In the Viking Period itself, we have numerous symbolic allusions to houses in mortuary contexts. Meanwhile, in the early tenth-century in northern England we find the use of 'hogback stones' (house-shaped stone grave-markers) often interpreted as 'houses for the dead'.[19]

The written sources also show a close set of connections between the house, death and burial. In the Icelandic sagas it is told that graves were placed close to houses, and sometimes a barrow is called a house.[20] In

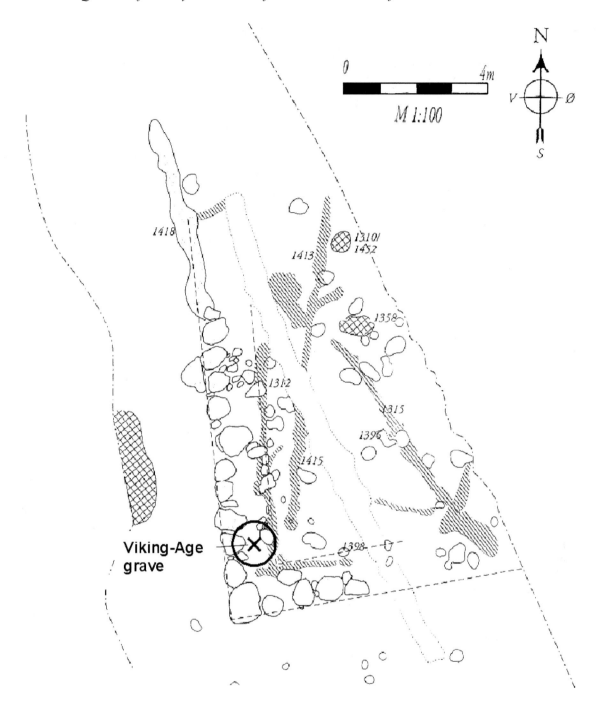

Figure 4. Location of the Viking-Age burial on the foundation wall of house no. 7 at Gausel, Stavanger kommune, Rogaland in Norway (after Børsheim & Soltvedt 2002, 107, fig. 79). With kind permission of the Arkeologisk museum i Stavanger

the Landnámabók (the 'Book of Settlements' – written in the 13th century AD) people were sometimes buried in barrows close to their living places, and there is one case where a man was interred in the yard of his farm.[21] In the Laxdæla Saga (written about AD 1250) a man named Hrappr wanted to be buried under the doorway of the living room of his house. The saga records that his intention was that: 'then I shall be able to keep a

more searching eye on my dwelling'.[22] Since Hrappr was of evil character he frightened the whole family off after his death; this was finally stopped by exhuming his remains and cremating his body.[23] In King Olaf Trygvesson's saga, Thorvald Ericsson – the brother of Leif Ericsson who discovered Vinland – wanted to be buried at the 'beautiful' spot where he had wished to build his farm before: 'Now I advise you to make ready with all the speed to return; but ye shall carry me up to the point which I thought would be so convenient for a dwelling [...] Ye shall bury me there [...]'[24] Here, a link between house and grave shows up again, although in a more abstract form.

Returning to the archaeological evidence, some of the re-used houses in Norway had been burnt down after being abandoned (all houses at Ullandhaug, and at least the Late Roman Iron Age house at Espeland), which would agree with the prehistoric evidence in Denmark and Sweden (as well as Germany[25]) to suggest a deliberate, ritualised destruction of houses, maybe at the death of an important individual[26], perhaps enacted when family lineages extincted or when people moved without the intention of returning. Norwegian archaeologists, however, prefer to explain this evidence as a possible consequence of war.[27] In the Icelandic sagas, sometimes high-status people were burnt in their houses, an act which may have had ritual connotations. King Olaf the Tree-Feller, for instance, was burnt in his house by his own people as a sacrifice to Odin to achieve better crops.[28]

The hall surrounded by flames seems to be a mythological image which appears in Fáfnismál (Elder Edda):

'A hall stands high on Hindarfjall;
All around it is wrapped in flame;
......
On the mount, I know, a war-spirit sleeps,
And around her flickers the lime-tree's foe [i.e. fire].'[29]

A passage in Saxo[30] suggests that sometimes a house 'died' when an individual died: The woman Signe and her maids committed suicide (a form of 'suttee') because Signe's lover Hagbarðr was going to be hanged. At the same time, the house where Signe stayed was set on fire.[31] Probably people believed that a burnt house would be available in the otherworld, much like grave goods placed on a pyre, according to Odin's law which said 'that all dead men should be burned, and their belongings laid with them upon the pile, and the ashes be cast into the sea or buried in the earth' and that 'every one will come to Valhalla with the riches he had with him upon the pile...'[32] Alternatively, could it be that the house was meant as a pyre, just as boats were sometimes used as ready-made pyres upon which the dead were cremated? Myhre has noted that late eleventh-and early twelfth-century mortuary houses in northern Norway were sometimes placed on graves and set on fire as part of the burial rite.[33]

The precise locations of graves within the houses discussed above may serve to contradict an expedient or practical explanation for the custom. The preference of certain locations within the houses and the re-use of building material suggests an intentionality to the practice. The graves were mainly located on the walls of buildings (see Table 1, 'location 1'). In four cases graves were placed close to entrances (see Table 1, 'location 3'). Sometimes graves were made from parts of the house; stones from house 1 at Ullandhaug were re-used for the ship setting beneath barrow 11. Meanwhile at Gausel stones of the building were re-used for the cairn which was superimposed on the burial and at Espeland one longitudinal wall of house 1 became part of the Viking Age stone cist. The only case which is doubtful is the round barrow on the transverse wall of house 6 at the site of Storsheia. However, this barrow fits into the context of two other burials from the same site that clearly and deliberately overlay buildings.

Having reviewed both the archaeological and the written sources, we can suggest that the house had a central importance in Viking-Period mortuary practices from Norway, and that the house was closely connected to death both directly and metaphorically. Unfortunately the sagas do not tell us anything explicit about the significance of the house itself, and none of the texts refers to the re-use of ruined buildings.

Table 1. Re-using grave structures and their location in earlier houses

Site	*grave*	*structure*	*alignment*	*re-use stones*	*location 1*	*location 2*	*location 3*
Ullandhaug	11	barrow	yes	yes	near wall	north	
Ullandhaug	12	barrow	yes		on wall	south-east	on entrance
Ullandhaug	1	barrow?			in corner / on wall?	south-east	near entrance
Ullandhaug	2	cairn			on wall	west	
Espeland	house II	stone cist		yes	on wall	north-east	
Espeland	house I	stone cist	yes	yes	attached to wall	west	
Storsheia	house 1	earth grave	yes		on wall	south	near entrance
Storsheia	house 2	earth grave	yes		on wall	north	near entrance
Storsheia	house 6	barrow			on wall	west	
Gausel	house 7	cairn		yes	on wall	south-west	
Buckquoy	house 3	barrow?			on wall	west	

Reasons for the re-use of houses

Yet we still have to explain the precise significance of why did people re-use houses for burial in Rogaland in the Viking Period after two or three hundred years of abandonment. It is also puzzling why ancient barrows were sometimes totally ignored while in other cases both houses and barrows were re-used.

A purely religious or metaphorical explanation for house-burials appears to be part of the picture. A ruin may have symbolized the idea of death because it is, in a manner of speaking, a 'dead house'. Moreover, the placing of graves close to or upon the entrances of houses probably represented the transition between the places of the living and the otherworld. There are indications in written sources (see for instance the report of Ibn Fadlan in the tenth century)[34] and in the archaeological evidence of the Viking Age that the door symbolised a boundary between life and death.[35] Richard Bradley has pointed out that the house itself combines domestic and sacred elements. He has based this argument on a comparison of the Scandinavian feasting hall with cult buildings in ancient Greece and an ethnographic case, the *marae* (meeting house) of the Maori in New Zealand: 'Indeed, they [the sacred and secular functions; E. T.] are so completely integrated with one another that such a neat distinction becomes meaningless.'[36]

However, a religious interpretation raises the question why house-burials are rather exceptional and why only individual, high-status graves occur associated with houses. One should expect more graves if burials in houses had been a common custom and were the focus of substantial cemeteries used by households and communities over long periods of time. Apart from that, a religious interpretation cannot explain why houses were preferred to other available monuments that might have held comparable associations with the past and with the ancestors.

It is likely that a more profane reason played a role related to the social and political importance of social memories evoked by linking the dead, houses and land. The idea of legitimating one's position by linking oneself to the ancestors through monument re-use for burial is a well-known theory. There is clear evidence from written sources that the ancestors must have been very important for people in Viking-Age Norway. This, in turn, focuses our attention on the Norwegian concept of the '*odal*'. The concept of the 'odal' is defined as "the family ownership of land and the right to own it", and this word is also used for the land itself.[37] The odal was always inherited by the oldest son,[38] and the odal law was strictly upheld to prevent the random distribution of land. It had to be offered first to other odal-men.[39] There were different kinds of odal land, but the first category listed in the Gulathing law was land which had 'passed from man to man for five successive generations.'[40]

Consequently, the ancestors were important to the claiming of odal rights, but ancestors were also connected to land and the house in other ways. Drawing upon historical and folklore evidence, Emil Birkeli has argued that the first builder of a farm who established a special claim to the land could become the focus of an ancestor-cult. This cult was still performed at some places in Norway in the eighteenth century, and according to Birkeli this custom is found widely throughout Europe.[41] This would agree with a historical source, the *Indiculus superstitionum et paganiarum* which mentions the pagan custom of regarding the dead as a saint: '[...] *quod sibi sanctos fingunt quoslibet mortuos*'.[42]

There was certainly a close relationship between the ancestors and the living which is apparent from incidents of offerings made on grave mounds – a custom that was forbidden by the Gulathing law.[43] Another custom was the '*utesitje*' which means 'sitting out' on the grave mound at night to ask the forebear for advice.[44] These are examples which show that the idea of the ancestral odal-man was closely linked to the burial mound. The word '*haugodalsman*' ('barrow-odal-man') which appears in a land-law from 1274, emphasizes this connection, too.[45] Consequently, if someone wanted to show his genealogical affiliation with his kin in order to legitimate his claim to odal rights after death, it would have made sense to use the burial mound of an ancestor for his own grave.

What to do if there were no local ancestors because the new owner of the land came from a different kin-group? Would a foreigner who came into possession of odal land have been allowed to link himself to the burial mound of the former owner of the farm to show his legal claim to the odal? The abandonment of a house for 200 or 300 years is a long time, but probably names of former odal-men were still known, and therefore it was clear that the new owner was not a member of the kindred. If such a person wanted to legitimate his position he might have chosen a more neutral place to express his rights, and sections of the Gulathing law suggest that this was the house.

Since the farmer had the right of jurisdiction (and, according to Burström, 'ruled like a king over his farm')[46] there should have been a place for dispensing justice. This was apparently the so-called 'high seat', the most prominent seat in the house which was occupied by the head of the household. Birkeli calls it a place of 'judicial sanctity'[47]. This seat was also important for the legitimization of the successor of the former odal man. The Gulathing law says: 'When a man is dead, his heir shall take his place in the high seat [...]'.[48] So the law itself linked death, succession and highseat. The highseat also became relevant when land was sold: According to the Gulathing law the buyer '...must take earth as the law prescribes; he shall take it from the four corners of the hearth and from under the highseat.'[49]

There was also another location of 'judicial sanctity'.

The '*dyradómr*', the 'door-court', was a Norwegian civil law, and court was held in front of the so-called 'men's-door', the main entrance. Meier suggested that such an event was connected with a so-called 'stone of justice' which was linked to the ancestor, and placed in front of this door.[50] The door was significant when odal land was reclaimed. According to the Gulathing law 'the doom shall be set outside the door of the defendant's house; the claimant shall place his men facing the principal door, and the defendant [his men] with their backs to the door [...]'[51] Several of the aforementioned graves were placed near the entrances of the houses, which was probably determined by the legitimating aspect of this custom.

The judicial meaning of the door in Norway agrees with its role in medieval Europe. The 'red door' was significant as a place for dispensing justice (the earliest examples derive from the twelfth century AD). Most of these doors were parts of sacral buildings such as churches and monasteries, but doors of secular buildings were apparently used in such a way, too.[52]

It seems that the house comprised more general aspects of law and jurisdiction while the barrow was more closely linked to a probably still known ancestor or former owner of the property. After all, the concept of the odal is associated with the barrow, and not with the house.

An Interpretation of Choices: Two Case Studies

Espeland, Norway

With these ideas in mind, let us now return to one of the sites discussed above to explore the implications of this explanation for understanding the selective re-use of houses and burial mounds. The evidence at Espeland (Fig. 2) suggests that probably not everybody was allowed to be buried in the odal mound 'Medhaug'. It is interesting that in the Early Migration Period and in the Viking Age both this barrow and two houses were re-used. In the first phase, barrow 22 (fourth or fifth centuries AD) was superimposed on house II. The size of the gravemound may suggest a competitive behaviour since it was bigger than the 'Medhaug' which was used for secondary burials. Maybe the individual in barrow 22 was not allowed to link himself to the 'odal mound', and chose to have a bigger barrow built for himself. It is also possible that for some reason the owner of a farm wished to separate himself from the former odal – and as a founder of a farm become a focus of cult himself.

In the Viking Age it was the 'Medhaug' which was re-used again, not barrow 22. This is surprising, for barrow 22 was bigger, and one could imagine that it had been more inviting for secondary burials. So the choice of the 'Medhaug' seems to have been deliberate. The Viking Age grave in this barrow, however, was not linked to the secondary grave of the Migration Period which was placed close to the periphery of the barrow. It was situated in the centre of the barrow, right above the original grave of the pre-Roman Iron Age. Both, its location and its size give the impression as though somebody wanted to make his affiliation obvious.

The other Viking Age burial which was attached to house I belonged to a man and appears somewhat richer than the grave in the 'Medhaug'. A barrow was not visible, but may have been existent. Probably it was the same situation as in the early Migration Period: one man could link his genealogy to the 'odal-mound' while the other individual (although of high status himself) could not take this position and had to look for another way to demonstrate his rights.

Buckquoy, Orkney

Having demonstrated the importance of this evidence for understanding the selective re-use of houses in Viking-Period Norway, let us turn elsewhere to illustrate the wider significance of the practice. In Orkney we find instances where houses were built over earlier dwellings as well as instances where burials were inserted into abandoned buildings.[53] At the site of Buckquoy, Bay of Birsay, Mainland Orkney, an inhumation burial of the tenth century was found on top of a ruined Viking Age farmstead. A man was buried here in the deposits of a house (house III) which had been abandoned at the end of the ninth century AD. Similar to the Norwegian evidence the grave was located above a wall; in this case the western wall of an earlier building. In contrast to the finds in Norway, the stones of the building had apparently not been re-used for any kind of grave structure. Compared to other graves in the surroundings this burial was quite wealthy and suggests that the man was of high (odal?) status.[54] According to Graham-Campbell and Batey there were some possible Viking Age barrows close to the site,[55] showing that houses were only one among many locations which could be used to commemorate the dead and emphasize links to the past through burial.

Could this man have been part of the family of the former owner? If so, why had he not just re-built the house and used it during his life-time just as the first settlers had done with the earlier Pictish farm at this place? Perhaps he had shifted the farm to a different location (as was common in Norway).[56] In that case, the farmer may have tried to establish a link to the former farm-house and his ancestors. However, he did not re-use a burial mound, but the house. So I suggest that he was a new owner who had built his farm somewhere else, but demonstrated his entitlement to the property by placing his grave on top of the settlement mound.

Conclusion

This paper has drawn upon archaeological and written evidence to suggest a metaphorical and socio-political significance for re-using abandoned houses in both Viking-Period Norway and Orkney. A descendant of a new landowner without ancestral links to the land may have chosen the house as a burial site for numerous inter-connected reasons:

> First, he may have used the ruin as a symbol to highlight the end of the lineage of the former odal man (symbolized by the destroyed house).

> At the same time he used the legal aspect of the house to legitimize his own position, whilst he avoided linking his burial to the odal mound of his predecessor.

> As the barrow had some legal aspects, too, the placing of a burial mound on the ruin of a house like at Ullandhaug could probably have doubled the effect of the demonstration of rights.

> All of this does not exclude the possibility that a new owner of the land could have tried to establish a link to the former owner by re-using stones of the house in order to make it part of his possession.

Overall, the evidence strongly suggests that the re-use of houses did not happen randomly, and that this custom had its own meaning which was different from the more common tradition to place the deceased in an already existing burial mound. In this way, the abandoned structure was the focus for complex choices; the choice of where to bury the dead was connected to the selective remembering or forgetting of the past. As such, the evidence presented here illustrates the importance of identifying monument re-use for understanding early medieval mortuary practices, but also it highlights the significance of *how* different monument types were re-used at particular times and in particular places.

Acknowledgements

I would like to thank Howard Williams for inviting me to give this paper at the 'Early Medieval Burial Practices' conference in Exeter in February 2004, and for his friendly help and comments concerning its publication.

I am grateful to Heinrich Härke for commenting on earlier drafts of this paper, and to Bjørn Myhre for encouraging me to write about this topic and for supplying me with references and information when I did research for my PhD in Stavanger.

Many thanks to Olle Hemdorff from the *Arkeologisk museum i Stavanger* for interesting discussions and for giving information and support whenever needed. I would also like to thank Friedrich Scheele from the *Ostfriesisches Landesmuseum Emden* for his help and for sending articles which were difficult to get hold of.

This may also be the best opportunity to express my gratitude to the staff of the *Arkeologisk museum i Stavanger* for their friendly support, especially Grete Lillehammer, Lotte Selsing, Jenny-Rita Næss, Paula Utigard Sandvik and Nina Elisabeth Ingebretsen. All of them made me feel welcome and being a part of museum's life.

Notes

1. *E.g.* Semple 1998; Thäte 1996; id. 2004 Williams 1997.
2. Cf. Boysen and Andersen 1983.
3. Sweden: Baudou 1991; Lindeberg 1995; Liedgren 1984; Lindell 1994; Denmark: Rasmussen 1993; Boysen and Andersen 1983.
4. Dag Widholm pointed out in an article on the Bronze Age in Kalmarsund, that there seems to have been a close connection between ship settings and house-symbolism: Gotland has got a remarkably high number of house urns. Three quarters of the total number has been found in ship settings (Widholm 2001, 194). The site of Ullandhaug still seems to indicate a context between ship and house. This is supported by the fact that chamber graves which according to Herschend (2001, 65) resembled the most important part of the house, were sometimes placed on ships (cf. Ellis 1943, 17). The close linkage between houses and ships is probably best demonstrated by the ship-shaped form of some Viking Age houses.
5. Helliesen 1901, 44–6; Møllerup 1974; Myhre 1980; Myhre 1992.
6. Myhre 1980, 113.
7. Espedal 1966; Bang Andersen 1967; Myhre 1965; Magnus and Myhre 1966, 30–4, no. 9141; Myhre 1980, 313; Innberetning om befaring på Espeland (Stavanger, Arkeologisk museum i Stavanger, Topographical Archive, 725 Sandnes, Espeland gnr. 26: (gnr. 26,4 og 5) Höyland s. og p. 19/3 1965).
8. Cf. Petersen 1933, 38–54.
9. *Ibid.*, 54.
10. *Ibid.*, 52.
11. Børsheim and Soltvedt 2002, 107–8, 177 and 226–8.
12. Børsheim 2001.
13. Cf. Boysen and Andersen 1983; Nielsen 1987, 184–6, no. 336; Baudou 1991; Broadbent 1985; Ramqvist 1983, 10, fig. 2,2; Ramqvist 1988; Lindell 1994, 1 and 4–8; Lindeberg 1995; Liedgren 1984, 100 ff; Liedgren 1988, 87 ff; Liedgren 1989, 75 ff; Løken 1978, 163.
14. Bradley 2001.
15. Schmidt and Sterum 1987, 120–1, no. 347.
16. Bradley 2005, 50–1.
17. Cf. Andersen 1951, 134; Jeppesen 1986; Häßler 1978, 307ff., Abb. 1–2; Laux 1983, 116–8; Løken 1971; Myhre 1976; Nilsson 1994; Nielsen and Stidsing 1986.
18. Myhre 1976.
19. Cf. Nilsson 1994.
20. Cf. Birkeli 1943, 114; Ellis 1943, 34, 92 and 57.
21. Ellis 1943, 37.
22. *The Laxdale Saga*, xvii, Foote and Press 1965, 42.
23. Ellis 1943, 37 and 91.
24. *King Olaf Trygvesson's Saga (Appendix)*, iv, Laing and Beveridge 1930 b, 107
25. Cf. Härke 1979, 95, fig. 27; 96.
26. See also Bradley 2005, 79.
27. Myhre 1980, 146; also explanation on the information board at the site of Ullandhaug.
28. *Ynglinga Saga*, xlvii, Laing and Beveridge 1930 a, 38.

29. Ellis 1943, 180–1; cf. also *The Lay of Fafnir (Fáfnismal)* 42–3, Terry 1978, 164–5, verse 42–3.
30. *The History of the Danes*, vii, Ellis Davidson and Fisher 1979, 216–17.
31. Cf. Ellis 1943, 53–4.
32. *Ynglinga Saga*, viii, Laing and Beveridge 1930 a, 12–13.
33. Myhre 1976, 14–5.
34. Reprinted in Foote and Wilson 1970, 408–11.
35. Cf. Andrén 1992 and also Arrhenius 1970.
36. Bradley 2005, 50; cf. also Bradley 2003; concerning the combination of domestic and sacred elements of the farm cf. also Andersson 1986 and Olsen 1928.
37. The Gulathing Law, Larson 1935, 424.
38. *Ibid.*, ciii, 108.
39. *Ibid.*, cclxxvi, 180.
40. *Ibid.*, cclxx, 178.
41. Birkeli 1938, 183, 189 and 201–2; cf. also Baudou 1991, 74;

Burström 1995, 173; Lindeberg 1995, 14.
42. *Indiculus superstitionum et paganiarum* 25, Boretius 1883, article 25.
43. The Gulathing law, xxix, Larson 1935, 57.
44. Zachrisson 1994, 222.
45. *Magnus Lagabøters Landslov*, vi, 16, Taranger 1915, 107.
46. Burström 1995, 166.
47. Birkeli 1944, 27; Birkeli 1932; cf. Baudou 1991, 74–5.
48. The Gulathing law, cxv, Larson 1935, 112.
49. *Ibid.*, ccxcii, 186–7.
50. Meier 1950, 23.
51. The Gulathing law, cclxvi, Larson 1935, 171.
52. Deimling 1998, 505.
53. Cf. Ritchie 1993, 25.
54. Ritchie 1977, 177 fig. 3, 184, 190 and 192.
55. Graham-Campbell and Batey 1998, 57.
56. Cf. Løken 1982, 75.

Bibliography

Andersen, H. 1951. Tomme Høje, *Kuml*, **1951**, 9–135.

Andersson, T. 1986. Germanisch Hof – Hügel, Hof, Heiligtum, in K. Hauck, K. Kroeschell, St. Sonderegger, D. Hüpper and G. von Olberg (eds), *Sprache und Recht. Beiträge zur Kulturgeschichte des Mittelalters. Festschrift für Ruth Schmidt-Wiegand zum 60. Geburtstag*, Band 1, 1–9, Berlin, New York: de Gruyter.

Andrén, A. 1992. Doors to Other Worlds. Scandinavian Death Rituals in Gotlandic Perspectives, *Journal of European Archaeology*, **1**, 33–56.

Arrhenius, B. 1970. Tür der Toten, *Frühmittelalterliche Studien*, **4**, 384–94.

Bang Andersen, S. 1967. Oldsaksamlingens tilvekst 1966, *Stavanger Museums Årbok*, **1966**, 5–40.

Baudou, E. 1991. Helgedom, hus och hög, in A. Lagerlöf (ed.), *Gravfältundersökningar och gravarkeologi, Rapport från riksantikvarieämbetet seminarium om „Gravmaterialet som källa för kunskap om människans hivsvillkor, religiösa och sociala värderingar" 26–27 oktober 1988*, 71–82, Forskning för kulturmiljövård, 3, Stockholm: Riksantikvarieämbetet.

Birkeli, E. 1932. *Høgsætet. Det gamle ondvege i religionshistorisk belysning*, Stavanger.

Birkeli, E. 1938. *Fedrekult i Norge. Et forsøk på en systematisk-deskriptiv fremstilling*, Skrifter utg. av Det Norske Videnskaps-Akademi i Oslo, II. Hist.-Filos. Klasse, No. 5, Oslo: Det Norske Videnskaps-Akademi i Oslo.

Birkeli, E. 1943. *Fedrekult. Fra norsk folkeliv i hedensk og kristen tid*, Oslo: Dreyer.

Birkeli, E. 1944. *Huskult og hinsidighetstro. Nye studier over fedrekult i Norge*, Skrifter utgiv. av Det Norske Videnskaps-Akademi i Oslo, kl. 1943: No 1, Oslo: Det Norske Videnskaps-Akademi i Oslo.

Boretius, A. (ed.) 1883. *Indiculus superstitionum et paganiarum*, Monumenta Germaniae Historica, Legum sectio II, Capitularia regum Francorum, tomus I, no. 108, 222–3, Hannover: Hahn.

Børsheim, R. L. 2001. Gausel – en forhistorisk storgård. *Frá haug ok heiðni*, **2001** (1), 25–31.

Børsheim, R. L. and Soltvedt, E.-C. 2002. *Gausel – utgravningene 1997–2000*, AmS-Varia, 39, Stavanger: Arkeologisk museum i Stavanger.

Boysen, A. and Andersen, S. W. 1983. Trappendal. Barrow and House from the Early Bronze Age, *Journal of Danish Archaeology*, **2**, 118–26.

Bradley, R. 2001. Orientations and Origins: a Symbolic Dimension to the Long House in Neolithic Europe, *Antiquity*, **75**, no. 287, 50–6.

Bradley, R. 2003. A Life Less Ordinary: the Ritualization of the Domestic Sphere in Later Prehistoric Europe, *Cambridge Archaeological Journal*, **13** (1), 5–23.

Bradley, R. 2005. *Ritual and Domestic Life in Prehistoric Europe*, London: Routledge.

Broadbent, N. 1985. New Knowledge of Early Iron Age Settlement in Northern Sweden. Cooperation between the University of Umeå and the Västernorrland County Museum, in M. Backe *et al.* (eds) *In Honorem Evert Baudou*, 387–93, Archaeology and Environment, 4, Umeå: Department of Archaeology, University of Umeå.

Burström, M. 1995. Gårdstankar. Kognitiva och sociala perspektiv på forntidens gårdar, in H. Göthberg, Ola Kyhlberg and Ann Vinberg (eds), *Hus & gård i det förurbana samhället – Rapport från ett sektorsforskningsprojekt vid Riksantikvarieämbetet*, 163–77, Riksantikvarieämbetet Arkeologiska Undersökningar, Skrifter nr 14, Stockholm.

Deimling, B. 1998. Ad Rufam Ianuam. Die rechtsgeschichtliche Bedeutung von „roten Türen" im Mittelalter, *Die Zeitschrift der Savigny-Stiftung für Rechtsgeschichte – Germanistische Abteilung*, **115**, 498–513.

Ellis, H. R. 1943. *The Road to Hel. A Study of the Conception of the Dead in Old Norse Literature*, Cambridge: Cambridge University Press.

Ellis Davidson, H. (ed.) and Fisher, P. (transl.) 1979. *The History of the Danes by Saxo Grammaticus*, Vol. 1, Cambridge: D. S. Brewer, New Jersey: Rowman and Littlefield.

Espedal, O. 1966. Espeland. *Frá haug ok heiðni*, **1966** (3), 237–41.

Foote, P. (ed.) and Press, M. (transl.) 1965. *The Laxdale Saga*, Everyman's Library 597, repr., London: J. M. Dent, New York: E. P. Dutton.

Foote, P. and Wilson, D. 1970. *The Viking Achievement. The Society and Culture of Early Medieval Scandinavia*, London: Sidgwick & Jackson.

Graham-Campbell, J. and Batey, C. E. 1998. *Vikings in Scotland. An Archaeological Survey*, Edinburgh: Edinburgh University Press.

Härke, H. G. H. 1979. *Settlement Types and Settlement Patterns in the West Hallstatt Province. An Evaluation of Evidence from Excavated Sites*, BAR International Series 57, Oxford: British Archaeological Reports.

Häßler, H.-J. 1978. Das Gräberfeld von Liebenau, in C. Ahrens (ed.) *Sachsen und Angelsachsen. Katalog der Ausstellung des Helms-Museums, Hamburgisches Museum für Vor- und Frühgeschichte, 18. November 1978 bis 28. Februar 1979*, 307 ff., Hamburg: Helms Museum.

Helliesen, T. 1901. Oltidslevningen i Stavanger amt, *Stavanger Museums Aarshefte*, **1900**, 31–62.

Herschend, F. 2001. *Journey of Civilization. The Late Iron Age View of the Human World*, Occasional Papers in Archaeology, 24, Uppsala: Department of Archaeology and Ancient History.

Jeppesen, J. 1986. De dødes huse, *Skalk*, **1986** (3), 27–30.

Laing, S. (transl.) and Beveridge, J. 1930 a. *Heimskringla. The Norse King Sagas by Snorre Sturlason*, Everyman's Library 847, London, Toronto: J. M. Dent.

Laing, S. (transl.) and Beveridge, J. 1930 b. *Heimskringla. The Olaf Sagas by Snorre Sturlason*, Everyman's Library 717, repr., London, Toronto: J. M. Dent.

Larson, L. M. (transl.) 1935. *The Earliest Norwegian Laws Being the Gulathing Law and the Frostathing Law*, Records of Civilization, Sources and Studies, 20, New York: Columbia University Press.

Laux, F. 1983. Der Reihengräberfriedhof in Oldendorf, Samtgemeinde Amelinghausen, Kr. Lüneburg / Niedersachsen. Ein Beitrag zu den frühgeschichtlichen Gräberfeldern im Bardengau, *Hammaburg*, **5** (1978–80), 91–147.

Liedgren, L. 1984. Iron Age Settlements in Hälsingland, in E. Baudou (ed.) *Papers in Northern Archaeology*, 93–112, Archaeology and Environment, 2, Umeå: Department of Archaeology, University of Umeå.

Liedgren, L. 1988. Synpunkter på den sedentära bebyggelsens etablering i Norrland, *Bebyggelshistorisk Tidskrift*, **14**, 83–104.

Liedgren, L. 1989. Bebyggelseutveckling i Forsa, Hälsingland, under den äldre jernåldern, *Arkeologi i norr*, **2**, 45–83.

Lindeberg, M. 1995. 'Högen och huset. Överlagrade husgrunder på Högomsgravfältet', unpublished uppsats i arkeologi, Påbyggnadskurs ht 1995, Institutionen för Arkeologi, Stockholms Universitetet, (Handledare: Torun Zachrisson).

Lindell, M. 1994. 'De levandes gravar och de dödas hus. En studie av gravar som överlagrar hus och huslämningar under järnålder i Sverige och Norge', unpublished C-uppsats i Arkeologi, Arkeologiska Institutionen Lunds Universitet, (Handledare: Påvel Nicklasson).

Løken, T. 1971. Dødehus over vikingtids flatmarksgraver? *NICOLAY. Arkeologisk tidsskrift*, **9**, 17–21.

Løken, T. 1978. Nye funn fra et gammelt gravfelt. Kan gård og gravplass gå tilbake til eldre bronsealder? *Viking*, **41**, 133–65.

Løken, T. 1982. Folkevandringstidsboplassen på Forssandmoen – detaljer i byggeskikken klarlagt, *Frá haug ok heidni*, **1982** (3), Bind 9, 75–83.

Magnus, B. and Myhre, B. 1966. Oldsaksamlingens tilvekst 1965, *Stavanger Museums Årbok*, **1965**, 5–51.

Meier, J. 1950. *Ahnengrab und Rechtsstein*, Deutsche Akademie der Wissenschaften zu Berlin. Veröffentlichungen der Kommission für Volkskunde, 1, Berlin: Akademie-Verlag.

Møllerup, O. 1974. Jernaldergarden på Ullandhaug, *Frá haug ok heiðni*, **1974** (3), 145–64.

Myhre, B. 1965. Vårens Feltarbeider, *Frá haug ok heiðni*, **1965** (2), 110–7.

Myhre, B. 1976. Hus over grav? *ARKEO*, **1976**, 14–8.

Myhre, B. 1980. *Sola og Madla i førhistorisk tid*, AmS-Småtrykk, 10, Stavanger: Arkeologisk museum i Stavanger.

Myhre, B. 1992. Funderinger over Ullandhaugs bosetningshistorie, in Anne Kari Skår (ed.) *Gammel gård gjenoppstår. Fra gamle tufter til levende museum*, 47–67, AmS-Småtrykk, 26, Stavanger: Arkeologisk museum i Stavanger.

Nielsen, B. H. and Stidsing, E. 1986. Flere Gravhuse, *Skalk*, **1986** (5), 7–10.

Nielsen, S. 1987. Byhøy, Hyllerup, sb. 39, St. Peders landsogn, in Nationalmuseet og de danske naturgasselskaber (ed.) *Danmarks længste udgravning. Arkæologi på naturgassens vej 1979–86*, København: Poul Kristensens Forlag, 184–6.

Nilsson, T. 1994. Sjælens hus, *Skalk*, **1994** (6), 3–7.

Olsen, M. 1928. *Farms and Fanes of Ancient Norway. The Place-Names of a Country Discussed in their Bearings on Social and Religious History*, Oslo: Aschehoug.

Petersen, J. 1933. *Gamle gårdsanlegg i Rogaland fra forhistorisk tid og middelalder*, Institutet for sammenlignende kulturforskning, Serie B: Skrifter XXIII, Oslo: Aschehoug

Ramqvist, P. H. 1983. *Gene. On the Origin, Function and Development of Sedentary Iron Age Settlement in Northern Sweden*, Archaeology and Environment,1, Umeå: Department of Archaeology, University of Umeå.

Ramqvist, P. H. 1988. Mellannorrland under äldre järnålder. Några aspekter på samhällsstrukturen, *Bebyggelshistorisk tidskrift*, **14**, 105–23.

Rasmussen, M. 1993. Gravhøje og Bopladser. En Foreløbig Undersøgelse af Lokalisering og Sammenhænge, in L. Larson (ed.), *Bronsålderns Gravhögar. Rapport från ett symposium i Lund 15.XI.–16.XI. 1991*, 171–85, University of Lund, Institute of Archaeology, Report Series, 48, Lund: Arkeologiska Institutionen och Historiska Museet.

Ritchie, A. 1977. Excavation of Pictish and Viking-age farmsteads at Buckquoy, Orkney, *Proceedings of the Society of Antiquaries of Scotland*, **108**, 174–227.

Ritchie, A. 1993. *Viking Scotland*, London: BT Batsford.

Schmidt, O. A. and Sterum, N. T. 1987. No. 347 Denstrupvej I, 14.04.01 Dalbyneder, Randers amt (RAS P. 983/86; KHM 89/86), *Arkæologiske udgravningar i Danmark*, **1986**, 120–21.

Semple, S. 1998. A Fear of the Past. The Place of the Prehistoric Burial Mound in the Ideology of Middle and Later Anglo-Saxon England, *World Archaeology*, **30** (1), 109–26.

Taranger, A. (transl.) 1915. *Magnus Lagabøters Landslov*, Kristiania: Forlagt av Cammermeyers Boghandel.

Terry, P. (transl.) 1978. *Poems of the Vikings. The Elder Edda*, 5th edit., Indianapolis: Bobbs-Merrill Educational Publishing.

Thäte, E. 1996. Alte Denkmäler und frühgeschichtliche Bestattungen. Ein sächsisch-angelsächsischer Totenbrauch und seine Kontinuität. *Archäologische Informationen*, **19** (1 and 2), 105–16.

Thäte, E. 2004. *Monuments and Minds. Monument Re-use in Scandinavia in the Second Half of the First Millenium AD*. Unpubl. PhD thesis, Reading: University of Reading.

Widholm, D. 2001. Bronsålder kring Kalmarsund, in Gert Magnusson and Susanne Selling (eds), *Möre historien om ett småland. E22 projektet*, Kalmar: Kalmar läns museum, 185–202.

Williams, H.M.R. 1997. Ancient Landscapes and the Dead. The Reuse of Prehistoric and Roman Monuments as Early Anglo-Saxon Burial Sites, *Medieval Archaeology*, **41**, 1–32.

Zachrisson, T. 1994. The Odal and its Manifestation in the Landscape, *Current Swedish Archaeology*, **2**, 219–39.

The Garden Gives up its Secrets: the Developing Relationship between Rural Settlements and Cemeteries, *c.* 750 –1100

Dawn Hadley

Anglo-Saxon archaeologists are becoming increasingly aware that following the decline of the deposition of grave goods in the seventh and eighth centuries burial did not become uniform.[1] They have begun to explore the diversity found in burial form, grave furniture, cemetery geography and aboveground markers, and to address the ways in which burial remained an arena of social display into the later Anglo-Saxon period.[2] This paper focuses on the relationships of rural cemeteries to the settlements in which they were located, between roughly the late eighth and eleventh centuries. It reveals that later Anglo-Saxon cemeteries were often ephemeral features in the rural landscape, prone to abandonment and often given over to domestic occupation or agriculture. Examination of the available evidence has much to reveal about the complexity of the emergence of the medieval pattern of churchyard burial, the processes by which parish communities were consolidated and the stages by which medieval nucleated villages emerged.

Rural Cemeteries, *c.* 750–1100

In order to place this discussion in context it is necessary to provide a brief overview of later Anglo-Saxon rural cemeteries, of which there were four main types. First, there are cemeteries associated with the religious communities founded in the seventh and eighth centuries. Excavated examples include the cemeteries at Repton (Derbyshire) and Ripon (Yorkshire). Although there is some debate about how quickly such churches came to provide burial for the laity, it is unquestionably the case that many dominated burial provision in their locality in the later Anglo-Saxon period.[3] Second, there are newly established cemeteries, some of which initially appear not to have had a church, but which subsequently acquired one (such as at Barton-upon-Humber and Holton-le-Clay, Lincolnshire), others of which were apparently secondary developments at a newly founded church (such as at Raunds, Northamptonshire and Trowbridge, Wiltshire).[4] Third, there are cemeteries of

varying size seemingly unconnected with a church throughout their period of use. Some of these are apparently newly founded in the late Anglo-Saxon period (such as Templecombe, Somerset, Thornton Steward and Riccall, Yorkshire), while others have earlier origins (such as Bevis Grave, Hampshire and Saffron Walden, Essex).[5] Finally, there are execution cemeteries (including the long-lived examples at Walkington Wold, Yorkshire and Staines, Middlesex).[6] This pattern of burial provision was not, however, particularly stable, not even where burials associated with churches were concerned, and, as we shall see, this has implications for our understanding of the origins of churchyard burial as the norm.

The Relationship between Cemeteries and Settlements in the Later Anglo-Saxon Period

A survey of published and unpublished sites permits a number of tentative observations about the relationships between later Anglo-Saxon cemeteries and earlier, contemporary and later settlements – relationships that were more dynamic than is generally supposed throughout the period under consideration.[7] First, many later Anglo-Saxon cemeteries, both with and without associated churches, are located on, or adjacent to, land previously, and apparently relatively recently, used for domestic occupation. This has been demonstrated at Trowbridge where in the tenth century a church and cemetery in a rectangular enclosure were added to a site occupied from the seventh century onwards, while a churchyard was added to the manorial complex and church at Raunds in the tenth century.[8] At Barton-upon-Humber a deliberately built-up middle Saxon layer of uncertain function was used by the ninth or early tenth century for burial. In the earliest phases burial respected a middle Saxon bank and ditch to the east, but by the late tenth or eleventh century it had been abandoned as a boundary feature and graves were cut into its fill, and this cemetery subsequently acquired a church.[9] At

Portchester (Hampshire) a phase of domestic occupation dating from the fifth to the eighth century, represented by buildings and pottery sequences, was superseded by a rubbish layer incorporating large quantities of domestic refuse. Over this layer was a tenth-century phase of buildings, including successive halls and a masonry tower to which burials were added in the mid-eleventh century, some of which occupied the site of one of the tenth-century halls.[10] At Thorpe-by-Norwich (Norfolk) a burial antedating the twelfth-century church post-dated a tenth-century occupation layer, while elsewhere in Norfolk at North Elmham the cathedral cemetery was extended in the early eleventh century over part of the adjacent settlement.[11] At Shepperton Green (Middlesex) a small cemetery, apparently of tenth-century date, and seemingly unaccompanied by a church, was added to an earlier occupation site producing early, mid- and later Anglo-Saxon pottery and a series of associated, if difficult to date, post-holes, pits and buildings.[12]

Tenth-century burials at Fillingham (Lincolnshire), located over 250 m from the parish church, appear to have been interred in a former occupation site, as mid-Saxon pottery was recovered from the fills of several graves and a short section of a ditch (roughly 2 m long, 1 m wide and around 30 cm deep) cut into the bedrock adjacent to the burials contained over 30 sherds of mid-later Saxon pottery (Fig. 1).[13] At both Holton-le-Clay and Cumberworth (Lincolnshire), later Anglo-Saxon burials associated with a church were cut through former occupation sites. At Holton occupation is indicated by a chalk layer, interpreted as a pathway, incorporating animal bones, oyster shells and sherds of mid-Saxon pottery, through which burials and the foundations of the church were later cut. At Cumberworth a sunken-featured building with associated mid-Saxon pottery was overlaid by a soil layer incorporating what has been interpreted as domestic refuse, including animal bones and shells, and which indicates occupation in the vicinity if not directly on the site. Through this layer burials were later cut, and a timber building, perhaps a church, and a stone church were later constructed over the excavated site.[14] Warwick Rodwell has commented on the amounts of mid-late Anglo-Saxon pottery recovered during grave digging on the sites of medieval churchyards in Norfolk, one interpretation of which is that there was domestic occupation preceding these cemeteries. Meanwhile the work of Tony Brown and Glenn Foard on the churchyards of Northamptonshire indicates that many may have been located within earlier, middle-Saxon settlement enclosures.[15] The recovery of some form of earlier settlement evidence from excavated later Anglo-Saxon cemeteries seems, thus, to be extremely common. Only rarely, however, is the nature and extent of the occupation pre-dating later Anglo-Saxon cemeteries extensively excavated, and it is often difficult to determine whether the burials occupied the precise site of a former dwelling, its associated yard or enclosure or an area adjacent to it. Nonetheless, at many of the sites highlighted

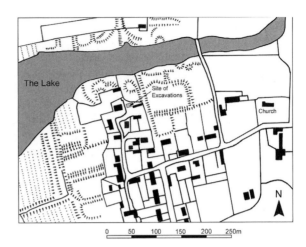

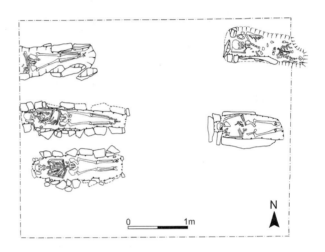

Figure 1. A late Anglo-Saxon cemetery excavated at Fillingham (Lincolnshire). Top: location of the excavation conducted in 2000 within the present village, where other burials had previously been uncovered; below: plan of those burials excavated in situ *(much of the cemetery had been disturbed by post-medieval quarrying). Illustration prepared by Oliver Jessop from original drawings by Andrew Chamberlain and Alex Norman*

here, especially where there has been excavation of pits, ditches and buildings, we can be confident that the burials were inserted into an area adjacent to contemporary occupation. While demonstrating continuity of occupation is difficult, later Anglo-Saxon cemeteries commonly appear to have been added to, or relocated within, pre-existing settlement sites.

The second notable feature of the archaeological record is the large numbers of later Anglo-Saxon cemeteries, or parts thereof, that were abandoned, and often subsequently either built upon or given over to agriculture or some other activity between the tenth century and the decades after the Norman Conquest. This sequence of events has been encountered in cemeteries associated with churches, such

Figure 2. Excavation of an eighth-century cemetery in the rear garden of a house in the village of Whitton (Lincolnshire). Excavation of mid- to later Anglo-Saxon cemeteries in such locations is becoming increasingly common. Photograph by Oliver Jessop

as Aylesbury (Buckinghamshire), Shipton-under-Wychwood (Oxfordshire), Rivenhall (Essex), Raunds, Cherry Hinton (Cambridgeshire), Dacre (Cumbria), Kirkdale, Addingham, Crayke (Yorkshire) and North Elmham, where part of the cemetery served as the village green in the late eleventh or twelfth century, and cemeteries apparently without churches, such as Milton Keynes (Buckinghamshire), Fillingham, Whitton (Lincolnshire), Templecombe and Mawgan Porth (Cornwall) (Figs 1, 2 and 3).[16]

In interpreting this evidence it is important not to conflate the evidence for quite distinct developments in the relationship between later Anglo-Saxon cemeteries and settlements. In some cases, such as Templecombe, Mawgan Porth and Cherry Hinton, the associated settlement appears to have been relocated, and this may account for the cessation of burial, but in other cases settlement was continuous and other factors must account for the disappearance of burial areas. At a number of burial grounds associated with major religious communities, an explanation for burial giving way to other activities can be sought in the reduced size of these cemeteries in the later Anglo-Saxon or early post-Conquest period. For example,

at Shipton-under-Wychwood around 30 later Anglo-Saxon burials have been identified outside the churchyard boundary, in and around the probably twelfth-century Prebendal House.[17] Similarly, at Aylesbury late eighth- to early tenth-century burials were discovered in an area that had apparently ceased to be a burial ground by the end of the eleventh century.[18] In his discussion of these burials, John Blair has suggested that the shrinkage of the cemeteries of minster churches was a common phenomenon in the period, citing similar developments nearby at Charlbury and Marsham (Oxfordshire), and Brixworth (Northamptonshire).[19] Indeed, this development can be paralleled elsewhere in the country, for example, at the early religious foundations at Dacre, Kirkdale, Addingham and Crayke.[20] There are several possible interrelated factors that may explain this trend. A church may have experienced a change in status, from that of a sizable religious community, to that of, effectively, a parish church, thus reducing the numbers of people seeking burial there. Alternately, irrespective of the status of the church concerned, the lay population for which it provided burial had declined in size following the foundation of other churches in the vicinity that acquired burial rights. The reduction in the size of cemeteries may also, as Helen Gittos has recently observed, have been related to the process of enclosing consecrated ground, which appears from the documentary and limited archaeological evidence to have been occurring in the later Anglo-Saxon period.[21]

This phenomenon of shrinking minster cemeteries appears real enough, but there is a danger of conflating evidence for this process with that for another, that is the abandonment of one or more discrete cemeteries and the transition to burial nearer a minster church. Major churches founded in the middle Anglo-Saxon centuries seem not uncommonly to have had multiple burial foci, often for the religious community itself and for members of the laity respectively, as has been demonstrated at Monkwearmouth, Hartlepool (County Durham), Repton and Ripon.[22] The abandonment of such burial areas is doubtless accounted for by the factors previously discussed concerning the shrinkage of large minster cemeteries, although in some cases the disruptions attendant on Scandinavian raids and settlement during the ninth and tenth centuries may have prompted reorganization of the layout of religious communities, if not the abandonment of part or all of the site. Whatever the dynamics behind the reduction of the burial area at minsters to a smaller site around the church, it is perhaps not surprising that the former areas of burial should eventually give way to settlement or cultivation.

However, reduction of the size of minster burial grounds is not the only explanation for the presence of later Anglo-Saxon burials underneath later settlement or cultivation. The presence and subsequent abandonment of one or more small, short-lived cemeteries located within and among rural settlements appears to be a relatively common phenomenon between at least the late eighth and tenth centuries, both within surviving and subsequently abandoned settlements. At Kilham (Yorkshire), for example, two areas of unaccompanied, pre-medieval burials have been encountered within the village some distance from the parish church, with skeletons from one of these sites recently yielding radiocarbon dates between the eighth and tenth centuries. This village has also produced clusters of fifth-, sixth- and seventh-century burials, suggesting a long sequence of occupation and successive relocations of the associated burial ground (Fig. 4).[23] At Trowbridge there are two burials, probably of the tenth century, beyond the limits of the cemetery, outside the entrance to the manorial enclosure.[24] Small, relatively short-lived cemeteries have been encountered among or adjacent to a number of subsequently abandoned occupation sites dating to somewhere between the eighth and tenth centuries at Templecombe, Shepperton Green, Thwing (Yorkshire), Bramford (Suffolk), Yarnton (Oxfordshire) and Gamlingay (Cambridgeshire).[25] Finally, consultation of the SMR or HER for just about any region produces examples of scattered, unaccompanied, and clearly pre-medieval burials within the confines of

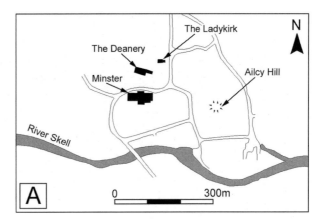

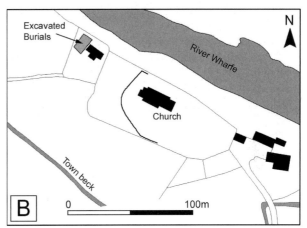

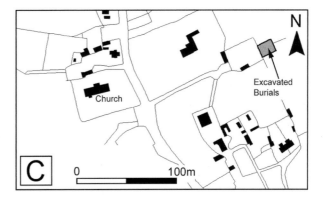

Figure 3. The location of excavated later Anglo-Saxon cemeteries that had been abandoned by the eleventh or twelfth century. A: Ripon (Yorkshire). Burials of the sixth to tenth centuries have been excavated at Ailcy Hill, and burials in the vicinity of the Ladykirk may date to the eighth to tenth centuries. Undated burials have also been excavated in the gardens of The Deanery and at two other sites within 200m of the Ladykirk. B: Addingham (Yorkshire). In 1989–90 55 graves dating to the between the eighth and tenth centuries were excavated to the west of the churchyard. C: Milton Keynes (Buckinghamshire). In 1992–3 100 burials were excavated adjacent to an area in which seven burials had been discovered during gravel digging in 1967. Radiocarbon dating suggests that the cemetery spans the tenth century. Drawn by Oliver Jessop

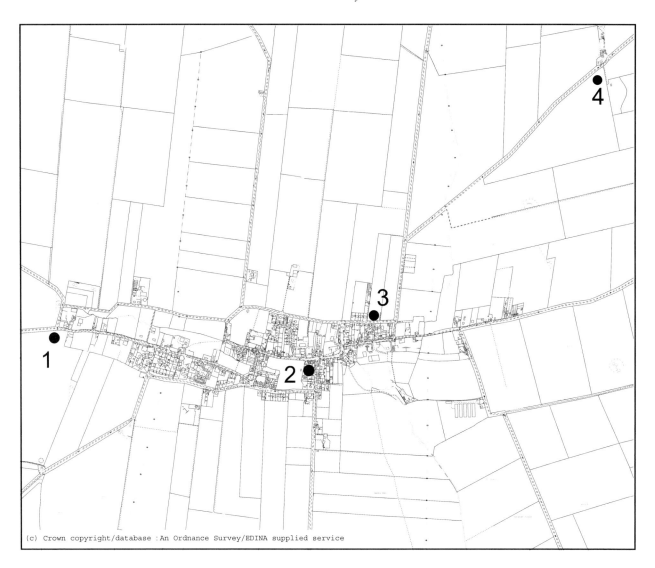

Figure 4. Burials at Kilham (Yorkshire): 1. Six unaccompanied burials, some in coffins, were excavated at the west end of the village in 1956; 2. Excavations in 1976 and 1989 recovered ten articulated burials and the disarticulated remains of at least 29 further individuals. Radiocarbon dating suggest that the burials date to between the eighth and tenth centuries. Over 100 skeletons had been excavated in the vicinity here in 1819, and a further 40 were found in 1907; 3. A child burial was excavated to the north of Back Lane in 1979, and the accompanying grave goods, including two annular brooches, suggest that it dates to the late sixth or seventh century; 4. Urns, bones and grave goods were recovered in 1814, and in 1824 a burial with grave goods was recovered. The grave goods from this site have been dated to the fifth and sixth centuries. Produced with the assistance of Elizabeth Chamberlin of Humber Archaeology Partnership, and Jo Buckberry. ©Crown Copyright/database right 20 (yy). An Ordnance Survey/ EDINA supplied service

medieval settlements. Any or all of these graves may be broadly contemporary with the cemeteries of known date in those villages. At Barrow-upon-Humber (Lincolnshire), for example, there is a cemetery founded in the tenth century, and at least three other areas of unaccompanied, pre-medieval burial have been located. A recently acquired radiocarbon date indicated that one of those cemeteries dates to the eighth century.[26] Similar examples of such scattered burials in and among rural settlements have been encountered elsewhere in Lincolnshire at, for example,

North Kelsey, Little Bytham, Brigg, and Threekingham.[27]

Such scattered and transitory burial grounds consisting of largely unaccompanied burials, in both surviving and abandoned settlements, are often assumed to date to the seventh century. Yet recent radiocarbon dating of some examples from within surviving villages (for example, at Kilham, Fillingham, Whitton, Great Hale (Lincolnshire) reveals that they date to somewhere between the eighth and tenth centuries, and it is becoming clear that the presence of these small clusters of short-lived, non-churchyard burials in and around settlements is not uncommon after the seventh century.[28] This appears to be a phenomenon common to north-west Europe, and has recently been discussed by Elisabeth Zadora-Rio with respect to northern France, and Frans Theuws who has examined comparable examples from The Netherlands.[29] As Zadora-Rio observes, this phenomenon casts doubt on the assumptions still held in some quarters that by the eighth century the Church had a firm grip on burial practices, that the close relationship between burial places and settlements from the seventh century onwards was invariably dictated by the Church or that churchyard burial quickly became the norm.[30] In his study of seventh- and eighth-century cemeteries in well-excavated settlement contexts in the southern Netherlands, Frans Theuws has suggested that some burials within settlements were those of the 'founding fathers of the farms', particularly those burials of males accompanied by elaborate assemblages of artefacts positioned next to a (their?) house. He concludes that other members of this man's family and subsequent generations were sometimes buried at various locations within the settlement, but others were buried in cemeteries located elsewhere.[31] It is certainly possible that in Anglo-Saxon England members of particular rural communities were buried in a diverse range of locations, some within or adjacent to the settlement and others in a cemetery or churchyard located elsewhere. The concept that some burials represent 'founding fathers' of settlements is, however, more difficult to substantiate although not inherently implausible. The multiple burial foci at some sites may, of course, have been successive, but it is possible that they relate to different social groups or families within communities. The use of former occupation sites may, then, have had some social or symbolic function, although the evidence from England is too sketchy to elaborate upon this suggestion convincingly. These developments in cemetery location bring to mind Andy Boddington's argument that the factors leading to the decline of grave goods from burials during the seventh century may be as much social and economic as religious.[32] These same factors may account for some aspects of the relocation of cemeteries from the eighth century to perhaps as late as the tenth, for the use of former settlement areas for burial and for the subsequent abandonment of burial sites.

Yet, we should also allow for the possibility that some isolated burials within or immediately adjacent to settlements are of individuals excluded from burial in consecrated ground, at a time when churchyard burial had become the norm. Such a conclusion is reinforced by such examples as grave 10 at North Elmham, which was distinguished by burial outside the boundary of the churchyard, by the fact that the individual was interred with the head to the east rather than the west, as was the norm for this period, and by the physical deformity of the individual. Grave 171 of the same cemetery was also unusual, as it was located beneath the line of the churchyard boundary wall and the deceased had met a violent

death.[33] At Ripon the tenth-century interments in what had once apparently been a monastic cemetery consisted of an individual with a severely distorted spine, and a multiple burial, and this phase of the cemetery has been interpreted as catering for the socially excluded.[34]

Evidently, scattered burial areas within settlements were eventually abandoned. The near universality of churchyard burial by the eleventh century, with the exception of felons and others specifically excluded from burial in consecrated ground, may represent the increased role of the Church in local society, a growing ecclesiastical concern to regulate burial, and the increasing legal and spiritual requirement to demarcate consecrated from unconsecrated ground. These are all developments mirrored in law codes of the tenth and eleventh century, which have hitherto been thought to conflict with the archaeological evidence for the abandonment of 'pagan' cemeteries and the supposed advent of churchyard burial by the eighth century. In fact, the late Saxon re-organisation of minster burial grounds and the appearance and subsequent abandonment of a whole series of other cemeteries suggests a gradual transition to churchyard burial for the majority.[35] As Zadora-Rio has said, this eventual transition may mark 'an important phase in the conceptualization of the parish community'.[36] That this was influenced by the Church is certain, but the close association of churches and manorial sites suggests lordly influence on the ground, as does the superimposition of churches and churchyards on settlements. Nonetheless, the variations present in grave construction (including a wide range of coffins and grave linings) and above-ground marking of graves, as well as other evidence such as the clustering of graves at prominent locations within churchyards, suggests considerable influence from members of the wider community over funerary practices in later Anglo-Saxon England.[37]

Churchyard Burial becomes the Norm

Although churchyard burial had become the norm for most people by the end of the tenth century in many regions of England, this, however, is not the whole story. Even once churchyard burial had commenced it did not invariably persist very far into the post-Conquest period if at all. This phenomenon is most well-known at Raunds, but has also been demonstrated at Thorpe-by-Norwich, Barrow-upon-Humber and Ketton Quarry (Rutland).[38] At Cherry Hinton a church and cemetery of over 600 burials dating to the later Anglo-Saxon period were deserted by the twelfth century, with burial apparently transferring to the medieval church of St Andrew, although it is not certain whether this church was contemporary with, or a successor to, the excavated church.[39] At Trowbridge the church and cemetery were incorporated within the early twelfth-century castle, the cemetery eventually going out of use later in that century.[40] Although beyond the remit of this paper, it is notable that many cemeteries and even churches were also abandoned in urban contexts following the construction of castles in the decades after the Norman Conquest, as has been demonstrated at Norwich, Newark (Nottinghamshire), Barnstaple (Devon), York and Newcastle-upon-Tyne (Northumberland).[41]

That lords played a part in the disappearance or relocation of churches and their cemeteries during the later Anglo-Saxon period should not be doubted. Lordly intervention may have been a particularly important factor in regions such as East Anglia and Lincolnshire, where multiple manors within settlements often gave rise to more than one church and churchyard, and where changes in manorial structure may have led to the abandonment of churches and their churchyards.[42] At Cherry Hinton, not only the cemetery but also an adjacent area of later Anglo-Saxon settlement, identified on the basis of ditches, pits, gullies and considerable amounts of late Saxon pottery, had been abandoned by the twelfth century, and it is possible that changes in lordship after the Norman Conquest, when the estate was divided into two manors, played a part in the reorganisation of the settlement and its burial ground.[43] At a later date it can sometimes be shown that seigneurial initiative contributed to the disappearance of a church. For example, at Sutton-in-Holland (Lincolnshire) in the later twelfth century a stone church was built at a new location to replace the existing wooden structure, and the lord who granted the land for the new building specified that the bodies buried there should be taken to the new church.[44] Similar developments may also have occurred in the pre-Conquest period, which, after all, was a time when it was necessary to formulate legislation to protect the financial interests of the old minsters in the face of thegnly foundations, when the presence of both a church and a churchyard on a thegn's land were marks of status, and when, reading between the lines, local people may have found themselves torn between both ecclesiastical and lordly pressure to bury their dead in what each force within local society deemed to be an appropriate location.[45] Rural settlements were part of complex social and economic networks, and these undoubtedly influenced their layout, including the location of peasant dwellings, seigneurial residences, church(es) and burial ground(s).

Conclusions

Burials came to be associated with churches gradually from the seventh century onwards. We can no longer assume that small transitory cemeteries of unaccompanied burials are unlikely to date to any later than the seventh century. Some of these burials appear to belong to a period when burial was not routinely restricted to churchyards, nor, seemingly, even to a single cemetery. A range of factors may account for this, including the exclusion of members of rural communities from churchyard or other community cemeteries by the local elite. Conversely, it may have been a conscious choice on the part of some members of rural communities to avoid larger cemeteries. This may have been an expression of local social standing or, perhaps, it derived from a desire on the part of rural communities to resist the centralising forces of kings, religious communities and the secular elite, as many of the latter becoming increasingly closely associated with individual communities, and to keep the dead of the community within the settlement rather than taking them to the churchyards of the elite for burial.[46]

The social and psychological impact of transformations in land use may have varied according to whether the cemetery was relatively recently abandoned prior to being put to alternative uses or had long since ceased to be remembered as a burial ground, and whether the reorganisation of burial was through choice or coercion. Unfortunately, the available evidence is rarely able to resolve these matters. The efforts made at Sutton-in-Holland at a later date to exhume the bodies of ancestors when the church and cemetery were moved and the archaeological evidence from Barton-upon-Humber for the careful exhumation of bodies prior to the building of the church indicate that burial grounds were not invariably abandoned or disturbed lightly or without due consideration of the dead and their surviving families.[47] What remains difficult to judge is whether small, short-lived burial areas of the later Anglo-Saxon period were consciously founded with the intention of accepting burial for a short period or for select groups, or whether events conspired to render the cemetery redundant within the local community.

We have also seen that even once burial at churches had begun it did not invariably persist. In the tenth and eleventh centuries the extent of minster burial grounds was often reduced, in part because of changes in the status and role of the churches concerned, but also because of developments in ecclesiastical attitudes, which required burial much closer to churches in enclosed spaces. The latter factor also seems to have extended to other settlements contexts, leading to the abandonment of scattered burial sites and the restriction of burial to areas around a church. Throughout the period between the eighth and tenth centuries settlements and associated cemeteries came into and went out of use, perpetuating a pattern observable at an earlier date, with settlements and cemeteries often succeeding each other, in which, it seems, both lords and churches played a part. There has long been a perception that after the seventh century burial locations became increasingly stable features in the landscape, while settlements continued to be relocated – but the present study has revealed that cemeteries continued to be relocated through the later Anglo-Saxon period, often within the context of the reorganisation of adjacent occupation areas.[48] At the same time, the cemeteries of minster churches appear to have been more stable centres of burial through the middle and later Anglo-Saxon period, albeit with occasional reductions of the scale of their cemeteries. At the other end of the spectrum, execution cemeteries are also increasingly being shown to have been long-lived. For example, three burials from the execution cemetery at Walkington Wold produced radiocarbon dates of 640–775 AD, 775–980 AD and 900–1030 AD (cal 2 sigma) respectively, while at Staines the three skeletons chosen for radiocarbon dating yielded dates of 684–893 AD, 999–1186 AD and 1024–1222 AD (cal 2 sigma).[49]

So far burial evidence has been used to address mortuary geography in later Anglo-Saxon England, but these patterns also shed new light on the processes of settlement nucleation in the period. It has become an orthodoxy that the tenth and eleventh centuries are a key phase in the emergence of nucleated villages in many regions, and it is certainly the case that the characteristic features of many villages – the church, churchyard and manorial enclosure – appear at this time. However, this brief survey suggests two significant issues in need of further investigation. First, there is, as Andrew Reynolds has also recently observed, a growing number of medieval villages with evidence of middle-Saxon occupation – often, as it happens, recovered during the excavation of cemeteries.[50] Second, although occupation in nucleated villages can often be traced back to the seventh century or even earlier, it was commonly subject to several major transformations, with manorial

enclosures, churches and churchyards often relative latecomers, and even then not necessarily static entities. Archaeologists studying the later medieval rural landscape have become accustomed to evidence that the allocation of space within settlements could sometimes change radically. For example, at Wharram Percy (Yorkshire) the twelfth-century manorial complex was succeeded by peasant tofts, and at Whythemail (Northamptonshire) a building was constructed across former property boundaries.[51] Yet, there is now also evidence, as we have seen, for the reallocation of space within continuously occupied sites of mid-later Anglo-Saxon date. Therefore, it is apparent that comments on the transition to churchyard burial have, until recently, tended to oversimplify the process, both hampering our understanding of the emergence of this important element of medieval religious life and obscuring our understanding of the dynamic changes in the layout of later Anglo-Saxon rural settlements. One final observation may be made. Archaeologists of the later period have often lamented the lack of excavated evidence for later pre-Conquest settlements. I would like to suggest that, in fact, there is considerable evidence in the form of mortuary remains. This evidence is not only more numerous than excavated buildings of the same period, but is also potentially more readily datable and has the capacity to throw important light on both continuity and change in later Anglo-Saxon rural settlements and the landscapes in which they were situated.

Notes

1. See Buckberry this volume.
2. See, for example, Hadley 2000; Hadley 2002; Thompson 2002; 2004; Zadora-Rio 2003; Buckberry 2004; Cherryson 2004.
3. Biddle and Kjølbye-Biddle 2001, 50–3, 60–7; Hall and Whyman 1996; Hadley 2000, 202–3.
4. Rodwell and Rodwell 1982, 290–2, 299–303; Sills 1982; Boddington 1996, 5–6; Graham and Davies 1993, 21–56.
5. Newman 1992; Adamson and Abramson 1997; Wenham 1960; Buckberry 2004, 464–5; Geake 1997, 154; Bassett 1982, 13.
6. Bartlett and Mackey 1973; Buckberry and Hadley 2007; Hayman and Reynolds 2005. The classification outlined here differs from that offered in Lucy and Reynolds 2001, 20–1, in which rural cemeteries are divided into three types: *Archaic* (cemeteries with a long lifespan and apparently unassociated with a church throughout their existence); *Adaptive* (cemeteries of tenth-century or earlier origins within which a church was subsequently constructed); and *Pioneer* (cemeteries added to an existing church, typically a thegnly foundation). They also identify execution cemeteries as a further category of Anglo-Saxon burial site. In the classification adopted in the present paper the cemeteries of minster churches have been identified as a separate category, my second category (of newly-founded churches) encompasses both the *Adaptive* and *Pioneer* categories of Lucy and Reynolds, while my third category (of cemeteries unassociated with a church) equates to the *Archaic* cemeteries.
7. The study area for this research includes northern England, the east midlands, East Anglia and the counties of the southern coast from Kent to Cornwall, plus a small number of published sites from other regions. Preliminary enquires at the Sites and Monuments Record for the rest of England indicates that many

more, later Anglo-Saxon cemeteries have been identified but not yet published.
8. Graham and Davies 1993, 21–56; Boddington 1996, 5–7.
9. Rodwell and Rodwell 1982, 289–90.
10. Cunliffe 1976, 14–61, 121–7, 301–4 and figs 98–100.
11. Darling and Gurney 1993, 254, where few details of this 'occupation layer' are given, other than the discovery of a 'silver pin of Viking type'; Wade-Martins 1980, 37–151, 185–7, 627–34.
12. Canham 1979, 103–10.
13. Buckberry and Hadley 2001.
14. Sills 1982; Green 1997.
15. Rodwell 1989, 151; Brown and Foard 1998.
16. Allen and Dalwood 1983, 6–8; Blair 1992; Rodwell and Rodwell 1985, 80–4, 90; Boddington 1996, 11–15; Geake 1997, 148; Rahtz and Watts 1998; Adams 1996; Adams 1990; Wade-Martins 1980, 633; Parkhouse, Roseff and Short 1993; Buckberry and Hadley 2001; Hadley 2003; Newman 1992; Bruce-Mitford 1997, 63–70, 87–9. I am grateful to Quinton Carroll for providing me with a copy of his research on Cherry Hinton in advance of publication.
17. Blair 1992.
18. Allen and Dalwood 1983, 6–8.
19. Blair 1994, 72–3.
20. Geake 1997, 148; Rahtz and Watts 1998; Adams 1996; Adams 1990.
21. Gittos 2002, 202–4.
22. Cramp 1969, 33; Daniels 1999, 108–11; Biddle and Kjølbye-Biddle 2001, 50–3; Hall and Whyman 1996.
23. Buckberry 2004, 429–31.
24. Graham and Davies 1993, 43.

25. Newman 1992; Canham 1979, 103–10; Geake 1997, 159; Nenk, Margeson and Hurley 1995, 284–5; Hey 2003; Reynolds 2003, 123.
26. Hadley 2003; Boden and Whitwell 1979; Buckberry 2004, 342–4, 411.
27. Buckberry 2004, 350, 381, 387–8, 404–5; the same point has been made about Oxfordshire in Blair 1994, 72.
28. Buckberry 2004, 430, 366; Buckberry and Hadley 2001, 13; Hadley 2003.
29. Zadora-Rio 2003; Theuws 1999.
30. Zadora-Rio 2003, 7, 9–13, 18–19.
31. Theuws 1999, 340–7.
32. Boddington 1990; see also Hamerow 2002, 123.
33. Wade-Martins 1980, 188–9.
34. Hall and Whyman 1996, 123–4.
35. Gittos 2002, 202; Hadley 2000, 211–12, 215.
36. Zadora-Rio 2003, 9.
37. On the diversity of later Anglo-Saxon burials see Hadley 2000, 2002; Buckberry 2004; Thompson 2004, 117–31.
38. Boddington 1996, 11–15; Darling and Gurney 1993, 254; Boden and Whitwell 1979; Meadows 1998.
39. Bradley and Gaimster 2000, 252.
40. Graham and Davies 1993, 144, 147–8.
41. Ayers 1985; Samuels 1998; Miles 1986; Hall 2004, 497; Lucy 1999, 42–3; Cherryson *this volume.*
42. See, for example, Williamson 1993, 154–61; Everson, Taylor and Dunn 1991, 46
43. Bradley and Gaimster 2000, 252; Quinton Carroll, pers. comm.
44. Owen 1990, 5.
45. Blair 1988, 8–13.
46. I am grateful to Howard Williams for prompting me to consider this range of possibilities.
47. Owen 1990, 5; Rodwell and Rodwell 1982, 294.
48. For example, Faull 1976; Boddington 1990, 194–7
49. Buckberry 2004, 445–6; Buckberry and Hadley 2007; Hayman and Reynolds 2005.
50. Reynolds 2003, 131.
51. Hurst 1979, 26–41; Hurst and Hurst 1969, 181; Lewis, Mitchell-Fox and Dyer 1997, 15. I am grateful to Annia Cherryson, Chris Dyer, Howard Williams and an anonymous reviewer for comments on an earlier draft of this paper. Quinton Carroll also generously provided information on Cherry Hinton in advance of publication. The illustrations were drawn by Oliver Jessop. Aspects of the research on which this paper was based were funded by the British Academy and NERC.

Bibliography

Adams, K. A. 1990. Monastery and village at Crayke, North Yorkshire, *Yorkshire Archaeol. Jnl.*, **62**, 29–50.
Adams, M. 1996. Excavation of a pre-Conquest cemetery at Addingham, West Yorkshire, *Medieval Archaeology,* **40**, 151–91.
Adamson, C. H. and Abramson, P. 1997. *Thornton Steward to Sowden Beck water pipeline. Archaeological excavation and watching brief for Yorkshire Water Services Ltd,* unpublished excavation report, available at Northallerton (Yorkshire) SMR.
Allen, D. and Dalwood, C. H. 1983. Iron Age occupation, a Middle Saxon cemetery and 12th to 19th-century urban occupation: excavations in George Street, Aylesbury, 1981, *Records of Buckinghamshire,* **25**, 1–60.
Ayers, B. 1985. *Excavations within the North-East Bailey of Norwich Castle,* East Anglian Archaeology, 28, Gressenhall: East Anglian Archaeology.
Bartlett, J. and Mackey, R. 1972. Excavations on Walkington Wold, *East Riding Archaeologist,* **1**(2), 1–93.
Bassett, S. R. 1982. *Saffron Walden: excavations and research 1972–80,* CBA Research Report, 45, London: Council for British Archaeology.
Biddle, M. and Kjølbye-Biddle, B. 2001. Repton and the 'great heathen army', 873–4, in J. Graham-Campbell, R. A. Hall, J. Jesch and D. Parsons (eds), *Vikings and the Danelaw: Select papers from the proceedings of the Thirteenth Viking Congress,* 45–96, Oxford: Oxbow.
Blair, J. 1988. Introduction: from minster to parish church, in J. Blair (ed.), *Minsters and Parish Churches. The local church in transition 950–1200,* 1–20, Oxford: Oxford University Committee for Archaeology.
Blair, J. 1992. The origins of the minster church at Shipton under Wychwood: human burials from Prebendal House, *Wychwoods Hist.,* **7**, 4–9.
Blair, J. 1994. *Anglo-Saxon Oxfordshire,* Stroud: Alan Sutton Publishing.
Boddington, A. 1990. Models of burial, settlement and worship: the final phase reviewed, in E. Southworth (ed.), *Anglo-Saxon Cemeteries: a reappraisal,* 177–99, Stroud: Alan Sutton Publishing.
Boddington, A. 1996. *Raunds Furnells : the Anglo-Saxon church and churchyard,* London: English Heritage.
Boden, J. M. and Whitwell, J. B. 1979. Barrow-upon-Humber, *Lincolnshire Hist. and Archaeol.,* **14**, 66–7.

Bradley, J. and Gaimster, M. 2000. Medieval Britain and Ireland in 1999, *Medieval Archaeology,* **44**, 235–354.
Brown, T. and Foard, G. 1998. The Saxon landscape: a regional perspective, in P. Everson and T. Williamson (eds), *The Archaeology of Landscape,* 67–94, Manchester: Manchester University Press.
Bruce-Mitford, R. 1997. *Mawgan Porth. A settlement of the late Saxon period on the north Cornish coast. Excavations 1949–52, 1954 and 1974,* English Heritage Archaeological Report, 13, London: English Heritage.
Buckberry, J. L. 2004. 'Later Anglo-Saxon Cemeteries in Lincolnshire and Yorkshire', unpublished PhD thesis, Sheffield University.
Buckberry, J. L. and Hadley, D. M. 2001. Fieldwork at Chapel Lane, Fillingham, *Lincolnshire Hist. and Archaeol.,* **36**, 11–18.
Buckberry, J. L. and Hadley, D. M. 2007. An Anglo-Saxon execution cemetery at Walkington Wold, *Oxford Jnl. of Archaeol.,* **26**(3), 309–29.
Canham, R. 1979. Excavations at Shepperton Green 1967 and 1973, *Trans. of the London and Middlesex Archaeol. Soc.,* **30**, 97–124.
Cherryson, A. 2004. Dating the dead of Saxon Southampton, *The Archaeologist,* **52**, 26–7.
Cramp, R. 1969. Excavations at the Saxon monastic sites of Wearmouth and Jarrow, co. Durham: an interim report, *Medieval Archaeology,* **13**, 21–66.
Cunliffe, B. 1976. *Excavations at Portchester Castle, Vol. II: Saxon,* London: Society of Antiquaries.
Daniels, R. 1999. The Anglo-Saxon monastery at Hartlepool, England, in J. Hawkes and S. Mills (eds), *Northumbria's Golden Age,* 105–12, Stroud: Alan Sutton Publishing.
Darling, M. J. and Gurney, D. (eds) 1993. *Caister-on-Sea: excavations by Charles Green 1951–55,* East Anglian Archaeology, 60, Gressenhall: East Anglian Archaeology.
Everson, P., Taylor, C. C. and Dunn, C. 1991. *Change and Continuity. Rural settlement in North-West Lincolnshire,* London: HMSO.
Faull, M. 1976. The location and relationship of the Sancton Anglo-Saxon cemeteries, *Antiquaries Jnl,* **56**, 227–33.
Geake, H. 1997. *The Use of Grave-Goods in Conversion-Period England, c. 600–c. 850,* BAR British Series, 261, Oxford: British Archaeological Reports.
Gittos, H. 2002. Creating the sacred: Anglo-Saxon rites for consecrating cemeteries, in S. Lucy and A. Reynolds (eds), *Burial in Early Medieval England and Wales,* 195–208, Society for Medieval Archaeology Monograph, 17, London: Society for Medieval Archaeology.

Graham, A. H. and Davies, S. M. 1993. *Excavations in the Town Centre of Trowbridge, Wiltshire 1977 and 1986–8*, Wessex Archaeology Report, 4, Salisbury: Wessex Archaeology.

Green, F. J. 1997. *St Helen's Cumberworth. Assessment Report*, unpublished excavation report, available at Lincoln SMR.

Hadley, D. M. 2000. Burial practices in the northern Danelaw, *c.* 650–1100, *Northern Hist.*, 36 (2) (2000), 199–216.

Hadley, D. M. 2002. Burial Practices in Northern England in the later Anglo-Saxon period, in S. Lucy and A. Reynolds (eds), *Burial in Early Medieval England and Wales*, 209–28, Society for Medieval Archaeology Monograph, 17, London: Society for Medieval Archaeology.

Hadley, D. M. 2003. Whitton, Lincolnshire, *Current Archaeol.*, **186**, 234–7.

Hall, R. A. 1994. The topography of Anglo-Scandinavian York, in R. A. Hall (ed.), *Aspects of Anglo-Scandinavian York*, 488–97, The Archaeology of York, 8/4, York: Council for British Archaeology.

Hall, R. A. and Whyman, M. 1996. Settlement and monasticism at Ripon, North Yorkshire, from the 7th to 11th centuries A.D., *Medieval Archaeology*, **40**, 62–150.

Hamerow, H. 2002. *Early Medieval Settlements. The archaeology of rural communities in north-west Europe 400–900*, Oxford: Oxford University Press.

Hayman, G. and Reynolds, A. 2005. Executions at Staines: regional and national perspectives, *Archaeol. Jnl*, **162**, 1–41.

Hey, G. 2003. Yarnton: Saxon and medieval, unpublished report available at http://www.oxfordarch.co.uk/yarnton/index.html.

Hurst, J. 1979. *Wharram: A Study of Settlement in the Yorkshire Wolds*, Society for Medieval Archaeology Monograph Series, 8, London: Society for Medieval Archaeology.

Hurst, J. and Hurst, D. G. 1969. Excavations at the deserted medieval village of Wythemail, Northamptonshire, *Medieval Archaeology*, **13**, 167–203.

Lewis, C., Mitchell-Fox, P. and Dyer, C. C. 1997. *Village, Hamlet and Field: Changing Medieval Settlements in Central England*, Manchester: Manchester University Press.

Loveluck, C. 2001. Wealth, waste and conspicuous consumption: Flixborough and its importance for middle and late Saxon rural settlement, in H. Hamerow and A. MacGregor (eds), *Image and Power in the Archaeology of Early medieval Britain: essays in honour of Rosemary Cramp*, 79–130, Oxford: Oxford University Press.

Lucy, S. J. 1999. Changing burial rites in Northumbria AD 500–750, in J. Hawkes and S. Mills (eds), *Northumbria's Golden Age*, 12–43, Stroud: Alan Sutton Publishing.

Lucy, S. J. and Reynolds, A. 2002. Burials in early medieval England and Wales: past, present and future, in S. J. Lucy and A. Reynolds (eds), *Burial in Early Medieval England and Wales*, 1–23, Society for Medieval Archaeology Monograph, 17, London: Society for Medieval Archaeology.

Meadows, I. 1998. Ketton Quarry, *Medieval Settlement Research Group Ann. Report*, **13**, 46–7.

Miles, T. J. 1986. The excavation of a Saxon cemetery and part of the Norman castle at North Walk, Barnstaple, *Proc. of the Devon Archaeol. Soc.*, **44**, 59–84.

Nenk, B. S., Margeson, S. and Hurley, M. 1996. Medieval Britain and Ireland in 1995, *Medieval Archaeology*, **40**, 234–318.

Newman, C. 1992. A late Saxon cemetery at Templecombe, *Proc. of the Somerset Archaeol. and Nat. Hist. Soc.*, **136**, 61–72.

Owen, D. M. 1990. *Church and Society in Medieval Lincolnshire*, History of Lincolnshire, 5, 3rd edition, Lincoln: Society for Lincolnshire History and Archaeology.

Parkhouse, J., Roseff, R. and Short, J. 1993. A late Saxon cemetery at Milton Keynes village, *Records of Buckinghamshire*, **38**, 199–221.

Rahtz, P. and Watts, L. 1998. Kirkdale Anglo-Saxon minster, *Current Archaeol.* **155**, 419–22.

Reynolds, A. 2003. Boundaries and settlements in later sixth to eleventh-century England, in D. Griffiths, A. Reynolds and S. Semple (eds), *Boundaries in Early Medieval Britain*, Anglo-Saxon Studies in Archaeology and History, 12, Oxford: Oxford University School of Archaeology.

Rodwell, W. 1989. *Church Archaeology*, London: English Heritage.

Rodwell, W. and Rodwell, K. 1982. St Peter's church, Barton-upon-Humber: excavation and structural study, 1978–81, *Antiquaries Jnl*, **62**, 283–315.

Rodwell, W. and Rodwell, K. 1985. *Rivenhall: investigations of a villa, church, and village, 50–1977*, CBA Research Report, 55, London: Council for British Archaeology.

Samuels, J. 1998. Newark Castle, *Current Archaeol.*, **156**, 458–61

Sills, J. 1982. St Peter's church, Holton-le-Clay, *Lincolnshire Hist. and Archaeol.*, **17**, 29–42.

Theuws, F. 1999. Changing settlement patterns, burial grounds and the symbolic construction of ancestors and communities in the late Merovingian southern Netherlands, in C. Fabech and J. Ringtved (eds), *Settlement and Landscape. Proceedings of a conference in Århus, Denmark*, 337–49, Moesgård: Jutland Archaeological Society.

Thompson, V. 2002. Constructing salvation: a homiletic and penitential context for late Anglo-Saxon burial practice, in S. Lucy and A. Reynolds (eds), *Burial in Early Medieval England and Wales*, 229–40, Society for Medieval Archaeology Monograph, 17, London: Society for Medieval Archaeology.

Thompson, V. 2004. *Dying and Death in later Anglo-Saxon England*, Woodbridge: Boydell Press.

Wade-Martins, P. 1980. *Excavations in North Elmham Park 1967–72*, 2 vols, East Anglian Archaeology, 9, Gressenhall: East Anglian Archaeology.

Wenham, L. P. 1960. Seven Archaeological discoveries in Yorkshire, *Yorks Archaeol. Jnl*, **40**, 298–328.

Williamson, T. 1993. *The Origins of Norfolk*, Manchester: Manchester University Press

Zadora-Rio, E. 2003. The making of churchyards and parish territories in the early-medieval landscape of France and England in the 7th–12th centuries: a reconsideration, *Medieval Archaeol.*, **47**, 1–19.

Anglo-Saxon Studies in Archaeology and History 14, 2007

Rescue Excavation of an Early Anglo-Saxon Cemetery at Gunthorpe, Peterborough

Philippa Patrick, Charles French and Christine Osborne
with a contribution by Bob Middleton
with illustrations by C. French, R. Parkin, P. Patrick
and A. Pluskowski

The day after the last Early Bronze Age skeleton was removed from beneath the barrow at the A15 Glinton-Northborough Bypass excavations in late August 1987,[1] the early Anglo-Saxon cemetery at Gunthorpe was discovered by contractor's box scrapers on the site of new playing fields between Coniston Road and the northern ring road, Peterborough (Figs 1 and 2). By the next morning a full archaeological response had been organised and salvage excavations had begun. These continued for ten days, using three staff members from Fenland Archaeological Trust and a host of local volunteers. The excavations were sponsored by Peterborough Development Corporation; and both the PDC and the contractors were extremely co-operative. English Heritage funded the conservation of the iron and bone artefacts, and the post-excavation analysis of the human bone assemblage.

Thirty-two skeletons were excavated from thirty grave pits and one stone coffin of probable Roman date, with fragments of four to seven more bodies present. Remnants of two other disturbed inhumations were found when the contractors finished the earth-moving a month later. Only one definite cremation in an Anglo-Saxon pot was recovered. Nevertheless, the promontory was observed to have numerous small 'shadows' containing charcoal, which may have been the last vestiges remaining of several former cremations. Sadly, the combination of thin topsoil cover, ploughing and heavy earth-moving machinery had largely destroyed this evidence by the time that salvage rescue excavations had begun.

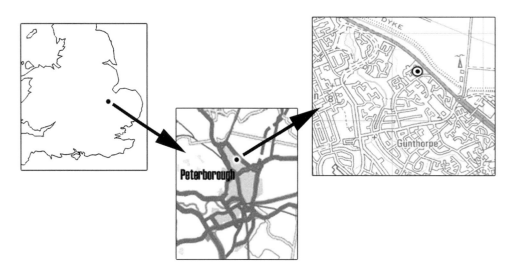

Figure 1. Location map (A. P.)

Figure 2. General view from the southeast looking across the machined and excavated area (C.F.)

Introduction

C. French

This rescue excavation was more of a ten-day salvage excavation and was prepared for publication through the goodwill and dedication of Pip Patrick and a small team. Consequently, there has been little attempt to contextualise and explore the wider context of the site due to severe limitations on time and funding. Nonetheless, as this is a rare example of a largely complete, but small, early Anglo-Saxon cemetery site that demonstrates quite a variety of different rites, it was considered important that publication of a basic descriptive outline of the excavation and findings was achieved. This ensures that this interesting cemetery does not remain within the 'grey literature.'

This small cemetery site is situated on a low knoll of gravel terrace at *c.* 10 m OD overlooking Newborough Fen to the northeast. It appears that the low promontory on which the cemetery was sited had previously seen some Bronze Age activity. Several pits and gullies were excavated, with small quantities of flint, pot and bone recovered, possibly of this period. A small, shallow ring gully of *c.* 4 m in diameter, possibly of the Romano-British period, was also excavated.

It remains somewhat uncertain whether the whole cemetery was excavated. Certainly the grave assemblage plan (Fig. 3) exhibits a strongly delimited edge on its northern side which appears artificial (although there may well have been an organic boundary such as a hedge along this alignment), whereas the other sides exhibit more 'feathered' edges. Moreover, many of the graves contained a gravelly backfill, which was extremely difficult to differentiate from the local drift geology and thus some graves may have gone undetected. This paper sets out to present the skeletal and grave assemblage data, before discussing the demography and spatial aspects of the human group represented.

Summary Chronology

C. French

The area of land occupied by the cemetery site witnessed some activity within the later Bronze Age and the Romano-British periods. The Bronze Age activity lead to a consistent but low abundance of worked flint within the surviving soil profile and possibly a few small pits in a cluster in the northern sector of the site (Fig. 31), although the Bronze Age flintwork may well be residual. Much later, in the Roman period, a small and shallow ring-ditch and a few associated small pits/postholes and short lengths of gully are suggestive of a small occupation of the southern sector of the excavated site, as well as one human burial in a stone sarcophagus. Interestingly, the bulk of the early Anglo-Saxon graves are situated between these two zones of early human activity on the site (Fig.

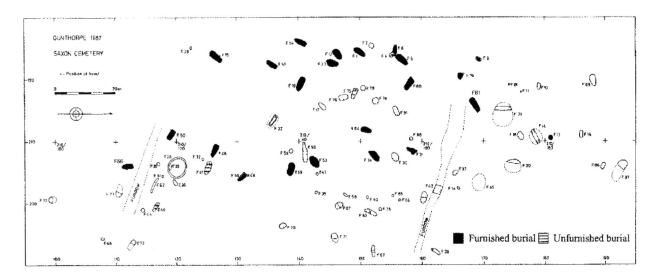

Figure 3. Plan of all excavated features, with furnished and unfurnished burial indicated (C. F./P. P.)

3). Chronologically, the assemblage of grave goods consistently points to an early Ango-Saxon date in the sixth century AD.[2]

The Excavations[3]

C. French

The Non-Saxon Features

In addition to the early Anglo-Saxon period cremations and inhumation graves which were the main focus of this salvage excavation, a number of other features were evident (Appendix 1). These included small and large pits, postholes, gullies and ring gullies. In most cases, their dating was problematic as they contained only one or two flints or abraded pieces of pottery, and in many cases no artefactual remains whatsoever.

In some cases, the small and shallow pits (*i.e.* F25), may have been the bases of pits which held cremations (*e.g.* F29). The short lengths of small gullies (*i.e.* F52, 62, and 63), small ring gully (F26) and the numerous small pits and possible bases of postholes that were found (Figs 3 and 4; Appendix 1) could represent a settlement of some kind, possibly of later prehistoric or Romano-British date. These features appeared to concentrate along the southern side of the cemetery (Fig. 3). The larger pits could just represent quarry pits for gravel, and the smaller pits and posthole features could represent some kind of emphemeral structure, whether contemporary with the use of the cemetery or of some other period. At the time of excavation, most of the larger to medium sized pits were suspected of being Bronze Age based on the typlogy of the few flints found within their fills. Nonetheless, the small Bronze Age artefact assemblage recovered from these features is only sufficient to suggest

a presence in the later 2nd millennium BC. These artefacts may of course have been re-incorporated into later fills.

Finally, the one small but complete ring gully, F26, was believed to be of the Romano-British period at the time of excavation (Figs 3 and 4) based on the presence of a few sherds of pottery. This was apparently a respected area, with no Saxon burials located within about 10m of it, so some remnant knowledge of this structure/former activity may have existed several hundred years later.

The Flint Assemblage

R. Middleton

This report concerns a total of thirty-seven worked flint artefacts from the Gunthorpe excavations (Table 1). The small number of artefacts has meant that detailed analysis has not been possible, so the following report aims to give a description of the assemblage and attempts to highlight trends which both date and suggest the origin of the material.

The assemblage derived from the ploughsoil and from the features cut into the subsoil. No sealed context produced more than three flints and, due to the nature of the excavation, no systematic collection of the surface material was possible. Both the infrequency of the finds and their generally undiagnostic nature meant that none could be satisfactorily used to date any of the context from which they derived.

All of the pieces were made of flint which, by the thin and abraded nature of the cortex, was probably collected from the vicinity of the site or from the neighbouring Nene and Welland river valleys where deposits of small flint nodules are plentiful. The flint was of good quality, with very few major flaws visible; the pieces of irregular workshop waste, however,

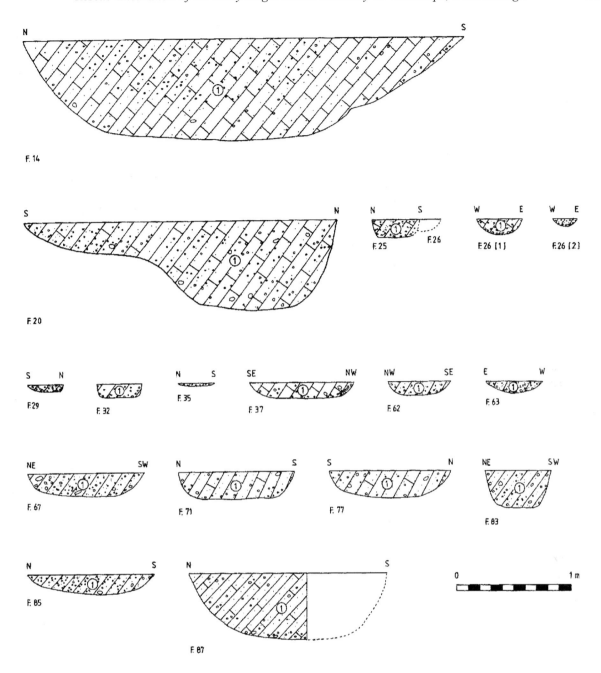

Figure 4. Sections of undated and non-Saxon pits and post-holes (C. F.)

represented pieces which split off planes of weakness during knapping, suggesting some faults in the raw material were encountered in the early stages of core preparation.

Most of the pieces were unpatinated, although two pieces had a slight off-white surface discolouration and on one piece the patination was too thick for the raw material colour to be seen. With the exception of the last piece, the degree of surface alteration does not appear to have been temporally significant. The heavily patinated piece, an abraded blade, may be part of the earlier component of the assemblage.

Most of the pieces exhibited some of post-depositional edge-damage; for the majority this took the form of small breaks along the thinner edges. The ploughsoil material was, however, much more extensively damaged, with comprehensive flaking on all edges. In some cases, notably features 18, 62, 72, and 76, the flints were extremely fresh, having totally undamaged edges. This may be a reflection of both the length of time the flints lay on the surface prior to incorporation into covered deposits, or the number of times the pieces have been reworked by later activity. Without a definite, sealed deposit for comparison,

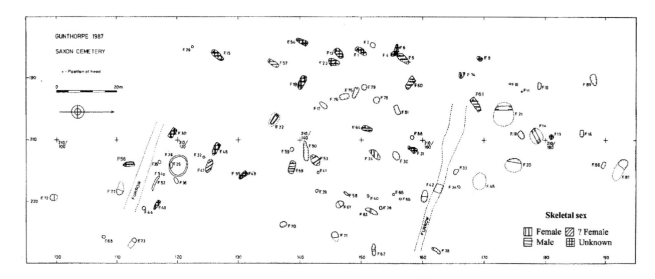

Figure 5. The skeletal sex distribution of the graves (C. F.)

Table 1. The flint typology

Flint type	Number	%
Unretouched flakes	21	63.6
Trimming flakes	4	12.1
Preparation flakes	2	6.1
Irregular workshop waste	4	12.1
Cores	2	6.1
Total debitage	33	100
Utilised flake	2	50
Scraper	1	25
Denticulate	1	25
Total implements	4	100

however, the precise implications for the variability in edge-damage must remain unknown.

Although small assemblages of this size, particularly those discovered by accident in contexts where the chance of later re-deposition is extensive, are notoriously difficult to date, there are a number of pointers to suggest that it may be possible in this case. This has been aided by recent excavations in the area, such as Fengate (Newark Road)[4] and Etton Landscape site 5,[5] which have allowed the main characteristics of local Bronze Age flintworking traditions to be defined.

An early component within the assemblage is indicated by a few pieces suggesting the use of a blade technology, including the patinated piece mentioned above. These pieces were generally in the same condition as the remainder of the assemblage and so the precise numbers involved was difficult to determine: the small number of blades (3) and pieces exhibiting dorsal blade scars (2) would suggest that this component was small. A finely-made scraper from the ploughsoil may also belong to this part of the assemblage. On subjective

grounds, this material, particularly the quality of blades, bears a resemblance to the earlier Neolithic material from Etton[6] and may be of a similar date.

The bulk of the assemblage were by-products from a technology which appears to be based on the use of flakes selected from *ad hoc* knapping, rather than core reduction aimed at the production of pre-determined flake forms. Flakes were removed using hard hammers, indicated by the predominance of hertzian cones of percussion (86.4%), associated with large, plain platforms. Similarly, most of the pieces exhibited multi-directional flaking. The technology, one hinge-fractured piece was present and most exhibited evidence of platform trimming to remove irregularities prior to removal from the core. The use of this technology suggests that most of the material dates to the middle Bronze Age or later.

The implements, particularly the two utilised flakes, being largely expedient in nature, do not provide any good dating evidence, although the presence of a crude denticulate, may be suggestive of a Bronze Age date.[7]

Given the re-deposited nature of the assemblage and the small quantity of the material, it is likely that most of it was originally deposited within the topsoil and incorporated into later features upon their construction. In the case of the fresh flints, the time between deposition and incorporation may have been extremely short. Unfortunately, the fact that most of the topsoil had been removed prior to the discovery of the site meant that the presence of further material of a similar nature in the ploughsoil outside the area of the features was untestable. The assemblage from Gunthorpe, therefore, may represent part of the wider spread of Bronze Age flints that covers the gravel landscape of both the Welland and Nene valleys, representing the extensive use of the landscape.[8] This material is, however, defined by its high implement : by-product ratio, (bearing in mind the

Table 2. The grave pits, their dimensions, the presence/absence of grave goods and sex as indicated by the bone and artefactual evidence

Feature number	Dimensions (m)	Bone sex	Age at death	Grave goods	Sex indicated by grave goods
1	2.2×1.4×0.2	? male	adult	yes	male
4	1.15×0.6×0.05	–	under 16	no	n/a
5	0.7×0.6×0.1	male	adult	yes	male
6	1.4×0.9×0.05	–	12–13	yes	?
7	1.0×0.6×0.05	female	adult	yes	? female
8	0.95×0.62×0.05	–	2–6	yes	?
9	0.75×0.7×0.05	–	no age given	no	n/a
12	1.9×0.75×0.008	–	9–13	yes	?
13 (cremation)	0.7×0.24	–	no age given	no	n/a
15	2.3×0.9×0.15	–	adult	yes	–
17	1.35×0.65×0.12	? male	adult	no	n/a
19	1.8×0.9×0.2	–	adult	yes	male
22 (sarcophagus)	2.2×1.4×0.7	female	mature adult	yes	female
23	1.8×1.06×0.15	–	mature adult	yes	? female
24	1.75×0.6×0.2	female	adult	yes	female
28	1.6×0.45×0.12	–	6–10	yes	female
31	1.5×0.6×0.08	–	adult	yes	?
36	1.0×0.52×0.2	–	no age given	no	n/a
39	0.5×0.37×0.28	–	no age given	no	n/a
46	1.45×0.68×0.1	–	no age given	yes	?
47	2.1×0.85×0.25	? female	adult	no	n/a
48	1.80.9×0.18	–	mature adult	yes	?
49	1.75×0.55×0.05	–	immature	no	n/a
53 (double)	1.95×1.1×0.15	–	adult (2)	yes	female
54	2.0×0.85×0.18	?	adult	yes	male
55	1.8×0.9×0.15	–	mid-teens	yes	female
56	1.8×0.65×0.08	male	adult	yes	male
57	1.95×0.75×0.3	male	adult	yes	male
60	2.1×0.95×0.3	male	young adult	yes	male
61	2.5×1.05×0.5	male	young adult	yes	male
64	1.7×0.8×0.15	male	adult	yes	male
69	2.0×0.9×0.35	male	young adult	yes	?
74	1.5×1.0×0.4	female	young adult	yes	female
75	1.75×0.7×0.08	–	young adult	no	n/a
80	1.5×0.8×0.3	–	9–14	yes	female
90	Unknown	–	adult	no	female

problems of implement numbers distorted through plough damage), a feature which this assemblage does not share. This, associated with the concentration of material in a relatively small area, may suggest that the Gunthorpe site lay close to a place where knapping was undertaken. The function of such a site and the elucidation of the meaning of this small number of flints must await further work in the area.

The Early Anglo-Saxon Graves

Burial survival, orientation and associations

Of the thirty-two skeletons recovered from thirty features (Figs 5–7), with fragments of another 4–7 individuals. Twelve skeletons were well preserved and nineteen had

suffered previous plough damage. The better preserved skeletons were located in deeper, rectilinear grave pits up to 75 cm deep, 1 m in width and 2 m in length. The other burials were placed in very shallow pits, c. 20–40 cm deep (Figs 8 and 9) (Table 2).

The early Anglo-Saxon activity would appear to be quite limited, both spatially and temporarily (Fig. 3). The graves are present in three rough rows: the westernmost 'row' 1 of c. 14 graves is ostensibly oriented southwest to northeast, the central row 2 of c. 10 graves exhibits graves in several orientations but with several having a similar orientation to those in row 1, and the easternmost 'row' 3 with a very dispersed group of c. 7 graves positioned in all orientations.

Twenty of the skeletons were laid out in an extended position, and nine in slightly flexed positions (Figs 6

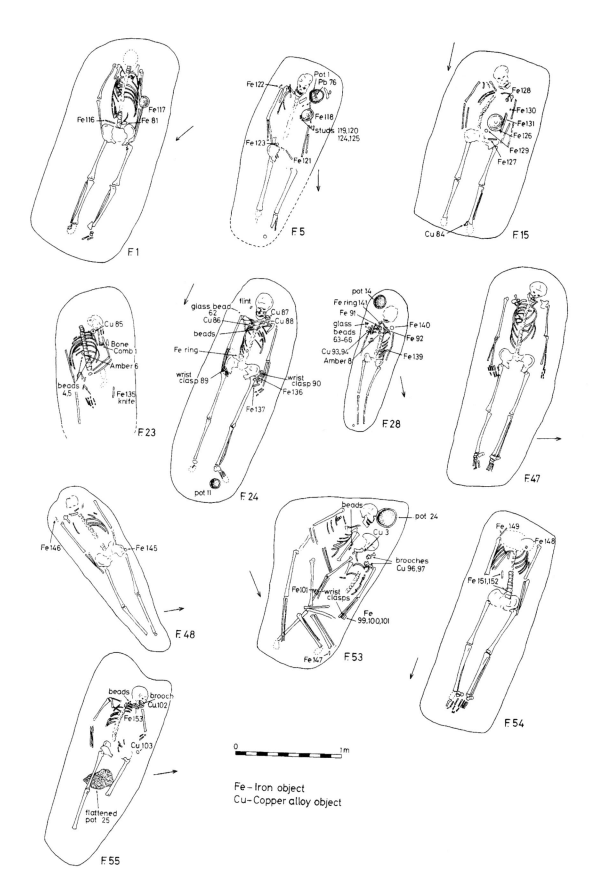

Figure 6. Plans of the skeletons and grave goods found in inhumation graves F1, 5, 15, 23, 24, 28, 47, 48, 53, 54, and 55 (C. F.)

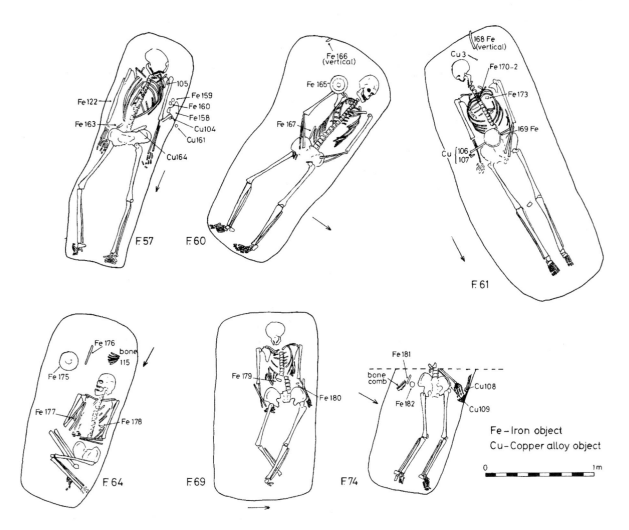

Figure 7. Plans of the skeletons and grave goods found in inhumation graves F57, 60, 61, 64, 69, and 74 (C. F.)

and 7). Although there was no systematic orientation to the graves, the skulls were generally placed at either the western or southern end of the grave pit. The stone coffin was aligned east-west, and contained an extended skeleton with the head at the western end (Fig. 10). In several cases the deeper grave pits appeared to have been deliberately back-filled with gravel pebbles, as if to disguise their location.

Field and osteological analyses (see Osborne below) suggested that there were nine definite male graves, five female graves, two young children and sixteen unidentified (Fig. 5; Table 3). Each of the probable male graves characteristically contained an iron shield boss, generally one or more iron spearheads and often a small iron knife (Table 4). The shield bosses tended to be positioned on the left or right upper arm, and in one instance on the lower chest. Remnants of the metal straps, rivets and in one case the iron grip behind the boss, were also recovered. The spearheads were usually

positioned parallel to the left or right arm, and often lay beneath the boss itself. In two instances, the spearhead was placed vertically behind the head.

The probable female graves contained a variety of bronze, iron and bone artefacts as well as beads and pottery (Fig. 5; Tables 3 and 4). Plain and decorated cruciform brooches, generally placed on the upper chest area, were common, as were strings of glass and amber beads (Fig. 28). Bronze swastika, disc, annular and penannular brooches were also present (Fig. 22). Two decorated bone combs were found (Figs 29 and 30). Complete pottery bowls (Fig. 31), placed near the head, were found with both male and female graves.

One grave pit (F53) contained two female skeletons, which were both flexed (Fig. 27; Tables 3 and 4). The burial in the Roman sarcophagus (Fig. 10, F22) may have been re-used, although a small bronze fibula brooch was found behind the head.

The grave goods, the skeletal remains, and their

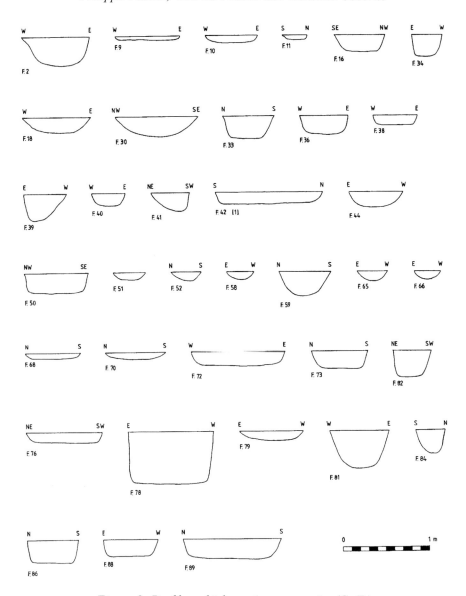

Figure 8. Profiles of inhumation grave pits (C. F.)

associations and parallels will be discussed by Osborne and Patrick below. Nonetheless, the generally consistent nature of the grave goods assemblage suggests that the cemetery is of the early Anglo-Saxon period can be placed in the sixth century AD. The shield bosses (Figs 15 and 16) and cruciform brooches (Figs 19–21) with the foot in the style of a horse's head are especially characteristic of this period.

The Human Skeletal Remains

C. Osborne

The human bones in this group represent at least thirty-two individuals (Figs 3 and 5–7), with a few remains possibly indicating up to seven others. After the second stage of analysis, a total of thirty-six inhumation graves

were evident. All are inhumations except for F13, which consists of cremated bone. The skeletal material is without exception in a very poor state of preservation. The bones are broken and fragmented, and this limits the amount of information to be obtained.

Sexing

The best indicators of sex are those characteristics of the skull and pelvis which differ between males and females. Also used, though not as accurate, are other features of the skeleton such as long-bone measurements (principally that of femoral head diameter) and general robusticity of the bones. As the characteristics of sexual dimorphism only develop during puberty, the sexing of immature individuals is not possible. Within this group the condition of the bones was such that sexing was not

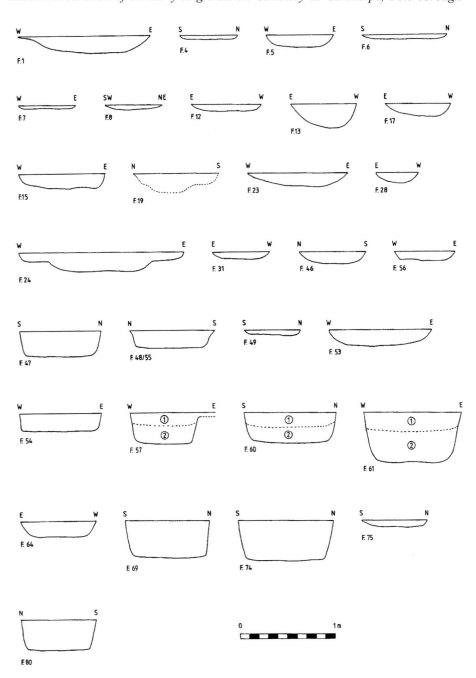

Figure 9. Profiles of other small features (C. F.)

often possible. Of the twenty-four adults, six were males, three were ?males, three were females and two were ?females (Figs 5 and 11). The uncertainty in sex arises if only very few of the sexual characteristics survive or if a skeleton exhibits both males and female characteristics.

Ageing
The ageing of adults is an uncertain business, and recently some of the methods used have come under severe criticism. For example, age was often based on the attrition (wear patterns) of molar teeth, although

this can vary greatly depending upon diet. A more reliable method of ageing is that based upon the changes to the pubic symphysis of the pelvis. This method is, however, only reliable in the ageing of males. In the female pubis, changes which arise as a result of pregnancy and childbirth can obscure those related to ageing. Unfortunately, within this group, none of the pubic symphyses survived. Other indicators such as degenerative disease of the skeleton and visible epiphyseal fusion lines can give a general idea of age.

The ageing of immature individuals is much more accurate than that of adults if the dentition is present, as

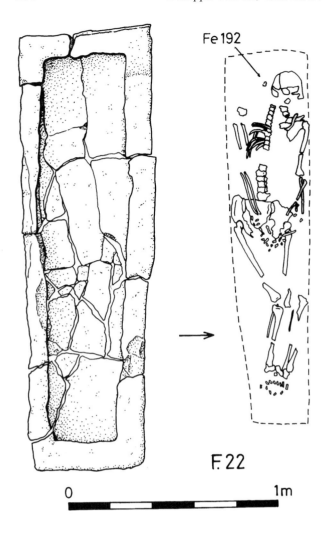

Figure 10. The Roman burial and sarcophagus (F22) (C. F.)

age can be estimated from the different stages of tooth development. In adolescents the different stages of epiphyseal union are used. If all the epiphyses of a skeleton are fused, it can be classed as adult. Within this group, twenty-four individuals have been recorded as such (Fig. 11). Of these, five have been estimated as younger adults and three as older adults. Further age divisions cannot be made. Seven immature individuals were present.

Stature
Usually the stature of an individual is calculated, basing the calculations upon measurement of complete long-bones. However, within this group the preservation of bone was such that no measurements of this type were possible.

Dentition
When present, the dentition was recorded using a standard system which notes the presence of absence (either through ante-mortem or post-mortem loss) of

teeth, along with any pathology and dental anomalies. Twenty-five individuals had varying degrees of surviving dentition: four had suffered from caries, two from ante-mortem tooth loss and one from an abscess.

Pathology

It should be noted that because of the poor conditions of the skeletal material, any pathology has been detected on broken fragments of bone. Much has obviously been lost and so the pathology recorded does not indicate the true pattern either for the individual or for the group as a whole. Some of the lesions found within the group are discussed below.

Eight individuals displayed varying degrees of degenerative disease, identified by bony lipping, pitting and eburnation (polishing) of the bone. It can be found throughout the skeleton although it occurs most frequently in the spine.

Seven skeletons exhibited Schmorl's nodes on their vertebral bodies. These are lesions on the surface of the body, caused by a herniation of the inter-vertebral disc into the adjacent body surface.

Five individuals have lesions in areas of muscle and ligament insertions. The cause of these lesions is unknown but they could be degenerative in nature or related to activity, particularly when they occur in the young.

One of the skeletons displays osteochondritis dissecans in both knees. In this condition, there is fragmentation and separation of a piece of articular surface, usually consisting of cartilage and underlying bone. The bone fragment can become re-attached, or remain as a loose body within the joint cavity. The knee is the most common joint affected and the cause is often traumatic. It occurs predominantly in adolescents and young adults.

The Grave Artefact Assemblages

(See Tables 3 and 4, and Appendix 4 for a catalogue of illustrated artifacts by figure no. and Appendix 5 for a complete catalogue of all the artifacts by find and feature number)

P. Patrick

Of the thirty-six Anglo-Saxon burials at Gunthorpe, twenty-six (72.2%) were furnished (Fig. 3). Typologically, the artefacts were in keeping with an 'Anglian' assemblage[9] of the sixth century AD and follow the standard dichotomy of weapon burials (namely spears and shields in this case) for men and jewellry with female burials. The majority of the artefacts are currently held in Peterborough Museum although unfortunately a number (30) of the copper alloy finds went missing prior to being fully studied. However, at least half of these were drawn before they were lost (Figs 19, 22, and 23).

Preservation of materials was variable. Iron objects

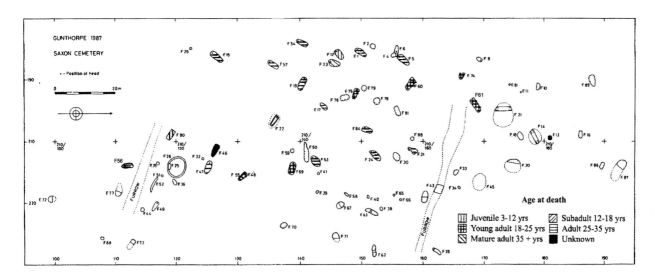

Figure 11. The age at death of the inhumation burials (P. P./C. F.)

Table 3. Summary list of grave goods as found in each inhumation pit

Feature/ grave no.	Iron shield	Iron spear	Iron knife	Iron brooch	Bronze pin	Bronze brooch	Bronze wrist clasp	Bone comb	Beads
1	1	–	1	–	–	1	–	–	–
5	1	–	1	1	–	–	–	–	–
6	–	–	–	1	–	–	–	–	–
7	–	–	–	–	–	2	–	–	–
8	–	–	1	–	–	–	–	–	–
12	–	–	–	1	–	–	–	–	–
15	1	1	–	–	1	–	–	–	–
19	1	1	1	–	–	–	–	–	–
23	–	–	1	–	–	1	–	1	3
24	–	–	1	2	–	3	2	–	5
28	–	–	1	1	–	4	–	–	5
31	–	–	1	1	–	–	–	–	–
46	–	–	1	–	–	–	–	–	–
48	–	–	2	–	–	–	–	–	–
53	–	–	2	–	1	2	2	–	24
54	1	2	1	–	–	–	–	–	–
55	–	–	1	–	–	2	–	–	11
56	–	2	1	–	–	–	–	–	–
57	1	–	1	–	–	–	–	–	–
60	1	1	1	–	–	–	–	–	–
61	1	1	–	–	–	–	–	–	–
64	1	1	2	–	–	–	–	–	–
69	–	–	–	–	–	–	–	–	–
74	–	–	1	1	–	–	1	1	–
75	–	–	–	–	–	–	–	–	–
80	–	–	–	–	–	4	–	–	23
Totals	**9**	**9**	**21**	**8**	**2**	**17**	**5**	**2**	**71**

were generally poorly preserved, and often very fragmentary. Copper alloys were generally much better preserved. Preservation of bone artefacts was variable; as with the skeletal material, some bone items were extremely fragile, although others survived in fairly good condition. Conservation work was carried out on the

artefacts by English Heritage. Analysis of mineralised organic remains from the site was carried out by Jacqui Watson at English Heritage's Ancient Monuments Laboratory. These findings are recorded in the site archive.

In this section the grave good assemblages accompanying each burial shall be summarised initially, and

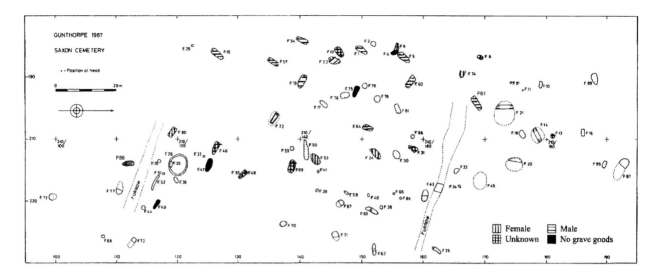

Figure 12. The sex of the burials as indicated by the grave goods assemblages (P. P./A. P.)

then different artefact classes will be discussed in greater detail. The grave good assemblages from each burial are described in Table 4 along with basic age and sex data for each burial. Italicised entries indicate that sex has been assigned on the basis of grave goods rather than skeletal markers (Fig. 12). Grave good sex is not a wholly reliable means of sexing bodies,[10] and there are occasionally disagreements between skeletal and grave good sex. However, these discrepancies are extremely rare,[11] and at Gunthorpe there are no disagreements between skeletal and grave good sex where both could be assessed.

Iron Artefacts

Weapon Burials
Ten of the twelve identified adult male burials (83.3%) contained weapons. This is quite a high figure compared with Härke's estimation[12] that in the Anglian area around 50–65% of adult males were buried with weapons. However, not too much emphasis should be placed on this discrepancy, because the Gunthorpe sample was fairly small and the skeletal material exceptionally poorly preserved. Therefore the number of weapon burials has been skewed to appear particularly high because in a number of cases, skeletal sex was indeterminate, making it impossible to know what proportion of the unfurnished, unsexed burials were of males.

Spearheads
Ten spearheads were recovered from nine graves of adult males (Figs 13 and 14). Most of these were fairly similar[13] with the exception of find 155 (grave F56), which was leaf-shaped, and find 168 (F60), which was an exceptionally long form. Seven of the spearheads retained mineral preserved remains of their shafts. Of these, four were of ash, one of willow or poplar, and two of unidentifiable wood.[14]

Table 5 shows the position of the spearheads within the graves. The most common arrangement, occurring in seven instances was for the spear to be laid within the grave, parallel to the body. There were three exceptions to this: in F15, the spearhead was placed across the stomach, suggesting the spear must have been broken prior to burial in order to fit it in the cut, which is not unprecedented.[15] In two cases (F60 and F61) the spears were placed vertically in the grave at the head end (Fig. 13).

Shield Bosses
Unfortunately the shield bosses were poorly preserved as a result of the aerobic and circum-neutral soil conditions on the site such that they were only photographed (Figs 15 and 16). Nonetheless, nine shield bosses were recovered from nine burials (Table 6). All of the shields have associated mineralised organic remains: eight retained fragments of the wooden shield board, while seven retained remains of the leather which covered the shield board. Of the shield boards, four were of willow or poplar, one of ash, one of lime, and two of unidentifiable wood.[16]

The shield bosses were all of comparable type and similar to Dickinson and Härke's groups 1.1 (*e.g.* in grave F60) and 2 (*e.g.* in grave F57),[17] although one (find 169 in grave F61) had a different form of grip on the rear of the shield, incorporating an iron bar spanning across the back of the shield (Fig. 16). Most shields were laid horizontally in the grave, usually laid on the body. In one case the shield was laid in a space by the head (F64), and in one case the shield was placed vertically at the side of the burial (F57).

Comparing the relative positions of the shields and spears in graves containing both items, a pattern emerges in which the spear and shield are often on opposite sides to each other. Härke notes that 'factors such as handedness and mode of carrying influenced the position of

Table 4. The grave good assemblages for each burial (note: italicised entries indicate that the sex was assigned on the basis of grave goods, not the skeletal data)

Grave	Sex	Age	Grave goods
F1	Male	Adult	Brooch/shroud pin; knife; shield
F4	Unknown	<16	No grave goods
F5	Male	Adult	Lead syringe-like object; pot; knife; spear; Shield; ?buckle
F6	Unknown	12–13 yrs	?Buckle
F7	Female	Adult	2 × brooch (penannular & trefoil-headed)
F8	Unknown	2y6m–6y4m	Brooch/shroud pin
F9	Unknown	Unknown	Pot
F12	Unknown	9–13 yrs	Knife
F13	Unknown	Unknown	Pot (cremation urn)
F15	Male	Adult	Pin; shield; spear; knife
F17	?Male	Adult	No grave goods
F19	*Male*	Adult	Pot; knife; spear; shield
F23	Female	Mature Adult	Comb; 5 × bead; knife; anuular brooch (?part of a pair)
F24	Female	Adult	Pot; 3 × brooch (2 swastika, 1 florid cruciform); 2 × wrist clasp; knife; buckle & strap end; 5 × bead
F28	Female	6–10 yrs	Pot; 5 × bead; perforated coin pendant; 2 × cruciform brooch; knife; 2 × Fe brooch; belt fitting
F31	Unknown	Adult	Tweezers; knife; buckle
F36	Unknown	Unknown	No grave goods
F39	Unknown	Unknown	No grave goods
F46	Unknown	Unknown	Knife
F47	?Female	Adult	No grave goods
F48	Unknown	Mature Adult	Knife; belt fittings
F49	Unknown	Unknown	No grave goods
F53/L	Female	Adult	No grave goods
F53/R	Female	Adult	Pot; 3 × wrist clasps; 29 × bead; CuAlloy needle; bone pin; 2 × knife; 2 × brooch; shroud pin
F54	*Male*	Adult	Knife; spear; shield; buckle
F55	*Female*	Mid-teens	Pot; 10 × bead; 2 × brooch (small-long & annular)
F56	Male	Adult	2 × spear; knife; buckle
F57	Male	Adult	Pot; spear; shield; knife; buckle
F60	Male	Young Adult	Spear; shield; knife
F61	Male	Young Adult	Spear; shield; knife; pin
F64	Male	Adult	Animal bones (food offering); spear; shield; strap-end; buckle; 2 × knife
F69	Male	Young Adult	Knife; buckle
F74	Female	Young Adult	Comb; knife; 2 × wrist clasps; Fe ring-shaped object to side of body (NB: burial truncated)
F75	Unknown	Young Adult	No grave goods
F80	*Female*	9y6m–14yr	Pot; 3 × scutiform pendant; cross-potent brooch; strap-end; 23 × bead
F90	Unknown	Adult	No grave goods

[most] weapon types',[18] the shield often being an exception. At Gunthorpe, however, four of the eight burials with both shields and spears have the spear on opposing sides to the shield (F5, F19, F54, and F57). In each case the set-up is is of a right-handed person. The remaining four burials with both shields and spears are more unusual. In F60 and F61 (Fig. 13), the spears have been placed in the ground vertically near the head rather than laid in the grave. In the other cases, the all the

'weaponry' is collected together in one place; in F15 it is all positioned on the stomach of the deceased, while in F64, the body is tightly flexed towards the 'bottom end' of the grave, and all the weapons, along with other grave gifts, are collected in the space to the right of the body.

Knives

Knives were buried with individuals of both sexes, from

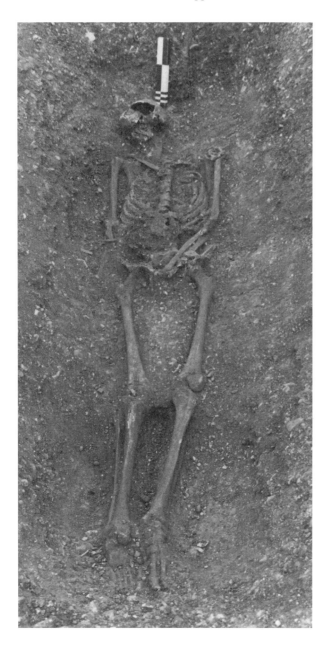

Figure 13. The fully extended skeleton in F61 with the vertically placed spearhead behind the head

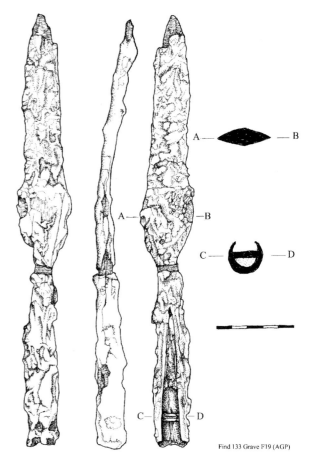

Find 133 Grave F19 (AGP)

Figure 14. Spearhead 133 in grave F19 (drawn at 1:1) (A. P.)

children to mature adults. They were most common in adult male burials; eleven of the twelve adult male burials (91.7%) contained knives, compared with four out of six adult female burials (66.7%), two out of seven sub-adult burials (28.6%). Two out of eight burials (25%) for which age and sex are uncertain also contain knives. Watson established that seven of the knives had associated mineralised remains of wood, leather sheaths, horn handles or other organic materials.[19]

Although poorly preserved, the knife types present at Gunthorpe were similar to Type 1 such as found at Dover with both back and cutting edge curved to a point, and to Type 2 at Dover with a straight back and curved cutting edge (Evison 1987).[20]

Härke has suggested that there might be a link between the length of knife blades and age or sex of individuals.[21] Not all the knives from Gunthorpe were in good enough condition to be measured, but the length of those that were is listed in Table 7.

Three knives from female burials were complete enough to be measured. The mean length was 110.3mm, and the range 107–16mm. Seven knives from male burials were measurable. The average length was 116.4mm, and the range 84–160mm. None of the knives from the sub-adult burials were complete enough to be measured, so Härke's theories regarding age and knife length[22] cannot be tested on the basis of this assemblage. But the Gunthorpe knives fall into Härke's (1989)[23] small and medium size classes, and Härke's assertion that knives over 126 mm long are only found in men's burials[24] is borne out by the Gunthorpe assemblage, with three adult males being buried with knives over this length, and female knives all being shorter.

Figure 16. The iron handle and shield boss over the adominal region of the skeleton in grave F61 (C. F.)

Figure 15. The shield boss on the right shoulder of the skeleton in grave F60 (C. F.)

Table 5. The position of spearheads in the graves

Grave	Find no.	Swanton typology	Position
F5	122	Fragments only	Horizontal, right shoulder
F15	131	Missing	Horizontal, across stomach
F19	133	C3	Horizontal, right shoulder
F54	149	Socket only	Horizontal, right shoulder
F56	154	C3	Horizontal, left shoulder
F56	155	D1	Horizontal, left shoulder
F57	162	C2	Horizontal, right shoulder
F60	166	Socket only	Vertical, head end
F61	168	E4	Vertical, head end
F64	176	C2	Horizontal, right shoulder

Table 6. The position of shield bosses in the graves

Grave	Find no.	Position
F1	117	Horizontal, centred over left elbow
F5	118	Horizontal, centred over left humerus/chest
F15	126	Horizontal, centred over left hand side of stomach
F19	132	Horizontal, centred over left hand side of stomach
F54	148	Horizontal, centred over left shoulder
F57	158	Vertical, beside left elbow
F60	165	Horizontal, centred over right shoulder
F61	169	Horizontal, centred on middle of stomach; elaborate grip
F64	175	Horizontal, in space to right of head

Table 7. The length of the knives in the graves

Grave	Find no.	Age/sex	Length (mm)
F1	116	Adult, male	92
F5	121	Adult, male	104
F12	186	9–13, sex unknown	Fragmentary
F15	127	Adult, male	160
F23	135	Mature adult, female	Fragmentary
F24	136	Adult, female	107
F28	139	6–10, female	Fragmentary
F31	143	Adult, sex unknown	Fragmentary
F46	144	Age and sex unknown	Fragmentary
F48	191	Mature adult, sex unknown	Fragmentary
F53/R	147	Adult, female	Fragmentary
F53/R	187	Adult, female	116
F54	151	Adult, male	Fragmentary
F56	156	Adult, male	128
F57	164	Adult, male	130
F60	167	Young adult, male	117
F61	174	Young adult, male	Fragmentary
F64	177	Adult, male	84
F69	171	Young adult, male	Fragmentary
F74	181	Young adult, female	108

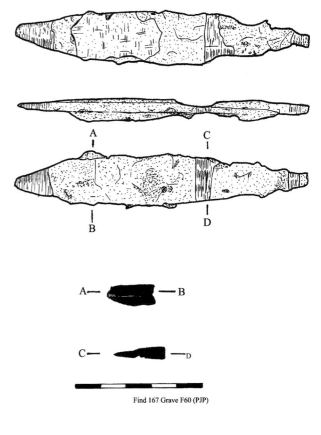

Figure 17. Knive 167 in grave F60 (drawn at 1:1) (P. P.)

Other Iron Artefacts

Other iron artefacts include a set of tweezers, buckles and shroud pins. In many cases these iron items are particularly fragmentary, and the interpretation of what they might be is based upon their position within the grave plan. Therefore iron ring-like items in the vicinity of the waist area are interpreted as probable buckles, while items positioned in more unusual areas, particularly in the vicinity of the lower legs or feet, are likely to be shroud fastenings. The iron ring placed beside the right hip of burial F74 among a collection of objects perhaps represents the fastening of a bag containing grave gifts.

Copper Alloy Artefacts

Roman Objects

There are three Roman copper alloy objects. One of these was a fibula (find 192) from grave F22, which accompanied the body of a mature adult female within a stone coffin (Fig. 10). Although re-use of Roman objects in Anglo-Saxon graves is not unprecedented, grave F22 contained no post-Roman material within the burial, suggesting that the burial was of Roman date, rather than re-use of Roman material in an Anglo-Saxon context. This hypothesis is not unreasonable; metal detector finds from the area around Gunthorpe produce ample evidence of Roman activity in the area, and there are probable Roman features within the excavated area at Gunthorpe. Unfortunately, the fibula is among the missing objects, and there are no drawings or photographs of it, so it cannot be described in detail or typologically dated.

Two Roman coins were also recovered. Both had been perforated and reused as pendants. One of these (find 80), although found on the surface (at 197E/137N; not clearly associated with any grave, presumably moved significantly out of context by machine drag), had a textile impression indicating that it had been worn as jewellry and associated with a burial.

The first coin (find 80) (Fig. 18) was in fairly poor condition, with much of the converse side corroded or obscured by textile impression. Comparison with similar coins shows that at 6.91g, the coin had lost around half its original weight in corrosion and wear. Despite the poor condition of the coin, identification was possible. It is a bronze *As* minted in the reign of the Emperor Domitian (AD 81–96). This particular example was minted between AD 85–96 as indicated by the letters

'GERM' on the obverse of the coin. Domitian gained the title 'Germanicus' in AD 84.[25]

The other Roman coin (find 93; grave F28) (Fig. 18) was a later example. It is perforated with a single hole, and its position on the chest in the grave suggests it was worn as a pendant. The converse of the coin carries an image of Romulus, Remus and the wolf. This is the design of the *Urbs Roma* issue (AD 330–34) minted during the reign of Emperor Constantine I (no further information about the coin itself is available as it is now missing).

Anglo-Saxon Artefacts

Jewellery

Brooches

A variety of different kinds of brooches were recovered the grave assemblages from Gunthorpe (Figs 19–21), although a large percentage of the brooches are now unfortunately missing from the collections in Peterborough Museum. The brooches are generally typical of sixth-century Anglian assemblages, including such types as cruciform brooches, both small cruciforms, and a larger florid cruciform brooch, small-long brooches, trefoil-headed brooches and cross-potent brooches. The pair of swastika brooches in grave F24, presents a less common form (Figs 20–2).

It is generally recognised that brooches served as dress fastenings on Anglo-Saxon women's' clothing; often a pair of small brooches at the shoulder fastening a 'peplos-style' dress. It is interesting to note that the pairs of brooches, with the exception of the swastika brooches (finds 86 and 87), were not matching pairs as might be expected, but rather a mix-and-match of common brooch forms.

Wrist Clasps

Seven wrist clasps were recovered; these were associated with three individuals (F24, F53/R and F74) (Fig. 23) (Table 8). In each case they were associated with adult females. Each of the clasps is of Hines' Form B,[26] and they all have lugs to be sewn onto clothing. There are examples present that are similar to Hines' form 7 (find 100 in grave F53R) and mainly form 20 (*e.g.* finds 89 and 90 in grave F24, and finds 99 and 101 in grave F53R, and finds 108 and 109 in grave F74) such as are found at Little Wilbraham (Hines 1993, 12–66).[27] Decoration is stamped, and in some cases incised, on the clasps.

Pendants

There were two kinds of pendants among the Gunthorpe assemblage: firstly perforated Roman coins (see above), and secondly specifically manufactured pendants. Grave F80 contains three copper alloy scutiform pendants (finds 111–13) (Fig. 24). Scutiform pendants are small flat discs with a raised boss in the centre, and a grip at the

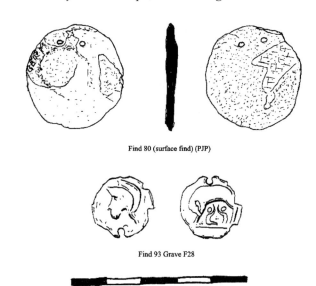

Find 80 (surface find) (PJP)

Find 93 Grave F28

Figure 18. The coin of Emperor Domitian (find 80; excavated surface) and the coin of Constantine I (find 93; Grave F28) (drawn at 1:1) (P. P.)

Table 8. The typology of the wrist clasps in the graves

Grave	Find no.	Hines typology
F24	89,90	B20
F53/R	99, 100, 101	B7 (100) B20 (99; 101)
F74	108, 109	B20

back, resembling a miniature shield, the grip also serving to thread onto a necklace. Hines[28] notes that although scutiform pendants are often made of silver, there are a number of copper alloy examples from the Anglian region. It is interesting to note that pendants were only found in graves of juvenile females. The implications of this observation are uncertain. On the one hand it could simply be a coincidence, but on the other hand, it has been suggested that girls wore their dowries prior to marriage, which could account for certain patterns of different adornments between adult females and juvenile females.[29]

Other items

Grave 53 contained a copper alloy needle (find 98), which, based upon its position in the grave (across the face of the flexed, richly furnished right-hand burial) seems to have been used as a 'shroud-pin'. The use of an item such as this, which is both unusual and made of a more valuable material than the standard bone needles, is an example of conspicuous display in this particular burial; even if much of the deceased's impressive array of dress accessories were enclosed within a shroud and

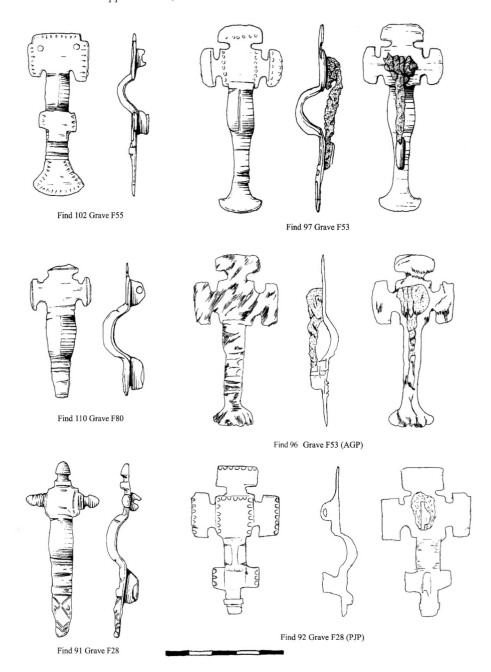

Find 102 Grave F55

Find 97 Grave F53

Find 110 Grave F80

Find 96 Grave F53 (AGP)

Find 91 Grave F28

Find 92 Grave F28 (PJP)

Figure 19. Brooches 91 and 92 (grave F28), 96 and 97 (grave F53) and 102 (Grave F55) (drawn at 1:1) (R. P.)

hidden from view when the body was placed in the ground, there was still scope for display in terms of the shroud and its means of fastening.

Some small fragments of copper alloy were recovered in association with the shield in grave F57 (finds 104 and 105). These were recovered in an extremely fragmentary conditions with some mineralised wood still adhered to them. The form of the copper alloy fittings could not be identified as a result of their fragmentary nature, but they could have been decorations of some sort, or perhaps washers fitted to rivets or studs which held the boss in place.

Lead Artifact

In addition to a standard male weapon assemblage, the grave goods accompanying burial F5 included an unusual lead artefact (Fig. 26), which was placed within a pot near the deceased's head. The item is at first glance 'syringe-like' in appearance, insofar as it incorporates a tube and a plunger, although its tapered shape means that it could not have functioned as a syringe does.

The artefact is formed out of two pieces of lead: a sheet bent into a tapered tube and secured with a tin-based solder, and a round piece of lead acting as the plunger. The taper has a rim at its wider end. The plunger

Figure 20. The long cruciform and two swastika brooches in the neck and upper chest area of the skeleton in grave F24 (C. F.)

Figure 21. Close-up view of the long cruciform brooch and two swastika brooches found in the neck and upper chest area of the skeleton in grave F24 (C. F.)

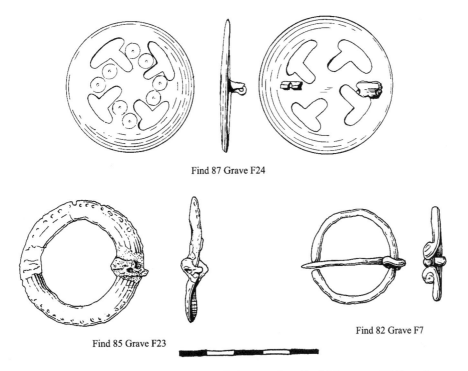

Find 87 Grave F24

Find 85 Grave F23

Find 82 Grave F7

Figure 22. The swastika brooch 87 from grave F24, and the annular (find 85; grave F23) and penannular (find 82; grave F7) brooches (drawn at 1:1) (R. P.)

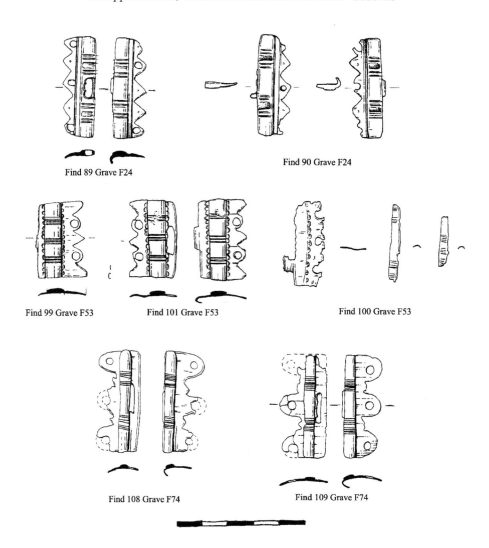

Find 89 Grave F24

Find 90 Grave F24

Find 99 Grave F53

Find 101 Grave F53

Find 100 Grave F53

Find 108 Grave F74

Find 109 Grave F74

Figure 23. The wrist clasps 89 and 90 (grave F24), 99–101 (grave F53), and 108 and 109 (grave F74) (drawn at 1:1) (R. P.)

is bent; this appears to have occurred prior to burial, and was thus presumably intentional.

Interpretation of this artefact is extremely difficult, as there are no parallels for it in the archaeological record. The most feasible explanation is that the object was a piece of medical equipment. There are certain similarities in form between the object and Roman 'tubes to prevent adhesion', although there are notable differences in material (the Roman examples are copper alloy), finesse (a 2–3 mm thick sheet of lead was used to make the Gunthorpe object), and also to an extent, form with the presence of the plunger in the Gunthorpe artefact. If the Gunthorpe artefact was indeed a piece of medical equipment, its most likely function was to prevent adhesion, and facilitate drainage of, a soft tissue infection. However, further investigation of the artefact is necessary.[30]

Beads

Both monochrome and polychrome glass and amber beads were found in graves of six girls and women at Gunthorpe, along with one bead that appeared to be ceramic. The assemblage was dominated by translucent blue glass small annular beads, while other monochrome and polychrome beads were opaque in appearance. The number and type of beads associated with individual burials varied, and is summarised in Table 9, while further details of the form and colours of beads based on Guido's typologies[31] can be found in the full catalogue of finds at the end of this report.

There seem to be no particular patterns relating frequency of beads with the age of individuals, although other authors such as Brugmann (2004)[32] have shown that this is possible to determine. In terms of material, both glass and amber are to be found in burials of all age groups, although the majority of the amber beads were found in grave F53/R (Figs 27 and 28).

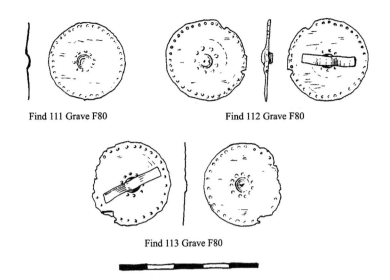

Find 111 Grave F80   Find 112 Grave F80

Find 113 Grave F80

Figure 24. The copper alloy scutiform pendants (finds 111–13 in grave F80) (drawn at 1:1) (P. P.)

Find 98 Grave F53

Figure 25. The copper alloy needle (find 98) in grave F53 (drawn at 1:1) (R. P.)

Bone Artefacts

The bone artefacts can be divided into two broad groups: fairly rough bone pins, presumably used as shroud pins, and combs. Two combs were recovered, both from graves containing adult females. Find 1 (grave F23) is extremely fragmentary, but a fair amount can be discerned from photographs taken during excavation of the grave of this adult female (Fig. 29). The comb was double-sided and of composite form. It was 158.3 mm long × 58.3 mm wide, with a 133.3 × 16.7 mm bar of bone riveted along the centre between the two rows of teeth. The comb was undecorated.

Find 2 (grave F74 of a young female) (Fig. 30) was much better preserved than the other comb from Gunthorpe. It is a single-sided composite comb with a triangular form, and two triangular panels riveted on. The comb is decorated on both sides with small circular stamped motifs, and a notch has been cut out of each end, also presumably for decorative purposes. The comb is 137 mm long, with a maximum width of 50mm, and 24 mm wide at the ends. The additional panels were 98 × 24 mm in size.

Two graves contained bone pins, the position of which, both being in the head area, were probably used as shroud fastenings; although they may also have been used as headdress fastenings for women, one of the burials with a bone pin in the same position was of a male.

The 'Rack of Ribs'

Grave F64 contains a collection of animal ribs, probably from a sheep, placed above the head of the deceased in the grave. Although appearing somewhat like a fan at the time of excavation, this appears to have been the outcome of soil pressure on a side of meat buried with the deceased. There are some comparable cases found in Anglo-Saxon graves in the East of England with joints of meat occasionally left as probable food offerings.[33] For example there is a good example from Sewerby in Yorkshire, where, and as with F64, the grave containing a food offering was comparatively richly furnished.[34]

Pottery

Pottery was recovered from several features at Gunthorpe (Fig. 31), including several cases in which pot sherds were recovered from features not directly identified as part of the cemetery (for example F42 yielded sherds of later medieval glazed pottery) (Table 10). In terms of the cemetery itself, it is possible to look at two distinct categories of pottery, namely pottery vessels which accompany burials in the form of grave goods, and vessels containing cremated remains. Preservation and complete-

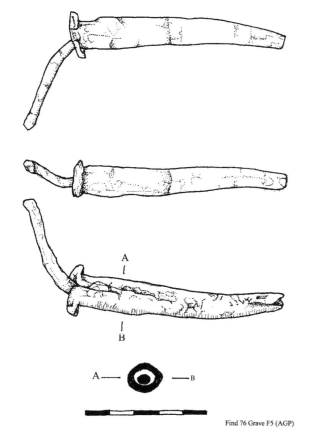

Find 76 Grave F5 (AGP)

Figure 26. The possible syringe of lead (find 76) found in the pottery vessel 1 in grave F5 (drawn at 1:1) (A. P.)

Although Gunthorpe was a mixed-rite cemetery, only one positively identified cremation (F13) was recovered from the excavation of the site. The pot in which the cremated remains were interred (Fig. 31, no. 4) was a flint tempered ware, dark brown in colour, and none of the surviving fabric is decorated. The pot was broken at its widest point at which the diameter was 233mm, and the upper section is missing. The base was approximately 60 mm in diameter.

The pottery recovered from graves at Gunthorpe is listed in Table 10. This only describes pottery which may be classed as grave goods, and does not include single sherds recovered from grave fills.

Patterns of Age And Sex

Certain artefact classes can be clearly linked with certain age groups in the Gunthorpe assemblage. The main artefact classes attached to particular age and sex groups are summarised in Table 11 below. One-off items such as the food offering, tweezers, and syringe-like object are excluded from the table. The bronze needle in grave F53/R (Fig. 28) can be viewed as belonging to the class of 'pin' in terms of its function as a shroud fastening.

Evidence for Conspicuous Display in Burials

There are some graves in which it might be argued there is evidence for conspicuous display in the mode of burial. Although in the past, processualist archaeologists such as Arnold[35] have suggested that wealth can be estimated on the basis of the artefacts associated with the body itself, such ideas are problematic, both in a general sense, especially in terms of the ability for females without a particularly elaborate assemblage of grave goods to accrue a massive wealth score simply because each individual bead is scored, and because survivability of materials can affect their score. For example, a sword scores lower than a wooden vessel and although it is conceivable that the wooden vessel was worth more in terms of status, these objects of course are rarer in the

ness of pottery artefacts was variable. Pots were hand made, and not kiln fired, the differential firing temperature manifested as variable colouring on the pot's surface, and the lack of intensity of firing heat evident from the soft, fragmentary nature of the pottery. In many cases, the pottery vessels are damaged, and often missing their top sections, presumably as a result of machine damage while removing the topsoil, or due to soil pressure on the weakened apex of the pots.

Table 9. The number and type of beads associated with individual burials

Grave	Age	Glass	Amber	Ceramic?	Missing	Total
F23	Mature adult	4	1	0	0	5
F24	Adult	3	1	1	0	5
F28	6–10 years	4	1	0	0	5
F53/R	Adult	23	4	0	2	29
F55	Mid-teen	7	1	0	2	10
F80	9y6m – 14 years	22	0	0	1	23
	Total	**63**	**8**	**1**	**5**	**77**

Figure 27. The double interment in F53 showing the upper two-thirds of the bodies and their 'embracing' arrangement (C. F.)

Figure 28. Close-up view of the double interment in F53 showing the position of the beads, copper pin, copper brooches and pottery bowl (C. F.)

Figure 29. The undecorated bone comb (find 1) found over the left upper arm and rib cage of the skeleton in grave F23 (C. F.)

archaeological record due to the conditions of pre-servation. Arnold's system is also problematic in relation to Gunthorpe, because it was a system based upon southern English sites which lacked a number of artefact classes represented in the Anglian region. Thus rather than trying to quantify wealth, it is perhaps more helpful to qualify conspicuous display. Therefore it is important to look at both the ritual and the items around the body itself and to focus upon the unusual artefacts that do not figure in Arnold's wealth score system.

What can be classed as conspicuous display? As with conspicuous consumption, the chief element is the dis-posal of valuable or rare items, usually in a context in which they could be seen during the ritual of burial: conspicuous display would have been more for the benefit of those witnessing the burial than for the deceased. Once shrouded ready for burial, it is probable that most of bodies looked similar and the amount of jewellry and so forth concealed within the shroud would not be visible to those witnessing the burial ritual. The paraphernalia surrounding the body would, however, be visible and would present opportunity for display.

Potential examples of conspicuous display at Gun-thorpe include grave F64, in which the body of the deceased was placed in the grave in a tightly flexed position in the bottom right corner of the grave (as one looks at the plan), laying on his right hand side with the grave goods (a food offering of a joint of meat, a spear and a shield) placed in the top left corner of the grave. The grave cut was not abnormally large but the space

was used very differently to other graves in the cemetery.

Grave F53 is also an interesting case-study. It comprises a double burial containing the remains of two adult females, one with many grave goods, the other with very few (Figs 27 and 28). Stoodley[36] notes that multiple burials were relatively unusual, and suggests that the special rite served in an amuletic capacity, in response to the presumably rare occurrence of two people dying more or less simultaneously (as must have been the case where the burials are contemporary and side by side, *e.g.* F53). When compared with Stoodley's data set, the Gunthorpe double burial is revealed as relatively uncommon. Multiple burials of adult females accounted for only 8.2% of Stoodley's sample (the most common being female and child at 20%),[37] while the arrangement of bodies, one extended and the other crouched is paralleled in only 4.2% of the sample.[38] The discrepancy in furnishings is matched by grave 391 at Dover Buckland (Kent) containing two adult females, one of which was exceptionally richly furnished.[39]

As in grave F64 the burial position of the richly furnished individual is unusual – lying on her right-hand side, flexed in the bottom right corner. The second individual was buried in an extended position, slightly angled to her left. The former was buried with an unusual item on display in the form of a copper alloy needle which appears to have been used to fasten the shroud around her face. This is a utilitarian item, but made from a more valuable material than normal. To dispose

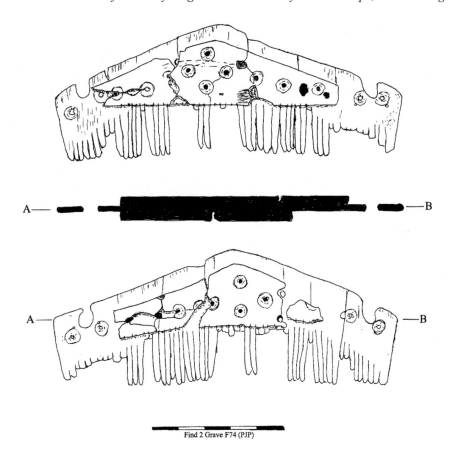

Find 2 Grave F74 (PJP)

Figure 30. The decorated bone comb (find 2) found to the right-hand side of the pelvis in grave F74) (drawn at 1:1) (P. P.)

Table 10. The type and position of pottery vessels found in the graves

Grave	Pottery no.	Description	Position
F5	1	Brown/black flint tempered, rim 140mm, contained 'syringe like object'	Left of head
F9	2	Black flint tempered pot fragments	Plan missing
F13	4	Cremation urn, brown, flint tempered, upper part missing, max. diameter 233mm	Cremation
F19	9	Brown/black flint tempered, bossed, incised & stamped decoration, max. diameter 280mm	Left of head
F24	11	Dark brown flint tempered large fragments, 9mm thick	Below left foot
F28	14	Dark brown flint tempered, fragmentary, top missing, max. diameter 140mm	Right of head
F53/R	24	Mid-dark red-brown/orange grog tempered pot fragments. Relatively fine ware: 4mm thick	Above head
F55	25	Brown-orange/black flint or grog tempered pot fragments, base almost complete	Flattened, beneath femurs
F57	26	Dark brown/orange brown, ? grog tempered fragments	Not marked on plan
F80	33	?Burnished brown/black flint tempered rounded based slightly irregular pot, complete, rim 140mm	On side, diagonally above/right of head

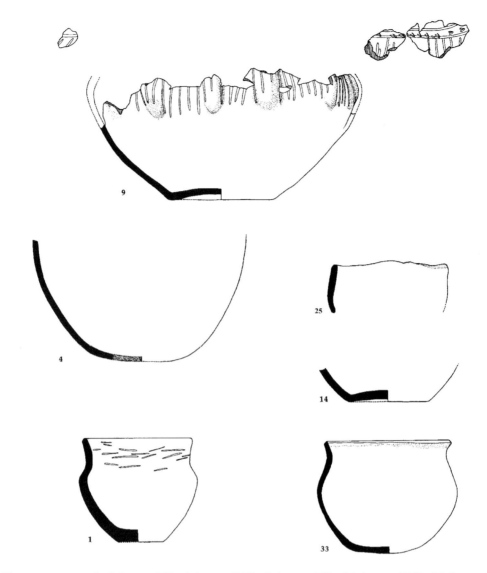

Figure 31. The pottery vessels 1 (grave F5), 4 (grave F13), 9 (grave F2), 14 (grave F28), 25 (grave F55) and 33 (grave F80) (scale 1/3 actual size) (R. P.)

of the needle in the grave and in a visible position implies a certain level of conspicuous display, in so far as such items could be spared, rather than been passed on to the living.

Burial F5 was buried with a pot (Fig. 31, no. 1), which contained an extremely unusual, and probably functional, item: a lead syringe-like object (find 76) (Fig. 26). The unique nature of the artefact and the comparative rarity of the material from which it was made would, as with the needle in grave F53 (Fig. 25), add to the sense of conspicuous display.

It is possible that the vertical position of the spearhead in graves F60 and F61 (Fig. 13) may indicate that the spear shaft was used as a form of grave marker after the deceased had been buried. Although soil conditions have not provided the opportunity to check for the organic remains of the shaft, it is a possibility. On a practical

level, it would be difficult to maintain a spear's vertical position prior to backfilling the grave. Furthermore, the shape of the spearhead in F61 (find 168) (Fig. 13) suggests that it was driven into the ground with some considerable force, probably bending on the gravelly subsoil material at the base of the grave cut.

Demography

P. Patrick

Gunthorpe highlights many of the problems inherent in palaeodemography and little can be said about the living who buried their dead in this cemetery. Waldron demonstrates how in all skeletal populations there are losses in numbers at every stage from death through to the osteologist's desk, leaving an unknown proportion of

Table 11. The main artefact classes attached to a particular age and sex group in the graves

Adult male	Adult female	Adult both sexes	Sub-adult female	All age Female	All ages & sexes
Spear	Wrist clasps	Pin	Pendant	Brooch (multiple)	Knife
Shield	Comb			Beads	Brooch (single)
					Pottery
					Belt fittings

the actual living population available for study.[40] Boddington summarised five particular factors which may distort the representation of a living population provided by a cemetery excavation: post-depositional disturbance, post-depositional decay, incomplete excavation, spatial variability and differential burial.[41]

At Gunthorpe, the circumstances of salvage excavation, with machine damage to the site and poor preservation of skeletal remains means there are limitations to the demographic usefulness of the assemblage. The density of burials in the west of the cemetery does not represent partial excavation – a much larger surrounding area was cleared by machine with no evidence of burials produced. It is probable the cemetery's extent has been identified. Only one cremation was positively identified, but some have undoubtedly been missed – a problem of the mixed burial rite.

The age profile of the cemetery (Table 12; Figs 32 and 33), based upon Osborne's analysis of the skeletal material (see above) is extremely unfeasible as a reflection of the total living population. Not only is the infant category in which we usually expect high mortality,[42] not represented at all but the majority of skeletons have been categorised as aged between twenty-five to thirty-five years at death. This is an age group in which such a high mortality rate is relatively uncommon – mortality is usually higher in children under ten years of age and in older adults.

This may represent methodological difficulties in terms of ageing remains accurately given the poor preservation of the skeletons. Chamberlain notes that ageing of skeletons is fallible even at the best of times;[43] with poorly preserved skeletons it is likely to have been even more problematic. Alternatively, the age profile may indicate that the cemetery contained considerably more burials than were recovered during the excavation and that these missing burials may have redressed the balance in terms of the age profile. There is no reason to believe that skeletons of older adults would have been significantly less-well preserved than those of under thirty-five's. One possibility is a different choice of burial ritual: if the older individuals in the society were cremated rather than inhumed, there may have been more problems inherent in locating, recovering, and analysing their remains.

Although Härke notes that infants aged under two to three years are often absent from early Anglo-Saxon

Table 12. The age profile of the bodies in the cemetery

Age group	Number	%
Infant (0–3)	0	0
Juvenile (3–12)	5	14.29
Sub-adult (13–18)	2	5.71
Young adult (18–25)	5	14.29
Adult (25–35)	16	45.71
Mature adult	2	5.71
Unknown	5	14.29

burial assemblages and uses this observation to support a claim that infants were held in low esteem by Anglo-Saxons,[44] it is possible to seek more practical reasons for their absence. The lack of infants may be associated with the nature of the site and the soil: gravel creates poor preservation conditions for human bone, and also makes small bones hard to locate, positively identify, and excavate. Guy *et al.* observed that the graves of young children were often shallower than those of other age groups, rendering their burials more susceptible to ploughing out either through agriculture after the cemetery went into disuse, or potentially during the machining prior to excavation.[45] Crawford cites similar reasons for a general lack of infant remains in Anglo-Saxon cemetery contexts.[46]

Plotting the distribution of age at death for males, females and individuals of unknown sex reveals that positively identified males tended to die between the ages of eighteen and thirty-five years, while positively identified females were dying with less frequency in adulthood some living into mature adulthood and others dying before maturity was reached. This phenomenon may be more related to the difficulties in identifying younger males; the female juveniles and sub-adults were sexed on the basis of their jewellry assemblages, while younger males did not have a distinctive grave good assemblage. The poor skeletal preservation at Gunthorpe also leaves a relatively large number of individuals for whom both age and sex cannot be accurately determined.

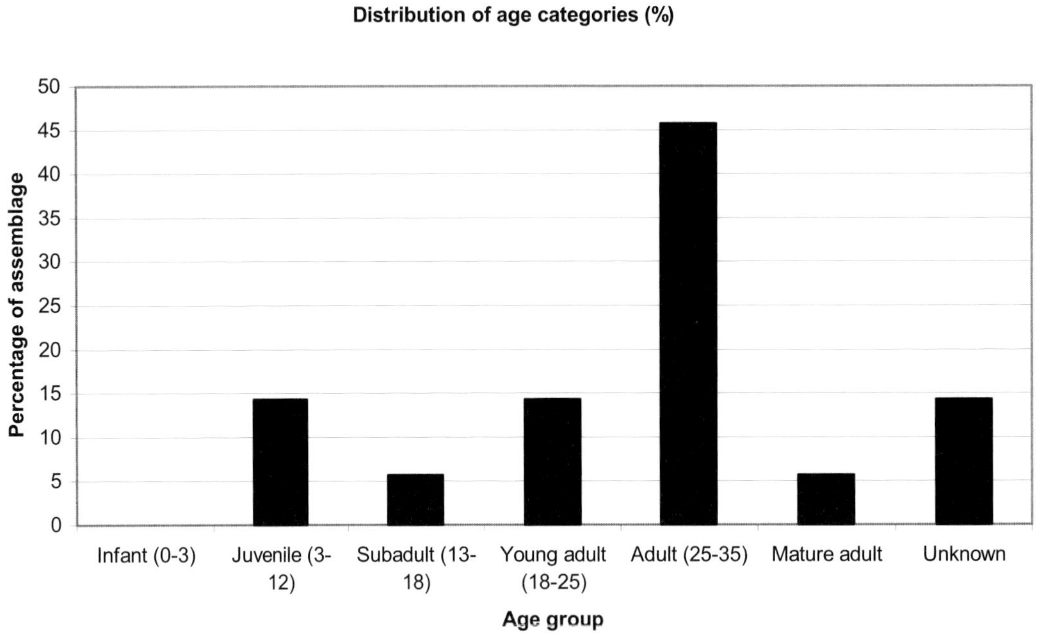

Distribution of age categories (%)

Figure 32. The distribution of age categories (in %) for the cemetery (P. P)

Spatial Analysis

P. Patrick

The site plan of Gunthorpe shows the cemetery was fairly small and compact (Fig. 3). The graves are concentrated in a rectangular area approximately 60m by 35m in size, with cremation F13 and other possible cremations occurring outside this focal area of inhumations. Within the cemetery, there are two concentrations of burials, firstly a concentration towards the centre of the excavated area, along with a secondary concentration of burials in the south of the site (near the Romano-British ring gully F26). There are no consistent patterns in terms of grave alignment and there are a few cases in which graves were truncated by subsequent burials, however, in general graves respect one another.

Grave F22 (Fig. 10) is situated within the focal area of inhumations despite the fact that the evidence points towards it being an earlier burial from the Roman period. Perhaps the Anglo-Saxons burying their dead at the site had no idea that the Roman coffined burial existed. There are no Anglo-Saxon burials within *c.* 10m and therefore there is no reason why it should have been disturbed in the process of creating the sixth-century cemetery. It is, however, interesting to note that other Roman features were respected, possibly indicating that the site was used for burial in more than one historical period, albeit with a lapse of some centuries in its ritual use.

Burial Position

The majority of burials were in a supine, extended position. Usually the legs are quite straight and close together, perhaps indicative of shrouding, while in some cases, such as F57 and F69 (Fig. 7), the legs are more widely spread, perhaps indicative of a coffined burial which allowed for more movement of the limbs. The positioning of the shield in F57, vertical at the side of the grave cut might also suggest that it was slotted down the side of the coffin. No wood staining or other physical evidence of coffins was observed, however, during excavation. Six of the burials were on their sides, with their legs slightly flexed, indicating a shrouded body or no wrapping rather than a coffin. Two burials: F53/R (Fig. 27) and F64 (Fig. 7) were tightly flexed, almost crouched. In these cases the grave goods were arranged around the body in the rest of the grave space.

Comparison with the cemetery at Great Chesterford where there was detailed work on the position and orientation of the skeletons in the graves is informative (Evison 1994, 36–44).[47] There, 76 out of 106 skeletons were positioned on their backs, with a great variety of positions of the head, arms and legs, but few were actually supine, whereas only 28 bodies were on their sides, usually with their legs drawn up. In addition, as in many other early Anglo-Saxon cemeteries, the heads were mostly to the south (in S-N graves) or to the west (in W-E graves), just as at Gunthorpe (Figs 6 and 7).

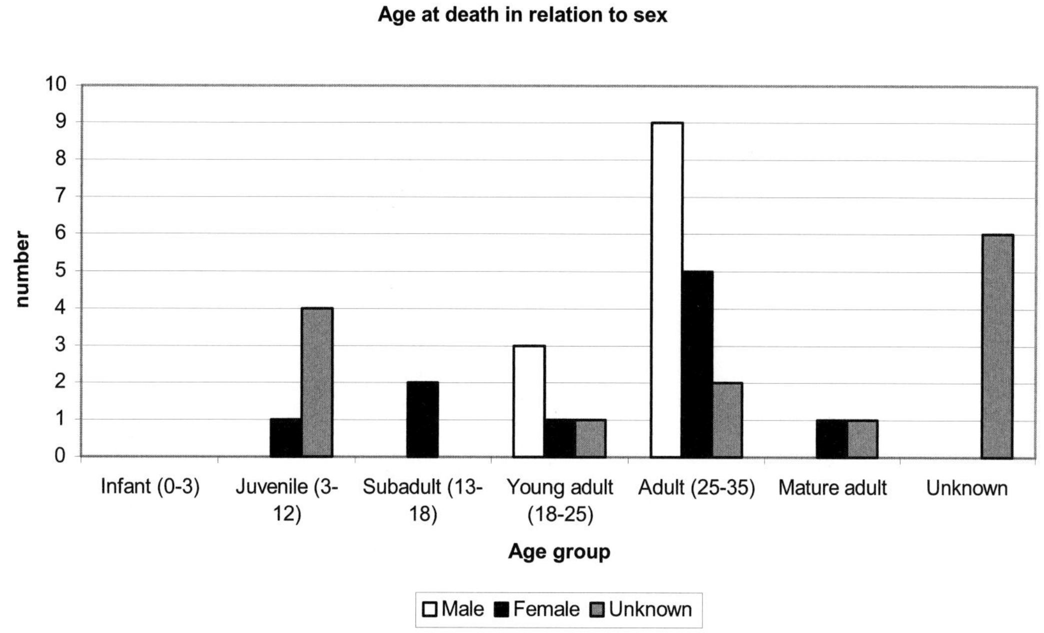

Age at death in relation to sex

Figure 33. The age of death in relation to sex (in numbers) for the cemetery (P. P)

Distribution of Graves in Relation to Sex

Although there are a number of cases in which the sex of individuals is uncertain, especially in terms of skeletal sex, Figures 5 and 12 show the distribution of sex according to skeletal and grave goods indicators. The plans show that there is a concentration of male burials in the western part of the site, while female burials are quite dispersed in their distribution, tending more towards the east of the site. There is no strict segregation of the sexes, however, as there are males to the east of the site and *vice versa*.

Distribution of Graves in Relation to Age

The distribution of different age groups is shown in Figure 11. The age groups used are the arbitrary categories used by Osborne (see above) in her analysis of the skeletal remains. All age groups are fairly evenly distributed throughout the site, although the absence of infants and younger children is noted. In Anglo-Saxon cemeteries, there are usually very few juvenile graves, except unusually at Great Chesterford where there were 86 non-adults of less than 15 years of age (Evison 1994, 31).[48]

The Position of Multiple Burial F53

Although Stoodley notes that multiple burials are sometimes confined to the outskirts of cemetery sites,[49] the multiple burial F53 (Fig. 27) does not seem to have

been especially marginalised. Although towards the eastern edge of the burial group, F53 is not especially picked out for a marginal position in relation to other burials and there are a number of burials in line with, or further east than F53.

Discussion and Conclusions

C. French and P. Patrick

The early Anglo-Saxon cemetery at Gunthorpe was small and its use seems to have been restricted to a relatively brief period of time in the sixth century. Despite the fact that there is evidence of Roman activity in the area, both in the form of Romano-British features in the excavated area, and metal-detector finds from nearby Werrington End Farm, there is no evidence for occupation of the site in the fifth century.

Gunthorpe represents a cemetery comprising approximately thirty-six inhumations and one cremation but was probably once slightly larger with a few fragments of other bodies and possible shadows of former cremations being observed during the exavations and clearance of the site. It was situated overlooking the contemporary fen edge. This was the southwestern edge of the Newborough/Borough Fen embayment in northwest Cambridgeshire, just inland of the route of the Car Dyke which marked the landward/southern edge of the growing peat fen in Roman times.[50]

The grave goods assemblages with the inhumations

Table 13. The burial positions in each grave (note: italicised entries indicate that the sex was assigned on the basis of grave goods, not the skeletal data)

Grave	Sex	Age	Position
F1	Male	Adult	Extended, supine
F4	Unknown	<16	Flexed on side, facing left
F5	Male	Adult	Extended, supine
F6	Unknown	12–13 yrs	Extended, supine
F7	Female	Adult	?
F8	Unknown	2y6m–6y4m	Supine, flexed facing left
F9	Unknown	Unknown	?
F12	Unknown	9–13 yrs	Extended, supine
F13	Unknown	Unknown	Cremation
F15	Male	Adult	Extended, supine
F17	?Male	Adult	Flexed on side, facing right
F19	*Male*	Adult	Extended, supine
F23	Female	Mature Adult	Extended, supine
F24	Female	Adult	Extended, supine
F28	*Female*	6–10 yrs	Extended, supine
F31	Unknown	Adult	Flexed on side, facing left
F36	Unknown	Unknown	?
F39	Unknown	Unknown	?
F46	Unknown	Unknown	Extended, supine
F47	?Female	Adult	Extended, supine
F48	Unknown	Mature Adult	Extended, supine
F49	Unknown	Unknown	Extended, supine
F53/L	Female	Adult	Extended, supine, facing left
F53/R	Female	Adult	Tightly flexed on side, facing right
F54	*Male*	Adult	Extended, supine
F55	*Female*	Mid-teens	Extended, supine
F56	Male	Adult	Extended, supine
F57	Male	Adult	Extended, supine
F60	Male	Young Adult	Extended, supine
F61	Male	Young Adult	Extended, supine
F64	Male	Adult	Tightly flexed on side, facing right
F69	Male	Young Adult	Extended, supine, with legs crossed
F74	Female	Young Adult	Supine, slightly flexed facing left
F75	Unknown	Young Adult	?
F80	*Female*	9y6m–14yr	Supine, flexed facing left
F90	Unknown	Adult	?

are typical of the sixth century in the Anglian period (after Penn and Brugmass in press). Twenty-six out of the thirty-six graves were furnished (*c.* 72%). The female graves contained a variety of of bronze, iron and bone artefacts. Plain and decorated cruciform bronze brooches often in the upper chest area were common, as were strings of glass and amber beads. Bronze swastika, disc, annular and penannular brooches were also present, as well as two bone combs and occasionally complete pottery vessels, placed near the head. The male graves contained mainly iron shield bosses placed to the right or left of the upper arm; spearheads placed either parallel to the arms or beneath the shield boss and pots placed near the head. Thirteen (or 36%) of the graves were unsexed. In terms of preservation, the bone was very poorly preserved and fragmentary, as were the iron artefacts, whereas the bronze finds were in excellent condition.

From this assemblage of human remains, it is hard to say much about the living population. The age profile is unrealistic as a reflection of a total living population. Certainly, it is curious that no infant nor older adult burials were recovered, but instead mainly adults in the twenty-five to thirty-five years of age group. The male graves appear to concentrate in the western part of the cemetery and the female graves are more dispersed but are situated towards the east with all age groups fairly evenly distributed across the site. The burials do seem to respect the presence of earlier features of possible Romano-British and Bronze Age dates.

This sixth-century cemetery is a very rare occurrence around the fen-edge in Cambridgeshire, let alone in the greater fenland region. Indeed, Hall noted that the Fenland Project Survey discovered very little Anglo-Saxon evidence in the Fens and along the fen-edge.[51] Although place-name evidence in the Peterborough area, including the suffix '-thorpe' show Germanic influence, the physical evidence for early Anglo-Saxon settlement and activity is extremely sparse. This may be related to difficulties that would be experienced cultivating land in and around the edges of the Fens if compared with more cultivatable land in areas Lincolnshire, the Midlands and southern Cambridgeshire where Anglo-Saxon settlement evidence is more abundant.

Nonetheless, there are cemeteries of the same period elsewhere, such as at Edix Hill, Barrington, in south Cambridgeshire,[52] and Castledyke South, Barton-on-Humber, to the north[53] which are of similar date and types of grave goods. There are also somewhat later cemetery sites at the new site of Littleport on the southern fen-edge of Cambridgeshire (T. Lane, pers. comm.) and at Burwell[54] and at Melbourn,[55] Shudy Camps[56] and Great Chesterford (Evison 1994)[57] in south Cambridgeshire/north Essex area, but these latter sites are regarded as more of the 'final phase' of the early Anglo-Saxon period sites.[58] Thus at present, it appears that Gunthorpe stands alone in Cambridgeshire as a wholly sixth-century cemetery.

Although inhumation was the predominant rite, there was a great deal of variation within the burial ritual in terms of the position of the body within the grave, and the positioning of artefacts in relation to the body of the deceased. The range of artefacts was largely a standard Anglian assemblage, showing some Scandinavian influences in the form of the scutiform brooches. There were also some unusual artefacts, especially the lead 'syringe-like' object, for which there are no known parallels in the archaeological record.

Overall, this was an unexpected and informative discovery undertaken in salvage conditions. It has provided previously unattested evidence of a sixth-century population along the fen-edge, however, the wider context of this cemetery in relation to contemporary settlements and other cemeteries on the northern Cambridgeshire fen-edge and the Peterborough remains to be explored.

Acknowledgements

Peterborough Development Coporation are owed a great debt for sponsoring the rescue excavation within days of its accidental discovery during the creation of a sports ground in late August, 1987. Subsequently, English Heritage sponsored the study of the human remains, some of the illustrations of the grave goods, the conservation of the ironwork, and the analysis of the mineralised remains by Jacqui Watson. It is really the research interest and persistence of Pip Patrick, however, that has led to this publication and her efforts are to be applauded. Numerous diggers from Fenland Archaeological Trust and a host of volunteers and students helped to excavate the graves in extremely rushed, hot and hard ground conditions – all of whom must be heartily thanked. Adrian Challands is thanked for co-directing the excavation, as well as Peterborough Museum, Ruth Parkin, Dr Catherine Hills, Dr Aleks Pluskowski and Ted Buttry, Fitzwilliam Museum, for their support in bringing this publication to fruition.

Notes

1. French and Pryor 2005.
2. Penn and Burgmann in press.
3. The actual digging was extremely hard due to dry weather and local subsoil conditions. It should be noted that the skeletons were not that well preserved (*e.g.* Figs 13, 15, 20 and 28), due to the circum-neutral pH of the local subsoil and disturbance by later ploughing, as well as the subsoil surface being compacted by the box scrapers. Also, the hard and dry subsoil conditions meant that it was impossible to excavate and remove the skeletal remains without sustaining some damage. After the box scraper had inadvertently revealed the site, the whole area was cleaned with hoes and base-planned at 1:50 prior to excavation taking place by hand. Excavation was undertaken using trowels, small chisels and brushes.

   All fully excavated skeletons in grave pits were photographed in colour and black and white, and drawn at 1:10. As each skeleton was lifted, each body part received a separate number for separate bagging, all artefacts received a small finds number at this stage and had their location marked on the 1:10 plan. Once the skeleton had been lifted, the remainder of the grave pit was excavated by trowel, planned at 1:50 and a section profile drawn at 1:10. All other features were similarly treated, photographed, planned at 1:50 and with sections drawn at 1:10. Cremations were bagged by feature in their entirety for wet-sieving at the laboratory.
4. Pryor 1980, 106–25.

5. Middleton 2005.
6. Middleton 1998.
7. Pryor 1980, 121.
8. Pryor 1982, 134–5.
9. The term 'Anglian' can carry certain implications in terms of ethnicity (Lucy 2002, 73), however in the context of this paper it is used to refer to the area of Eastern England typically referred to as the 'Anglian region': Norfolk, Suffolk, Cambridgeshire, *etc.*
10. Lucy 1998, 34.
11. Härke 1997, 132.
12. Härke 1989a, 50.
13. Cf. Swanton 1973.
14. Watson 1994.
15. Lucy 2000, 95.
16. Watson 1994.
17. Dickinson and Harke 1992.
18. Härke 1993, 64.
19. Watson 1994.
20. Evison 1987.
21. Härke 1989b and 1997.
22. Härke 1989b.
23. Harke 1989b.
24. Härke 1997, 133.
25. Buttry 1998 and pers. comms.
26. Hines 1993.
27. Hines, 1993, 12–66.

28. Hines 1984, 221 and 226.
29. Hills 1980, 198.
30. Patrick in preparation.
31. Guido 1999.
32. Brugmann 2004.
33. Lucy 1998, 74.
34. Hirst 1985, 94.
35. Arnold 1980.
36. Stoodley 2002, 120–21.
37. *Ibid.*,113.
38. *Ibid.*, 108.
39. *Ibid.*, 118.
40. Waldron 1994, 13.
41. Boddington 1987.
42. Mensch 1985, 309–27.
43. Chamberlain 2000, 105.

44. Härke 1997, 127.
45. Guy *et al.* 1997, 223.
46. Crawford 1991, 21.
47. Evison 1994, 36–44.
48. Evison 1994, 31.
49. Stoodley 2002, 120.
50. Hall 1987, fig. 12.
51. Hall 1987, 11.
52. Malim 1998.
53. Drinkall and Foreman 1998.
54. Lethbridge 1931.
55. Duncan *et al.* 2003.
56. Lethbridge 1931.
57. Evison 1994.
58. Cf. Leeds 1936.

Bibliography

Arnold, C. 1980. Wealth and social structure: a matter of life and death, in P. Rahtz, T. Dickinson and L. Watts (eds), *Anglo-Saxon Cemeteries 1979*, 81–142, BAR British Series, 82, Oxford: British Archaeological Reports.

Boddington, A. 1987. From bones to population: the problem of numbers, in A. Boddington, A. N. Garland and R. C. Janaway (eds), *Death, decay and reconstruction: approaches to archaeology and forensic science*, 180–97, Manchester: Manchester University Press.

Brugmann, B. 2004. *Glass beads from Early Anglo-Saxon graves. A Study on the provenance and chronology of glass beads from Anglo-Saxon graves based on visual examination*, Oxford: Oxbow.

Chamberlain, A. 2000. Problems and prospects in palaeodemography, in M. Cox and S. Mays (eds), *Human osteology in archaeology and forensic science*, 101–15, London: Greenwich Medical Media.

Crawford, S. 1991. When do Anglo-Saxon children count?, *Jnl. of Theoretical Archaeol.*, **2**, 17–24.

Dickinson, T. and Härke, H. 1992. *Early Anglo-Saxon Shields, Archaeologia 110*, London: Society of Antiquaries.

Drinkall, G. and Foreman, M. 1998. *The Anglo-Saxon Cemetery at Casteledyke South, Barton-on-Humber*, Sheffield Excavation Reports, 6, Sheffield: Sheffield Academic Press Ltd.

Duncan, H., Duhig, C. and Phillips, M. 2003. A Late Migration/Final Phase cemetery at Water Lane, Melbourn, *Proc. Camb. Antiq. Soc. XCII*, 57–134.

Evison, V. 1987. *Dover: the Buckland Anglo-Saxon cemetery*, HBMCE Archaeological Report, 3, London.

Evison, V. 1994. *An Anglo-Saxon Cemetery at Great Chesterford, Essex*, York: Council for British Archaeology Research Report, 91.

French, C. and Pryor, F. 2005. *Archaeology and Environment of the Etton Landscape*, Peterborough, EAA, 109, Peterborough: East Anglian Archaeology.

Guido, M. 1999. *The glass beads of Anglo-Saxon England c. AD 400–700: a preliminary visual classification of the more definitive and diagnostic types*, Woodbridge: The Boydell Press.

Guy, H., Masset, C. and Baud, C-A. 1997. Infant taphonomy, *International Jnl. of Osteoarchaeol.*, **7**, 221–29.

Hall, D. 1987. *The Fenland Project number 2: Cambridgeshire survey Peterborough to March*. EAA, 35, Norwich: East Anglian Archaeology.

Härke, H. 1997. Early Anglo-Saxon social structure, in J. Hines (ed.), *The Anglo-Saxons from the migration period to the eighth century: an ethnographic perspective*, Woodbridge: Boydell Press.

Härke, H. 1989a. Early Anglo-Saxon Weapon Burials: frequencies, distributions and weapon combinations, in S. C. Hawkes (ed.), *Weapons and warfare in Anglo-Saxon England*, 29–61, Oxford University Committee for Archaeology Monograph no. 21, Oxford: Oxford University Committee for Archaeology.

Härke, H. 1989b. Knives in early Saxon burials: blade length and age at death, *Medieval Archaeol.*, **33**, 144–8.

Härke, H. 1993. The shield in the burial rite, *Archaeologia*, **110**, 63–70.

Härke, H. 1997. Early Anglo-Saxon social structure, in J. Hines (ed.), *The Anglo-Saxons from the migration period to the eighth century: an ethnographic perspective*, 125–70, Woodbridge: Boydell Press.

Hills, C. 1980: Anglo-Saxon cremation cemeteries, with particular reference to Spong Hill, Norfolk, in P. Rahtz, T. Dickinson and L. Watts (eds), *Anglo-Saxon cemeteries 1979*, 197–207, BAR British Series, 82, Oxford: British Archaeological Reports.

Hines, J. 1984. *The Scandinavian character of Anglian England in the pre-Viking period*, BAR British Series, 124, Oxford: British Archaeological Reports.

Hines, J. 1993. *Clasps – hektespenner – agraffen: Anglo-Scandinavian clasps of classes A–C of the 3rd to sixth centuries AD typology, diffusion and function*, Stockholm: Kungl. Vitterhets Historie Och Antikvitets Akademien.

Hirst, S. 1985. *An Anglo-Saxon cemetery at Sewerby, East Yorkshire*, York: York University Archaeological Publications 4.

Leeds, E. T. 1936. *Early Anglo-Saxon Art and Archaeology; being the Rhind lectures delivered in Edinburgh, 1935*, Oxford: Clarendon Press.

Lethbridge, T. C. 1931. *Recent Excavations in Anglo-Saxon Cemeteries in Cambridgeshire and Suffolk*, Cambridge: Cambridge Antiquarian Society.

Lucy, S. 1998. *The early Anglo-Saxon cemeteries of East Yorkshire. An analysis and reinterpretation.*, BAR British Series, 272, Oxford: British Archaeological Reports.

Lucy, S. 2000. *The Anglo-Saxon Way of Death*, Stroud: Sutton Publishing.

Malim, T. 1998. *The Anglo-Saxon Cemetery at Edix Hill (Barrington A), Cambridgeshire*, CBA Research Report, 112, York: Council for British Archaeology.

Mensch, B.S. 1985. Child mortality, contraceptive use and fertility in Columbia, Costa Rica and Korea, *Population Stud.*, 39, 309–27.

Middleton, R. 1998. Flint and chert artefacts, in F. Pryor, *Etton: Excavations at a Neolithic Causewayed Enclosure near Maxey, Cambridgeshire*, 215–50, HBMC Archaeological Report,18, London: English Heritage.

Middleton, R. 2005. The Lithic Assemblage, in C. French and F. Pryor, *Archaeology and Environment of the Etton Landscape,* Peterborough: East Anglian Archaeology 109, 49–71.

Patrick, P. in preparation. An unusual syringe-like object from early medieval Peterborough, *Medieval Archaeol.*

Penn, K. and Brugmann, B. in press. *Anglo-Saxon cemeteries: Morning Thorpe, Spong Hill, Bergh Apton and Westgarth Gardens,* Norwich: East Anglian Archaeology.

Pryor, F. 1980. *Excavations at Fengate, Peterborough, England: The Third Report*, Northamptonshire Archaeological Society Monograph 1/Royal Ontario Museum Monograph 6, Northampton/Toronto.

Pryor, F. 1982. Problems of Survival: later Prehistoric Settlement in the Southern East Anglian Fenlands, *Analecta Praehistorica Leidensia,* **XV**, 125–43.

Stoodley, N. 2002. Multiple burials, multiple meanings? Interpreting the early Anglo-Saxon multiple interment, in S. Lucy and A. Reynolds (eds.) *Burial in early Medieval England and Wales*, 103–21, Society for Medieval Archaeology Monograph, 17, London: SMA.

Swanton, M. J. 1973. *The spearheads of the Anglo-Saxon Settlements*. London: The Royal Archaeological Institute.

Waldron, T. 1994. *Counting the dead.* Chichester: John Wiley and Sons.

Watson, J. 1994. Organic material associated with metalwork from the Anglo-Saxon cemetery at Gunthorpe, Ancient Monuments Laboratory Report 41/92.

Minerva: an Early Anglo-Saxon Mixed-Rite Cemetery in Alwalton, Cambridgeshire

Catriona Gibson
with specialist contributions from
Ian Baxter, Jane Cowgill, Nina Crummy, Andrew Fawcett, Val Fryer,
Peter Guest, Jonathan Last, Tom McDonald,
Jacqueline McKinley, Berni Sudds and Tony Waldron
Illustrations by Donna Cameron, Amy Goldsmith
and Kathren Henry

PART I INTRODUCTION

Summary

During the late spring and summer of 1999 an archaeological excavation was carried out on *c.* 1.25 ha of land by Hertfordshire Archaeological Trust at Minerva Business Park, Alwalton, near Peterborough (Cambridgeshire) (NGR TL 136 962), in advance of site development (Figs 1–2). Two separate areas (Area A and B) were excavated.[1] The former produced evidence predominantly of Iron Age date, comprising pits, ditches and a post hole structure. An early Anglo-Saxon cemetery formed the main component of the Area B excavation. Twenty-eight urned and two unurned cremation burials dating to between the fifth and sixth centuries AD and thirty-four inhumations, dating to between the late fifth and early seventh centuries AD, were uncovered. Both cremation burials and inhumation burials were provided with pyre or grave goods, and some of the burials were richly furnished.

Introduction

The site is located approximately 6 km south-west of Peterborough to the south of Alwalton (Fig. 1). The trenches lay 400 m north-east of Alwalton church on land between Oundle Road and the River Nene at approximately 10 m OD, positioned on land that slopes down gently north-eastwards towards the river.

Geologically, the site lies on Cornbrash limestone partly overlain by tertiary river terrace gravels and clay deposits. Geological features such as ice wedges were encountered during the excavation, making recognition of archaeological features difficult. Variations in topsoil thickness were attributed to a combination of recent soil dumping and the presence of ridge and furrow.[2] A dark grey silty topsoil between 0.2 and 0.3 m thick overlay the orange/brown silty clay subsoil that was deeper in the northern part of the site.

The site was excavated in two stages (Areas A and B), and followed an earlier evaluation of Area A by CCC AFU[3] and Area B by HAT (Fig. 2).[4] The evaluation of Area A found multi-period features, including ditches containing Roman and middle Anglo-Saxon material, implying the presence of Anglo-Saxon and earlier activity in the vicinity. The second phase of evaluation assessing the northern part of the site (Area B) revealed early Anglo-Saxon cremation burials and inhumation burials.[5]

The early Anglo-Saxon cemetery formed the main component of the Area B excavation. Twenty-eight cremation burials dating between the fifth and sixth centuries AD were excavated and were found to be predominantly located across the southern and western part of this (Fig. 4). Although several cremation burials had been damaged in antiquity, the majority were truncated by medieval ploughing and several had been lost particularly in the central part of the site, where gaps in the distribution of cremation burials coincided with medieval furrows. Two cremation burials were unurned and lacked grave goods. Thirty-four inhumation burials were excavated. Although there was some overlap with the cremation burials, the majority of inhumations were found in the eastern and southern parts of Area B (Fig. 4). Two possible, fragmentary inhumations were also identified.

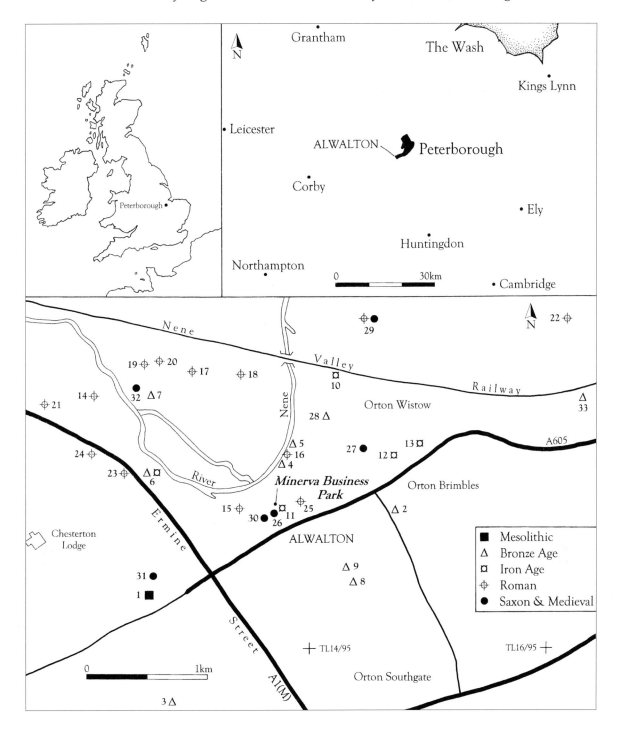

Figure 1a. LOCAL SITES
1. Mesolithic flint scatter; 2. Five Bronze Age ring ditches; 3. Possible Bronze Age tumulus; 4. Late Bronze Age leaf-shaped sword from river; 5. Late Bronze Age dagger from river; 6. Possible Bronze Age ring-ditch associated with ?Iron Age enclosures and field system; 7. Bronze Age ring ditch; 8. Possible Bronze Age ring ditch; 9. Possible Bronze Age ring ditch; 10. Iron Age settlement (ditch contained two undated cremation vessels); 11. Iron Age settlement; 12. Possible Iron Age-Roman enclosure; 13. Possible Iron Age-Roman enclosure; 14. Roman small town of Durobrivae; 15. Roman villa; 16. Roman quarry; 17. Castor Roman villa; 18. Possible Roman villa; 19. Mill Hill – four large Roman villas; 20. Roman kiln; 21. Roman kiln; 22. Roman fort; 23. Roman burials; 24. Roman burials; 25. Roman burials; 26. Anglo-Saxon inhumation (sixth century); 27. Anglo-Saxon cremations within possible barrow (fifth century); 28. Bronze Age ring ditch; 29. Lynch Farm. Settlement that shows possible continuity from Roman to Saxon period; 30. Possible evidence of Roman and Saxon domestic activity; 31. Medieval church; 32. Possible site of 7th century church; 33. Neolithic-Bronze Age inhumation and ditched enclosure

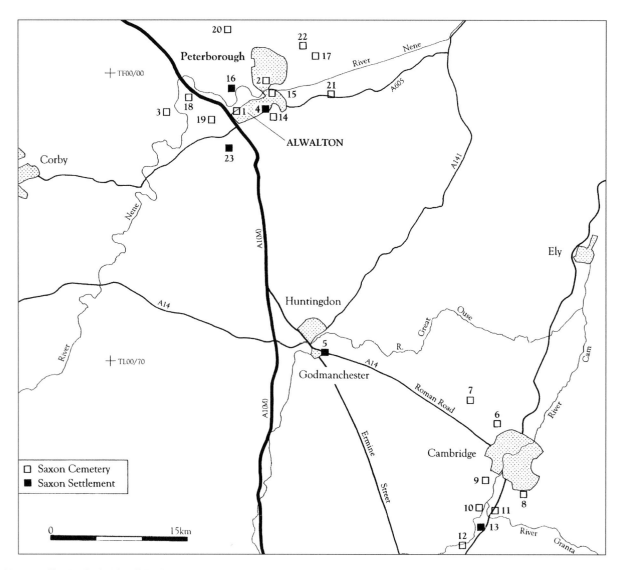

Figure 1b. REGIONAL SITES

1. Minerva Business Park, Alwalton. Early Saxon mixed-rite cemetery; 2. Longthorpe. Early Saxon mixed-rite cemetery (predominately cremation); 3. Nassington. Early Saxon mixed-rite cemetery (mainly inhumation); 4. Orton Hall Farm. Roman to early Saxon settlement site and Orton Longueville early Saxon settlement; 5. Cardinal Distribution Park, Godmanchester. Early Saxon settlement; 6. Girton. Early Saxon mixed-rite cemetery; 7. Oakington. Early Saxon mixed-rite cemetery; 8. Trumpington. Early Saxon inhumation cemetery; 9. Grantchester. Early Saxon inhumation cemetery; 10. Haslingfield. Early Saxon mixed-rite cemetery; 11. Hauxton. Early Saxon mixed-rite cemetery; 12. Barrington A and B. Early Saxon inhumation cemetery; 13. Harston (Mill and Manor Farm). Early Saxon settlements; 14. Old Fletton. Early Saxon inhumation cemetery (see Fig. 1a); 15. Woodston. Early Saxon inhumation cemetery and settlement (see Fig. 1a); 16. Castor. Middle Saxon settlement; 17. Gunthorpe. Early Saxon mixed-rite cemetery; 18. Sibson. Single early Saxon inhumation burial; 19. Chesterton. Possible early Saxon inhumation cemetery; 20. Helpston. Early Saxon inhumation cemetery; 21. Whittlesey. Early Saxon inhumation cemetery; 22. Eye. Early Saxon inhumation cemetery; 23. Haddon. Early Saxon settlement (reoccupation of Roman settlement)

PART II THE EXCAVATION

Natural features

A number of geological features such as rivulet ice wedges and tree throws were located across Area A (Fig. 3). One of these, 1113, produced three struck flints, including a button scraper and a retouched flake, a sherd of possible early Iron Age pottery and an iron nail. In Area B, most of the natural features were tree throws and many were associated with the cremation burials (Figs 4–5, 11). They indicated that the site had been quite densely wooded in the past and the presence of Saxon pottery sherds in some suggests that they may have been broadly contemporary with the use of the

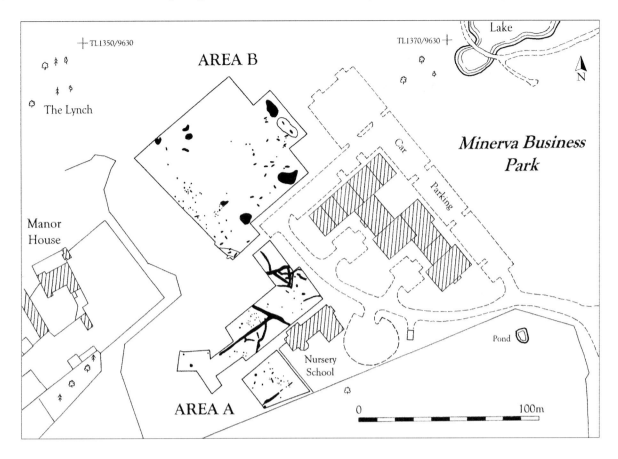

Figure 2. Trench location plan

cemetery. One further large natural hollow over 6 m in diameter lay in the southern part of the site (1417). This contained a small quantity of early Saxon pottery and butchered animal bone as well as fragments of horse bone and the remains of a small dog.

Unphased

A large number of undated features were found in Area A, consisting mostly of postholes (Fig. 3). Some could be dated by their stratigraphic relationships with other features. Ditch 1226 contained a few small fragments of animal bone. Only one of the seven undated pits contained any finds – pit 1056 contained the remains of a large, old male dog.

In the centre of the excavation trench, a group of fifteen postholes appeared to form a small pen or enclosure (Structure 2) situated within the south-western corner of a field system and measuring *c*. 6 m in diameter (Fig. 3). No packing or post pipes were identified in any of the postholes, although four contained charcoal. Two additional postholes, a stake hole and a pit formed part of an internal arrangement to Structure 2. Most of the postholes were 0.35–0.50 m in diameter and few were deeper than 0.10 m. It is suggested that Structure 2 may be Saxon (see Features in Early Anglo Saxon Area A below).

Three undated pits, 1038, 1269 and 1334 were

identified in Area B (Fig. 4–5). All were roughly oval in shape and measured *c*. 1 m in diameter and 0.25 m in depth. Although they did not contain any datable material these pits may potentially be phased to the early Saxon period on the basis of their spatial association with cemetery features. All three pits showed a close correlation with cremation burials and the contents imply that they may have been linked to practices associated with cremation. Pits 1038 and 1269 both contained quantities of charcoal and fragments of burnt limestone; pit 1269 also contained sparse burnt human bone. The contents may have been the residues left after the raking of the bone from the pyre and the subsequent separation of cremated bone from the ashy waste. One of the pits, 1269, truncated cremation burial 1271, although it is unlikely to be significantly later in date. Unlike pits 1038 and 1269, pit 1334 contained small quantities of charcoal and a large number of limestone blocks and chips.

The only other features in Area B that yielded no finds were a cluster of postholes (1277, 1291, 1443, 1445, 1447) located around a group of Saxon cremation burials (1257, 1266, Figs 4 and 5). Again, their spatial association with the cremation burials suggests that they may have been contemporary, possibly acting as grave markers. This argument is supported by the presence of a sherd of early Saxon pottery in posthole 1313, which lay adjacent to cremation 1293 (Fig. 4). However, with

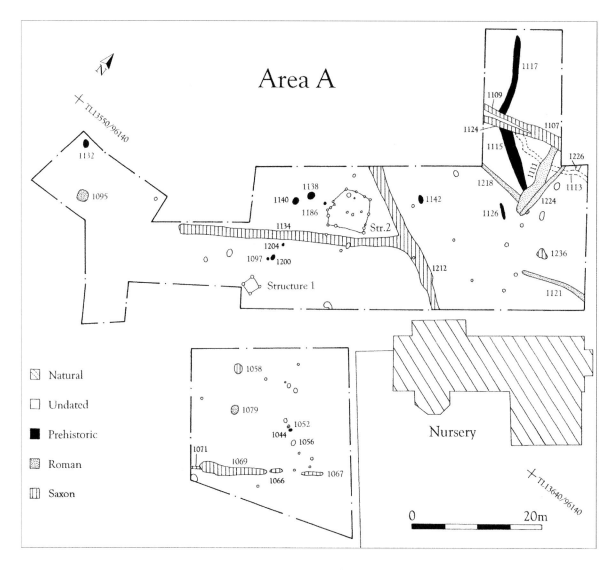

Figure 3. Area A phase plan

the exception of 1277, which is potentially related to cremation 1257, the remaining four postholes formed an arc around cremation burial 1266. These could be the remains of a post-built grave structure or canopy, although no coherent or discernible pattern was identified (see The cremation graves: morphology and layout below). Alternatively, they may have formed a small protective fence around the cremation grave. One other undated posthole (1317) lay in an isolated position in the centre of the excavation with no obvious relationship with any other features. Medieval ploughing in this part of the excavation area may have removed any associated cremations (see Introduction above).

Prehistoric
Neolithic-Bronze Age

Re-deposited Neolithic and Bronze Age material was found in later features and occurred as residual material

from the topsoil and subsoil in Area A. With the exception of one sherd of possible Bronze Age pottery from oval pit 1142 in Area A (Fig. 3), the material comprised struck flints. These included two notched flakes, three end-scrapers and a finely retouched serrated blade from the subsoil. Several struck flints were recovered from later features such as ditches 1107 and 1117 and well 1058.

Early Iron Age

A number of features in Area A, comprising postholes, pits, gullies and ditches, were dated to the early Iron Age. The ditches were situated in the north-western sector of Area A, while the other features were mainly centrally located within the excavation area (Fig. 3). Ditch 1117 was initially dated to the early to middle Saxon period,[6] although further dating evidence recovered during excavation strongly suggested it was of an early Iron Age

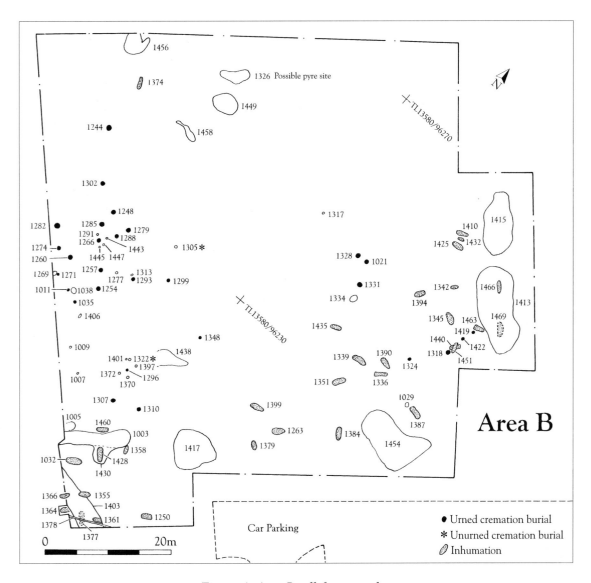

Figure 4. Area B, all features plan

date.[7] Ditch 1115, located south-east of Ditch 1117, was dated to the late pre-Roman Iron Age.[8]

Two circular pits, 1138 and 1140, measuring *c.* 1 m in diameter and 0.1 m deep, were located 1.5 m apart in the central-north part of the excavation area (Fig. 3). The former produced one sherd (13 g) of pottery dated to the early-middle Saxon period in the CCC AFU evaluation,[9] although during the excavation it produced eleven sherds of early Iron Age pottery (68 g), while adjacent pit 1140 produced eighty-three sherds of early Iron Age pottery (788 g). A nearby posthole, 1186, also produced a single sherd of Iron Age pottery. Three other postholes (1097, 1200 and 1204), originally identified during the Area A evaluation, also produced pottery of this period when re-excavated during the excavation (Fig. 3).

An undated four-post structure located in the centre of Area A (Fig. 3) was provisionally dated to the early Iron Age on the basis of form.[10] The postholes were all

roughly circular in shape (*c.* 0.35 m in diameter and 0.15 m to 0.25 m deep) and were set *c.* 1 m apart (Fig. 3, Structure 1). The function of such structures is not yet clear, although they may be associated with cereal storage in low-lying clay areas such as Alwalton. A single struck flint was recovered from the fill of one posthole.

Roman

In Area A, Roman pottery was recovered from five ditches (1111, 1115, 1121, 1215 and 1224) as well as the subsoil (Fig. 3). The dating of the ditches is tentative. Ditch 1111/ 1128 cut ditch 1115. Ditch 1121 contained a single Roman sherd and a Roman iron nail. Ditch 1215 and its recut, ditch 1218, were cut by ditches 1111/1128 and 1224. The former produced pottery which may have been Roman or Anglo-Saxon. However, both the latter ditches produced only Roman pottery and hence they are also provisionally assigned to the Roman period. Ditch 1224 also contained

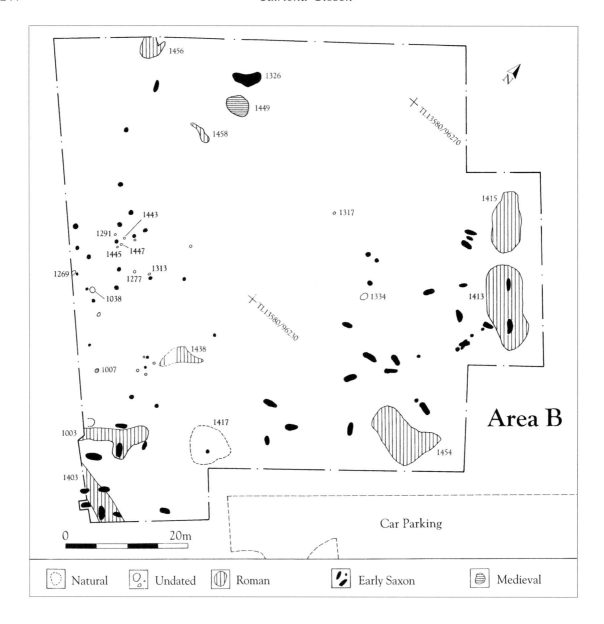

Figure 5. Area B phase plan

animal bone fragments, including cattle. Pit 1095 contained Roman pottery and a ram cranium with both horn cores attached.

A few sherds of Roman pottery were recovered from the topsoil and the subsoil in Area B, mostly from its western area. However, the few features that contained Roman pottery were not all located in this western area. Roman features included ditch 1003, orientated east-north-east – west-south-west (Fig. 5) and ditch 1403 (late Iron Age to late 1st century AD), orientated north-west – south-east and which continued through the southern and western baulks. The latter was wider and deeper than ditch 1003 (0.80 m deep as opposed to 0.45 m). Several later inhumations cut ditch 1403 but none respected the ditch alignment, contrasting with the cemetery layout at Barrington.[11]

A number of later features also produced Roman pottery, including graves 1361 and 1466, tree throw 1438 (which contained predominantly Roman finds and animal bone including cattle bone and a goat horn core) and pit 1449. The latter also contained medieval sherds. The pottery dates suggest that most of the Roman activity on the site is relatively late, between the third and fourth centuries AD.

A group of three large, oval quarry pits lay on the eastern side of the site (1413, 1415 and 1454). The most northerly, pit 1415, was elongated, measuring nearly 10 m in length, 4.5 m in width and over 1 m in depth. It contained a large quantity of cattle bone and one pottery sherd (AD 375–410), which joined with a sherd from adjacent quarry pit 1413. Pit 1413 was over 13 m long, 6 m wide and 1 m deep. A large quantity of Roman pottery (47 sherds), dated from the late fourth to early fifth centuries, was retrieved from its single fill along with over 3 kg of animal bone. This included the remains of two large dogs, sub-adult pig remains, horse and goose bones. Two Saxon inhumations (1466 and 1469) cut pit 1413 and were aligned roughly north-west – south-east within it.

The third pit, 1454, was located in the south-eastern corner of the site. It was sub-oval in shape and of similar dimensions to pits 1415 and 1413 although shallower (0.75 m deep). Two small sherds of mid-second to fourth century Roman pottery were retrieved from its fill, along with a small quantity of animal bone which included fragments of horse.

Features in Early Anglo-Saxon Area A

The majority of features of this phase were ditches and, as with the Roman ditches, their dating is tentative. Ditches/ gullies 1067, 1066 and 1071 are part of the same alignment as ditch 1069 and therefore are assigned to the early Anglo-Saxon period (Fig. 3). Ditches 1109 and 1124 are clearly related to 1107. Together, these ditches may have formed part of a complex of enclosures or a field system. An interrupted ditch (1066, 1067 and 1069), over 20 m long and tapering from 1.55 m wide in the west to only 0.5 m in the east, may have formed one side of an enclosure. It was also deepest in the western section (0.30 m). Although it was slightly irregular in shape, the three interrupted sections ran very straight. They were orientated roughly west-south-west – east-north-east, broadly parallel to an adjacent modern field boundary and to ditch 1134, situated *c.* 35 m to the north-west. The interrupted ditch and 1134 may have been contemporary, originally forming parallel sides of an enclosure. Datable finds were only retrieved from 1069, comprising a single sherd of early Anglo-Saxon pottery. Ditch 1134 was over 34 m long, 1.40 m wide, but less than 0.07 m deep, probably due to heavy truncation. Ditch 1134 was abutted by ditch 1212 which ran north-west – south-east across the trench. 1212 was of similar width and depth to 1134 and it is likely that these two ditches were roughly contemporary. Both contained single fills and produced sparse finds, comprising small quantities of struck flint and animal bone.

A series of four intercutting ditches were identified in the north-eastern part of the trench, one of which was certainly of early Anglo-Saxon date (1107/1109), demonstrating the long and complex process of boundary/enclosure marking in this area (Fig. 3). Ditch 1107/1109 cut the Iron Age ditches 1117 and 1115, as well as Roman ditch 1111/1128. The relationship between some of these ditches is difficult to establish: if their lines are projected it is clear that 1107/1109 and 1212 do not meet since neither was attested in CCC AFU evaluation trench 6. Thus, either both ditches stop and show no association, or else there may have been an entrance at this point.

Since Structure 2 was located in the corner of this

potential Anglo-Saxon field system, it is possible that it was associated with it (Fig. 3). It is unlikely that the structure represents the remains of an Iron Age roundhouse since these tend to have gullies, nor is it likely to be a late Bronze Age roundhouse as there is no associated pottery of this date. Its arrangement is quite irregular and although this may be to do with truncation and removal of postholes, it does not have a convincing circular shape. Two of the postholes (1144 and 1160) are slightly larger than the others and could potentially be associated with a porch or doorway. However it is more likely that this structure was a small animal pen or enclosure.

A well shaft, 1058, was recorded in the southern part of Area A. It was relatively shallow and would have drawn water from the natural limestone, 1.73 m below the present ground surface. Its primary fill of clay and silt was capped with a deliberate, compact backfill over 1 m thick, which contained early Saxon pottery and animal bone.

Early Anglo-Saxon Mixed-Rite Cemetery in Area B

This area was located to the north of Area A (Fig. 2). The main component of this excavation area comprised a mixed-rite early Anglo-Saxon cemetery that dated between the early fifth and late sixth to early seventh centuries AD (Figs 4–5). A full catalogue of inhumation and cremations graves is contained in the appendices, and further details regarding human remains can be found below.

Twenty-eight urned and two unurned cremation burials were mainly located across the southern and eastern parts of the site. Most of the urned cremation burials were decorated and the majority contained grave or pyre goods. Thirty-three inhumations were also excavated, just under half of which contained grave goods. A small number of the graves were stone-lined (grave 1263, Fig. 13; grave 1336, Fig. 17, grave 1355, Fig. 19 and grave 1435, Fig. 30) which may have been related to status. The distribution of stone-lined graves and other possibly high-status burials has been plotted in Figure 8. Some of the skeletons were well-preserved, but several had been disturbed by ploughing (see Introduction above) and some may been robbed of grave goods (*e.g.* grave 1435, Fig. 30).

Inhumation Graves: Morphology and Layout

The cemetery was relatively well spread out with large spaces between the graves (Fig. 5), *c.* 5 m, suggesting that this part of the cemetery never reached a stage of overcrowding. There was only one instance of intercutting: grave 1451 cut grave 1440. This implies the use of grave markers, although no evidence was encountered for this. A double inhumation grave (grave 1387, Fig. 30) contained a male and a female skeleton.

Table 1. Body positions of the inhumations

		Skeleton No	1032	1250	1263	1336	1339	1342	1345	1351	1355	1358	1361	1364	1366	1374	1377	1379
LEGS	Extended, parallel	A	X					X		X	X		X	X	X			
	Flexed to the right	B																
	Flexed to the left	C		X														X
	Crossed at ankles	D							X									
	Feet meet	E			X	X						X				X		
	Extended to right	F																
	Extended to left	G																
ARMS	Left extended	1			X	X									X			
	Right extended	2	X		X								X			X		
	Extended parallel	3							X									
	Left flexed over chest	4						?		X								
	Right flexed over chest	5				X									X			X
	Both flexed over chest	6																
	Left flexed to pelvis	7	X									X	X					X
	Right flexed to pelvis	8		X						X				X				
	Both flexed to pelvis	9										X						
HEAD	Tilted to left	L		X														
	Tilted up	U																
	Tilted down	D														X		
	Tilted to right	R	X			X			X	X	X	X			X			
NOTE					?		disart									disart		

The graves were mainly cut into the natural clay subsoil, although eight cut Roman pits and ditches. There was no evidence for any coffin burials, such as wood or discolouration of the soil from decomposed wood or metal coffin fittings. Most of the graves were relatively shallow and several had been severely truncated by ploughing and other activities. The graves ranged from 0.95 m – 2.1 m in length (average 1.71 m), from 0.34 m – 0.9 m in width (average 0.62 m) and from 0.06 m – 0.6 m in depth (average 0.22 m). They were either sub-oval or sub-rectangular in shape. There was no obvious correlation between the size of the grave cut and the age or sex of the deceased; however as most were adults, this may not be surprising. Three of the largest graves, graves 1387.2, 1399 and grave 1460 (respectively measuring 1.95 m – 0.85 m, 2.1 m – 0.7 m and 2.1 m –

0.7 m) contained adult males of twenty-five to thirty-five years of age. One other grave (1387.1) measuring 1.95 m – 0.85 m, contained a female of forty-five years of age or more of age.

Burial Positions

Most of the graves contained extended supine inhumations (Table 1). The predominance of this general body position is in keeping with other early Anglo-Saxon cemeteries, such as Barrington A (Cambridgeshire), where two-thirds of the burials had been laid out this way.[12] There were no examples of prone burials. Some of the inhumations, however, were partly or fully disarticulated (*e.g.* 1364, Fig. 22) and their burial positions could not be determined.

Table 1., cont.

	Skeleton No/ Grave No.		1 3 8 4	1 3 8 9	1 3 9 3	1 3 9 0	1 3 9 4	1 3 9 9	1 4 1 0	1 4 6 9	1 4 2 5	1 4 2 8	1 4 3 2	1 4 3 5	1 4 4 0	1 4 5 1	1 4 6 3	1 4 6 7
LEGS	Extended, parallel	A	X										X	?	X			
	Flexed to the right	B		X								X						
	Flexed to the left	C				X	X											
	Crossed at knees	D																
	Feet meet	E			X			X	X		X					X	X	X
	Extended to right	F								X								
	Extended to left	G																
ARMS	Left extended	1					X						X					
	Right extended	2	X	X		X			X		X						X	X
	Extended parallel	3														X		
	Left flexed over chest	4				X											X	
	Right flexed over chest	5					X	X										
	Both flexed over chest	6																
	Left flexed to pelvis	7	X	X					X		X							X
	Right flexed to pelvis	8											X					
	Both flexed to pelvis	9			X					X					X			
HEAD	Tilted to left	L	X	X		X		X	X							X	X	X
	Tilted up	U																
	Tilted down	D								X					X			
	Tilted to right	R			X							X	X					
NOTE														disart				

There were six examples of flexed inhumations – graves 1250 (Fig. 12), 1379 (Fig. 26), 1387 (Fig. 30), 1394 (Fig. 27), 1425 (Fig. 30) and 1410 (Fig. 30), but none were tightly flexed. While most of these were lying on their backs, the skeletons in graves 1250 (Fig. 12) and 1410 (Fig. 30) were in crouched positions on their sides. Sk 1469 was buried with her legs straight but at an obtuse angle to her torso, a position which may have been determined by the shape of the pit in which she was buried (Fig. 30). Where arm positions could be identified, nearly all of the examples had one or both arms flexed over the body, usually over the chest (in eight cases it was the left arm and in six cases it was the right). In only two cases the arms were fully extended by the sides of the body. The most common position for the legs was to be fully extended (twenty-one examples) and in eleven of these cases the feet met. The head was commonly tilted to the right (ten examples) or the left (a further nine examples). Grave goods were not restricted to the torso but frequently were placed by the arms, next to the skull or even between the legs.

There was no obvious correlation between the arrangements of the body positions in relation to age, sex and status at Alwalton. At Barrington A, it was noted that leg positions often reflected elements of gender: males had legs flexed to the right and females to the left.[13] Another position – that of straight legs, left arm crooked over stomach and right arm slightly bent to rest the hand over the right innominate – was a group almost exclusively composed of females. These burial positions may have been associated with the display of sexually differentiated grave goods.

Disarticulated and Disturbed Bone

Five deposits of disarticulated bone were also collected

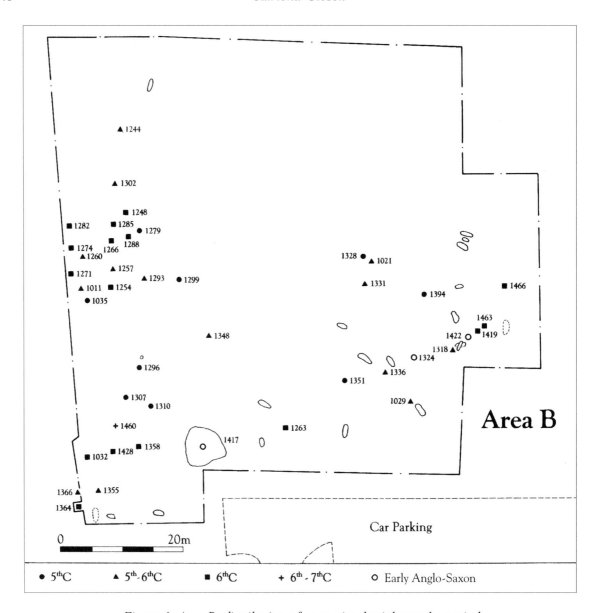

Figure 6. Area B, distribution of cremation burial urns by period

from the site. These included fragments of a child's skull discovered during the evaluation, associated with a fragmentary vessel (1029, Sk 1030) (Fig. 40). This may represent the remains of a severely truncated child inhumation, buried more shallowly than an adult (see Human skeletal remains below). If so, it lies close to double burial 1387 and was perhaps originally part of a family group.

The cremation graves: morphology and layout

In comparison to the inhumations, the cremation burials were generally placed more closely together, separated by an average distance of 2.5 m. Like the inhumations, there was no obvious pattern to their layout, although six were placed in a straight line (cremation burials 1244, 1302, 1285, 1266, 1257 and 1254) that followed a north-west to

south-east orientation (Fig. 6). This line may have been a deliberate row. However, they were not all of the same date, but ranged from the fifth to mid-sixth centuries AD. Evidence for grave markers was identified, since four cremation graves were located adjacent to postholes. These included posthole 1313 with cremation grave 1293 and posthole 1277 with cremation grave 1257 (Fig. 4).

The cremation grave cuts were all circular or sub-circular in plan and most were relatively shallow (Table 2). Many of the cremation vessels had lost their rims or upper parts as a result of truncation in antiquity. It was clear that others had been lost during medieval ploughing, with the greatest damage occurring to those situated within furrows (see Introduction above). The pit cuts ranged from 0.17 m to 0.59 m in diameter (average 0.35 m) and 0.09 m to 0.24 m in depth (average 0.14 m). There was no correlation between the depth of the cut and the age of the

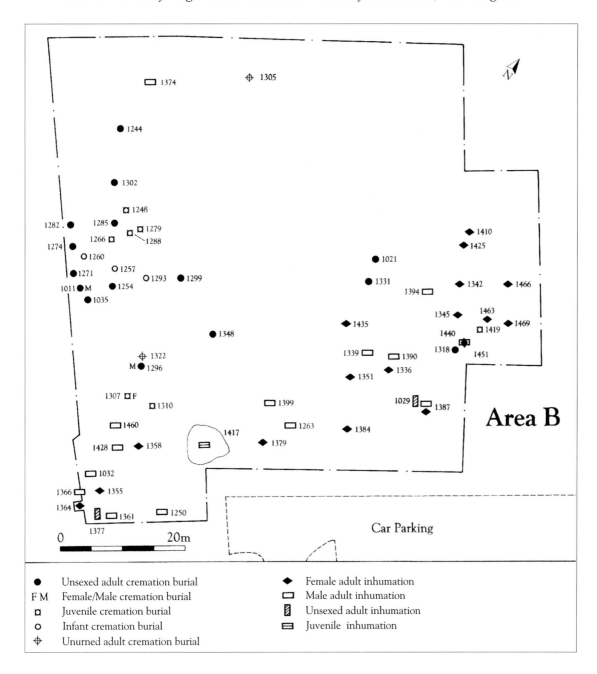

Figure 7. Age and sex of cremations and inhumations

individual interred, but the later truncation may have affected any pattern.

The two unurned cremation burials (1305 and 1322) may represent token, rather than complete cremation deposits and both included a quantity of charcoal (Fig. 7). The majority of the cremation burial vessels were decorated. The pits into which the cremation urns were inserted were generally sub-circular with rounded or concave bases, although seven (1011, 1271, 1285, 1293, 1296, 1348 and 1419) were circular and one (1318) was oval in plan. The only construction related to the cremation graves was a four-post structure enclosing cremation 1296 (Fig. 4).

Many of the cremation burials had grave or pyre goods. The most common items were combs, made of either antler or bone. These were predominantly unburnt token deposits that had been deliberately snapped off the comb (thirteen fragments as opposed to only three complete examples were retrieved, and only one burnt fragment was noted). The occurrence of broken unburnt combs deposited in cremation urns was observed at Millgate cemetery, Newark-on-Trent (Nottinghamshire), and Spong Hill (Norfolk), with end tooth segments dominating the assemblage.[14] Other artefacts recovered from Minerva include pyre goods, such as copper-alloy (brooches, beads etc), iron nails and some toilet items

Table 2. Depths of grave cuts

Depth of grave cut (cm)	Inhumations	Cremations
0–10	5	9
11–20	16	15
21–30	4	3
31–40	4	0
41–50	0	0
51–60	1	0
>60	1	0

(see Grave goods from the cremation burials, below).

Cremation grave 1296 was situated within a four-post structure. This cremation burial is noteworthy not only because it may have been placed within a wooden funerary house, but the cremation urn also included a small quantity of animal bone and three items unique to the site (see Grave goods from the cremation burials and Cremation burial 1296 below; Fig. 35). These items were a pair of iron shears, a razor and a hone stone. Spatially, however, cremation grave 1296 was not located centrally within the main cluster of cremation graves, but lay *c.* 15 m to the south-east, although of course the full extent of this funerary landscape is unknown.

The possible wooden funerary house around cremation 1296 measured *c.* 2.3 m × 1.67 m. Funerary houses have been noted at other cremation cemeteries. For example, at Apple Down (Sussex)[15] most of the cremation burials were contained within four-post structures, ranging in dimensions from 1 m² to 2.7 m × 2.5 m. Single examples, as at Alwalton, are known from Croydon (Surrey)[16] and Berinsfield (Oxfordshire).[17] A reconstruction of one of the structures at Apple Down[18] suggests that it had a pitched roof, perhaps with wattle and daub sides, and some may have housed the cremation burials of an entire family. The structure at Alwalton may have been associated with a second, unurned cremation, 1322.

A possible funerary pyre site (1326) was identified in the northern part of the excavation trench (Fig. 4). It was irregular in plan and measured over 4 m in length and 2.4 m in width. It was initially described as a large burning pit and contained a large quantity of charcoal and ash, in association with burnt fragments of human bone. A barbed and tanged arrowhead was retrieved from one of the upper burnt layers within this feature (Fig. 37 No. 9). This may have been deliberately curated and placed in the pyre pit as part of a ritual closure deposit. The presence of a funeral pyre site at Alwalton is important and unusual as they are rarely identified in Anglo-Saxon cemeteries. A possible pyre site was recorded at the Snape mixed-rite cemetery (Suffolk). It lay at the southern end of the cemetery within the Anglo-Saxon topsoil and consisted of a two metre square layer of burnt flints, cremated human bone, charcoal and metal fragments.[19]

Population structure

Height of the population

Although the heights of all of the skeletons could not be determined, from the eighteen that were sufficiently well preserved to enable analysis, the average female height was 1.61 m and male height was 1.75 m. The females appear to have been significantly shorter than the males, particularly in comparison with other cemeteries. For example at Barrington A, the mean height for females was 1.63 m, while males were 1.73 m.[20] However, the overall average for the population was similar (1.68 m for Alwalton and 1.69 m for Barrington A), though the small size of the sample from Alwalton may not reflect the true mean height of the whole population.

Demography and mortality

No definite juvenile, child or infant inhumations were identified at Alwalton, although disarticulated bone of these age groups were retrieved. This is a relatively unusual feature. Although early Anglo-Saxon cemeteries tend to be unrepresentative of infant mortality (with the exception of Great Chesterford (Essex)),[21] on average the juvenile population tends to form about a third of the overall cemetery population, as at Portway and Worthy Park (Hampshire) and Polhill (Kent).[22] More males than females tended to die in the younger adult age group, between fifteen and twenty-five years of age (*e.g.* Barrington A),[23] while female deaths peaked between the ages of twenty-five and thirty-five (*e.g.* Barrington (Cambridgeshire), Great Chesterford). These two peaks may be related to death through warfare and childbirth respectively. However, Alwalton exhibited a quite different demographic profile, although this may be biased by the partial sample of the cemetery excavated. From the three cremated and twenty-six inhumed individuals that could be aged and sexed, males most commonly died between the ages of twenty-five and thirty-five, while the majority of females lived into older age, dying after forty-five years. A large proportion also died between the ages of fifteen and twenty-five.

PART III SPECIALIST REPORTS
Struck and Burnt Flint (Fig. 37.9)

Tom McDonald

Eighty-four residual struck flints were recovered from late Iron Age, Roman and Anglo-Saxon features and one lump of burnt flint from the subsoil. Retouched pieces include a fine serrated blade, a small barbed and tanged arrowhead, a spurred implement, end and side scrapers, and two button scrapers. The barbed and tanged arrowhead had been broken during production; the projectile point is unfinished and shallow scale flaking (thinning) is absent down one side (Fig. 37.9). The raw material varies from light grey to dark grey brown/black. Flaws, frost fractures, are apparent on four pieces. The condition of the flint varies from battered to sharp. Six pieces are sharp, twenty-six pieces are patinated and re-use of patinated flint is evident on one example.

Evidence for *in situ* knapping was not recorded during the excavation and only a very few spalls were recovered. The presence of four blade cores suggests that, although knapping may not have occurred on site, it was undertaken nearby. Secondary flakes predominate from later industries which also suggest that knapping occurred elsewhere. Evidence for both soft and hard hammer core reduction strategies are present. The former predominate and are evidenced by the occurrence of narrow platforms and diffused bulbs of percussion.[24]

Two industries are represented; the early Neolithic by a few true blades, blade cores and a bladelet core. The majority of the pieces fall within the flake-dominated later Neolithic and Bronze Age periods, the presence of hard hammer struck flakes may also suggest later Bronze Age activity. The near absence of burnt flint suggests that there is little evidence for prehistoric settlement and that the mixed assemblage spanning more than one period is 'background' material.

Prehistoric Pottery (Fig. 38)

Jonathan Last

The significant contexts are postholes 1044 and 1097 and adjacent Pits 1138 and 1140 in Area A. These produced eighty-five per cent of the total pottery by weight (not including topsoil and subsoil finds). The pottery from these features is all handmade and has been assigned to the early Iron Age (EIA). Similar material was found in the gravel pits at Fengate, Peterborough, a few kilometres down the River Nene.[25] However, consideration is given to the possibility that some of it may be Anglo-Saxon in date, given the nature of the site and the initial interpretation of pottery from pit 1138 (partly excavated during the evaluation) as being of early/middle Anglo-Saxon date.[26] The early Anglo-Saxon and EIA periods are often hard to distinguish within small assemblages because vessel forms are rather similar.

Fabrics

Most of the pottery is shell-tempered, the inclusions varying in size and density. In some cases the shell particles on the surface have been dissolved, leaving platy voids. Differences in inclusion size, along with vessel wall thickness, allow a distinction between 'finewares' (mainly in posthole 1097 and pit 1138) and 'coarsewares' (posthole 1044, pit 1140). Surface colours are frequently mottled among both groups, although the few strongly oxidised and wholly dark-faced sherds are all thin-walled. A number of the sherds with relatively sparse shell appear to also contain particles of grog, which is rare, but not unknown, in the early/middle Iron Age (for Northamptonshire).[27] A single quartz-tempered sherd was present in pit 1140 but there is a complete absence of flint tempering, which seems unusual since the EIA pottery from the Fengate gravel pits includes flint-, shell- and chalk-tempered fabrics. However, shell is by far the predominant inclusion type for the Iron Age phases at the more recent Fengate excavations.[28]

Forms

The principal forms evidenced are coarseware shouldered jars with everted rims and fineware angular (carinated) bowls with upright or flaring rims and straight or concave necks. Angular profiles are a characteristic feature of the EIA, as opposed to the late Bronze Age or the middle Iron Age (MIA). MIA pottery at Fengate is characterised by globular forms and scored decoration, while the late pre-Roman Iron Age (LPRIA) assemblage is predominantly wheelmade.

Rim sherds of at least eleven vessels have been recovered. Those in posthole 1097 and pit 1138 are all thin-walled finewares. The vessel in posthole 1097 (unoxidised) has an upright neck and outward-curving rim above an open body. An unoxidised vessel with incised decoration in pit 1138 may be of similar form, while the two plain forms there, both thin-walled and part oxidised, are a carinated bowl with upright rim and a simple bowl. A distinctive situlate jar in posthole 1044, for which there is a complete profile (Fig. 38), has a sharp, high shoulder with a short neck, everted rim and internal bevel above a straight, slightly angled body and a thick, flat base. Another large jar in pit 1140 has a flaring, flat-topped rim with an applied cordon on the neck and a relatively weak shoulder. Four other rims were recovered from the fill of pit 1140: two open bowls, one (oxidised) with an expanded rim and two probable jar rims. Finally a small, oxidised, flat-topped rim, probably of a shouldered bowl, from posthole 1052 may also belong to the EIA.

Other diagnostic forms include two shoulders/carinations from the fill of posthole 1097, both probably from bowls with short concave necks, like the rim from that context. Part of the neck zone of a second jar in pit 1140 was also found. Two base junctions are present in pit 1140 and part of a flat base in posthole 1097, possibly from the same vessel as one of the shoulders.

The bowl forms are paralleled in a number of EIA assemblages,[29] including Fengate gravel pits; the high-shouldered jar is less obvious there although one vessel (X1)[30] is similar, if less pronounced. Open bowls are also unusual, although they are present, for example, at Sandown Park, Esher (Surrey).[31] However, there is no positive evidence at Alwalton for omphalos bases, which might be expected in assemblages of this date.

Surfaces and decoration

The division between coarseware and fineware extends also to decoration, the former with fingernail impressions and the latter incised or plain burnished. This is characteristic of late Bronze Age/early Iron Age assemblages. All the sherds in posthole 1097 are plain, although the rim has a moderate burnish inside and out. The chevron pattern on the dark-faced incised vessel in pit 1138 is reminiscent of Fengate EIA designs, although these usually occur lower on the shoulder (see below). This sherd also has a finer finish than the other rims, which are merely smoothed.

Among the coarsewares, the large jar in pit 1140 has three rows of fingernail impressions – on the rim, applied neck-band and shoulder angle. This is typical of the coarseware situate jars from the Fengate gravel pits[32] although this vessel is less angular. The jar in posthole 1044 and another rim in pit 1140 have fingernail impressions on the rim only, respectively on the exterior and the top. One body sherd in pit 1140 has shallow vertical scoring marks; these may show an affinity with Cunliffe's Breedon-Ancaster group of fifth century BC and later date,[33] or merely be the effect of wiping the vessel with coarse vegetable matter, a practice that goes back to the Bronze Age.

Use, breakage and discard

Charring from cooking is present on the interior walls of the jar from the fill of posthole 1044 and one large body sherd from pit 1140. The underside of the base of the former vessel is also somewhat worn. Therefore the pottery clearly represents a domestic assemblage. Both of these contexts also contain large, joining sherds. Those from pit 1138 and posthole 1097 are much smaller, although they come mainly from smaller vessels, but both contexts still include joining fragments. Hence the assemblage, despite its small size, also has a relatively high integrity, which suggests this is 'fresh' refuse that has not been re-deposited. The vessels may even represent deliberate (votive) deposition.

Other features

Other shell-tempered sherds that are probably of Iron Age date came from the fills of ditches 1109, 1113, 1126 and posthole 1186. These small fragments could easily be residual. Certainly residual in subsoil L1001 were a rim and a base junction. Sherds with grog and shell temper, which resemble the fabrics present in posthole 1097 and posthole 1044, came from L1001, pit 1079 (which also produced Roman pottery) and ditch 1117. Grogged sherds with sand which might be of LPRIA date came from L1001, ditches 1115 and 1121, which yielded a simple handmade rim that may in fact belong with the EIA group. A handmade partly oxidised

grog and sand-tempered sherd from pit 1142 might be earlier still, possibly dating to the Bronze Age.

Discussion

The assemblage comes from a group of dispersed features, each with rather different characteristics, and is not straightforward to interpret. The analysis made the assumption that the four major features are contemporary, although this is not necessarily the case. An EIA date is favoured, with the absence of characteristic features, such as flint-gritted fabrics and omphalos or footring bases, perhaps reflecting local preferences or simply the small number of vessels represented. The presence of some grog along with the shell in sherds recovered from the fills of postholes 1044 and 1097 seems unusual. The fabric and decoration of the jar in the posthole 1044 is rather reminiscent of LPRIA (Belgic) wares, although the sharp-shouldered form does not seem appropriate. However, fragments of Roman tile were retrieved from this feature.

A third possibility, especially given the facts rehearsed above, is that some of the material is Anglo-Saxon in date. However, while the jar fabric from posthole 1044 bears some resemblance to pottery from context 2101 (03) (ESSS or MAX) at Gamlingay (Cambridgeshire),[34] no Maxey ware or other shell-tempered wares are recorded from the early Anglo-Saxon features in Area B at Alwalton and the four jars there are of different, mineral-gritted, fabric types.[35] Moreover, the vessels in posthole 1044 and pit 1140 are not typical Anglo-Saxon forms, nor would the use of grog temper or fingernail impressions be expected.

More crucially, Spoerry suggests the small assemblage from the evaluation, which comes largely from pit 1138, is Anglo-Saxon in date and includes Maxey fabric G.[36] The most diagnostic element in this group is the carinated bowl with incised decoration. The decoration and form of this vessel tend to link it with the EIA assemblage from Fengate, as mentioned, although the presence of incision on the neck zone rather than the shoulder is not directly paralleled there, and appears closer to some examples at West Harling.[37] Anglo-Saxon parallels could be found with the fifth century carinated bowls that are relatively widespread in eastern England; burnishing and incision is also common on early Anglo-Saxon pottery. However, the neck appears rather too upright for these forms, so the resemblance is again far from exact. Moreover, the typical early Saxon bosses and stamps are entirely absent at Alwalton.

Roman Pottery (Fig. 39)

Andrew Fawcett

Archaeological work at Alwalton revealed twenty-seven contexts containing Roman pottery. This is derived mainly from the subsoil and archaeological features such as pits and ditches. The majority of the Roman pottery is small, abraded and non-diagnostic with many contexts containing three sherds or less. Some sherds were residual. Not surprisingly, a large number of contexts are considered unreliable in terms of dating. Only two contexts contained relatively large pottery assemblages (Possible pyre 1326 and pit 1413).

Methodology

All of the pottery was identified at ×20 magnification. The ceramic fabrics were divided using codes based upon the national system.[38] Full descriptions were only employed if the fabric was unsourced. Form matches were obtained from the nearest relevant sites, which were Durobrivae (Water Newton, Cambridgeshire)[39] and Orton Hall Farm (Cambridgeshire).[40] The site archive contains a comprehensive listing and description of all the pottery and contexts.

Fabric descriptions

LGF SA   La Graufesenque samian ware.
Description: Tyers,[41] Webster,[42] Tomber and Dore.[43] Source: La Graufesenque in southern Gaul. Date: *c.* AD 40 to AD110/120. Comments: Only two small and very abraded sherds are represent this fabric. Both are bases.

LMV SA   Les Martres-de-Veyre samian ware.
Description: Tyers,[44] Webster,[45] Tomber and Dore.[46] Source: Les Martres-de-Veyre in central Gaul. Date: AD100 to AD120/5. Comments: One small and abraded sherd accounts for this fabric.

LEZ SA 2   Lezoux samian ware Category 2.
Description: Tyers,[47] Webster,[48] Tomber and Dore.[49] Source: Lezoux in central Gaul. Date: *c.* AD120 to the later second century AD. Comments: All three sherds in this fabric are small and very abraded. None are from a well dated context. One form is recognisable, a Drg18/31 base.

LNV CC   Lower Nene Valley colour-coated ware.
Description: Howe *et al.*,[50] Tomber and Dore,[51] Perrin.[52] The decorative techniques are fairly narrow comprising of brown and dark grey colour coats with rouletting and white painted barbotine scrolls. Source: Lower Nene Valley area, for instance Chesterton, Sibson-cum-Stibbington, Stibbington and Water Newton. Date: *c.* AD150 to *c.* AD410. Comments: In total fifty-one sherds, weighing 398g, with a r.eve of 0.07 are present. The one diagnostic sherd is a dish form dated from the late third to fourth centuries AD. Forms identified through body sherds are a flagon, beaker and an imitation of the samian bowl form Drg38.

SOB GL   Southern-British glazed ware.
Description: Tomber and Dore.[53] The fabric (represented by one sherd) is fairly hard, sandy with a slight soapy feel. The surfaces are orange/brown with a faint light grey core. It consists of abundant fine, well sorted quartz, accompanied by common fine black iron ore and silver mica. The other notable inclusions are sparse rounded clay pellets and fine red iron ore. Source: Unknown, but possibly the south-east. Date: *c.* late first to early/mid second century AD.

LNV WH   Lower Nene Valley white ware.
Description: Tomber and Dore.[54] The single sherd still displays some very abraded black slag grits. Source: See above. Date: AD110 to AD410.

UNS WH   Unsourced white ware.
Description: This fabric appears to be a coarse variant of the Nene Valley industry. Essentially it is hard, sandy with a hackley fracture. The surface colour is creamy-white whilst the outer is fumed around the rim and neck. The fabric is composed of fairly well sorted clear quartz, common ill sorted sub-angular red iron ore and fine common silver mica. Source: Probably local. Date Roman. Comments: A single jar rim represents the fabric. Its style, like the fabric, shows some affinities with the Nene Valley jar range.

HAD OX   Hadham oxidised ware.
Description: Harden and Green,[55] Tomber and Dore,[56] Fawcett.[57] The sherds display the classic 'salt n pepper' arrangement. This mineral trait was first associated with the oxidised finewares that were produced at the kilns in the later Roman period. However, recent work undertaken by the author has demonstrated that this fabric analogy does not satisfactorily account for all of the oxidised wares and, in particular, the reduced wares. There is a greater degree of variation.[58] Source: The Hadhams, east Hertfordshire. Date: The examples noted at Alwalton are dated to the late fourth century AD. Comments: A frilled narrow neck jar is the only form. Two similarly decorated types are known from Verulamium[59] and Baldock[60] in Hertfordshire. Both are dated from the late fourth to early fifth century AD. It is a classic export of the late period.

UNS OX   Unsourced oxidised wares.
Description: One sherd displays a fairly silty fabric with common ill sorted, mostly rounded calcite and quartz. The fabric is orange with a grey core and has a slight soapy feel. There are few sherds, all are non-diagnostic. Source: Unknown. Date: Roman.

BSW   Black surfaced or Romanising grey wares.
Description: Going,[61] Fawcett.[62] The fabric displays a variety of colours, hardness and range of inclusions. However, at Minerva the fabrics are fairly unified. The surfaces are either black, dark grey with a grey or brown core, often with orange or brownish margins. The main trait that all of the fabrics follow is the presence of grog, either common or sparse, though never to the extent of the grog tempered fabrics. It occurs alongside quartz and other subsidiary inclusions such as red iron ores or mica. Source: Local or regional. Date: Roman.

It is most common from the mid/late first to mid/late second century AD. The fabric continues to the end of the Roman period, but in drastically reduced numbers. In Hertfordshire[63] and Essex[64] the fabric generally replaces the late Iron Age style between the late first and early second century AD. Comments: No diagnostic sherds are noted in the fabric.

GRS   Unsourced sandy grey wares.
Description: Two fabric divisions are noticeable. The first is simply a basic quartz mix with no other notable inclusions. It is hard, sandy with a medium grey core and lighter surface, one sherd displays burnishing. The second is soft, fine in a medium grey colour (a coarser version is also present). The quartz is abundant and well sorted, it is distinguished by ill sorted, rounded and sparse black iron ore, frequently larger than the quartz. Sparse calcite is also noted. Source: Local or regional. Date: Roman. Comments: Only two sherds are diagnostic, although not beyond the point of basic form of jar or dish.

LNV RE   Lower Nene Valley reduced ware.
Description: Perrin.[65] This is a reduced version of the colour-coated fabric. The examples have a dark to medium grey surface colour with white margins, the core being thick, light grey, dark grey or off white. Source: Lower Nene Valley. Date: AD150 to late third / early fourth century AD. Comments: Two forms are noted, a flat rimmed bowl alongside a beaded and grooved dish.

HAR SH 1 and 2 Harrold shell tempered ware (early and late).
Description: Fawcett,[66] Tomber and Dore,[67] Tyers,[68] Brown.[69] Source: The best known kiln evidence for this industry is from Harrold, Bedfordshire, though the shell gritted industries of the Roman period are not well sourced or understood. In particular the ceramics that represent Harrold present a complicated picture. They seem to depict a wide regional trend, however with little kiln evidence to go on it is difficult to draw definite conclusions. Nevertheless there is a clear distinction in form and fabric from those produced up to the second century AD and those in the third and fourth century. The later period form range coincides with the major expansion of the shell gritted style that we associate with the Harrold industry. Due to the large number of variants in shell tempered fabrics that occur in this area during the Roman period,[70] and in particular the later centuries, it is more practical to use Harrold as an umbrella term. However, several of the fabrics listed as HAR SH appear to be true Harrold products. Date: Throughout the Roman period, although major expansion starts in the third century AD with the fourth century AD accounting for the largest output in growth. Comments: The best example on the site is from fill 1327 of possible pyre 1326. The jar is virtually complete although the upper half of the vessel

was detached at some point in antiquity (Fig. 39 No.1). It is decorated with a wide zone of riling between the base and shoulder, a typical Harrold style. However, the form is not typical of Harrold. The rim type has more in common with Bourne-Greetham products than the Bedfordshire industry. Nonetheless some of the less common jar types in the Harrold corpus hint at this style. This example may be a product of a kiln(s) yet to be discovered that are related to the Harrold industry.

UNS SH   Unsourced shell tempered ware.
Description: The first fabric is a fairly hard hand-made fabric. It has a sandy but also slightly soapy feel, especially on the surfaces. The break is hackley, the surface is fairly smooth, uneven and is red-brown with a dark grey and black core. The inclusions are generally ill sorted and consists of abundant shell (some up to 5 mm), common limestone, sparse quartz and red iron ore. Brown rounded grog is noted, however it is only easy to detect at the outer surface area. The second fabric is hard with a soapy feel. The surfaces are black with an orange brown core. The break is also hackley. This fabric is composed almost entirely of ill sorted shell and is at least wheel finished. The only other inclusions are sparse mica and black iron ores. Clay pellets/grog are hard to detect but are present. The fabric does seem to share some similarities with the Bourne-Greetham fabrics. Source: Local. Date: Without diagnostic examples it is always difficult to suggest accurate dates. However, the general make-up of the fabrics suggests a transitional or early Roman date. Furthermore the fabrics do equate to those identified at Orton Hall Farm as transitional and early.[71] Comments: Only non-diagnostic sherds are present and some examples are no more than crumbs.

SOB GT   Southern British grog tempered ware.
Description: Thompson,[72] Tomber and Dore.[73] Source: Local. Date: This fabric (just two small and abraded sherds) continues from the late Iron Age (c. 20BC onwards) to the late first century AD (into the early second century on some rural sites). Comments: The fabric is not particularly common in this area of the country and Orton Hall Farm confirms this trend.[74] To the east, Cambridge is considered to be on the fringe of the distribution of this style whilst to the west the Northampton area seems to be the limit.[75]

Discussion

In total 232 sherds, weighing 2569 g, with a r.eve of 1.67 were recovered. Excluding storage jar fabrics (eight sherds at 453 g and a r.eve 0.24) the average sherd weight is 9.4g. Two contexts contained relatively large assemblages (Area B, possible pyre 1326 and quarry pit 1413), but still insufficient to merit quantification (although they are consistent in date see below).

Samian and other imports

The samian assemblage is negligible and, with the exception of one sherd, it was found in the topsoil. It is all small and very abraded (six sherds weighing 49 g). A base fragment belonging to the transitional plate/bowl form Drg18/31 is the only diagnostic sherd. No amphorae fabrics or other imports are present.

Romano-British finewares

Probably due to the close proximity of the Nene Valley industry, its products are the sole Romano-British fineware on the site (nineteen per cent by weight). There is only one truly diagnostic sherd within the assemblage. Later assemblages would not necessarily have contained other finewares (such as Oxfordshire red/brown slipped ware), as Peterborough is on the edge of their distribution area and presumably, the sites were well supplied by the local kilns. For instance Oxfordshire ware is recorded at the nearby site of Werrington (Cambridgeshire).[76] At Orton Hall Farm it is not until Period 5 (AD 375+) that Oxfordshire fabrics are recorded and then in very small quantities.[77] The status and function of a site might also influence the supply and quantity of this fabric.

Coarsewares

The coarseware assemblage is basic. GRS accounts for nineteen per cent by weight and shell tempered wares sixty-four per cent. The majority of coarsewares are unsourced, although most are probably local. If one accepts that the HAR SH sherds may have been produced closer to Peterborough, then the furthest travelled fabric is the Hadham oxidised ware. All of the HAD OX sherds, except one, belong to a late frilled jar form. A number of reduced fabrics from the Nene Valley industry are also present. The few forms represent a very limited range, just seven jar types, two dishes, a bowl and doubtful flagon (forty per cent of forms are only allocated a general class due to their small and abraded state).

Dating

Although the pottery spans the entire Roman period, the majority of pottery is late Roman. Possible Anglo-Saxon Pyre 1326 contained pottery dated from the third to fourth century AD a combination of LNV CC and HAR SH. The pottery is in good condition, however of the 126 sherds, 116 belong to a Harrold jar (Fig. 39 No. 1). Pit 1413 (A.17) contained a consistent range of Roman ceramics dated from AD 375 to 410 (see below). These are divided between HAD OX, LNV CC and HAR SH. The Hadham form joins with a sherd from pit 1415. Other features containing pottery of the same period are pit 1438 and hollow 1458. Although some minimal early Roman activity is recorded most appears to relate to the third and fourth centuries AD. In fact many of the features listed second to fourth century (due to the presence of non-diagnostic, long-lived wares) may also represent this period.

Oxidised or colour coated sherds account for twenty-five per cent of the assemblage. The majority of these are from single context features and the subsoil. Only pit 1413 contained a primary ceramic assemblage. The rest of the pottery is coarse and in poor condition, suggesting that its presence within Anglo-Saxon features is accidental. Nonetheless, curation of Roman pottery was noted at West Stow (Suffolk). Here, seventy-seven per cent of the assemblage comprised colour-coats with the majority of sherds being rims and bases.[78] There is no clear evidence for curation at Minerva, and no diagnostic Roman sherds were present in contexts of Anglo-Saxon date.

In conclusion it appears that Roman activity is mainly restricted to the late period and was found in possible Anglo-Saxon pyre 1326 and pit 1413. The limited form range and lack of both regional and continental imports tentatively suggests a fairly inward looking, rural assemblage. The lack of good ceramic groups means that definitive issues of status and function are beyond our reach.

Vessels From the Cremation and Inhumation Graves (Figs 40–42)

Berni Sudds

In total, thirty-three semi-complete or complete vessels were recovered from the evaluation and excavation at Alwalton (amounting to 1286 sherds weighing 28,675 g). The group is comprised primarily of vessels derived from cremation burials, although ceramic accessory containers were recovered from five inhumation graves. It should be noted, however, that the group is only likely to represent a sample of the whole cemetery that potentially lies beyond the area of excavation. Indeed, three contemporary cremation burials were discovered just 700 yards to the south-west in 1975, at least nine in the vicinity of Woodston and Fletton and twenty-two at Longthorpe approximately three miles to the north-east.[79]

Medieval ploughing, and to a lesser extent, machine stripping, have truncated most of the vessels to varying degrees but where undisturbed, the condition of the pottery is excellent. Some of the more severely damaged examples have only the lower half of the vessel remaining and the majority have lost at least some of the neck or rim. Indeed, a r.eve of just 4.47 was recorded for all thirty-three funerary vessels. Fortunately, enough of the rim survives, often having collapsed inside of the vessel, to allow a complete profile to be reconstructed.

Fabrics

As the vessels are handmade and consequently highly variable, they have been divided into very broad fabric groups based upon major inclusion type.

Table 3. Summary of vessels

Vessel	Type	Fabric	Form	Profile	Size	Deco	Sex	Age
1001	–	ESLDM	Jar	Biconical	Very small	P	–	–
1011	CRM	ESQ	Jar	Biconical	Large	P	M	A
1021	CRM	ESQGRN	Jar	Sub-biconical	Large	P	–	A
1029	IH	ESQL	–	Sub-biconical	Medium	LB	–	J
1032	IH	ESQL	Shallow bowl	Splay-sided	Very small	P	M	A
1035	CRM	ESQL	Jar	Biconical	Very large	LD	F*	A
1244	CRM	ESQL	Jar	–	Large	LB	–	A
1248	CRM	ESQL	*Schalenurne*	Biconical	Medium	L	–	J
1254	CRM	ESQL	Jar	Globular	Large	LS	–	A
1257	CRM	ESQL	Jar	Sub-biconical	Medium	P	–	I
1260	CRM	ESQGRN	Jar	–	Medium	L	–	I
1266	CRM	ESQL	–	Biconical	Medium	LBS	–	J
1271	CRM	ESQO	Squat jar	Biconical	Large	LS	–	A
1274	CRM	ESQL	Jar	Biconical	Large	LS	F*	A
1279	CRM	ESQGRN	–	–	–	LB	–	J
1282	CRM	ESQL	Jar	Shouldered	Large	LBS	F*	A
1285	CRM	ESQL	Squat jar	Shouldered	Large	LS	M*	A
1288	CRM	ESQL	Jar	Sub-biconical	Medium	LBS	–	J
1293	CRM	ESQL	Jar	Shouldered	Medium	LB	–	I
1296	CRM	ESQL	Jar	Shouldered	Large	LBD	M	A
1299	CRM	ESQL	–	Sub-biconical	Large	L	–	A
1302	CRM	ESQL	Jar	Sub-biconical	Very large	–	–	A
1307	CRM	ESSIRL	*Schalenurne*	Biconical	Medium	L	F*	J
1310	CRM	ESQO	Jar	Sub-biconical	Medium	LBD	–	J
1318	CRM	ESQGRN	Jar	Biconical	Small	P	–	A
1324	CRM	ESFQ	–	–	–	–	–	A
1328	CRM	ESFQO	–	–	Small	–	M	A
1331	CRM	ESQL	Jar	Sub-globular	Large	P	–	A
1348	CRM	ESQL	Jar	Shouldered	Large	LS	–	A
1419	CRM	ESL	Medium bowl	Hemispherical	Small	P	–	J
1422	CRM	?ESQ	–	Globular	Small	–	–	–
1428	IH	ESFQ	–	–	Very small	LBS	M	A
1463	IH	ESL	Shallow bowl	Hemispherical	Very small	P	F	A
1466	IH	ESORG	Deep bowl	Straight-sided	Medium	P	F	A

Key – CRM / IH: Inhumation / L: Line / LB: Line and boss / LBD: Line, boss and dot / LS: Line and stamp / LBS: Line, boss and stamp / P: Plain / M: Male / F: Female *Sex implied by grave goods / I: Infant (0–4 years) / J: Juvenile (5–14 years) / A: Adult (15+)

ESQ Abundant coarsely crushed quartzite/ meta-quartzite up to 2 mm. Rare siltstone up to 8 mm.

ESQL Abundant coarsely crushed quartzite/ meta-quartzite up to 2 mm, occasional to moderate calcareous (shelly limestone) inclusions up to 2.5 mm and occasional to moderate organics (chaff). Rare red and black iron ore.

ESQGRN Abundant coarsely crushed quartzite/ meta-quartzite and occasional to moderate granite both up to 2 mm (rarely up to 3 mm). Most examples in this group also contain occasional to moderate dark mica and organics (chaff), rare calcareous (shelly limestone) inclusions up to 3 mm and rare iron ore.

ESQO Abundant coarsely crushed quartzite/ meta-quartzite up to 2 mm, moderate oolitic limestone and ooliths up to 1 mm, occasional organics (chaff) and rare feldspar up to 3 mm.

ESFQ Abundant finely crushed quartzite/ meta-quartzite and calcareous (shelly limestone) inclusions both up to 0.75 mm. Rare organics (chaff).

ESFQO   Abundant finely crushed quartzite/ meta-quartzite up to 1 mm and moderate organic (chaff) inclusions.

ESSIRL   Abundant rounded clear, white and iron-stained quartz up to 0.5 mm (occasionally up to 1 mm), moderate calcareous (shelly limestone) inclusions up to 1.5 mm, occasional red iron ore up to 1 mm and rare organics (chaff).

ESORG   Abundant elongated voids left from burnt out/ leached organics, probably chaff. Occasional calcareous inclusions.

ESL   Abundant crushed shelly limestone up to 4.5 mm. The limestone includes many well-rounded fragments mostly up to 0.5 mm. Some appear to have the concentric structure of ooliths. Rare to moderate quartzite up to 1 mm and rare organics.

ESLDM   As above but also containing occasional dark mica.

ESST*   Crushed sandstone tempered fabric. Moderate sandstone up to 3 mm and abundant sand up to 0.2 mm. Occasional to moderate shelly limestone up to 4 mm, red iron ore up to 2.5 mm and quartz/ quartzite up to 1 mm.

ESIRN*   Abundant sub-rounded to angular red iron ore up to 1.5 mm, moderate calcareous inclusions (shelly limestone) up to 3 mm and occasional rounded to sub-rounded clear, white and iron-stained quartz up to 0.5 mm.

Fabrics not encountered in-situ as cremation vessels but likely disturbed from other burials in the vicinity.

Provenance

In attempting to address broader issues of vessel production and trade little can be concluded with any authority. The mechanisms of production and exchange of ceramics in the early Anglo-Saxon period are poorly understood. Nonetheless the vessels from Alwalton do fall into distinctive groups which can be paralleled both more locally and further afield, indicating trade or cultural links with the east and north Midlands.

In composition the assemblage demonstrates close affinities to those from settlement and cemeteries immediately to the east at Orton Hall Farm, Peterborough, to the west at various sites in the vicinity of Rutland Water and in the Nene Valley in general.[80] The most frequently identified fabric is dominated by crushed quartzite in varying degrees of coarseness, often with moderate calcareous inclusions; probably shelly limestone. Granitic tempered vessels, also containing crushed quartzite, form the second largest group, with a few oolitic limestone, sandstone, quartz sand, ironstone and organic tempered vessels accounting for the remainder of the assemblage.

The vessels that contain shelly limestone, and certainly those containing ooliths, are likely to originate from further up the Nene Valley into Northamptonshire where the Jurassic limestone and oolite series outcrop

(Hunter 1979). It is possible these vessels were manufactured in the upper Nene valley and traded down river, although more localised production cannot be entirely ruled out. Indeed, an oolitic limestone tempered fabric is known to have been produced at Oundle (Northamptonshire) located some eight miles further up the river that may provide a possible source for examples at Alwalton.[81] The few ironstone and sandstone tempered fabrics identified may also find a source local to Northampton or more broadly within the east Midlands.[82]

The granitic tempered group includes a small number of sub-groups, perhaps indicating more than one provenance. Those containing igneous inclusions and biotite or dark mica (vessels 1021, 1279, 1318) are likely to derive from an area around the Mountsorrel granodiorite in the Charnwood Forest region of north Leicestershire.[83] Other examples, including vessel 1260, contain occasional to moderate granite but in addition to abundant organic inclusions or increased quantities of limestone. These, however, could represent examples of the Charnwood and chaff fabric also identified in the region.[84]

Products attributed to the Charnwood area are found all over the midlands and eastern England. Indeed, they have been recovered in some number further to the south of Cambridgeshire at Godmanchester and Gamlingay.[85] As closer to Leicestershire, although still at a significant distance, it is unsurprising to find products from this region at Alwalton. The distribution of Charnwood Forest-type wares has formed the focus of some debate, principally focusing on how or why this fabric in particular should be found over such a broad area.[86] One suggestion, given the incidence of large cremation cemeteries in the area where the fabric is found, is that the vessels could have been exchanged and distributed at religious gatherings.[87]

It is clear, however, when viewed in contrast to contemporary assemblages from further south and east that Alwalton falls within a distinct fabric tradition with close links to both the west and north.[88] As early as the fifth- or sixth-century the ceramic tradition in Nene Valley not only included extensive trade in local types from south Lincolnshire to south Northamptonshire, but also regional exchange with Leicestershire.[89]

Dating

In the years since the publication of Myres's extensive typology of early Anglo-Saxon pottery in 1977 it has become increasingly apparent that it is dangerous to ascribe precise dating to vessels or establish a chronology solely on the basis of decoration or form.[90] Many of the fifth century forms and decorative styles, in particular, can now be seen to extend into the sixth century and beyond.[91] Myres indicated himself that although chronological development in decoration can be observed, falling under three general stylistic groups (line, plastic or boss and stamp), each can be found throughout period of settlement.[92] Changes in style are proportional rather than absolute and dating individual vessels can be problematic.[93] Nonetheless, through decoration, parallel and importantly, associated finds it has been possible to narrow the dates for a number of the funerary vessels.

The 'line and groove' and 'line and dot' decoration attributed by Myres to the fifth and possibly early sixth century, primarily of Anglian affiliation, is largely confirmed by evidence from a number of settlement and cemetery sites.[94]

The simple horizontal decoration and squat *Schalenurne* profile of vessel 1307 may suggest it represents one of the earliest recovered (Fig. 40).[95] An early date is derived from the appearance of similar vessels in the final phase of occupation at Feddersen Wierde, pre-dating AD 450. This represents the end date of site, however, and not necessarily the pottery style, so a broad fifth century date remains possible.[96] The large sub-biconical urn 1299 (Fig. 40) is decorated above the carination with massed diagonal slashes below well-defined horizontal linear grooves. This is also a style paralleled by Myres to the fifth century but may continue into the early sixth.[97]

The simple chevron and dot design of the very large biconical jar 1035 (Fig. 40) is also likely to be early. This example may represent a combination of the styles outlined on Myres figs 285, 286 and 288 depicting vessels with single dots, triangles of three dots and finger-tip rosettes between the chevrons, all thought to be early in the decorative series.[98] The double-sided Romano-British antler comb (Fig. 31) found within the vessel substantiates a date during the first half of the fifth-century (see Grave and Pyre Goods from the Cremation Burials below). The use of chevron and rosettes or simple dots is rare in England but parallels can be found at Spong Hill (Norfolk) where associated with a fifth-century Frisian comb[99] and at Thurmaston (Leicestershire).[100] A footed base further corroborates the fifth century date of this vessel.[101]

Vertical, horizontal and diagonal grooves decorate the upper part of vessel 1260 but too little survives to securely determine the style represented. From associated finds simple chevron designs are known to be common to the fifth century although they were still in use in the sixth (Figs 33 and 40).[102] Similarly, vessel 1328 was accompanied by a triangular comb with a decoratively shaped edge probably dating to the fifth century (Fig. 36). As only the lower half of the vessel survives any decoration that may have been present is now missing.

Vessels with plastic or boss decoration represent the second major group identified by Myres and were thought to be most popular during, although not restricted to, the late fifth century.[103] Bosses do occur on plain vessels but are more commonly found in conjunction with other types of decoration, predominantly line but also stamp, which can influence their dating. Indeed, at Mucking bossed pottery was found in fifth- and sixth-century areas of the settlement.[104]

Three of the cremation vessels and one inhumation accessory vessel are all line and boss (or hollow) decorated in a similar arrangement (nos. 1029; 1244; 1248; 1279 – Figs 40–41). Pairs, groups or massed vertical lines demarcate, or extend over (in the case of vessel 1279), spaced linear bosses or hollows. The latter extend over the carination or maximum girth of the vessel and often extend from a horizontal linear zone of decoration above (1029; 1248). This style is typically Anglian in influence and is thought to date primarily to the fifth century although the evidence at Alwalton is a little more mixed.[105]

Vessel 1279 was deposited with a triangular comb with a decoratively cut edge dating to the fifth century and both vessels 1029 and 1248 have squat profiles, further indicating an early date. Vessel 1248 particularly resembles the rounded *Schalenurne* profile commonly dated to the second half of the fifth century but was found in association with a long brooch dating to the early sixth century.[106] Vessel 1244 is less diagnostic and could date from the fifth to early sixth century. The distribution of line and boss decorated vessels is suggested to have been primarily focused on Norfolk and the lower Trent Valley of Lincolnshire and East Yorkshire but similar examples are evident locally at the Longthorpe cemetery, dated to the fifth century, and to the west at Thurmaston.[107]

No direct parallel can be found for the elaborately decorated cremation vessel 1310 but it would appear to fall under the *Buckelurnen* group identified by Myres (Figs 36 and 40).[108] Only the lower two thirds remain but the vessel is decorated with at least two zones of chevron and dot decoration and at least two types of decorated boss, one linear and one circular. The vessel, therefore, falls under Group II, dated with the majority of other *Buckelurnen* in Britain to the second half of the fifth century.[109] Group I and II examples can, however, date into the early sixth century and the decorated bosses on the Alwalton vessel resemble Group V variants from Girton and Little Wilbraham (Cambridgeshire) also dated to the sixth century.[110]

The large shoulder boss jar 1296 with a tall neck and footstand base is also likely to date to the latter part of the fifth century although a date into the early sixth century cannot be ruled out. Shoulder boss urns are characteristic of the late fifth and early sixth century and the line, boss and dot decoration would be in keeping with this date.[111] This vessel is perhaps the most competently made and decorated of the entire group with a very even wall thickness and regular finish. The hone stone accompanying the cremation compares favourably with a late fifth century example from the cemetery at Great Chesterford (Essex) (Fig. 35).[112] A similar example was recovered from Little Wilbraham.[113] The remaining bossed vessel, cremation 1293, is a medium shouldered jar with irregular and poorly executed decoration (Figs 34 and 40). As shoulder bossed and line and stab decorated this is likely to date from the late fifth to early sixth century.

The final stylistic group isolated by Myres is re-presented by vessels incorporating stamped decoration. Again, as evident with bossed vessels, the combination of decorative elements used will influence dating but, as corroborated at Mucking (Essex), there is a marked increase in the use of stamps during the sixth and seventh centuries.[114]

A mid to late fifth-century date is conceivable for the large shouldered jar 1348 (Fig. 41) but a date into the sixth century cannot be excluded. The vessel is line, boss and stamp decorated, possibly in the *stehende Bogen* (standing arches) or hybrid *stehende* and *hangende Bogen* (hanging arches) style as seen on vessels from Rothley (Leicestershire) and Elkington (Lincolnshire).[115] Vessels with a combination of line, boss and a limited number of stamps identified to the east of Alwalton, at Orton Hall Farm, were also dated into the early sixth century.[116] Accessory vessel 1428 (Fig. 41) similarly combines line, boss and simple stamp decoration but is more firmly dated to the early sixth century through parallel to a similar example from Loveden Hill and association with a Swanton F1–type spear.[117]

Biconical jar 1271 is fairly unusual with line and stamp decoration in a pendant-cross design (Figs 33 and 42). A single, multiple circle, stamp has been used. Unenclosed pendant-triangle schemes are generally dated to the sixth century although have been seen on late fifth century vessels.[118] The example from Alwalton has a cross as opposed to a triangular design but the hollow neck and use of just one stamp may suggest a date around the turn of the century or in the early half of the sixth.

Vessel 1274 (Figs 33 and 41) is decorated above the carination with a single panel of enclosed chevrons entirely filled with a single gridded rectangular stamp. This type of enclosed zone decoration, in conjunction with the use of multiple stamp dies developed during the sixth century.[119] As with vessel 1271, however, the biconical form, pedestal base and use of a just one stamp may indicate the vessel dates from as early as the late fifth century, although restrained stamping can be a particular feature of the early sixth century.[120]

The enclosed horizontal stamped zones that appear on cremation vessels 1282 (Fig. 41), 1285 and 1254 (Fig. 42) generally date to the sixth century.[121] It is difficult to find a parallel for the bossed stamped panel decoration of vessel 1282. The preponderance of bosses, use of multiple stamps and panel arrangement are features commonly found during the sixth century, a date confirmed by the associated cruciform brooch.[122]

Vessels 1285 and 1266, although the latter does not incorporate an enclosed horizontal stamped zone, are decorated with stamped pendant triangles (Fig. 42). Few continental parallels can be determined for this style and it has been suggested the scheme represents an indigenous development to England during the sixth century.[123] Associated finds from a number of regional sites corroborate this date.[124] It is possible, although by

no means certain, that the angular, shouldered profile of vessel 1285 (Figs 34 and 42) indicates a date earlier within this range.[125]

Using a similar but increased range of stamps to vessel 1285, vessel 1254 (Fig. 42) is decorated with a stamped chevron design also dated to the sixth century.[126] The rounded form would verify a later date but the recovery of an early double-sided comb is problematic unless it represents an heirloom or 'curated' item (see Grave and Pyre Goods from the Cremation Burials below).

Stamped pendant triangles also decorate vessel 1288 (Fig. 42) but they are unenclosed and separated by seven equally spaced bosses. Examples with no linear ornament are potentially late in the typological series.[127] Un-enclosed stamped pendant triangles appear on a vessel at Great Chesterford dated to the second half of the sixth century by an associated brooch.[128] Unlike 1288, however, the vessel is unbossed and globular in form. Unenclosed triangles of dots are seen at beginning of period, however, and the substitution of these with stamps may have occurred earlier in the sixth century as stamped decoration became more popular.[129]

The vessel from the subsoil (1001) and cremation urns 1318, 1011, 1302, 1257 and 1021 are plain with biconical or sub-biconical profiles (Fig. 41). They are consequently difficult to date precisely. In the absence of datable small finds, a date from the fifth to sixth centuries, and potentially beyond remains possible although the hollowed necks of vessel 1318 and the example from L1001 may indicate a date earlier in this range. Vessel 1331, a wide-mouthed, sub-globular jar with an asymmetrical profile, can also be only broadly dated from the fifth to sixth centuries (Fig. 41).

A sixth-century date is tentatively suggested for a group of four plain hemispherical, straight and splay sided bowls.[130] The first three are accessory vessels within inhumation graves (1466 – Figs 29 and 42; 1032 – Figs 12 and 42; 1463 – Figs 29 and 42) and the fourth from a small cremation (1419 – Fig. 42). The 'rectangular' shaped bowl 1466 is very crudely made and finished in particular contrast to the other accessory vessels. The chaff-tempered fabric of this vessel would substantiate a sixth century date, when this fabric became more prevalent.[131]

Chronology, distribution and vessel selection

The transition from cremation to inhumation remains an imperfectly understood aspect of early Anglo-Saxon burial practice although it is observed that it is generally a chronological process and that there is often a considerable degree of overlap between the two methods. In Cambridgeshire, however, it has been argued that there is no consistent difference in date or status between the rites, but rather that they reflect cultural distinctions.[132] In this way the east of the county reveals greater affinities with the East Anglian tradition of cremation and the west with the Saxon rite of inhumation.[133] The location of Alwalton, on a rather ambiguous boundary between cultural groups, may indeed explain why mixed rite burial is evident within the cemetery but ultimately the transition to inhumation should be seen as a chronological phenomenon, with 'Germanic' communities beginning to assume elements of British culture.[134]

The presence of contemporary cremation and inhumation at Alwalton complicates any discussion of chronology and the small sample of burials and relatively short use of the cemetery prevent the observation of any significant patterns. Nonetheless, it is apparent that both cremation and inhumation were in evidence at Alwalton from the fifth century. Furthermore, there appear to be a greater proportion of cremations to inhumations during the fifth century with a reversal of this trend during the sixth century. In the area excavated all but one of the accessory vessels appear in inhumations dated to the sixth century. This may indicate that mixed cultural groups were using the cemetery from the outset but that the proportional increase in inhumation, paralleled across the region, represents the gradual disappearance of strictly 'Gemanic' rites.[135] It is certainly evident that cemeteries in the vicinity of Alwalton but founded later, such as Wakerley (Northamptonshire), predominantly favour inhumation.[136]

There appears to be no obvious chronological distribution of the dated vessels across the site. The apparent grouping of cremations to east and west may thus reflect social affiliations. The cluster to the east are all plain whilst those to the west are predominantly decorated. The percentage of decorated vessels in early Anglo-Saxon assemblages does appear to decrease during sixth and seventh centuries but the division at Alwalton is not chronological with contemporary sixth-century cremations represented in both groups.[137] Gender could not be determined for the majority of the small group to the east but, in keeping with the rest of the cemetery, both adults and juveniles were identified, potentially representing a separate family or kin group.

The extent to which vessels used in cremation cemeteries were drawn from domestic stock or specifically made for burial remains largely unclear.[138] The same fabrics have been encountered both within cemeteries and settlements, but this does not necessarily rule out the existence of targeted production. Cremation vessels can generally be demonstrated to be larger than domestic vessels and a far higher proportion are decorated than is observed in settlement assemblages.[139] A greater level of care and skill can also be evidenced in production of most funerary vessels.

An apparent distinction between household or domestic and ceremonial production has been recognised by Brisbane.[140] Chaff-tempered pottery rarely appears in funerary contexts but became increasingly popular in domestic assemblages as the early Anglo-Saxon period progressed.[141] The absence of chaff-tempered cremation

vessels could in part be explained by the simultaneous decrease in cremation burial, in favour of inhumation, at exactly the time chaff-tempered fabrics began to dominate assemblages. If this were the case, however, more chaff-temper might be expected in sixth-century cremations than is apparent. A more fundamental reason has been suggested, however. As often simply constructed and incorporating the agricultural by-product of dung, chaff-tempered pottery was likely produced by occupants of a settlement or household for domestic use.[142] This may also be true for the single ironstone vessel recovered. Although not directly related to a burial the general absence of this fabric may verify a later date as indicated elsewhere, or like the chaff-tempered ware that it was generally not selected for funerary use.[143]

The different spatial groupings of the burials at Alwalton may highlight, for whatever reason, that at least two levels of production and vessel selection were taking place. The urns clustered to the west of site are generally larger, with a greater proportion finely finished and decorated than encountered in contemporary settlement assemblages elsewhere in Cambridgeshire.[144] Although deposited at same time the majority of the vessels interred to the east of the cemetery are simple plain forms, including the only chaff-tempered example recovered, and would not be out of place in a domestic context. Furthermore, no other grave-goods were recovered, from either the cremations or inhumations to the east, yet those to the west were relatively well adorned.

It is tempting to suggest that this dichotomy may reflect the varying affluence or status of different groups within a single settlement or between different settlements using the cemetery. Vessels may have been specifically made or acquired for many of the individuals buried to the west of site, whereas to the east they are perhaps more likely to have been selected from what was available in the settlement or household. Certainly, the re-use of pottery in the cemetery appears to be indicated by the presence of a vessel repaired with a lead plug, although the latter cannot be directly attributed to a burial (Fig. 42).

There would also appear to be some symbolism behind the selection of vessels at Alwalton. Detailed quantification and analysis of funerary assemblages has revealed certain significant correlations between the pottery vessel used in a burial and the individual buried.[145] The shape of the vessel, for example can correlate with the sex of the individual or the patterning on the urn.[146] The size of the cremation vessel can also correspond to the age of the individual cremated and to some extent the gender.[147]

Despite the relatively small number recovered it can be argued that the age of the deceased and the size of the vessel are linked at Alwalton, with adults predominantly interred in large vessels and infants and juveniles contained within small or medium urns (Table 4). A link between the age of the individual and the size of the vessel used was also identified at Spong Hill within the cremations and at Wakerley with the accessory vessels of inhumations.[148]

Within the adult burials at Spong Hill, however, there appeared to be no correlation between quantity of bone collected and either sex or age but it was apparent that the urns were rarely filled to capacity, probably indicating the size of vessel was symbolic rather than purely practical.[149] Very few of the cremations at Alwalton could be assigned a gender but where identified adult males were associated with large vessels and adult females with medium and large urns. With such a small sample no secure correlation could be determined between the decoration of vessels and either age or gender.

Vessel groupings, possibly indicating family or kin groups, have been identified within the western cluster of cremations, primarily through grave-goods. The significance of this is discussed elsewhere but it is worth noting that these links are not necessarily compatible with the grouping of vessels suggested by the use or combination of similar stamps, namely 1266, 1254, and 1285. These three vessels are near neighbours within the western group and of a similar date, perhaps suggesting they represent members of same social or settlement group as opposed to the same family (as intimated through the grave-goods).

In keeping with fabric, the decoration of the vessels at Alwalton and the Peterborough vicinity, can be more readily affiliated with the north and west, namely Northamptonshire, Leicestershire, Lincolnshire and Nottinghamshire, with a lesser but apparent connection to East Anglia and Cambridgeshire (see catalogue (Appendix 3) for individual parallels).[150]

The presence of a re-fired fragment of pottery within vessel 1282 may indicate the presence of food, drink or some other organic based material as a pyre offering for this cremation.[151] As pyre sites were often re-used, however, it may have accidentally been collected.

Illustrations of pottery not directly associated with inhumations or cremations

Fig. 40.6. 1001/1029: Fragmented medium sub-biconical vessel found adjacent to grave [1029]. Black fabric and surfaces. Burnished. Anglian style – Myres 1977, Figs 218/9, 220, 223/4/5; Hills, Penn and Rickett 1987, Fig. 25.2422; Evison 1994, 20.

Fig. 41.2 1001: Very small plain biconical jar with an upright rim. Dark grey to black fabric with a dark grey-brown to black surface. Burnished. Myres 1977, Fig.10.

Fig. 41.4 1011: Large plain biconical jar with a concave base and slightly everted rim. Largely dark grey throughout with occasional light grey-buff and light grey external fuming. Burnished. Myres 1977, Fig. 2.3250 (Loveden Hill, Lincolnshire).

Fig. 42.12 U/S: Dark grey fabric with dark grey to black surfaces. Burnished. Repaired with a lead plug.

Fig. 42.13 1438: MAX; Slightly flaring pierced lug. Black fabric with pinkish-buff surfaces. Smoothed.

Grave and Pyre Goods from the Cremation Burials

Nina Crummy

The small finds have been divided into three groups: grave goods from the cremations, grave goods from the inhumations, and other site finds. The division by burial rite allows major differences to be discerned in patterns of deposition, for example the marked preference for depositing a comb, or a token fragment of a comb, with a cremation, and the complete absence of combs from inhumations.

The inhumation graves range in date from the first half of the fifth century to the late sixth or early seventh, giving a minimum period of use from *c.* 440 to *c.* 600 AD. The cremations date between the early fifth and late sixth centuries. This is interesting since they demonstrate not only a spatial, but also considerable chronological overlap with the inhumation burials.

Though a degree of economic status is exhibited by two cremation graves, one of a male containing a toilet set (cremation 1296, Fig. 35), the other of a female containing an ivory bag hoop (cremation 1274, Fig. 33), the overall impression given by the cremation assemblage superficially is not one of wealth (Table 5). In contrast, several of the inhumations suggest that the deceased enjoyed a degree of status, and in some cases, real economic wealth. However, more cremations than inhumations contained deposits (seventy per cent as opposed to forty-one per cent). Thus, any observed distinction given by the grave goods between the two rites can only be an impression, many objects having been wholly destroyed on the pyres, as evidenced by a few pieces of refrozen metal recovered from some cremations.

Table 4. Correlation between vessel size and age for cremation burials (excludes accessory vessels within inhumations)

Age	Small	Medium	Large	Very large
Up to 4 years		3		
Juvenile (5 – 14 years)	1	5		
Adult (15+ years)	2		12	2

Grave goods from the cremation burials

Nineteen of the twenty-seven urned cremation graves contained deposits (seventy per cent), ranging from brooches burnt on the pyre, to fragments of combs deposited as 'token' representations of complete items, to a man's toilet set, shears, razor, and hone.

Table 5 shows that among the grave deposits, combs and comb fragments predominated, and were deposited in sixteen graves. This amounts to fifty-nine per cent of the total number of graves and eighty-four per cent of graves with deposits. The consistency provides a base line for comparison with deposit practice within the Alwalton cemetery and in other cremation cemeteries both in the immediate area and in the wider region.

All but one of the cremations containing a comb lay in the main cluster on the western side of the excavated area. The exception is cremation 1328, which is one of three cremations located to the north-west of the main inhumation group (Fig. 7).

Two of the sixteen 'comb' cremations contained complete double-sided combs. One is a Romano-British form (that from cremation 1035, Fig. 31), while the other is a form that occurs in both late Roman Britain and in Anglian cemeteries. Both were in the main cremation cluster, in adjacent graves on its southern edge (cremations 1035 and 1254). This proximity is

unlikely to be accidental and allows a strong argument to be put forward for considering these two graves as members of one family, as well as reasonably close in date (Fig. 9). A third nearly complete double-sided comb, of regular straight-ended Anglo-Saxon form, came from a slight outlier to the north of the main cluster (cremation 1244), and two straight-ended end-plate fragments came from neighbouring grave pits on the north of the group (cremation 1285, Fig. 34; cremation 1302, Fig. 36). These graves too may be closely associated, with that containing the complete comb probably pre-dating those with only token fragments.

The rest of the comb deposits were token corner fragments from triangular combs, possibly ubiquitous enough to be considered a community practice rather than that of close relations, but another potential family can be detected in the small sub-cluster of three (cremations 1296, 1307 and 1310) to the south of the main cremation group (Fig. 9). All three contained a corner fragment from a triangular comb and, while combs could be deposited in both male and female graves, two of these three may be sexed by the deposit of specific gender related items. However, it should be noted that cremation grave and pyre goods are often more ambiguous in meaning by nature. Several archaeologists have demonstrated a much weaker link between gender and grave good association in cremation assemblages as

Table 5. Grave goods from urned cremations

Grave	Brooch	Bead	Comb	Tweezers	Toilet set	Bag fitting	Spindle–whorl	Nail	Melted copper alloy
1011			X						
1035		X	X						
1244			X						
1248	X		X						
1254			X						X
1260			X						
1266			X						
1271									X
1274		X	X			X			X
1279			X						X
1282	X								
1285			X	X					
1293			X						
1296			X		X				
1299				X				X	
1302			X					X	
1307			X				X		
1310			X					X	
1328			X					X	

Some miscellaneous items have not been included.

opposed to inhumations.[152] In spite of this, these analyses have upheld a few specific links between sex and artefact (in particular brooches).

Four cremations contained goods that have a stronger link with sex. One contained a male toilet set consisting of shears, razor and hone, a very rare deposit in itself, and this individual was also marked out as of some importance within the community by a possible structure erected above the cremation pit (cremation 1296, Fig. 35). The other held a spindlewhorl, a typically female deposit (cremation 1307, Fig. 36). One, possibly two, other females can be detected on the basis of grave goods. Cremation 1274 contained an ivory ring from a cloth bag of the type deposited in female inhumation graves (cremation 1274, Fig. 33). The contents of the bag have not survived, though a tiny droplet of refrozen copper alloy from an object melted on the pyre was also found in the grave, and a scorched bead may have come from either the bag or from a bead string. Cremation 1035, which also held the comb of Romano-British form, contained a fragment of a bead, and may also be female, although the possibility that the fragment may have come from a sword bead should be borne in mind (Fig. 31).

Within the region, no other cemetery appears to have emphasised the comb as an important funerary deposit to the same extent as Alwalton. Of about 300 cremations at Caistor-by-Norwich (Norfolk) only twenty-seven (nine per cent) contained combs, in Sancton Trench A only thirteen of approximately sixty-seven cremations (nineteen per cent), and only fifty out of 595 cremations from the 1976–7 season of excavations at Spong Hill (eight per cent). At these sites often only a single token fragment was deposited and burning was rare, and miniature comb tokens were also used.[153] Similarly, at Great Chesterford (Essex), only one cremation out of thirty three (three per cent) contained a comb fragment, the unburnt end of a double-sided comb, again probably a token deposit.[154]

Strong variation in the use of combs as deposits in early Migration Period cremation graves is likely to be the result of different family or community practices, but may also be a reflection of the availability of the combs themselves. Similarly, an interruption to comb supply or a diminution of an existing settlement assemblage is likely to have been the reason for the use of token fragments or miniature combs. The triangular combs predominating at Alwalton, Spong Hill and Caistor-by-Norwich are likely to be continental imports, perhaps in the main brought over during the Anglian migration or for some years afterwards through continuing trade links. Without the possibility of replacement, the deposit of a complete comb could be considered to be a form of conspicuous consumption beyond the means of the early settlements. The balance between preserving necessary personal equipment and meeting the exigent demands of religious practice could thus be met by the deposit of a single corner fragment from a comb, or by the manufacture of a simply-made miniature.

The other grave goods from Alwalton occur in insufficient numbers for worthwhile comparisons with the practice of other cemeteries to be made, but are of standard types. The toilet set (cremation 1296, Fig. 35) and tweezers (cremations 1285 and 1299, Fig. 34) are matched in many cremations at Spong Hill and Caistor-by-Norwich, though the inclusion of a hone with the shears and razor is rare.[155] Interestingly, many of the shears and razors at Caistor are miniatures.[156] Ivory rings from bag hoops also occur at both sites.[157]

The recovery of individual nails in early cremations is usually explained by assumptions that they are either residual or lone survivors from decayed or burnt grave deposits or (?house)-timbers used as pyre fuel. [158] However, comparison with Roman cremations, where bent and broken nails of many sizes among pyre debris can easily be seen as coming from reused timbers or pyre deposits (personal observation of at least 100 early and late Roman cremations at Colchester excavated in recent years), marks out the undamaged examples from Alwalton and other Anglo-Saxon sites as very different. They appear to be good quality examples deliberately selected for deposition (cremation 1299, Fig. 35) and must have had a significance that is now not immediately obvious. A connection to Thor the hammer god seems most likely, not only because a hammer was used both to produce and use nails, but also by comparison with the God's-nails driven into the pillars of Thorolf Most-Beard's high seat, set up in a temple he raised to Thor following his successful migration to Iceland.[159] Nails were also used in amuletic magic in the eighth century on the continent, and may have been considered generally beneficent because they were made of iron.[160]

Brooches

Both brooch fragments (cremations 1248 Fig. 32 and 1282 Fig. 34) have been burnt and can be presumed to have been worn by the deceased on the pyre. One is a small-long brooch, the other cruciform, and neither can be closely assigned to a type, though the rudimentary lappets on the cruciform brooch suggest it is a Mortimer Type D.[161] Both are probably early sixth century in date.

Beads

Two glass beads were recovered, one a scorched pyre deposit, the other only a fragment. The latter is not burnt and may be a token burial deposit similar to the corners of antler combs described above. This fragment, from cremation 1035 (Fig. 31), is a fragment of a green cylinder bead of Guido's Type 5iib, which, though concentrated in Kent, has a distribution along the east coast stretching as far north as County Durham.[162] It is possible that this example is of late Roman date. The type also occurs in late Roman graves[163] and here is accompanied in the grave by an antler comb of late Roman form. The blue glass annular bead from cremation 1274 (Fig. 33) is of Guido's Type 6i, a very common form throughout Anglo-Saxon England and possibly an indication of low status. [164]

Combs

All the combs are composite, five are double-sided and eleven triangular. Where the teeth survive, all show the beading characteristic of wear. On the smaller pieces from triangular combs this enables them to be identified as coming from used full-size, rather than miniature, examples.

Only one comb has been burnt, and is now a dark brown in colour (cremation 1302 Fig. 36). The remainder have been deposited as grave, rather than pyre, goods. Two of the double-sided combs are complete apart from some slight damage consistent with wear (cremation 1035, Fig. 31; cremation 1254, Fig. 32), and two are fragmentary, perhaps through wear or post-depositional decay (cremation 1244, Fig. 32; cremation 1285, Fig. 34), though the possibility of deliberate damage on deposition should be considered. The fifth double-sided fragment is a burnt end-plate (cremation 1302, Fig. 36). The eleven fragments from triangular combs all consist of a single piece broken from a corner, and this consistency of retrieval, coupled with the lack of burning, is a clear indication that in these graves a fragment has been deposited as a token representing the whole. This burial rite was also used at Caistor-by-Norwich and Spong Hill where many combs were recovered as small fragments only, often just a corner. Few of these combs were burnt, and token deposits were also made in the form of miniature combs. [165] The use of token deposits may be an indication of economic poverty. A corner fragment could be removed from a comb without preventing its future use. However, the symbolic connotations of these deposits should also be considered.

The comb from cremation 1035 (Fig. 31) is of late Roman double-sided form, and though small, is not miniature, but within the parameters of size for Roman combs. The end-plate design is found on combs from Winchester,[166] Poundbury,[167] and Colchester,[168] and the plain convex connecting-plates occur at Winchester,[169] Colchester[170] and Portchester.[171] Such combs fall within a date range of *c.* AD 365–410 in Britain, but the end date is conventional, rather than precise, and could be extended for some years further into the fifth century. This example may therefore simply have survived longer than most, or it may be a collected item, along with the many other Roman objects found deposited within Migration Period graves.[172]

The concave ends of the comb from cremation 1254 (Fig. 32) relate this example as well to late Roman combs, with a close parallel coming from Winchester.[173] However, the varying forms of its corners and the irregular spacing of its rivets (although the latter might be from a repair) suggest that this comb is not Romano-British. Similar combs, though with rather less concave ends, come from the Anglo-Saxon cemeteries of Spong Hill and Sancton.[174]

The three straight-ended double sided combs are of regular Anglian form, in use from the fifth to seventh centuries. There are no diagnostic features on the end-plate fragment from cremation 1302 (Fig. 36), but those from cremations 1244 (Fig. 32) and 1285 (Fig. 34) share characteristics with combs from Spong Hill, West Stow, and Empingham.[175]

Triangular combs also developed in the late fourth century and continued into the sixth. Those with decoratively carved edges are early in the series (cremation 1279, Fig. 34; cremation 1328, Fig. 36). The fragments of connecting-plates surviving on four of the pieces all have marginal parallel grooves, a common feature also found on combs from Spong Hill, West Stow, and Sancton.[176]

Tools and personal equipment
Tweezers
Sprung tweezers are generally identified as toilet instruments and in the early Anglo-Saxon period often form part of male toilet sets.[177] While the form changes little over time, those of the Anglo-Saxon period tend on the whole to be slightly longer and stouter than their Roman predecessors, and are more frequently found in iron as well as copper-alloy (cremation 1285, Fig. 34; cremation 1299, Fig. 35).

As well as being used for depilation, tweezers are also essential items in surgical kits, used for, among other things, pulling teeth and extracting splinters.[178] Neither of these uses is incompatible with the inclusion of tweezers in a male toilet set. Tweezers as single deposits were recovered from male graves at Great Chesterford,[179] from female graves at Empingham,[180] and from graves of both sexes at Edix Hill.[181] They cannot therefore be taken as secure indications of gender.

Toilet set
This suite of objects consisted of a piece of a triangular comb (see above), fragments from a possible razor, a pair of shears, and a hone for sharpening (cremation 1296, Fig. 35). The inclusion of the hone is unusual. The shears are small, suitable only for personal grooming rather than shearing or trimming cloth.[182] The form, with straight arms and simple bow, is well represented in the early Anglo-Saxon period[183] and is also found in the Iron Age and Roman periods.[184]

Two fragments of iron, one tanged, are probably from a razor (cremation 1296 Fig. 35.3). On the tanged fragment the blade curves sharply away from the line of the tang, implying a sickle-shaped object, which is echoed in the second fragment which terminates in a slight hook. On both the section is thicker on the inner side of the curve, with the edge outermost. This section, coupled with the strong blade curvature shown on the tanged piece and implied on the other, is highly idiosyncratic, but not incompatible with the hand/object movements used in shaving.

Several toilet sets with similar shears, some miniature,

were recovered from cremations at Caistor-by-Norwich and Spong Hill, usually associated with knives or razors, some of which are of similar form to the razor from this grave. The strong curve, hooked tip, and edge on the outer curve of the blade is found on knives/razors from Caistor-by-Norwich in graves X23, M43, and N56,[185] and on several examples from Spong Hill.[186]

The hone is small and well-made, and is quite well worn on the two narrow sides of its rectangular section (cremation 1296, Fig. 35.4). Greensand hones were produced in considerable quantities during the Roman period and had a wide-spread distribution throughout southern Britain. They also occur on pagan Anglo-Saxon sites such as West Stow and Sutton Courteney.[187] There is then a possibility that this may be a re-used Roman object, but the degree of wear is not excessive and need not be other than contemporary with the use of the shears and razor.

A fifth century grave at Great Chesterford held a similarly well-made hone together with items of Frankish origin, and the ceramic evidence from Cremation 1296 also suggests a fifth century date for the Alwalton grave, though late.[188] It has been suggested, in connection with the Sutton Hoo sceptre, that whetstones were associated with both royalty and the gods Odin and Thor, a connection that may be reinforced by the recovery of a hone in a late fifth-century child's grave at Sancton, which also contained iron shears and a pot decorated with swastikas – the symbol of the wheel of the sky-god.[189] This need not be taken to imply that either the Alwalton, Great Chesterford, or Sancton burials were those of even minor royalty, but could be an indication that in all three cases the people or their families held a degree of status within their communities.

Bag ring

A group of burnt and laminated elephant ivory fragments is all that remains of an ivory bag ring, used to provide a solid frame for the mouth of a cloth bag and to enable the bag to be attached to a belt (cremation 1274, Fig. 33.2). The only other objects from cremation 1274 are a scorched bead, a triangular comb fragment, and a pellet of resolidified copper-alloy from a burnt pyre deposit (Fig. 33). The sections of the fragments vary from rectangular to a low D-shape, and some pieces are narrower than others. The outer face on one large fragment is ridged. The narrower rounded fragments have been more heat-affected than those of rectangular section.

Similarly fragmented bag hoops are widely spread on the continent and in early Anglo-Saxon England, with a large proportion of those known recovered from cremations, as burning affects the ivory in such a way that it has a greater chance of survival than in an inhumation (though here see inhumation graves 1263, 1358 and 1364). The hoops, if not the bags themselves, have been linked to a trade in elephant ivory probably centred on the kingdom of Aksum, in Ethiopia, with the ivory either sourced locally, or from southern Africa, or from India.[190]

Spindlewhorl

This antler spindlewhorl is of simple form, with no decoration discernible where the original surface survives (cremation 1307, Fig. 36.2). Spindlewhorls of antler/bone, shale and recycled Roman pottery sherds have been found in cremations at *e.g.* Caistor-by-Norwich, Norfolk[191] and in inhumations at Burwell and Edix Hill, Cambridgeshire, and Empingham, Rutland.[192] A whorl from Woodstone, near Peterborough, is illustrated but its fabric not given.[193] Its shape suggests that it is probably shale.

The spindles used would have been made of wood, and the spindle hole diameter of this example falls near the centre of the range recorded for whorls of fired clay and recycled Roman sherds at Mucking, Essex,[194] West Stow, Suffolk[195] and Pennylands, Buckinghamshire.[196]

In inhumations spindlewhorls are specifically female items, and in cremations can be taken as indications of gender.

Tube

The purpose of this bone object is not certain (cremation 1254, Fig. 32). It is too fine and curved for use as a handle and bears no trace of any means of fixing a tang inside. It may perhaps be an amulet, the hollow centre seeming appropriate for suspension, but a possible interpretation for a curved bone tube, externally square, is as a needlecase.[197] However, Evison and Hill have offered another explanation, since their open ends makes them unsuitable for containing needles.[198] They suggested that they may have been a cosmetic aid, functioning as brushes. This tube may therefore represent the equivalent in bone of the sheet-metal copper-alloy brush holders dating from the late fifth into the mid or late sixth century.[199]

Miscellaneous iron objects

Neither arm of the iron clip from cremation 1285 is complete (Fig. 34.3), and originally both would have turned inwards, as with the clips from Caistor-by-Norwich,[200] Holywell Row, Suffolk, Little Wilbraham, Cambridgeshire, and Great Chesterford, Essex.[201] Often found in pairs, the function of these objects is not certain. Many retain traces of wood, and MacGregor and Bolick suggest that they were used to repair wooden vessels.[202] A pair were found with a maple vessel placed inside a bucket at Edix Hill.[203] However, the frequent, though not exclusive, association of pairs of these clips with the skull suggests that they may also have been used on some form of dress accessory.

Nails

Five nails came from four cremations (1299, Fig. 35; 1302, 1310 and 1328, Fig. 36). Most are complete or very nearly so, but only a fragment came from cremation 1328. None appears to have been burnt. This good state of preservation suggests that these nails are not individual survivors from otherwise decayed wooden objects, but grave deposits in their own rights.

At Great Chesterford, Essex, several cremations also

contained only one well-preserved nail, as did inhumations both there and at Edix Hill, Cambridgeshire, but at both sites it was assumed that they represented a destroyed or decayed wooden object.[204] However, it seems rather more likely that these nails were placed among the grave deposits with some specific meaning credited to them. Tokenism has already been demonstrated by the inclusion in some cremations of corners of combs rather than whole examples, and these nails too may therefore be tokens of a larger object, or perhaps of a degree of wealth in a society where iron would have considerable economic importance. A religous or amuletic purpose may also lie behind their deposition (see above).

Pyre Debris

Fragments of scorched or refrozen melted copper-alloy came from four cremations (1254, 1271, 1274 and 1279). The fittings from cremation 1271 (Fig. 33) may be from a belt-suite.

Grave goods from the inhumations

Thirty-three skeletons were excavated, of which thirteen, possibly fourteen, were accompanied by grave goods (forty-one to forty-four per cent; see Table 6 below). A fragment of an iron strip from grave 1440 is unlikely to be a deliberate deposit, though its position adjacent to the right hip suggests that it might (Fig. 28). It is included in this section as deriving from an inhumation whether or not it was deliberately placed there. It may perhaps have been a token deposit as fragments of combs were in many of the cremations.

The deposits range from single items, such as the knife in grave 1379 (Fig. 26), to full suites of jewellery with a girdle group as in grave 1364 (Figs 22–24). This range allows some assumptions about economic status to be made, as do some specific items.

Grave 1394, dated to the fifth century by a buckle of Hawkes and Dunning's Type IIIb, contained two awls with bone handles, and possibly a third with a wooden handle (Fig. 27). This early grave may be that of a leatherworker, and a long, well-sharpened knife in the grave might also be a craft tool. The deposit points to the importance credited to leatherworking, which is also shown by a grave containing three awls at Buckland, Dover, Kent.[205]

Similarly, the shield in grave 1366 (Fig. 25) and the spear in grave 1428 (Fig. 28) both occur in burials of males aged forty-five years or more, who can be presumed to have attained a certain status within their community, and their age conforms to the broad rule that single weapon graves denote males below the age of eighteen and above that of forty.[206] The Alwalton assemblage has markedly few weapon graves, as well as an absence of multiple weapon graves, falling well below the East Anglian average of fifty to sixty-five per cent noted by Härke.[207] However, the clustering of weapon graves noted

at both Edix Hill and Empingham suggests that the low number at Alwalton may simply mean that they lay in an area that was not threatened by development.[208] Several single weapon graves at Edix Hill lay on the periphery of a shield plus spear group and, as graves 1366 and 1428 both lay in the south-west corner of the site, it is possible that a concentration of double weapon graves lies beyond them.

Among the female graves, status is much clearer. Three are clearly of high status, with one, grave 1263, being particularly richly-furnished (Figs 13–16). It contained three brooches, two small-long brooches for the dress and a cruciform brooch for the cloak, a bead string of nineteen amber and 114 glass beads, wrist-clasps, and a girdle group with a bag ring of elephant ivory, a knife, and at least one latchlifter. The glass beads were a mix of small monochrome blue, crimson and green pieces, with some larger polychrome and monochrome terracotta items.

Girdle groups with a bag ring of elephant ivory, a knife, and latchlifters were also found in graves 1358 and 1364 (Figs 20–24). Grave 1358 had in addition two gilt applied disc brooches for the dress, a long pin for the cloak, and a bead string of 21 beads, mainly of glass but with one of amber and a possible amulet of soapstone. The glass beads were mainly monochrome blue and polychrome, the latter chiefly with a terracotta matrix. Grave 1364 had only an annular brooch, probably used for a cloak, wrist-clasps, and a bead string of nineteen amber beads, but the high status of this woman is shown not only by her bag but also by a pair of copper-alloy girdle-hangers, two silver finger-rings, and an amulet of a Roman melon bead in a copper-alloy sling suspended from the bead string.

Three other female graves, 1336, 1351, and 1355 have no bags but still show a degree of wealth. Grave 1351 is early in date (Fig. 19). The burial of an elderly female, it contained an iron penannular brooch, a gilt applied disc brooch, and three beads. The disc brooch has a star motif, which suggests a date for the grave in the fifth century. While the penannular brooch is generally suggestive as an indication of low status, the applied disc brooch is an indication of some wealth, as is an unusual cuboid bead of white glass with green frame and red dots, for which no parallel is known. It was accompanied by two simple blue glass beads.

Grave 1336 is distinguished by a bead string of seventeen beads of amber and colourless monochrome glass, wrist-clasps and belt-fittings (Figs 17–18). The same punch was used on the clasps and belt-stiffeners, making the two groups a matching suite (Fig. 17). That the ensemble had been in use for some time is shown by the replacement of one half of one clasp, though with a piece also decorated with the same punch marks, and by a non-matching buckle-plate, brightly-silvered, but of fairly crude manufacture.

Grave 1355 (Fig. 19) contained only two non-matching

Table 6. Grave goods from inhumations

Grave	Sex	Brooch	Bead/Amulet	Pin	Finger Ring	Wrist–Clasps	Belt–Fittings	Girdle hangers	Bag Fittings	Box Fittings	'Treasures'	Latch–Lifter	Knife	Toilet Set	Tools	Shield	Spear	Other
G1250			X										X					
G1263	F	XXX	X x 133			X	X		X			X	X					
G1336	F		X x 25			X	X											
G1351	Elderly F	XX	X x 3		X								X					
G1355	F	XX	X	X														
G1358	F	XX	X x 23	X			X		X			XX	X					
G1364	F	X	X x 20		XX	X	X	X	X		X	XX	X					
G1366	M												X			X		
G1374							X						X					
G1379													X					
G1394	M						X						X		XX			
G1428	M						X						X				X	
G1440																		X
G1460										X	XXX		X					

small-long brooches, a small loop-headed pin, and a single globular blue glass bead, a very common form, fifty-four of which came from grave 1263 (Fig. 16).

For most of the graves only a general date range can be offered, though a progression can be seen from the fifth through to the late sixth or early seventh century. The fixed-plate buckle in the male grave 1394 belongs to the fifth century, perhaps the first half (Fig. 27.1), while the star-motif applied disc brooch in the female grave 1351 is of mid-fifth-century date (Fig. 19.1) and unlikely to have been deposited later than the end of the century. Grave 1358, with a pair of applied disc brooches with Style 1 zoomorphic decoration, belongs in the first half of the sixth century (Fig. 20). A wrist-clasp stored in the girdle bag in grave 1364 dates to later than *c.* AD 525 (Fig. 22), while the cruciform brooch in grave 1263 is probably mid sixth century (Fig. 13). Wrist-clasps in grave 1336 date the grave to within the sixth century (Fig. 17), while the latest grave may be grave 1460, which contained a disc-headed pin, possibly stored as 'treasure', dating to the late sixth or early seventh century (Fig. 29).

In terms of distribution, it is interesting to note that the richly-furnished grave 1263 is in the same general area (the eastern half) of the site as the two lower-status graves 1351 and 1336 (Fig. 6). The trio range in date, at the broadest, from the mid fifth to mid or later sixth century, with the least wealthy being the earliest and the most wealthy probably the latest, while the other two high-status female graves 1358 and 1364 lie in the south-western corner of the site with the lower-status and earlier grave 1355 between them. This division may point to family areas within the cemetery, the less richly-furnished female graves equating with earlier date, and wealth being accumulated over time.

The idea of family areas may be supported by the proximity of the early male grave 1394 to the early female grave 1351 in the first group described above, but may conflict with the suggestion above that the two male single-weapon graves in the south-west corner might denote the edge of a cluster of weapon burials.

Punchmarks on the metalwork

Applied decorative features on the metalwork consist of punchmarks of various forms (*e.g.* Figs 13–14), incised linear grooving, white-metal plating, and gilding. The gilt applied disc brooches from grave 1358 have central insets of blue glass and nail-headed rivets made of a different alloy to the main body of the brooch (Fig. 20).

The punchmarks (see Table 7 below) are defined by the classification used by Mortimer for the Edix Hill assemblage.[209] Most are of Group C, the design based upon a punch tip of simple solid geometric shape with fine detailing added to it by another much smaller punch. The exceptions are a Group B punch with more complex basic design and detailing added by a file and two Group D punches, with internal divisions added by a file or engraving tool.

In grave 1336 the same punch, with a tiny half ring-and-dot design, was used for the wrist-clasps and the belt-stiffeners, therefore the belt-fittings formed part of a complete ensemble with the dress-fittings (Fig. 17). Elements of both had been repaired. Part of one wrist-clasp had been replaced, though with a piece that also had the same punchmarks. The buckle-plate was made by a much poorer craftsman than the one responsible for the other metal fittings and must be a replacement for a well-made original. It is fashioned from a belt-stiffener, thicker than the originals, bent over at one end to hold the buckle loop and with a slot cut out for the tongue. The stamps decorating this piece are large and of simple design, and have been carelessly applied to the margins.

The horseshoes on this buckle-plate are angular, while those on the girdle hangers from grave 1364 are much smaller and well-formed (Fig. 23).

Brooches
The high-status female in grave 1263 wore a brooch suite consisting of a pair of identical small-long brooches and a cruciform brooch, the former on the shoulders of the dress, the latter fastening the cloak (Fig. 13). A pair of identical gilt copper-alloy applied disc brooches came from grave 1358, with a long pin used instead of a third brooch (Fig. 20), and a pair of small-long brooches, not matching, came from grave 1355, also with a pin for the cloak (Fig. 19). A single annular brooch in the high-status female grave 1364 may have been used for a cloak (Fig. 22), while an iron penannular brooch and an applied disc brooch in grave 1351 may both have been used on a dress (Fig. 19).

The cruciform brooch in the female grave 1263 (Fig. 13) is of Leeds and Pocock's Florid type, Group V and Mortimer's Type Z.[210] The side lappets are fully-developed bird's heads, the collar above the animal-head foot has two bands of transverse ridges separated by a groove, and the scrolled nostrils of the animal mask have developed into a pair of bird's heads on elongated necks. However, the head decoration lacks the developed masks on the top and sides, and instead consists of plates with rudimentary masks and tiny knobs. These features, and the side panels of the head, owe more to Group IVb brooches, as does the restrained marginal punched decoration. Together with the brooch's association with a pair of wrist-clasps belonging to a developed form of Hines B12, its character suggests a date towards the middle of the sixth century. The small-long brooches in the same grave, found on either shoulder, are products of south Cambridgeshire, derivatives of Leeds' cross potent form, with rebated upper corners, two perforations, and basal notches, and triangular foot.[211] Their date is probably late rather than early,[212] and association with the cruciform brooch suggests that this pair belong firmly in the sixth century.

Applied disc brooches with star patterns, such as that from grave 1351 (Fig. 19) occur in the early fifth century on the continent, where they are found in male graves, and probably from the mid fifth century in Britain, where they have been recovered from both male and female (but mainly female) graves and over a wide area from Portchester to Yorkshire.[213] The scalloped border of the brooch is a continental feature, also found on a pair that are an exact match for this brooch from a fifth or possibly early sixth century grave at Harnham Hill, Wiltshire,[214]

and on a very similar brooch from a female grave at Holywell Row, Cambridgeshire.[215]

Grave 1351 also contained a fragmentary iron penannular brooch of Fowler's Type C (Fig. 19) with simple coiled terminals.[216] Penannular brooches in early Anglo-Saxon graves are always from female graves, such as the pairs from Holywell Row, Suffolk, and Wakerley, Northamptonshire[217] and single brooches from Wakerley, Edix Hill, Cambridgeshire, Great Chesterford, Essex, and Morning Thorpe, Norfolk.[218] Type C penannulars were initially thought by Fowler to have been produced continuously from the late Iron Age through to the Anglo-Saxon period, but the form with circular-section hoop is now known to have died out during the early Roman period, only to commence again with either a circular-section segmented hoop or a flat-section decorated hoop in the fourth century.[219] Iron penannular brooches are not common in the late Roman period, though they do occur in the earlier phase of production, and those found in Anglo-Saxon graves can be considered to belong to that period.

The unmatched pair of small-long brooches from grave 1355 are square- and trefoil-headed (Fig. 19). The square-headed brooch, found on the right shoulder, has incised double-ring-and-dots on the head and the slightly-expanded foot. Ring-and-dot decoration occurs on small-long brooches of many forms on the continent, across southern Britain and into the Midlands.[220] A large double ring-and-dot is also set on the centre of the trefoil-headed brooch found on the left shoulder, which is further ornamented by carefully-applied marginal punchmarks. The pair belong somewhere in the late fifth or sixth century.

The identical pair of applied disc brooches with Style 1 zoomorphic decoration found on the shoulders of the female in grave 1358 probably belong in the first half of the sixth century (Fig. 20). Similar central nail-headed rivets occur on brooches from Nassington and Wakerley, Northamptonshire, though the inner and outer borders and zoomorphic decoration is different.[221]

Grave 1364, that of a high-status female, contained a single annular brooch of Ager's Type E found on the left shoulder, presumably used to fasten a cloak rather than on the dress (Fig. 22.4). Type E brooches are a long-lived form,[222] but this grave can be dated by a wrist-clasp in a bag collection to after *c.* AD 525.

Beads and amulets
Seven graves contained beads, most of which were glass, but four had amber beads. Two graves (1250 and 1355) contained only single beads and one only three (grave 1351). Grave 1351, with three beads, also contained an applied disc brooch of early form (Fig. 19.1) and a large finger-ring (Fig. 19.2), probably too large to be considered as a female item. Most of the beads were found on the upper chest, but the single bead in grave 1250 was deposited near the waist.

Table 8 (below) lists the beads, with the glass beads put into the groups defined in Guido.[223] This breaks the beads down by base colour, then within colour by form and decoration. Beads not found in Guido are put in their appropriate base colour group.

The amber beads are in a range of sizes and shapes, the majority quite large and irregular, but with some well-made discs and a few small lozenge-shaped/biconical pieces. Amber, a fossil resin, is mainly sourced to submarine deposits around the coast of the Baltic. Like jet, it was prized in antiquity for both its appearance and its electro-static, seemingly magical, qualities. Though amber beads are known from Roman Britain, they are not common, while they occur frequently in pagan Anglo-Saxon Britain. At Edix Hill, Cambridgeshire, they formed nearly eighty per cent of the bead assemblage.[224] Calculations of the total weight of amber beads in each grave group at Edix Hill hints at their being sold in weight groups of approximately 10–12 g. This may be borne out here by the groups from graves 1263 and 1364, though the former is slightly 'overweight'.

The glass beads also come in a wide range of forms and colours. In many cases only one or two examples are present, the exceptions being the groups of small mono-chrome beads of blue, crimson, and green glass found in grave 1263 (Fig. 16), of colourless glass in grave 1336 (Fig. 18), and of blue glass in grave 1358 (Fig. 21). These, no doubt, were considerably cheaper than the larger or more ornate items and in the case of the blue and green beads, were also produced over a very long period.[225] Small crimson beads appear to be continental Anglian in origin, arriving in Britain in the mid fifth century or slightly earlier, though here they have a wide distribution and are often found in sixth century graves.[226]

Many of the polychrome beads also have a wide distribution and general pagan Anglo-Saxon date. Some have been set within the sixth and early seventh century, but evidence from graves at Mucking suggests that their starting date may be earlier. For example, though those of Group 3iiic, opaque white with blue crossed waves and red dots, are chiefly dated AD 500–650, an early example occurs in a fifth-century grave at Mucking, Essex.[227] Similarly, opaque yellow beads of Guido's Group 4vi with green, rather than the more usual terracotta, crossed waves and dots, appear to have been popular principally in East Anglia in the sixth century, though again one in a grave from Mucking may be fifth century.[228]

The Roman melon bead set in a copper-alloy sling from grave 1364 (Fig. 23.18) belongs to a form of amulet found in sixth-century graves. The suspended object was often crystal, as at Chessell Down, Isle of Wight, Bifrons and Deal, Kent, and Frénouville, Normandy,[229] though other materials were also used, such as an oak gall from a grave at Little Wilbraham, Cambridgeshire, and an unpolished quartzite pebble in a grave at Wakerley, Northamptonshire.[230] The crystal amulets from Britain and the oak gall were found in association with a spoon, and may have been used for divination. The Wakerley pebble and the melon bead from grave 1364 were on bead strings and were probably treasured either as curiosities or for apotropaic powers. Roman melon beads are occasionally found on early Anglo-Saxon necklaces.[231]

An unpierced cylinder of soapstone(?) from grave 1358 is probably an amulet (Fig. 21.22). It came from the same area as a group of beads and may have been suspended from the bead string by a sling of now decayed organic material such as thread or a leather thong. The same grave also produced a single amber bead which may also have been added to the string for its reputed magical qualities.

Finger-rings

The large cast ring from grave 1351 was among a group of objects laid on the right shoulder/chest (Fig. 19.2). This may be a finger-ring or possibly a belt-fitting. It is rather large for a female finger or thumb, though the grave also contained an iron penannular brooch, a female item. An applied disc brooch from the grave also carries a star motif, and its recurrence on this ring is unlikely to be a coincidence.

Coiled silver finger-rings are a form found in high-status female graves, as here in grave 1364 (Fig. 22). They occur, for example, in grave 11 at Holywell Row.[232]

Table 7. Punchmarks

Grave	SF no	Object	Stamp	Group
G1263	83	cruciform brooch	solid triangle with internal divisions	d
G1263	84–85	pair of small-long brooches	keyhole with central boss	c
G1355	125	small-long brooch	ring-and-dot & notched V	c, b
G1336	137–138	pair of wrist-clasps	half ring-and-dot	c
G1336	48	belt-stiffeners	half ring-and-dot	c
G1336	48	buckle-plate	Horseshoe	c
G1364	97	annular brooch	solid circle with central raised bar	d
G1364	101	pair of girdle hanger	Horseshoe	c
G1366	126	Tweezers	half ring and full dot	c

Pins

Long pins such as that from grave 1358 (Fig. 20.3) often form part of the jewellery suites in high-status female graves, used instead of the third brooch to fasten a cloak. They are occasionally decorated with spangles suspended from the pierced head by a suspension ring. This pin had a pair of spangles set back to back and fixed closely together, perhaps soldered. Single and double spangles (now separate) were found on several pins from Oxfordshire,[233] and a single spangle was found on a pin from Morning Thorpe, Norfolk.[234]

The pin in grave 1355 was also found between a pair of brooches (Fig. 19.3). Small loop-headed pins are more frequently found in iron, as at West Stow, Suffolk, and Great Chesterford, Essex,[235] though they are found in both materials at Wakerley, Northamptonshire.[236] No close date can be offered for the form. The disc-headed pin from grave 1460 (Fig. 29.1), however, is a type found in copper-alloy, bone and iron that belongs to the late sixth or early seventh century.[237] This particular example may have been stored as 'treasure' in a bone-veneered wooden box (Fig. 29.22).

Wrist-clasps

Three graves contained pairs of wrist-clasps for fastening sleeve ends, and in one of these graves, grave 1364, a single clasp of a particularly decorative form was among the objects stored in a bag (see 'Treasures', below) (Fig. 22.3). A clasp fragment, possibly from the disturbed grave 1377 (Fig. 26), is also described under the section on other site finds below.

Graves 1263 and 1364 are clearly of high-status females, but the only other objects found in grave 1336 were a necklace of amber beads and a girdle with silvered strap-fittings (Figs 17–18). Both these items indicate a degree of wealth, but one well below that demonstrated in the other two graves. It is therefore particularly interesting to note that the clasp from the right sleeve in 1336 has been repaired, using a hook of the same form and with similar punchmarks, but not a direct match and lacking its cast bar. Mismatched pairs of clasps were also found at Wakerley, Northamptonshire, Empingham, Rutland, and Edix Hill, Cambridgeshire.[238] This implies that these accessories were luxury items and at Edix Hill there is also a parallel for the treasuring of broken clasps shown here by grave 1364.[239]

In both 1336 and 1364 the clasps are of Hines Form B17a, with applied cast bars and shaped outer edge.[240] Those in grave 1263 (Fig. 14) are of Form B12, cast and with pierced lugs on the upper and lower ends, but belonging to a sub-group where the central feature, in this case hammerheads, providing a strong similarity to the cast cruciform B11s.[241] This sub-group of B12 developed in the sixth century, while the B17a clasps may belong in the late fifth or sixth century.[242]

Belt-fittings

The belt-fittings varied from a single buckle as in grave 1358 (Fig. 20), to the suite of stiffeners with a buckle and strap-end in grave 1336 (Fig. 17). Most came from female graves, but single buckles came from the male graves 1394 (Fig. 27) and 1428 (Fig. 28). The suite of fittings in grave 1263 includes two unusual triangular fittings (Fig. 14). One is considerably larger than the other. They were found close together on the right side of the waist area, together with fragments of a probably latchlifter.

The suite from grave 1336 (Fig. 17) consists of long silvered tongue-ended fittings of a form found in many other cemeteries of the period, such as Edix Hill.[243] Three belt-stiffeners with punched decoration were found on the right side, one on the left side with a rectangular strap-end, and a buckle and belt-plate rested on the lower spine. The buckle loop was of iron, fitted onto a stiffener similar to the others but of stouter construction and with different punchmarks.

The buckles in graves 1374, 1394 and 1428 all lay at waist level and were not accompanied by any other fittings. The buckle in grave 1358 was also found at waist level, and a large cast ring found near a bag in this grave may be another buckle (Fig. 20.4). The strap-end in grave 1364 (Fig. 22.6) lay close to the bag deposited on the legs and may have been stored within it or fitted to the straps attaching it to the girdle. The former is most likely as a fragment of a second strap-end came form the same area. The tiny doubled-over strip fragment in this grave lay close to the spine and may be a dress- or belt-fitting.

The large cast copper-alloy ring found in grave 1358 may have been among the objects stored in the bag, or may have been a simple buckle (Fig. 20.4). It belongs to a group of objects described by MacGregor and Bolick as probably either belt- or harness fittings.[244] A well-defined band of discolouration on the hoop of this example opposite the 'bezel' and knobs suggests it was attached to a leather or fabric strap 16 mm wide. In the grave it lay adjacent to an ivory bag hoop. It may have been sewn to one end of the strap to which the bag was fixed, the other end passing through it at least twice and perhaps knotted. It may alternatively have been sewn to the outside of the bag and used to secure a short strap on a lid flap. While reconstruction drawings of bags do not show them as having the potential to be closed, this none the less seems a desirable feature for containers in which personal possessions were stored (see below).

The buckle in grave 1394, with zoomorphic decoration and with the plate cast in one with the loop (Fig. 27.1), belongs to Hawkes and Dunning's Type IIIb, Marzinzik's Type II.1a and Böhme's Haillot type, which he dates to the first half and the middle of the 5th century.[245] It was clearly in use at the time of burial and, although it may be a survival into the second half of the fifth century, is not excessively worn and need not have been particularly old when buried. Böhme dates smaller buckles of similar form, his Krefeld-Gellep type, to the middle of the fifth century into the second half.[246] Taking the two Böhme types together as one, from Britain there are two examples from Sarre, Kent, an unprovenanced example in Canterbury Museum also probably comes from Kent, one from Long Wittenham, Oxfordshire, two from graves at Mucking, Essex, and one each from Alfriston, East Sussex and Nunburnholme, Yorkshire.[247] All can be accommodated with a date in the fifth century, but the Long Wittenham burial may be as late as the early sixth century. Yet another example of the form was recently found in a grave at Dartford, Kent.[248]

Girdle groups

Three female graves contained girdle groups (1263 Fig. 14; 1358 Figs 20–21; 1364 Figs 22–23), strings of items worn suspended on a strap or belt and found in the grave on or close to the lap of the corpse. All three of these groups consisted of a bag with an elephant ivory frame used to store and carry personal possessions and a knife. Those in graves 1358 and 1364 also contained iron latchlifters and a latchlifter was recovered from grave 1263, but lay on the right hand side of the body close to a strap-fitting. The bag in grave 1263 lay between the left arm and the hip and also contained a ring made from an antler burr and an earring of

probable Roman date. Its ivory hoop had been repaired with an iron band. The girdle groups in graves 1358 and 1364 were found between the leg bones and the bag in grave 1364 also held iron rings and a broken wrist-clasp. Strap-fittings (see above) and a pair of girdle-hangers were found close to the bag in grave 1364. The origin of these cloth bags with elephant ivory frames is described above in the section dealing with the cremations; in inhumations they are usually an indicator of a high-status burial. This is borne out by these three inhumations, all of which also contained a wide range of jewellery.

Reconstructions of bags and the method of suspension are illustrated in Myres and Green, Malim and Hines, and Meaney.[249] The rigidity of the hoop and the weight of the objects in the bag were presumed to force the hoop to hang down against the body and so hold it closed to some extent. However, a better method of closure seems needed, especially considering the importance of the bag's contents in both personal and social terms. If bags were fitted with a flap, they could be more securely closed, and a large cast ring found close to the bag in grave 1358 (Fig. 20.4) has been suggested as a means of securing such a flap (see above).

Latchlifters and girdle hangers are also strong

Table 8. Glass bead types

Type	G1250	G1263	G1336	G1351	G1355	G1358	G1364
amber – all forms		20 (27 g)	17 (3 g)			1 (2 g)	19 (10 g)
1i, colourless, all forms			8				
— colourless with red trail		2					
1iii, lightly coloured melon						1	
— black uncertain form						1	
3iiic, white with blue crossed waves & red dots		1					
3iiid, white with green crossed waves & red dots		1					
3vi, white with coloured bands						2	
— white with green frame & red dots				1			
4vi, yellow with green crossed waves & dots		2					
5i, green		13					
5vii, green with red crossed waves & yellow dots		1					
6i, blue		54		2	1	10	
6xi, blue with coloured specks						1	
7, crimson		37					
8i, terracotta		2					
8xivc variant, terracotta with double green wave						1	
8xvi variant, terracotta with yellow band						1	
8xviiic, terracotta with green and yellow marbled dots						1	
8xixa, terracotta with green and yellow stripes	1					2	
— terracotta & yellow						1	
amulet						1	1
Totals	**1**	**133**	**25**	**3**	**1**	**23**	**20**

indications of status in Anglian female graves. The latchlifters, usually either L-shaped or of 'finger-crooked' form, often occur in groups of three, but the Alwalton examples are too fragmentary for the exact number present to be determined. Girdle hangers are usually found as pairs. They are essentially T-shaped, but in some cases the terminals are joined to the shank as they are here.[250]

The bag in the high-status female grave 1263 contained an antler ring (Fig. 14.10), and that in grave 1364 two iron rings (Fig. 23 Nos. 15 and 16). Similar antler rings, made from the burr, have been found at Sancton, Spong Hill, Empingham and Edix Hill. Timby suggests that the Empingham example may be an armlet,[251] but these rings, with internal diameters generally between 25 and 35 mm, are too small to pass over a hand. One ring from Sancton is rather larger, about 45 mm internally, but is still too small to be an adult bracelet.[252] The Edix Hill antler ring seems to have been tied to a group of iron rings,[253] and a pair of iron rings were also found in the bag in grave 1364. Many other bags were found to contain rings, often of iron, but also of copper alloy and decorated antler.[254]

Iron rings may be simply interpreted as part of the suspension method for latchlifter groups,[255] but some also, as with latchlifters, held further significance in terms of wealth and status.[256] This may also be true of antler burr rings.

Box and treasures
Fragments of decoratively cut bone strips and long iron rivets from Grave 1460 may derive from a wooden box (Fig. 29), though there are problems with this interpretation. The box was placed on the right hip of the deceased. A well-preserved silver denarius of Elagabalus (AD 218–22), a copper-alloy disc-headed pin, and a tinned fragment of sheet copper alloy were also found in the grave and were probably stored in the box (Fig. 29). The pin is a late sixth- or early seventh-century form.

The bone pieces consist of two long strips, now partly decayed and fragmented, and parts of two lozenges (Fig. 29.2). Each of the latter had a large central perforation, while the strips had pairs of perforations with a rivet set between them to form part of the decorative scheme. The veneer was probably laid out with the long strips on the long sides of the box (front and back) with the lozenges set in the centre. The lengths of the strips suggest a box over 150 mm long, while the rivets give a board thickness of about 22 mm. The lack of other fittings point to jointed construction with either a sliding or push-on lid. However, this identification is only tentative. One rivet has small chips of bone attached to each end, which suggests that the veneer was fixed on either side of a solid rectangular wooden object. The small number of rivets recovered, their length, and the number of rivet holes support this idea. Such an object could not work as a box, though it is difficult to imagine what its purpose might have been. Moreover, this alternative does not make use of the veneer lozenges.

'Treasures'
The earring from grave 1263 came from the bag in that grave and is probably a collected and curated antique Roman item (Fig. 14).[257] The fragment of sheet metal from grave 1460 (Fig. 29.3) was probably stored in a box with a silver *denarius* of Elagabalus and a late sixth to early seventh-century pin. The treasuring of scrap metal in a box, perhaps for future recycling into a piece of jewellery, was also noted at Burwell, Cambridgeshire.[258]

The bag in grave 1364 contained an oval composite wrist-clasp of which the eye catch is broken (Fig. 22.3) and that plate also lacks its applied repoussé plate. The form is Hines' Form B13c, but is oval not rectangular. The design is exactly the same as that on a similarly treasured half clasp from Nassington (Northamptonshire).[259] A similar oval clasp with fragmentary repoussé plates came from the right sleeve of Skeleton A in Grave 85 at Empingham (Rutland). The clasp on the left sleeve was of Hines Form B12. The surviving decoration on the Empingham clasp is sufficient to show that it differed from that here, but both designs employed segmented raised curves.[260] Hines dates Form B13c no earlier than the second quarter of the sixth century, giving a *terminus post quem* of *c.* AD 525 for grave 1364. The surviving applied plate of the Alwalton clasp is not much worn, and it need not have been in use long before being added to the bag collection.

Grave 1364 also contained a two-piece strap-end and part of another (Fig. 22) (see above) found lying across the right leg and close to the contents of the bag. In view of the presence of the fragment these items may also have been stored in the bag, but it is also possible that they were fitted onto the straps that attached the bag to the girdle.

The treasuring of broken clasps is also found at Edix Hill, where the broken halves of a mismatched pair on one sleeve in Grave 3 were found in the purse group in the grave.[261]

Toilet set
A copper-alloy toilet set consisting of a pair of tweezers and an ear-scoop came from the male grave 1366 (Fig. 25). As noted above tweezers are not necessarily gender-related, although sets of toilet instruments can be, depending upon their composition.[262]

Knives, awls and weapons
Knives
The knives have been described by back type and length group, as at Edix Hill.[263] Type A is curved-backed, B is straight-backed; and C has an angle on the back near to the point. Length Group 1 covers 45–99 mm, Group 2 covers 100–129 mm, Group 3 covers 130–75 mm.

The blades from graves 1250 (Fig. 12) and 1394 (Fig. 27) are the largest in the assemblage, with that from grave 1250 at the upper range of length Group 3. Both have straight backs and the S-shaped profile typical of frequent sharpening. They may have been used for butchery, though that from grave 1394, which was found with at least two bone-handled awls or punches, may have been a craft tool. This knife retained a considerable amount of mineral-replaced wood from the handle, but none of the disassociated fragments could be identified to species. A buckle from the grave dates it to the first half of the fifth century.

One other knife, from grave 1374 (Fig. 25), probably belongs in length Group 2. Though it is incomplete it is clearly more substantial than those of Group 1, to which the remainder of the blades belong.

Only one blade appears to have an angled back, that from the early female grave 1351 (Fig. 19). As angled-back blades are usually seventh century in date, this identification is suspect. The blade has been stripped of its corrosion products and no pre-conservation X-ray is available. The present line of the back may not be an accurate reflection of the original form, which may instead have been curved, as on a knife from Wakerley (Northamptonshire).[264] The remainder of the knives are between about 80 and 130 mm long, and exhibit a range of forms.

Awls
A pair of well-made plain circular-section bone handles was found together with a number of fragments of iron shafts between the left arm and left side of the skeleton in grave 1394 (Fig. 27), dated to the first half of the fifth century. These probably represent two, possibly three, awls. These tools were found with the second largest knife in the assemblage, which may also have been used as a craft tool.

Allocation of iron fragments to the appropriate handle has been complicated by the absence of pre-conservation X-rays and by the iron corrosion products having being stripped off. One handle (Fig. 27.2) is fully perforated and empty, and is likely to belong with the iron fragments of Figure 27.5, though these are much thinner than the handle hole and too short to project more than a little. Part of the length must have been lost. The rough bone tissue inside the hole will have served to some extent to grip the tang, but it may also have been packed with some fibrous material. If the pairing of No. 2 and No. 5 is correct, the fragments of No. 4 belong with handle No. 3 which is only partially perforated and retains part of the iron tang. The shouldered fragment No. 5 may, however, represent a third tool with a wooden handle, now decayed and missing.

Given the state of preservation, identification of these tools as awls can only be tentative. However, the most likely alternative for the form of the surviving iron is that they might be punches, though these are unlikely to have been fitted with bone handles, which would have suffered from repeated hammering.

A well-preserved awl with a roughly-shaped bone handle and with the tang projecting slightly at the end was found in the sixth-century sunken-featured building

56 at West Stow (Suffolk)[265] and awls without surviving handles have also been found at Mucking (Essex) and Shakenoak (Oxfordshire).[266]

Unidentified object
This strip fragment, found by the right hip of the skeleton in grave 1440 (Fig. 28.1), is almost certainly residual. It is well-preserved and so must have been broken before the time of burial. The section suggests it may be a mount of some kind, though no rivet hole remains at the surviving end.

Shield
The shield in grave 1366 is represented by a boss and grip (Fig. 25). No mounts or studs were found. The boss is of Dickinson and Härke's Group 1, the commonest form in England and characterised by its low height and concave walls.[267] The grip is of Type 1a2, narrow and plain. The date range for the group is long, *c.* AD 450 to 600, but may terminate before AD 575.[268]

No weapon was deposited with the shield, which lay beneath the skull. The only other grave goods were a copper-alloy ear-pick and pair of tweezers. Shields can be seen as an indication of warrior status, even when deposited with juveniles. The proportion of graves with shields but lacking a spear is often low, for example one per cent at Morning Thorpe (Norfolk), three per cent at Wakerley, Empingham and here at Alwalton, six per cent at Edix Hill, and seven per cent at Nassington (Northamptonshire). None were found at Great Chesterford.

Spears
One spear was deposited in grave 1428 (Fig. 28), set against the wall of the grave to the right of the head. It is of Swanton's Series F Type 1, with a long socket and small angular blade. No accompanying ferrule was found. Graves containing this type of spearhead are often poorly-furnished and date to before the mid sixth century.[269] In addition to the spear, grave 1428 contained only a small frequently-sharpened knife and a strap-end.

While shield-only graves usually represent a low proportion of inhumations, spear-only graves tend to be more frequent, seven per cent at Great Chesterford, Essex, eight per cent at Edix Hill and Wakerley, nine per cent at both Nassington, and Morning Thorpe and thirteen at Empingham. At three per cent, this single spear from Alwalton therefore represents a very low recovery rate.

Other small finds
The other small finds from the site cover a wide date range, from the early Iron Age through to the early post-medieval period. They are arranged as far as possible chronologically below, with items of uncertain date grouped at the end in context number order.

The bone double-pointed tool from the early Iron

Age pit 1140 may be a weaving implement (Fig. 37.7). It is similar to the much later pinbeaters, though not worked to a smooth finish. One face is rough with cancellous tissue, and there are several transverse nicks close to one point. It is, however, rather better made than most bone tools of the period.

The fragments of lava quern from ditch 1107 and pit 1148 are of Roman date but may have been re-used in the early Anglian period. The stone was less hard-wearing than the native British querns of Milltone Grit and Hertfordshire Puddingstone, and similar small fragments to these are often found in early Anglo-Saxon contexts, probably re-used as rubbing-stones. Though interrupted during the Migration Period, the trade in lava querns from the Eifel Hills of Germany was re-established in the middle to late Saxon periods and continued to at least the end of the medieval period. The upper-stone fragment from pit 1269 is an early medieval form (Fig. 37.10).

The copper-alloy penannular brooch recovered from the spoil heap is unfinished and points to manufacture in the area (Fig. 37.2). One terminal is a simple incomplete coil, the other has been flattened and its end clinched. The marks of the clinching tool continue around the hoop for a short distance. Type C brooches with rectangular section and decorated hoop are generally of late Roman date, and this example may be contemporary with the fourth century coins from the site. It may, however, be an early Anglo-Saxon product.

The cruciform brooch fragment is of early form, with raised lines prefiguring the later scroll-shaped nostrils (Fig. 37.1). Broken across the humped bow, it may have been intended for use as a funerary deposit. The Hines Form B7 wrist-clasp fragment from modern feature 1378 may have come from the disturbed inhumation grave 1377. The form is the commonest in Britain, with a generally sixth century date. Also of Anglo-Saxon date is the ferrule from hollow 1417.

The unstratified hooked tag fragment is an example of the late medieval revival of a less ornate Saxon form (Fig. 37.4). The open-work relief-decorated plate and rectangular slot for the strap or ribbon are typical of the later form.[270]

Other finds included a number of fragments of lava quern fragments, siltstone fragments and iron nails. The tip of a bone pin was also recovered from the subsoil.

Illustrations

Fig. 37.1 SF 166. (1000). Topsoil. Fragment from the foot of a cruciform brooch. The animal mask is of undeveloped style, with slightly expanded rounded terminal, simple raised bosses for the eyes, and raised lines marking the snout. Length 52.5 mm.

Fig. 37.2 SF 176. From spoil heap. Unfinished copper-alloy penannular brooch of Fowler Type C (1960, 152), slightly distorted. One terminal is curled at right angles to the plane of the ring, the other has been flattened, its end crossed by the marks of a clinching tool which continue onto the rectangular-section hoop for a short distance. Maximum diameter 26.5 mm.

Fig. 37.3 SF -. Unstratified. Copper-alloy shape of simple folded tapering form with a hole for attachment on each side. From the scabbard of a single-edged blade, with one side straight, the other rounded. Length 34 mm, maximum width 18 mm. The quality of the metal suggests an early post-medieval date.

Fig. 37.4 SF -. Unstratified. Copper-alloy circular hooked tag with decorative moulded open-work panel beneath a rectangular slot for the strap or ribbon. The hook is missing. Length 22 mm, width 17 mm. Late medieval.

Fig. 37. 5 SF -. (1001). Subsoil. Rectangular copper-alloy plate, probably a buckle-plate, with rivet hole at one end, and staining from iron rivet. Geometric incised decoration, plain central panel, triangles on either side, with those with base line on edge filled with rocker-arm ornament. Length (bent) 30.5 mm, width 22 mm.

Fig. 37.6 F 63. (1001). Subsoil. 1) Fragment of copper-alloy strap-fitting, with decoratively-shaped end and incised grooves. There are two holes for rivets at the end. Length 21 mm, width 17 mm. Probably from a belt or book-clasp. late medieval or early post-medieval. 2) Not illustrated. Crumpled fragment of decayed copper-alloy sheet. Maximum dimensions 25 by 20 mm.

Fig. 37. 7 SF. Pit 1140 (1141) Early Iron Age. Fill of early Iron Age pit. Double-ended bone tool with angled entasis set off-centre. The shorter end is slightly polished, the longer shows facets from manufacture and has a series of transverse nicks close to the point. Rough tissue from the marrow cavity shows it to have been made from a long bone. Length 64 mm.

Fig. 37.8 SF -. Unstratified. Small socketed spear head with a narrow blade no wider than the socket. Length 132 mm. Probably Roman, of Manning's Type III (1985, 166).

Fig. 37.10 SF -. Pit 1269 (1270). Fill of pit. Fragment of a lava quern upper-stone of early medieval form, Röder's Type 7.[271] The grinding surface is smooth, the upper surface rough, and with a raised lip around the hopper hole. Diameter approximately 400 mm, thickness 20 mm.

Coins

Peter Guest

Twelve coins were recovered during the investigations, including a silver groat struck for Henry VII (1000, SF11) recovered from the topsoil. The remaining eleven coins were of Roman date and included three large bronzes of the first or second centuries AD, a denarius of Elagabalus (1462, SF71), two third-century radiates and four bronze coins of the fourth century. Although the number of coins from this site is rather small, it is significant that the assemblage covers the entire Roman period and that the first two hundred years of Roman rule produced as many coins as the fourth century, an unusual situation for Roman Britain.

Slag

Jane Cowgill

Introduction and Methodology

A total of 287g of smithing slags and associated materials (seventeen pieces) were recovered. The slag was identified solely on morphological grounds by visual examination, sometimes with the aid of a ×10 binocular microscope. A note of probable fuel type has been recorded when fragments or imprints were incorporated within the slag. The soil in all the bags containing slag was checked with a magnet for evidence of hammerscale but none was found.

Discussion

The small assemblage of slag comprises only seventeen pieces. With the exception of the piece from cremation 1286, all the pieces were generated by the smithing of iron, namely the fabrication, repair or recycling of iron objects (secondary smithing). Charcoal was the sole fuel noted within the slags. Most of the pieces appear to be abraded, which with such hard dense material such as slags suggests that it has been extensively reworked and/ or has been weathered on the ground surface. Post-depositional processes, however, can effect slags although how is poorly understood at present.

The largest assemblage (still only thirteen pieces) is from ditch fill 1225 (ditch 1224), one of the intercutting ditches in the north-eastern sector of Area A. Few datable finds were recovered from these features so they are tentatively dated Roman, Anglo-Saxon or later periods. The only datable find from ditch 1224 is a sherd of Roman pottery (4 g). The slag from this feature visually appears to be iron-rich (although none responded to a magnet) and two pieces, a plano-convex hearth bottom and proto-hearth bottom, are very dense, thin and an unusual purple red colour. The best parallel for these, seen by the author, are from the Anglian settlement at West Heslerton (West Yorkshire).[272] Some of those slags have, through microstructural analysis, been uniquely identified as having been generated by bloom smithing (primary smithing) in association with secondary smithing slags.[273] As a cautionary note smithing slags are, however, inherently undatable and a wide range of factors effect their form and appearance and therefore on the basis of so few pieces a direct comparison cannot be made. The small size of the assemblage and indeed of the individual pieces is more typical of an Anglo-Saxon assemblage than a Romano-British one.

Cremated Human Remains

Tony Waldron

The cremated remains of thirty individuals from the site were examined. All the remains were weighed and the fragments were examined for anatomically identifiable elements from which the age and sex of the individual could be determined. The fragments were also examined for signs of pathological change but none were found. The colour of the fragments was recorded as was the length of the longest fragment.

The results of the examination are shown in Table 11 (below) from which it will be seen that none of the cremations is complete. Only two weighed in excess of a kilogram and even this represents a relatively small proportion of the total weight expected from an adult cremation. The average weight of an adult cremation is between 2.5 – 3.0 kg.[274] Most were very much smaller than this showing that, in most cases, only a token amount of the cremated remains were taken for disposal – assuming that the amount recovered was the amount buried.

Colour

Virtually all the fragments were white or white/black in colour suggesting that the majority of the cremations had been conducted at the same, relatively high temperature. Cremated bones become lighter in colour as the temperature of the pyre increases and in a large assemblage it may be possible to determine the position of the body within the pyre from the colour of the different elements of the skeleton.[275]

Age and sex

The age and sex of the cremated individuals could be determined in many cases from the survival of anatomically recognisable elements; recovery of some molar crowns in three cases allowed the individual to be aged within narrow limits. In other cases, the thickness of cortical bone or the morphology of the sutures on surviving skull fragments at least allowed one to determine whether the individual was juvenile or adult. Anatomical elements that might have allowed the sex of the individual to be determined were almost entirely lacking, but in two cases, a fragment of the occiput had survived and in both, the morphology suggested that that it was from a male.

One interesting feature of the assemblage was the relatively large number of children and immature individuals present. Of the twenty-four individuals to whom an age at death could be assigned (albeit in many cases merely to state that they were adult), thirteen were less than twenty-five years at death and the majority of these were less than fifteen. Three very young children were present, their ages being confirmed by the presence of partly formed molar crowns. This proportion of young individuals is greater than usually found in a burial assemblage from the period but whether it truly reflects a difference in disposal of the young is dubious is view of the small numbers involved.

Identifiable elements

As expected, the majority of the fragments came from the skull and the long bones; there were very few recognisable vertebral or rib fragments which may merely reflect the greater ability of the skull and long bones to resist thermal destruction. Very few of the fragments could be identified to element but where a positive identification could be made, the majority of the bones came from the hands. The distribution of the surviving bones from the hand is shown in Table 11 below.

The fact that in so many cases, bones of the hand were recovered suggests that the hands may have come to lie outside the main area of the pyre when the body was placed on it, or the arms may have moved during the cremation; in either case they escaped destruction. It may also be the case that when picking through the ashes, fully recognisable bones were taken preferentially as being obviously part of the individual who had been cremated. The fact that no bones of the feet were recognisable seems to indicate that the feet were well within the pyre, which is rather to be expected.

Intrusive elements

A single vertebral body from an infant was found among the fragments from juvenile cremation 1283 and three other contexts contained animal fragments. Cremation burial 1294 contained a virtually complete sheep molar and cremation 1318, three sheep molar fragments; all were burnt. In addition, cremation 1318 contained a small fragment of cockle shell as did context 1421 (Cremation burial 1419). It was not possible to determine whether the shell fragments had been burned or not.

Cremation Burial 1296

Jacqueline I. McKinley

The large intact burial urn with in situ contents (context 1296) was processed as part of the *Meet the Ancestors* television programme. Although the top of the vessel had been truncated by about 4 cm as a result of plough damage, none of the contents of the vessel had been lost.

Method

The contents of the vessel were excavated in a series of ten spits, each of 2 cm in depth. As soon as cremated remains were encountered (spit 5), each spit was sub-

Table 9. Catalogue of coins

Context	Denom.	Date	Obverse	Reverse	Mint	Ref/ remarks
U/S SF1910	AE3	388–402	House of Theodosius	Salus Reipublicae	//[…]	
U/S SF1911	AE2	1st–2nd C	Illegible	Illegible		
U/S SF1912	AE3	330–335	Urbs Roma	Wolf & twins	//TrdotP	HK:65
1000 SF4	AE1	1st–2nd C	Illegible	Illegible		
1000 SF11	Groat	1485–1509	Henry VII			
1000 SF162	AE3	367–375	Gratian	Gloria Novi Saeculi	OF/I//[….]	Pierced
1001 SF2	AE1	1st–2nd C	Illegible	Illegible		
1001 SF12	AE1	Mid–late 4th	Illegible	Illegible	//[….]	11 mm diam.
1001 SF13	Radiate	270–74	Tetricus I	Illegible		
1259 SF20	Barb. Radiate	270–90	As Tetricus I	Illegible		
1418 SF15	AE3	Late 3rd–4th	Illegible	Illegible		12 mm diam.
1462 SF71	Denarius	218–22	Elagabalus	Libertas Augusti		RIC:115

divided into four quadrants and bagged separately for sieving (to 1 mm fraction) and analysis.

Results

A total of 1176.9 g of cremated bone was recovered. The bone was in good condition, with a relatively fresh appearance. Despite the compact nature of the soil matrix, minimal additional fragmentation occurred during excavation and ther was none of the toal crumbling of spongy bone as has occasionally been observed by thwe writer during excavavtion of other cremation urns.[276] The cremation comprised the remains of an older mature adult (*c.* thirty to forty-five years), probably male, along with skeletal elements from an immature female pig.[277] A number of minor pathological lesions were noted including a dental abscess in the maxillary left M3 (1/20 sockets); slight osteophytes (new bone growth at articular surface margins) at three sites (cervical, thoracic and patella) and mild to moderate exostoses (new bone growth at tendon/ ligament insertions) at three sites (iliac crest, femur shaft, patella). One extra-sutural ossicle and the site of at least one other in the lambdoid suture were also noted. The individual appears to have been relatively large and of robust build, the noted lesions being indicative of a

relatively strenuous lifestyle. Osteological analysis followed the writer's standard procedure for the examination of cremated bone.[278] Age was assessed from the stage of skeletal and tooth development[279] and the general degree of age-related changes to the bone.[280] Sex was ascertained from the sexually dimorphic traits of the skeleton.[281]

Pyre technology and cremation rituals
Cremation

With very few minor exceptions, the cremated bone was uniformly the buff/white colour associated with a high degree of oxidation.[282] Rare minor variations were noted in a few odd fragments from the lower limbs and extremities, which were slightly blue inside. This may indicate a slight shift of certain parts of the body in the later stages of cremation to areas of the pyre, such as the edges, where the heat was insufficient to complete the combustion of the bone.

Bone weights, fragmentation and skeletal elements

The total weight of bone recorded is slightly lower than was actually recovered due to it not being feasible to weigh all the <2 mm fraction, although the excluded fragments would not have accounted for more than *c.* 50 g. Of the 1176.9 g recorded, 35.5 g was identified as

Table 10. Catalogue of slag

Context/Area	Feature	Type	Description	Weight (g)
1001 A	–	Subsoil	1 piece of cinder rich iron smithing slag; abraded	12
1070 A	1069	Early Anglo–Saxon Ditch Fill	1 small fragment of an iron smithing lump	7
1225 A	1224	Roman Ditch Fill	1 small fragment of a plano-convex hearth bottom generated by iron smithing but maybe residual (or weathered) because it appears abraded.	15
			1 fragment of a plano-convex hearth bottom. Thin and dense with a small inclusion resembling tap slag, also an unusual purple red colour but not rusty. Mass charcoal imprints on top. Probably abraded.	81
			A probable proto-hearth bottom. Length 33mm, width *c.*45mm, height 15mm. Again dense and a purple-red colour. Charcoal imprints, probably abraded	16
			3 fragments of a plano-convex hearth bottom. More normal in section but very abraded. Charcoal inclusions.	53
			2 iron rich pieces of slag. One has a large vitrified stone inclusion.	21
			3 small smithing slag lumps. All probably iron rich and quite dense; all abraded.	20
			1 piece of cindery smithing slag lump.	16
			2 blobs of totally vitrified hearth lining.	10
			SF5, a possible hearth bottom fragment. Iron rich and corroding, abraded? Charcoal imprints.	12
			1 small fragment of a hearth bottom. Probably a normal type, the large crystals on the upper surface indicate that it cooled rapidly.	15
1286 B	1285	Early Anglo–Saxon Cremation	SF148, a lump of molten glass? Not associated with metal working.	9

Catriona Gibson

animal bone. The human remains recovered represent *c.* fifty to seventy-three per cent of the expected weight of cremated bone from an adult male.[283] The weight is above the average of *c.* 800–900 g recorded from undisturbed burials from other Anglo-Saxon cremation cemeteries,[284] although greater weights have been recovered for both sexes.

The vast majority of fragments (*c.* eighty-four per cent) were recovered from the 10 m sieve fraction, with maximum fragment sizes of 57 mm for skull and 68 mm for long bones. These figures are within the range of maxima recorded from modern crematoria prior to cremation (pulverisation) of the remains, of 45–95 mm for skull and 68–195 mm for long bone.[285] The role of the urn in providing added protection to the cremated bone within the burial environment has been discussed elsewhere,[286] as has the amount of undetectable fragmentation (often along dehydration fissures formed during cremation) which may occur due to disturbance and during excavation. A certain degree of the latter was observed during removal of the bone from the vessel, despite care taken in excavation. There is no evidence to suggest deliberate fragmentation of bone prior to burial, although a certain amount of incidental breakage may have resulted from tending the pyre and during recovery of bone for burial.

Skeletal elements from all areas of the body were included in the burial. Whilst it may appear, as is commonly the case, that there was a preference for collecting skull elements over others, this must be tempered by the fact that skull fragments are far easier to identify than fragments from other parts of the body.[287] This is illustrated by the fact that only *c.* fifty-eight per cent of the remains were classified as 'identifiable', the rest comprising unplaced fragments of long bone and trabecular bone. The percentage of upper limb elements within the burial is slightly lower than expected, but all the bones of the upper limb are represented. There was a noticeable absence of tooth roots (only one was recovered), which are generally more common; the apparent exclusion may not have been deliberate, but simply fortuitous or related to the mode of recovery of remains from the pyre for burial.

Table 11. Identifiable elements from cremation burials

Anatomical element	Number of cases	Number of elements
Carpals	1	2
Metacarpals	2	2
Proximal phalanges	8	10
Middle phalanges	2	4
Distal phalanges	6	6

Pyre goods and grave goods

Elements of an immature female pig were recovered within the burial, including parts of the mandible and maxilla, ribs and shoulder.[288] The inclusion of animal remains on the pyre was a common characteristic of the Anglo-Saxon cremation rite. Between twenty-one and forty-eight per cent of burials from seven major British cemeteries of this period contain animal remains.[289] As do up to eighty per cent of contemporary European burials.[290] Pig does not tend to be the most common species recovered. For example, only 8.5 per cent of the cremated animal bone from Spong Hill was pig.[291] Pig accounted for only 9.5 per cent of animal bone from Sancton.[292] At Spong Hill, the pig remains occurred very slightly more frequently with adult females than with other groups.[293] Where pig bone has been recovered, the animal is generally immature and only selected parts of the carcass were placed on the pyre.[294]

Although no other pyre goods were recovered from the burial, there are indications of the possible presence of some copper alloy on the pyre. A very small globule of melted copper alloy was recovered from spit 5c and a fragment of skull vault from spit 6b shows a small area of green staining on the exocranial surface, suggesting the presence of copper alloy. In view of the fact that not all the cremated human remains were collected for burial, it is likely that not all fragments of pyre goods were collected either. A small assemblage of iron artefacts, including a set of shears and part of a razor, were recovered from the burial together with a hone stone and a fragment of a triangular antler/bone comb. None of these items showed any evidence of having been on the pyre. This, combined with their close proximity to each other at the top or in the upper levels of the cremated bone urn fill, suggests that they were added after the deposition of the cremated remains within the urn.

Burial formation processes

One aim of the detailed division of the burial remains into horizontal and vertical sub-contexts was to try and distinguish any ordered deposition of individuals, skeletal elements, pyre and grave goods, or any other formation processes associates with burial.

The remains of the burial were encountered from spit 5 down. Associated fragments of bone (1.2 g, less than 0.1 per cent of the total) recovered from spits 1 to 4 were probably moved there by worm action. The division of bone within the remaining spits was not equal, both as a consequence of the shape on the vessel and the uneven horizontal distribution. The horizontal distribution was a major factor: thirty-six per cent of the bone was recovered from quadrant a, 23.3 per cent from quadrant b, 11.3 per cent from c and 20.3 per cent from d. These figures show that the bone was substantially angled in its distribution within the vessel. Since the vessel was upright in the grave, the angling of the contents can only have occurred during the deposition of the bone and indicates that the vessel was laid over to one side to enable the bone to be inserted, presumably from an adjacent surface on which it was heaped. This angled deposition may represent evidence against two possible theories related to the collection and deposition of cremated bone. Firstly, the theory that individual pieces of bone were immediately inserted into the burial urn during recovery from the pyre site, since this would not have necessitated tipping the vessel to this extent; secondly, bone was initially stored in another receptacle and was transferred into the urn at a later date, as there would be little advantage in placing the vessel at such an acute angle to effect the transfer.

The largest fragments were recovered from spits 6 (skull) and 8 (long bone). With the exception of spit 7c (the first level in quadrant c at which any quantity of bone was recovered) it was only in the lowest spit (10) that less than seventy-five per cent of the bone was recovered from the 10 mm sieve fraction, *i.e.* the smaller bone fragments had tended to work their way towards the base of the vessel.

Skeletal elements from all areas (skull, axial skeleton, upper and lower limb) were represented within each level of the fill. Elements of upper and lower limb were distributed throughout, with no observed significant variation. Slightly higher than average amounts of axial skeleton were recorded in spit 7 (34.4 per cent of identified axial fragments) but fragments from all areas of the spine, ribs and pelvis were observed in all levels. Higher than average percentages of skull fragments were recorded in spit 6 (forty six per cent of all recorded skull fragments) with lower than average amounts in spit 10 (1.4 per cent). Some specific areas of the skull were also very limited in distribution, with the majority of the mandible, all the maxilla and other facial bones being recovered from spits 6 and 7. Although the evidence does not suggest that skeletal elements were inserted into the vessel in any specific order, the slight variations in percentage distribution probably being largely fortuitous, the very limited distribution of the anterior bones of the skull does imply that they were at least amassed together during collection and remained together during deposition.

The fragments of cremated pig bone were recovered from spits 6–10 and were spread across the quadrants. The majority of fragments (ninety-six per cent) comprised elements of the ribs and jaw. Although fragment from both were recovered in the upper and lower parts of the burial, the rib fragments were predominantly recovered from spits 6 and 7 (sixty-two per cent) while fragments from the mandible and maxilla were predominantly from spits 8–10.

Conclusion

Some of the formation processes associated with the cremation and subsequent burial have been suggested by the detailed analysis of the burial remains. A single adult, probably male, was cremated together with portions of a dismembered immature female pig and some copper alloy object(s) were probably also included on the pyre. After cremation, which was executed efficiently, substantial proportions of the remains were gathered together into a heap for burial. Collection may have comprised recovery of individual bone fragments by one or more individuals, the remains being deposited together in a heap beside the pyre. Such a mode of collection would have been performed easily and rapidly, provided that the pyre had cooled.[295] If the pyre was still hot (the ash base still retaining heat for some considerable time) the cremated bone may have been raked off the top of the pyre to form a heap on one side. Both methods would result in a relatively random and mixed selection of skeletal elements, although hand-collection would be more likely to mass together the anterior bones of the skull in the way suggested by their position in the urn. The burial urn was placed on its side adjacent to the bone heap and fragments were 'shovelled in' by hand. Grave goods were inserted on top of the bone. One other possibility is for the inclusion of some organic material which assisted in maintaining the position of the bone in the vessel once it was returned to an upright position. The position of the bone and grave goods suggest that there was no attempt to level the contents once the vessel was righted.

Human skeletal remains

Tony Waldron

The skeletal remains from this site consisted of thirty-three adult inhumations and a small amount of dis-articulated material. This included a femur fragment of an adult male from an unstratified horizon in Area A; in Area B, an unfused femur fragment and unfused skull from a juvenile (1029/1030). A pottery vessel was also found in this feature and may have been a grave good (Fig. 40). Another juvenile femur fragment came from natural hollow 1417. This evidence suggests that juvenile inhumations may originally have been present on the site, but being shallow, were subsequently truncated by ploughing activities.

The inhumations were generally in poor condition. Some were rather fragmentary and most had suffered some post-mortem damage. Many of the skeletons had green staining on one or more of the bones, from contact with copper objects in the grave.

The skeletons were examined to determine the age and sex of the skeleton using standard anthropological techniques,[296] to look for any pathological changes and diagnose these changes wherever possible.

Age and sex

All but two of the skeletons could be assigned a sex and all but two of the males and three of the females were given an age at death. There were more females than males in the assemblage (eighteen compared to thirteen), giving a male to female ratio of 0.72. Normally one would expect the ratio to be close to unity, but given the small number in the assemblage, no particular significance should be given to this observation. It has undoubtedly been affected by the fact that the entire cemetery was not excavated. The demographic distribution of the assemblage is shown in Table 12 below. This shows that the sample contained a substantial proportion of young men – half were aged under thirty-five years at the time of their death. On the other hand, the age distribution of the females was much more in line with expectation, with the majority of the deaths in the oldest age group. It is interesting that there were no juvenile skeletons in the assemblage (although there were possible truncated, disarticulated and fragmentary juveniles). These normally account for up to a third of the burials at the site. Some foetal and juvenile bones were found, from unstratified horizons, natural hollows and pits as well as intrusive with one of the adult female inhumations. These included the unfused skull of a child from the subsoil and an infant femur from hollow 1417, suggesting that children had been buried on the site, although outside the area of the present excavation, or else were from shallow graves, now completely destroyed.

An estimation of height was possible in eighteen of the skeletons, using the regression equations published by Mildred Trotter.[297] There is little overlap between the heights of the two sexes. The differences in the mean heights (1.75 m for the males and 1.61 m for the females) was highly significant ($p<0.001$); the mean scale is weighted by two exceptionally tall individuals, one of 1.80 m and another of 1.85 m (5 ft 11 in and 6 ft 1 in, respectively). The heights were estimated from the maximum length of the extant long bone with the smallest standard error and this may have resulted in the mean heights of the males being underestimated,[298] which would make this small sample of males even more unusual.

Dental health

Several of the skeletons lacked skulls or mandibles or both and so the number of sets of teeth available for examination was relatively small. The total number of teeth which should be present in thirty three adults is 1056 (33×32), but in fact, only 672 (63.6 per cent) could be accounted for. This total was made up of 614 extant teeth, forty-two sockets from which teeth had been lost post-mortem, twelve teeth lost ante-mortem and two unerupted third molars. Eight individuals had dental disease, including caries, ante-mortem tooth loss and there was a single case with a dental abscess (Table 13 below).

The state of the mouths of the individuals from Alwalton was reasonable and certainly considerably better than that generally seen at other Anglo-Saxon or medieval sites. At Barrington, seventy-five per cent of the adults of forty-five plus years of age had ante-mortem tooth loss, as well as fifty per cent caries.[299] The most frequent occurrence was the loss of teeth during life, whether as a result of primary tooth or gum disease, or from trauma is difficult to tell, but the fact that in only a single case was tooth loss associated with dental caries, suggests that it was more likely to be due to gum disease or trauma.

Pathology

A number of pathological conditions were noted in this group of skeletons, including osteoarthritis and rotator cuff disease, spondylolysis, trauma and possible infection. The most common finding (in eleven cases) was of Schmorl's nodes in either the thoracic or lumbar regions of the spine. They occurred at all ages and in both sexes. Schmorl's nodes are recognised in the skeleton as indentations of various shapes in the end plates of the vertebrae. They are caused when the gelatinous inner part of the intervertebral disc ruptures through the outer fibrous layers to cause a pressure defect in the bone. They usually cause no symptoms and the affected individuals generally are completely unaware of their presence during life.

There were four cases of osteoarthritis, all in females aged at least forty-five years at the time of their death, and all were in common sites. One had osteoarthritis of the spine, another of the left acromio-clavicular joint and a third of the proximal interphalangeal joints of the hand. The final case had osteoarthritis of the patello-femoral joint of the left knee and of the left acromio-clavicular joint. In addition, this woman had rotator cuff disease during life. This is a condition which is caused by inflammation of some or all of the tendons which form the capsule of the shoulder joint. In some cases the capsule ruptures, allowing the head of the humerus to impinge on the under surface of the acromion, which if continued for long, results in eburnation of the superior surface of the humerus and the inferior surface of the acromion. Although the humerus was missing, the undersurface of the acromion was eburnated, indicating that the humeral head must have rubbed against it for a considerable time. There was a second case of rotator cuff disease, this time of the right shoulder as shown by the presence of new bone on the point of insertion of the subscapularis muscle on the anterior surface of the top of the humerus; this was another 'elderly' female.

Rotator cuff disease is a common cause of shoulder and arm pain in the modern population and is highly age-related. It is most likely that the two women who had the condition in the Alwalton assemblage would also have noticed some pain and, in the case of the woman with impingement syndrome, some limitation of movement at the shoulder as well.

There were no cases of primary bone infection but, in a single case, a male of twenty-five to thirty-five, two of the left ribs (number 2 and number 3 or 4) had periosteal new bone on their inner surfaces (grave 1032). While there are many causes of periostitis, in this position, it is likely to have been caused by an infection in the periphery of the lung; either pneumonia or pleurisy could have affected these changes.

One man, aged twenty-five to thirty-five at death, had a well-healed fracture in the upper quarter of his left tibia (grave 1387.2). The fracture had clearly occurred several years before his death as it was completely remodelled. The bones had healed in good alignment, suggesting that he had received some treatment at the time of the break. Although there were no other fractures, an adult male was found with the right distal tibia fused to the talus, which could also have been the result of trauma. In the same man, a raised area of new bone was found at the distal end of the left tibia which was probably caused by the presence of a varicose ulcer in the overlying soft tissue of the ankle.

An interesting finding was of four cases of spondylolysis, three in females and one in a male. Spondylolysis is caused by a fracture, usually through the pars interarticularis, which results in the lamina of the vertebra becoming separated from the body. The lesions almost always occur in the lumbar vertebrae, usually L5, and the condition is thought to be a form of stress fracture. In the present series, three of the cases were at the L5 and the fourth at the L4. The rates of spondylolysis vary considerably between countries and there has been some variation over time; in the Anglo-Saxon period in Britain the prevalence rate has been calculated to be approximately five per cent with an approximately equal sex ratio.[300] The prevalence rate at the Alwalton cemetery is considerably greater than this and the sex ratio is substantially different since three of the four cases were in females. The prevalence rate is approximately sixteen per cent (four in twenty-five cases with extant lumbar vertebrae). However, consideration of the ninety-five per cent confidence intervals, that is, the range within which the 'true' prevalence is likely to lie, shows how little credence should be given to results based on small samples. The ninety-five per cent confidence intervals are 4.5–36.1 per cent, which encompasses the 'expected' value of five per cent, suggesting that this is not an unusual cluster of cases, but an artefact caused by the size of the sample.

identified/recorded fragments were recovered from Area A and 153 identified/recorded fragments from Area B. The condition of the animal bone was, in general, fair to good. The Number of Identifiable fragments of bones of each Species (NISP) for each period in Area A is presented in Table 14. NISP for each phase of Area B is given in Table 15.

Methodology

Bone was identified by comparison with reference material in the collection of the author and published descriptions. The recording system is based on Davis,[301] Albarella and Davis[302] and Albarella, Beech and Mulville.[303] In brief, a restricted set of fragments identifiable to species is recorded. That provides all available evidence for ageing and metrical analysis and eliminates unnecessary replication and the recording of redundant information. Vertebrae and ribs are not recorded (although a note is made of their general frequency in any given deposit). An exception has been made with regard to the dog skeletons where each element recovered is recorded and counted.

Notes on the species

Horse

In Area A, a distal equid metapodial fragment was found in Roman ditch 1111, femur fragments in Anglo-Saxon pit 1236 and an axis fragment in Anglo-Saxon well 1058.

In Area B, horse remains are found in Roman and Anglo-Saxon contexts and comprise seven per cent of animal bones identified to species. In Roman quarry pit 1413 seven isolated upper and lower teeth were found belonging to one, or possibly two, animals aged between eight and twelve years.[304] A distal tibia fragment and a calcaneum belonging to a single individual were found in Roman quarry pit 1454. In natural hollow 1417 distal tibia and astragalus fragments belonging to a single individual were recovered.

Cattle

The remains of cattle are more frequent than those of any other taxon, accounting for thirty-one per cent of identified fragments recovered from Area A and twenty-

Animal Bone

Ian L. Baxter BA MIFA

Introduction

A total weight of 18 kg of animal bone representing 1089 fragments was recovered from Areas A and B. Of this total, 225 'countable' fragments were identified to species (see Methodology below). A total of seventy-one

Table 12. Age and sex distribution of skeletons

Age (years)	Male	Female	Unknown
		Sex	
15–25	2	3	
25–35	5	2	
35–45	1	1	
45+	3	9	
Unknown	2	3	2
Total	**13**	**18**	**2**

six per cent from Area B. All the cattle bones are extensively butchered and provide little information on size and conformation from any period, although beasts ranging from calves to elderly animals are represented in the Roman and early Anglo-Saxon deposits in both areas. The horncore of an adult female was found together with the tips of two other cores in medieval pit 1449. The complete core came from a short horned beast with forward curving horns. An innominate fragment found in Area A Anglo-Saxon well 1058 came from a cow based on the low acetabular rim height and sharp ilio-pubic ridge.[305] The only complete bones from stratified deposits suitable for providing withers heights came from Area B Roman quarry pit 1415 and tree throw 1438. These came from beasts 1.30 m and 1.01 m high at the shoulder.[306] An ischium fragment from Area A ditch 1224 has a polished (eburnated) acetabulum suggestive of arthritis.[307] Two first phalanges from Area B natural hollow 1417 have cut marks, in one case above the lateral distal articulation and in the other multiple transverse cut marks on the anterior surface distal to the proximal articulation.

Sheep/Goat

Sheep/Goat remains account for fourteen per cent of fragments found in Area A and twenty-four per cent found in Area B. Only one identifiable goat fragment was recovered, a horncore from Area B tree throw 1438. This derived from a male based on its basal dimensions. In all other cases where species could be identified the bones belonged to sheep. Sheep were positively identified in Roman, Anglo-Saxon and medieval deposits in Areas A and B. A posterior cranium with both horncores belonging to a ram were found in Area A Roman pit 1095. There are cut marks across the occipital above the foramen magnum. In the same Area the horncore of a ewe was found in Anglo-Saxon well 1058. This is marked with 'thumb prints' (eidellungen). The available evidence suggests that horncore depressions are due to a resorption of calcium in completely developed cores, most frequently

affecting ewes and probably caused by a combination of environmental stresses, such as malnutrition, repeated pregnancies and excessive milking.[308] At the early Anglo-Saxon site of Cardinal Distribution Park, Godmanchester (Cambridgeshire) 10.5 per cent of sheep horncores had 'thumb prints'.[309] A sheep metacarpus and metatarsus from medieval pit 1449 came from animals 0.564 m and 0.592 m high at the shoulder.[310]

Pig

Pig remains were infrequent in Area A accounting for six per cent of identified bone, but more common in Area B at fourteen per cent. A calcaneum from Area A Anglo-Saxon well 1058 came from an animal approximately 0.676 m high at the shoulder.[311] A male lower canine fragment was found in Area B Roman quarry pit 1413. This may belong with the other pig remains from the same feature which are all sub-adult. A male maxilla fragment and a male mandible, possibly from the same individual, were found in Area B medieval pit 1449. This animal was a young adult.

Dog

The remains of domestic dog were frequent in both Areas and include partial skeletons. In Area A undated pit 1056 contained twenty-four bones belonging to a single animal. This dog stood around 0.67 m high at the shoulder, and the recovery of its baculum or os penis indicates that it was male.[312] Three of the thoracic vertebrae possess ventral osteophytes (stage 3) and four have pitted and eburnated centra. The animal suffered from spondylosis deformans (spinal arthritis) probably resulting in stiffness of the shoulder area. This condition is quite common in older dogs.[313] A humerus fragment belonging to a large dog was found in Area A Anglo-Saxon well 1058. Roman pit 1413 in Area B contained the remains of two large dogs. The only suitable bone complete enough to indicate shoulder height is a Mt. V which came from an animal that stood approximately 0.60 m high at the withers.[314] Mandible and humerus

Table 13. Dental disease in skeletons

Context No.	Sex	Age	With caries	Number of teeth Missing ante mortem	With abscess
1352	Female	45+	1	6	
1368	Male	45+	2		
1375	Male	45+	1		
1381	Female	35–45		4	
1405	Male	45+	1		1
1452	Female	45+		1	
1464	Female	45+	1		
1469	Female	45+		1	

fragments of a slightly smaller dog were found in hollow 1417 in Area B. The humerus fragment is gnawed.

Birds
The bones of domestic birds were infrequent in both areas but fowl fragments occurred in Area A ditch 1224 and tree throw 1438 in Area B. Goose bones were found in Area A Anglo-Saxon well 1058 and Area B Roman quarry pit 1413.

Discussion

Not enough material was recovered from either area to provide any detailed evidence of husbandry practices during any period of the site's occupation. However, horses, cattle, sheep, pigs and dogs were all kept during the Roman and early Anglo-Saxon periods. The dogs were large and doubtless used for both hunting and herding, although there is no evidence for the exploitation of natural resources. There is evidence that goats, chickens and geese were kept during the Roman period and geese in the early Anglo-Saxon.

Charred Plant Macrofossils and other Remains

Val Fryer

Samples for the extraction of plant macrofossils were taken from across the excavated area and thirty-three were submitted for assessment. The samples were processed by the excavators, collecting the flots in a 500 micron mesh sieve. The dried flots were scanned under a binocular microscope at magnifications up to ×16. Nomenclature follows Stace.[315] All plant remains were preserved by charring.

Modern contaminants including fibrous roots, seeds/fruits and arthropod remains were present in all samples.

Plant macrofossils

Cereals and seeds/fruits of common weed species were noted at extremely low densities in eleven samples. Preservation of the material was very poor; cereal grains and seeds had become extremely puffed and distorted during charring and many specimens were also abraded and fragmentary.

Cereals
Grains were noted in only nine samples. Oats (*Avena* sp.), barley (*Hordeum* sp.) and wheat (*Triticum* sp.) were recorded. Chaff elements were not present. A cotyledon fragment from a large indeterminate pulse (Fabaceae) was recovered from Sample 64 (grave 1425, fill 1426).

Wild flora and other plant macrofossils
Seeds/fruits of common weeds were extremely rare; single specimens were present in only eight samples. Taxa noted included brome (*Bromus* sp.), black bindweed (*Fallopia convolvulus*), redshank/pale persicaria (*Persicaria maculosa/lapathifolia*), chickweed (*Stellaria* sp.) and vetch/vetchling (*Vicia/Lathyrus* sp.). Small fragments of hazel (*Corylus avellana*) nutshell were recovered from Samples 16 (early Iron Age pit 1140, fill 1141) and 20 (Bronze Age pit 1142, fill 1143).

Charcoal fragments were present at varying densities throughout and formed the sole component of the assemblages from Samples 7 (pit 1038, fill 1039), 22 (Area A, evaluation posthole 1119, fill 1120), 80 (cremation 1257, fill 1259) and 84 (cremation 1285, fill 1287). Other plant macrofossils included fragments of heather (Ericaceae) stem and indeterminate seeds and tubers.

Table 14. Area A. Number of identifiable fragments of bones of each species

Taxon	Early Iron Age	Romano–British	Anglo–Saxon	Undated	Total
Horse (*Equus caballus* L.)	–	1	2	4	7
Cattle (*Bos* f. domestic)	–	7	12	3	22
Sheep/Goat (*Ovis/Capra* f. domestic)	3	2	4	1	10
Sheep (*Ovis* f. domestic)	–	(1)	(1)	–	(2)
Pig (*Sus* f. domestic)	1	–	2	1	4
Dog (*Canis familiaris* L.)	–	–	1	24*	25
Domestic Fowl (*Gallus* f. domestic)	–	2	–	–	2
Domestic Goose (*Anser* f. domestic)	–	–	1	–	1
Total	4	12	22	33	71

Key * skeleton (MNI = 1) 'Sheep/Goat' also includes specimens identified to species. Numbers in parentheses are not included in the total of the period.

Other materials

The fragments of black porous 'cokey' material and black tarry material are probably derived from the combustion of organic materials at very high temperatures. The fragments of burnt bone are all probably related to the early Anglo-Saxon cremations.

Molluscs

Mollusc shells were common or abundant in the majority of samples although most appear to be modern contaminants. A single burnt specimen, which may be contemporary with the deposits, was recorded from Sample 34 (cremation 1244, fill 1246)

Discussion

For the purposes of the discussion, the material will be divided by period.

Pre-Roman deposits

Two samples of probable pre-Roman date were submitted, one from a pit fill of possible early Iron Age date (pit 1140) and another from a pit containing one sherd of Bronze Age pottery (pit 1142). Both contain material (including cereals, seeds, nutshell fragments and charcoal) which is probably derived from a very low-density scatter of refuse of unknown origin.

Early Anglo-Saxon deposits

Three samples were taken from the fills of well 1058. Cereals, weed seeds and charcoal fragments were present but rare and it appears likely that all are probably derived from wind-blown detritus that became accidentally incorporated within the fills.

A total of twenty samples were taken from cremation and/or inhumation deposits. Of these, only six contained material other than charcoal, indeterminate plant macrofossils and burnt bone fragments. Grave 1425 contained very few plant macrofossils and were reduced to a single cereal grain, a fragment of a large pulse, charcoal fragments and small pieces of charred root, rhizome or stem, all of which were probably accidentally incorporated within the grave fill.

Cereals and seeds are also extremely rare within the cremation deposits, occurring in only three samples. Although the cereals may be derived from offerings to the deceased, which were included within the pyre, the quantity recovered is so low that it appears more likely that they were accidentally introduced. The grasses and grassland herbs, heather stems and indeterminate tubers may be derived from material used as fuel or kindling for the fires. Similar assemblages, also interpreted as fuel residues, were noted from contemporary cremation deposits at, for example Tranmer House, Sutton Hoo (Suffolk) and RAF Lakenheath (Suffolk).[316]

The sample from the pyre deposit contained a single burnt shell of *Vallonia costata*, a species of mollusc indicative of open dry land habitats. This may either have been introduced on the kindling materials or incorporated beneath the pyre.

Undated Contexts

Two samples were taken from the fills of undated postholes 1154 and 1170. The assemblages are typical of those seen elsewhere on the site in that they contain a low density of cereals and weed seeds and are probably derived from a low density scatter of refuse.

Table 15. Area B. Number of identifiable fragments of bones of each species

Taxon	Romano-British	Anglo-Saxon	Med	Undated	Total
Horse (*Equus caballus* L.)	9	2	–	–	11
Cattle (*Bos* f. domestic)	25	4	9	2	40
Sheep/Goat (*Ovis/Capra* f. domestic)	20	3	6	7	36
Sheep (*Ovis* f. domestic)	(1)	(2)	(2)	(1)	(6)
Goat (*Capra* f. domestic)	(1)	–	–	–	(1)
Pig (*Sus* f. domestic)	8	–	12	1	21
Dog (*Canis familiaris* L.)	41*	3	–	–	44*
Domestic Fowl (*Gallus* f. domestic)	1	–	+	–	1
Domestic Goose (*Anser* f. domestic)	+	–	–	–	+
Total	104	12	27	10	153

*Key * skeleton (MNI = 1) 'Sheep/Goat' also includes specimens identified to species. Numbers in parentheses are not included in the total of the period.*

Conclusions

In summary, the assemblages from this site typically contain an extremely low density of material. Although some macrofossils from the cremations may be derived from the fuel or kindling used for the pyres, the remaining material appears to comprise very small quantities of refuse of unknown origin which have become accidentally incorporated into the features. None of the samples contained quantifiably viable assemblages (*i.e.* 200+ specimens).

PART IV DISCUSSION

Catriona Gibson

The local and regional context of Alwalton cemetery

The excavations at Alwalton produced substantial and significant remains of an early Anglo-Saxon mixed-rite burial ground. A fuller understanding of this site can be appreciated through placing it within its local and regional context.

Evidence for activity in the vicinity of Alwalton dates back to the Mesolithic, with the presence of a flint scatter identified *c.* 1 km to the south-west of the site (Fig. 1a.1). It was in the early Bronze Age, however, that this landscape became moulded, as attested by the creation of funerary mounds, many of which have been identified from aerial photographs. The site itself is to some extent surrounded by barrows and these features were probably instrumental in influencing the location of the later Anglo-Saxon cemetery (Fig. 1a.2, 3, 6–9). It is argued that such re-use of monumental landscapes is common to approximately twenty-five per cent of all known Anglo-Saxon cemetery sites.[317]

In the late Bronze Age, the spectacular site of Flag Fen, on the eastern fringe of Peterborough, attests to a high level of ritual and settlement activity in the area. A number of late Bronze Age deposits of weaponry have been recovered from the River Nene, just to the north of Minerva Business Park (Fig. 1a.4–5). These include a leaf-shaped sword and a small dagger, and may suggest a continuation of the Flag Fen ritual landscape associated with watery votive deposits to the west.

There is a wealth of Iron Age settlement evidence, although most dates to the middle or late phases. This may be a bias of archaeological visibility rather than reality and Pryor has suggested it reflects the development from a dispersed occupation in the early Iron Age such as that revealed at Fengate, to more obvious nucleated settlements in the landscape.[318] A late Iron Age settlement, known as Monument 97, lies in the vicinity of Minerva Business Park, at Orton Longueville (Fig. 1a.11). This was composed of a number of roundhouses and ditched yard enclosures.[319] The Iron

Age evidence from the Area A excavation may be associated with this settlement. There are a number of other cropmarks and earthworks dotted around the landscape. Although many are undated, several are undoubtedly of this period and a Roman settlement to the east of the site appears to have originated in the late Iron Age (Fig. 1a.12).

During the Roman period, the site would have lain in the hinterland of the small town at Water Newton (Durobrivae), only 1.5 km to the north-west, and the fort of Great Casterton to the north. The evidence demonstrates that this region was very prosperous, with activity and occupation stretching along the line of Ermine Street outside the town wall in both directions, with the river acting as a major bridging point. It would appear that these suburbs extended to within 500 m of the site. The production of Nene valley pottery was an important industry in this area. Many kilns are known, but seem to be distributed predominantly on the north side of town. To the east of the site, the nature of the Roman occupation is more rural in character, with features such as yards, ditches and burials having been recorded in the vicinity.

During this time, the Nene Valley was characterised not only by industrial sites, but also by opulent villas. Durobrivae reached its apogee during the second and third centuries AD, with the large and impressive villa of Castor and the Water Newton silver hoard. It was in the fourth century that the site suffered a severe decline, consequently becoming deserted. To the north-east of Minerva Business Park, the late Roman farmstead of Orton Hall Farm attests to potential continuity between the Roman and Anglo-Saxon periods, through the mixture of Roman and Anglo-Saxon pottery.[320]

It is into this context that the burials at Minerva Business Park, Alwalton, may be placed. A number of other fifth and sixth century Anglo-Saxon cemeteries are attested along the Nene valley. Remains of urns found during pipe-laying in 1975, only 800 m to the north-east of the Minerva site, were thought to have come from the remains of a ploughed-out barrow, rather than part of a flat cemetery.[321] It is likely, however, that this formed part of the same funerary landscape as the mixed rite cemetery at Minerva Business Park. Notebooks held at Peterborough Museum suggest the pots were in the upper fill of a large quarry pit, perhaps similar to features encountered in Area B. An earlier watching brief immediately to the west had found evidence of Anglo-Saxon inhumations along with skull fragments, Roman and Anglo-Saxon pottery (Fig. 1.26). These finds clearly indicate that the Alwalton cemetery continues to the west.

Several more substantial cemeteries are known within a few kilometres of Alwalton. The first finds came to light intermittently during the nineteenth and early twentieth century in Peterborough itself and thus their locations are not precisely known. Two main areas of burials were uncovered. The larger site lay on the boundary between Woodston and Fletton, and covered an area of at least 200 × 100 m; a second cemetery of uncertain extent was located about 800 m further west.[322] This latter site, in the vicinity of Woodston Hill, may be the same as that on the north side of Oundle Road, where Abbott excavated in 1911.[323]

A further early Anglo-Saxon cemetery was excavated in 1942, also by Abbott, at Nassington, about 7 km upstream from Alwalton.[324] As with the Peterborough cemeteries, cremation appears to have been just a minor element, but at Nassington many more cremations than the three excavated are likely to have been destroyed. Some 2.5 km north-east of Alwalton, on the north side of the river, the mid fifth- to late sixth-century cemetery at Longthorpe contained twenty-two cremations, some accompanied by objects, and just two inhumations.[325] Many of these cremation urns were decorated with similar motifs to those noted at Minerva and although grave goods were less frequent than at the latter site, fragments of antler/bone combs were the most common items. More recent excavations at Gunthorpe, *c.* 8 km north-east of Alwalton, revealed some thirty inhumation graves, probably of sixth-century date, and one urned cremation – although, as at Nassington, the excavators suspected further cremations had been destroyed.[326]

Individual burials from the vicinity of Alwalton are known at Sibson (Fig. 1a.18) to the west and Castor to the north. Another possible cemetery is also recorded at Chesterton (Fig. 1a.19) just 2 km west of the site. Further afield, a number of cemeteries are known from the Welland valley to the north, including one at Helpston, 11 km from Alwalton; and on the east side of Peterborough at Eye and Whittlesey, 12–15 km away.[327]

Settlement sites which complement the burial information remain relatively sparse, although one would expect these gravels to be attractive for occupation. At Alwalton, some middle Saxon evidence potentially related to occupation was found to the south of the cemetery in Area A. This may have been part of a shifting settlement pattern, with early Saxon settlement evidence lying in the vicinity. Only 3 km to the north-east of Alwalton, early Anglo-Saxon occupation is attested on the Roman site at Orton Hall Farm, apparently lasting into the early sixth century AD. Its demise then may be related to a fresh migration attested in the annals for the time.[328] A number of other Roman sites in the area show fifth to sixth century reoccupation, including settlements at Haddon, south of Alwalton, and Marholm Road, Peterborough; the latter included a possible Grubenhaus. Early twentieth century excavations in Peterborough produced sixth to seventh century settlement evidence from sites at Woodston and Orton Longueville. Subsequently, occupation producing Middle Saxon Ipswich ware (*c.* AD 650–850) has been discovered north of the river at Castor, again on an old Roman site, associated with the nunnery mentioned below.

Documentary evidence from the seventh-century Tribal Hidage suggests the presence of small tribal units in the Nene valley, with the lands of the North and South Gyrwa or 'Fen Dwellers' to be found either side of the river. This was a time of the creation of larger kingdoms and polities, however, and by the end of the century the Peterborough area lay within the kingdom of the Middle Angles, a tributary of Mercia. It was also the time when the Church came to prominence, with a number of early monasteries founded in Mercia. King Wulfhere (AD 657–674) endowed a monastery at Medehamstede (Peterborough) while the daughters of King Penda (AD 632–654), Cyneburgha and Cynethryth, allegedly founded the nunnery at Castor. Occupation of the period has, as mentioned, been excavated at the latter site, while seventh-century burials in the present Cathedral close seem to attest to the former.[329]

Thus, the setting in which the Alwalton cemetery formed a part was complex and multi-layered. It was located within earlier prehistoric and Roman landscapes and strands of continuity may be witnessed between the Roman and Anglo-Saxon periods. Earlier Bronze Age barrows, Iron Age and Roman settlements all moulded and transformed this cultured space. The Nene valley acted as a focus for burial places, particularly in the early Anglo-Saxon period, when numerous small cemeteries were dotted along the river.

To date, the burial ground at Alwalton is one of the largest excavated along this valley dating between the fifth and sixth centuries. Although some of the cremation burials are slightly earlier in date than the inhumations, both show considerable chronological overlap. Other mixed-rite cemeteries are known elsewhere in the region. Further south in Cambridgeshire, cemeteries of sixth-century date are known at Oakington, Haslingfield and Hauxton, while a fifth-century example was discovered at Girton.[330]

Cemeteries with both inhumation and cremation burials are not uncommon and published examples include Longthorpe and Nassington (Peterborough), Beckford (Hereford and Worcester), Mucking and Great Chesterford (Essex), Spong Hill (Norfolk), Snape (Suffolk) and Portway (Hampshire). However, they often have a majority of one particular type of burial, and there tends to be little overlap in date between cremation and inhumation burials, with the former generally being earlier.[331] For example, at Great Chesterford, inhumations predominated, and the same was true at Beckford.[332] At Beckford, most of the cremations were situated close to the inhumations, although one was in an isolated position at the eastern edge of the cemetery.

Alwalton is unusual in that comparable numbers of cremations and inhumations were found (thirty-three inhumations and thirty cremations), although it is important to note that the sample is biased as the cemetery was only partially excavated. To some extent, cremations and inhumations overlapped chronologically, with examples of both types dating to between the late fifth and early sixth century. Figure 6 illustrates the distribution of cremation graves on the site over time, showing fairly even development over time rather than development in any particular direction. A similar number of inhumation and cremation burials have been identified at Snape (forty-seven and fifty-one respectively) which also overlapped in date from the late fifth to the seventh century.[333]

While the inhumation burials from Alwalton were on the whole spatially separate from the cremation burials, a certain degree of overlap can be identified, particularly in the eastern part of the site. For example, cremation burials 1324, 1318, 1422 and 1419 show close spatial association with inhumation graves 1390, 1451, 1440 and 1463 respectively, with only a few metres separating them (Fig. 4). Interestingly, these four cremation burials were all unfurnished and were placed in plain vessels (Fig. 9). Plain vessels are significantly more common in the eastern part of the site, while decorated vessels and a mixture of decorated and plain vessels are more common in the west of the site (Fig. 9).

There is also a mixture of cremation and inhumation burials in the south-western part of the site, although they are not located so closely together (Fig. 4). In general, however, most of the cremation burials are concentrated in the west, while the inhumations nearly all lie in the southern and eastern parts of the site. A single outlying inhumation was noted in the far north-western area (grave 1374, Fig. 4), but this was also located well away from the main cluster of cremations. This was the grave of an adult male lacking in grave goods, but there was no other indication as to why it lay so far from contemporary burials. The distribution of cremations predominately to the west and inhumations to the east was also noted at Portway, Andover (Hampshire)[334] and Lucy [335] noted a similar distribution pattern in cemeteries in East Yorkshire.

Only a few more inhumation than cremation burials were recovered, yet twice as many grave goods were retrieved from the former (mean of 2.7 grave goods per inhumation and 1.6 grave goods per cremation burial). However, this average hides some other important statistical variations. Firstly, more cremation burials than inhumations were furnished (seventy per cent as opposed to fifty per cent). This number may have been skewed by grave robbing and other disturbance, and certainly some of the more poorly preserved and disarticulated skeletons lack grave goods. However, pyre goods once associated with the cremations may have been burnt or melted beyond recognition, or may not have been collected with the cremated bone at the time of burial. Thus, direct comparisons between the number of grave goods in inhumation and cremation burials will not provide accurate reflections. Over half the total number of grave goods came from only three inhumation burials (graves 1263, 1358 and 1364), implying a greater disparity in wealth with respect to the inhumations.

Location of the cemetery

The social and political background to the Alwalton cemetery can be explored further through an understanding of its geographical context. The burial ground is located only 150 m to the south of the River Nene and lies at only 10 m AOD. As already mentioned, further Anglo-Saxon cemeteries have been found along the Nene valley, and proximity to water appears to be a consistent feature of many Anglo-Saxon burial sites.[336] River valleys tend to provide excellent agricultural land and although it may seem wasteful to inter the dead within prime land, the fertility of the soil may in itself provide a metaphor for the dead – implying a link between fertility and rebirth. Rivers often delimit territorial units and a number of archaeologists have advocated that Anglo-Saxon cemeteries are connected with this idea of boundary formation and delimitation.[337]

It is hard to determine whether we can call the cemetery at Alwalton a bounded 'field cemetery', within well demarcated limits, since only part of the site was excavated. However, previous findings of other inhumation and cremation burials in the vicinity might suggest that the people buried at Alwalton were interred within part of a broader funerary landscape, lacking defined limits and stretching in both directions along the river. This may help to explain why the cemetery was not particularly crowded, with both cremation and inhumation burials being generally well spaced and respecting natural features in the landscape rather than man-made barriers.

Layout and internal arrangement of the cemetery

The internal arrangement of the exposed part of the cemetery at Alwalton at first glance would appear to be haphazard and random. Many early Anglo-Saxon cemeteries show clear internal organisation, with graves laid out in rows, lines[338] or radiating spirals.[339] In other cases, burial may be aligned along earlier features in the landscape, such as the Iron Age ditch at Barrington A.[340]

However, on closer inspection, there may have been a conscious organisation of the cemetery. In the first place, some of the inhumation and cremation burials are clustered together, suggesting that they are part of small family groupings (Fig. 8). This idea is supported by the grave goods, in particular fragments of the same bone combs being retrieved from different cremation burials (see Grave Goods from the Cremations above). Other key indicators of kinship relationships include the proximity and alignment of certain graves. Pairs of burials such as graves 1355 and 1366, or trios, such as graves 1410, 1425 and 1432, were undoubtedly related. There was less certainty with others but grave 1389, containing two inhumations (a forty-five year old female and a twenty-five and thirty-five year old male) may also have been part of the same kinship group (Fig. 8).

Catriona Gibson

Some form of social affiliation is also possible given the predominance of plain cremation vessels to the east and decorated to the west.[341]

Other levels of organisation may also be identified. When taken as a group, the layout of the inhumation burials respects the course of the adjacent river. With one exception, they form a rough meandering line oriented roughly north-east/south-west, mirroring the River Nene. Conversely, the cremations bear a close relationship to the tree throws (Fig. 11)[342] and if the trees were indeed contemporary with the cemetery, perhaps some marked or shaded the urns.

Some 'gaps' in the cemetery were also identified at Alwalton and may have defined pathways, to the south and east of putative cremation pyre 1326. Furthermore, with the exception of grave 1374, there were no burials in the vicinity of pyre 1326. This may have been because this area was wooded, or because it was kept as an open space, where groups of people would gather to perform death ceremonies (Fig. 11).

Orientation of the inhumations

Most of the burials were orientated in a roughly east-facing direction; predominantly approximately south-west – north-east (fifty-six per cent). The others were aligned north-west – south-east (nineteen per cent), south-east – north-west (twelve per cent) or east-west (nine per cent). Orientation does not appear to have been related to age, sex or supposed status at the cemetery of Alwalton, although the small number of burials excavated may mask any discernible patterns. Only one burial, grave 1399, was laid directly opposite to the standard alignment, with the head to the north-east. This contained an adult male, between twenty-five and thirty-five years of age. He was buried without grave goods and was also in a rather unusual position, lying on his side with his body twisted (Fig. 30). Although in the south-eastern part of the excavation area, he was in slight spatial isolation with respect to the other in-humation burials. At Great Chesterford, reverse direction graves were argued to represent the presence of strangers in the community.[343]

The predominant orientation at Alwalton suggests that, as at other cemeteries such as Barrington A, there was no obvious connection between alignment and astronomical events such as sunrise. Natural and other topographical factors were perhaps deemed more relevant. In the case of Alwalton, the main orientation may have been related to the large Bronze Age tumulus on Chesterton Hill, *c.* 1.8 km south-west of the site. Chesterton Hill is the highest point in the vicinity (54 m AOD), overlooking the Nene valley to the north and the low-lying fens to the east.

Population profiles

With the exception of Great Chesterford, where eighty-six non-adults were present, infants and even juveniles are often lacking or at least under-represented in most early Anglo-Saxon cemeteries.[344] For example at Polhill and Dover in Kent, infant burials were completely absent from the two cemeteries.[345] This is also true at Alwalton, at least with respect to the inhumation burials. Several theories have been put forward to explain this under-representation of the younger members of society.

The youngest individuals may have been buried in very shallow graves and therefore may have been more susceptible to ploughing and other disturbance. This may have been a contributing factor in the survival of infant remains at Alwalton since the three possible juvenile interments (graves 1029, 1417 and 1432) were heavily disturbed and truncated. When coupled with the fact that infant bones, being smaller and more fragile, are less likely to be preserved, this may account for some bias in the record.

However, there is also the possibility that infants were conceptualised as a different category within society. High child mortality within Anglo-Saxon communities may have acted as a deterrent to the adults, so that they refrained from becoming emotionally attached to their offspring until an age when their chance of survival was considered good.[346] However, the fact that infants are occasionally buried with quite wealthy grave assemblages implies that the situation is more complex than this.[347]

An interesting and potentially complex pattern also emerges when we compare the different age categories from Alwalton. While no infants and only three possible juveniles were represented in the inhumation record, the cremation burials included three infants, seven juveniles and one adolescent. This indicates a different selective process with respect to the two burial traditions (Table 16). The same is true at the opposite end of the age spectrum – mature adults are not represented in the cremation burials. Again this skewing of age according to burial rite may be a result of the fact that only part of the cemetery was excavated. Nonetheless, it may be significant. Furthermore, a number of people survived until over forty-five years of age at Alwalton (nine females and three males). This is a relatively high figure in comparison to other cemeteries. For instance, at Barrington A, only eight males and six females survived to the age of forty-five years (out of 194 inhumation and cremation burials).

The different age ranges for the two burial types may support the idea that cremation rites were slightly earlier than inhumation practices. This argument is put forward by Nina Crummy who suggests that the inhumation grave goods demonstrate an increase of wealth within the society.[348] If the associated settlement had become more affluent, this may have resulted in an improved diet, producing a healthier population with fewer members

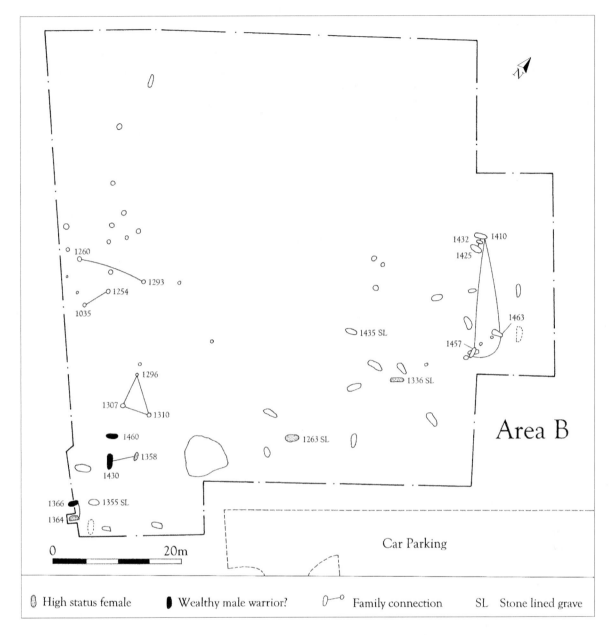

Figure 8. Cremation and inhumation burials

dying young and more people living well into old age.

However, one should not simply couple the increased number (and preservation) of grave goods in inhumations with elevated wealth. Cremation burials were undoubtedly also elaborate affairs and may only have been possible for people of high status. Building up a large cremation pyre may have been both a time-consuming and costly enterprise, since wood was an expensive commodity. Furthermore, the cremation burial rite, on practical grounds, demands that only small, 'token' or broken, or melted goods be incorporated into the urn, since there is little space to place, for instance, an entire sword. Thus 'scoring' the richness of the burials on the basis that inhumations demonstrate more obvious or overt wealth need not be an accurate depiction. However, the presence of a repaired vessel and the possibility that some of the vessels used at Alwalton originally had a domestic purpose may indicate that cremation was not beyond the reach of all the population.[349]

An idea of how elaborate the cremation pyre was may be gained from the condition of the cremated bones and how completely burnt they were. Another factor to take into consideration with cremation burials is that it may have been weather-dependent. A wet Spring or Autumn may have made it difficult to get the cremation pyre going. Thus the tradition may have been only seasonal with the population being interred in the wetter months.

The demographics of the cemetery at Alwalton (section Age and sex above) demonstrate that more females than males were interred in the area excavated. However, it must also be remembered the under-representation of males might be partially affected by men dying away from the settlement – perhaps during warfare or raids abroad. Most of the individuals buried were quite healthy, with few incidences of crippling disease or illness. At the cemetery of Beckford A, Wells suggested that the fact that the males were more robust than the females indicated that they had a better diet.[350] This would not appear to be the case at Alwalton, since equal numbers of females and males were robust. Furthermore, more females than males were living into old age (a ratio of 3:1).

Some of the medical conditions suffered by the population included Schmorl's nodes. These are indicative of disc degeneration as a result of load-bearing stresses on the spine and are often age-related, with most older people (over forty years) having them.[351] What is interesting about the cases from Alwalton is that they were more common in females than males (sixty-seven per cent) and also tended to occur more often on younger adults, under the age of forty. This may indicate that some of the younger women were used to undertaking arduous work, which involved lifting heavy weights. One male, aged twenty-five to thirty-five years (grave 1390), had a case os acromiale on his left scapula. This occurs from severe shearing stresses and was found on several of the Mary Rose longbow-men.[352] The general wear and tear of individuals suggests that the early Anglo-Saxon population at Alwalton, as at other cemeteries, was used to a physically active lifestyle, from heavy agricultural work. Furthermore, out of the four individuals with spondylolysis (grave 1410, 1451, 1463 and 1428), three were females. A relationship between spondylolysis and genetic tendency and trauma has been suggested by some.[353] The incidence at Minerva was quite high (for instance at the Barrington A cemetery, almost four times its size, only four cases were identified). Since three of these skeletons (graves 1410, 1463 and 1451) occurred in spatial association, this may be indicative of a family cluster (Fig. 8).

There was evidence for only one possibly hurried burial – a female in an unusual position at the base of a pit (Sk. 1469 from pit 1413, Fig. 30). There was no evidence for

malnutrition and only one individual exhibited signs of trauma. This was a twenty-five to thirty-five year old male who had a well-healed fracture on the upper part of his lower leg (grave 1387.2). This is unlikely to have been a result of warfare and more likely was caused from a trip or fall accident. Only one shield and two spears (one of which was unstratified) were recovered from the excavated male graves at Alwalton. This low number may indicate that the role of warfare, physical or ideological, real or surrogate, was not as significant to the Alwalton community as it may have been to others. At Barrington A, males with weapons only slightly outnumbered those without (twenty-four to twenty-three).[354] However, at Beckford B only half of the males had weapons (nine out of twenty-seven).[355]

Funerary ritual, grave goods and symbolism

A study of sociological and anthropological sources clearly indicates that death and funerals are generally times for strong emotional, social and obviously ideological responses.[356] Following Van Gennep and others, death can be viewed as a transition between states.[357] Liminal zones are often places where reality is revoked and ideology is reversed. Durkheim has argued that death is a time when the individual becomes transformed and integrated within a communal life of the ancestors.[358] Death and funerals are imbued, perhaps more than any other aspects of the human lifecycle, with potent symbolism and representation.

An understanding of the evidence from Alwalton, or for that matter, any other Anglo-Saxon cemetery site, cannot be attempted without taking on board some theoretical constructs. Positions of skeletons, orientation of graves and provision of grave goods should not be taken at face value, without a deeper appreciation of the possible complex patterns behind their manifestation. In the past, the reasons as to why the grave goods were there in the first place were left undiscussed. Their presence had little meaning beyond providing archaeologists with useful indicators concerning gender, identity, occupation and social position.

The complex symbolism of the artefacts that were placed with the Anglo-Saxon dead has led archaeologists in recent years to move away from the rather simplistic coupling of rich grave goods with richer members of

Table 16. Age of individual at death in accordance with burial rite

Age	Infant	Juvenile	Adolescent	Young adult	Adult	Old adult
Burial type						
Cremation	XXX	XXXXXXX	X	XX	XXXXXXXXXXX	0
Inhumation	0	?XXX	0	XXXXX	XXXXXXXXXXXXXXXX	XXXXXXXXXXX

society, jewellery specifically with women and weapons with men. However, comparisons of physiological sex with grave goods at cemeteries such as Barrington A,[359] Great Chesterford[360] and others has indicated that in general, the correlation of specifically female and male items with women and men is consistent, although it can occasionally be misleading.[361]

The meaning and function of grave goods in early Anglo-Saxon inhumations have been debated over the years. It has often been assumed that they were objects used by the deceased during his/her life and therefore they reflect the status of the owner. Certainly some of the dress accessories from Alwalton, for instance, were clearly quite worn and show signs of reuse. This includes the copper alloy pin from grave 1358 (Fig. 20) and the repaired right sleeve wrist clasp from grave 1336 (Fig. 17). Other examples, such as a leper with spina bifida from Great Chesterford with a spearhead, unlikely to have been in military service in life, suggests more complex symbolism in the grave good ritual. It should not be forgotten that these items were chosen by the deceased's kin for the funeral display and may have been selected for numerous reasons. While some items may have been used to establish status, others may have been appropriate only to that individual and therefore could not be inherited (perhaps being too potent or carrying too much memory).

Burning or burying? The relationship between inhumation and cremation burials

Although Anglo-Saxon burial theory has been developed substantially in recent years,[362] there has as yet been relatively little dialogue concerning the reasons behind mixed-rite cemeteries, where cremation and inhumation were undoubtedly contemporary.[363] It is generally accepted that inhumation replaced the tradition of cremation, with the latter rite dying out relatively quickly, although Ravn[364] and Williams[365] both note the use of both rites at the same time. This leads to the question of how two quite contrasting, potentially contradictory burial rites could be enacted on the same site and landscape at Alwalton over a period of possibly up to two hundred years. A number of explanations can be put forward. The first possibility is that, for whatever reason, a single community was employing two separate burial rites to dispose of its dead. An analysis of the evidence suggests that cremation was employed predominantly for the younger members of the community, while inhumation was a rite for the adult population. An alternative suggestion is that this cemetery (or rather funerary landscape) was being utilised by at least two separate communities who came to the same sacred ground to inter their dead. With the idea of a dispersed settlement pattern in the early Anglo-Saxon period, a relatively widely spaced, dispersed cemetery may fit well into this context.

The distribution of the burials allows two separate patterns to be distinguished. As stated above, the inhumations form a roughly linear arrangement running roughly north–south and perhaps mirroring the meander of the River Nene. On the other hand, although a few of the cremation burials in the south-east of the excavation area overlap spatially with the inhumations, the majority are situated in a separate part of the cemetery. It is true that in several cases only a few metres separate the two types of burial, but the picture changes when the evidence for the location of the tree throws is superimposed. The trees show a strong association with the cremations and also the probable cremation pyre site in the north-western area of the site. If the trees are roughly contemporary with the cemetery, they imply the presence of both a wooded glade (cremation zone) and a more open area that formed the inhumation burial ground. Perhaps the sharing of space by two separate communities using two separate ideologies was possible because the two areas of the funerary landscape were segregated, with the cremation graves secluded and screened off from the processes of inhumation. In particular, the wooded zone around the funerary pyre would have permitted a quite dramatic effect through the funnelling of smoke up into the air (Fig. 11).

On the other hand, a more pragmatic reason may have been responsible for the correlation between trees and cremation burials. It would make sense to have the cremation ground located near an area where plentiful supplies of fuel were available. Analysis of environmental samples indicates that there was generally a low density of cereals and weeds. However, the scant material did not suggest a heavily wooded area, but rather, scrubby grassland in the vicinity of arable fields producing oats, barley, wheat and pulses.[366]

The differences between cremation and inhumation need to be considered in understanding the dynamics behind the death rituals and other experiences performed at the cemetery of Alwalton. In an inhumation ceremony, the dead person was carried to the grave and lowered into it as a recognisable member of the community, laid out with objects that were meant to reflect the status and identity of that person. This may have been a communal ceremony where the deceased was presented in full view for people to come and pay their last respects. The careful arrangement of the body within the grave and the placement of the artefacts on the body were also undoubtedly imbued with hidden (to us) meanings. The rich and varied grave goods that the inhumations were buried with highlights the striking visual importance of the burial rite.

The cremation rite contrasts with that of inhumation, not only visually but presumably also ideologically, with the physical transformation of the body[367] perhaps allowing the soul to rise into the sky rather than going into the ground. The rite was potentially more dramatic to the eye. Additionally, there is also a second 'post-cremation' rite to consider, where the cremated remains of the body and any pyre goods were collected (or selected) and deposited, often into a vessel, sometimes with additional unburnt goods. Thus, the act of cremation actively destroys the physical identity of the deceased while the post-cremation rite recreates or reinforces it.[368]

The cremation and inhumation burials were provided with different arrays of grave goods (Fig. 10). The percentage of cremation goods (seventy per cent of the urns contained goods) from Alwalton is a relatively high figure compared to other cremation cemeteries. For example at Sancton, only sixty per cent of the cremation burials were furnished and this ratio dipped to only thirty-four per cent at Illington and twenty-one per cent at Lackford.[369] Furthermore, the cremation burial accompaniments at Alwalton were dominated by antler/ bone combs, again more common than at other cremation cemetery sites, although a number of examples were recorded at Millgate (Newark-on-Trent)[370] (see Grave Goods from the Cremation Burials, above). Combs are often linked with feminine identity, although this tends to be an association restricted to inhumations (*e.g.* Barrington).[371] Combs were not found in the inhumation graves at Alwalton and items such as the spindle whorl (cremation 1307, Fig. 36) and the hone stone (cremation 1296, Fig. 35) were also unique to the cremations. A number of artefact categories were restricted to the inhumations. These included many of the jewellery types and the knife blades. The only objects that occurred infrequently in both types of burial are copper brooches, iron nails, ivory pouch hoops, bone handles, coins, copper hoops and tweezers.

The most obvious grouping of the cremation burials at Alwalton is on the basis of the urns. There is a clear distinction between decorated and undecorated urns, especially regarding their location (Fig. 9). Of the plain vessels, some seventy per cent (seven examples) lie in the eastern part of the site and only thirty per cent (three examples) to the west, while seventeen decorated vessels (ninety-four per cent) were situated in the west, within the main cluster of cremation burials (Fig. 9). There was also some correlation between decoration of vessels and grave goods. Only three of the plain vessels contained other artefacts – excluding disturbed burial 1324 – compared to fifteen of the decorated vessels. The tendency for plain unaccompanied urns in the east of the site and the decorated urns with burial goods in the west might be indicative of two phases of use of the cemetery. On the other hand, it might reflect distinctions based on other criteria such as wealth, status or ethnic/ social affiliation. It may also reflect differences in the funerary rites: the decorated vessels tend to contain considerably more cremated bone on average than the plain pots (726 g as opposed to 370 g). This may denote that different types of cremation practices were being conducted at Alwalton.

The differences discerned when comparing the type and range of grave goods recovered from cremations and inhumations suggests that gender-related items, such as jewellery and weapons, were more strongly affiliated with inhumations.[372] In cremation it would appear that most grave goods are not exclusively associated with one sex, although some showed stronger tendencies (*e.g.* ear scoops, shears, tweezers, razors with men and spindle whorls and bone and antler rings with women).[373] These are guiding and not structuring principles, however. For example, the one sword found in a cremation burial with sexable remains from Spong Hill was with a female.[374]

Stoodley has recently proposed that the grave-goods interred with early Anglo-Saxon inhumations had specific age associations.[375] He argued that the different age and gender thresholds in life impacted upon the construction of the Anglo-Saxon lifestyle. Indicators included the number of beads and the complexity of necklaces which increased from puberty until middle age, only to decline again in old age.[376] The key stage in the female life-cycle, as indicated by the introduction of specifically female-related grave goods, appeared to be around ten to twelve years of age.

Again, similar patterns related to age could not be identified from cremation goods, although Huggett and Richards have suggested that the decoration on the cremation vessels may have fulfilled this role.[377] Richards has been able to demonstrate that the size of the urn was proportionate to the age of the occupant, while the different types of decorative motifs were also closely tied to the status and identity of the deceased.[378] Most of the cremation urns were made specifically to act as containers for the remains of the dead person. Some however, at most cemeteries do show signs of wear, such as lead plugs, abrasion, residues or sooting. The indicators that some of the vessels were in fact reused were also noted at Alwalton.[379]

The cremation goods themselves, however, were undoubtedly employed in aspects of mortuary symbolism. On further analysis, interesting binary oppositions may be discerned through the structured deposition of the cremation pyre and grave goods. These oppositions include:

Body and grave goods – Integrity:
Complete   vs   Broken/token

Body and grave goods – Pre-depositional processing:
Melted/burnt   vs   Unburnt

Burial contents:
Human   vs   Animal

This implies that meaning may have been conveyed through the dichotomy between burnt, melted and broken objects and those that remained unburnt and/or complete. These oppositions may underlie part of a relatively complex structured ideology of the cremation process. For instance, most of the combs were fragmentary or token items that were rarely burnt. On one level this may be read as a sign of poverty, whereby the next of kin could not afford to put the whole object in the cremation urn. However on another level, the snapping of a bit of a comb may have been deliberate tokenism, whereby every time a member of the family died, a fragment of the ancestral comb was placed within the urn. This would allow the family connections to be retained between members of the living and the dead (Fig. 8). Several pairs of cremations with parts of the same combs were identified at Minerva.

McKinley has studied the differences between pyre and grave goods at Spong Hill, where she noted that the vast majority of the cremation grave goods had been burnt to some extent.[380] McKinley argued that 'to assume automatically that the lack of apparent burning of an object illustrates that it was not on the pyre shows a lack of understanding of pyre cremation'.[381] This is a fair point but at both Spong Hill and Alwalton there were certain artefact categories that consistently remained unburnt. This seems too coincidental unless these objects were always placed on the same part of the body – a part that was not subjected to intensive heat/ flames.

McKinley suggested that this might be the case with the combs.[382] She proposed that some of the combs may have been placed in the hair and thus could have fallen off early on in the cremation, once the hair was burnt. However, if we consider the evidence from another point of view, we can offer alternative reasons for the lack of burning on the combs. Firstly, the combs are normally considered as brushes for the hair since most are too large and heavy to be used as hair ornaments. Secondly, even if they were placed on the hair as part of the funerary rite, it is likely that at least some would have fallen down into the heart of the pyre, rather than off the edge. The fact that none are burnt does suggest that they were never on the pyre in the first place. Thirdly, from the cremations at Alwalton, only two of the sixteen combs were complete. The rest were small fragments deliberately broken off – 'token deposits'. It is unlikely that any of these would have been placed as ornaments in the hair, particularly as some did not even have teeth. Fourthly, many of the combs from Spong Hill were either near the base or the top of the vessel, suggesting they had been placed in the urn either first or last.[383]

In sum, the evidence would support the idea that these combs were probably part of a separate ritual, whereby, at least at Alwalton, fragments of family or 'ancestral' combs were snapped off and added to the cremation. Thus the burnt / unburnt dichotomy may well be indicative of two separate rituals being enacted during a cremation ceremony. The first was a personal one, involving the deceased and his / her personal belongings. The second was a family ritual, whereby part of a family treasure or heirloom was snapped off as a token and added later.

It is in this context that perhaps we should consider the cremation urns themselves. As mentioned previously, there is often a close correlation between the size of the vessel and the type of decoration and the identity of the person interred within it.[384] It is worth questioning whether these rich decorative schemes were only for the act of interment when the cremation vessel was put in the ground. It might seem more likely that such visually impressive pots were meant also to be put on communal display for a time before being buried. It was perhaps during this time that the second funerary ritual was undertaken.

Often the iron objects were not burnt, although it can be difficult to recognise the effects of burning. Perhaps specific objects were selected for inclusion with the cremation rite and rules may have governed what could and could not be burnt with the individual. Some items may have gained potency through the act of burning, melting or transformation; others may have lost power. Some of the pyre goods, through their melting, warping and deformation, may have acted as a metaphor for the whole cremation process. Through the act of cremation, the complete body was broken up and fragmented and became unrecognisable as a human being; perhaps to become reborn as part of the ancestral community.

The presence of nails was interesting, since they are more common in the cremation than the inhumation burials. Crummy has suggested that the nails may have formed a symbolic, non-functional element of grave goods.[385] Nails, which did not give the appearance of coffin structures, have been identified at other Anglo-Saxon cemetery sites. For example at Barrington A, Malim and Hines argued that the nails from the inhumations were too few and irregular to have been part of coffin construction.[386] At Great Chesterford, it was noted that nails tended to occur in male graves without weapons.[387] The nails had been transformed through being broken up, fragmented ('tokenism') or through the warping and melting on the pyre. Thus these goods were significant and symbolic in different ways from the inhumation grave goods.

Conclusions

Rescue excavations at Alwalton have revealed part of an early Anglo-Saxon mixed-rite cemetery and evidence for contemporary agricultural field systems, possibly related to settlement to the south. This site is located within the rich archaeological landscape of the Nene valley, which was heavily populated and supported flourishing pottery and metalworking industries and villa estates by the fourth century AD. Although the nature and intensity of Roman decline are not yet clear, there is some evidence for continuous occupation through the late Roman to post-Roman period. The River Nene was an important route for extensive early Anglo-Saxon penetration from the mid-fifth century onwards.

Rich Anglo-Saxon grave-fields have been discovered in the Nene valley, possibly reflecting a developing hierarchy and an increasing expression of material wealth. However, Alwalton is the largest fifth- to sixth-century cemetery to have been excavated in the area to date. Although excavations only revealed part of the cemetery, there appeared to be comparable numbers of contemporary cremation and inhumation burials. While mixed-rite cemeteries are not uncommon, they usually show a majority of one type of riter.

The relationships between the ideologies behind cremation and inhumation are imperfectly understood. These can be teased out through an appreciation of the social, historical and geographical contexts in which these cemeteries were created and developed, along with a deeper comprehension of the complex symbolism of both types of mortuary behaviour. Although the contemporary meaning of such symbolism may never be fully understood, it may be possible to deduce symbolic references to underlying elemental and cosmological oppositions – the enduring parameters of the human life cycle. The significance of grave goods and cemetery layout in Anglo-Saxon cemeteries is not clear. It is possible that furnished burials displayed material wealth and social power, but this cemetery does not conclusively reveal any standardised scheme based on sex, age and 'rank'. Although grave goods may have been personalised tokens reflecting the living roles of the deceased, they may reflect the beliefs and self-perception of living community and the bereaved, rather than those of the dead.

The individuals buried in the cemetery appear to have been fairly healthy, with few incidences of crippling disease or illness. They appear to have been engaged in a physically active lifestyle, possibly involving heavy agricultural work. There is no evidence of injury through violence or warfare. There is little evidence for any sex-based differentiation in diet, with significantly more females than males were living into old age and equal numbers of females and males being robust. However, a significant proportion of younger women suffered from lumbar disc degeneration, which may indicate that they habitually undertook arduous, weight-bearing physical labour.

The layout of the cemetery appears to have been influenced by practical and topographical factors. Located away from any known focus of settlement, graves were aligned with the course of the River Nene and may also have been directed towards a Bronze Age barrow on Chesterton Hill; such reference to earlier monuments is common to many Anglo-Saxon cemeteries. The position of the cemetery on the low-lying southern bank of the Nene would have made it visible to passing river traffic. The site may have been sparsely wooded, with cremations shaded by trees and occasionally marked with posts or sheltered by post-built grave structures. The probable pyre was located in the northern part of the cemetery, lying close to the river and some distance away from the excavated concentration of cremations.

Although numerous early Anglo-Saxon cemeteries have been excavated along the valley of the River Nene, settlement remains have thus far proved to be more elusive (Fig. 2). This lack of known settlement sites makes it difficult to link cemeteries to a 'living' landscape and it is not clear where the individuals buried at Alwalton would have lived and worked. Evidence for the early Anglo-Saxon occupation has been found south of the Nene at Haddon, Orton Hall Farm and Orton Longueville. These sites straddle Roman Ermine Street, which was presumably still an important communication route at the time. Spatial analysis suggests that the cemetery continued to the west, while the presence of early Anglo-Saxon field boundaries and a well in Area A suggest that the cemetery adjoined farmland. Environmental evidence indicates that this was probably pasture rather than arable land, so the cemetery appears

Table 17. Dichotomies between cremations and inhumations

Cremation	Inhumation
Burning	Interring
Body burns into air (sky)	Body buried under ground (earth)
Gender and sex destroying	Gender preserving (Brush 1988)
Act of wet to dry: Quick process	Act of wet to dry: Slow process
Visually impressive with pyre	Visually impressive with body laid out with all finery and funerary costume
Broken up disarticulated remains contained within a vessel	Intact remains placed in a grave (sometimes lined with a coffin)
In general few grave goods	Often many grave goods
Double funerary ritual. 1st is the burning & the 2nd is the interring. Both may be associated with a different set of processes associated with burning/lack of burning. The first is personal; the second may be affiliated with the wider kin group	Single funerary ritual

to have lain beyond the outfield system of any putative associated settlement(s).

Excavations have offered a tantalising glimpse into the lives and beliefs of early Anglo-Saxons buried at Alwalton. However, the results of the excavation raise further questions regarding these people. Although their physical remains provide information about their diet and lifestyle, it is not yet known where they lived and what part they played in the post-Roman social and economic landscape. Individuals buried at Alwalton may not all have lived in the same settlement – several dispersed communities practising different burial rites may have occupied the same burial ground. Inhumations and cremations extend to the west and any further work may elucidate questions regarding the layout and zonation of the cemetery as a whole.

To conclude, excavations at the cemetery of Alwalton have added to our understanding of the nature of early Anglo-Saxon burial practices in Cambridgeshire and elsewhere. Analysis of the layout and date of the site has enhanced knowledge regarding the interaction between the rites of cremation and inhumation.

Acknowledgements

Archaeological Solutions (formerly Hertfordshire Archaeological Trust) is grateful to KingChem Ltd for commissioning the archaeological desk-based assessment, evaluations and excavations. AS is also pleased to acknowledge their archaeological consultant, Oxford Archaeological Associates (OAA), in particular Martin Petchey. AS would like to thank Tim Reynolds, Simon Kaner and Andy Thomas (Cambridgeshire County Council, County Archaeological Office) and the staff at Huntingdon Record Office for their assistance. AS would also like to acknowledge the BBC and '*Meet the Ancestors*' programme, in particular Dr Julian Richards, for showing an interest in the cemetery and filming it as part of the series. AS is grateful to Jacqueline McKinley for undertaking a detailed analysis of one of the cremation urns excavated for the programme.

The evaluation of Area A was undertaken by Judith Roberts of Cambridgeshire County Council Archaeological Field Unit. The evaluation of Area B and the excavation of Areas A and B was carried out by Tom Vaughan of Hertfordshire Archaeological Trust. The project was managed for HAT by Tom McDonald. The evaluation report was written by Jon Murray, the Interim excavation report for Area A by Tom McDonald and Tom Vaughan, and the Area B report by Tom McDonald and Jonathan Last. The post-excavation assessment and updated project design was written by Jonathan Last. The report was written in 1999–2001 and has not been significantly updated since. Leonora O'Brien and Alexandra Grassam assisted with the post-excavation analysis. The illustrations were prepared by Donna Cameron, Amy Goldsmith and Kathren Henry. The finds were managed by Berni Sudds, Corinna Hattersley and Hannah Firth.

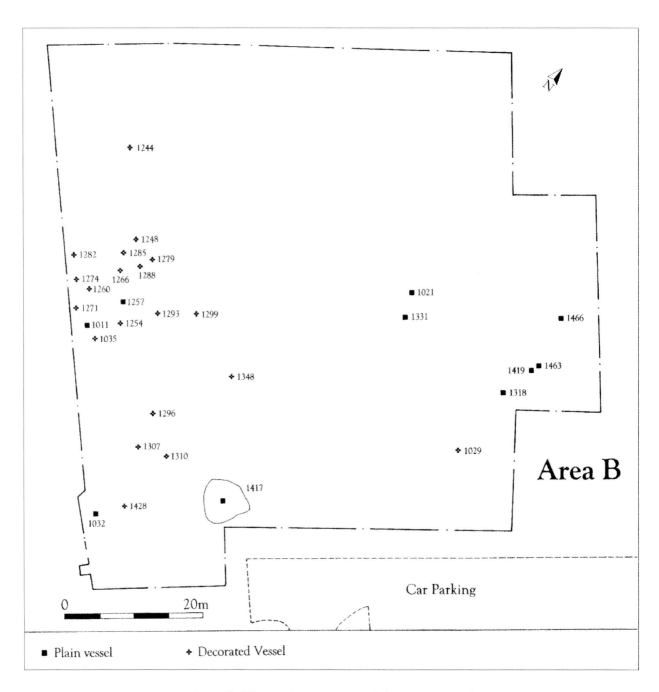

Figure 9. Distribution of plain and decorated vessels

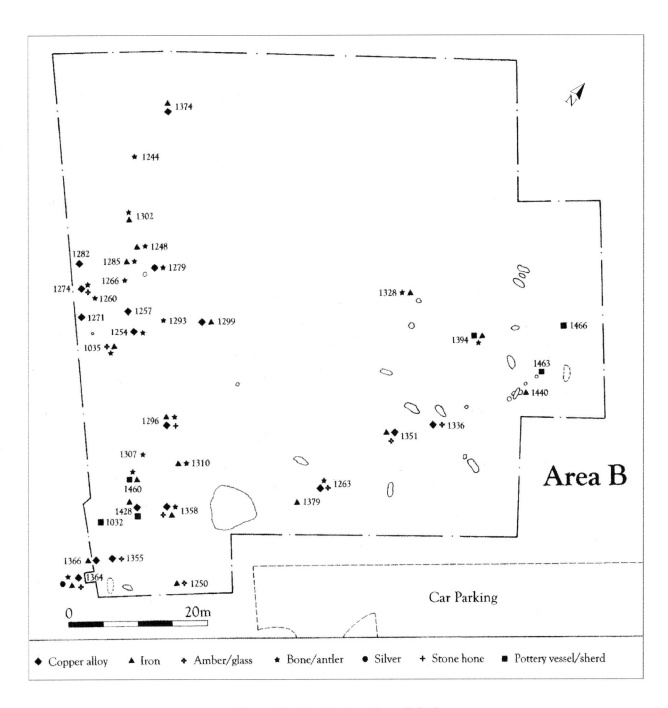

Figure 10. Distribution of small finds

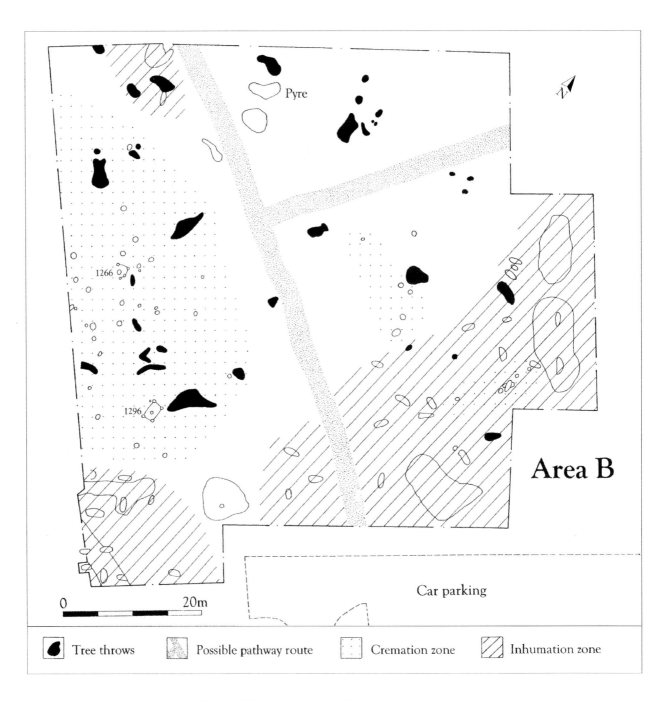

Figure 11. Interpretative plan of cemetery layout

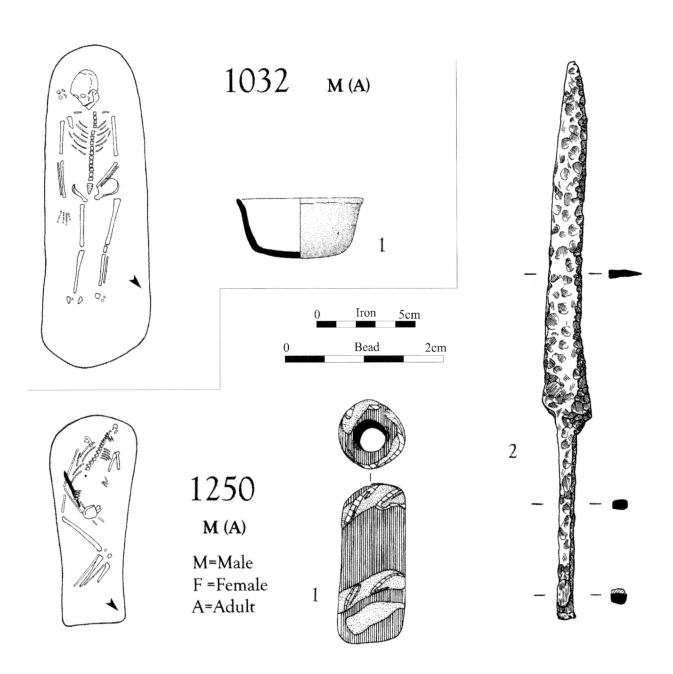

Figure 12. Grave goods from graves 1032 and 1250

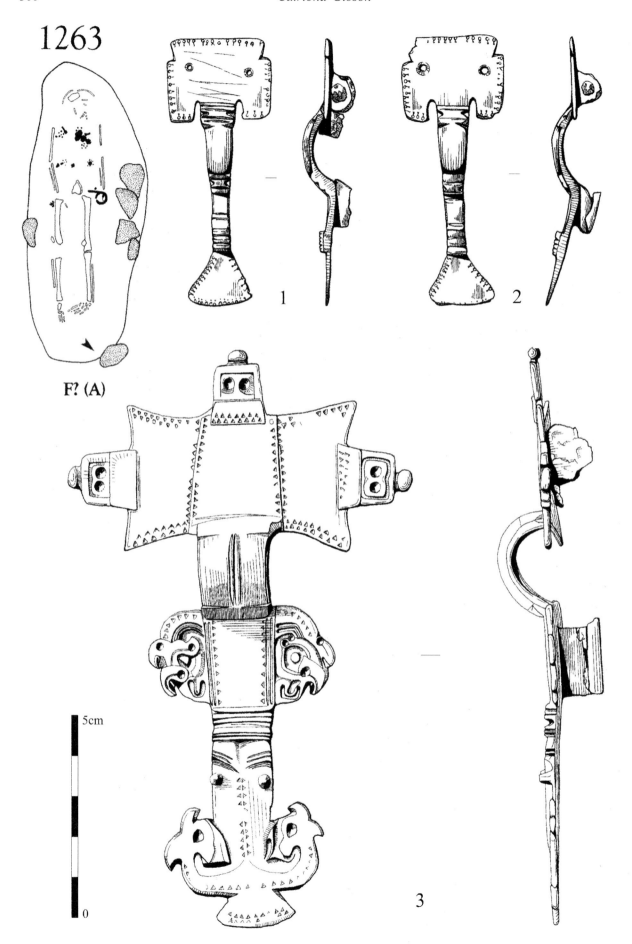

1263

F? (A)

5cm

0

1

2

3

Figure 13. Grave goods from grave 1263

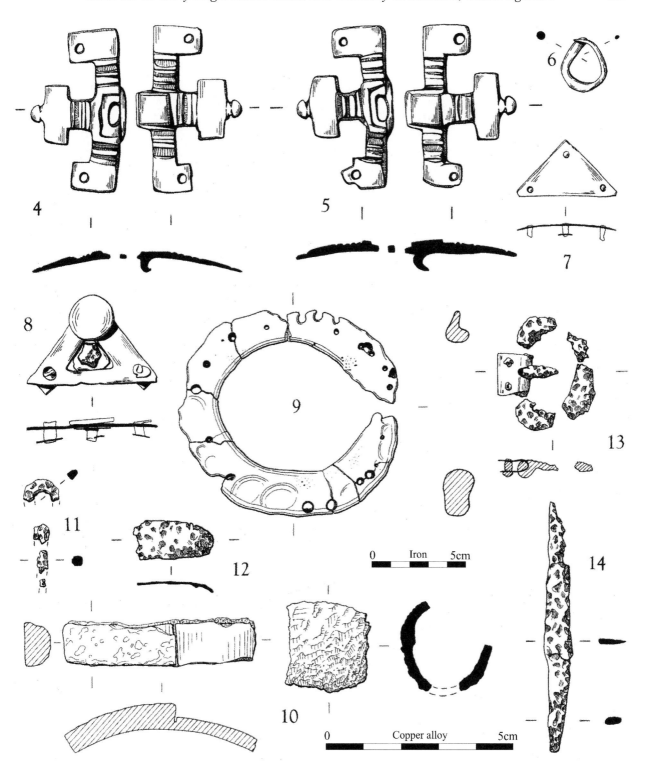

Figure 14. Grave goods from grave 1263

Catriona Gibson

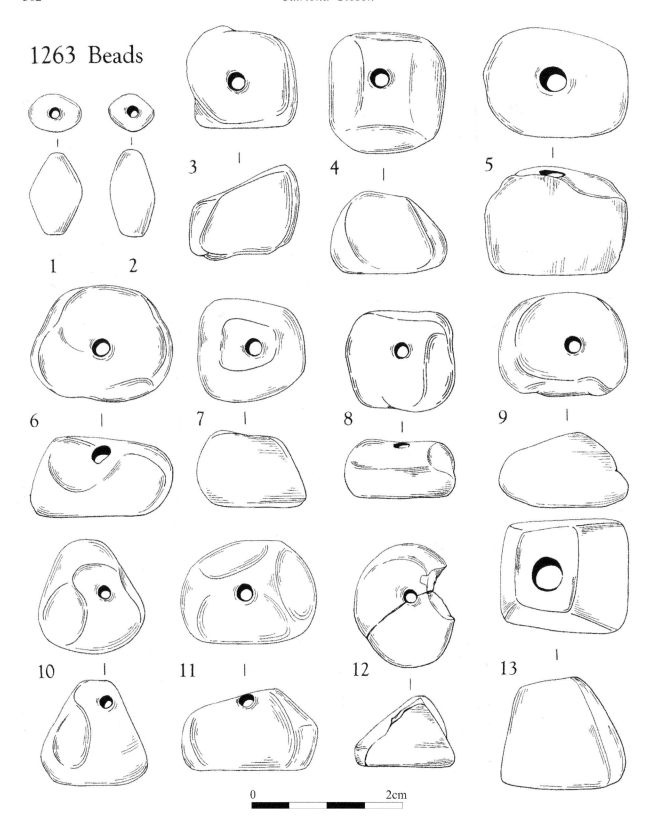

1263 Beads

Figure 15. Beads from grave 1263

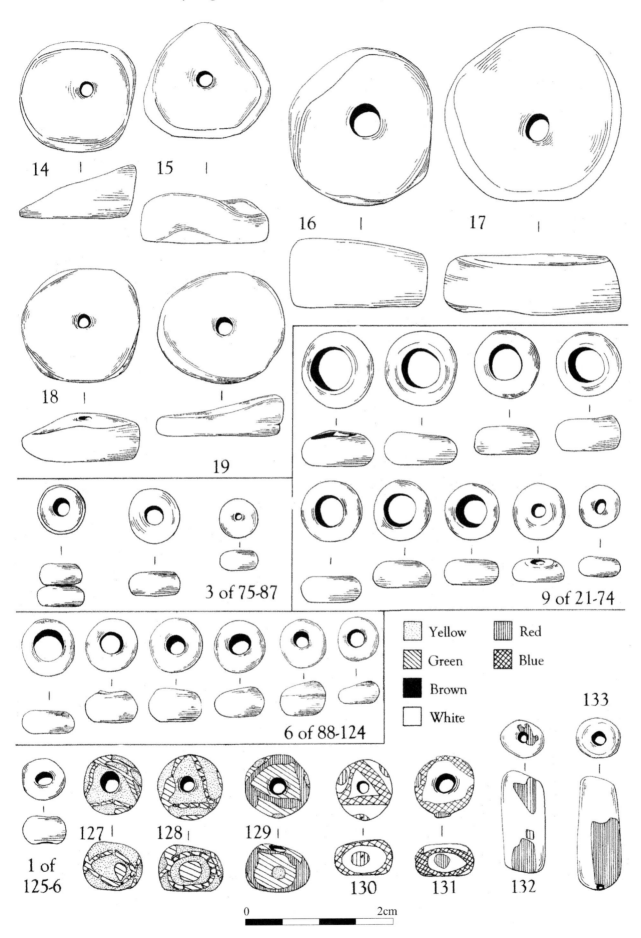

Figure 16. Beads from grave 1263

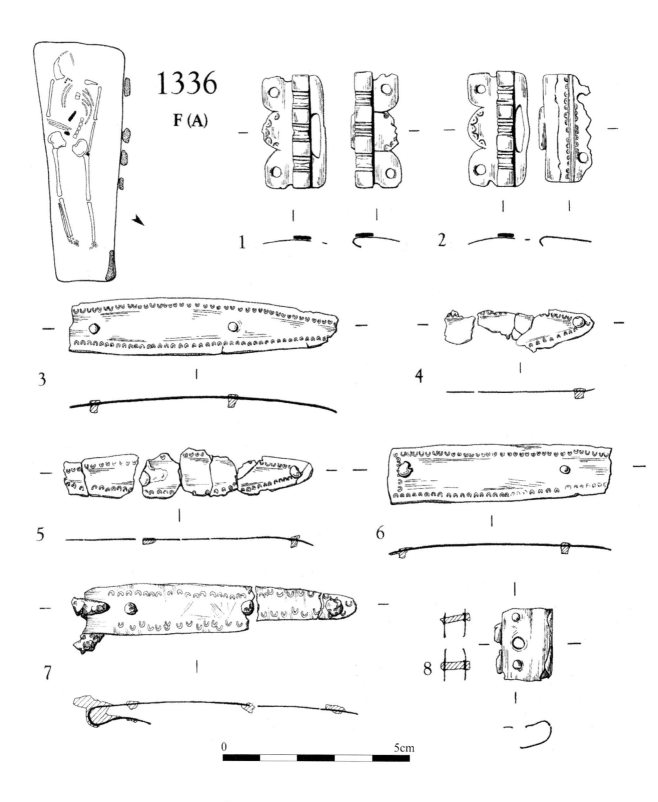

Figure 17. Grave goods from grave 1336

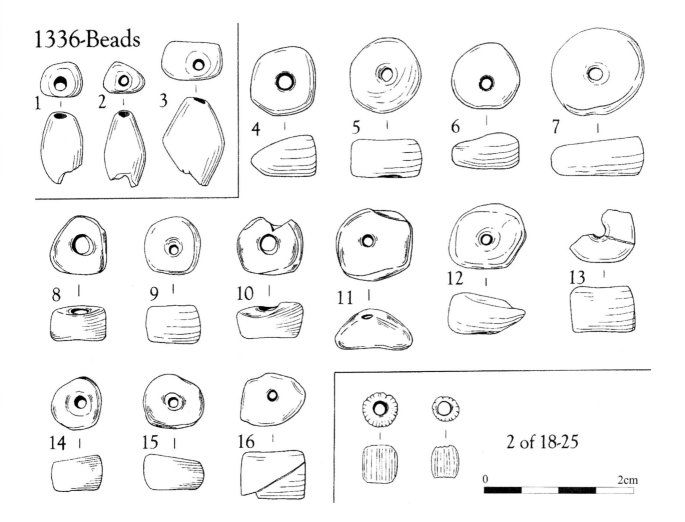

Figure 18. Beads from grave 1336

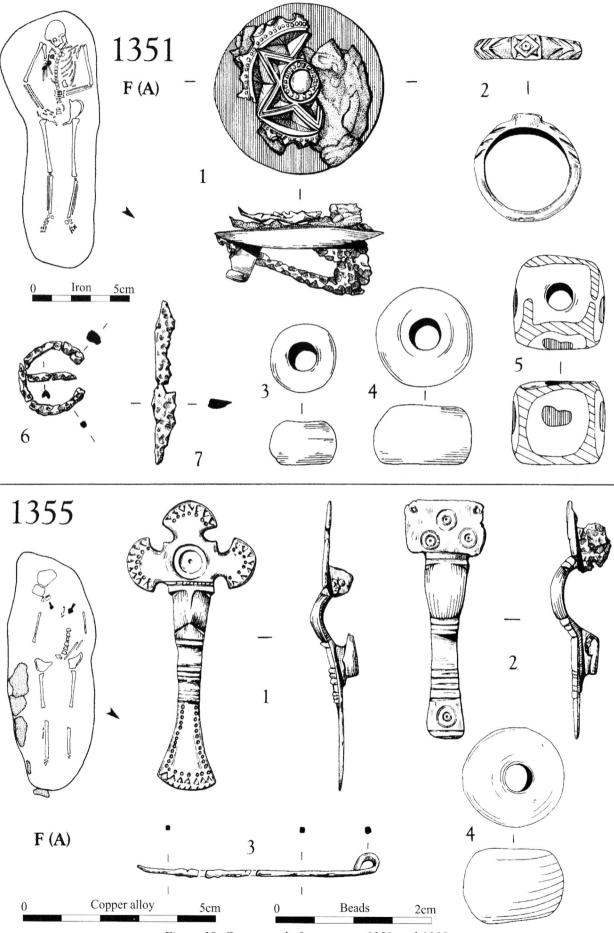

Figure 19. Grave goods from graves 1351 and 1355

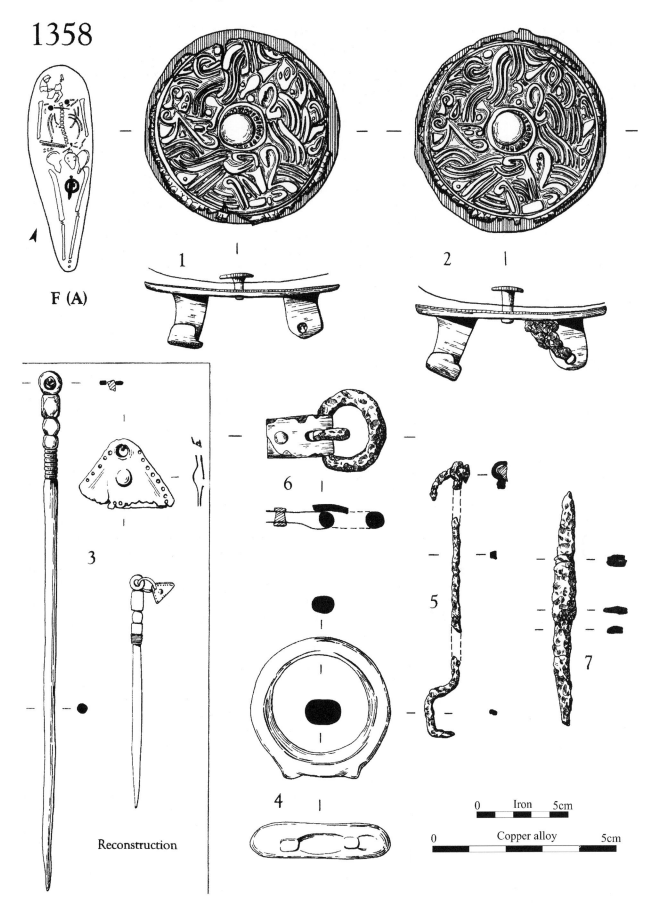

Figure 20. Grave goods from grave 1358

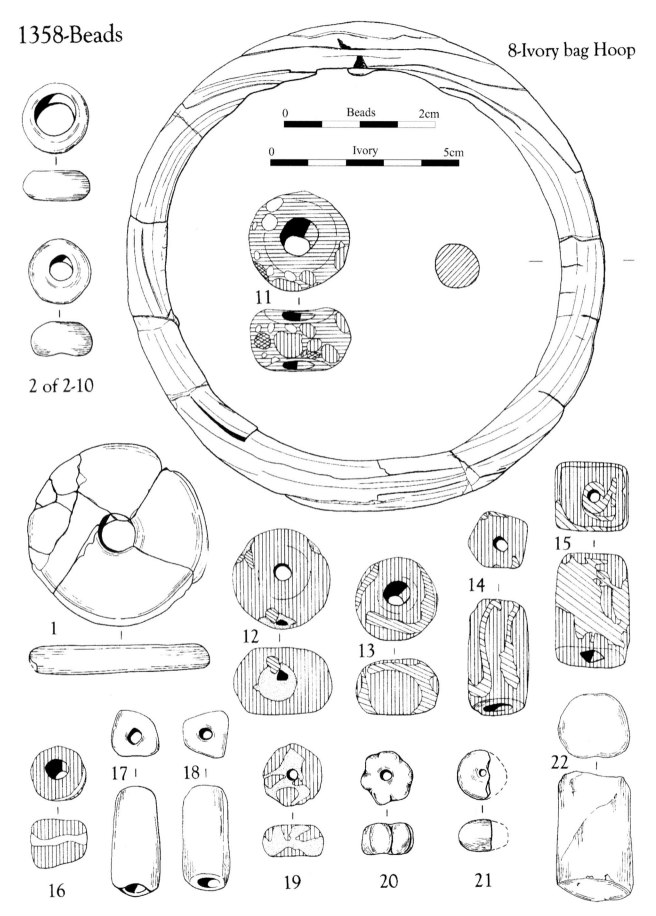

1358-Beads

8-Ivory bag Hoop

Figure 21. Beads and ivory bag hoop from grave 1358

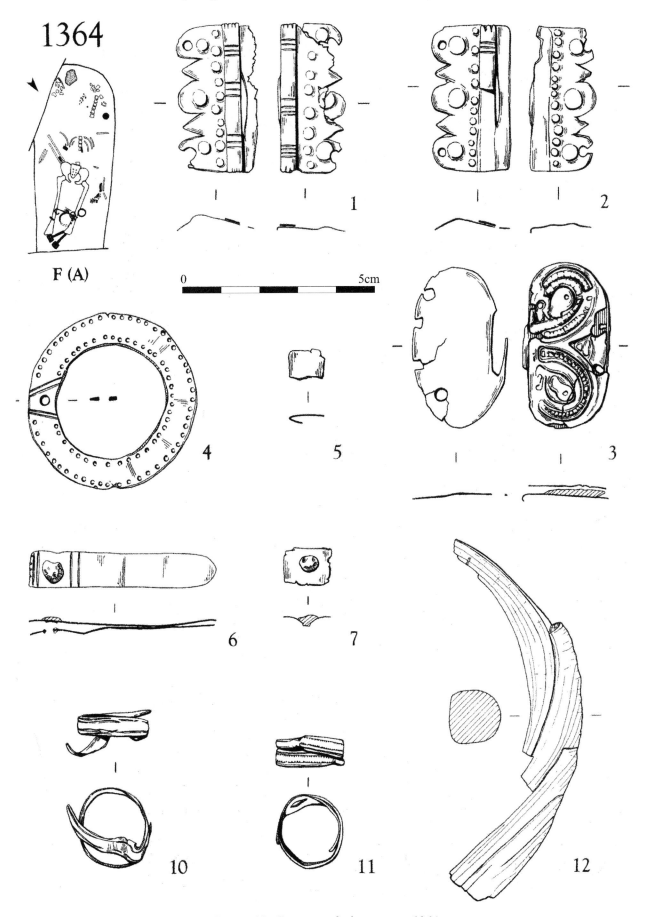

Figure 22. Grave goods from grave 1364

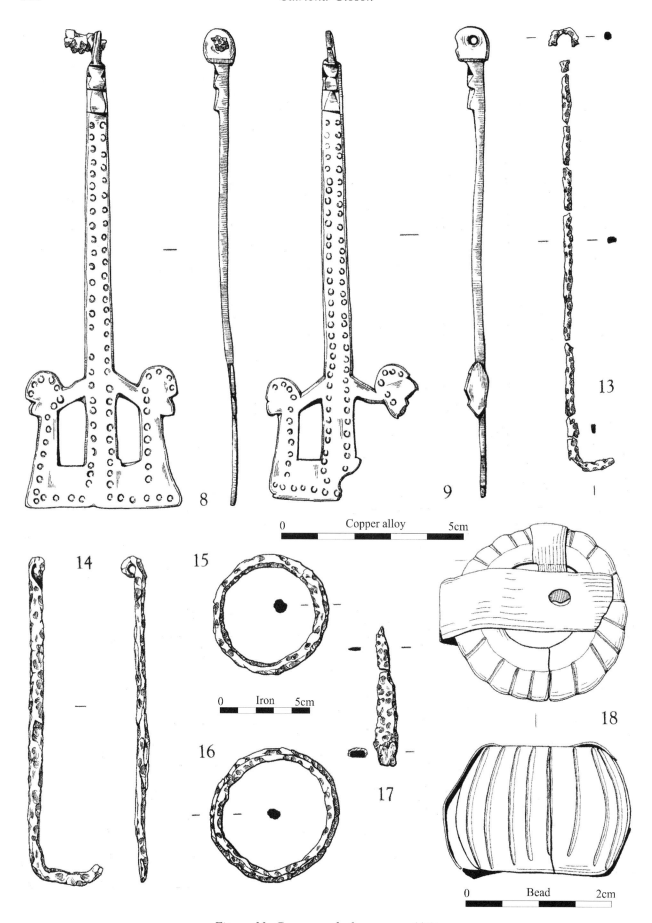

Figure 23. Grave goods from grave 1364

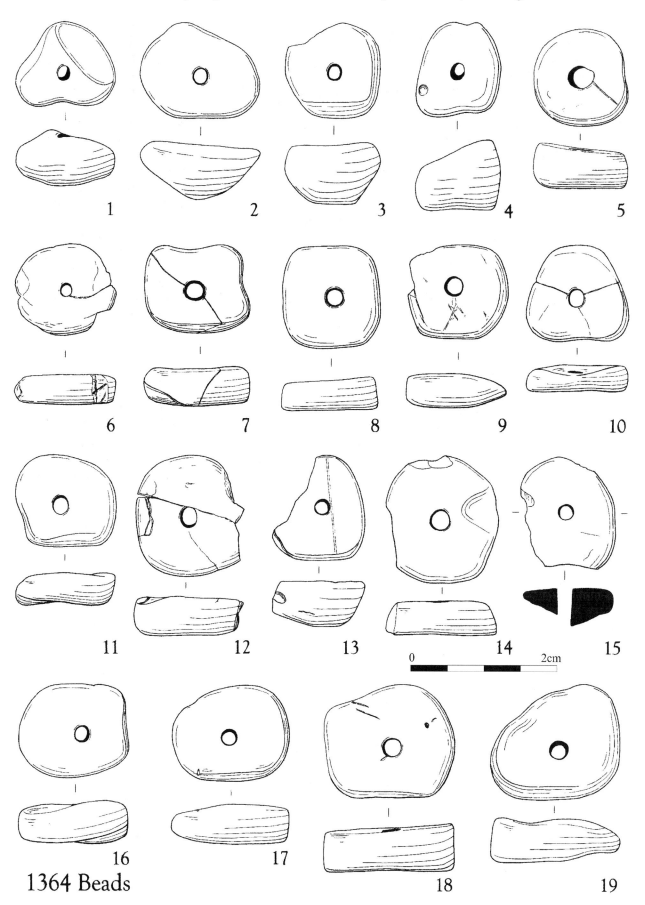

1364 Beads

Figure 24. Beads from grave 1364

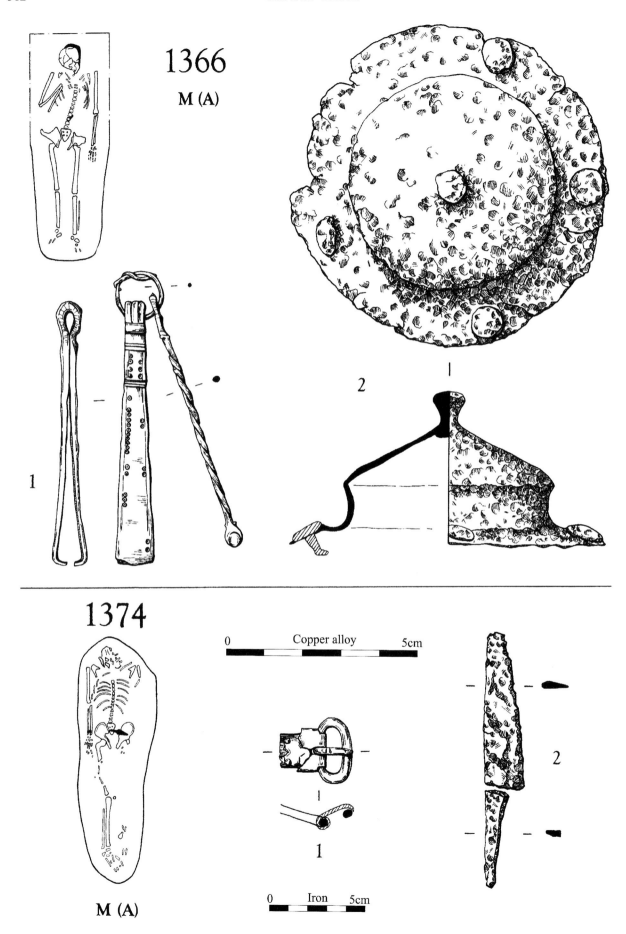

Figure 25. Grave goods from graves 1366 and 1374

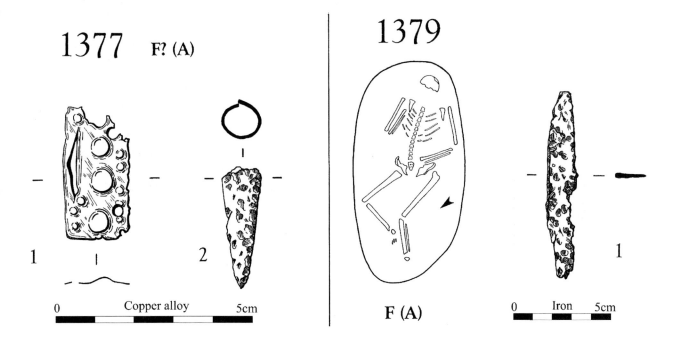

Figure 26. Grave goods from graves 1377 and 1379

1394

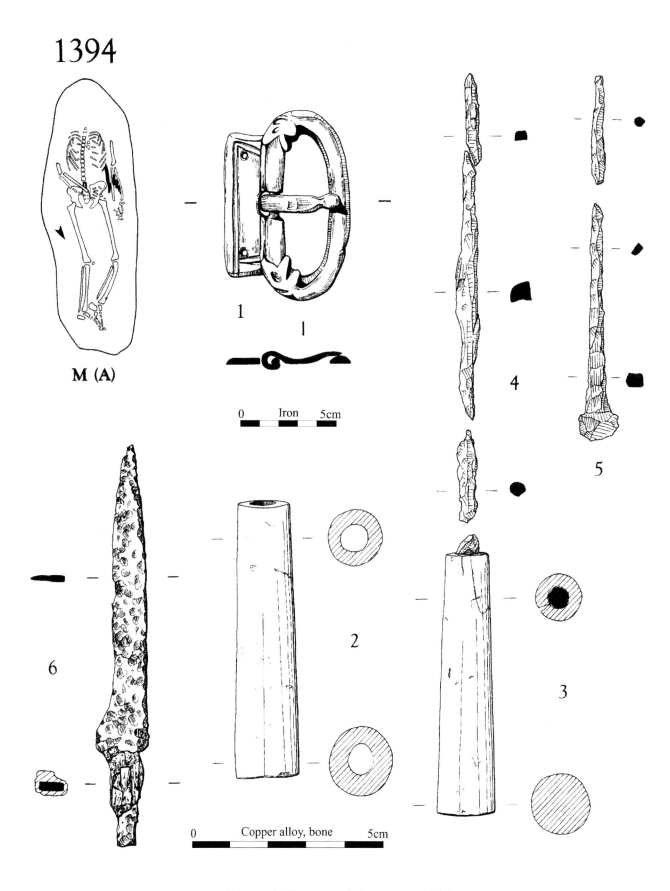

M (A)

1

0   Iron   5cm

4

5

6

2

3

0   Copper alloy, bone   5cm

Figure 27. Grave goods from grave 1394

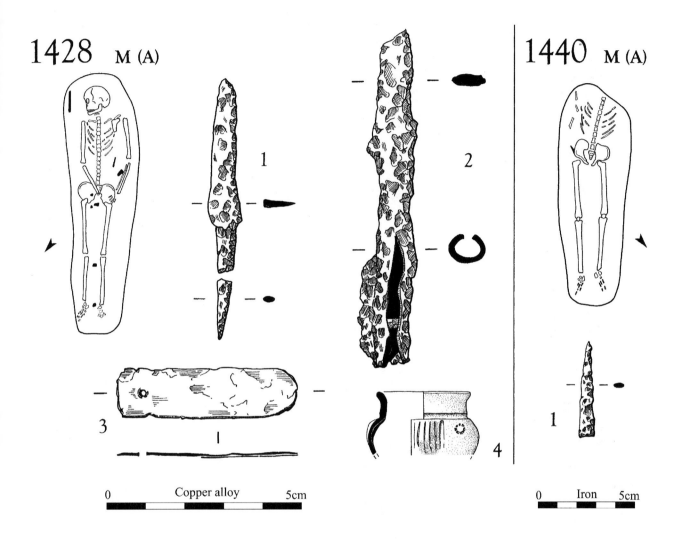

Figure 28. Grave goods from graves 1428 and 1440

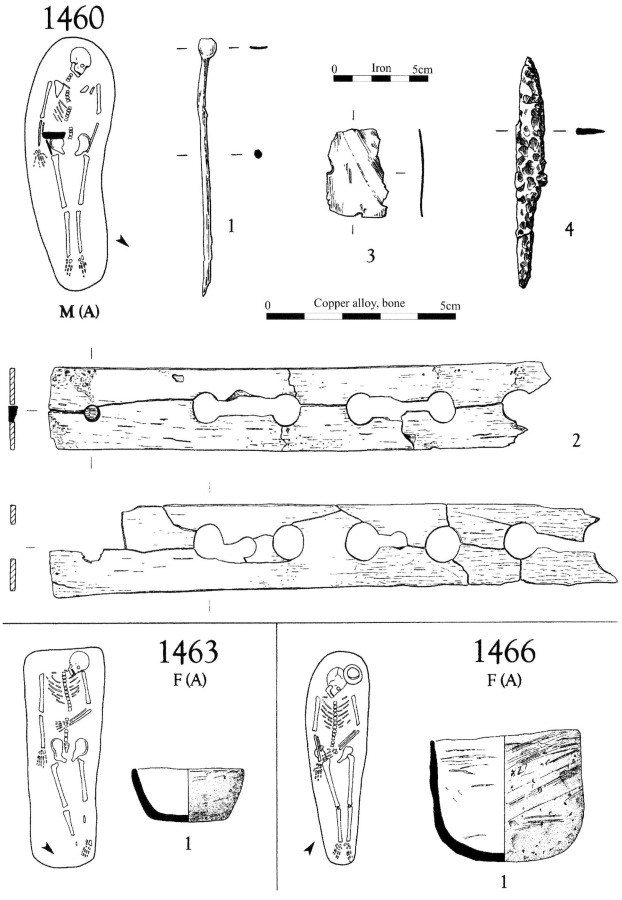

Figure 29. Grave goods from graves 1460 and 1466

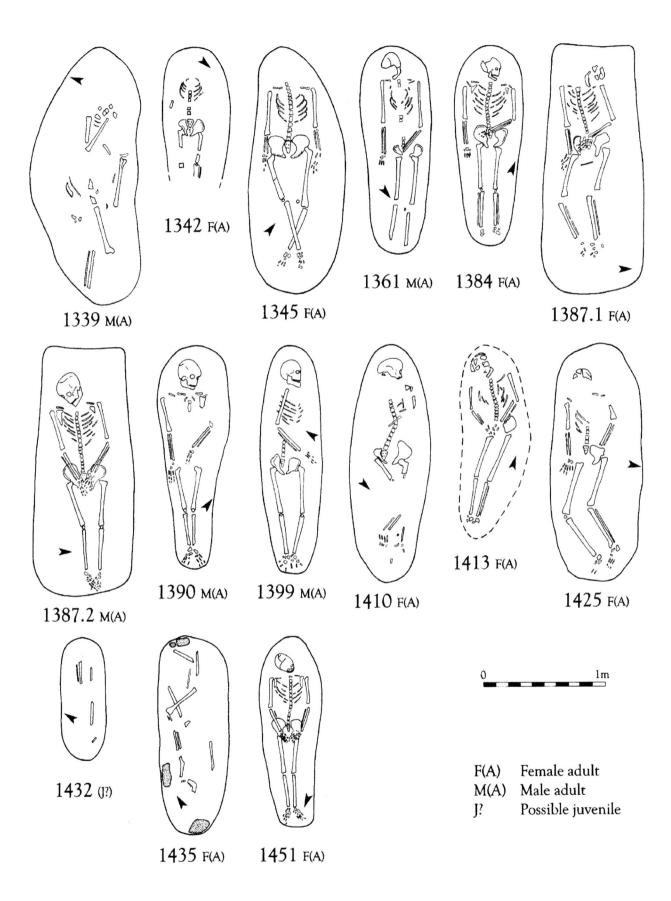

1342 F(A)

1339 M(A)

1345 F(A)

1361 M(A)

1384 F(A)

1387.1 F(A)

1387.2 M(A)

1390 M(A)

1399 M(A)

1410 F(A)

1413 F(A)

1425 F(A)

1432 (J?)

1435 F(A)

1451 F(A)

0   1m

F(A)   Female adult
M(A)   Male adult
J?   Possible juvenile

Figure 30. Inhumations without grave goods

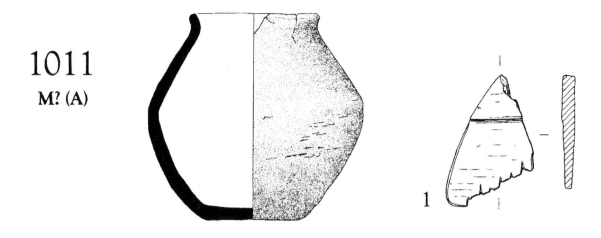

1011
M? (A)

1

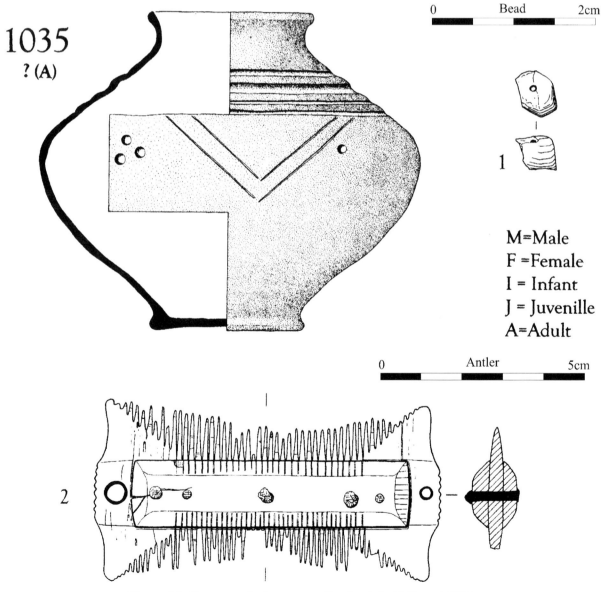

1035
? (A)

0   Bead   2cm

1

M=Male
F =Female
I = Infant
J = Juvenille
A=Adult

0   Antler   5cm

2

Figure 31. Grave goods from cremation burials 1011 and 1035

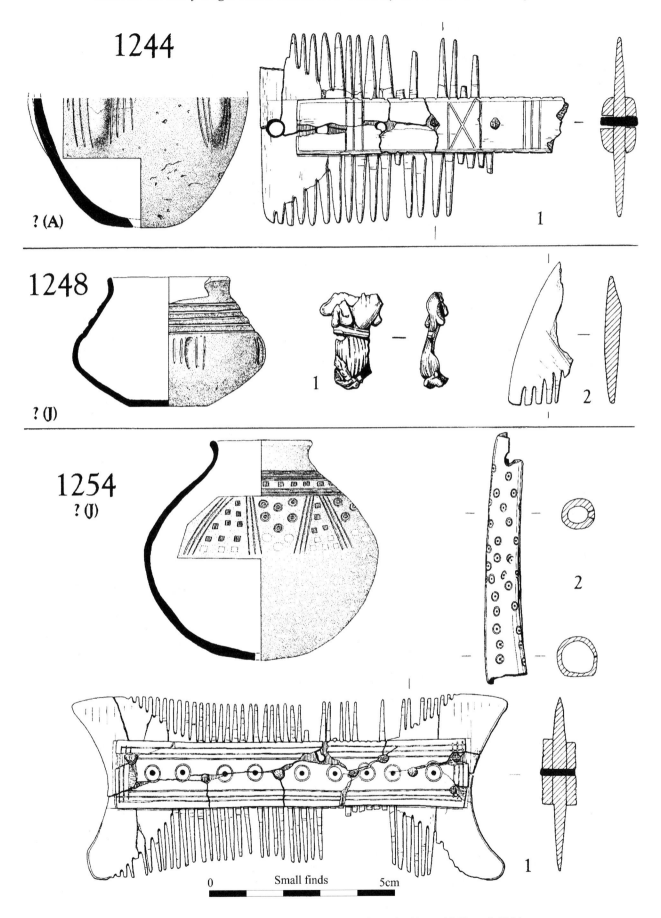

Figure 32. Grave goods from cremation burials 1244, 1248 and 1254

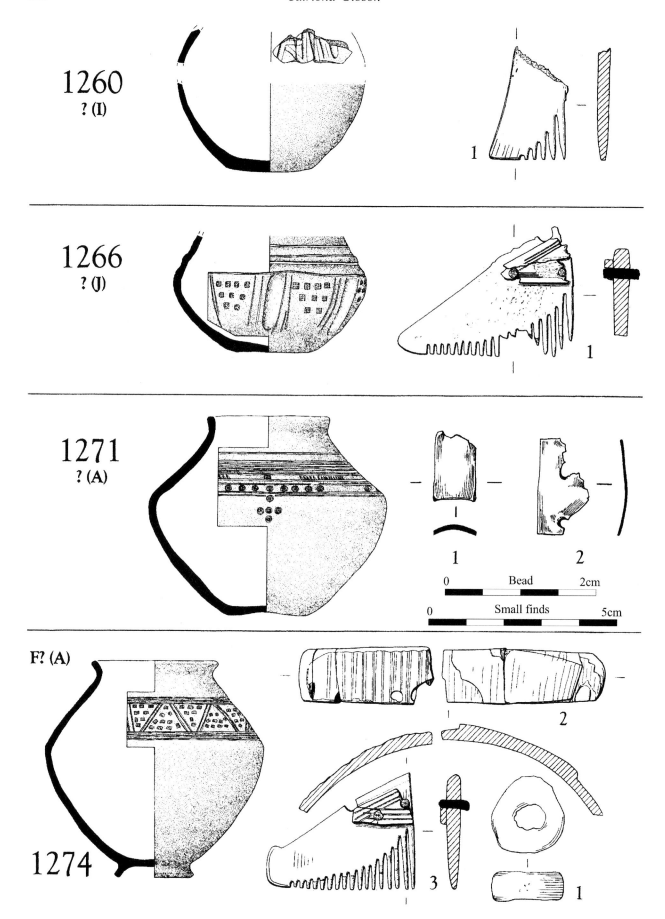

Figure 33. Grave goods from cremation burials 1260, 1266, 1271 and 1274

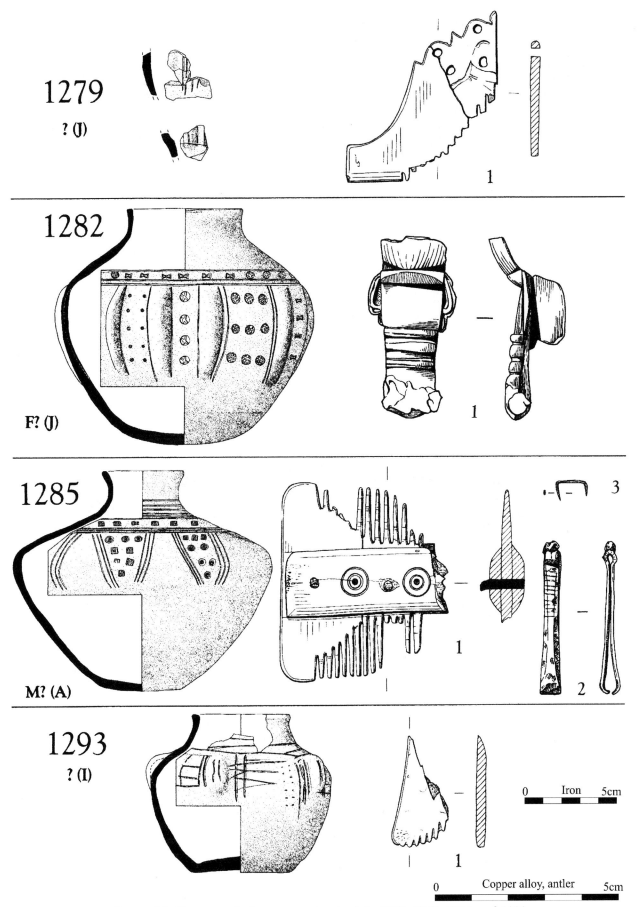

Figure 34. Grave goods from cremation burials 1279, 1282, 1285 and 1293

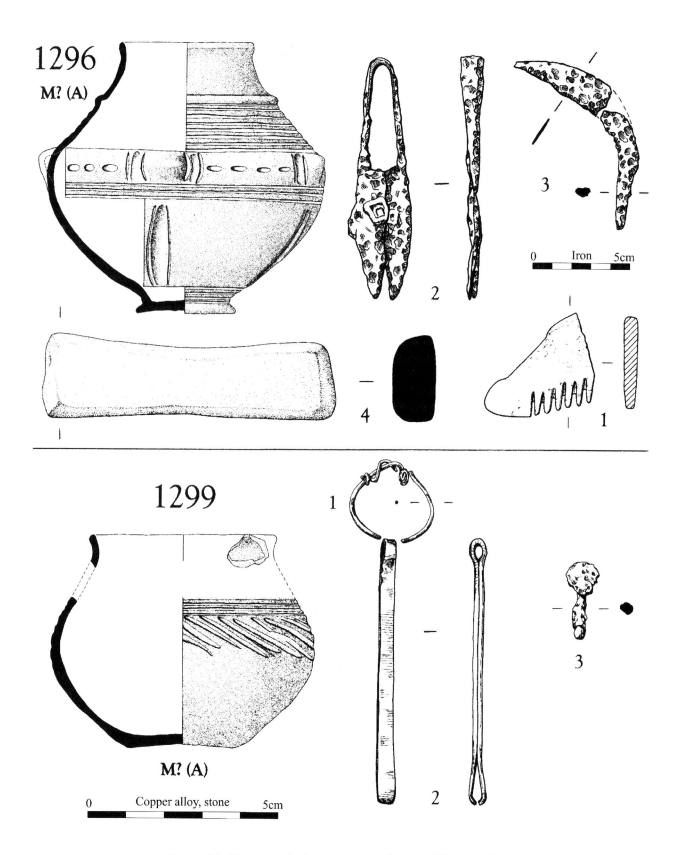

Figure 35. Grave goods from cremation burials 1296 and 1299

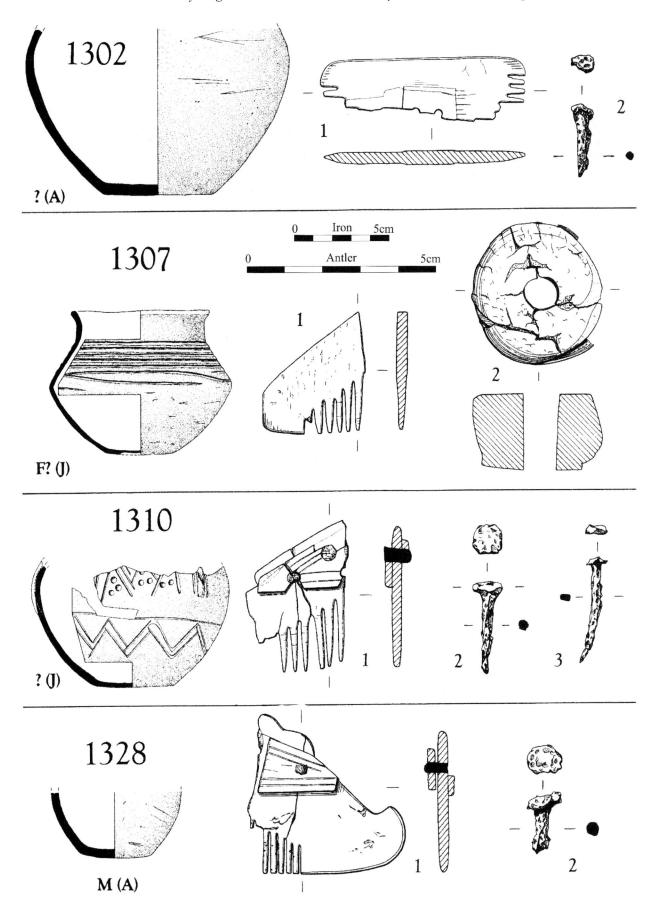

Figure 36. Grave goods from cremation burials 1302, 1307, 1310 and 1328

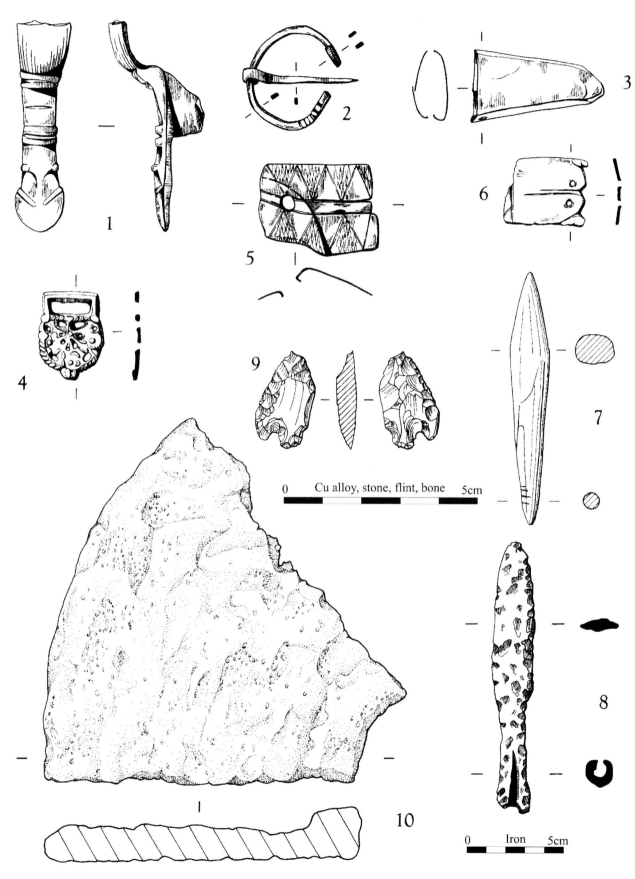

Figure 37. Small finds not from graves

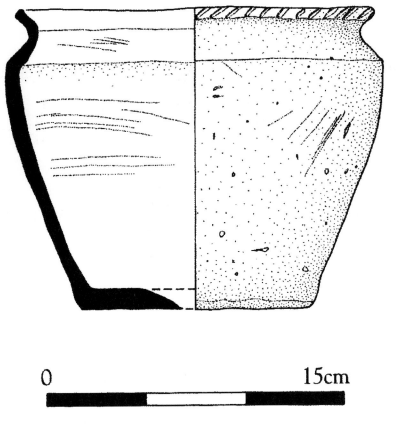

0   15cm

Figure 38. Prehistoric pottery

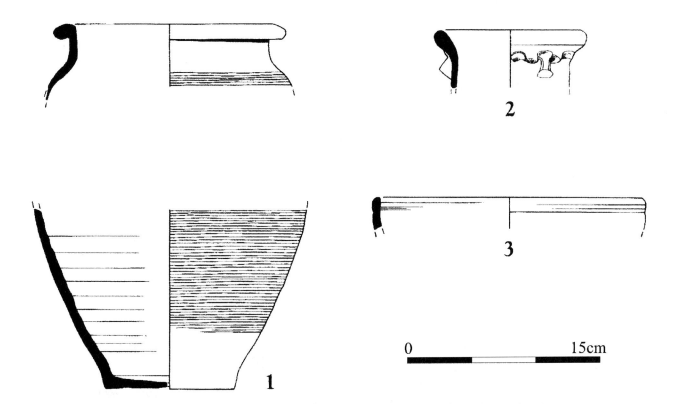

0   15cm

Figure 39. Roman pottery

Catriona Gibson

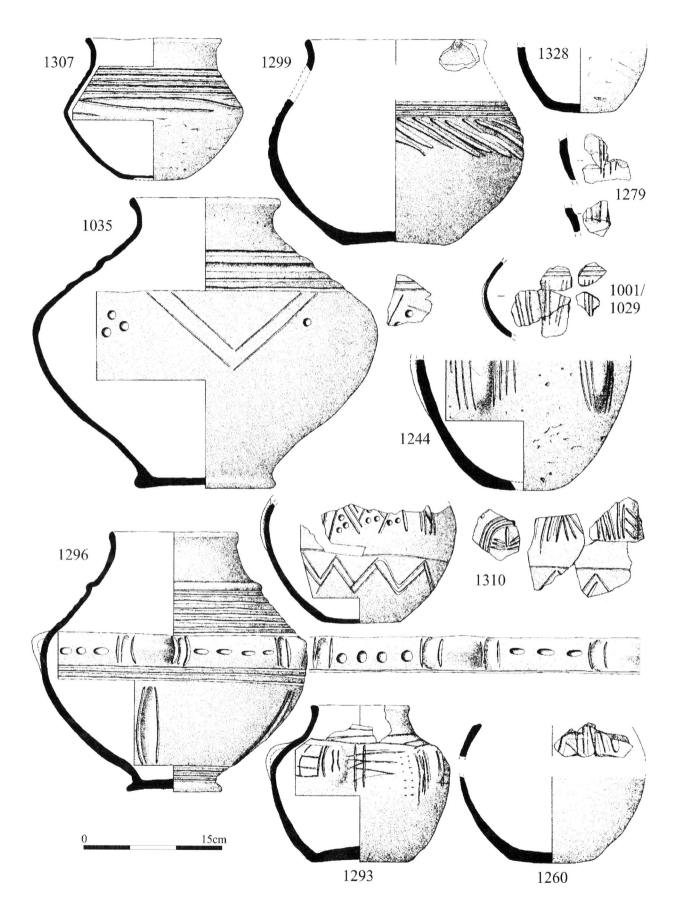

Figure 40. Saxon pottery

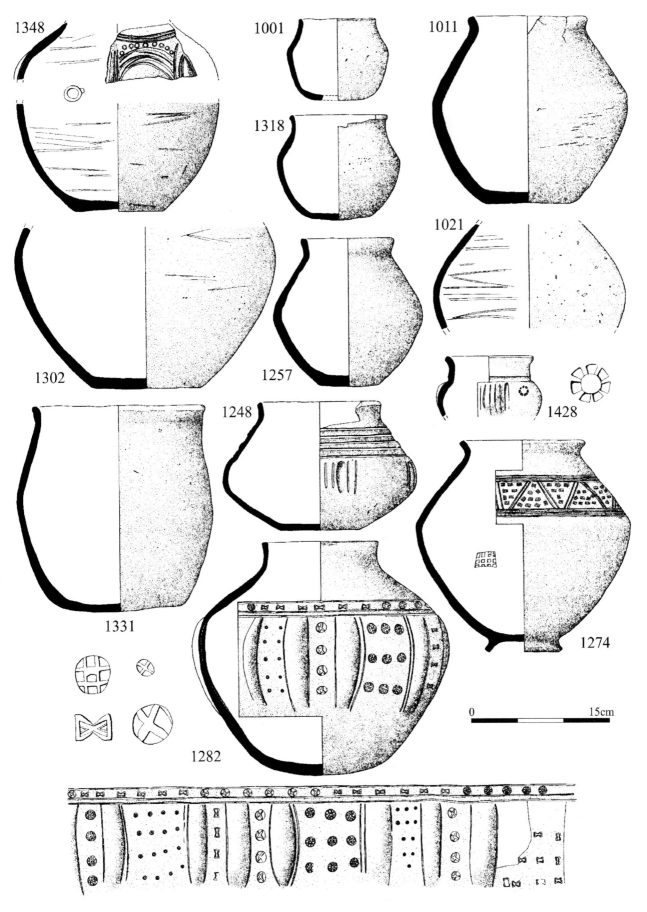

Figure 41. Saxon pottery

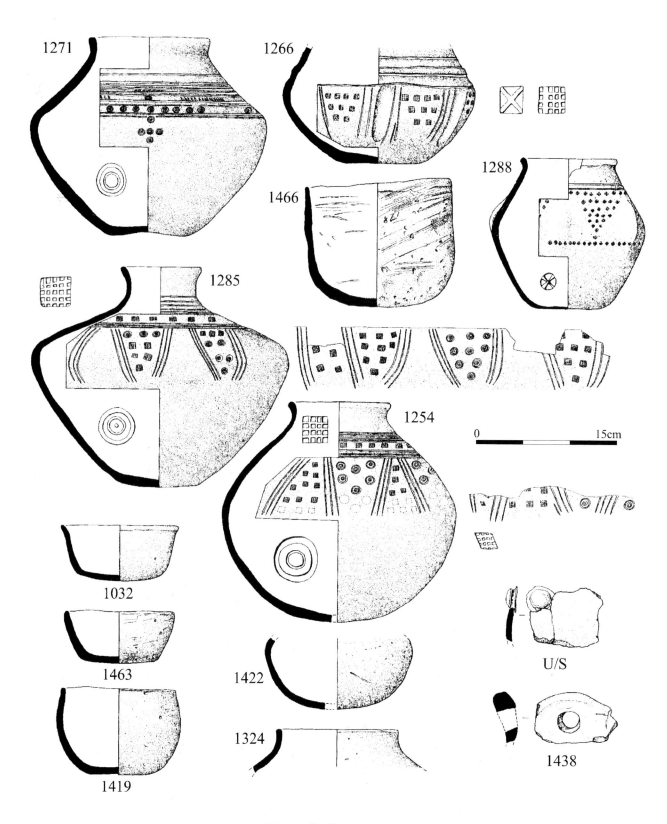

Figure 42. Saxon pottery

Notes

1. According to briefs prepared by OAA in association with Cambridgeshire County Council County Archaeology Office (CCC CAO) and specifications compiled by HAT.
2. French 1999.
3. Roberts 1999.
4. Murray 1999.
5. Murray 1999.
6. Spoerry in Roberts 1999.
7. McDonald and Vaughan 1999, 4.4.5.
8. *Ibid.*
9. Spoerry in Roberts 1999.
10. Ellison and Drewett 1971, 190–2.
11. Malim and Hines 1998.
12. Malim and Hines 1998.
13. *Ibid.,* 34–41.
14. Kinsley 1989, 19.
15. Down and Welch 1990, 25–33.
16. Nielsen 1992, 6–7.
17. Webster and Cherry 1975, 227.
18. Down and Welch 1990, 29.
19. Filmer-Sankey and Pestell 2001, 252.
20. Duhig 1998, 154.
21. Evison 1994.
22. Crawford 1991, 125–133.
23. Duhig 1998, 160; Malim and Hines 1998, 292.
24. Holgate 1988.
25. Hawkes and Fell 1945.
26. Roberts 1999.
27. D. Jackson, pers comm.
28. Williams in Pryor 1984, 134.
29. See Cunliffe 1991.
30. Hawkes and Fell 1945, 213.
31. Burchell and Frere 1947, fig. 16.9.
32. Cf. Hawkes and Fell 1945, 204, G1.
33. Cunliffe 1991.
34. Anderson 1998.
35. Anderson in Murray 1999.
36. In Roberts 1999.
37. *E.g.* Cunliffe 1974, fig. A4: 10–11.
38. Tomber and Dore 1998.
39. Perrin 1999.
40. *Ibid.*, 114–204.
41. Tyers 1996, 107–114.
42. Webster 1996.
43. Tomber and Dore 1998, 28–29.
44. Tyers 1996, 107–114.
45. Webster 1996.
46. Tomber and Dore 1998, 30–31.
47. Tyers 1996, 107–114.
48. Webster 1996.
49. Tomber and Dore 1998, 32–33.
50. Howe *et al.* 1980.
51. Tomber and Dore 1998, 117–118.
52. Perrin 1999, 87–106.
53. Tomber and Dore 1998, 213.
54. *Ibid.*, 119.
55. Harden and Green 1978, 170.
56. Tomber and Dore 1998, 151.
57. Fawcett unpublished and forthcoming.
58. Fawcett unpublished, forthcoming and 2006.
59. 2155: Wilson 1984, 220.
60. 845: Rigby 1986, 379.
61. Going 1987, 9.
62. Fawcett unpublished and forthcoming.
63. Fawcett unpublished and forthcoming.
64. Going 1987, 9.
65. Perrin 1999, 78–87.
66. Fawcett unpublished and forthcoming.
67. Tomber and Dore 1998, 115.
68. Tyers 1996, 192.
69. Brown 1994, 19–107.
70. Perrin 1996, 119–120.
71. *Ibid.*, 119.
72. Thompson 1982.
73. Tomber and Dore 1998, 214.
74. Perrin 1996, 121.
75. Thompson 1982, 16.
76. Perrin 1988, 131–141.
77. Perrin 1996, 164–177.
78. Tyers 1996, 79.
79. Howe 1984 and unpublished; Walker 1899; Myres 1974.
80. Walker 1978; Pearson 1988–9; Mackreth 1996; Blinkhorn 2000.
81. Pearson 1985; 1988–9.
82. Denham 1985, 122; Vince 2000, 168; Blinkhorn 2000, 104.
83. Walker 1978; Williams and Vince 1997.
84. Vince 2000, 168.
85. Anderson 2003; Sudds 2005.
86. Williams and Vince 1997; Hall 2000.
87. Williams and Vince 1997.
88. West 1985; Anderson 2003; Sudds 2005.
89. Pearson 1985 and 1988–9.
90. Hamerow 1993; Arnold 1997, 17.
91. Hamerow 1993.
92. Myres 1969, 34.
93. Hamerow 1993, 52.
94. Hamerow 1993, 45; Evison 1994, 20; Mackreth 1996, 207; Blinkhorn 2000, 100.
95. Myres 1977, 17–18.
96. Williams 1983.
97. Myres 1977, 40.
98. *Ibid.*, 48–50.
99. Hills 1977, Figs 49/50.
100. Williams 1983, Fig.10.98.
101. Evison 1994, 20.
102. Myres 1977, 45.
103. *Ibid.*, 6 and 39.
104. Hamerow 1993, 45.
105. Myres 1977, 39; Evison 1994, 20.
106. Evison 1994, 20–21 and Fig. 55.148/1; Crummy, this volume.
107. Myres 1974; Williams 1983.
108. Myres 1969, 45–8; 1977, 31–4.
109. *Ibid.*, 46.
110. Myres 1977, 31–4, Fig. 199.
111. *Ibid.*; Blinkhorn 2000, 100.
112. Evison 1994, 20–1.
113. Myres 1977, Fig. 201.2650.
114. *Ibid.*; Hamerow 1993, 52.
115. Myres, 1977, Fig. 170.3722 and 653 respectively.
116. Mackreth 1996, 210.
117. Myres 1977, 22 and Fig. 119.3241; Crummy, this volume.
118. *Ibid.*, 56; Fig. 327.3687.
119. *Ibid.* 1977.
120. Blinkhorn 2000, 100.
121. Myres 1977, 27.
122. *Ibid.* 35 and 42–3.
123. *Ibid.* 1977, 27.
124. *Ibid.* 54–6; Evison 1994, 21.
125. Myres 1977, 53.
126. *Ibid.*, 51.
127. *Ibid,* 56.
128. Evison 1994, 21 and Fig. 28.
129. Myres 1977, 56.
130. *Ibid.*, 7–8.
131. Sudds 2005.
132. Taylor 2000.
133. *Ibid.*

134. Dark 2000, 77–8.
135. *Ibid.*
136. Adams and Jackson 1988–9.
137. Hamerow 1993, 52.
138. Arnold 1997, 96.
139. Richards 1987; McKinley 1994a; Arnold 1997.
140. Brisbane 1981.
141. Sudds 2005.
142. *Ibid.*
143. Blinkhorn 2000.
144. Anderson 2003; Sudds 2005.
145. Richards 1987.
146. *Ibid.*
147. *Ibid.,* 195–6.
148. McKinley 1994a, 101–2; Pearson 1988–9, 165.
149. McKinley 1994a, 85.
150. Howe 1984, 60; Myres 1974.
151. McKinley 1994a, 91.
152. Brush 1988; McKinley 1994a; Lucy 2000.
153. Myres and Green 1973, 91; Timby 1993, 276; Hills and Penn 1981, figs 168–75.
154. Evison 1994, fig. 60, C12/2.
155. Hills and Penn 1981, figs 146–60; Myres and Green 1973, 103.
156. *Ibid.,* 108.
157. *Ibid.,* 100–3; Hills and Penn 1981, fig. 266.
158. *E.g.* Evison 1994, 24–5; Fitzpatrick 1997, 105.
159. Davidson 1964, 78–9; *Eyrbyggja Saga* IV.
160. Meaney 1981, 12.
161. Mortimer 1990.
162. Guido 1999, 43, 239–40.
163. *E.g.* Crummy 1983, fig. 36, 1426–9.
164. Guido 1999, 48.
165. Myres and Green 1973, 91; Hills 1977, figs 133–4; Hills and Penn 1981, figs 170–2.
166. Galloway 1979, fig. 31, 64; Crummy *et al.* forthcoming, Victoria Road SF 705.
167. Greep 1993, fig. 78, 2–3.
168. Crummy 1983, fig. 58, 1855.
169. Galloway 1979, fig 31, 479, 482.
170. Crummy 1983, fig. 58, 1853.
171. Webster 1975, fig. 117, 104.
172. White 1988.
173. Crummy *et al.* forthcoming, Victoria Road SF 776/941.
174. Hills and Penn 1981, fig. 174, 2192; Timby 1993, illus. 34.
175. Hills and Penn 1981, fig. 174; West 1985, figs 252–30; Timby 1996, 61.
176. Hills 1977, figs 132–4; Hills and Penn 1981, figs 171–3; West 1985, fig. 13, passim; Timby 1993, illus. 35, 38.
177. Myres and Green 1973, 82–3; Stoodley 1999a, 33.
178. Jackson 1997, 1472.
179. Evison 1994, 44.
180. Timby 1996, 64–5.
181. Malim and Hines 1998, 218.
182. Cowgill *et al.* 1987, 58–60.
183. *E.g.* Hamerow 1993, fig. 89, 5, fig. 138, 1.
184. Manning 1985, 34.
185. Myres and Green 1973, figs 9, 25, 34.
186. Hills and Penn 1981, fig. 148, 1989, fig. 153, 1696, fig. 157, 2199, fig. 158, 2233.
187. Evison 1975, 72.
188. Evison 1994, 26.
189. Simpson 1979; Timby 1993, 336, Illus. 39–40; Green 2004, 44, 55.
190. Hills 2001, 139–40, 143.
191. Myres and Green 1973, 112–13.
192. Lethbridge 1931, fig. 37; Malim and Hines 1998, 219; Timby 1996, 61–2.
193. Walker 1899, pl. 2.
194. Hamerow 1993, 64–5.
195. West 1985, fig. 30 passim.

196. Williams 1993, 119–21.
197. Hills and Penn 1981, fig. 179, 1976.
198. Evison and Hill 1996, 10.
199. Brown 1974; Boyle *et al.* 1995, 89; MacGregor and Bolick 1993, 227–8.
200. Myres and Green 1973, fig. 1.
201. Lethbridge 1931, fig. 9, 5, fig. 14, J2, K, fig. 39, 9; Evison 1994, 97, fig. 27, 36b.
202. MacGregor and Bolick 1993, 263.
203. Malim and Hines 1998, 52, fig. 3.38, 1.
204. Evison 1994, 24–5; Malim and Hines 1998, 227.
205. Evison 1987, 116.
206. Härke 1989, 59; Malim and Hines 1998, 300–1.
207. Härke 1989, 50.
208. Malim and Hines 1998, 300–1; Timby 1996, 15.
209. Mortimer 1998, 259–61.
210. Leeds and Pocock 1971, 27–9; Mortimer 1990.
211. Leeds 1945, 20–2, fig. 10.
212. Malim and Hines 1998, 201.
213. Evison 1979a, 91; 1979b, 261, 269.
214. *Ibid.,* 261–2, pl. 54, c.
215. Lethbridge 1931, fig. 11, F2.
216. Fowler 1960, 152.
217. *Ibid.,* fig. 19, A3–4; Adams and Jackson 1990, fig. 21, G21/1–2.
218. *Ibid.,* 149; Malim and Hines 1998, fig. 3.43, 20:12; Evison 1994, figs 26, 29:1, 37, 79:1; Green *et al.* 1987, table 5, passim.
219. Fowler 1983.
220. *E.g.* Leeds 1945, fig.1 passim; MacGregor and Bolick 1993, 127 passim.
221. Leeds and Atkinson 1944, pl. 23a, 33; Adams and Jackson 1990, fig. 39.
222. Ager 1985, fig 17.
223. Guido 1999.
224. Malim and Hines 1998, 207.
225. Guido 1999, 42–3, 48.
226. *Ibid.,* 56, 277–82.
227. *Ibid.,* 33.
228. *Ibid.,* 40.
229. White 1990, fig. 12, 2; Jessup 1950, pl. 33; Parfitt 1991, 217; Pilet 1980, pl. 157, 603/3.
230. White 1990 fig. 12, 1; Adams and Jackson 1990, 152, fig. 41, e.
231. *E.g.* Lethbridge 1931, fig. 3.
232. *Ibid.,* 1931, fig. 2, 6.
233. MacGregor and Bolick 1993, 185–7.
234. Green *et al.* 1987, fig. 436, N.
235. West 1985, fig. 246, 7; Evison 1994, 19.
236. Adams and Jackson 1990, 156.
237. West 1985, 123.
238. Adams and Jackson 1990, fig. 48; Timby 1996, figs 105, 122, 135; Malim and Hines 1998, 216.
239. *Ibid.,* fig. 3.31, 10, 17.
240. Hines 1984, fig. 2.1.
241. *Ibid.,* 78, fig. 2.1.
242. *Ibid.,* 79, 86.
243. Malim and Hines 1998, fig. 3.45.
244. MacGregor and Bolick 1993, 258–9.
245. Hawkes and Dunning 1962, 60; Marzinzik 2003, 35; Böhme 1986, 492, 495.
246. Böhme 1986, 508–9.
247. Hawkes and Dunning 1962, fig. 19 bis, b, fig. 20, g–h; Evison 1981, 145.
248. O'Brien 2006.
249. Myres and Green 1973, 102–3, Malim and Hines 1998, fig. 6.9 and Meaney 1998, fig. 6.9.
250. Adams and Jackson 1990, fig. 18; MacGregor and Bolick 1993, 231, nos 42.8–10.
251. Timby 1996, 122–3, fig. 149, 11.
252. Timby 1993, illus. 32.
253. Meaney 1998, 269.

254. *E.g.* Lethbridge 1931, fig. 32; Timby 1996, fig. 110.
255. *E.g.* Malim and Hines 1998, fig. 3.57, 15.
256. Meaney 1998, 275.
257. White 1988, 100–1.
258. Lethbridge 1931, 61.
259. Leeds and Atkinson 1944, pl. 29, 13.
260. Timby 1996, fig. 77, grave 85, fig. 135, 5–6, 5a–6a.
261. Malim and Hines 1998, fig. 3.31, 10, 17.
262. Stoodley 1999a, 33.
263. Malim and Hines 1998, 217.
264. Jackson and Ambrose 1978, fig. 65, 14.
265. West 1985, fig. 188, 1.
266. Hamerow 1993, 69; Brodribb *et al.* 1972, fig. 52, 315, 1973, fig. 58, 400.
267. Dickinson and Härke 1992, 10.
268. Evison 1994, 5.
269. Swanton 1974, 15–16.
270. Goodall 1985, fig. 27, 25; Hinton 1990, 549.
271. Crawford and Röder 1955, fig 1.
272. Powlesland *et al.* 1986.
273. Mack and McDonnell 1999.
274. Evans 1963.
275. McKinley 1994.
276. *E.g.* McKinley 1997, 245.
277. P. Smith, pers. comm.
278. McKinley 1994a, 5–21.
279. Beek, 1983; McMinn and Hutchings 1985; Webb and Suchey 1985.
280. Bass 1987.
281. Bass 1987.
282. Holden *et al.* 1995 a and b.
283. McKinley 1993a.
284. *E.g.* McKinley 1993a and b, 1994a.
285. McKinley 1993a.
286. McKinley 1993b, 1994b.
287. McKinley 1994a, 5–6.
288. P. Smith, pers comm.
289. McKinley 1994a, 92.
290. *Ibid.*, 92; Wahl 1988.
291. McKinley 1994a, table 5; Bond 1994.
292. McKinley and Bond 1993, table 9.
293. McKinley 1994a, 99.
294. *Ibid.*, 92–100; Bond 1994.
295. McKinley 1997a and b.
296. Workshop of European Anthropologists 1980.
297. Mildred Trotter 1970.
298. Waldron 1998.
299. Duhig 1998, 172.
300. Waldron 1991.
301. Davis 1992.
302. Albarella and Davis 1996.
303. Albarella, Beech and Mulville 1997.
304. Barone 1980; Levine 1982.
305. Grigson 1982, Fig. 1.
306. Matolcsi 1970.
307. Baker and Brothwell 1980, 114–117.
308. Albarella 1995, 703–4.
309. Baxter unpublished.
310. Teichert 1975.
311. Teichert 1990.
312. Harcourt 1974.
313. Morgan, Ljunggren and Read 1967; Harris 1977.
314. Clark 1995.
315. Stace 1997.
316. Fryer 2001; Fryer and Murphy 1999.
317. Williams 1998, 92.
318. Pryor 1984, 231.
319. *Ibid.*, 232.
320. Mackreth 1996.
321. Howe 1984.
322. Walker 1899.
323. Smith 1926.
324. Leeds and Atkinson 1944.
325. Frere and St Joseph 1974, 112–121.
326. Patrick *et al.* forthcoming.
327. information from Peterborough Sites and Monuments Record.
328. Mackreth 1996, 239.
329. Peterborough SMR 585; Prosser 1999.
330. Malim and Hines 1998, 320.
331. Cf. Ravn 2003, 94.
332. Evison and Hill 1996.
333. Filmer-Sankey and Pestell 2001.
334. Cook and Dacre 1985, 52.
335. Unpublished dissertation 1995, quoted in Ravn 2003.
336. *E.g.* Lucy 1995, quoted in Ravn 2003.
337. *E.g.* Goodier 1984; Reynolds 1999.
338. Great Chesterford; Evison 1994.
339. Beckford, Hereford; Evison and Hill 1996.
340. Malim and Hines 1998, fig. 3.1a and 3.4.
341. Sudds this volume.
342. Last and McDonald 1999, fig. 3.
343. Evison 1994, 35.
344. *Ibid.*
345. *Ibid.*, 31.
346. Stoodley 2000, 458.
347. Crawford 1993, 85.
348. Crummy this volume.
349. Sudds this volume.
350. Wells 1996, 47.
351. Duhig 1998, 167–168.
352. Stirland 1993.
353. *E.g.* Duhig 1998, 10
354. Malim and Hines 1996.
355. Evison and Hill 1996, 23.
356. See Metcalf and Huntingdon 1991.
357. Van Gennep 1960.
358. Durkheim 1965.
359. Malim and Hines 1998.
360. Evison 1994.
361. See Lucy 1997; Holst 1993.
362. *E.g.* Pader 1982; Richards 1984; 1987; Huggett 1996; Stoodley 1997; 2000; Lucy 1998.
363. See Williams 2002; Ravn 2003.
364. Ravn 2003, 94.
365. Williams 2002, 61.
366. Fryer this volume.
367. *Ibid.*
368. *Ibid.*, 68; Ravn 2003, 131.
369. See McKinley 1994a.
370. Kinsley 1989.
371. Malim and Hines 1998.
372. See Brush 1988.
373. Richards 1987.
374. Lucy 2000, 110.
375. Stoodley 1999b.
376. *Ibid.*, 462.
377. Huggett and Richards 1990, 77–78.
378. Richards 1987.
379. Sudds this volume.
380. McKinley 1994a.
381. *Ibid.*, 90.
382. *Ibid.*, 91.
383. see McKinley 1994a, figs 20 and 24; Lucy 2000, fig. 4.2.
384. Richards 1984; 1987; 1988.
385. Crummy this volume.
386. Malim and Hines 1998, 42.
387. Evison 1994, 35.

Bibliography

Adams, B. and Jackson, D. 1988/9. 'The Anglo-Saxon cemetery at Wakerley, Northamptonshire'. *Northamptonshire Archaeology*, **22**, 69–183.

Adams, B. and Jackson, D. 1990. 'The Anglo-Saxon cemetery at Wakerley, Northamptonshire. Excavations by Mr D Jackson, 1968–9', *Northamptonshire Arch*, **22**, 69–183.

Ager, B. M. 1985. 'The smaller variants of the Anglo-Saxon quoit brooch', *ASSAH*, **4**, 1–58.

Albarella, U. 1995. 'Depressions on sheep horncores', *Jnl of Arch Science*, **22**, 699–704.

Albarella, U. and Davis, S. J. M. 1994. *The Saxon and Medieval Animal Bones Excavated 1985–1989 from West Cotton, Northamptonshire*, London: English Heritage AML Report 17/94.

Albarella, U., Beech, M. and Mulville, J. 1997. *The Saxon, Medieval and Post-medieval mammal and bird bones excavated 1989–1991 from Castle Mall, Norwich (Norfolk)*, London: English Heritage AML Report 72/97.

Anderson, S. 1998. *Station Road, Gamlingay: the pottery*, Hertfordshire Archaeological Trust Unpublished Assessment Report

Anderson, S. 2003. 'Post-Roman Pottery', in C. Gibson with J. Murray, An Anglo-Saxon Settlement at Godmanchester, Cambridgeshire, *ASSAH*, **12**, 174–83.

Arnold, C. J. 1997. *An Archaeology of the early Anglo-Saxon Kingdoms: New Edition*, Routledge, London and New York.

Baker, J. and Brothwell, D. 1980. *Animal Diseases in Archaeology*, London: Academic Press

Barone, R .1980. *Anatomia Comparata dei Mammiferi Domestici*, Vol. III, Bologna: Splancnologia.

Baxter, I. L. 2003. Animal Bone, in C. Gibson with J. Murray, An Anglo-Saxon Settlement at Godmanchester, Cambridgeshire. *ASSAH*, **12**, 190–7.

Blinkhorn, P. 2000. 'The early Anglo-Saxon Pottery' in N. J. Cooper (ed.), 'The Archaeology of Rutland Water: Excavations at Empingham in the Gwash Valley, Rutland, 1967–73 and 1990', *Leicester Archaeology Monograph*, **6**, 98 – 104.

Bond, J. 1994. 'The cremated bone', in J. McKinley (ed.), *The Anglo-Saxon Cemetery at Spong Hill, North Elmham. Part VIII: The Cremations*, 121–35, East Anglian Archaeology, 69, Dereham: Field Archaeology Division, Norfolk Museums Service.

Böhme, H. W. 1986. 'Das Ende der Römerherrschaft in Britannien und die angelsächsische Besiedlung Englands im 5. Jahrhundert', *Jahrbuch des Römisch-Germanischen Zentralmuseums Mainz* **33.2**, 469–574.

Boyle, A., Dodd, A., Miles, D. and Miles, A. 1995. *Two Oxfordshire Anglo-Saxon cemeteries; Berinsfield and Didcot*, Thames Valley Landscapes Monograph 8, Oxford: Oxford Archaeological Unit.

Brisbane, M. 1981. 'Incipient Markets for early Anglo-Saxon Ceramics: Variations in Levels and Modes of Production', H. Howard and E. L. Morris (eds), BAR International Series, 120, 229 – 242, Oxford: British Archaeological Reports.

Brodribb, A. C. C., Hands, A. R. and Walker, D. R. 1972. 'Excavations at Shakenoak Farm, near Wilcote, Oxfordshire: III, Site F', *Jnl of Roman Stud.*

Brown, A. 1994. 'A Romano-British Shell-Gritted Pottery and Tile Manufacturing Site at Harrold, Bedfordshire', *Bedfordshire Arch. Jnl.*, **2**, 19–107.

Brown, P. D. C. 1974. 'So-called "needle cases"', *Medieval Archaeology* **18**, 151–4.

Brush, K. A. 1988. 'Gender and mortuary analysis in pagan Anglo-Saxon archaeology', *Arch. Rev. from Cambridge*, **7**(1), 76–89.

Burchell, J. and Frere, S. 1947. 'Sandown Park, Esher (Surrey), Occupation during the Stone Age, early Iron Age, and Anglo-Saxon period', *Antiquaries Jnl*, **27**, 24–46.

Clark, K. M. 1995. 'The later prehistoric and protohistoric dog: the emergence of canine diversity', *Archaeozoologia*, **7/2**, 9–32.

Cook, A. M and Dacre, M. W. 1985. *Excavations at Portway, Andover 1973–1975*, Oxford: Oxford University Committee for Archaeology Monograph 4.

Cowgill, J., de Neergaard, M. and Griffiths, N. 1987. *Medieval finds from excavations in London: 1. Knives and scabbards*, London: HMSO.

Crawford, O. G. S. and Röder, J. 1955. 'The quern-quarries of Mayen in the Eifel', *Antiquity*, **29**, 68–76.

Crawford, S. 1991. 'When do Anglo-Saxon children count?', *Jnl. of Theoretical Arch.*, **2**, 17–24.

Crawford, S. 1993 'Children, Death and the Afterlife in Anglo-Saxon England' in Filmer-Sankey, W. (ed.) *ASSAH* **6**, 83–91.

Crummy, N. 1983. *The Roman small finds from excavations in Colchester 1971–9*, Colchester Archaeological Report 2.

Crummy, N., Ottaway, P. and Rees, H. forthcoming. *Small Finds from the Suburbs and City Defences* Winchester Museum Publication 6.

Cunliffe, B. 1974. *Iron Age Communities in Britain*, 1st edition. London: Routledge.

Cunliffe, B. 1991. *Iron Age Communities in Britain*, 3rd edition. London: Routledge.

Dark, K., 2000. *Britain at the end of the Roman Empire*. Tempus Publishing Ltd, Gloucestershire.

Davidson, H. R. E. 1964. *Gods and Myths of Northern Europe*, Harmondsworth: Penguin Books

Davis, S. M. J. 1992. *A Rapid Method for Recording Information about Mammal Bones from Archaeological Sites*, London: English Heritage AML report 19/92.

Denham, V. 1985. 'The Saxon Pottery' in H. Bamford 'Briar Hill: Excavation 1974–1978'. *Northampton Development Corporation; Archaeological Monograph* No. **3**, 122–124 and microfiche

Dickinson, T. and Härke, H. 1992. 'Early Anglo-Saxon shields', *Archaeologia* **110**

Down, A. and Welch, M. 1990. *Chichester Excavations VII: Apple Down and the Mardens*, Chichester: Chichester District Council.

Duhig, C. 1998. 'The human skeletal material', in T. Malim and J. Hines (eds), *The Anglo-Saxon Cemetery at Edix Hill (Barrington A), Cambridgeshire*, 154–99, CBA Report 112 York: Council for British Archaeology.

Durkheim, E. 1965 (1912). *The Elementary Forms of the Religious Life*, New York: Free Press.

Ellison, A. and Drewett, P. 1971. 'Pits and postholes in the British early Iron Age: some alternative explanations', *Proc. of the Prehistoric Soc.* **37**, 183–194.

Evans, W. E. D. 1963. *The Chemistry of Death* Springfield, Massachusetts: CC Thomas.

Evison, V. I. 1975. 'Pagan Anglo-Saxon whetstones', *Antiquaries Jnl.* **55/1**, 70–85.

Evison, V. I. 1979a. 'early Anglo-Saxon applied disc brooches I: on the continent', *Antiquaries Jnl.* **58**, 88–102.

Evison, V. I. 1979b. 'early Anglo-Saxon applied disc brooches II: in England', *Antiquaries Jnl.* **58**, 260–78.

Evison, V. I. 1981. 'Distribution maps and England in the first two phases', in V. Evison (ed.), *Angles, Saxons and Jutes Essays presented to JNL Myres*, 126–167, Oxford: Clarendon Press.

Evison, V. I. 1987. *Dover: The Buckland Anglo-Saxon Cemetery*, London: English Heritage Archaeological Report 3.

Evison, V. I. 1994. *An Anglo-Saxon Cemetery at Great Chesterford, Essex*, Council for British Archaeology Research Report, 91, York: CBA.

Evison, V. I. and Hill, P. 1996. *Two Anglo-Saxon Cemeteries at Beckford, Hereford and Worcester*, Council for British Archaeology Research Report, 103, York: CBA.

Eyrbyggja Saga, trans. H. Palsson and P. Edwards in 1973, UNESCO collection of representative works. Icelandic Series, Edinburgh: Southside (Publishers) Ltd.

Fawcett, A. R. unpublished. 'The Roman pottery from Sandridge and Turners Hall Farm', in T. McDonald and A. Pearson (eds) in prep. *Two Romano-British Settlements in Hertfordshire: Turners Hall Farm and Sandridge*.

Fawcett, A. R. forthcoming. *The End of Roman Britain – Continuation*,

Assimilation or Isolation: a ceramic viewpoint.

Fawcett, A. R. 2006. 'The Roman pottery', in J. Murray with T. McDonald 'Excavations at Station Road, Gamlingay, Cambridgeshire', *ASSAH* **13**, 213.

Filmer-Sankey, W and Pestell, T. 2001. *Snape Anglo-Saxon cemetery: excavations and surveys 1824–1992*, East Anglian Archaeology, 95, Bury St Edmunds: Suffolk County Council Archaeological Services

Fitzpatrick, A. P. 1997. *Archaeological excavations on the route of the A27 Westhampnett Bypass, West Sussex, 1992, 2: the late Iron Age, Romano-British, and Anglo-Saxon cemeteries*, Wessex Archaeology Report 12.

Fowler, E. 1960. 'The origins and development of the penannular brooch in Europe', *Proc. of the Prehistoric Soc.* **26**, 149–77.

Fowler, E. 1983. 'Note on the Type C brooches', in N Crummy (ed.), *The Roman Small Finds from Excavations in Colchester 1971–9*, Colchester Archaeological Report 2.

Frere, S. and St Joseph, J. K. S. 1974. 'The Roman fortress at Longthorpe', *Britannia* **5**,1–129.

Fryer, V. 2001. *Charred Plant Macrofossils and Other Remains from Tranmer House, Sutton Hoo, Suffolk (BML 018): An assessment for Suffolk County Council Archaeological Service.*

Fryer, V. and Murphy, P. 1999. *Charred Plant Macrofossils and Other Remains from Lakenheath, Suffolk (ERL 104): An assessment for Suffolk County Council Archaeological Service.*

Galloway, P. 1979. 'Combs', in G. Clarke (ed.), *The Roman Cemetery at Lankhills*, Winchester Studies 3.

Going, C. J. 1987. *The Mansio and Other Sites in the South-Eastern Sector of Caesaromagus: The Roman Pottery,* Council for British Archaeology Research Report 62 London: Chelmsford Archaeological Trust.

Goodall, A. R. 1985. 'Personal equipment', in C. M. Cunningham and P. J. Drury (eds), *Post-medieval Sites and their Pottery: Moulsham Street, Chelmsford*, 40–1, Chelmsford Archaeological Trust Report 5, CBA Research Report 54.

Goodier, A. 1984. 'The formation of boundaries in Anglo-Saxon England: a statistical study', *Medieval Arch* **28**, 1–21.

Greep, S. 1993. 'Bone combs', in D. E. Farwell and T. I. Molleson (eds), *Excavations at Poundbury 1966–80, vol. 2, the cemeteries,* 105–10, Dorset Natural History and Archaeology Society Monograph Series **11**.

Green, B., Rogerson, A. and White, S. G. 1987. *The Anglo-Saxon Cemetery at Morning Thorpe, Norfolk. 2 vols* East Anglian Archaeology Report 36 Gressenhall: Norfolk Archaeological Unit.

Green, M. 2004 (first published in 1986). *The Gods of the Celts*, Stroud: Sutton.

Grigson, C. 1982. 'Sex and age determination of some bones and teeth of domestic cattle: a review of the literature', in B. Wilson, C. Grigson and S. Payne (eds), *Ageing and Sexing Animal Bones from Archaeological Sites*, 7–24, BAR British Series, 109, Oxford: British Archaeological Reports.

Guido, M. 1999. *The glass beads of Anglo-Saxon England c. AD 400–700* Woodbridge: Boydell Press for Society of Antiquaries.

Hall, D. 2000. 'The Ceramic Sequence' in R. Mortimer 'Village Development and Ceramic Sequence: The Middle to Late Saxon Village at Lordship Lane, Cottenham, Cambridgeshire', *Proc. of the Cambridge Antiquarian Soc.,* **LXXXIX**, 21–32.

Hamerow, H. 1993. *Excavations at Mucking 2: the Anglo-Saxon settlement*, English Heritage Archaeological Report 21.

Harcourt, R. A. 1974. 'The dog in prehistoric and early historic Britain', *Jnl. of Arch. Science* **1**, 151–75.

Harden, D. and Green, C. 1978. 'A late Roman grave-group from Minories, Aldgate', in J. Bird, H. Chapman and J. Clark *Collectanea Londiniensia: studies in London archaeology and history presented to Ralph Merrifield*, 163–75, London: London and Middlesex Archaeological Society.

Härke, H. 1989. 'early Anglo-Saxon weapon burials: frequencies, distributions and weapon combinations', in S. C. Hawkes (ed.), *Weapons and warfare in Anglo-Saxon England*, Oxford University

Committee for Archaeology Monograph 21, 49–61, Oxford, Oxford University Committee for Archaeology.

Harris, S. 1977. 'Spinal Arthritis (Spondylosis Deformans) in the Red Fox, *Vulpes vulpes*, with some methodology of relevance to zooarchaeology' *Jnl. of Arch. Science* **4**, 183–95.

Hawkes, C. and Fell, C. 1945. 'The early Iron Age settlement at Fengate, Peterborough', *Archaeol. Jnl.* **100**, 188–223.

Hawkes, S. C. and Dunning, G. C. 1962. 'Soldiers and settlers in Britain, fourth to fifth century', *Medieval Arch* **5**, 1–70.

Hills, C. M. 1977. *The Anglo-Saxon Cemetery at Spong Hill, North Elmham, Part I*, East Anglian Archaeology Report, 6, Gressenhall: Norfolk Archaeological Unit.

Hills, C. M. and Penn, K. 1981. *The Anglo-Saxon Cemetery at Spong Hill, North Elmham, Part II*, East Anglian Archaeology Report, 11, Gressenhall: Norfolk Archaeological Unit.

Hills, C. 2001. 'From Isidore to isotopes: ivory rings in early medieval graves', in H. Hamerow and A. MacGregor (eds), *Image and Power in the Archaeology of Early Medieval Britain: essays in honour of Rosemary Cramp*, 131–46, Oxford: Oxbow Books.

Hinton, D. A. 1990. 'Hooked tags', in M. Biddle (ed.), *Object and Economy in Medieval Winchester* Winchester Studies, 7/2, Oxford: Oxford University Press.

Holden, J. L., Phakey, P. P. and Clement, J. G. 1995. 'Scanning electron microscope observations of heat-treated human bone', *Forensic Science International* **74**, 29–45.

Holgate, R. 1988. *Neolithic Settlement of the Thames Basin*, BAR British Series 194, Oxford: British Archaeological Reports.

Holst, M. 1993. *Comparing the Relationship of Biological Sexing and Evidence for Gender from Grave Goods in Anglo-Saxon Burials.* Unpublished BA Dissertation, Department of Archaeology, University of Leicester.

Howe, M. D. 1984. 'Three Anglo-Saxon burials from Alwalton, Cambridgeshire', *Northamptonshire Arch.* **19**, 53–61.

Howe, M. D., Perrin, J. R. and Mackreth, D. F. 1980. *Roman Pottery from the Nene Valley: a guide.* Occasional Paper 2 Peterborough City Museum and Art Gallery, Peterborough.

Howe, M. D. unpublished report. *Anglo-Saxon cemeteries from Woodston*, Peterborough Museum Archive.

Huggett, J. 1996. 'Social Analysis of early Anglo-Saxon Inhumation Burials: archaeological methodologies', *Jnl. of European Arch.* **4**, 337–65.

Huggett, J. and Richards, J. 1990. 'Anglo-Saxon burial: the computer at work', in E. Southworth (ed.), *Anglo-Saxon Cemeteries. A reappraisal*, 65–86, Stroud: Alan Sutton.

Jackson, D. A. and Ambrose, T. 1978. 'Excavations at Wakerley, Northants, 1972–75', *Britannia* **9**, 115–242.

Jackson, R. 1997. 'An ancient British medical kit from Stanway, Essex', *The Lancet* **350**, 1471–3.

Jessup, R. F. 1950. *Anglo-Saxon Jewellery*. London: Faber.

Kinsley, A. G. 1989. *The Anglo-Saxon cemetery at Millgate, Newark-on-Trent, Nottinghamshire.* Nottingham: Nottingham Archaeological Monographs 2.

Last, J. and McDonald, T. 1999. *Minerva Business Park, Alwalton, Cambridgeshire. Area B interim excavation report*, Hertfordshire Archaeological Trust Unpublished Report 599.

Leeds, E. T. 1945. 'The distribution of the Angles and Saxons archaeologically considered' *Archaeologia* **91**, 1–106.

Leeds, E. T. and Atkinson, R. J. C. 1944. 'The Anglo-Saxon cemetery at Nassington, Northants', *Antiquaries Jnl.* **24**, 100–28.

Leeds, E. T. and Pocock, M. 1971. 'A survey of the Anglo-Saxon cruciform brooches of florid type', *Medieval Arch.* **15**, 13–36.

Lethbridge, T. C. 1931. 'Recent excavations in Anglo-Saxon cemeteries in Cambridgeshire and Suffolk', *Proc. Cambridge Antiquarian Soc.* (Quarto Publication) 3.

Levine, M. A. 1982. 'The use of crown height measurements and eruption-wear sequences to age horse teeth', in B. Wilson, C. Grigson, and S. Payne (eds), *Ageing and Sexing Animal Bones from Archaeological Sites*, 223–50, BAR British Series, 109, Oxford: British Archaeological Reports.

Lucy, S. 1995. *The Anglo-Saxon cremations of East Yorkshire*, unpublished dissertation, University of Cambridge.

Lucy, S. 1997. 'Housewives, warriors and slaves? Sex and gender in Anglo-Saxon burials', in J. Moore and E. Scott (eds), *Invisible People and Processes: writing gender and childhood into European archaeology*, 150–68, Leicester: Leicester University Press.

Lucy, S. 1998. *The early Anglo-Saxon Cemeteries of East Yorkshire. An analysis and reinterpretation*. British Archaeological Reports, British Series, 272, Oxford: BAR.

Lucy, S. 2000. *The Anglo-Saxon Way of Death*, Stroud: Sutton Publishing.

Lyne, M. 2003 'The Roman Pottery', in D. Griffiths, A. Reynolds and S. Semple (eds) *Boundaries in Early Medieval Britain*, 154–6, *ASSAH*, **12**.

McDonald, T. and Vaughan, T. 1999. *Archaeological Excavations at Minerva Business Park, Alwalton, Peterborough, Cambridgeshire. Area A interim excavation report*, Hertfordshire Archaeological Trust Unpublished Report 531.

MacGregor, A. and Bolick, E. 1993. *A Summary Catalogue of the Anglo-Saxon collections in the Ashmolean Museum*. BAR British Series, 230, Oxford: British Archaeological Reports.

McKinley, J. I. 1993a. 'Bone fragment size and weights of bone from modern British cremations and the implications for the interpretation of archaeological cremations', *International Journal of Osteoarchaeology* 3, 283–7.

McKinley, J. I. 1993b. 'Cremated Bone', in J. Timby (ed.) 'Sancton I Anglo-Saxon Cemetery excavations carried out between 1976 and 1980'. *Archaeological Journal* **150**, 243–365.

McKinley, J. 1994a. *The Anglo-Saxon Cemetery at Spong Hill, North Elmham. Part VIII: The Cremations*, East Anglian Archaeology, 69, Dereham: Norfolk Museums Service, Field Archaeology Division.

McKinley, J. I. 1994b. 'Bone fragment size in British cremation burials and its implications for pyre technology and ritual', *Jnl. Archaeological Science* **21(3)**, 339–42.

McKinley, J. I. and Bond, J. 1993 'Summary discussion' in J. Timby (ed.), 'Sancton 1 Anglo-Saxon cemetery. Excavatons carried out between 1976 and 1980' *Archaeological Jnl* **150**, 308–9.

McKinley, J. 1997a. 'Bronze Age barrows and funerary rites and rituals of cremation', *Proc. of the Prehistoric Soc.* **63**, 129–45.

McKinley, J. I. 1997b. 'Pyre Technology and Ritual', in A. Fitzpatrick (ed.) *Archaeological Excavations on the Route of A27 Westhampnett Bypass, West Sussex. Volume 2 The Iron Age, Romano-British and Anglo-Saxon Cemeteries*, 65–6. Salisbury: Wessex Archaeology Report 12.

Mack, I. and McDonnell, G. 1999. 'Report on the Analysis of Slags and Stock material from West Heslerton, North Yorkshire', in C. Haughton and D. Powlesland (eds) *West Heslerton: The Anglian Settlement*. Archaeological monograph series (Landscape Research Centre), 1, Yedingham : Landscape Research Centre.

Mackreth, D. F. 1996. *Orton Hall Farm: A Roman and early Anglo-Saxon farmstead* East Anglian Archaeology, 76, Manchester [England]: Nene Valley Archaeological Trust.

Malim, T. and Hines, J. 1998. *The Anglo-Saxon Cemetery at Edix Hill (Barrington A), Cambridgeshire* Council for British Archaeology Report, 112, York: CBA.

Manning, W. H. 1985. *Catalogue of the Romano-British iron tools, fittings and weapons in the British Museum*, London: British Museum Publication.

Marzinzik, S. 2003. *early Anglo-Saxon Belt Buckles, late 5th to early 8th century AD: their classification and context*, BAR British Series 357, Oxford: British Archaeological Reports.

Matolcsi, J. 1970. 'Historische Erforschung der Körpergröße des Rindes auf Grund von ungarischem Knochenmaterial', *Zeitschrift f. Tierzüchtg. u. Züchtungsbiologie*, Hamburg **87**, 89–137.

Meaney, A. L. 1981. *Anglo-Saxon Amulets and Curing Stones*, BAR British Series 96, Oxford: British Archaeological Reports.

Meaney, A. 1998. 'Girdle groups: reconstruction and comparative study', in T. Malim and J. Hines (eds), *The Anglo-Saxon Cemetery at Edix Hill (Barrington A), Cambridgeshire*, 268–275, Council for British Archaeology Report 112, York: CBA.

Metcalf, P. and Huntingdon, R. 1991. *Celebrations of Death*, Cambridge: Cambridge University Press.

Morgan, J. P., Ljunggren, G. and Read, R. 1967. Spondylosis deformans (vertebral osteophytosis) in the Dog, *Jnl. of Small Animal Practice* **8**, 57–66.

Mortimer, C. 1990. *Some aspects of early medieval copper-alloy technology, as illustrated by a study of the Anglian cruciform brooch*, unpublished DPhil thesis, Oxford University.

Mortimer, C. 1998. 'Punchmarks on the copper-alloy artefacts', in T. Malim and J. Hines (eds) *The Anglo-Saxon Cemetery at Edix Hill (Barrington A), Cambridgeshire,* Council for British Archaeology Report 112, 258–261, York: CBA.

Murray, J. 1999. *Minerva Business Park, Alwalton, Cambridgeshire: an archaeological evaluation (Area B)*, Hertfordshire Archaeological Trust Unpublished Report 510.

Myres, J. N. L. 1969. *Anglo-Saxon pottery and the settlement of England*, Oxford: Clarendon Press.

Myres, J. N. L., 1974. 'The Anglo-Saxon Pottery' in S. S. Frere and J. K. St. Joseph 'The Roman Fortress at Longthorpe'. *Britannia*, Vol. **5**, 113 – 121

Myres, J. N. L. 1977. *A Corpus of Pagan Anglo-Saxon pottery 2 vols* Oxford: Clarendon Press.

Myres, J. N. L and Green, B. 1973. *The Anglo-Saxon cemeteries of Caistor-by-Norwich and Markshall, Norfolk*. Report of the Research Committee of the Society of Antiquaries, 30, London: Thames and Hudson.

Nielsen, R. 1992. 'Early Anglo-Saxon burials in Croydon', *London Arch* **7**, 6–7.

O'Brien, L. 2006. *An Iron Age Settlement, Roman Shrine and early Anglo-Saxon cemetery at St Edmunds Church and Vicarage, St Edmunds Road, Temple Hill, Dartford, Kent*. Archaeological Solutions Unpublished Report 2141.

Pader, E. J. 1982. *Symbolism, social relations and the interpretation of mortuary remains*, BAR International Series, 130, Oxford: British Archaeological Reports.

Parfitt, K. 1991. 'Deal', *Current Arch.* **11**(5) (XI, 5), 215–20.

Patrick, P., French, C. and Osborne, C. forthcoming *Rescue excavation of a pagan Saxon cemetery at Gunthorpe, Peterborough.*

Pearson, T. 1985. 'Saxon and Medieval Pottery: An outline of the evidence from Raunds, Furnells' in G. Foard and T. Pearson 'The Raunds Area Project: First Interim Report'. *Northamptonshire Archaeology*, **20**, 9–21.

Pearson, T. 1988/9. 'The Anglo-Saxon Pottery' in B. Adams and D. Jackson 'The Anglo-Saxon cemetery at Wakerley, Northamptonshire'. *Northamptonshire Archaeology*, **22**, 160 – 168.

Perrin, J. R. 1988 'Roman Pottery from Two Pits at Werrington, Cambridgeshire', in D. F. Mackreth (ed.), 'Excavation of an Iron-Age and Roman Enclosure at Werrington, Cambridgeshire', *Britannia* **19**, 120–141.

Perrin, J. R. 1996. 'The Roman Pottery', in Mackreth, D. F. (ed.), *Orton Hall Farm: a Roman and early Anglo-Saxon farmstead*, East Anglian Archaeology, 76, 114–204, Manchester: Nene Valley Archaeological Trust.

Perrin, J. R. 1999. 'Roman Pottery from Excavations at and near to the Roman Small Town of Durobrivae, Water Newton, Cambridgeshire, 1956–58' *Jnl. of Roman Pottery Stud.* **8**.

Pilet, C. 1980. *La nécropole de Frénouville*, BAR International Series, 83, Oxford: British Archaeological Reports.

Powlesland, D., Houghton, C. and Hanson, J. H. 1986. 'Excavations at Heslerton, North Yorkshire 1978–82', *Archaeol. Jnl.* **143**, 53–173.

Prosser, L. 1999. *Minerva Business Park, Alwalton, Cambridgeshire. An archaeological desk based assessment*, Hertfordshire Archaeological Trust Unpublished Report 587.

Pryor, F. M. M. 1984. *Excavation at Fengate, Peterborough, England: the Fourth Report*, Northamptonshire Archaeological Society Monograph 2; Royal Ontario Museum Archaeological Monograph 7.

Ravn, M. 2003. *Death, Ritual and Germanic social structure (c. AD 200–600)*, BAR International series, 1164, Oxford: British Archaeological Reports.

Reynolds, A. 1999. *Later Anglo-Saxon England. Life and landscape*, Stroud: Tempus.

Richards, J. 1984. 'Funerary symbolism in Anglo-Saxon England: further social dimensions of mortuary practices', *Scottish Arch Rev.* **3**, 42–55.

Richards, J. 1987. *The Significance of Form and Decoration of Anglo-Saxon Cremation Urns*, BAR British Series, 166, Oxford: British Archaeological Reports.

Rigby, V. 1986. 'The Stratified Groups of Iron Age and Roman pottery', in I. M. Stead and V. Rigby (eds), *Baldock: The excavation of a Roman and Pre-Roman settlement, 1968–72*, 257–380, Britannia Monograph Series, 7, London: Society for the Promotion of Roman Studies.

Roberts, J. 1999. *Multi-period Features on Land at Minerva Business Park, Alwalton*, Cambridgeshire Archaeology Unpublished Report 155.

Simpson, J. 1979. 'The King's whetstone', *Antiquity* 53/208, 96–101.

Smith, R. A. 1926. 'Anglo-Saxon remains', in W. Page and G. Proby (eds) *Victoria History of the County of Huntingdonshire*, 1, 271–9, London: St Catherine's Press.

Soil Survey of England and Wales 1983 *Legend for the 1:250,000 Soil Map of England and Wales. A brief explanation of the constituent soil associations*, 7–8, Harpenden: SSEW.

Stace, C. A. 1997. *New Flora of the British Isles*. Second edition Cambridge: Cambridge University Press.

Stirland, A. J. 1993. 'Asymmetry and activity-related change in the male humerus', *International Journal of Osteoarchaeology* 3(2), 105–113.

Stoodley, N. 1997. *The spindle and the spear: a critical enquiry into the construction and meaning of gender in the early Anglo-Saxon inhumation burial rite*. Unpublished PhD thesis, University of Reading.

Stoodley, N. 1999a. *The Spindle and the Spear*, BAR British Series 288, Oxford, British Archaeological Reports.

Stoodley, N. 1999b. 'Burial rites, gender and the creation of kingdoms: the evidence from seventh-century Wessex', *ASSAH* **10**, 99–107.

Stoodley, N. 2000. 'From the cradle to the grave: age organisation and the early Anglo-Saxon burial rite', *World Arch*, **31**(3), 456–472.

Sudds, B. 2005. 'The Saxon Pottery' in J. Murray with T. McDonald (eds),'An Anglo-Saxon settlement at Gamlingay, Cambridgeshire', *ASSAH*, **13**, 213–222.

Swanton, M. J. 1974. *A corpus of Pagan Anglo-Saxon Spear-Types*, BAR, 7, Oxford: British Archaeological Reports.

Taylor, A. 2000. 'Anglo-Saxon Cemeteries' in T. Kirby and S. Oosthuizen (eds), *An Atlas of Cambridgeshire and Huntingdonshire History*, section 25, Cambridge: Anglia Polytechnic University.

Teichert, M. 1975. 'Osteometrische Untersuchungen zur Berechnung der Widerristhöhe bei Schafen'. In A. T. Clason (ed.) *Archaeozoological Studies*, 51–69, Amsterdam and Oxford: North-Holland/New York: Elsevier.

Teichert, M. 1990. *Withers Height Calculations for Pigs. Remarks and experience*, Handout distributed at the 6th ICAZ Conference, Washington D.C. May 1990

Thompson, I. 1982. *Grog-Tempered 'Belgic' Pottery of South-Eastern England*, BAR British Series, 108, Oxford: British Archaeological Reports.

Timby, J. R. 1993. 'Sancton I Anglo-Saxon cemetery. Excavations carried out between 1976 and 1980', *Archaeol. Jnl.* **150**, 243–365.

Timby, J. R. 1996. *The Anglo-Saxon cemetery at Empingham II, Rutland*, Oxbow Monograph, 70, Oxford: Oxbow.

Tomber, R. and Dore, J. 1998. *The National Roman Fabric Reference Collection: A handbook*, MoLAS Monograph, 2, London: Museum of London Archaeology Service.

Trotter, M. 1970. 'Estimation of stature from intact limb bones', in T. D. Stewart (ed.), *Personal Identification in Mass Disasters*, Washington: Smithsonian Institution.

Tyers, P. 1996. *Roman Pottery in Britain* London: Batsford.

Van Gennep, A. 1960 (1908). *The Rites of Passage*. Chicago: University of Chicago Press.

Vince, A., 2000. 'The Petrology of the Anglo-Saxon Pottery' in J. Albone and K. Leahy 'The Anglo-Saxon Cemetery at Tallington, Lincolnshire'. *ASSAH*, **11**, 168.

Wahl, J. 1988. *Süderbrarup: a Roman and Migration period cemetery in Angeln. II: Anthropological research*, Offa-Bücher, 64, Neumünster: Wachholtz.

Waldron, H. A. 1991. 'Variations in the prevalence of spondylolysis in early British populations', *Jnl. of the Royal Soc. of Medicine* **84**, 547–49.

Waldron, T. 1998. 'A note on the estimation of height from long-bone measurements', *International Jnl. of Osteology* **8**, 75–7.

Walker, J. 1978. 'Appendix: Anglo-Saxon Traded Pottery: Analysis of sherds from Orton Hall Farm, Peterborough, and other sites' in M. Todd (ed.), *Studies in the Romano-British villa*, 224–228, Leicester University Press.

Walker, T. J. 1899 'Notes on two Anglo-Saxon burial places at Peterborough', *Jnl of the British Arch Assoc*. **5**, 343–49.

Webster, J. 1975. 'Objects of bone and antler', in B. W. Cunliffe, *Excavations at Portchester Castle Vol. I*, Roman Society of Antiquaries Research Reports, 32, London: Thames and Hudson.

Webster, L. and Cherry, J. 1975. 'Medieval Britain in 1974', *Medieval Arch* **19**, 220–59.

Webster, P. 1996. *Roman Samian Pottery in Britain*. Council for British Archaeology Practical Handbooks in Archaeology 13, York: Council for British Archaeology

Wells, C. 1996. 'The human burials', in V. Evison and P. Hill (eds), *Two Anglo-Saxon Cemeteries at Beckford, Hereford and Worcester*, Council for British Archaeology Research Report, 103, 41–61, York: CBA.

West, S. 1985. *West Stow, the Anglo-Saxon village*. East Anglian Archaeology, 24, Ipswich: Suffolk County Planning Dept.

White, R. 1988. *Roman and Celtic Objects from Anglo-Saxon Graves*. BAR British Series, 191, Oxford: British Archaeological Reports.

White, R. 1990. 'Scrap or substitute: Roman material in Anglo-Saxon graves', in E. Southworth (ed.) *Anglo-Saxon Cemeteries: A reappraisal*, 125–52, Stroud: Alan Sutton.

Williams, D., and Vince, A. 1997. 'The characterization and interpretation of early to middle Saxon granitic tempered pottery in England' in *Medieval Arch.*, **XLI**, 214 – 220.

Williams, H. M. 1998. 'Monuments and the past in early Anglo-Saxon England', in R. Bradley and H. Williams (eds), *The Past in the Past: the reuse of ancient monuments*, *World Arch.* **30**(1), 90–108.

Williams, H. 2002. 'Remains of Pagan Saxondum? – The study of Anglo-Saxon cremation rites', in S. Lucy and A. Reynolds (eds), *Burial in early medieval England and Wales*, 47–71, Leeds: Society of Medieval Archaeology Monograph 17.

Williams, P. W., 1983. 'IV. The Pottery' in *An Anglo-Saxon Cemetery at Thurmaston, Leicestershire*. Leicestershire Museums, Art Galleries and Records Service: Archaeological Reports Series, No. 8, 9–15.

Williams, R. J. 1993. *Pennyland and Hartigans: two Iron Age and Saxon sites in Milton Keynes*. Buckinghamshire Archaeological Society Monograph, 4, Aylesbury: Buckinghamshire Archaeological Society.

Wilson, M. G. 1984. 'The other pottery', in S. Frere (ed.) *Verulamium Excavations Vol. III*, Oxford University Committee for Archaeology Monograph, 1, 200–66, Oxford: Oxford University Committee for Archaeology.

Workshop of European Anthropologists, 1980. 'Recommendations of age and sex diagnosis of skeleton', *Jnl. of Human Evolution* **9**, 517–49.

Appendix 1: Catalogue of Inhumations

Cut No.	Fig	Grave Dimensions (L × W × D)	Orientation	Shape 1	Sex2	Age (years)	Skeleton Position 3	Pathology	Notes	Grave goods (SF)
1032	12	1.9 × 0.69 × 0.3 m	235°	Sr	M	25–35	Ex A D 2 7 R. 85% remaining	New bone on internal surface of two left ribs, possibly due to lung infection	Partial skeleton with much post mortem damage. Lacking mandible	119
1250	12	1.52 × 0.6 × 0.1 m	250°	So	M	35–45	Cr B 8. Little of the left arm remained. Legs bent at the knee. 60% remaining	Schmorl's nodes in thoracic vertebra.	Very fragmentary skeleton with much post mortem damage	17, 18
1263	13, 14, 15 & 16	2 × 0.9 × 0.2 m	217°	So	?F	45+	Ex E 1 2. Left foot pointing inwards.	—	Bone in poor condition Cranium crushed from above (by the stone lining of the grave). No ribs or vertebrae and little survived of the pelvis and hands.	23, 55, 83, 84, 85, 86, 87, 88, 89, 90, 91, 92, 93, 94, 105a, 105b,
1336	17, 18	1.56 × 0.67 × 0.18 m	141°	Sr	F	45+	Ex E 1 5 R. Fragmentary skull rolled to the right. Feet turned inwards. 95% remaining.	—	Substantial female inhumation – height 1.67 m (right radius)	48, 137, 138, 139
1339	30	1.8 × 0.6 × 0.2 m	240°	Sr	M	15–25	–	—	Badly disturbed and robbed grave – almost completely disarticulated. Substantial male inhumation – height 1.79 m (right humerus)	None
1342	30	0.95 × 0.36 × 0.2 m	225°	Ov	F	Adult	Ex A. Missing the skull and most of the arms and lower legs. 30% remaining	—	Much truncated supine burial. Very fragmentary.	None
1345	30	1.65 × 0.7 × 0.13 m	330°	So	F	Adult	Ex D 3. Skull missing 80% remaining	—	Incomplete skeleton	None
1351	19	1.85 × 0.75 × 0.18 m	222°	So	F	45+	Ex A 4 8 R. Left arm flexed over lower vertebrae, right arm flexed over the lower pelvis. 100% remaining	Dental disease	Height 1.63 m (right humerus)	50, 133, 134, 135, 136
1355	19	1.7 × 0.5 × 0.13 m	218°	So	F	45+	Ex A 7 R. 50% remaining	—	Skeleton in poor condition with most of the smaller bones and extremities missing. Legs and	51, 123, 124, 125

Cut No.	Fig	Grave				Skeleton				Grave goods (SF)
		Dimensions (L × W × D)	Orientation	Shape 1	Sex2	Age (years)	Position 3	Pathology	Notes	
1358	20–21	1.85 × 0.8 × 0.18 m	340°	Int	F	25–35	Ex E 9 R. 100% remaining	Schmorl's nodes in thoracic and lumbar regions.	extended by sides. Much post mortem damage. Much post mortem damage. Substantial female inhumation	52, 75, 76, 77, 78, 79, 80, 81, 82
1361	30	1.58 × 0.56 × 0.2 m	220°	So	M	15–25	Ex A 2 7 R. 70% remaining	—	Partial and damaged skeleton. Epiphysis of upper humerus not fused.	None
1364	22, 23 & 24	1.5 × 0.8 × 0.3 m	230°	Int	F	Adult	Ex A 8. Skull and much of upper body missing. 70% remaining	—	Incomplete skeleton. Intrusive juvenile skull (aged 4–6 years) and foetal first rib, clavicle and vertebral fragments).	14, 53, 54 , 95, 97, 98, 99, 100, 101, 102/103, 106, 107, 109, 110, 110, 112, 113/108.
1366	25	1.75 × 0.5 × 0.3 m	228°	Sr	M	45+	Ex A 1 5 R 100% remaining	Dental disease	Height – 1.75 m (left femur and tibia).	57, 126
1374	25	1.7 × 0.7 × 0.1	145°	So	M	45+	Ex E 2. Much of the left hand side of the body missing. Cranium crushed. Left arm probably flexed over pelvis and right arm fully extended at side. Right leg slightly flexed 75% remaining	Dental disease	Substantial male inhumation but with much post mortem damage, and lacking most of left arm and hand. Height – 1.70 m (right tibia).	56, 127
1377	26	No grave cut identified	SE–NW	–	?F	Adult	Almost completely disarticulated. 30% remaining	—	Very incomplete and disturbed. However, green staining on right clavicle suggests that a copper alloy ornament (possibly a brooch) was once part of the funerary outfit.	60, 62
1379	26	1.4 × 0.65 × 0.12 m	145°	Ov	F	35–45	?Cr C 5 7. Some truncation to skull 80% remaining	Schmorl's node lumbar region. Dental disease.	Height – 1.62 m (right tibia).	58
1384	30	1.7 × 0.5 × 0.16 m	344°	So	F	15–25	Ex A 2 7 L. 90% remaining	Schmorl's nodes T12 and L1.	Substantial female inhumation. Height 1.53 m (right radius).	None
1387.1 (1389)	30	1.95 × 0.85 × 0.32 m	269°	Sr	F	45+	Ex B 2 7 L 60% remaining	Osteoarthritis on left knee and shoulder. Schmorl's nodes lumbar and thoracic areas.	Much damaged	None
1387.2	30	1.95 × 0.85	270°	Sr	M	25–35	Ex E 9 R	Well-healed fracture in the upper	Height – 1.67 m (left humerus).	None

Cut No.	Fig	Grave Dimensions (L × W × D)	Orientation	Shape 1	Sex 2	Age (years)	Skeleton Position 3	Pathology	Notes	Grave goods (SF)
(1393)		× 0.32 m					95% remaining	quarter of the right tibia.	Much post mortem damage.	
1390	30	1.78 × 0.58 × 0.15 m	324°	So	M	25–35	Ex E 2 4 L 80% remaining	*Os acromiale* on left scapula. Schmorl's nodes in thoracic area.	Substantial male. Height – 1.69 m (left femur).	None
1394	27	2 × 0.7 × 0.06 m	212°	So	M	Adult	Ex C 1 5. Cranium missing 70% remaining	Osteophytes in thoracic and lumbar regions. Schmorl's nodes in thoracic region. Small oval lesion on outer surface of left tibia, probably the result of a varicose ulcer. Right distal tibia fuesd to talus and navicular, possibly the result of infection or trauma.	Substantial male inhumation. Height – 1.74 m (left femur).	59, 128, 129, 130, 131, 132
1399	30	2 × 0.7 × 0.35 m	63°	So	M	25–35	Ex E 5. Positioned onto the left hand side, with pelvis twisted round about 30° so legs extended. Left forearm pointed upwards, humerus under the body. 90% remaining	Schmorl's nodes in lumbar region.	This male is orientated in completely the opposite direction to the majority of others, with head pointing to the north-east. Substantial male inhumation. Height – 1.75 m (left femur and tibia)	None
1410	30	1.8 × 0.6 × 0.09 m	220°	So	F	15–25	?Ex B 2 7 L 60% remaining	Spondylolysis of L5.	Fragmentary skeleton	None
Pit 1413	30	Found in a pit at 1.1 m depth	353°	n/a	F	45+	Ex F E 9 D 80% remaining	Dental disease. Osteoarthritis of left acromio-clavicular joint	Substantial inhumation but very damaged. Height – 1.50 m (left humerus).	None
1425	30	1.46 × 0.47 × 0.15 m	262°	Sr	F	15–25	Ex B 2 7. Fragmentary cranium 60% remaining	–	Substantial inhumation but poorly preserved. Height – 1.67 m (both tibiae).	None
1428	28	1.9 × 0.4 × 0.6 m	134°	Sr	M	45+	Ex A 1 8 R 80% remaining	Dental disease. Spondylolysis of L4.	Substantial male inhumation. Height – 1.71 m (left femur).	61, 96, 118, 122
1432	30	0.9 × 0.4 × 0.06 m	SW-NE	So	Int	Child judging by the grave cut	Very little of skeleton preserved (15%). Probably a supine extended inhumation.		–	None
1435	30	1.32 × 0.34 × 0.18 m	–	So	F	Adult	Badly disturbed and robbed grave – disarticulated. 5% remaining		Very fragmentary skeleton	None
1440	28	1.5 × 0.5 × 0.1 m	223°	So	M	Adult	Ex A. Missing skull, neck, shoulders and much of arms. Right arm probably straight at the side, while the left arm would appear to be bent at		Truncated grave, directly overlying another grave cut on a slightly different alignment. Height – 1.80 m (right tibia).	178

	Grave						Skeleton			
Cut No.	Fig	Dimensions (L × W × D)	Orientation	Shape 1	Sex2	Age (years)	Position 3	Pathology	Notes	Grave goods (SF)
1451	30	1.7 × 0.75 × 0.3 m	143°	So	F	45+	Ex E 9 D 85% remaining. [...] the elbow and placed across the pelvis. 70% remaining	Dental disease. Osteoarthritis of the spine. Rotator cuff disease of right shoulder. Osteophytes and Schmorl's nodes in thoracic region. Spondylolysis of L5.	Substantial female inhumation. Height – 1.53 m (left femur).	None
1460	29	2.1 × 0.7 × 0.2 m	230°	So	M	25–35	Ex E 3 L 80% remaining	–	Robust and substantial male inhumation. Height – 1.85 m (left radius).	68, 69, 70, 71, 72
1463	29	1.65 × 0.55 × 0.55 m	218°	Sr	F	45+	Ex E 2 4 L 80% remaining	Dental disease. Spondylolysis L5.	Partial skeleton.	Shallow bowl
1466	29	1.7 × 0.5 × 0.2 m	330°	Sr	F	25–35	Ex E 2 7 L 80% remaining	Impacted upper third molar.	Lacking most of the vertebral column. Height – 1.54 m (both tibiae).	167

1 Shapes: Sr = sub-rectangular; Ov = oval; So = sub-oval; Int = indeterminate

2 Sex: M = male; F = female; Int = indeterminate

3 BODY POSITION: Ex = Extended; Cr = Crouched. LEGS: A = Extended, parallel; B = Flexed to the right; C = Flexed to the left; D = Crossed at ankles; E = Feet meet; F = Extended to right; G = Extended to left. ARMS: 1 = Left extended; 2 = Right extended; 3 = Both extended parallel; 4 = Left flexed over chest; 5 = Right flexed over chest; 6 = Both flexed over chest; 7 = Left flexed to pelvis; 8 = Right flexed to pelvis; 9 = Both flexed to pelvis. HEAD: L = Tilted to left; U = Tilted up; D = Tilted down; R = Tilted to right.

Appendix 2: Catalogue of Grave Goods associated with Inhumations

Grave No.	SF No.	Fig. No	Description of Grave Good	Position in Grave
1032	119	12.1 42	Very small shallow splay-sided bowl with a slightly everted rim and rounded base. Dark grey to black fabric with predominantly oxidised mid buff to mid orange-buff surfaces. Burnished.	To right of head
1250	17	12.2	Iron Knife with slightly curved back. Total length 275 mm. Blade length 173 mm	Located at an angle across the right hip
	18	12.1	Terracotta glass cylinder bead with green and yellow spirals (Guido 8xixa). Length 19.5 mm; diameter 8.5 mm.	Centre of the waist
1263	23 & 55	14.4-5	Pair of cast cruciform copper-alloy wrist-clasps (SFs 23 & 55). The lateral arms of the cross terminate in hammerheads. Hines Form B12. Length 42 mm, width (joined) 49 mm.	23 by right waist / 55 by left waist
	83	13.3	Copper-alloy cruciform brooch (SF 83) with the head and side-knobs replaced by small knobbed subrectangular plates with rudimentary masks. The side lappets are well-formed bird heads. The animal-head lower foot has two double-grooved bands above the furrowed forehead, eye bosses, and crescentic terminal. The nostrils have become upturned bird-head finials. Only traces of the iron spring mechanism remain. Lines of triangular punchmarks emphasise the features of head and foot. Length 142 mm.	On upper chest
	84 & 85	13.1–2	Pair of identical copper-alloy small-long brooches, one with a small part of the iron spring and pin remaining. The head is square and perforated with the upper corners rebated and basal notches flanking the bow. This is marked by notched and faceted and grooved transverse mouldings. The foot, below further mouldings, is triangular with in curving sides and rounded base. The edges of both head and foot are decorated with keyhole-shaped punch marks with a raised dot in the centre of the circular element. On the base and one side of the foot of SF 84 these are applied to close to the edge and blundered. Length 67 mm	84 on right shoulder / 85 on left shoulder
	86	14.14	Iron knife with rectangular section tang. Both back and edge are straight. The edge rises to the point, the very end of which is missing. Total length 129 mm, length of blade 83 mm. Back Type B, length Group 1	By left hip
	87	14.8	Copper-alloy open triangular fitting, with rivets in each corner. That at the top has a large head. Each has a square washer on the opposite end. Height 23 mm, length 35 mm. Also a small roughly triangular scrap of sheet copper-alloy with traces of an iron rivet in the centre. This fits fairly well inside the open centre of the main fitting. Maximum dimensions 8 by 10 mm.	Right of waist
	88	14.12	Fragment of an iron tongue-shaped strap-end back-plate. Length 43 mm, maximum width 19.5 mm.	Right of waist
	89	14.11	Small fragment from an iron ring or suspension loop, and three iron shaft fragments. Probably from a latch-lifter.	Right of waist
	90	14.6	Copper-alloy earring made of tapering wire. Length 14 mm, diameter 12 mm.	By left hip
	91	14.7	Copper-alloy triangular fitting (SF 91), with rivet in one corner and a rivet hole in the other two. Height 14.5 mm, length 25.5 mm.	Centre of waist
	92	14.13	Iron buckle, in fragments, with a copper-alloy strap-plate. The buckle is probably D-shaped, and has traces of mineral-replaced textile on the surfaces. The strap-plate is of folded one-piece form with a cut-out for the iron tongue. There are two iron rivets at the outer end for attaching the strap. Length (with tongue extended) 32.5 mm, width 22 mm.	Left of waist
	93/94	15–16	Twenty amber beads, total weight 27 g, and 113 glass beads. Fig.15 Nos 1–2) lozenge (as G1336), the largest 11.5 mm long, 6 mm wide, 4.5 mm thick; Fig.15 Nos 3–13) with (sub)rectangular base, one incomplete, the most regular measures 13.5 mm long, 15 by 17 mm maximum section; Fig.16 Nos 14–19) discs, largest is 24 mm diameter, 8 mm thick; Fig.16 No. 20) amber bead, not illustrated. Fig.16 Nos 21–74) annular/globular blue glass, various sizes (Guido 6i); Fig.16 Nos 75–87); annular/globular/short segmented cylinder green glass, various sizes (Guido 5i); Fig.16 Nos 88–124) annular/globular dark crimson glass, various sizes (Guido 7); Fig.16 Nos 125–6) globular terracotta glass, 3.5 mm long, 6.5 mm diameter (Guido 8i); Fig.16 Nos 127–8) globular yellow glass with green crossed waves and dots (Guido 4vi), length 6 mm, diameter 9 mm; Fig.16 No. 129) globular green glass with red crossed waves and yellow dots (Guido 5vii), length 6.5 mm, diameter 8.5 mm; Fig.16 No. 130) globular white glass with blue crossed waves and red dots (Guido 3iiic), length 4.5 mm, diameter 8.5 mm; Fig.16 No. 131) globular white glass with green crossed waves and red dots (Guido 3iiid), length 4.5 mm, diameter 8 mm; Fig.16 Nos 132–3) colourless glass with red trail, partly internal, length 12 mm, diameter 6 mm.	On right shoulder/chest

Grave No.	SF No.	Fig. No	Description of Grave Good	Position in Grave
1336	105a	14.10	1) Fragments of a laminated ivory bag hoop (only the largest is illustrated). Internal diameter approximately 80 mm, D-shaped section, 13 mm thick. 2) Fragments of an iron band. Diameter approximately 18 mm, height 21.5 mm. Possibly used to attach it to the girdle, or possibly among the bag's contents.	By left hip
	105b	14.9	Fragmentary antler ring, internal diameter 34 mm, hoop 12 mm maximum width.	On waist
	48	17.3–8	Copper-alloy belt fittings. Silver-plated long belt stiffeners with copper-alloy rivets and marginal lines of half ring-and-dot punchmarks. Two of the stiffeners are very fragmentary and none is complete. Maximum length 77.5 mm, width 14.5 mm. Fig. 17.7 Silver-plated buckle-plate, tongue-ended at each end, one bent round and pierced to take an iron buckle loop and tongue (both partly missing), with iron rivets and irregularly-applied marginal lines of horseshoe-shaped punchmarks. The difference in craftsmanship points to this plate being a repair. Length 77 mm, plate width 13.5 mm. Fig. 17.8 Rectangular strap-end made from folded sheet metal, the ends fixed with two iron rivets, probably replacments for a single central larger rivet, now missing. Length 15 mm, width 18 mm.	
	137 & 138	17.1–2	Pair of copper-alloy wrist-clasps half ring-and-dot punchmark decoration. The same punch was used on the belt-stiffeners from the grave. The one for the right sleeve is repaired. Hines Form B17a. Length 29 mm, width (joined) 28 mm.	By right and left wrists
	139	18	String of amber and colourless glass beads. Total weight of amber 3 g. No. 17 is fragmentary and not illustrated	Around throat
1351	50	19.2	Large copper-alloy finger-ring with chevrons leading to a small square bezel marked with a 6-pointed star with inner circle design. Internal diameter 21.5 mm.	Right breast
	133	19.1	Fragmentary copper-alloy applied disc brooch. The gilt disc has a raised 5-pointed star motif within a border with small bosses and serrated edge. The spandrels have sharp sunk facets. A border of small bosses surrounds a central blue glass stud. The back-plate retains its iron pin. Diameter 43 mm.	Right breast
	134	19.3–5	Three glass beads. Fig.19.3 & 4 Bun-shaped blue glass, lengths 7.5 mm/5.5 mm, diameters 12.5/8.5 mm (Guido Group 6I); Fig.19.5 cuboid white glass with green frame on each face and red dots on the unpierced faces, length 11.5 mm, section 11.5–12 mm	Right breast
	135	19.6	Fig.19.6. Fragments of a circular section penannular brooch with coiled terminals (Fowler Type C, 1960).	Right shoulder
	136	19.7	Small iron knife with short tang. Total length 80 mm, blade length 62 mm. Back Type C, length group 1.	Right breast
1355	51	19.4	Globular blue glass bead, Guido Group 6i, diameter 13 mm, length 9.5 mm	By skull (on neck)
	123	19.3	Fragmentary copper-alloy pin with loop head (SF 123). Length 60 mm	On sternum
	124 & 125	19.1–2	Pair of two non-matching small-long copper-alloy brooches. No. 2 has a square head decorated with a triangle of incised double ring-and-dot motifs and with a small perforation in each upper corner. A double ring-and-dot motif is set on the foot below transverse mouldings. Length 60.5 mm. No. 1 Small-long brooch with trefoil-shaped head. The margins of the lobes are decorated with a row of ring-and-dot punchmarks set inside a row of V-shaped punchmarks, with tiny notches on the open side. The margins of the foot have a row of ring-and-dots with an outer row of notched Vs along the bottom edge, which is also notched. The centre panel has a large double ring-and-dot motif. A transverse moulding between head and bow has slanting grooves. There are slight incised lines at the base of the facetted bow. Only a tiny part of the spring iron pin remains. Length 73 mm.	SF 124 on right shoulder SF 125 on left shoulder
1358	52 & 75	20.1–2	Pair of gilt copper-alloy applied disc brooches, with central copper-alloy stud. The Style 1 zoomorphic decoration is identical on each brooch. The rims survive but are detached and fragmentary. Only fragments of the iron spring mechanisms remain. A nail-headed rivet is set in the centre of each. There is a ribbed inner and outer border. Diameters 52–3 mm.	SF 52 on left shoulder SF 75 on right shoulder
	76	20.3	Long copper-alloy pin with pierced disc head above three mouldings and eight close-set grooves. Length 136 mm. A short part of an iron loop embedded in the head served to attach a pair of spangles set back to back (soldered). The spangles have a raised central boss and marginal impressed dots. On one plate the boss has worn through. There are traces of iron in both suspension holes from the wire loop. Height 18 mm, width about 29 mm.	On sternum
	77	21.8	Ivory bag hoop (SF 77), internal diameter 107 mm, circular section, 12.5 mm	Between thighs
	78	20.4	Copper alloy ring	In or on bag

Grave No.	SF No.	Fig. No	Description of Grave Good	Position in Grave
	79/82	21	One amber and twenty-one glass beads, and an unpierced cylinder of soapstone. Fig.21.1) large amber disc, diameter 24 mm, 3.5 mm thick, weight 2 gm; Fig.21.2–10) annular blue glass, Guido Group 6i, diameter 9 mm. Fig.21.11) bun-shaped blue glass with white, terracotta and other-coloured specks, Guido Group 6xi, diameter 13 mm, length 8.5 mm; Fig.21.12) bun-shaped terracotta glass with green and yellow marbled dots, Guido Group 8xviiic, diameter 13 mm, length 9 mm; Fig.21.13) bun-shaped terracotta glass with double green wave (colour variant of Guido Group 8xivc), diameter 10.5 mm, length 7.5 mm. Fig.21.14) terracotta glass cylinder, round section, with yellow and green trail along the length (Guido Group 8xixa), diameter 8.5 mm, length 14 mm; Fig.21.15) terracotta glass cylinder, square section, with yellow and green trail along the length (Guido Group 8xixa), length 13 mm, width 10 mm; Fig.21.16) bun-shaped terracotta glass with yellow band (variant of Guido Group 8xvi), length 6 mm, diameter 7 mm; Fig.21.17–18) degraded glass cylinders of uncertain colour, subsquare section, probably banded blue and white, Guido Group 3vi, length 12mm; Fig.21.19) bun-shaped degraded terracotta and yellow glass, the pattern uncertain, length 4.5 mm, diameter 8 mm; Fig.21.20) gadrooned bead of light blue-green glass, Guido Group 1iii, length 4 mm, diameter 7 mm; Fig.21.21) fragment, globular black glass, length 4 mm, diameter 6 mm; Fig.21.22) soapstone cylinder, circular section, ends unworked, length 15 mm, diameter 10 mm.	Round neck/on sternum
	80	20.7	Iron knife with traces of mineralised organic material on the rectangular-section tang. The blade has a straight back and straight edge. Total length 122 mm, blade length 65 mm. Back Type B, length group 1.	In bag
	81	20.5	Fragments of at least two iron latch-lifters. Only one end remains, but there are two suspension loops on the girdle ring. Length uncertain.	In bag
	82	20.6	Iron buckle with a copper-alloy strap-plate. The buckle hoop is a rounded D-shape. The strap-plate is of folded one-piece form, with a large cut-out for the iron tongue and a copper-alloy rivet at the outer end for fixing the strap. Length 32 mm, width 20 mm.	On waist
1364	14	23.15	Iron ring. Internal diameter 52 mm, subcircular section, maximum thickness 8 mm.	In bag
	53	24.1–19	Nineteen amber beads, total weight 10 gm and an amulet. 1–4) Very roughly pyramidal, largest 7 mm, maximum width 16 mm; 5–19) roughly-shaped discs ranging from circular to square to triangular, largest length 5 mm, maximum width 17.5 mm	Round neck/on sternum
	54	23.16	Iron ring. Internal diameter 69 mm, subcircular section, maximum thickness 7 mm	By left thigh
	95	23.14	Iron L-shaped latch-lifter, the top looped for suspension. Length 173 mm	In bag
	97	22.4	Copper-alloy annular brooch of Ager's Type E (1985), with lines of marginal punchmarks and incised transverse slanting lines flanking the pin hole. The punchmarks are solid circles with a slight raised bar not quite projecting right across the centre. Diameter 45 mm, width of hoop 8 mm.	On left shoulder
	98	22.11	Coiled silver finger-ring, decorated with lines of small incised nicks and mouldings. Beyond small transverse mouldings the terminals are plain and tapering. Internal diameter 16 mm, height 8 mm, width 1 mm	On left hand
	99	23.18	Amulet consisting of a broken Roman blue melon bead held in a sling of copper-alloy strips (now in fragments), length 17 mm, diameter 24 mm	Round neck/on sternum
	100	22.3	Copper-alloy wrist-clasp (found in bag) with applied repoussé plate attached to the hook half by lead-based solder. The decoration shows confronting zoomorphs. Length 42 mm, width (joined) 44 mm. Similar to Hines Form B13c, but oval.	In bag
	101	23.8–9	Pair of copper-alloy girdle hangers, one damaged. Both are decorated with horseshoe-shaped punchmarks. The returned ends are joined with copper-alloy strips. The top of each shaft is moulded and perforated for suspension. One retains a small part of an iron loop. Lengths 128 and 126 mm.	By left knee
	102/103, 106	22.1–2	Pair of copper-alloy wrist-clasps with applied cast bars (mostly missing on one clasp), decorated with large and small repoussé dots and with a decoratively-shaped outer edge. Length 37 mm, width (joined) 34 mm. Hines Form B17a.	SF102/103 on right wrist SF 106 on left wrist
	107	22.5	Copper-alloy strip, folded back at one end. Length 9 mm, width 7.5	On spine/waist/hips

Grave No.	SF No.	Fig. No	Description of Grave Good	Position in Grave
	109	22.6–7	Copper-alloy two-piece tongue-ended strap-end and a fragment of another. The blunt end was fixed together with an iron rivet, the other ends may have been soldered together. The front-plate has pairs of incised lines to either side of the rivet, the back-plate one pair on the inner side. Length 48 mm, width 9 mm.	On right thigh
	110	22.12	Fragments of a laminated ivory bag hoop (only the largest is illustrated). Internal diameter approximately 75 mm, D-shaped section, 14 mm thick.	Between thighs
	111	22.10	Distorted coiled silver finger-ring with tapering terminals, decorated with mouldings. Internal diameter 19 mm, height 9 mm, width 1 mm.	On left hand
	112	23.17	Two fragments of an iron knife with curved back and concave edge. There are traces of mineralised organic material on the short tang. Total length 75 mm, length of blade 65 mm. Back Type A, length group 1.	In bag
1366	113/108	23.13	Iron L-shaped latch-lifter, the top looped for suspension. In fragments. Approximate length 215 mm.	In bag
	57	25.2	Iron shield boss with grip. The boss has concave walls, a low cone, and a blunt discoid apex. There were five rivets on the flange. Height 80 mm, diameter 157 mm. The ends of the grip are missing, but parts of the fixing nails survive. Length of grip 101 mm, width 16 mm.	Under head
	126	25.1	Copper-alloy tweezers and ear-scoop on a wire suspension ring with twisted join. The tweezers have transverse mouldings below the loop and a faceted panel with paired half ring and full dot punchmarks between transverse grooves. Length 67 mm. The scoop has a twisted shaft hammered flat and pierced for suspension at the top. The scoop is round and dished. Length 69 mm.	On lower chest/centre waist
1374	56	25.1	Small copper-alloy buckle with oval hoop and one-piece folded strap-plate, fixed to the strap by three copper-alloy rivets. Length 29 mm, width 17 mm.	On right wrist
	127	25.2	Tang and blade fragments from a large iron knife. The tang is rectangular in section, slightly narrower on one side. The back is straight, the edge is also straight and rises to meet it. Length of tang fragment 48 mm, length of blade fragment 79 mm. Back Type B, length group probably 2 when blade complete.	Across hips
Disturbed Skeleton	60	26.1	From F1378. Modern feature. The eye half of a wrist-clasp, decorated with large and small repoussé dots. Length 33 mm, width 17 mm. Hines Form B7.	Unstratified, out of context
	62	26.2	From F1417, L1418. Fill of natural hollow. Iron ferrule from the butt of a spear shaft (SF 62). Length 61 mm. – possibly from disturbed burial 1377, because 1378 cut this burial	Unstratified, out of context
1377	58	26.1	Iron knife, tip and end of rectangular-section tang missing (SF58). Back curved, edge straight. Total length 90.5 mm, blade length 50 mm. Back Type A, length group 1.	Not recorded
1379	59	27.6	Iron knife and fragments of mineral-replaced wood from the handle. The knife has a very slightly curved back and curved edge running up to the point. The edge has a low S-shaped profile at the upper end from much sharpening. The tang is rectangular and set at the centre of the blade. Total length 201 mm, blade length 153 mm. Back Type A, length group 3.	Against left side between body and arm
	128	27.3	Probably a pair of bone-handled iron awls: Bone handle with solid upper end and retaining part of an iron tang. Length 70.5 mm..	On left arm
1394	129	27.2	Bone handle fully perforated along its length, 66 mm.	On left arm
	130	27.4	Three iron shaft fragments, lengths 68, 23.5, and 23 mm.	On left arm
	131	27.1	Large copper-alloy buckle with integral strap-plate. The oval hoop shows two animal heads biting the inner upright. The plate has double marginal grooves. Length 32 mm, width 47 mm.	Centre of waist
	132	27.5	Two fragments of an iron shaft with roughly pyramidal head, subsquare in section apart from the circular-section tapering tip, lengths 59.5 and 26.5 mm.	On left arm
1428	61	28.2	Iron knife with slightly angled back and tang set below its line. Edge has an S-shaped profile at the upper end from much sharpening, before rising in a straight line to the point. Total length 129 mm, blade length 76 mm. Back Type A, length group 1.	On left side of chest
	96	28.3	Copper-alloy two-piece convex-ended strap-end, with most of one plate missing. Length 45 mm, width 13 mm.	Against inside of left arm

Grave No.	SF No.	Fig. No	Description of Grave Good	Position in Grave
	118	28.4 41	Very small ?biconical or shouldered vessel with an everted rim. Dark grey fabric, dark grey to black surfaces with occasional external dark buff fuming. Burnished. Single divided circle stamp (Briscoe type A 5di). Not enough of the vessel to survives to demonstrate direct parallels but from the elements present the arrangement may resemble something similar to Myres 1977, Fig.119.3241 (Loveden Hill, Lincolnshire).	At legs and feet
	122	28.1	Iron spearhead with blade and long socket. The tip of the blade is missing. The socket rivet survives. Swanton's F1. Length 165 mm	Against wall of grave cut to right of head
1440	178	28.1	Tip of long thin iron strip of plano-convex section. Length 47 mm. Purpose unknown.	By right hip
1460	68	29.2	Bone veneer fragments and iron rivets. Probable lozenge-shaped pieces with central perforation. One has iron staining at one end. Lengths 47 and 44 mm, widths 21 and 20 mm. Rectangular strips with large perforations set in pairs flanking smaller rivet holes. Part of a terminal rivet remains in one end. Lengths 134 and 141 mm, widths 21 and 22 mm. 5–8) Iron rivets and rivet fragments. Lengths 23, 20, and 22 mm.	Across right side of waist
	69	29.4	Iron knife with straight back and curved edge. The tang is of rectangular section. Total length 119 mm, blade length 68 mm. Back Type B, length group 1.	By right hip
	70	29.1	Copper-alloy disc-headed pin in two fragments and with tip missing. Length 66 mm.	Not planned
	71		Silver denarius	Not planned
	72	29.3	Fragment of copper-alloy sheet plated with white metal. One long side has broken across a rivet hole. Maximum dimensions 22 by 15 mm. Probably from a belt-fitting.	Not planned
1463	–	29.1 42	Very small shallow hemispherical bowl with a simple rim and flat base. Dark grey to black throughout with a smoothed finish (possibly once burnished). Myres 1977, Fig.67 (Nassington, Northamptonshire).	–
1466	167	29.1 42	Medium straight-sided deep bowl with a simple rim and rounded base. Very crude. Dark grey to black throughout with occasional light / mid grey and mid orange-brown fuming. Grass wiped. Myres 1977, Fig.71.2702 (Little Wilbraham, Cambridgeshire), 71.3794 (Mundesley, Norfolk)	Left of the grave by head

Appendix 3: Catalogue of Cremations and Associated Vessels

Cremation No.	Fig	Dimensions (L × W × D)	Grave — Description of Cremation Vessel	Skeleton — Sex	Age	% remaining	Burnt Grave Goods	Unburnt Grave Goods
1011	31 41	0.35 × 0.34 × 0.25 m	Large plain biconical jar with a concave base and slightly everted rim. Largely dark grey throughout with occasional light grey-buff and light grey external fuming. Burnished. Myres 1977, Fig.2.3250 (Loveden Hill, Lincolnshire). Decorated but burnished	M	Adult	1032 g	–	Antler comb
1021	41	0.3 × 0.3 × 0.09 m	Large plain sub-biconical jar. Dark grey fabric and surfaces. External surface occasionally oxidised buff to mid orange. Smoothed. Not decorated	Int	Adult	357 g	–	–
1035	31 40	0.59 × 0.55 × 0.16 m	Very large biconical jar with a flared rim and footstand base. Dark grey to black fabric with a mottled dark buff, orange-buff but predominantly dark grey to black surface. Occasional light to mid grey and orange fuming. Upper two thirds burnished, lower third wiped. Partial external off-white residue. Simple chevron and dot design (Briscoe type A 1ai). Not clear in illustration but the chevrons are comprised of linear hollows, demarcated by an incised line on either side. No direct parallel. Combination of the styles outlined on Myres 1977, Figs.285, 286 and 288; Hills 1977, Fig.48.1545; Hills, Penn and Rickett 1987, Fig.25.2430.	Int	15–25 yrs	599 g	–	Glass bead, antler comb, iron object (SF 157)
1244	32 40	0.38 × 0.34 × 0.12 m	Large jar with a slightly rounded base. Dark grey fabric with a dark grey / black surface demonstrating moderate light grey / buff fuming. Burnished. Anglian style – Evison 1994, Fig.67.20; Myres 1977, Figs.224.392, 224.2989 (Lackford, Suffolk); Hills 1977, Fig.40.1139. Decorated.	Int	25–35 yrs	485 g	–	Antler comb
1248	32 41	0.38 × 0.34 × 0.11	*Schalenurne* – Medium biconical bowl with an upright rim and flat base. Dark grey / black throughout. Burnished. Decorated with five well defined horizontal grooves above pairs of vertical incised lines delineating vertical indents. No direct parallel but similar to Myres 1977, Fig.213.4030, 214.3456 (both Newark, Nottinghamshire); West 1985, Fig.92.3.	Int	Juvenile	1298 g	Cu alloy brooch	Antler comb
1254	32 42	0.53 × 0.47 × 0.24 m	Large narrow mouthed globular jar with a slightly everted rim and rounded base. Dark grey to black fabric. Dark grey, dark grey-brown to black surface demonstrating occasional mid grey to buff fuming. Partial external off-white residue. Burnished. Stamped chevron decoration. Three alternating stamps; concentric circles and two squared/ diamond cross-hatched (Briscoe types A 2 bi; C 2aiii; F 2aii). Myres 1977, Figs.303–305; Hills, Penn and Rickett 1987, Fig.55.2715.	Int	Juvenile	940 g	Fragment of curved bone tube	Antler comb
1257	41	0.37 × 0.36 × 0.1 m	Medium plain sub-biconical jar with everted rim and rounded base. The vessel is predominantly dark grey with a patchy oxidised pink-orange to buff external surface. The vessel also demonstrates some internal oxidisation. Burnished (deteriorated). Myres 1977, Fig.28.2166. Undecorated.	Int	2 yrs	91 g	–	–
1260	33	0.36 × 0.24 × 0.1 m	Medium sized jar with a slightly rounded base. Dark grey to black throughout with a smoothed surface. No direct parallel. Possibly chevron based – Myres 1977, Fig.277.	Int	2 yrs	16 g	–	Antler comb

Cremation No.	Fig	Dimensions (L × W × D)	Grave Description of Cremation Vessel	Sex	Age	Skeleton % remaining	Burnt Grave Goods	Unburnt Grave Goods
1266	33 42	0.29 × 0.28 × 0.1 m	Medium biconical vessel with a flat base. Mid grey to black fabric with a mid grey / black and occasionally mid greyish-brown external surface. Burnished. Decorated in the pendant-triangle style. Alternating squared cross-hatched and divided square stamps and separated by linear depressions and incised lines (Briscoe types C 2aiv; C 3bii). No direct parallel; similar to Myres 1977, Fig.318.2790 (Lackford, Suffolk), 319.2226 (Illington, Norfolk).	Int	Juvenile	658 g	–	Antler comb
1271	33 42	0.33 × 0.33 × 0.14 m	Large, squat biconical jar with a slightly hollowed neck, short upright rim and concave base. Dark grey fabric. Predominantly black external surface with moderate orange, buff and light to dark grey fuming. Burnished. Single concentric circle stamp (Briscoe type A 2ai). No parallel is forthcoming in Myres for this arrangement although the style appears to broadly encompass elements of the horizontal stamped schemes on Figs. 98 and 102 and to the pendant-triangles examples on Figs. 327/8 (1977).	Int	Adult	1258 g	2 fragments of Cu alloy fittings	–
1274	11 41	0.4 × 0.4 × 0.18 m	Large, finely made and finished, decorated biconical jar with a short everted rim and footring base. Mid grey fabric with a buff-orange external margin. Predominantly dark grey / black surface with moderate, feathery light to dark grey and light buff fuming restricted to the lower half of the vessel. Burnished. Single squared cross-hatched stamp (Briscoe type C 2aiii). No direct parallel but the design is similar in layout and execution to Myres 1977, Fig.142.1871, 142.2252 and 142.2316; Hills 1977, Fig.66.1200.	F*	15–25 yrs	946 g	Glass bead, fragments of ivory bag hoop	Antler comb
1279	34 40	0.43 × 0.36 × 0.1 m	Fragmented vessel. Dark grey fabric with a mottled grey-buff, light grey to dark grey surface. Burnished. Decorated with massed vertical lines that extend over spaced linear bosses and onto the panels between. Parallel: Myres 1977, Fig.226; Hills 1977, Fig.40.1093.	Int	Juvenile	115 g	–	Antler comb
1282	34 41	0.38 × 0.38 × 0.2 m	Large shoulder-boss jar with a well formed upright rim and rounded base. Dark grey fabric and black surfaces with very occasional light grey-buff fuming. Burnished. Four clusters of three vertical linear bosses extending down from an enclosed horizontal line of stamps running around the shoulder of the vessel. The panels are filled with four alternating stamps in a rectangular or linear arrangement (cross in circle, circular cross-hatched and bow stamps; Briscoe types A4 ai; D 2aii; D 4ai; E 4bii). Very well made, finished and decorated. No direct parallel but similar combination of elements to Myres 1977, Figs.244/5/6; Hills 1977, Fig.61.1689.	Int	Juvenile	794 g	Brooch fragment	–
1285	34, 42	0.37 × 0.34 × 0.21 m	Large shouldered squat jar with slightly everted rim. Dark grey fabric with a mid orange-buff external margin and dark grey surface. ?Smoothed. Partial internal and external white residue. Enclosed	M*	Adult	1387 g		Antler comb, Iron tweezers, clip, slag

Cremation No.	Fig	Dimensions (L × W × D)	*Grave* Description of Cremation Vessel	Sex	Age	*Skeleton* % remaining	Burnt Grave Goods	Unburnt Grave Goods
			stamped pendant-triangles. Two stamps; concentric circles and squared cross-hatched (Briscoe types A 2ai; C 2av). Myres 1977, Figs.320, 322, 324, 325.2453.					fragment (SF 148)
1288	42	0.37 × 0.34 × 0.23 m	Medium sub-biconical jar with a short rim and flat base. Dark grey fabric and internal surface. Predominantly oxidised mid orange external surface with occasional light to dark buff, buff-brown and light to dark grey / black fuming restricted to the lower half of the vessel. Burnished (now mostly deteriorated). Single stamp; cross in circle (Briscoe type B 1bii). Myres 1977, Fig.339.290 (St Johns, Cambridgeshire).	Int	12–15 yrs	450 g	–	–
1293	34, 40	0.34 × 0.3 × 0.14 m	Medium shouldered jar with a short, upright rim and slightly concave base. Dark grey fabric with a mottled surface ranging in colour from buff through brown to dark-grey / black. Smoothed. Even wall thickness and fairly well made but the decoration is very irregular and poorly executed. The shoulder is marked by five regularly spaced bosses delineated on either side by pairs of vertical lines and decorated with pairs of roughly vertical incisions. The panels between the bosses are decorated with three to four horizontal lines that occasionally continue onto the boss itself. The decoration on one panel appears to have broken down and with irregular lines terminating at two vertical lines of small stab marks (Briscoe type M 1ai). No direct parallel but similar decorative elements to Myres 1977, Fig.184.849 (Lackford, Suffolk).	Int	1 yr	150 g	–	Antler comb
1296	35, 40	0.36 × 0.36 × 0.19 m NB 4-post structure arranged above this cremation pit	Large shoulder bossed jar with a tall neck and footstand base. Predominantly dark grey to black with occasional mid buff-grey external fuming. Burnished. Five bosses of uniform shape and spacing extend around the shoulder of the vessel separating five panels decorated with alternating combinations of circular and lozenge shaped dots (Briscoe types A 1ai; D 1ai). Five linear indented bosses, also demarcated with incised lines, decorate the lower body. Competently made and decorated; very even wall thickness and regular finish. No direct parallel but similar to another Little Wilbraham example – Myres 1977, Fig.201.2650, 230/1.	M*	35–45	1177 g	–	Antler comb, Fe shears, Fe razor, hone
1299	35, 40	0.38 × 0.34 × 0.11 m	Large sub-biconical urn with slightly everted rim and concave base. Dark grey fabric and surfaces with occasional external mid buff-grey fuming. Burnished. Anglian style – Myres 1977, 40; Fig.209.1411 (Loveden Hill, Lincolnshire), 209.1557, 212.1546; Hills 1977, Fig.23.1485, 23.1544. Decorated.	M*	Adult	1659 g	–	Cu alloy hoop, Cu alloy tweezers, Cu alloy wire ring, Fe nail.
1302	36, 41	0.35 × 0.28 × 0.17 m	Very large plain ?sub-biconical or shouldered urn with a flat base. Dark grey fabric and black surfaces with occasional light grey / buff fuming. Burnished. Undecorated.	Int	Adult	980 g	Antler comb	Fe nail
1307	36, 40	0.27 × 0.28 × 0.09 m	Medium biconical bowl with slightly flaring rim. Dark grey fabric with brown-black to black surfaces. Burnished. Occasional internal and external residue. Parallel for form Evison 1994, *Schalenurne*, Fig.67.19. Decorated	?F*	Juvenile	486 g	Spindlewhorl	Antler comb

Catriona Gibson

Cremation No.	Fig	Dimensions (L × W × D)	*Grave* Description of Cremation Vessel	Sex	*Skeleton* Age	% remaining	Burnt Grave Goods	Unburnt Grave Goods
1310	36, 40	0.3 × 0.25 × 0.1 m	Medium ?sub-biconical jar. Dark grey to black fabric with mottled light to dark grey/ black, buff, orange but predominantly mid buff-grey external surface. Burnished. *Buckelurnen* decorated with at least two zones of line (chevron) and line (chevron, vertical) and dot decoration (Briscoe type A1 ai). A least two types of boss are also evident, one linear (vertical) and one circular. No direct parallel but similar boss decoration to examples from the Girton/ Little Wilbraham, Cambridgeshire – Myres 1977, Figs.185, 195, 199.	Int	Juvenile	262 g	–	Antler comb, 2 Fe nails
1318	41	0.26 × 0.22 × 0.14 m	Small plain biconical jar with a slightly hollow neck, wide-mouth, slightly everted rim and rounded base. Black throughout with a smoothed finish. Myres 1977, Fig.27.1201 (Worthy Park, Hampshire), 31.503 (Ruskington, Lincolnshire), 47.1988 (Aston Remenham, Berkshire). Undecorated.	Int	Adult	–	–	–
1324	42	No defined cut	Upright rim. Dark grey fabric with dark grey to dark brown surfaces. Burnished	Int	Adult	–	–	–
1328	36 40	0.25 × 0.23 × 0.09 m	Small vessel with a slightly rounded base. Black fabric and surfaces with partial mid to dark grey external fuming. Smoothed. Undecorated.	M	Adult	1050 g	–	Antler comb, Fe nail
1331	41	0.39 × 0.36 × 0.14 m	Large plain sub-globular jar. Dark-grey to black although the external surface ranges from black through grey to buff and to pink-buff towards the base. The rim, neck and shoulder of the vessel have been smoothed but the rest has a fairly rough feel and finish. Myres 1977, Fig.63.961. Undecorated.	Int	Adult	418 g	–	–
1348	41	0.17 × 0.17 × 0.13 m	SF 49 Large shouldered jar with concave base. Dark grey fabric. Predominantly dark brown to black external surface with moderate light grey, light orange and orange-brown fuming. Smoothed. Single annular stamp (Briscoe type A 1bi). Myres 1977, Figs.177.941 (Lackford, Suffolk), 162–177, 170.653 and 170.3722 (Elkington, Lincolnshire and Rothley, Leicestershire respectively)	Int	Adult	390 g	–	–
1419	42	0.24 × 0.23 × 0.13 m	Small hemispherical bowl with an upright rim and a slightly concave base. Black throughout with a burnished surface. Myres 1977, Fig.67.3636 (Hassocks, Sussex).	Int	Juvenile	5 g	–	–
1422	42	0.32 × 0.28 × 0.09	Small globular vessel with a rounded base. Black fabric with a mottled, predominantly black but also dark grey and buff external surface. Burnished.	Int	Int	–	–	–

* sex assigned on basis of accompanying grave goods

Appendix 4: Catalogue of Grave Goods associated with Cremations

Cremation No.	Fig. No	Description of Grave Good	Condition of goods
1011	–	Found during evaluation. Triangular antler comb fragment, unburnt. Corner tooth-plate fragment, one face slightly reduced on the line of the connecting-plate. Length 22 mm, height 31 mm. The tooth line is a straight slope.	Unburnt
1035	31.1	Fragment of a green opaque glass cylinder bead with polygonal section. Length (incomplete) 3.5 mm, diameter 4 mm.	Interesting that the antler comb is complete. All the other grave goods are fragmentary
1035	31.2	Double-sided antler comb, unburnt. Complete, apart from some damage to the teeth and the end of one connecting-plate. The end-plates have a raised central area, notched on the edge, flanked by a concave sweep to straight end sections. There is a large hole set at the centre at one end, with a smaller hole in the same position at the other end. The convex connecting-plates are plain. There are five iron rivets, two set close to each end, one in centre. Length 86 mm, width 44 mm.	
1244	–	SF 157 iron object.	Complete – certainly not a token deposit
1244	32.1	Double-sided antler comb, unburnt. One end and parts of the connecting-plates are missing. The end-plate is straight, with a centrally-placed hole. The tooth line is a straight slope. The connecting-plates are decorated with groups of three transverse lines alternating with a cross between transverse lines. Length 84 mm, width 50.5 mm, plates 15 mm wide.	
1248	32.1	Burnt copper-alloy small-long brooch fragment (6th C). Length 25 mm.	One object is burnt and the other one is not – interesting oppositions. Both are fragmentary and may be tokens
1248	32.2	Triangular antler comb fragment, unburnt. Corner-plate fragment, slightly convex. The tooth line is slightly concave. Length 17 mm, height 38 mm.	
1254	32.1	Double-sided antler comb, unburnt. Complete apart from some teeth. The end-plates are concave, with asymmetrical corners. On one side they are rounded, but not equal-sized at each end. On the other side they are pointed. The tooth-line is a straight slope. The flat connecting-plates run to the edges of the end-plates. They are decorated with a frame of three incised grooves around a line of single ring-and-dot motifs. There are two rivets at each end, four down the centre, and two on one edge. Length 117 mm, width 47 mm, plates 17.5 mm.	
1254	32.2	Fragment of a burnt curved bone tube, partly missing. Four lines of single ring-and-dot motifs run up from the thickest end, but are irregularly set on the main body. Length 66 mm, maximum diameter 11.5 mm.	Burnt and fragmentary.
1260	33.1	Triangular antler comb fragment, unburnt. Corner-plate fragment. The upper edge and the tooth line are gently concave. Similar to the fragment from G1293 and to a comb from West Stow (West 1985, fig. 251, 11). Length 21 mm, height 28.5 mm.	Only a fragment and unburnt
1266	33.1	Triangular antler comb fragment, unburnt. Corner tooth-plate fragment, with a small part of one connecting-plate and two iron rivets. This is decorated with close-set triple marginal grooves, as SF 172. The toothplate corner is long and projects well beyond the connecting-plate, both characteristics seen on a comb from West Stow (West 1985, fig. 207, 9). The upper edge is decoratively shaped above the line of the connecting-plate. The tooth line is gently concave. Length 47 mm, height 33 mm.	A fragment of comb unburnt
1271	33.1–2	Two fragments of burnt copper-alloy fittings. 1) Strip, burnt and now transversely convex in section. Length (incomplete) 18 mm, width 11 mm. 2) Plaque, broken across two rivet holes. Length 25 mm, width (incomplete) 13.5 mm. Probably from a buckle-plate (a belt suite).	
1274	33.1	Scorched blue glass annular bead. Length 4 mm, diameter 9.5 mm. (Guido's type 6I – said to be indicative of low status).	Contained an ivory ring from a cloth bag of the type deposited in female inhumation graves. The contents of the bag have not survived, though a tiny droplet of refrozen copper alloy from an object melted on the pyre was also found in the grave, and a scorched bead may have come from either the bag or from a bead string.
1274	33.2	Many fragments (sample only illustrated) of a burnt ivory bag hoop.	
1274	33.3	Triangular antler comb fragment, unburnt. Corner-plate fragment with part of one connecting-plate. This has triple marginal grooves (as SF 26). Two iron rivets remain. The edge is notched by the end of the connecting-plate, and has a hook at the corner. The tooth line is a reverse curve. Length 40.5 mm, height 30 mm.	
1279	34.1	Triangular antler comb fragment, unburnt. End-plate fragment, with decoratively cut edge of alternating points and curves, the latter pierced, above a concave sweep down to a short blunt end. There are two rivet holes and	

Cremation No.	Fig. No	Description of Grave Good	Condition of goods
		one side is stained with iron corrosion. Length 40.5 mm, height 43 mm. Possibly quite early 5th C because of the decorated edge.	
1282	34.1	Burnt copper-alloy cruciform brooch fragment. There are small lappets on either side of the foot-plate and traces of the zoomorphic foot mask survive. Length 48 mm.	Burnt and fragmentary (at least 2 frags)
1285	34.1	Double-sided antler comb fragment, unburnt. End-plate and part of one tooth-plate, with parts of the connecting-plates. The end is straight with the connecting-plates set close to the edge. They are decorated with double ring-and-dot motifs alternating with iron rivets. The tooth line is concave. Length 45 mm, width 52 m, plates 18.5 mm wide.	The tweezers are complete, the comb & clips are fragmentary
	34.2	Iron tweezers with slight constrictions from a clenching tool below the suspension loop. The blades are very slightly waisted before they flare out. Transverse lines decorate the upper part of each blade. Length 76 mm.	
	34.3	Iron clip, arms only slightly tapering, tips missing. Width 17 mm, length 11 mm.	
	—	Slag fragment. Not illustrated.	
1293	34.1	Triangular antler comb fragment, unburnt. End-plate fragment, very slightly concave. The tooth line is concave, with teeth cut right to the corner. Similar to the fragment from G1260. Length 15 mm, height 28.5 mm.	Could it be part of the same comb as that from Grave 1260 – a family or some kind of link. Male toilet set
1296	35.1	Triangular antler comb fragment, unburnt. End-plate fragment, with a step at the point where the connecting-plates ended and a slightly enlarged rounded corner. The tooth line is a straight slope. Length 28 mm, height 26 mm.	
	35.2	Pair of iron spring shears with straight-sided arms bent into a simple bow and with curved backs to the blades. Length 123 mm.	
	35.3	Two iron fragments, probably from a razor. One is tanged, with a blade curving sharply below the tang. The inner edge is thicker than the outer. Length 59 mm. The second is much wider and thinner, but again has a thicker inner edge. Its tip is slightly hooked. Length 50.5 mm.	
	35.4	Hone of greensand, stained by contact with iron corrosion products. Rectangular section. Length 74 mm, maximum width 19 mm.	
1299	35.1	Copper-alloy hoop.	Cu alloy hoop fragmentary. The others almost complete
	35.2	Copper-alloy tweezers and a wire suspension ring. The tweezers are plain. Length 67 mm. Diameter of ring 19 mm.	
	35.3	Iron nail, bent, tip missing. Head flat and circular. Length 34.5 mm	
1302	36.1	Double-sided antler comb fragment, burnt. End-plate fragment with straight end, broken across two rivet holes, which are set almost side by side across, not along, the comb. The connecting-plates are missing. One face of the end-plate is slightly raised where the connecting-plate would have been fitted. The teeth are cut almost right up to corners, and the line was probably concave. Length 17 mm, width 53.5 mm.	Comb is burnt and fragmentary. Iron nail more or less complete
	36.2	Iron nail, tip missing. Head damaged, probably circular and flat. Length 33 mm.	
1307	36.1	Triangular antler comb fragment, unburnt. End-plate fragment, with a marked shoulder at the corner. The tooth line is more or less a straight slope. Stained with copper-alloy on one side, with some penetration through to the other side. Length 27 mm, height 31 mm.	Unburnt fragmentary comb and burnt complete spindlewhorl
	36.2	Burnt antler discoidal spindlewhorl. Diameter 36 mm, height 20 mm; diameter of perforation 9.5 mm.	
1310	36.1	Triangular antler comb fragment, unburnt. Very similar to the comb from 1266. Fragment of a corner tooth-plate but missing the corner itself, which projected beyond the end of the connecting-plates. The upper edge is stepped at the tip of the connecting-plates. Parts of both connecting-plates survive, each has marginal grooves. On the best preserved they are triple on the angled side, double and wide-spaced on the straight side. Two iron rivets remain, and the comb has broken across the hole for a third. The teeth are big, wide-spaced, and cut on a straight slope. Length 27 mm, height 38 mm.	Bent although almost complete nails; fragmentary comb. All unburnt
	36.2–3	Two iron nails. 2) Tip missing. Head flat and subrectangular. Length 47.5 mm. 3) Complete, bent. Head damaged, domed and probably subrectangular. Length 56 mm.	
1328	36.1	Triangular antler comb fragment, unburnt. Corner tooth-plate fragment with parts of both connecting-plates. The angled edge is decoratively shaped, with a hook upwards at the projecting end. The connecting-plates have double marginal lines. One iron rivet remains. Length 42.5 mm, height 42 mm. The tooth line is a straight slope. (Early in date – 5th C because of the decoration.)	Unburnt & fragmentary comb. Unburnt fragmentary nail
	36.2	Iron nail, lower part of shaft missing. Subrectangular head, slightly domed. Length 34 mm.	